HISTORY OF THE CATHOLIC DIOCESE OF DUBLIN

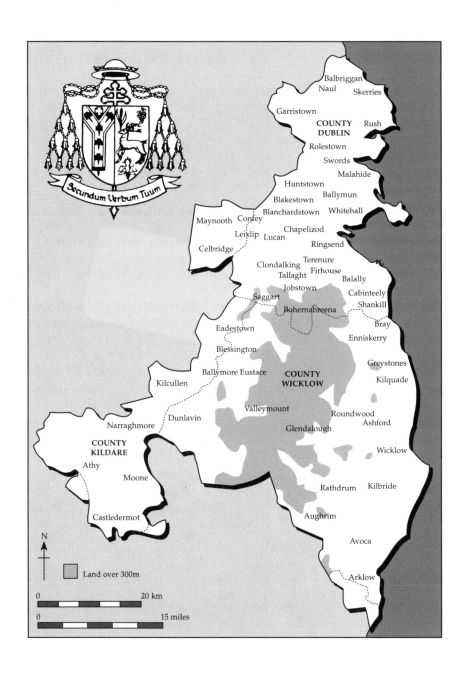

The archdiocese of Dublin

History of the Catholic Diocese of Dublin

James Kelly and Dáire Keogh

EDITORS

FOUR COURTS PRESS

Set in 10.5 on 12.5 Ehrhardt for
FOUR COURTS PRESS LTD
Fumbally Lane, Dublin 8, Ireland
e-mail: info@four-courts-press.ie
and in North America by
FOUR COURTS PRESS
c/o ISBS, 5804 N.E. Hassalo Street, Portland, OR 97213.

A catalogue record for this title
is available from the British Library.

ISBN 1–85182–248–8

Printed in Great Britain
by MPG Books, Bodmin, Cornwall

Contents

Illustrations appear between pages 22 and 23; and 246 and 247.

Preface

Since the demise of the journal *Reportorium Novum* in the early 1970s, the diocese of Dublin no longer possesses an outlet devoted to the exploration of its long and complex history. Obviously, a once-off publication such as this is no substitute for a serial publication. Its purpose is to provide a historical perspective on the diocese from the introduction of Christianity to the death of Archbishop McQuaid based upon the collective expertise of a body of scholars who possess a common interest in the history of religion in Ireland. What follows cannot claim to be a comprehensive history of the diocese over this extended time frame; it is not *the* history or even *a* history of the diocese, yet most of the major issues and the major personalities from that history feature on its pages. The object of the collection is to provide the reader with a modern account of the main features of the Christian experience in the region and in the diocese up to the Reformation and the particular experience of Roman Catholicism thereafter based upon the available documentary record.

This book has been long in gestation, and its preparation and publication have been greatly eased by support from a variety of quarters. In particular, the editors wish to acknowledge a generous grant in aid of publication from the archbishop of Dublin, Dr Desmond Connell, who has taken a keen interest in the project and whose support and encouragement has facilitated its completion. The Research Fund of St Patrick's College, Drumcondra, has also favoured a request for assistance that is gratefully acknowledged. The editors wish, in addition, to express their gratitude to departmental colleagues past and present – Dr Pauric Travers, Father Patrick O'Donoghue and Dr Carla King – for their continuing collegial support. Acknowledgment is due also to the publisher, Michael Adams, and all the staff at Four Courts Press for their efficiency and encouragement, and to Helen Litton who copy-edited the text. Furthermore, the editors wish to thank the contributors for their patience and courtesy. Each has his or her own story; we trust that the end result makes them feel their work was worthwhile.

James Kelly and Dáire Keogh
June 1999

Notes on contributors

HOWARD CLARKE lectures in Medieval History at University College Dublin. An expert in the history of early Dublin, he is the editor of *Medieval Dublin* (2 vols, Dublin, 1990) and other works.

SÉAMUS ENRIGHT is a priest in the Redemptorist Order. He is Director of the Marionella Centre and is completing a Ph.D. at the National University of Ireland, Maynooth.

HUGH FENNING is a priest of the Dominican Order; his many publications include *The Irish Dominican province 1698-1797* (Dublin, 1990).

RAYMOND GILLESPIE is senior lecturer in History at the National University of Ireland, Maynooth. His most recent book is *Devoted people: belief and religion in early modern Ireland* (Manchester, 1997).

MAURICE HARTIGAN is a secondary school teacher and the author of 'The Catholic laity of Dublin 1920-40' for which he was awarded a doctorate by St Patrick's College, Maynooth in 1992.

JAMES KELLY is Head of the History Department at St Patrick's College, Drumcondra. His most recent book is *Henry Flood: patriots and politics in eighteenth-century Ireland* (Dublin, 1998).

DÁIRE KEOGH lectures in History at St Patrick's College, Drumcondra. His most recent book is *A patriot priest: the life of James Coigly* (Cork, 1998).

DONAL KERR is a priest of the Society of Mary and emeritus Professor of Ecclesiastical History at St Patrick's College, Maynooth. He is author of *A nation of beggars: priests, people and politics in famine Ireland* (Oxford, 1994), among other books.

COLM LENNON lectures in History at the National University of Ireland, Maynooth. His most recent book is *An Irish prisoner of conscience of the Tudor era: Archbishop Richard Creagh of Armagh, 1523-86* (Dublin, 2000).

MICHAEL McCARTHY is Professor of History of Art, University College Dublin. He is the author of *The origins of the Gothic Revival* (London, 1987) and many articles on the history of architecture.

DEIRDRE McMAHON teaches History in Mary Immaculate College, Limerick. She is the author of *Republicans and imperialists: Anglo-Irish relations in the 1930s* (New Haven, 1984).

AILBHE MacSHAMHRÁIN teaches on the Medieval Irish Studies programme at the National University of Ireland, Maynooth. He is the author of *Church and polity in pre-Norman Ireland: the case of Glendalough* (Maynooth, 1996).

MARGARET MURPHY was awarded a Ph.D. by Trinity College, Dublin in 1987 for her thesis 'The archbishops and administration of the diocese and province of Dublin, 1181-1298'. She is based at the Centre for Metropolitan History, London.

JAMES MURRAY is assistant registrar at Dublin City University. His Ph.D., 'The Tudor diocese of Dublin: episcopal government, ecclesiastical politics and the enforcement of the Reformation, *c.*1534-1590', is to be published by Cambridge University Press.

CIARAN O'CARROLL is priest in the diocese of Dublin and lecturer in Church History at Holy Cross College, Clonliffe, Dublin.

DAVID C. SHEEHY is the Archivist to the Dublin Diocese.

The historiography of the diocese of Dublin

James Kelly

For a diocese of its size and national importance, Dublin possesses a modest historiography. Unlike many Roman Catholic dioceses in Ireland, it did not secure a major history during the 'golden age' of diocesan history that spanned the second half of the nineteenth and the early decades of the twentieth century when large, frequently multi-volumed, studies were fashionable. Thus, there is no Dublin equivalent to Anthony Cogan's pioneering work, *The diocese of Meath – ancient and modern*,[1] to James O'Laverty's encyclopaedic *Historical account of the diocese of Down and Connor ancient and modern*,[2] to Canon Carrigan's monumental *History and antiquities of the diocese of Ossory*[3] or even to more modestly conceived accounts such as Fahey's *Diocese of Kilmacduagh*, Grattan-Flood's *Diocese of Ferns* or Burke's *Catholic archbishops of Tuam*.[4] Likewise, the diocese was not the subject of an ambitious documentary compilation such as Comerford produced for the diocese of Kildare and Leighlin, and Canon Monahan for Ardagh and Clonmacnoise.[5] It may be that these works, and others such as Maguire's *Raphoe* and D'Alton's *Archdiocese of Tuam* dating from the 1920s,[6] are too confessionally

---

1 Published in three volumes in Dublin between 1862 and 1870 and reissued, accompanied by a biography of Cogan entitled *Faith, famine and fatherland in the nineteenth century Irish midlands: perceptions of a priest and historian Anthony Cogan 1826-1872* by Alfred Smyth, published by Four Courts Press, Dublin, in 1992. 2 Published in five volumes in Dublin between 1878 and 1895, and reissued by Davidson Books in 1980-3. 3 Published in four volumes in Dublin in 1905, and reissued by Roberts Books, Kilkenny in 1981. 4 J. Fahey, *The history and antiquities of the diocese of Kilmacduagh* (Dublin, 1893); W.H. Grattan Flood, *History of the diocese of Ferns* (Waterford, 1916); O.J. Burke, *The history of the Catholic archbishops of Tuam* (Dublin, 1882). 5 M. Comerford (ed.), *Collections relating to the dioceses of Kildare and Leighlin* (3 vols, Dublin [1883-86]); John Monahan, *Records relating to the united diocese of Ardagh and Clonmacnoise* (Dublin, 1886). 6 E. Maguire, *A history of the diocese of Raphoe* (2 vols, Dublin, 1920); E.A. D'Alton, *History of the archdiocese of Tuam* (3 vols, Dublin, 1928).

partisan and insufficiently rigorous methodologically to satisfy contemporary historiographal requirements, but they invariably provide a political narrative and basic information appertaining to diocesan succession, parish formation, church construction and other formative events and issues. Moreover, because the documents they cite are not always readily accessible or have been destroyed or lost, they are, in many instances, important sources of primary documentation.

The diocese of Dublin was not untouched by the enthusiasm manifested in the late nineteenth and early twentieth centuries for broad narratives. Indeed, it was the subject of such a study in microcosm in the form of Nicholas Donnelly's short histories of the parishes of Dublin city and county, published in seventeen parts between 1904 and 1917. The twenty- to fifty-page pamphlets in which Donnelly presented the results of his extensive researches, and which were subsequently published unaltered in four small volumes, explore the history of the Church in the county of Dublin from a parish perspective.[7] They are sometimes sketchy, but they have stood the test of time better than John D'Alton's inadequate biographical sketches of the lives of the archbishops of Dublin published in 1838,[8] and P.F. Moran's fuller but more obviously partisan *History of the Catholic archbishops of Dublin since the Reformation* published in 1864.[9]

The problem then, and it remains the case today, is that the retrieval of the complex history of the diocese of Dublin is too forbidding to be encompassed satisfactorily by one person. As a consequence, when others elsewhere were embarked on the more manageable task of preparing expansive histories of their chosen dioceses, the canvas that occupied those attracted by the challenge of exploring Dublin's particular experience was palpably more limited. They were encouraged to take this option by the greater availability of primary source material and by the emphasis placed in the late nineteenth and early twentieth centuries on the production of accurate and accessible editions of major manuscripts. The pre-Reformation history of the diocese of Dublin was certainly illuminated at this time by the publication of editions of important documents. Foremost among those engaged in this activ-

---

7 Nicholas Donnelly, *Short histories of Dublin parishes* (17 parts, Dublin, 1904-17). Significantly, Donnelly envisaged them as part of a projected, but never realised, larger work to include all the parishes in the diocese of Dublin and Glendalough: see obituary of Nicholas Donnelly, *Journal of the Royal Society of Antiquaries of Ireland* (henceforth, *JRSAI*), 51 (1921), pp 92-3. The seventeen published pamphlets were reissued as part of the chapbook series published by Carraig Books in the 1970s.   8 John D'Alton, *The archbishops of Dublin* (Dublin, 1838). This volume provides brief, and unsatisfactory, biographical sketches of the archbishops of Dublin from the twelfth century.   9 P.F. Moran, *History of the Catholic archbishops of Dublin since the Reformation* (Dublin, 1864).

ity was the great historian of Dublin, Sir John Gilbert, who prepared texts
of the chartularies of St Mary's abbey, the register of the abbey of St
Thomas and the register book of the archishops of Dublin before the
Reformation for publication in the 1880s and 1890s.[10] His efforts were complemented by Charles Plummer, who edited the life of Laurence O'Toole
for *Analecta Bollandiana*; by H.F. Berry, who prepared an edition of fif-
teenth-century wills and inventories; and by M.J. McEnery's calendar of
Christ Church deeds.[11] Parallel with this, the indefatigable P.F. Moran
embarked, with more evangelical purpose, on the preparation of editions of
documents from a later, more controversial, era whose purpose was to sustain the claim that the Irish Church was ever loyal to Rome and the majority of the Irish population ever committed Catholics. In the course of this
enterprise, Moran identified many important documents in Irish and Roman
archives though, regrettably, he was also prepared, as some of the partial
texts reproduced in the large three-volume collection entitled *Spicilegium
Ossoriense* attest, to bowdlerise material that did not reflect well on the
Catholic Church or its bishops.[12] If this casts something of a shadow over
the reliability both of this generally valuable collection and over Moran's
scholarship, it can be said in his defence that the proportion of documents
presented in less than their entirety is small, and that the substantial volume
of material he included appertaining to the diocese of Dublin in the seventeenth and eighteenth centuries ensures that *Spicilegium Ossoriense* remains
a standard source for all historians interested in ecclesiastical and religious
issues. Nor was this Moran's only contribution to the history of the diocese;
he also prepared a three-volume edition, running to near 2,500 pages, of the
public letters and pastoral statements of his uncle Paul, Cardinal Cullen
which, while intended primarily to affirm his political and pastoral message,
represents an important window into the political and pastoral endeavour of
that influential prelate.[13]

Though the size of the publication needed to accommodate his public
writings was appropriately monumental, Cullen was but the most towering

---

10 John T. Gilbert (ed.), *Chartularies of St Mary's abbey, Dublin* (2 vols, London, 1884);
idem, *Register of the abbey of St Thomas, Dublin* (London, 1889); idem, *Crede Mihi: the
most ancient register book of the archbishops of Dublin before the Reformation* (Dublin, 1897).
11 Charles Plummer (ed.), 'Vita Sanctii Laurencii Archiepiscopi Dublinensis', *Analecta
Bollandiana*, 33 (1914); H.F. Berry (ed.), *Register of wills and inventories of the diocese of
Dublin in the time of Archbishops Tregury and Walton* (Dublin, 1898); M.J. McEnery (ed.),
'Calendar of Christ Church deeds 1174-1684', *Report of the Keeper of Public Record Office
of Ireland*, vols 20-27 (1888-95).   12 P.F. Moran (ed.), *Spicilegium Ossoriense: being a col-
lection of original letters and papers illustrative of the history of the Irish Church* (3 vols,
Dublin, 1874-84).   13 P.F. Moran (ed.), *The pastoral letters and other writings of Cardinal
Cullen, archbishop of Dublin* (3 vols, Dublin, 1882).

of the three nineteenth-century episcopal leaders of the Catholic diocese of Dublin who were the subject of contemporary memorials in which documents appertaining to their life and work were published. Like Cullen's *writings*, the two-volume edition of the sermons of Archbishop Daniel Murray published in 1859 was also first and foremost an exercise in religious edification rather than historical scholarship, yet both it and Meagher's *Life of Archbishop Daniel Murray* provide important documentary insights into the career of one of the most overlooked archbishops of the modern era.[14] William Meagher's acknowledgment of his decision not to consult Murray's papers when preparing his 'life' serves as a stark reminder of the limitations of his short biography. Patrick Walsh, who had served Archbishop William Walsh as secretary for fifteen of his thirty-six years as archbishop (1885-1921), placed himself under no such constraint, and his biography is fuller and replete with documentary quotations as a result. However, it is first and foremost the life of a 'public man'; it has little to say about Walsh's 'pastoral work' and it is unsatisfactory as a consequence.[15]

The publication, shortly after their death, of biographies and of editions of their public pronouncements containing valuable information on key ecclesiastical figures from the nineteenth century was not matched by similar work on the bishops of earlier centuries. Those who sought in the 1920s to explore the early post-Reformation history of the diocese of Dublin were obliged, if Donnelly did not satisfy their curiosity, to content themselves with extracting pertinent information from works with a primarily national focus. One of the most useful was W.P. Burke's exploration of the impact of the penal laws upon Irish priests during the century 1660 to 1760, because it incorporated extensive documentary extracts then to be found in the Irish Record Office.[16] The insights offered there were extended and enhanced by parallel work published in serialised form in the *Irish Ecclesiastical Record* by Reginald Walsh on 'the penal times' and by Nicholas Donnelly on the diocese of Dublin in the eighteenth century.[17] This and an edition of a document listing the priests in the diocese in 1697 indicate that Donnelly was a historian of considerable energy and ability, but for all the usefulness of the 'short' histories of Dublin parishes that he published in the first two decades of the

14 *Sermons of the late ... Daniel Murray, archbishop of Dublin* (2 vols, Dublin, 1859); William Meagher, *Notices of the life and character of ... Daniel Murray, late archbishop of Dublin ...* (Dublin, 1853).   15 Patrick J. Walsh, *William J. Walsh, archbishop of Dublin* (London, 1928), p. v.   16 W.P. Burke, *Irish priests in the penal times* (Waterford, 1914). 17 Reginald Walsh, 'Glimpses of the penal times' in 14 parts in *Irish Ecclesiastical Record* (henceforth *IER*), 20 (1906), 22 (1907), 25 (1909), 26 (1909), 27 (1910), 28 (1910), 29 (1911), 30(1911); Nicholas Donnelly, 'The diocese of Dublin in the eighteenth century', parts 1-8, *IER*, 9 (1888), 10 (1889), 11 (1890).

twentieth century, neither they nor the texts of episcopal wills and other documents that also saw print during these years provided more than a series of disconnected snapshots of the history of the diocese.[18]

The essentially fragmented nature of the history written on the diocese of Dublin during the 'golden age' persisted thereafter. Thus, while historians elsewhere during the mid-twentieth century continued to produce ambitious diocesan surveys, the work published on Dublin was more specialised in its subject and theme. There was, in other words, nothing to equate with Philip O'Connell's comprehensive survey of the diocese of Kilmore published in 1937; with the second volume of John Begley's ambitious account of Limerick that appeared in 1938; with the pamphlets published by John Brady between 1937 and 1945 on the diocese of Meath that form the basis of the three-volume work completed by Olive Curran that saw print in 1995 or with James MacNamee's history of the united dioceses of Ardagh and Clonmacnoise which was published in 1954.[19] Dublin's most prolific historian during this period was Myles Ronan whose first major work, published in 1926, was a study of the Reformation in Dublin.[20] Four years later he extended and expanded on this with a companion volume which examined the Reformation from a national perspective during the reign of Elizabeth, and he reinforced his reputation as the diocese's major historian in the decades that followed with a series of articles in historical journals on a variety of topics over a broad time-span.[21] Because of the Catholic bias of his

18 N. D[onnelly], 'The diocese of Dublin in the year 1697', *IER*, 9 (1888), pp 407-13, 511-19. Canon William Carrigan published texts of episcopal wills; those relating to Dublin are in *Archivium Hibernicum*, 4 (1916), pp 66-95. The Dublin section of 'The report of the state of popery, 1731' is on pages 131 to 177 of the same number of that journal. 19 Philip O'Connell, *The diocese of Kilmore: its history and antiquities* (Dublin, 1937); John Begley, *The diocese of Limerick* (2 vols, Dublin, 1906-38); Olive Curran, *History of the diocese of Meath, 1860-1993* (3 vols, [Mullingar], 1995); James MacNamee, *History of the dioceses of Ardagh and Clonmacnoise* (Dublin, 1954). 20 Myles Ronan, *The Reformation in Dublin 1536-58* (London, 1926). 21 Myles V. Ronan, *The Reformation in Ireland under Elizabeth 1558-80 (from original sources)* (London, 1930). From the listing of Ronan's articles in Richard Hayes, *Sources for the history of Irish civilisation: articles in periodicals* (9 vols, Boston, 1970) he wrote and edited twenty-one articles on subjects appertaining to the history of Dublin diocese. These include 'The union of the dioceses of Glendalough and Dublin', *JRSAI*, 60 (1930), pp 56-62; 'The diocese of Dublin in its beginnings', *IER*, 42 (1933), 43 (1934); 'Anglo-Norman Dublin and Diocese', *IER*, 45 (1935), pp 148-64, 274-91, 46 (1935), 47 (1936), 48 (1936), 49 (1937); 'Religious life in old Dublin' *Dublin Historical Record*, 2 (1939-40), pp 46-54; 'Royal visitation of Dublin, 1615' *Archivium Hibernicum*, 8 (1941), pp 1-55; 'Archbishop Bulkeley's visitation of Dublin, 1630', *Archivium Hibernicum*, 8 (1941), pp 56-98; 'Catholic schools of Old Dublin' *Dublin Historical Record*, 12 (1951), pp 65-82. There is a bibliography of Ronan's work in *Reportorium Novum*, 2, no. 2 (1959-60), pp 225-7.

interpretation and approach, the parts of his extensive corpus most frequently referred to today are the editions of documents he published in journals like *Archivium Hibernicum*, but much of his work remains worthy of consultation on all periods from the twelfth to the nineteenth centuries. This is notably true of his study of Father Henry Young which, as well as providing the necessary biographical details of Young's life and work, offers a valuable perspective on 'Catholic life in Dublin between 1749 and 1869', and is especially useful for the insights it offers into clerical activity at parish level and into the role of lay parochial societies in 'promoting spiritual and corporal works of mercy'.[22]

Ronan's range and versatility mark him out as arguably the premier historian of the diocese in the twentieth century. At the same time, his work on the medieval period was surpassed during his lifetime by that of Aubrey Gwynn, whose biographical studies of the early archbishops of Dublin, and accounts of the origins of the see of Dublin and other subjects are only now being revised by, among others, contributors to this volume.[23] Ronan's work on the eighteenth and nineteenth century has also been revised; but it was complemented during his lifetime by that of Roland Burke Savage, whose 'chronicle' of Teresa Mulally and George's Hill school, published in 1940, provided a revealing perspective on the educational and religious motivations of the female religious who emerged to play an important part in the Catholic Church in the diocese at that time.[24] With the exception of the annals of the Dominican Convent of St Mary's, published just before the First World War, a number of essentially hagiographical accounts of Mary Aikenhead and her role in the founding of the Irish Sisters of Charity, and Margaret Gibbons' life of Margaret Aylward, the founder of the Holy Faith sisters, published in 1928, this phenomenon has received less attention than it deserves.[25] In

22 Myles V. Ronan, *An apostle of Catholic Dublin: Father Henry Young* (Dublin 1944). 23 Aubrey Gwynn, 'Henry of London, archbishop of Dublin: a study in Anglo-Norman statecraft', *Studies*, 38 (1949), pp 295-306, 349-402; 'Bishop Samuel of Dublin', *IER*, 60 (1942), pp 81-8; 'The origins of the see of Dublin', *IER*, 57 (1941); 'The medieval university of St Patrick's, Dublin', *Studies*, 28 (1938), pp 199-212, 437-54; 'The origins of St Mary's abbey, Dublin', *JRSAI*, 79 (1949), pp 110-25. For other work on Dublin by Father Gwynn and for his updating of some of the opinions see A. Gwynn, *The Irish Church in the eleventh and twelfth centuries* ed. Gerard O'Brien (Dublin, 1992). 24 Roland Burke Savage, *A valiant Dublin woman: the story of George's Hill (1766-1940)* (Dublin, 1940). 25 *Annals of the Dominican Convent of St Mary's, Cabra, with some account of its origin 1647-1912* [Dublin, 1912]; Margaret Gibbons, *The life of Margaret Aylward, foundress of the Sisters of the Holy Faith* (London, 1928); S.A., *Mary Aikenhead, her life, her work and her friends* (Dublin, 1879); *Letters of Mary Aikenhead* (Dublin, 1914); *The life and work of Mary Aikenhead, foundress of the Congregation of Irish Sisters of Charity 1787-1858 by a member of the congregation* (Dublin, 1925).

common with Ronan's life of Father Young, Burke Savage's study of Mulally provides an extensive contextual account of the eighteenth and early nineteenth environment, though both authors are too ready, perhaps, to interpret their subject's lives and deeds in heroic terms. The same can be said also of Burke Savage's study of Catherine McAuley, the founder of the Sisters of Mercy, but, as with the works on Aikenhead and Aylward referred to above, this is compensated for by the inclusion of extensive extracts from primary sources.[26] Moreover, collectively, these studies offered real insight into the work and motivation of the female religious who contributed in an important way to the expansion of Catholic activity in the realms of education, health and the care of the marginalised in Dublin in the nineteenth century. This work was complemented by a number of publications celebrating the achievements of the Christian Brothers, in which their educational role in the Dublin diocese was appropriately chronicled and of Holy Cross College, the diocesan seminary, which celebrated its centenary in 1959.[27]

Meanwhile, the tradition of editing important texts had not atrophied, and the publication of the court book of the liberty of St Sepulchre in 1930, the register of the hospital of St John the Baptist in 1936, Archbishop Alen's register in 1950 and its companion, the annotated list of churches known as the *reportorium viride*, in 1941, the 'Dignitas Decani' of St Patrick's cathedral in 1957 and the sixteenth-century precedent book known as the Registrum Diocesis Dublinensis in 1959 were important additions to the already significant corpus of such publications.[28] In addition, Aubrey Gwynn prepared a valuable edition of Dublin provincial and diocesan decrees during the Anglo-Norman period and Myles Ronan a transcript of Archbishop John Troy's correspondence with Dublin Castle, both of which appeared in *Archivium Hibernicum*; while Newport White's edition of the extent of Irish monastic lands prior to their dissolution, published in 1943 by the Irish Manuscripts Commission, also illuminated a little known area.[29]

26 Roland Burke Savage, *Catherine McAuley: the first sister of Mercy* (Dublin, 1949); for Margaret Aylward and Mary Aikenhead see note 25.   **27** [M. McCarthy], *Edmund Ignatius Rice and the Christian Brothers* (Dublin, 1926); J.D. Fitzpatrick, *Edmund Rice: founder of the Christian Brothers* (Dublin, 1945); *Holy Cross College, Clonliffe Dublin: College history and centenary record* (Dublin, [1962]).   **28** H. Wood (ed.), *Court book of the liberty of St Sepulchre within the jurisdiction of the archbishop of Dublin 1586-90* (Dublin, 1930); E. St John Brooks (ed.), *Register of the Hospital of St John the Baptist, Dublin* (Dublin, 1936); Charles McNeill (ed.), *Calendar of Archbishop Alen's register c.1172-1534* (Dublin, 1950); Newport B. White (ed.), *Extent of Irish monastic possessions* (Dublin, 1943); idem, 'The *reportorium viride* of John Alen, archbishop of Dublin, 1533', *Analecta Hibernica*, 10 (1941), pp 173-217; idem, *The 'Dignitas Decani' of St Patrick's cathedral, Dublin* (Dublin, 1957); idem, *'Registrum Diocesis Dublinensis': a sixteenth century Dublin precedent book* (Dublin, 1959).   **29** Aubrey Gwynn, 'Provincial and diocesan decrees of Dublin during the Anglo-Norman period', *Archivium Hibernicum*, 11 (1944), pp 31-117; M.V. Ronan, 'Archbishop Troy's correspondence with

Most Catholic diocesan history (including most of that appertaining to the diocese of Dublin) written in Ireland in the first half of the twentieth century was authored by clergymen of the Catholic Church. There were a number of reasons for this. The most obvious was the readiness of clergymen with an interest in history, and Church history in particular, to undertake this work. The fact that few religious institutions or organisations possessed archives or archivists was also consequential, since clerical historians were more likely than outsiders to be in a position to examine the material that was accessible. One must also take cognisance of the underdeveloped state of the historical profession in Ireland at this time; the number of professional historians working in Ireland remained small until the 1960s, and those that were in tenured employment had, with few exceptions, a modest research track record. As a result, it is clear that if the Church did not sponsor and churchmen did not write or, at the very least, oversee the writing of diocesan history, it would largely be left unwritten.

The clerical background of so many of those who published on the history of the diocese inevitably coloured the history they chose to write. Ideally, the history of any Church must encompass the laity as well as the clergy, and popular as well as institutional expressions of religiosity. It is fair to say that while none of these dimensions has been entirely overlooked in the corpus of work appertaining to the diocese of Dublin produced in the first half of the twentieth century, the clergy and the institution were the primary focus. Given the prominent place of the institutional Church in contemporary Irish society, the high social standing of the hierarchy, and the fact that many of the most able and energetic diocesan and Church historians were themselves figures of eminence in the Church, this is only to be expected. It is, to be sure, difficult to establish definitively how important a factor this was, but it is hardly just a coincidence that of the eminent diocesan historians already cited in this chapter, Patrick Francis Moran became a cardinal, James MacNamee a bishop, Nicholas Donnelly an auxiliary bishop, and John Monahan, William Carrigan and John Begley all canons. At the same time, that fact that the diocesan history written by lay Catholics was similar in tone and approach cautions one against making a simple causal link between the occupations of individual historians and the primarily institutional and clerical history they wrote. All who engaged in the writing of Catholic diocesan history, be they laity or clergy, shared a common vision of the role and place of the Church. Moreover, as the content, to offer but one example, of the *Journal of the Ardagh and Clonmacnoise Antiquarian Society* highlights, Church-sponsored outlets did not exclude work that took a non-institutional focus.[30]

Dublin Castle', ibid., pp 1-30; Newport B. White (ed.), *Extent of Irish monastic possessions* (Dublin, 1943).   **30** The *Journal of the Ardagh and Clonmacnoise Antiquarian Society* was

These caveats entered, there is no evading the conclusion that *most* of the religious and diocesan history produced in Ireland between 1850 and 1950 was preoccupied with the institutional Church and its concerns rather than with broader issues of religiosity, and that the religious experience of the people was inadequately accommodated in the narratives that resulted. Applying the taxonomy defined by Patrick Collinson, most of the religious history written was 'traditional ... vertical ecclesiastical history' whose primary focus was 'the descent and continuity of the Church as a visible organisation through its professional personnel'. This is manifestly the case in respect of what is arguably the most famous work on Dublin, Donnelly's *Parishes*. But, as Ronan's work on Father Young also attests, the history produced in that era was not entirely unmindful of what Collinson terms 'horizontal' religious history whose primary foci are 'relations and interactions and the place and role of religion in society'.[31]

As this suggests, the distinction drawn by Collinson between 'vertical' and 'horizontal' religious history is not something that most practitioners of the craft of writing diocesan history in Ireland in the first half of the twentieth century would have recognised. Their priority, simply, was to expand their knowledge base, and they were provided with an excellent opportunity to do precisely this in 1955 with the establishment of 'a journal in which could be set down historical findings proper to the diocese' in order to expand 'the published narrative of ecclesiastical Dublin' which, the then archbishop John Charles McQuaid admitted, was 'meagre in quantity'.[32] *Reportorium Novum's* primary function, its editor averred, was to serve as a 'source-book reproducing, or summarising, or editing unpublished records or those not easily accessible'.[33] The expectation was that the surviving papers of successive archbishops from Archbishop John Carpenter (1770-86) onwards would figure prominently in its pages, but while Monsignor Michael Curran, one of the key figures behind the journal, prepared four substantial articles from Carpenter's papers none of his predecessors or successors ever featured prominently.[34] Documents from a variety of quarters appertaining to a range of aspects and eras in the diocese's history were carried in every issue. A

founded in 1926 and was published, at somewhat irregular intervals, until the 1950s. 31 Patrick Collinson, 'The vertical and the horizontal in religious history: internal and external integration of the subject' in Alan Ford, James McGuire and Kenneth Milne (eds), *As by law established: the Church of Ireland since the Reformation* (Dublin, 1995), pp 15-32. 32 'Foreword' to the first issue of *Reportorium Novum* (1955), p. ix. 33 Ibid., p. xi. 34 M.J. Curran, 'Archbishop Carpenter's epistolae (1770-86), parts 1 and 2, 'Correspondence of Abp. Carpenter with Bp. Sweetman of Ferns', 'Instructions, admonitions, etc of Archbishop Carpenter 1770-86', *Reportorium Novum*, 1, nos 1 and 2 (1955-6), pp 154-72, 381-98, 399-406, 2, no. 1 (1957-8), pp 148-71.

number of little known medieval texts from English and Irish archives,[35] and a collection of letters from Mateo De Oviedo, the Spaniard who became archbishop of Dublin in 1600, were printed,[36] but the majority of the documents published date from the seventeenth and eighteenth centuries. These included, inevitably, several lists of clergy as well as a number of manuscripts from the diocesan archives,[37] additional to those of Archbishop Carpenter already mentioned, that reinforced rather than altered existing understanding of the diocese's history.

This was true also of the substantial number of articles on diocesan history that were published by the journal. The editors were prepared to be venturesome, as John Kingston's work on 'Catholic families of the Pale', the republication of the first Catholic Directory, Caoimhín Ó Danachair's inventory of holy wells and several short notes amply demonstrate, but the overall tone and focus was familiar and predictable.[38] Thus the first and second articles published by the journal were, appropriately enough, by Aubrey Gwynn (on 'The first bishops of Dublin') and Myles Ronan (on the 'Deanery of Taney).[39] There were a number of essentially political studies and essays in biography and bibliography, and many studies of individual religious orders.[40] Most are well-researched and worthwhile, but few registered as much impact as Patrick Corish's study of Cardinal Cullen and the National

---

35 Geoffrey Hand (ed.), 'The Psalter of Christ Church, Dublin (Bodleian Ms Rawlinson G.185)', 'Cambridge University Additional Ms 710' and William Hawkes (ed.), 'Cashel Ms 2: a thirteenth century liturgical document in Dublin', *Reportorium Novum*, 1, no. 2 (1956), pp 311-22; 2, no. 1 (1957-8), pp 17-32; 3, no. 1 (1961-2), pp 83-93; M.P. Sheehy, 'The Registrum Novum: a manuscript of Holy Trinity cathedral' parts one and two, ibid., 3, no. 2 (1963-4), pp 249-81; 4, no. 1 (1971), pp 33-42; G. MacNiocaill, 'The charters of John, lord of Ireland to the see of Dublin', ibid., pp 282-306.   36 P.P. McBride, 'Some unpublished letters of Mateo de Oviedo, archbishop of Dublin', *Reportorium Novum*, 1, nos 1 and 2 (1955-56), pp 91-116, 351-68.   37 W.M. O'Riordan, 'A list of the priests, secular and regular, of the diocese of Dublin, 1697', 'A list of 17th century Dublin diocesan priests', 'On two documents in the *Liber Decanatus I* in the Dublin Diocesan Archives', *Reportorium Novum*, 1, no. 2 (1956), pp 369-80; 2, no. 1 (1957-8), pp 109-20; 2, no. 2 (1959-60), pp 257-68; 3, no. 1 (1961-2), pp 137-52.   38 John Kingston, 'Catholic families of the pale' parts 1 and 2, *Reportorium Novum*, 1, nos 1 and 2 (1955-6), pp 76-90, 323-50; C. Ó Danachair, 'The holy wells of County Dublin', 'The holy wells of County Dublin: a supplementary list', ibid., 2, nos 1 and 2 (1957-60), pp 68-87, 233-5; 'The Catholic Directory for 1821' ibid., 2, no. 2 (1959-60).   39 *Reportorium Novum*, 1, no. 1 (1955), pp 1-26; no. 2 (1956), pp 263-84.   40 John Ryan, 'The ancestry of St Laurence O'Toole', Canice Mooney, 'The library of Archbishop Piers Creagh', Thomas Wall, 'Archbishop John Carpenter and the Catholic revival, 1770-86', *Reportorium Novum*, 1, no. 1 (1955), pp 64-75, 117-39, 173-82; Aubrey Gwynn, 'Archbishop John Cumin', ibid., no. 2 (1956), pp 285-310; John Kingston, 'Lord Dunboyne', Thomas Wall, 'An eighteenth-century Dublin life of St Patrick', ibid., 3, no. 1 (1961-2), pp 62-82, 121-36.

Association of Ireland published in 1962. This is significant, not least because
it suggested that the future of historical research by then lay increasingly
with university-based professionals and this conclusion is reinforced by the
fact that only two further numbers of the journal appeared.[41] Nonetheless,
over seven issues *Reportorium Novum* provided an outlet where amateurs and
professionals alike could present the results of their researches into a wide
variety of aspects of the history of the diocese of Dublin. Many feature
prominently in the footnotes to several essays in this volume but by 1971,
when the last issue of the journal saw print, only the work of the latter was
expanding.

   The professionalisation of Irish history that gathered pace in the 1960s
and 1970s did not produce any major early dividend for the diocese of
Dublin. The most ambitious work published during this time was a short
history by Canice Mooney which appeared in the *Dictionnaire d'Histoire et
de Géographie Ecclésiastiques*, volume 14, in 1960. However, this was little
noticed at the time because of the general unavailability of the publication in
which it appeared. Like most entries in reference works of this kind,
Mooney's narrative suffers from compression; nonetheless it remains, as Hugh
Fenning observes, 'the basic and best history of the diocese' in print.[42]
Elsewhere, during this time a number of important articles were published
by Jocelyn Othway-Ruthven, Geoffrey Hand, Colmcille Ó Conbhuí, Francis
Finnegan, Nuala Burke, Hugh Fenning, H.E. Peel and Brian Mac Giolla
Phádraig on particular aspects of the history of the diocese from the medieval
era to the eighteenth century.[43] These apart, the most significant additions
to knowledge about the diocese were provided, *en passant*, in works whose
focus was national. In this category belong the ambitious but incomplete

---

41 P.J. Corish, 'Cardinal Cullen and the National Association of Ireland', *Reportorium
Novum*, 3, no. 1 (1961-2), pp 13-61.   42 Canice Mooney, 'Dublin', *Dictionnaire d'Histoire
et de Géographie Ecclésiastiques*, 14 (1960), cc 830-936; Fenning, below, p. 175, note 1.   43
A.J. Otway-Ruthven, 'The medieval Church lands of County Dublin' in J.A. Watt (ed.),
Medieval studies presented to Aubrey Gwynn (Dublin, 1961), pp 54-73; G. Hand, 'Rivalry
of the cathedral chapters in medieval Dublin', *JRSAI*, 92 (1962), pp 193-206; idem, 'The
medieval chapters of St Patrick's cathedral, Dublin', *Reportorium Novum*, 3, no. 2 (1964),
pp 229-48; Colmcille Ó Conbhuí, 'The lands of St Mary's abbey, Dublin', *Royal Irish
Academy proceedings*, 62C (1962); Francis Finnegan, 'The Jesuits in Dublin 1660-1760',
Reportorium Novum, 4, no. 1 (1971), pp 43-100; Nuala Burke, 'A hidden Church? the
structure of Catholic Dublin in the mid-eighteenth century', *Archivium Hibernicum*, 32
(1974), pp 88-91; H.E. Peel, 'The appointment of Dr Troy to the see of Dublin',
Reportorium Novum, 4, no. 1 (1971), pp 5-17; H. Fenning, 'Letters from a Jesuit in Dublin
on the confraternity of the Holy Name 1747-48', *Archivium Hibernicum*, 39 (1970), pp
133-54; Brian Mac Giolla Phádraig, 'Dr John Carpenter, archbishop of Dublin 1770-86',
Dublin Historical Record, 30 (1976-77), pp 2-17.

History of Irish Catholicism edited by Patrick Corish, John Watt's two studies *The Church and the two nations* and *The Church in medieval Ireland*, and E.R.R. Norman's account of the Church and radicalism in the mid-nineteenth century.[44] Important new information was also made available in printed calendars of archival material. Pride of place in this respect belongs deservedly to the Franciscan journal *Collectanea Hibernica*, which has served Catholic religious history well over forty years through its policy of publishing expansive calendars in English of Irish material in such collections in the Vatican Archives as *Nunziatura di Fiandra, Scritture riferite nei congressi, Irlanda, Scritture riferite originali nelle congregazioni generali* and *Fondo di Vienna*. In addition, calendars and texts have also been presented from other important collections in Roman, Irish and Franciscan archives that frequently illuminate the history of the diocese at different moments between the mid-seventeenth and the early twentieth centuries.[45] These calendars complement and are complemented by John Brady's valuable collection of extracts on Catholics and Catholicism from the eighteenth-century press, published initially in the journal *Archivium Hibernicum*, and as a separate stand-alone volume in 1966.[46]

One of the major obstacles in the way of research into the history of the diocese in the modern era was the inaccessibility of the archives of the diocese. The conditions in which the diocesan records were stored were much improved in 1957 with their transfer from Archbishop's House to a purpose-built strong room in an annex to Holy Cross College, but access remained restricted. Though some historians, notably Emmet Larkin, were permitted to examine certain papers, the fact that the bulk of the material was inadequately catalogued and that there was no fulltime archivist obviously acted as a severe limitation, which the publication of extracts from the papers of Archbishops Carpenter and Troy in *Reportorium Novum* only partly alleviated.[47] The decision of Archbishop Dermot Ryan to appoint Father Kevin Kennedy as diocesan archivist in 1972, and the embarkation by Mary Purcell in 1975 on the listing of the collection were developments of enormous consequence, therefore, since they opened up the prospect of the modern history of the diocese, to which the archive's holdings almost exclusively relate, being written.[48]

---

44 J.A. Watt, *The Church and the two nations* (Cambridge, 1970); *The Church in medieval Ireland* (Dublin, 1972, reissued 1998); E.R.R. Norman, *The Catholic Church and Ireland in the age of rebellion 1859-73* (London, 1965).   45 *Collectanea Hibernica*, 40 vols (1958-98) passim. The main editors of these series have been Cathaldus Giblin and Benignus Millett.   46 John Brady, *Catholics and Catholicism in the eighteenth-century press* (Maynooth, 1966).   47 For Emmet Larkin's experience see Emmet Larkin, 'Archival Odyssey, 1958-1995', *New Hibernia Review*, 1, no. 2 (1997).   48 The history of the development of

One cannot claim that the decision of successive archbishops from Dr McQuaid to the present to establish, fund and, over time, to develop a policy of access to the diocesan archives that is among the most accommodating in the state, has occasioned a dramatic increase in historical research into the diocese in the quarter century since it was inaugurated, but it has contributed in no small way to the general expansion and deepening of understanding of the role of the Catholic Church in Irish history. It is of course true that much of the best-known and best-received work that has been informed by research conducted in the diocesan archives has had a national rather than diocesan focus, but the publications of Dáire Keogh on the late eighteenth century, Donal Kerr, Emmet Larkin, Desmond Keenan, Ambrose Macaulay on the nineteenth and Dermot Keogh and Mary Harris on the twentieth, to mention some of the most eminent of the current generation of scholars who have trawled in the diocesan archives, have clarified the political role played by successive archbishops of Dublin.[49] In a number of cases, individual archbishops have attracted more specific attention, and if the focus in each instance has primarily been political, the interpretations offered in recent biographies of John Thomas Troy and Paul Cullen are informed by an awareness of their pastoral activity and impact.[50] Much remains to be done in respect of these dominant figures, and in respect of those who have attracted less attention. In the case of Daniel Murray, whose political activity in the 1840s has been luminously described by Donal Kerr,[51] the availability in print of a calendar of his own episcopal papers and those of his secretary and vicar-

the diocesan archives is told in M.J. Curran, 'Dublin Diocesan Archives', *Reportorium Novum*, 2, no. 1 (1957-8) and David Sheehy, 'Dublin Diocesan Archives – an introduction', *Archivium Hibernicum*, 42 (1987), pp 39-47. **49** Dáire Keogh, *'The French disease': the Catholic Church and radicalism in Ireland, 1790-1800* (Dublin, 1992); Desmond Keenan, *The Catholic Church in nineteenth century Ireland: a sociological study* (Dublin, 1983); Donal Kerr, *Peel, priests and politics: Sir Robert Peel's administration and the Roman Catholic Church in Ireland* (Oxford, 1982); idem, *'A nation of beggars'; priests, people and politics in famine Ireland, 1846-52* (Oxford, 1994); Ambrose Macaulay, *William Crolly, archbishop of Armagh, 1835-49* (Dublin, 1994); Emmet Larkin, *The Roman Catholic Church and the creation of the modern Irish state, 1878-1885* (Dublin, 1995); idem, *The Roman Catholic Church and the emergence of the modern Irish political system, 1870-74* (Dublin, 1996); Mary Harris, *The Catholic Church and the foundation of the Northern Irish state* (Cork, 1993); Dermot Keogh, *The Vatican, the bishops and Irish politics 1919-39* (Cambridge, 1986). **50** V.J. MacNally, *Reform, revolution and reaction: Archbishop John Thomas Troy and the Catholic Church in Ireland, 1787-1817* (Lanham, 1995); Desmond Bowen, *Paul, Cardinal Cullen and the shaping of modern Irish Catholicism* (Dublin, 1983). For Troy, see also D. Keogh, 'Archbishop John Thomas Troy (1739-1823)', *Archivium Hibernicum*, 49 (1995), pp 105-11; for Cullen, see also Peadar MacSuibhne, *Paul Cullen and his contemporaries* (5 vols, Naas, 1961-77). **51** Kerr, as in note 49.

general, Archdeacon John Hamilton, should facilitate the task which Dr Kerr commences below.[52]

Because the archives' holdings are so thin prior to John Carpenter's archbishopric, improved access to the diocese's manuscript holdings has had relatively little impact on the exploration of the earlier history of the diocese. Despite this, the revision of understanding of its history continues. The essays presented in this volume aspire to contribute to this. The opening essay by Howard Clarke on the history of Christianity in the region up to the emergence of the archdiocese opens up an era that is still largely *terra incognito*. Clarke's careful assessment of the surviving evidence is emblematic of the approach of the contributors to this volume. The object is to provide a documented perspective on the evolving history of the diocese that reflects the vigor of contemporary scholarship. Like all approaches to historical reconstruction, this is not hermaneutically unproblematic but the intention is to move on from the primarily confessional character of much of the history referred to above. This can be illustrated by the essays on the medieval diocese by Ailbhe MacShamhráin and Margaret Murphy, both of whom completed their graduate study at Trinity College, Dublin. MacShamhráin is the author of a monograph on the diocese of Glendalough whose unification with Dublin he describes below,[53] while Dr Murphy, analyses the anglicising policies pursued by successive archbishops following the Norman Conquest arising out the work she did on the archbishops and the administration of the diocese in the twelfth and thirteenth centuries for her Ph.D. As well as their chapters in this volume, they are also the authors of a number of densely documented articles that expand on and modify Gwynn on the early history of the metropolitan see.[54]

Parallel with the reassessment of the foundation and emergence of the diocese in the twelfth and thirteenth centuries that is underway, the contours of the diocese's historical landscape during the sixteenth and early seventeenth centuries are also being redrawn based upon an intensive analysis of the existing documentation. The essays of James Murray and Colm Lennon

---

52 Mary Purcell and David Sheehy, 'The Murray papers', 7 parts, *Archivium Hibernicum*, 36-42 (1981-7); 'The Hamilton papers', 6 parts, ibid., 43 (1988), 45-9 (1990-5). 53 Ailbhe S. MacShamhráin, *Church and polity in pre-Norman Ireland: the case of Glendalough* (Maynooth, 1996); idem, 'Uí Muiredaig and the abbacy of Glendalough, eleventh to thirteenth centuries', *Cambridge Medieval Celtic Studies*, 25 (1993), pp 55-75. 54 Margaret Murphy, 'The archbishops and administration of the diocese and province of Dublin, 1181-1298' (Ph.D., Trinity College, Dublin, 1987); idem, 'Balancing the concerns of Church and state: the archbishops of Dublin 1181-1228' in T.B. Barry, et al. (eds), *Colony and frontier in medieval Ireland* (London, 1995), pp 41-56; idem, 'Ecclesiastical censures: an aspect of their use in thirteenth century Dublin', *Archivium Hibernicum*, 44 (1989), pp 89-98.

in this volume proffer a fundamentally different interpretation to that offered by Ronan and others that the Reformation failed because the Irish people were ever committed and loyal Roman Catholics. The outcome, the evidence now suggests, was far less clear cut, and the combined effects of the explanation for the Reformation's failure in Dublin offered by Murray and the vigour of the Counter-Reformation described by Lennon indicate conclusively that human agency ever played an important part. Murray's essay in this volume is based on his major study of the Tudor diocese of Dublin, which is scheduled for publication in the near future. This promises to provide a definitive assessment of the impact upon the Church in the diocese of the Reformation.[55] Colm Lennon's historical *oeuvre* is already extensive, and among his primary foci have been Dublin and the Counter-Reformation. Since his early reconstruction of the world of Richard Stanihurst, Lennon has produced a substantial body of work on the persistence and adaptation of Catholic beliefs in the sixteenth and early seventeenth centuries that identifies how the Counter-Reformation in Dublin pursued its ideological and organisational goals to lay the groundwork for the attempts to establish a Tridentine Church in the diocese in the early seventeenth century.[56]

There is no equivalently detailed assessment of the evolving religious history of the diocese in the seventeenth century currently taking place, though Raymond Gillespie's pioneering analysis of the religion of the people provides a model which he himself applies to the smaller canvas of Dublin in this volume.[57] As Gillespie's work manifests, religious history can be written from a number of perspectives, and it is to be anticipated that his example will prompt others to apply his innovative methodology, *mutatis mutandis*, to earlier as well as to later eras. Meanwhile, there remains much about the history of the diocese of Dublin in the seventeenth century that remains ill-explored, and it is to be hoped that it will not be long before it is possible to connect the detailed reconstruction of Catholic religious life achieved by Lennon for the late sixteenth and early seventeenth centuries with that achieved by Patrick Fagan and Hugh Fenning for the early eighteenth.

---

55 James Murray, 'The Tudor diocese of Dublin: episcopal government, ecclesiastical politics and the enforcement of the Reformation *c.*1532-1590' (Ph.D., Trinity College, Dublin, 1997). See also, idem, 'The sources of clerical income: the Tudor diocese of Dublin ca 1530-1600', *Archivium Hibernicum*, 46 (1991-2), pp 139-60.   **56** Colm Lennon, 'Recusancy and the Dublin Stanihursts', *Archivium Hibernicum*, 33 (1975), pp 100-10; 'Civic life and religion in early seventeenth-century Dublin', ibid., 38 (1983), pp 14-26; 'The chantries in the Irish reformation: the case of St Anne's Guild Dublin 1550-1630' in R.V.Comerford et al. (eds), *Religion, conflict and coexistence* (Dublin, 1991); *The lords of Dublin in the age of Reformation* (Dublin, 1989); 'The survival of confraternities in post-Reformation Dublin', *Confraternitas*, 6 (1995), pp 5-12.   **57** Raymond Gillespie, *Devoted people: belief and religion in early modern Ireland* (Manchester, 1997).

Between them, Fagan and Fenning have written a number of studies of individual Dublin priests and bishops, explored the changing demographic and economic fortunes of Catholics in Dublin life, described definitively such critical features of religious life as the novitiate question and the experience of the Dominican order, and illuminated a myriad other issues.[58] As a result of their very distinctive, and different, endeavours we now possess a complex, variegated, and fuller understanding of the Church in Dublin during the so-called 'penal era'. Significantly, this does not accord with the oppressive scenario painted a century ago by Walsh and Donnelly or with that of intermittent and ineffectual repression favoured in some quarters more recently. In respect of these issues, the chapters below by Kelly, Fenning and Keogh provide further perspectives, while Michael McCarthy's assessment of the role of Archbishop Troy in the construction of the Pro-Cathedral serves to emphasise the contribution of that prelate as the Church grew in confidence in the more tolerant atmosphere of the early nineteenth century.

Compared with the 'penal era', the diocese in the nineteenth and twentieth centuries has been the subject of less focused analysis. Indeed, it might be observed that the religious and administrative history of the diocese during this period has taken second place to the political careers of successive archbishops though much important detail about the diocese is made available in political works, some of which are cited above,[59] and in institutional histories such as *The missionary College of All Hallows* by Kevin Condon.[60] Building upon this work, the essays in this volume by Donal Kerr, Ciaran O'Carroll and David Sheehy begin the process of establishing the pastoral contributions of Archbishops Murray, Cullen and Walsh while Seamus Enright complements this by exploring the impact of female religious as they emerged as a major force in the diocese.

There remains, as these comments suggest, much to be done to clarify diocesan development in the nineteenth century. This is true also of the twentieth century, but the completion in recent years by Maurice Hartigan, Eamon Dunne, Enda Delany and others of theses on aspects of lay and clerical Catholic activity suggests that this may not remain the case for very long.[61]

58 Patrick Fagan, *Dublin's turbulent priest: Cornelius Nary 1658-1738* (Dublin, 1991); *Catholics in a Protestant country: the papist constituency in eighteenth-century Dublin* (Dublin, 1998); 'Luke Fagan – eighteenth century prelate', *Ríocht na Midhe*, 8 (1992-3); Hugh Fenning, *The undoing of the friars of Ireland: a study of the novitiate question in the eighteenth century* (Louvain, 1972); *The Irish Dominican province 1698-1797* (Dublin, 1990); 'Ten documents relating to Irish diocesan affairs 1749-84', *Collectanea Hibernica*, 20 (1978); 'Some problems on the Irish mission 1733-74', *Collectanea Hibernica*, 8 (1965); 'Dublin imprints of Catholic interest 1701-1739', *Collectanea Hibernica*, 39 & 40 (1997-8), pp 106-54. 59 See note 49. 60 Kevin Condon, *The missionary college of All Hallows 1842-1891* (Dublin, 1986). 61 Maurice Hartigan, 'The Catholic laity of Dublin 1920-40' (Ph.D.,

The account provided of the John's Lane confraternities by Thomas Butler in his history of the Augustinians at John's Lane complements the exploration provided by Maurice Hartigan in this volume of the active religious life of the Catholic laity in the 1920s and 1930s.[62] The laity were content to accept the guidance of the clergy and episcopacy during this period. The dominant ecclesiastical figure in the diocese in the twentieth century was John Charles McQuaid, and the timely release of his papers means it is at last possible to embark upon the task of providing a balanced assessment of his personality and career. Deirdre MacMahon begins this with the last essay in the volume in which she surveys his impact upon the diocese.

It is clear from this sketch of the historiography of the diocese of Dublin and of the content of this volume that the history of the diocese remains incomplete though much has been achieved. The reassessment of the medieval history of the diocese that is currently taking place is encouraging, but both the early Church and the later medieval eras remain palpably under-explored. Indeed, it is not until one reaches the sixteenth century that the contours of the history of the diocese are reasonably delineated. Much remains that is unclear about the sixteenth, seventeenth and eighteenth centuries, but the broad picture is better defined than it is for the nineteenth and twentieth centuries.[63] The availability of the papers of successive archbishops and others active in the diocese in the modern era,[64] the identification of surviving institutional collections,[65] and an active generation of research students should enable much to be clarified in the next quarter century. However, there seems little prospect in the short term either of a series of monographs or of a work of the scope of the histories of the diocese of Cork published between 1972 and 1993 by Evelyn Bolster, of modern Killaloe by Ignatius Murphy in the early 1990s or of the ambitious and, as yet, incomplete study of modern Achonry under way by Liam Swords.[66] Given this context, the present

St Patrick's College, Maynooth, 1992); Eamon Dunne, 'Action and reaction: Catholic lay organisations in Dublin in the 1920s and 1930s', *Archivium Hibernicum*, 48 (1994), pp 107-18; Enda Delany, 'Father Denis Fahy C.S.Sp. and Maria Duce 1945-54' (M.A. thesis, St Patrick's College, Maynooth, 1993); Dermot Quigley, 'The Catholic Church and the labour movement: Dublin and Clydeside 1906-32' (M.A. thesis, University College Dublin, 1991); P. Murray, 'The political involvement of the Catholic clergy in Ireland 1922-1937' (Ph.D., Trinity College Dublin, 1997). **62** T.C. Butler, *History of John's Lane Augustinians in Dublin 1280-1980* (Dublin, 1983). **63** The most recent addition to the literature is Jacinta Prunty's study of Margaret Aylward, published by Four Courts Press in 1999. **64** For a short guide see Sheehy, 'The Dublin Diocesan Archives' cited above, note 48. **65** Many are listed in S. Helferty and R. Refaussé (eds), *Directory of Irish archives* (3rd ed., Dublin, 1999). **66** Evelyn Bolster, *A history of the diocese of Cork* (4 vols, Cork, 1972-93); Ignatius Murphy, *The diocese of Killaloe* (3 vols, Dublin, 1991-5); Liam Swords, *A hidden Church: the diocese of Achonry 1689-1818* (Dublin, 1997).

volume of essays seeks to provide the interested reader both with a perspective on those aspects of the history of the diocese of Dublin on which research is currently being conducted and on the current state of knowledge of the diocese's history. It is certainly appropriate to mark the history of a diocese that has existed for nearly a thousand years as the anniversary of the founder of the Church of which it is a part approaches its two thousanth year with some work of historical reflection.

Conversion, Church and cathedral: the diocese of Dublin to 1152*

Howard B. Clarke

Writing in the 1180s Jocelin of Furness, in his Life of St Patrick, has the national apostle of Ireland make a triumphal progress to Dublin as a matter of course.[1] The country's foremost saint and foremost 'city' (*civitas*) had of necessity to be brought into contact with one another. That St Patrick would have bypassed Dublin was unthinkable by the twelfth century. Like many a later commentator, Jocelin could not conceive of Dublin before the Vikings and so his Patrician city is peopled with pagan Norwegians. Its king is duly converted to Christianity and its grammatically feminine name in Latin is derived pseudo-historically from the same king's daughter, Dublinia. Jocelin of Furness was not the first twelfth-century writer to make such a connection.[2] A series of 51 quatrains which may be dated to *c.*1121 or a little later and which is preserved in the Book of Uí Maine names the

---

* This is a vast and under-researched topic. To take one example, there is an urgent need for a detailed study of the medieval estates of the (arch)bishops, including the division between prelates and monks as well as between the two cathedrals after *c.*1220. Because of close links with Dublin in the eleventh and twelfth centuries, suitable models would be the following: R.A.L. Smith, *Canterbury cathedral priory: a study in monastic administration* (Cambridge, 1943); F.R.H. Du Boulay, *The lordship of Canterbury: an essay on medieval society* (London, 1966); Christopher Dyer, *Lords and peasants in a changing society: the estates of the bishopric of Worcester, 680-1540* (Cambridge, 1980). In the circumstances this essay can merely scratch the surface, discussing certain points briefly, hinting at others, and ignoring yet others altogether. I wish to thank my colleague, Charles Doherty, for invaluable bibliographical guidance and my fellow-contributor, Ailbhe MacShamhráin, for comments and suggestions. 1 Thomas Messingham (ed.), *Florilegium insulae sanctorum; seu, vitae et acta sanctorum Hiberniae* (Paris, 1624), p. 33; E.L. Swift (trans.), *The life and acts of Saint Patrick, the archbishop, primate and apostle of Ireland ...* (Dublin, 1809), p. 84. 2 Contrary to Joseph Szöverffy, 'The Anglo-Norman Conquest of Ireland and St Patrick: Dublin and Armagh in Jocelin's Life of St Patrick', *Reportorium Novum*, 2, no. 1 (1957-8), p. 6.

king of the 'foreigners' of Dublin (Áth Cliath) as Ailpín mac Aiúl and has Patrick bring his son back to life.[3] In return for the king's acceptance of the new faith, along with an annual payment of tribute to Armagh, Patrick promises good government, prosperity and security.[4] A slightly earlier text, the Book of Rights, contains a shorter version of the same poem.[5] Still earlier again, the cult of the national apostle was presumably being fostered during the episcopacy of Dublin's second Hiberno-Norse bishop, Gilla Pátraic, the 'servant of Patrick' (1074-84). There was, apparently, a church dedicated to St Patrick by the time of the c.1121 recension; it stood on an island between two branches of the river Poddle and near the strategic intersection of two long-distance routeways.[6] From the outset, therefore, we are enmeshed in a tangle of fact and fiction, of the credible and the credulous, of pious faith and equally pious fantasy.

CONVERSION AND SYNTHESISATION

In recent years, after centuries of pious deference to myths and myth-making, hallowed by repetition down the generations, a new sense of historical realism has begun to enter our understanding of the conversion process in early medieval Ireland. The stark truth is that 'we have no evidence to show by what means and in what manner Ireland received Christianity, for this is an

---

3 *The Book of Uí Maine, otherwise called 'The Book of the O'Kellys'*, with introduction by R.A.S. Macalister (Dublin, 1942), 125 d 53 to 126 c 6, beginning 'Ata sund in seancas seang', here at 126 a 1-17. Dating limits of *c*.1121 x *c*.1129, that is to say, between the deaths of Bishop Samuel of Dublin and Archbishop Cellach of Armagh, are suggested in Donnchadh Ó Corráin, 'Ireland, Wales, Man, and the Hebrides' in Peter Sawyer (ed.), *The Oxford illustrated history of the Vikings* (Oxford and New York, 1997), p. 107. I am considerably indebted to Dr Colmán Etchingham for allowing me to make use of his working translation of this difficult text.   4 *Bk Uí Maine*, 126 a 32-7.   5 *Lebor na Cert: the Book of Rights*, ed. and trans. Myles Dillon (Ir. Texts Soc., vol. 46, Dublin, 1962), pp 114-19. For a new edition of this version see D.N. Dumville, *Saint Patrick, A.D. 493-1993* (Studies in Celtic History, vol. 13, Woodbridge, 1993), pp 260-2. If the Book of Rights dates from the effective overlordship of Dublin by Muirchertach Ua Briain (1094-1114), the gap separating the two recensions would have been quite short. Given his own dating for the Book of Rights, it is difficult to understand how Dillon concluded that the legendary conversion of a supposed king of Dublin could have been derived from Jocelin of Furness (*Lebor na Cert*, p. 117 n. 2). More probably Jocelin was articulating existing traditions in Ireland, as was John de Courcy himself in the context of Downpatrick.   6 *Bk Uí Maine*, 126 b 51; H.B. Clarke, 'The topographical development of early medieval Dublin' in H.B. Clarke (ed.), *Medieval Dublin, i, The making of a metropolis* (Dublin, 1990), pp 52-69, reprinted from *Journal of the Royal Society of Antiquaries of Ireland* (hereafter *JRSAI*), 107 (1977), pp 29-51, here at pp 56, 57, 61.

area in which the statements of hagiography must be discounted'.[7] We do
not know how dioceses were organised by Patrick or by anyone else and the
process of conversion may have been considerably more intermittent and protracted than is sometimes supposed.[8] St Patrick has been portrayed as 'a
slightly disreputable Romano-British bishop set in a sub-Roman and patris-
tic milieu' and the see of Armagh itself cannot be traced further back than
the year 640.[9] The canonical text known as The First Synod of Patrick, which
dates from the sixth century, reveals a country that is still only partially
Christianised and 'in which the cleric and his flock are in regular contact
with pagans and paganism'.[10] But when Tírechán was writing around the year
670, contact with the real Patrician world had been lost sight of and at the
same time the claims of Armagh were being promoted. Its southern counterpart and rival, Kildare, was equally ambitious if ultimately less successful.
The hagiography associated with St Brigid included schematic provincial cir-
cuits and a second journey focused on the dynasties known later as the
Southern Uí Néill that brought her into personal contact with St Patrick.[11]
Moreover the strongly synthetic character of so much hagiographical writing is compounded by that of the annals themselves down to the 730s.[12]
Neither for the first time nor for the last time, Ireland in the seventh cen-
tury was being invented.[13]

    The site of Dublin lay at the interface of the Patrician and non-Patrician
missions to Ireland.[14] In Patrick's own day the kingdom of Leinster had
extended northwards to the river Boyne, but by the early sixth to seventh
century Uí Néill expansion had pushed the boundary to the Liffey and its
tributary the Rye Water.[15] Since the aggression was coming from the north,
the victors are hardly likely to have stopped short permanently at the Tolka,
which was not only a much less definitive boundary marker than the Liffey,
but also too insignificant to serve as a satisfactory east-west frontier.[16] The

7 Richard Sharpe, 'St Patrick and the see of Armagh', *Cambridge Medieval Celtic Studies*,
4 (1982), p. 55.   8 Richard Sharpe, 'Some problems concerning the organisation of the
Church in early medieval Ireland', *Peritia*, 3 (1984), p. 241.   9 Sharpe, 'St Patrick and
the see of Armagh', pp 34-5.   10 Fergus Kelly, *A guide to early Irish law* (Early Irish Law
Series, vol. 3, Dublin, 1988), p. 40. Cf. 'The First Synod of St Patrick', re-edited in D.N.
Dumville, *Councils and synods of the Gaelic early and central middle ages* (Quiggin Pamphlets
on the Sources of Mediaeval Gaelic History, no. 3, Cambridge, 1997), pp 6-17, §§ 6, 11,
12, 14, 18, 22.   11 Kim McCone, 'Brigit in the seventh century: a saint with three lives?',
Peritia, 1 (1982), pp 122-3.   12 Liam de Paor, 'The aggrandisement of Armagh' in T.D.
Williams (ed.), *Historical Studies VIII* (Dublin, 1971), pp 106-7; F.J. Byrne, *Irish kings
and high-kings* (London, 1973), p. 146.   13 Echoing Declan Kiberd, *Inventing Ireland*
(London, 1995).   14 For a map illustrating this point see Seán Duffy (ed.), *Atlas of Irish
history* (Dublin, 1997), p. 17.   15 A.P. Smyth, *Celtic Leinster: towards an historical geography of early Irish civilisation A.D. 500-1600* (Dublin, 1982), pp 10, 45.   16 Contrary to

contraction of the overkingship left dynastic segments stranded on the wrong side, including those in the vicinity of the Tolka and lower Liffey valleys.[17] The raid on northern Leinster conducted in 770 by the Ciannachta looks like a classic border incident, the Uí Téig defenders massing on the south bank of the Liffey and some of the raiders meeting their nemesis in the rising water of the tidal river.[18] This was not only a political boundary but also to some degree a cultural one, hence the interesting observation that the Uí Néill territories of Brega and Mide had a strong souterrain-building tradition, in contrast to Leinster.[19] At the same time travellers and influences must have crossed the border in both directions; thus churchmen from Ulster visited Glendalough in the seventh century and the cult of St Kevin (Cóemgen) may have been diffused northwards along the 'Brega corridor'.[20] South of the Liffey lay a great swathe of territory occupied by five segments of the Uí Dúnlainge confederation, some of which would monopolise the provincial overkingship from the beginning of the eighth century.[21] Ecclesiastically and politically, the identity of early Dublin would have been moulded by these people and by the settlement's border location and central-place potential.

This potential was derived partly from Dublin's locational advantage in being situated in the 'eastern triangle' of Ireland – effectively the naturally strategic core of the whole island.[22] The site of Dublin stood at the eastern terminus of the Slige Mór, the east-west highway that not only crossed the middle of the country at its narrowest point, but also symbolically divided it into two roughly equal halves, Leth Conn and Leth Moga.[23] By c.700, and

Geraldine Stout and Matthew Stout, 'Patterns in the past: County Dublin 5000 B.C.-1000 A.D.' in F.H.A. Aalen and Kevin Whelan (eds), *Dublin city and county: from prehistory to present* ... (Dublin, 1992), p. 15. Indications that the Tolka constituted the northern boundary of Leinster may relate to the Viking period after the initial settlement of 841. The early medieval period in Ireland was far from being static.   17 A.S. MacShamhráin, *Church and polity in pre-Norman Ireland: the case of Glendalough* (Maynooth Monographs, vol. 7, Maynooth, 1996), p. 207.   18 *The Annals of Ulster (to A.D. 1131)*, part 1, *Text and translation*, ed. Seán Mac Airt and Gearóid Mac Niocaill (Dublin, 1983), pp 224-5. For the basic chronology of events this chapter depends on the Annals of Ulster (henceforth *AU*); other annals are cited only for additional or alternative details. In the year 770 the head of the Uí Téig lineage was Tuathal, ruler of Uí Máil (726-78), the dynasty that was gradually superseded by Uí Dúnlainge in the course of the eighth century (MacShamhráin, *Church and polity*, pp 70-3).   19 Mark Clinton, 'The souterrains of County Dublin' in Conleth Manning (ed.), *Dublin and beyond the Pale: studies in honour of Patrick Healy* (Bray, 1998), p. 117. Lucan may have been an Uí Néill outlier south of the border (ibid., p. 125).   20 MacShamhráin, *Church and polity*, p. 69.   21 Smyth, *Celtic Leinster*, pp 123 (genealogical table), 148 (map).   22 J.H. Andrews, 'A geographer's view of Irish history' in T.W. Moody and F.X. Martin (eds), *The course of Irish history* (2nd ed., Cork and Dublin, 1984), p. 20 (map).   23 The remains of a bridge across the river Shannon at Clonmacnoise have been dated dendrochronologically to the year 804 (Fionnbarr Moore, 'Ireland's oldest

Fig. 1: 'The enthronement of St Romold as bishop of Dublin' by the Master of the Youth of St Romold (courtesy of the National Gallery of Ireland).

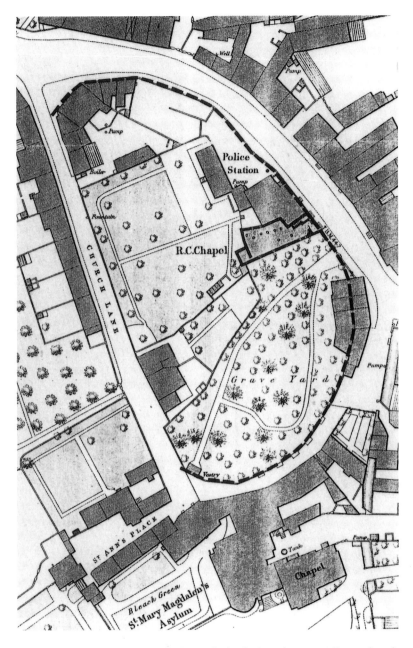

Fig. 2: Part of the outline of the ecclesiastical enclosure at Donnybrook
superimposed on the Ordnance Survey map (1865 revision), scale 1:1056 (by
permission of the Government of Ireland, permit no. MP001899). North is at
the top. Church Lane is now called Crescent Lane.

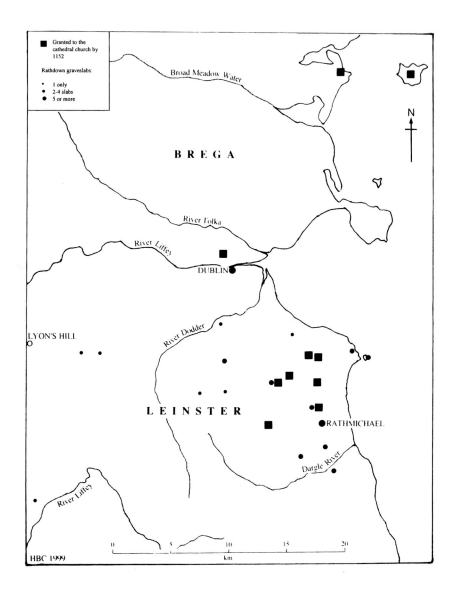

Fig. 3: Map showing the distribution of early land grants to Christ Church
Cathedral and of Rathdown graveslabs.

Fig. 4: 'The round tower of the church of St Michael le Pole', by an unknown artist, 1751 (courtesy of the National Library of Ireland).

Fig. 5: 'The round tower of the church of St Michael le Pole', by Gabriel
Beranger, 1766 (courtesy of the National Library of Ireland).

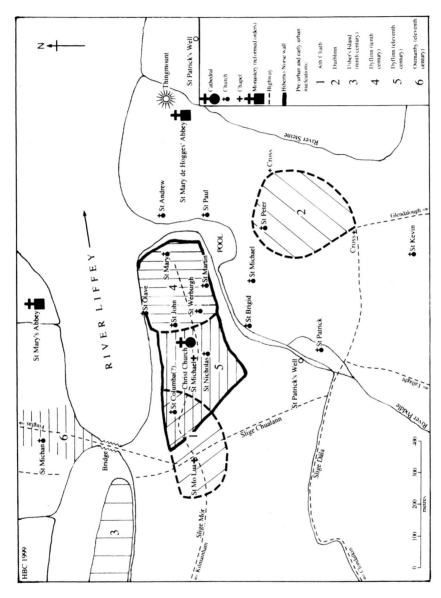

Fig. 6: Map showing the churches of Dublin c.1152 in relation to pre-urban and early urban nucleations.

probably much earlier, a number of long-distance routeways had been established in Ireland, as everywhere else in Europe. This we can deduce from the survival of a tract describing a hierarchy of roads ranging from highway (*slige*) to cow-track (*bóthar*).[24] The geographical logic of the pattern of highways was clearly to enable the inhabitants of Ireland to travel to the neighbouring island of Britain. This is exemplified in the story of Conall Corc from Munster to Dublin (Áth Cliath), where he saw ships about to sail.[25] Dublin was the focal point of four highways and it comes as no surprise that the Triads, for all their artificiality, include the ford across the Liffey at Áth Cliath as one of the most notable.[26] Such a strategic site must have been a focus of communication and exchange, most of it undocumented. Thus the main concentration of authentic Roman finds in Ireland has come from the coastal district between the Boyne and the Liffey, as well as from the valley of the former river.[27] Early medieval trading settlements were often located at river crossings and on small offshore islands, but many have been obscured by subsequent urban development.[28] In addition to material goods, beliefs and practices would have been communicated and exchanged.[29]

EARLY CHURCHES AND BISHOPS

The first Christian missions in Ireland came from Gaul and operated mainly in Leinster as it then was. Missionary churches were established in proxim-

bridge – at Clonmacnoise', *Archaeology Ireland*, 10, no. 4 (1996), p. 26). **24** Fergus Kelly, *Early Irish farming* (Early Irish Law Series, vol. 4, Dublin, 1997), pp 537-8. **25** Vernon Hull, 'The Exile of Conall Corc', *Publications of the Modern Language Association of America*, 56 (1941), pp 940, 942 and n. 13. The Cycle of Crimthann dates from the eighth or ninth century: see Myles Dillon, *The cycles of the kings* (Dublin, 1946), p. 35. **26** *The Triads of Ireland*, ed. and trans. Kuno Meyer (Dublin, 1906), pp 6-7; Clarke, 'Topographical development', pp 57-8. The idea of Tara as the epicentre of five highways is part of the synthetic tradition associated with five provinces. Tara had effectively, though not finally, been abandoned by the sixth century (Bernard Wailes, 'The Irish "royal sites" in history and archaeology', *Cambridge Medieval Celtic Studies*, 3 (1982), p. 5). Cf. Conor Newman, *Tara: an archaeological survey* (Discovery Programme Monographs, vol. 2, Dublin, 1997), pp 230, 235, 242. **27** J.D. Bateson, 'Roman material from Ireland: a reconsideration', *Proceedings of the Royal Irish Academy* (henceforth *PRIA*), 73C (1973), p. 31. **28** David Griffiths, 'The coastal trading ports of the Irish Sea' in James Graham-Campbell (ed.), *Viking treasure from the north west: the Cuerdale hoard in its context* (National Museums and Galleries on Merseyside Occasional Papers, Liverpool Museum, no. 5, Liverpool, 1992), pp 63-72; H.B. Clarke, 'Proto-towns and towns in Ireland and Britain in the ninth and tenth centuries' in H.B. Clarke, Máire Ní Mhaonaigh and Raghnall Ó Floinn (eds), *Ireland and Scandinavia in the early Viking age* (Dublin, 1998), pp 342-3. **29** An apt illustration is provided by the pre-Viking house with Anglo-Saxon parallels discovered at Copper Alley (Linzi Simpson, *Director's findings: Temple Bar West* (Temple Bar Archaeological Reports, no. 5, Dublin,

ity to power centres: examples are Dunshaughlin (Tara), Kilashee (Naas) and Kilcullen (Dún Ailinne).[30] Royal patronage probably played a major part in the foundation and endowment of churches, even though these processes cannot now be traced in detail. By the eighth century there appears to have been a balanced distribution of churches throughout the country, each *túath* possessing at least one principal church and a number of lesser ones.[31] Churches offered sacramental and intercessory services for the people – baptism, communion and burial rites – and laymen were insistent on the provision of proper pastoral care.[32] Confession may have been comparatively rare and 'confined in practice to those electing to reform their way of life and submit to a regular regime of continence in matrimony under a confessor's direction'.[33] Early texts such as *Córus Bésgnai* and *Bretha nemed toísech* refer to the functions of churches and to the failure to fulfil them.[34] Against this broad background, we may reasonably assume that the inhabitants of the aboriginal settlement at Dublin – Áth Cliath – came to participate in the Christian way of life. Reputedly the oldest church site in the city centre is St Audoen's (Church of Ireland) and its location in Cornmarket, at the hub of a whole network of roads, laneways and property boundaries, would support this belief despite the lack of archaeological confirmation.[35] The dedication to St Ouen (latinised as Audoenus), who died in 684, is probably of much later date, while the hypothesis attributed to Aubrey Gwynn that this church was previously dedicated to St Colum Cille (Columba) has been dismissed.[36] Nevertheless there does appear to have been such a church in

---

1999), pp 9-11, figs 4, 7 and plate II).   **30** Charles Doherty, 'The basilica in early Ireland', *Peritia*, 3 (1984), pp 303, 308, 309; Duffy (ed.), *Atlas of Irish history*, p. 17 (map).   **31** Thomas Charles-Edwards, 'The pastoral role of the Church in the early Irish laws' in John Blair and Richard Sharpe (eds), *Pastoral care before the parish* (Leicester, 1992), pp 64-5.   **32** Ibid., pp 69, 76. These functions need to be considered in relation to the form and size of early churches, which were probably bigger and more complex than the small oratories that have been investigated in western parts of Ireland. For seminal ideas see especially P.F. Wallace, 'Irish early Christian "wooden" oratories – a suggestion', *North Munster Antiquarian Journal*, 24 (1982), pp 19-28; Niall Brady, 'De oratorio: Hisperica famina and church building', *Peritia*, 11 (1997), pp 327-35.   **33** Colmán Etchingham, 'The early Irish Church: some observations on pastoral care and dues', *Ériu*, 42 (1991), p. 101.   **34** Ibid., pp 102-4.   **35** Clarke, 'Topographical development', pp 58-9; H.B. Clarke, *Dublin c.840 to c.1540: the medieval town in the modern city* (Dublin, 1978), where medieval sites are shown on a modern (1939) base-map. The 'old foss' opposite the churchyard of St John the Baptist's hospital cited in a document of *c.*1263 may have been a remnant of the boundary demarcating Áth Cliath ('Calendar to Christ Church deeds' in *Report of the Deputy Keeper of the Public Records Ireland*, 20-4 (Dublin, 1888-93), no. 511).   **36** G.A. Little, *Dublin before the Vikings: an adventure in discovery* (Dublin, 1957), pp 116-17 and n. 49; John Bradley, 'The topographical development of Scandinavian Dublin' in Aalen and Whelan (eds), *Dublin city and county*, p. 49.

*c.*1178; its Anglo-Norman priest, Richard, witnessed an important document along with many other priests in the town.[37] A second church at Áth Cliath cannot readily be explained except in terms of a wayside chapel dedicated to one of several saints called Mo Lua.[38] Its long-term survival illustrates the principle that 'the existence or tradition of a church on a particular site was a powerful factor in the decision to build again on the same site and to reinstate or to continue the tradition, in some cases over hundreds of years'.[39]

An early Christian presence in Dublin is indicated with far greater precision at a different nucleation called Duiblinn (normalised as Dubhlinn). The main evidence takes the form of the unmistakable outline of an ecclesiastical enclosure preserved in a curving pattern of streets and a former property boundary.[40] The dimensions of this enclosure place it well within Leo Swan's biggest size category of over 140m., which may be interpreted as a measure of its comparative importance.[41] Such enclosures are commonly associated with monastic sites, though not exclusively so. The monastic aspect of Duiblinn is confirmed by annalistic references to two abbots, Beraid who died in 650 and Siadal who died in 790.[42] The physical presence of this monastery may be hinted at in a ditch with an internal bank running roughly parallel to the curving line of Stephen Street Lower, although no finds predating the twelfth century were discovered.[43] Where such enclosures still sur-

---

37 'Cal. Christ Church deeds', no. 364; H.J. Lawlor, 'A calendar of the *Liber Niger* and *Liber Albus* of Christ Church, Dublin', *PRIA*, 27C (1907-9), p. 24, no. 42: *Ricardo presbitero de sancto Columba.* Among the other priests present were those of St Brigid's, St Mary's, St Patrick's, St Michael's, St Michan's and St Martin's. The citation of all these churches is consistent with other evidence.   38 J.T. Gilbert and R.M. Gilbert (eds), *Calendar of ancient records of Dublin in the possession of the municipal corporation* (19 vols, Dublin, 1889-1944), iii, 55-6; Clarke, 'Topographical development', p. 59. One of several possibilities is Mo Lua of Clonfertmulloe, County Laois, who had links with St Davids in Wales (Smyth, *Celtic Leinster*, pp 9, 72, 73 and fig. 37). His cult was being observed at Tallaght at the time of the ascetic revival *c.*800 (*Félire Óengusso céli Dé: the Martyrology of Oengus the Culdee* ..., ed. and trans. Whitley Stokes (Henry Bradshaw Society, vol. 29, London, 1905; reprinted Dublin, 1984), pp 56-7).   39 Máirín Ní Mharcaigh, 'The medieval parish churches of south-west County Dublin' in *PRIA*, 97C (1997), p. 248. Another research *desideratum* is for the entire diocese to be surveyed along the lines of this excellent model.   40 Clarke, 'Topographical development', pp 61-3 and fig. 6 (misaligned in relation to the caption).   41 Leo Swan, 'Enclosed ecclesiastical sites and their relevance to settlement patterns of the first millennium A.D.' in Terence Reeves-Smyth and Fred Hamond (eds), *Landscape archaeology in Ireland* (British Archaeological Reports, British Series, vol. 116, Oxford, 1983), p. 274 and fig. 4. The dimensions of the enclosure at Duiblinn are approximately 335m. north-south and 260m. east-west.   42 *AU*, pp 246-7; *Annála ríoghachta Éireann: Annals of the kingdom of Ireland by the Four Masters, from the earliest period to the year 1616*, ed. and trans. John O'Donovan (7 vols, Dublin, 1851) (henceforth *AFM*), i, 264-5, 392-3.   43 Peter Harbison, 'A shaft-fragment from Slane, County

vive in the Irish countryside (the great majority), their physical aspect is usually represented by hedges, banks and ditches. Some enclosures incorporate townland or other boundaries in their outline and the Duiblinn example was apparently durable enough to delineate the medieval parish of St Peter.[44] The off-centre position of this church is similar to that of the main church at Duleek, for example.[45] Centuries later this early Christian site would form part of an extensive ecclesiastical suburb on the south side of the medieval city.[46] Two stone crosses on or near the boundary and a market-place towards the south, pointing in the direction of the Slige Dála, could conceivably have been relics of the former monastery of Duiblinn.[47]

In early medieval Ireland monasteries served as royal chapels; the important ones were to be found near power centres such as Knowth, Lagore and Naas.[48] Many monasteries, far from being isolated from the world, were located on overland routeways, fording-places across rivers, and political boundaries. They also ministered to local communities.[49] One such community was headed by Uí Fergusa, a minor branch of the great Uí Dúnlainge dynasty. Their territory in the eighth century has been pinpointed as the district lying between the Liffey and the Camac to the north and north-west, and the Dodder to the south and south-east.[50] We do not know where their secular power base was situated but, if this historical reconstruction is correct, it is reasonable to suppose that the monastery of Duiblinn was under Uí Fergusa patronage.

Now at least one major church in every *túath* would have been associated with a bishop. Bishoprics may well have been founded initially in the sixth century: when referring to churches one of the *Liber Angeli*'s three categories is a 'city' of episcopal rank (*civitas ab episcopali gradu*).[51] The late Liam de Paor suggested that outbreaks of plague from *c.*540 onwards undermined these initial foundations and that there was a revival around the turn of the sixth century.[52] This may be the historical context for much later and highly

Meath, and other recent high cross discoveries' in Manning (ed.), *Dublin and beyond the Pale*, p. 175 (note by Alan Hayden).   **44** Nicholas Donnelly, *History of Dublin parishes* (3 vols, Dublin, [*c.*1905-12]), ii, 134.   **45** John Bradley, 'St Patrick's church, Duleek', *Ríocht na Midhe*, 7, no. 1 (1980-1), p. 40. The enclosure at Duleek was somewhat larger.   **46** H.B. Clarke, '*Urbs et suburbium*: beyond the walls of medieval Dublin' in Manning (ed.), *Dublin and beyond the Pale*, pp 51-4 and fig. 5.   **47** Ibid., p. 52, with references. Admittedly this is mere conjecture. One of the assembly places along the course of the Slige Dála ('highway of the assemblies') may have been the most important in Leinster, the Óenach Carman, on which see Smyth, *Celtic Leinster*, pp 34-5.   **48** Smyth, *Celtic Leinster*, pp 27-8.   **49** Ibid., p. 29.   **50** Ibid., p. 148, plate VIII; cf. plate XI.   **51** Ludwig Bieler (ed. and trans.), *The Patrician texts in the Book of Armagh* (Scriptores Latini Hiberniae, vol. 10, Dublin, 1979), pp 188-9; Colmán Etchingham, 'The implications of *paruchia*', *Ériu*, 44 (1993), p. 149.   **52** De Paor, 'Aggrandisement of Armagh', p. 99.

dubious traditions featuring bishops of Duiblinn.[53] The first of these is recorded in a latinised form as Livin(i)us, who is reputed to have died in the year 633.[54] A later bishop, Rumoldus, is also cited in the seventeenth-century Martyrology of Donegal.[55] In the case of St Rumold, continental hagiographical tradition forged a link with St Romold of Malines (Mechelen) and a painting of his enthronement as bishop of Dublin was executed by an unknown Brabantine artist towards the end of the fifteenth century.[56] Finally, Abbot Siadal of the late eighth century is also listed as a bishop in the martyrologies.[57]

Siadal's dual identity reminds us that the head church of a *túath* might be both episcopal and monastic at one and the same time; too sharp a distinction should not be drawn.[58] An eighth-century text, *Ríagal Phátraic*, implies that every *túath* had at least one bishop, whose tasks are prescribed as ordaining and supervising priests, consecrating churches, acting as a personal confessor, baptising and confirming adherents to the faith, and associated duties.[59] Accordingly the episcopal *paruchia* of the canonists amounted

---

53 A list of early bishops of Dublin was produced by John Colgan in the seventeenth century and it was followed by some later writers: for example, John D'Alton, *The memoirs of the archbishops of Dublin* (Dublin, 1838), pp 16-26; Henry Cotton, *Fasti ecclesiae hibernicae* ... (5 vols, Dublin, 1845-60), v, 7-8. Although his treatment of this material is completely unsatisfactory, Little's instincts may well prove to have been correct in this instance (*Dublin before the Vikings*, pp 96-102). A thorough investigation of these medieval and early modern traditions is another *desideratum* that lies beyond the scope of this essay.   54 John Colgan, *Triadis thaumaturgae, seu ... Hiberniae sanctorum insulae communium patronorum acta* (Louvain, 1647), p. 112, citing Flemish sources. For trenchant criticism of 'this fable' see John Lanigan, *An ecclesiastical history of Ireland* ... (4 vols, Dublin, 1822), ii, 470-1 n. 119.   55 *The Martyrology of Donegal: a calendar of the saints of Ireland*, ed. and trans. John O'Donovan, J.H. Todd and William Reeves (Dublin, 1864), pp 184-5. This work was compiled by Michael O'Clery and his associates and was completed in 1630 (ibid., pp xi, xxi). Cf. Colgan, *Triadis thaumaturgae*, pp 111-12. Again for cogent criticism see Lanigan, *Ecclesiastical history*, iii, 197-8 and nn 169-71.   56 Christiaan Vogelaar, *Netherlandish fifteenth and sixteenth century paintings in the National Gallery of Ireland* (Dublin, 1987), pp 53-9 and figs 52, 54-6. I am grateful to my colleague, Eileen Kane, for informing me of the existence of this painting, which is one of an extensive series. Continental hagiography took Romold from Ireland to Rome and then northwards to the Low Countries, where he became the first bishop of Malines, only to be murdered there in 775. For the hagiography of St Romold see Joseph Laenen, *Histoire de l'église métropolitaine de Saint-Rombaut à Malines* (2 vols, Malines, 1919-20), to which I have not had access.   57 *The Martyrology of Tallaght* ..., ed. and trans. R.I. Best and H.J. Lawlor (Henry Bradshaw Society, vol. 68, London, 1931), p. 16, at 12 February; *Martyrology of Donegal*, pp 46-7; *The Martyrology of Gorman*, ed. and trans. Whitley Stokes (Henry Bradshaw Society, vol. 9, Dublin, 1895), pp 34-5.   58 Charles-Edwards, 'Pastoral role', p. 67, where the remark that 'it would be unsurprising ... for the bishop to be head of the Church, *princeps*, and also in relation to the monks, *abbas*' might well apply to Siadal.   59 For text and translation see J.G.

in principle to a fairly compact territory over which its bishop exercised jurisdiction.[60] This is why boundary disputes were envisaged: one community's
diocese was surrounded by others.[61] It is worth reiterating the point that all
of the early references to, and later traditions about, abbots and bishops in
the immediate vicinity of Dublin relate essentially to Duiblinn rather than
to Áth Cliath.[62] Hypothetically at least, this was the chief church of Uí
Fergusa, who controlled the southern approach to the nearby ford. Who,
therefore, were their neighbours? To the south-east a diocesan centre probably existed at Tully, for which an early name Tulach na nEpscop, 'hill of
the bishops' is recorded.[63] Tully lay in the territory of Uí Briúin Chualann,
which corresponded roughly to the two half-baronies of Rathdown, and not
far from an Iron Age hillfort that may have continued in use as a power
centre.[64] To the south-west the Uí Dúnchada power centre was positioned
prominently on another elevated site at Liamain (Lyon's Hill), east of which
there was an important church at Newcastle Lyons.[65] A short distance to the
north of the river Tolka, at the 'monastic' site of Finglas, the text known as
The Monastery of Tallaght refers to a bishop of the Déisi called Caínchomrac.[66] With further study it ought to be possible to clarify the pattern
of major ecclesiastical and secular sites in their sometimes changing political
contexts during the seventh and eighth centuries.

For the moment we must content ourselves with the tentative proposition that the early medieval or pre-Viking diocese of Dublin extended broadly

O'Keeffe, 'The Rule of Patrick', *Ériu*, 1 (1904), pp 218-24. See also Etchingham, 'Early
Irish Church', pp 105-6 and for an extended discussion of this important source see
Sharpe, 'Organisation of the Church', pp 252-9.   **60** Etchingham, 'Implications of
paruchia', pp 141, 147, 162.   **61** Ibid., pp 141-3, with references to *Collectio canonum
hibernensis*.   **62** Cf. Clarke, 'Topographical development', p. 63.   **63** Liam Price, 'The
antiquities and place-names of south County Dublin', *Dublin Historical Record*, 2 (1939-
40), p. 129; Elizabeth O'Brien, 'Churches of south-east County Dublin, seventh to twelfth
century' in Gearóid Mac Niocaill and P.F. Wallace (eds), *Keimelia: studies in medieval
archaeology and history in memory of Tom Delaney* (Galway, 1988), p. 519.   **64** At
Rathmichael there is a ringfort (rath) and souterrain within an earlier hillfort (Stout and
Stout, 'Patterns in the past', pp 11, 15). The barony name Rathdown was presumably
derived from a site of this nature and quite possibly from this particular one.   **65** Leo
Swan, 'Newcastle Lyons – the prehistoric and early Christian periods' in Peter O'Sullivan
(ed.), *Newcastle Lyons – a parish of the Pale* (Dublin, 1986), pp 1-10; Ní Mharcaigh,
'Medieval parish churches', pp 272-4.   **66** E.J. Gwynn and W.J. Purton, 'The Monastery
of Tallaght', *PRIA*, 29C (1911-12), p. 130, § 7; Charles-Edwards, 'Pastoral role', p. 69 n.
37. For a description of this site see Leo Swan, 'Monastic proto-towns in early medieval
Ireland: the evidence of aerial photography, plan analysis and survey' in H.B. Clarke and
Anngret Simms (eds), *The comparative history of urban origins in non-Roman Europe* ... (2
parts, British Archaeological Reports, International Series, vol. 255, Oxford, 1985), i, 91
and figs 4.11, 4.16.

speaking from the Liffey-Camac to the Dodder. Within this territory there were other high-ranking churches, though none with episcopal associations. One was at Kilmainham, founded by the eponymous Maigníu in the late sixth or early seventh century on the narrow ridge that then separated the Camac from the Liffey.[67] A contemporary of Abbot Siadal of Duiblinn, the learned Lergus, died there in 787.[68] Further up the Camac, not far from the course of the Slige Dála and perhaps near or even beyond the western limit of Uí Fergusa territory, stood Clondalkin, a seventh-century foundation dedicated to St Mo Chua (Crónán).[69] His relics, together with those of St Kevin of Glendalough, were taken on circuit together in the year 790 – a sign of Uí Dúnlainge control over both houses.[70] In the opposite direction, near the left bank of the river Dodder, lay Donnybrook, whose barely recognised enclosure is still partially traceable. To judge from the place-name, this was a *domnach* site and therefore an early one.[71] Across the river a cemetery containing approximately 600 burials was discovered in the late nineteenth century.[72] Outside the petty kingdom of Uí Fergusa, there is a particularly impressive number of major church sites and associated monuments south of the Liffey.[73] The territory dominated by the Síl nÁedo Sláine lineage to the north was apparently less well endowed, but there were important foundations at Finglas, Glasnevin, Kilmartin, Lusk and Swords, all of which conserve traces of an ecclesiastical enclosure.

The learning of Lergus, the display of holy relics, and the sheer number of ecclesiastical establishments may be interpreted as signs of a flourishing Christian faith, yet there was also dissatisfaction and a critical spirit abroad during the last decades of the eighth century. At that time, as is well known, a 'reform movement' or 'religious revival' emerged whose followers called themselves *céli Dé* (Culdees).[74] Its main objective was to reinvigorate small

---

67 Colum Kenny, *Kilmainham: the history of a settlement older than Dublin ...* (Dublin, 1995), pp 10-17. A bell from Kilmainham is preserved in the National Museum of Ireland. 68 *AU*, pp 242-3.   69 Clondalkin's position relative to the political boundary between Uí Dúnchada and Uí Fergusa cannot easily be determined. The monastic site, whose outer enclosure is still well preserved in the street pattern, was on the right bank of the river. For early views and a recent survey see Ní Mharcaigh, 'Medieval parish churches', pp 264-5 and plates V, VI.   70 MacShamhráin, *Church and polity*, pp 173-4. At that time the provincial overking was Bran Ardchenn, of Uí Muiredaig. Clondalkin had strong links with Glendalough (ibid., p. 125).   71 Donnybrook (Domnach Brocc) is mentioned in the Martyrology of Tallaght at 30 September (*Martyrology of Tallaght*, p. 75).   72 William Frazer, 'Description of a great sepulchral mound at Aylesbury Road, near Donnybrook, in the county of Dublin ...', *PRIA*, 16 (1879-88), pp 29-55. On this site see now Elizabeth O'Brien, 'A re-assessment of the "great sepulchral mound" containing a Viking burial at Donnybrook, Dublin', *Medieval Archaeology*, 36 (1992), pp 170-3.   73 Stout and Stout, 'Patterns in the past', pp 14 (map), 33-7 (referenced list).   74 On the question of reform

monastic communities and to emphasise devotional life.[75] A striking fact about this movement is that it took root initially in the hinterland of Dublin, at Tallaght and at Finglas, in the general area of the lower Liffey valley. The site at Tallaght was probably granted to Máel Ruain by the provincial over-king, Cellach mac Dúnchada (760-76).[76] From the vantage-point of Liamain, Tallaght lay towards the south-eastern margins of Uí Dúnchada territory. The royal gift included 25 ringforts, whose dues and produce were presumably intended to assist the new ascetic community in its devotional life.[77] Finglas seems to have retained its episcopal status, for Bishop Caínchomrac died there in 791, the year before Máel Ruain himself.[78] The effect, if any, of this ascetic movement on the neighbouring Uí Fergusa diocese focused on Duiblinn cannot now be detected, but in general terms it appears to have been strongest in the southern half of Ireland.[79] In any case, reformed monasteries set their own individual standard and their influence was 'moral and spiritual rather than constitutional'.[80] Old ways died hard, too, as in 824 when Tallaght was attacked and plundered by men from the community at Kildare.[81] As Kathleen Hughes remarked, 'while one anchorite dwelt alone in his hermit's cell, renouncing this wretched world, another [Feidlimid mac Crimthainn, king-bishop in Munster], who held a kingdom, assumed abbacies, burned churches beyond his own borders, and slew their inhabitants'.[82]

THE IMPACT OF THE VIKINGS

In that sense, Vikings had little to teach the Irish; their main distinguishing features as people were their language and their paganism. This is how native annalists appear to have thought of them – as foreigners (*gaill*) and as Gentiles (*Geinte*). One of the first places in the Dublin area to be plundered by them was Clondalkin, in 833.[83] Even earlier, in 821, so-called Gentiles had attacked Howth and had taken away 'a great prey of women' (*praed mor*

or revival see Kathleen Hughes, *The Church in early Irish society* (London, 1966), p. 174 and n. 1. For a more specialised treatment see Peter O'Dwyer, *Célí Dé: spiritual reform in Ireland 750-900* (2nd ed., Dublin, 1981). 75 Sharpe, 'Organisation of the Church', p. 267. 76 MacShamhráin, *Church and polity*, p. 136. 77 Monks at Tallaght were expected to perform physical work, too, hence Máel Ruain's rejection of a particularly anorexic anchorite (Hughes, *Church in early Irish society*, p. 183). 78 *AU*, pp 246-9. His distinctive name makes it likely that he is to be identified with the bishop mentioned in The Monastery of Tallaght (above, p. 28). 79 Hughes, *Church in early Irish society*, p. 182. 80 Ibid., pp 183, 185. 81 *The Annals of Inisfallen (MS Rawlinson B 503)*, ed. and trans. Seán Mac Airt (Dublin, 1951) (henceforth *Ann. Inisf.*), pp 124-5. This event occurred during the provincial overkingship of the Ua Fáeláin Muiredach (808-29). 82 Hughes, *Church in early Irish society*, p. 193. 83 *AU*, pp 288-9.

di mnaibh).[84] Lusk was plundered and burnt in 827, after which the Boyne valley district in particular was laid waste.[85] Accordingly the hinterland of Dublin was to feel the impact of the Vikings before the settlement of 841. The first *longphort* is stated to have been at Duiblinn and it is quite possible that the monastery's buildings were occupied and its resources commandeered.[86] Soon afterwards, however, these aggressive sea pirates may have moved to a more defensible site on an island in the Liffey near the strategic ford at Áth Cliath.[87] Further upstream again, the neighbouring monastery at Kilmainham was used as a burial-place for pagans, together with a site by another ford at Islandbridge.[88] These are the graves of 'a military élite engaged in commerce'.[89] Other pagan graves have been discovered, including one in the Donnybrook burial-mound, reaching a total of between 80 and 90.[90] About 10 per cent of these graves are those of women – a significant proportion on one level,[91] yet indicative of a shortfall that was made up by the kind of incident recorded at Howth. An important circumstance can be deduced from these facts: from an early stage in Scandinavian involvement in Ireland, pagans were exposed to powerful and proximate Christian influences.

In recent archaeological excavations, a domestic environment for cohabiting Irish and Scandinavians in the second half of the ninth century has been uncovered at Essex Street West. Much of this has strong rural associations: a ploughing level, sunken-featured buildings (*Grubenhäuser*), wattle enclosures and pens.[92] The existence of houses close together should not in itself be interpreted automatically as proof of a specifically urban context, for this was a characteristic of tens of thousands of villages in medieval Europe. But if Patrick Wallace's Type 1 house is to be understood as a product of cultural interaction between natives and foreigners, then such interaction was already occurring at Dublin in the late ninth century.[93] A striking detail from this important site is the evidence for pagan burial rites in the form of cattle heads and the tops of two human skulls.[94] In the political sphere it has to be

---

84 Ibid., pp 276-7.   85 Ibid., pp 284-5.   86 A similar and simultaneous takeover of Annagassan, County Louth, resulted in the violent death of the local abbot in the following year (ibid., pp 298-301).   87 Clarke, 'Proto-towns and towns', pp 346-50 and figs 13.2, 13.3.   88 Elizabeth O'Brien, 'The location and context of Viking burials at Kilmainham and Islandbridge, Dublin' in Clarke, Ní Mhaonaigh and Ó Floinn (eds), *Ireland and Scandinavia in the early Viking age*, pp 203-21.   89 Raghnall Ó Floinn, 'The archaeology of the early Viking age in Ireland' in Clarke, Ní Mhaonaigh and Ó Floinn (eds), *Ireland and Scandinavia in the early Viking age*, p. 143.   90 Ibid., p. 142; O'Brien, 'Viking burial at Donnybrook'.   91 Ó Floinn, 'Archaeology of the early Viking age', pp 140-2.   92 Simpson, *Director's findings*, pp 11-28.   93 P.F. Wallace, *The Viking age buildings of Dublin* (2 parts, National Museum of Ireland, Medieval Dublin Excavations 1962-81, ser. A, vol. 1, Dublin, 1992), i, 65-95 for a full discussion.   94 Simpson, *Director's findings*, pp 16-17.

assumed that the Uí Fergusa dynasty was eliminated and that the early Scandinavian kingdom was its successor. When the first Scandinavian king, Amlaíb (Norse Ólåfr), built his stronghold (*dún*) at Clondalkin, he may have been defending the traditional frontier between Uí Fergusa and Uí Dúnchada.[95]

In the ecclesiastical sphere it has to be assumed that Duiblinn ceased to be a residence of bishops in 841 (if not earlier) and that episcopal functions for the local Christian community were transferred elsewhere. Of this we get a hint in 882, when an abbot of Clondalkin who is also described as a bishop died.[96] Most of the monasteries in the Dublin area appear to have survived and the great majority of ordinary churches, which would not have contained much or anything of value, are likely to have done so as well. The survival of the Church as a living institution within a few kilometres of Viking Dublin, coupled with the prevalence of Christian burial customs at the behest of most of the womenfolk, would explain the relative paucity of ostensibly pagan graves.

There is little evidence for Norse (so-called 'Viking') settlement in the Dublin area. Although the number of ninth-century pagan burials is by far the largest in Ireland, it is small relative to a time-span of about sixty years (841-902). Cremation may have been customary, as well as inhumation. No intensive pattern of rural place-names so characteristic of Scandinavian Scotland was created,[97] suggesting that both the nature and the purpose of Scandinavian settlement in Ireland were different. One of the few inland names of purely Norse type, Leixlip (Norse *laxhløypa*, 'salmon's leaping-place'), need be no more than descriptive of a prominent feature in a river that would remain a major fishing resource for centuries to come.[98] Even the main settlement in the tenth century was small and compact: the distribution of bronze stick-pins implies that the earliest Scandinavian inhabitants outside the eastern core (on the High Street and Winetavern Street sites) set-

95 Referred to only at its destruction in 867 (*AU*, pp 322-3). At some unknown date, Uí Dúnchada themselves established a boundary marker further east, judging by the reconstituted place-name Carn Ua nDúnchada which survives disguised outlandishly as Dolphin's Barn. The heap of rocks and stones, if that is what this monument was, survived for long enough to be immortalised in this way and may explain the curious southwestward projection in the boundary of the later liberty of Dublin (Clarke, '*Urbs et suburbium*', p. 47, fig. 2).   96 *AFM*, i, 528-9. His son became the next abbot, illustrating the continuation of well-worn practices in the Irish Church (Hughes, *Church in early Irish society*, pp 210-11).   97 Conveniently summarised in P.G.B. McNeill and H.L. MacQueen (eds), *Atlas of Scottish history to 1707* (Edinburgh, 1996), pp 64-70.   98 It is significant that this name was transmitted directly from Norse to English, without an intermediate Irish stage (Magne Oftedal, 'Scandinavian place-names in Ireland' in Bo Almqvist and David Greene (eds), *Proceedings of the seventh Viking congress ...* (Dublin, 1976), p. 131).

tled in the second half of that century.[99] The great majority of the local population must have been Irish as well as Christian.

The continuity of Christian burial rite has been revealed archaeologically at the two most extensive sites found so far, at Cabinteely on the south side and at Castleknock on the north side. At the former the dating range of almost a thousand human skeletons has been put between the sixth century and the twelfth or thirteenth centuries.[100] The skeletal remains of about 400 people, representing a third of the cemetery, were uncovered at Castleknock in 1938. Their estimated dating range was considerably shorter – from the mid-ninth to the mid-eleventh century – but it indicates continuity of well-organised Christian burial practices throughout the Viking period no more than 8km. from Norse Dublin.[101] This is but one of several grounds for believing that the impact of the Vikings has been exaggerated by most modern commentators.

THE FOUNDATION OF CHRIST CHURCH CATHEDRAL

The annalists continue to refer to Scandinavians as non-Christians down to the third quarter of the tenth century.[102] The last great 'Viking' raid out of Dublin was conducted to the Kells district of Mide in 951, when the warriors were led by an upstart during the absence in York of King Amlaíb Cúarán (945-80).[103] There were occasional raids thereafter, even well into the eleventh century, but Amlaíb's reign looks like a period of transition from an economy characterised by pillaging and slave-trading to one characterised by craft-working and commerce. In other words, Dublin was becoming a town with a genuinely urban economy as distinct from a military base and trading emporium.[104] Amlaíb Cúarán's baptism as a Christian struck a chord over in England, for the event was recorded in a rather jejune part of the Anglo-Saxon Chronicle.[105] The West Saxon ruler, Edmund, appears to have got the better of him and baptism may have been a condition of making peace, as it had

99 Celie O'Rahilly, 'A classification of bronze stick-pins from the Dublin excavations 1962-72' in Manning (ed.), *Dublin and beyond the Pale*, p. 32.   **100** *Irish Times*, 17 July 1998.   **101** E.P. Mc Loughlin, *Report on the anatomical investigation of the skeletal remains unearthed at Castleknock in the excavation of an early Christian cemetery in the summer of 1938* (Dublin, 1950), pp iii, iv, 71. Where the sex could be determined, in the case of 235 adults and adolescents, 42 per cent were female, a very different ratio from that of the pagan graves (ibid., p. v).   **102** For the literary evidence see Máire Ní Mhaonaigh, 'Friend and foe: Vikings in ninth- and tenth-century Irish literature' in Clarke, Ní Mhaonaigh and Ó Floinn (eds), *Ireland and Scandinavia in the early Viking age*, pp 381-402.   **103** *AU*, pp 396-7.   **104** Clarke, 'Proto-towns and towns', pp 333-4, 344-64.   **105** *Two of the Saxon chronicles parallel …*, ed. Charles Plummer (2 vols, Oxford, 1892-9), i, 110-11.

been for the Danish war-leader, Guthrum, after his defeat at Edington in 878.[106] Amlaíb's Christian faith may have been little more than skin-deep, despite the fact that he allegedly died as a penitent on Iona in 981.[107] As late as 995 there was residual paganism in Dublin, for on the occasion of his third capture of the town, Máel Sechnaill of Mide confiscated the ring of Thor.[108] This was probably a ceremonial oath-swearing artefact of considerable antiquity; there would have been no point in his taking possession of it (or in the annalists' recording of the fact) unless it still represented something of value to at least some of the leading inhabitants.

The adoption of the Christian faith by the Hiberno-Norse population of Dublin and its immediate hinterland was undoubtedly a gradual process, an unrecorded aspect of acculturation.[109] It is as well to remember that Christianisation in Scandinavia itself was hesitant and also more complex than is sometimes allowed for.[110] In the Dublin area the mass of the population, especially the womenfolk, continued to be Christian and the probability is that episcopal functions were maintained at major church sites in the vicinity, such as Clondalkin. For that very reason, as well as pagan opposition, the move to re-establish Dublin as a bishopric was long delayed. As is well known, it came towards the end of the reign of Amlaíb Cúarán's son, Sitriuc Silkbeard (Norse Sigtryggr *silkiskegg*). The traditional foundation date for Christ Church cathedral, 1038, is incorrect, as was argued nearly sixty years ago by Aubrey Gwynn.[111] The precise date is indeterminable, for the

---

106 Ibid., pp 76-7.   **107** *Chronicum Scotorum: a chronicle of Irish affairs, from the earliest times to A.D. 1135 ...*, ed. and trans. W.M. Hennessy (Rolls Series, vol. 46, London, 1866) (henceforth *Chron. Scot.*), pp 226-7; *AFM*, ii, 710-13. On Amlaíb's ambivalence see Charles Doherty, 'The Vikings in Ireland: a review' in Clarke, Ní Mhaonaigh and Ó Floinn (eds), *Ireland and Scandinavia in the early Viking age*, pp 304-5.   **108** *Chron. Scot.*, pp 234-5; *AFM*, ii, 732-3. O'Donovan traced this ring back to Tomrair, a Viking jarl who was killed in 848 (*AU*, pp 306-7; *AFM*, ii, 733 n. 1), whereas Todd saw this name as a common title given to kings of Dublin (*Cogadh Gaedhel re Gallaibh: the War of the Gaedhil with the Gaill ...*, ed. and trans. J.H. Todd (Rolls Series, vol. 48, London, 1867), p. lxvii n. 4). Máel Sechnaill's previous demand for a tax to be paid on Christmas night may also be interpreted as a Christian slight to a partly pagan population.   **109** On the possible role of Columban missionaries see Doherty, 'Vikings in Ireland', pp 298-301, while for the suggestion that the church at Skreen was founded or endowed by Amlaíb Cúarán see Edel Bhreathnach, 'The documentary evidence for pre-Norman Skreen, County Meath', *Ríocht na Midhe*, 9, no. 2 (1996), pp 41-3.   **110** Peter Sawyer, 'The process of Scandinavian Christianisation in the tenth and eleventh centuries' in Birgit Sawyer, Peter Sawyer and Ian Wood (eds), *The Christianisation of Scandinavia ...* (Alingsås, 1987), pp 68-87. For the tortuous relationship between Christians and pagans in Northumbria see W.S. Angus, 'Christianity as a political force in Northumbria in the Danish and Norse periods' in Alan Small (ed.), *The fourth Viking congress* (Edinburgh, 1965), pp 142-65.   **111** Aubrey Gwynn, 'The origins of the see of Dublin' in *The Irish Church in the eleventh*

event did not rate a mention in any of the surviving annals, but the presumed outer limits are Sitriuc's return from his Roman pilgrimage late in 1028 and his deposition as king in 1036.[112] Our best estimate, therefore, is c.1030 or a little later. The king's generosity to his new foundation was hardly lavish, extending as it did to a site in the town and land at Grangegorman.[113] There may have been opposition to his religious policy. His surviving son, Amlaíb, was murdered in England whilst on his way to Rome in 1034, two years before Sitriuc's deposition.[114] The location selected for the cathedral church is unlikely to have been a vacant plot and it may have been cleared of existing buildings down to, or even below, the original boulder clay surface.[115] According to one of the late medieval accounts the new bishop, Dúnán (Donatus), built the nave, two 'collateral structures' (? transepts), a chapel dedicated to St Nicholas on the north side, along with other buildings, but we have no means of assessing the accuracy of this information.[116]

The second royal, and therefore approximately datable, grant to Christ Church comprised Lambay Island and its access point from the mainland, Portrane. The grantor was the Uí Chennselaig underking of Dublin, Murchad, son of Diarmait mac Máel na mBó (1052-70).[117] Lambay, a Norse name, had probably long been a Scandinavian possession, but Portrane was in southern Brega and there may have been an element of staking a claim to territory north of the Liffey. Next came Clonkeen (in Kill of the Grange),

---

and twelfth centuries, ed. Gerard O'Brien (Dublin, 1992), pp 50-67, reprinted from Irish Ecclesiastical Record (henceforth IER), 5th ser., 57 (1941), pp 40-55, 97-112. The two late medieval accounts of the foundation of the cathedral and diocese, 'half legendary, half historical', are printed in Aubrey Gwynn, 'Some unpublished texts from the Black Book of Christ Church, Dublin', Analecta Hibernica, 16 (1946), pp 308-10.   112 Sitriuc's departure as a pilgrim, accompanied by the king of south Brega, took place in 1028 (AU, pp 466-7). His return is entered under the same year in The Annals of Tigernach, ed. and trans. Whitley Stokes (2 vols, Llanerch, 1993, reprinted from Revue celtique, 16 (1895), pp 374-419; 17 (1896), pp 6-33, 119-263, 337-420; 18 (1897), pp 9-59, 150-97, 267-303, 374-90 (henceforth Ann. Tig.) here at ii, 260; Chron. Scot., pp 266-7.   113 Calendar of Archbishop Alen's register c.1172-1534, ed. Charles McNeill (Dublin, 1950), p. 28. The document in question is a confirmation by King John, dated 6 March 1202, of all the lands of Holy Trinity cathedral and priory. Both personal names and place-names in this text are exceedingly corrupt and in many cases difficult or impossible to identify. The list of grants, judging by the occurrence of kings, appears to be in roughly chronological order, which implies that some kind of record of acquisitions was being kept from the 1030s onwards. According to the longer foundation narrative, Sitriuc also gave gold and silver for building the church (Gwynn, 'Some unpublished texts', p. 309).   114 AU, pp 472-3.   115 Recent investigations below the floor of the crypt, including beneath the choir and the south transept, have yielded nothing but boulder clay (Stuart Kinsella, personal communication).   116 Gwynn, 'Some unpublished texts', p. 309.   117 Alen's reg., p. 28. A lengthy praise-poem accompanies his death-notice in AFM, ii, 898-9.

the gift of Donnchad mac Domnaill Remair *c.*1088, which has been described as 'a conscious act of patronage by the new ruler'.[118] The Ua Briain over-kingship left little trace in the endowment of the cathedral at Dublin, despite their interest in promoting ecclesiastical reform. The one exception was a grant of *Balirodelf* by Domnall Gerrlámhach, son of Muirchertach Ua Briain and underking of Dublin in his father's declining years, *c.*1114-18.[119] Following Muirchertach's death, Uí Chennselaig made a successful come-back at Dublin, as is evidenced by the grant of *Realgeallyn* by Énna, son of Donnchad Mac Murchada and underking *c.*1122-6.[120]

Down to the middle of the twelfth century other properties were donated by men whose names bespeak an Hiberno-Norse social context. Two parts of Ballyogan, for example, were bestowed by Paul, son of Thorkell, and by Dormlagh, son of Paul, perhaps representing three generations of the same family.[121] In addition to Ballyogan the places that can be identified, at least tentatively, are (in order of citation in the 1202 confirmation) Tully, part of Cabinteely, part of Kiltiernan, another part of Kill of the Grange, and *Tech na Breatan* near Kilgobbin.[122] Accordingly most of the recognisable places that constituted the early endowment of Christ Church cathedral lay south of the Liffey and one of them, Tully, may once have been an episco-pal centre of Uí Briúin Chualann. This distribution pattern fits remarkably neatly with that derived from a specialised art-historical phenomenon – the Rathdown graveslabs.

The Rathdown slabs share a number of characteristics in common: cup marks, concentric circles, a centre band, herring bone patterning, radiating lines, vestigial cross-arms, semi-spherical bosses, and semicircular loops.[123] Not all of these features necessarily occur together and some of the survivors are incomplete. They have been variously dated in the past, but there now seems to be general agreement that they belong to the period from the tenth to the twelfth century.[124] While the difficulty of dating these objects is recog-nised, the six cross-slabs in St Patrick's cathedral have all been assigned to the tenth/eleventh century in a recent survey.[125] Stylistically these graveslabs

118 *Alen's reg.*, p. 28; Seán Duffy, 'Irishmen and Islesmen in the kingdoms of Dublin and Man, 1052-1171', *Ériu*, 43 (1992), p. 104.   119 *Alen's reg.*, p. 28. For context see Duffy, 'Irishmen and Islesmen', pp 115-16.   120 *Alen's reg.*, p. 28; Duffy, 'Irishmen and Islesmen', p. 118 n. 124. Énna was the older brother of the more famous Diarmait Mac Murchada.   121 *Alen's reg.*, p. 28.   122 Ibid. The next item relates to *Kembonnca* and Glasnevin, which are stated to have been purchased by the convent, perhaps soon after *c.*1163 when Laurence O'Toole established Augustinian canons regular at Holy Trinity priory.   123 Pádraig Ó hÉailidhe, 'The Rathdown slabs', *JRSAI*, 87 (1957), pp 75-6.   124 For example, O'Brien, 'Churches of south-east County Dublin', p. 515.   125 Heather King, 'The pre-1700 memorials in St Patrick's cathedral' in Manning (ed.), *Dublin and*

have strong Norse features,[126] with the result that they may justifiably be regarded as Hiberno-Norse artefacts. In distributional terms their centre of gravity is Rathmichael, with ten slabs,[127] but it is surely significant that the modern city centre is well represented by the six in St Patrick's, one in St Audoen's and one, found in Lower Mount Street, in the National Museum of Ireland. None has been discovered north of the Liffey. Taken in conjunction with the early endowment of Christ Church cathedral, the distribution of Rathdown graveslabs carries with it the implication that the Hiberno-Norse heartland of Dublin comprised territories formerly belonging to Uí Fergusa, the northern Uí Briúin Chualann and the southern Uí Dúnchada. This may have formed the original core of Fine Gall, first recorded as such in the annals in 1013.[128] No doubt there was some infiltration north of the Liffey, even as far as the Broad Meadow Water, but the rulers of Brega continued to be a force to be reckoned with well into the twelfth century.[129] In 1121, for instance, we find a king of southern Brega being killed by Dubliners, who appear to have been pursuing an aggressive policy in this district, while as late as 1146 the men of the same territory defeated the king of Dublin, Raghnall mac Torcaill, and his Leinster allies.[130]

To put beside the Rathdown graveslabs, many other objects that attest to a part-Scandinavian culture have been assembled from archaeological excavations. One substantial group consists of pieces of timber that reveal 'overwhelmingly that the Dublin ships and boats were in the mainstream of the Viking tradition'.[131] Most spectacularly the vessel found in Roskilde Fjord, Sjæland, Denmark and known as Skuldelev 2 has been interpreted as a warship built of oak from the Dublin region in the 1060s.[132] Graffiti and models of ships are in conformity with this evidence in representing vessels of Nordic

beyond the Pale, pp 82-4. A date 'some time between the late tenth century and the early twelfth century' is proposed in the textual discussion (ibid., p. 78). **126** Stout and Stout, 'Patterns in the past', p. 15. **127** Ó hÉailidhe, 'Rathdown slabs', p. 86. It will be recalled that Rathmichael may have been the power centre of Uí Briúin Chualann (above, p. 28). **128** *Ann. Inisf.*, pp 182-3. **129** Gilla Mo Chonna, the king of southern Brega who died in 1013 after a session of heavy drinking in Máel Sechnaill's house, is said picturesquely to have yoked the foreigners to the plough (*AU*, pp 444-5). Máel Sechnaill's burning of Swords in 994 could have been a response to a plundering expedition from Dublin in the previous year (ibid., pp 424-5; *Chron. Scot.*, pp 234-5; *AFM*, ii, 730-1). The attack on Swords in 1035 can certainly be understood to mean that it belonged to the kingdom of Dublin by that date (*AU*, pp 474-5; John Bradley, 'The medieval boroughs of County Dublin' in Manning (ed.), *Dublin and beyond the Pale*, p. 138). **130** *Chron. Scot.*, pp 342-3; *AFM*, ii, 1012-13, 1080-1; Duffy, 'Irishmen and Islesmen', p. 119 n. 125. The context of the 1121 incident is Drinan, near Swords. **131** Seán McGrail, *Medieval boat and ship timbers from Dublin* (National Museum of Ireland, Medieval Dublin Excavations 1962-81, ser. B, vol. 3, Dublin, 1993), p. 98. **132** Ibid., p. 87.

type on a consistent basis.[133] A third category of object is decorated wood, whose style has been described as 'an eclectic fusion of insular and middle Viking period elements'. Furthermore, 'even the very Vikings [sic] involved in the process must have been half-assimilated into the insular sphere'.[134] Five of these decorated pieces of wood have been classified as crooks and they could conceivably have been used in an ecclesiastical milieu. Two of the three examples found in datable contexts belong to the first half of the eleventh century.[135] A late eleventh-century cross-arm was also discovered.[136] A quite different artefact, the ringed pin, has been recovered in considerable numbers from the Dublin excavations; this is a fastening device that originated in Ireland at the beginning of the historic era and continued to evolve typologically during the Viking and Hiberno-Norse periods.[137] Unmistakably Norse influences are represented by a dozen runic inscriptions whose dating range has been put at c.950 x 1125.[138] In this collection there are signs of both West Scandinavian and East Scandinavian speech, indicative of Norwegian and Danish strains in the population, though the extent of Scandinavian-speaking is uncertain.[139] In broad terms the artefactual evidence amounts to a powerful Scandinavian cultural presence in Dublin down to the early twelfth century at least, which could have included elements of pagan belief if not of overt practice. Against this essentially mixed cultural background, the idea that *Brjáns saga* was composed, in Norse, in Dublin c.1100 makes perfectly good sense.[140] It would have found a receptive audience.

   Coincidentally Christianity in Dublin made gradual and unremarkable progress as an institution. As we have already seen, the bulk of the pre-Norman endowment of the cathedral was probably granted in the twelfth century rather than the eleventh. When the first Hiberno-Norse bishop, Dúnán, died in 1074, he was buried (if later tradition can be believed) on the right-hand side of the high altar.[141] According to the Black Book of Christ

---

133 A.-E. Christensen, 'Ship graffiti and models' in P.F. Wallace (ed.), *Miscellanea 1* (National Museum of Ireland, Medieval Dublin Excavations 1962-81, ser. B, vol. 2, Dublin, 1988), pp 13-26.   134 J.T. Lang, *Viking-age decorated wood: a study of its ornament and style* (National Museum of Ireland, Medieval Dublin Excavations 1962-81, ser. B, vol. 1, Dublin, 1988), p. 48.   135 Ibid., pp 63-5, plate XIII and figs 70-1.   136 Ibid., p. 75 and fig. 84.   137 Thomas Fanning, *Viking age ringed pins from Dublin* (National Museum of Ireland, Medieval Dublin Excavations 1962-81, ser. B, vol. 4, Dublin, 1994), pp 52-7.   138 M.P. Barnes, J.R. Hagland and R.I. Page, *The runic inscriptions of Viking age Dublin* (National Museum of Ireland, Medieval Dublin Excavations 1962-81, ser. B, vol. 5, Dublin, 1997), p. 13.   139 Ibid., pp 14-15.   140 Donnchadh Ó Corráin, 'Viking Ireland – afterthoughts' in Clarke, Ní Mhaonaigh and Ó Floinn (eds), *Ireland and Scandinavia in the early Viking age*, pp 449-52.   141 James Ussher, *The whole works of the Most Rev. J. Ussher ...*, ed. C.R. Elrington (17 vols, Dublin, 1847-64), reprinted from *Veterum epistolarum hibernicarum sylloge ...* (Dublin, 1632), here at iv, 488; Cotton, *Fasti*

Church, Dúnán founded a chapel dedicated to St Michael (the Archangel) and situated it in his 'palace'.[142] If this is an authentic late medieval tradition, an episcopal complex may have begun to form around the cathedral. Towards the north-east and the bank of the Liffey, a church dedicated to Norway's king-martyr, Óláfr (Olave), was built in Dublin some time after 1031. Possibly this was frequented by Christian sailors and traders, in contradistinction to the episcopal and royal foundation near the summit of the east-west ridge round which the town had been developing. An interesting parallel is that York's earliest documented pre-conquest church, apart from the Minster, was also dedicated to St Olave.[143] Moreover Chester, Dublin's closest overseas trading partner, had a church with the same dedication.[144] Among the relics of Christ Church cathedral was a part of the vestment of St Olave, possibly presented by Bishop Dúnán himself.[145]

Across the Liffey a church for the inhabitants of the transpontine suburb known to later generations as Oxmantown was founded in 1095 x 1106.[146] Its patron, Michan, was believed by Meredith Hanmer in the late sixteenth century to have been a Norseman (Dane), but it is possible that this name was derived from Mo Chainne, a hypochoristic form of Cainnech, the patron of Finglas.[147] The cathedral's own tradition was that Michan was an Irish saint, bishop and confessor.[148] At all events, by c.1100 there must have been a

ecclesiae hibernicae, v, 9.   **142** Gwynn, 'Some unpublished texts', p. 308: 'capellam sancti Michaelis in palacio suo'.   **143** A.P. Smyth, *Scandinavian York and Dublin: the history and archaeology of two related Viking kingdoms* (2 vols in 1, Dublin, 1987, reprinted from original ed. in 2 vols, Dublin and New Jersey, 1975-9), ii, 235. The D text of the Anglo-Saxon Chronicle attributes the foundation of this church to Siward, earl of Northumbria (c.1033-55), a Danish appointee of King Cnut (*Two Saxon chronicles*, i, 185).   **144** Bruce Dickins, 'The cult of S. Olave in the British Isles', *Saga-book of the Viking Society*, 12 (1937-45), pp 70-1.   **145** *The Book of Obits and Martyrology of the cathedral church of the Holy Trinity, commonly called Christ Church, Dublin*, ed. J.C. Crosthwaite with introduction by J.H. Todd (Dublin, 1844), p. 141.   **146** For a full discussion of the complicated traditions about the origins of this church see Emer Purcell, 'Oxmantown, Dublin: a medieval transpontine suburb' (M.Phil. thesis, N.U.I., Dublin, 1999), pp 17-18, 60-7.   **147** Meredith Hanmer, 'The chronicle of Ireland' in James Ware (ed.), *Ancient Irish histories: the works of Spencer, Campion, Hanmer and Marleburrough* (2 vols, Dublin, 1633; reprinted 1809), ii, 194; Ailbhe MacShamhráin, personal communication. A verse in the Book of Uí Maine (at 126 b 53-4) implies that in the district north of Dublin there were churches dedicated to SS Cainnech and Comgall (of Bangor).   **148** *Book of Obits and Martyrology*, pp lxx, 149. Hanmer states that the site itself was donated by 'Murchad, king of Leinster'. This may be a misrepresentation of Muirchertach (Ua Briain), overking of Dublin from 1094 to 1114. Much nearer to the time in question, the Anglo-Norman William of Malmesbury uses 'Murcardus' for 'Muirchertach' (*De gestis regum Anglorum* ..., ed. William Stubbs (2 vols, Rolls Series, vol. 90, London, 1887-9), ii, 484). If this hypothesis is correct, Hanmer's date of 1095 (derived from Stanihurst) suggests that the

Christian population on the northern bank of the river and it may be significant that the first reliable reference to a permanent bridge over the Liffey dates from 1112.[149] Accordingly, when territorial dioceses were established for the whole of Ireland at the synod of Ráith Bressail, conventionally dated to 1111, these and probably other churches existed in and near the Hiberno-Norse town.[150]

ENGLISH CONNECTIONS

The synod conducted at Ráith Bressail was held under the presidency of Ireland's most powerful king, Muirchertach Ua Briain, who was also the overking of Dublin. For complex reasons, partly related to the ambitions and personality of Bishop Samuel (1096-1121), the Hiberno-Norse diocese was incorporated in that of Glendalough.[151] Dublin's other episcopal neighbours at that time were Kildare to the south-west, Clonard to the west, and Duleek to the north. The diocesan boundaries were preserved by Geoffrey Keating in the seventeenth century as bipolar axes, the two northernmost co-ordinates of the diocese of Glendalough being Greenoge and Lambay Island.[152] These details suggest that the northern boundary of the diocese of Dublin was essentially the Broad Meadow Water, with Portrane and Lambay Island as outliers.[153] The southern limit was probably not well defined, but the distribution of Rathdown graveslabs does not extend much further south (at Kilbride, near Bray) than the later county boundary.[154]

foundation is an example of the exercise of royal authority over Dublin early in the new régime.   **149** *AFM*, ii, 994-5.   **150** On the date of this synod see Dumville, *Councils and synods*, p. 44 and n. 166.   **151** By a reversal of fortune a century later, the diocese of Glendalough was incorporated in that of Dublin (below, pp 65-70).   **152** *The History of Ireland by Geoffrey Keating, D.D.*, ed. David Comyn and P.S. Dinneen (4 vols, London, 1902-14), iii, 306-7; John Mac Erlean, 'Synod of Ráith Breasail: boundaries of the dioceses of Ireland (A.D. 1110 or 1118)', *Archivium Hibernicum*, 3 (1914), pp 3, 5, 11, 16. For a map see T.W. Moody, F.X. Martin and F.J. Byrne (eds), *A new history of Ireland*, ix, *Maps, genealogies, lists ...* (Oxford, 1984), p. 26, no. 24.   **153** A generation later, in 1133, the church at Lusk was burnt with all the people inside it by the men of Mide, implying that some diocesan boundaries were shifting in conjunction with political ones (*The Annals of Loch Cé: a chronicle of Irish affairs from A.D. 1014 to A.D. 1590*, ed. and trans. W.M. Hennessy (2 vols, Rolls Series, vol. 54, London, 1871; reprinted Dublin, 1939), i, 132-3; Duffy, 'Irishmen and Islesmen', p. 120 n. 135).   **154** The routeway represented by the Norse name Windgate, south of Bray, may be taken as a reflection of Hiberno-Norse settlement at an unknown date. It is described as 'perhaps the most likely instance of a purely Scandinavian placename' in north-east Wicklow in Colmán Etchingham, 'Evidence of Scandinavian settlement in Wicklow' in Ken Hannigan and William Nolan (eds), *Wicklow history and society: interdisciplinary essays on the history of an Irish county*

At this stage, then, the revived diocese of Dublin appears to have lacked the territorial precision and comparative stability of its English counterparts, yet English influences were undoubtedly strong. The most conspicuous is that Dublin's bishops-elect were consecrated in England by archbishops of Canterbury. There is no direct evidence that Dúnán was consecrated in this way, but the cathedrals of Canterbury and Dublin had the same dedication – to the Holy Trinity – and both were alternatively known as Christ Church. In his letter to King Gofraid of Dublin written in 1073 x 1074 Archbishop Lanfranc certainly expresses the belief that consecration by his predecessors was customary, but this may have been an attempt to lend the dignity of precedence to something that was essentially new.[155] The journeys of Dublin's bishops-elect took them to the far south-eastern corner of the neighbouring island and must have had some impact on their view of the Church as an institution. Indeed, Bishop Samuel seems to have learnt too much from Lanfranc's example, for he seized his chance after Anselm's exile in 1097 and presented himself as a metropolitan in his own right.[156] Anselm's letter of rebuke had no effect and Samuel went his own way, even to the extent of being buried in the church that he had helped to found (or refound) earlier in his episcopate, St Michan's across the river.[157]

The extant professions of obedience for Gilla Pátraic (1074), Donngus Ua hAingliu (1085), Samuel Ua hAingliu (1096) and Gréne (1121) represent

---

(Dublin, 1994), p. 131. For the proposition that Bishop Gilla Pátraic had jurisdiction over the Isle of Man see Duffy, 'Irishmen and Islesmen', p. 107 n. 68.   **155** Helen Clover and Margaret Gibson (ed. and trans.), *The letters of Lanfranc archbishop of Canterbury* (Oxford, 1979), pp 66-7 (*more antecessorum nostrorum*); Michael Richter, 'The first century of Anglo-Irish relations', *History*, 59 (1974), p. 199 n. 16. Gilla Pátraic, consecrated in 1074, had only one known Hiberno-Norse predecessor. For the Canterbury connection down to 1152 see M.T. Flanagan, *Irish society, Anglo-Norman settlers, Angevin kingship: interactions in Ireland in the late twelfth century* (Oxford, 1989), pp 7-38.   **156** Aubrey Gwynn, 'Bishop Samuel of Dublin', *IER*, 5th ser., 60 (1942), pp 82, 85-6; idem, 'Saint Anselm and the Irish Church' in *The Irish Church in the eleventh and twelfth centuries*, pp 110-11, 114. Curiously, in the last years of the eleventh century the obverse of many Hiberno-Norse coins features a crook or crozier in front of the bust (Michael Dolley, *Viking coins of the Danelaw and of Dublin* (London, 1965), p. 30). Could the Dublin mint have been operating in the cathedral precinct?   **157** H.J. Lawlor, 'Note on the church of St Michan, Dublin', *JRSAI*, 56 (1926), pp 17-21. The effigy that Lawlor and others believed to represent Samuel as a bishop has been dated *c.*1200-20 on art-historical grounds (John Hunt, *Irish medieval figure sculpture 1200-1600: a study of Irish tombs with notes on costume and armour* (2 vols, Dublin, 1974), i, 139, no. 42 and plate 64). If this effigy was nevertheless intended to portray Samuel, we may surmise that the Ostmen were engaged in a process of cultural revivalism at a time when their transpontine suburb was being developed as a township with its own identity. The style has been described as 'somewhat hesitating and provincial' (ibid.).

what Aubrey Gwynn described as 'a well-planned campaign of ecclesiastical imperialism' by the Normans then established in England.[158] Before they
were elected, three of these bishops had been trained as Benedictine monks
in England: Gilla Pátraic at the cathedral priory in Worcester, Donngus at
the cathedral priory in Canterbury, and Samuel at the abbey of St Albans.[159]
They were thus already acquainted with England and may well have been
able to speak English and/or Norman French. Evidence of an English presence has been recovered from archaeological sites near the cathedral. At
Fishamble Street an Anglo-Saxon griffin plaque made of walrus ivory was
found in a late tenth-century level.[160] One object from Christchurch Place
was a double-edged wooden comb bearing three personal names.[161] Part of a
leather scabbard came from the seating area of a stave-built house; the Latin
maker formula, composed of Anglo-Saxon capitals, indicates that it was made
by a man called Eadric.[162] Both of the Christchurch Place finds, like the house
itself, are of eleventh-century date. The third inscribed object from this site
was an iron sword from a post-and-wattle house discovered along with sherds
of a late Saxon tripod pitcher.[163] Such finds are mere straws in the wind, but
they are commensurate with the view that, down to the time of the Norman
Conquest of England, English and Irish monks shared a common cultural
world.[164] This world of regular, two-way contact between Dublin and the
neighbouring island becomes clearer still when we turn to one particular part
of England which would continue to have close links long after 1170 – the
west midlands, focused ecclesiastically on the diocese of Worcester.

It comes as no surprise, for instance, that relics of St Wulfstan, bishop
of Worcester from 1062 to 1095, were obtained for, and preserved in, Christ
Church cathedral.[165] The bishop of Dublin who received his Benedictine

---

158 Michael Richter (ed.), *Canterbury professions* (Canterbury and York Soc., vol. 67,
Torquay, 1973), pp 29, 31, 34, 39; Aubrey Gwynn, 'The first bishops of Dublin' in H.B.
Clarke (ed.), *Medieval Dublin*, ii, *The living city* (Dublin, 1990), pp 37-61, reprinted from
Reportorium Novum, 1, no. 1 (1955), pp 1-26, here at p. 44.   **159** According to Eadmer,
Samuel was the choice of Muirchertach Ua Briain, together with the clergy and people of
Dublin (*Eadmeri Historia novorum in Anglia ...*, ed. Martin Rule (Rolls Series, vol. 81,
London, 1884), p. 73). He was probably of the same lineage as his predecessor (Dumville,
Councils and synods, p. 55 n. 196).   **160** Janet Backhouse, D.H. Turner and Leslie Webster
(eds), *The golden age of Anglo-Saxon art 966-1066* (London, 1984), p. 126 and fig. 130.   **161**
Elizabeth Okasha, 'Three inscribed objects from Christ Church Place, Dublin' in Hans
Bekker-Nielsen, Peter Foote and Olaf Olsen (eds), *Proceedings of the eighth Viking congress
...* (Medieval Scandinavian Supplements, vol. 2, Odense, 1981), pp 45-7, where the possi-
bility of liturgical use is entertained.   **162** Ibid., pp 47-8.   **163** Ibid., pp 49-50.   **164** Denis
Bethell, 'English monks and Irish reform in the eleventh and twelfth centuries' in T.D.
Williams (ed.), *Historical Studies VIII* (Dublin, 1971), p. 125.   **165** Raymond Refaussé with
Colm Lennon (eds), *The registers of Christ Church cathedral, Dublin* (Dublin, 1998), p. 39.

training at Worcester, Gilla Pátraic, has left us a body of prose and poetry composed in Latin.[166] This is a pointer in the direction of a literate élite focused on the cathedral, despite contrary indications from the inscriptions on locally produced coins.[167] One of Gilla Pátraic's poems was sent to his friend and former fellow-monk at Worcester, Aldwin (= Ealdwine).[168] Gilla Pátraic was almost certainly responsible for establishing Benedictine monks at his cathedral and these were presumably Englishmen from Worcester or its diocese.[169] Their eventual expulsion by Bishop Samuel should not detract from the significance of this English and English-speaking presence in the heart of Dublin during the last quarter of the eleventh century.

We learn from a quite different source that, while Gilla Pátraic was probably still a monk at Worcester, Evesham abbey (in the same English diocese) was the resort of many pilgrims 'from Ireland' in the time of Abbot Æthelwig (1058-78).[170] For pilgrims from Ireland, whether Irish or Norse or both, even to have heard of Evesham, there must have been some kind of close contact.[171] The chief international port in Æthelwig's local justiciarship and in the diocese of Worcester was Bristol, which is known to have had commercial ties with Dublin.[172] Æthelwig, a collaborator with the new régime in England, was entrusted with the imprisonment of a former fellow-abbot, Godric of Winchcombe, a Benedictine house in the west midlands that had a definite connection with Dublin.[173] The Annals of Multyfarnham and part of the Black Book of Christ Church represent a set of annals brought from Winchcombe abbey to Dublin early in the twelfth century.[174] The great

---

166 Aubrey Gwynn (ed. and trans.), *The writings of Bishop Patrick, 1074-1084* (Scriptores Latini Hiberniae, vol. 1, Dublin, 1955).   **167** Dolley, *Viking coins*, pp 11, 28-9.   **168** Gwynn, *Writings of Bishop Patrick*, pp 102-5. For the suggestion that Aldwin may have been the monk of Winchcombe who led the reform of monasteries in northern England see Bethell, 'English monks and Irish reform', p. 127.   **169** Gwynn, *Writings of Bishop Patrick*, p. 7.   **170** *Chronicon abbatiae de Evesham ad annum 1418*, ed. W.D. Macray (Rolls Series, vol. 29, London, 1863), p. 91: 'Solebant illis temporibus multi peregrini de Aquitannia, de Hibernia, ac de aliis terris plurimis huc venire ...'. For the date of Æthelwig's death, usually given as 1077, see H.B. Clarke, 'The early surveys of Evesham abbey: an investigation into the problem of continuity in Anglo-Norman England' (Ph.D. thesis, University of Birmingham, 1977), pp 32-3.   **171** A possible, though unproven, link in the chain is Abbot Ælfweard (1014-44), who was also a bishop of London (1035-44) and a kinsman of King Cnut (*Chronicon de Evesham*, p. 83).   **172** The south aisle of St Michan's church was dedicated to St Osyth, part of whose dual identity may have reached Dublin via the north midlands of England and the port of Chester. For a penetrating analysis of the complexities see Denis Bethell, 'The Lives of St Osyth of Essex and St Osyth of Aylesbury', *Analecta Bollandiana*, 88 (1970), pp 75-127.   **173** *Chronicon de Evesham*, p. 90.   **174** Robin Flower, 'Manuscripts of Irish interest in the British Museum', *Analecta Hibernica*, 2 (1931), pp 317-19; Gwynn, 'Some unpublished texts', pp 313-16.

Benedictine houses of the diocese of Worcester, situated in the valleys of the Severn and Warwickshire Avon, appear to have complemented Canterbury as places that enjoyed a special relationship with Dublin in what has been called 'the first century of Anglo-Irish relations'.[175]

TWELFTH-CENTURY REFORM AND ITS INFLUENCES

During the episcopate of Gilla Pátraic a senior Irish cleric with metropolitan pretensions, Máel Ísu mac Amalgada, the abbot of Armagh (coarb of Patrick), may have come to Dublin bearing the insignium of his ecclesiastical superiority, the Bachall Ísu (Staff of Jesus).[176] The circumstances revolved round the establishment of a political hegemony by Toirrdelbach ua Briain and nothing of immediate ecclesiastical significance came of this visitation. With the creation of two Irish metropolitan sees at the synod of 1111, however, the question of archiepiscopal jurisdiction over Hiberno-Norse Dublin acquired a new dimension. Dublin and its territory were allocated to Cashel, but did not obtain official recognition as a suffragan see. The crisis came with the death of Bishop Samuel ten years later, when the Christian community in the town seems to have split into two factions. One may be described as pro-Irish and welcomed Archbishop Cellach of Armagh; the other was a pro-Norse group that elected Gréne, who was then only a young subdeacon, as Samuel's successor and sent him off to Canterbury for consecration. In a revealing letter to Archbishop Ralph, all the burgesses of the 'city' of Dublin and the whole assembly of clergy stated plainly that they wished to maintain the traditional bond with Canterbury.[177] In September 1121 Gréne was ordained to the priesthood by Roger, bishop of Salisbury, at Devizes Castle; on 2 October he was consecrated bishop at Lambeth; Gréne then made his profession of obedience to Archbishop Ralph at Canterbury; and on 24 October we find him in attendance at the consecration of Tewkesbury abbey, situated at the confluence of the rivers Severn and Avon, before embarking for Dublin at Bristol.[178] For

175 Richter, 'First century of Anglo-Irish relations', pp 195-210; cf. Bethell, 'English monks and Irish reform', pp 116-17, 127, 129-30. 176 Ann. Tig., ii, 305-6; Chron. Scot., pp 292-3. On the date and interpretation of this entry see Aubrey Gwynn, 'Pope Gregory VII and the Irish Church', IER, 5th ser., 58 (1941), p. 102. By another reversal of fortune about a century later, the Staff of Jesus was to return to Dublin and there to remain in Christ Church cathedral until its destruction at the Reformation (M.V. Ronan, 'St Patrick's Staff and Christ Church' in Clarke (ed.), Medieval Dublin, ii, The living city, pp 123-31, reprinted from Dublin Hist. Rec., 5 (1942-3), pp 121-9). 177 Historia novorum in Anglia, p. 297, trans. in Gwynn, 'First bishops of Dublin', pp 56-7: 'omnes burgenses Dublinae civitatis cunctusque clericorum conventus ...'. In all such contexts civitas should be understood in an ecclesiastical sense. 178 Gwynn, 'First bishops of Dublin', p. 57.

the time being, the Canterbury connection was maintained intact. Moreover, if the famous Worcester charter, *Altitonantis*, is now to be accepted as an outright forgery of the 1140s, ecclesiastical imperialism was alive and well elsewhere in England.[179] On behalf of King Edgar (959-75 as sole ruler), it claims jurisdiction over the greater part of Ireland, including 'its most noble "city" of Dublin' (*sua nobilissima civitate Dublina*).[180]

The counterblast to all of this may be heard in the claims made in the final section of the poem referred to earlier and preserved in the Book of Uí Maine. Whenever the abbot of Armagh paid a visit to Áth Cliath, we are told, he and his party were entitled to board and lodging.[181] Bishops of Dublin were to be provided by the church of Armagh, which was to be paid a tithe levied on horseloads of goods.[182] The poem ends with a list of churches in Dublin, at least one of which looks like pure invention – the *ceall mac nÉda*, 'church of the sons of Áed'.[183] On the other hand the church dedicated to St Patrick (*ceall P[hádraig]*) is probably not a mere conceit, for the Anglo-Norman sources say that Archbishop John Cumin selected the site of an existing parish church for his collegiate foundation.[184] A well with the same dedication is mentioned separately.[185] South of the town (*dún*) the cult figures alluded to are Máel Ruain (of Tallaght) and Michael.[186] The latter could well be an indication of the existence of the church known to later generations as St Michael le Pole's, situated near the pool of Dublin. Its chief claim to distinction was the round tower that survived down to the late eighteenth century. This structure has been compared with that of St Kevin's church at Glendalough, that is to say, it may have been incorporated into the west end of the nave, although eighteenth-century drawings depict a relatively tall tower.[187] The tower's location relative to the ancient enclosure was non-stan-

179 Julia Barrow, 'The community of Worcester, 961-c.1100' and Patrick Wormald, 'Oswaldslow: an "immunity"?' in Nicholas Brooks and Catherine Cubitt (eds), *St Oswald of Worcester: life and influence* (London and New York, 1996), pp 97, 122.   180 In the modern edition of Eric John, *Land tenure in early England: a discussion of some problems* (Leicester, 1964), p. 162.   181 *Bk Uí Maine*, 126 a 27-9. The place-name form Duiblinn also occurs (ibid., 126 a 21, 126 b 8, 126 b 50).   182 Ibid., 126 a 54-5, 126 b 13-15.   183 Ibid., 126 b 44.   184 Ibid., 126 b 50-1; *Alen's reg.*, pp 3, 4, 7, 18, 29, 42. Cf. W.M. Mason, *The history and antiquities of the collegiate and cathedral church of St Patrick, near Dublin* ... (Dublin, 1820), pp 2-4.   185 *Bk Uí Maine*, 126 b 42. One of the two traditional holy wells in central Dublin with this association was located by the Poddle northwest of St Patrick's cathedral (Caoimhín Ó Danachair, 'The holy wells of County Dublin', *Reportorium Novum*, ii (1957-58), p. 80, no. 54). A graveslab found nearby in 1901 belongs to the Rathdown group and is now preserved inside the cathedral (King, 'Pre-1700 memorials', p. 82, no. 1). The second well may still be seen below the Nassau Street entrance to Trinity College (Ó Danachair, 'Holy wells', p. 80, no. 55).   186 *Bk Uí Maine*, 126 b 52-3.   187 Stout and Stout, 'Patterns in the past', p. 24 n. 72; G.L. Barrow, *The round towers of Ireland: a study and gazetteer* (Dublin, 1979), p. 88. The two Beranger drawings

dard, however, and it may have been built in a spirit of Hiberno-Norse revivalism; it could also have served as a watch-tower overlooking the pool, especially if the latter sheltered the Dublin fleet. In competition with both Armagh and Glendalough, Dubliners may have felt in need of an ecclesiastical status symbol of their own.

According to the Armagh poet there were four churches inside Áth Cliath. First to be mentioned is one allegedly dedicated to SS Paul and Peter (*ceall Poil is Pedair*).[188] No such building is otherwise known to have existed at Dublin, but ironically a new stone church with the same dedication was consecrated by Archbishop Cellach in 1126 at Armagh itself.[189] This new-style abbey stood apart from Armagh cathedral and subsequently joined the Arroasian congregation.[190] At Dublin, on the other hand, there appear to have been separate churches in honour of these central figures in early Christianity. St Peter's, as we have seen, occupied an ancient site within the old monastic enclosure, whereas St Paul's, according to Archbishop Alen writing in the sixteenth century, may have been nearer to the river Poddle.[191] The latter was granted to Holy Trinity by a pious Hiberno-Norseman, Gillamichell ('servant of Michael'), probably in the twelfth century.[192] Next in the poet's list comes Christ Church (*ceall Crist*), although there is no hint of its primacy among the town's places of worship.[193] The cult of Mary, widespread in Europe by the twelfth century, is represented by a church in her honour (*ceall Muire*).[194] This building may reasonably be identified with the church of St Mary del Dam, due north of the later castle. Finally we come to St Brigid's (*ceall Brigdi*), purportedly inside the defences,[195] whereas the well-documented building of this name was located across the Poddle from the town a short distance to the south. This could have been yet another

show the tower emerging from the roof of what was then a schoolhouse, whose construction may have been the occasion for such an arrangement (G.A. Little, 'The provenance of the church of St Michael de le Pole [sic]', *Dublin Hist. Rec.*, 12 (1951), p. 12; idem, *Dublin before the Vikings*, p. 109). Archaeological excavations conducted in 1982 uncovered foundations tentatively identified as those of the medieval tower (John Bradley and H.A. King, 'Urban archaeology survey, part VIII: Dublin City' (unpublished report, 2 vols, [1988]), ii, 121).   188 *Bk Uí Maine*, 126 b 54-5.   189 *AU*, pp 570-1.   190 Aubrey Gwynn and R.N. Hadcock, *Medieval religious houses: Ireland* (London, 1970; reprinted Dublin, 1988), p. 157, where it is stated that the new monastery would have been founded before 1126.   191 *Alen's reg.*, p. 293. By this time St Paul's had been demolished and in its stead there was a garden belonging to Holy Trinity.   192 Ibid., p. 29.   193 *Bk Uí Maine*, 126 b 56.   194 Ibid. Another sign of the currency of this cult is that Gillamichell's father is given as Gillamurri (*Alen's reg.*, p. 29). Devotion to the Virgin Mary had been strong in the neighbouring island (Mary Clayton, *The cult of the Virgin Mary in Anglo-Saxon England* (Cambridge Studies in Anglo-Saxon England, vol. 2, Cambridge, 1990), passim).   195 *Bk Uí Maine*, 126 b 56-7.

Hiberno-Norse creation in the general area of monastic Duiblinn; alternatively such a foundation could have gone back as far as the days of Uí
Dúnlainge domination prior to 841. Certainly St Brigid's had royal associations, for it was later granted to Holy Trinity, together with some land in
the parish, by the last underking, Asculf mac Torcaill (1160-70).[196]

Like the Book of Rights, a poetic source with a strong line in propaganda
has very definite limitations as historical evidence. Churches that receive no
mention at all could well have been in existence by c.1121. As has already
been observed, St Audoen's is likely to occupy a nodal site and a graveslab
of the Rathdown type is preserved in its entrance chamber. Another church
with putative French connections was St Martin's, situated on sharply rising
ground overlooking the pool in the Poddle. Dedications to the great evange-
liser of late Roman Gaul can be exceedingly early, as at Canterbury, but it is
impossible to establish when his cult came to Dublin.[197] This church was
important enough to be among the first recorded parish centres in the town.[198]
English contacts, especially with Chester, are reflected in the nearby church
of St Werburgh, whose parish coexisted with that of St Martin's at the beginning of the thirteenth century.[199] The location of this church in the eastern
core of the Hiberno-Norse town is worth noting and its origins may have preceded the suggested dating limits of 1172 x 1178.[200] Yet another church with
probable mercantile patronage was dedicated to St Nicholas and positioned
prominently south of Christ Church cathedral. Like St Werburgh's it enjoyed
parochial status early in the Anglo-Norman period, but the date of foundation is unknown.[201] If the late medieval tradition of a chapel of St Nicholas
in the first cathedral building is correct, however, his cult in Dublin would
have gone back to the 1030s at least.[202] North-east of Christ Church, and
assigned to the canons by the time of Pope Alexander III's confirmation of
c.1179, stood the church of St John.[203] Like St Paul's outside the walls, this
intramural church was donated to Holy Trinity by Gillamichell, the son of
Gillamurri, and an Hiberno-Norse provenance is a reasonable supposition.[204]

In virtually all essentials, therefore, the pattern of intramural churches at
Dublin had been completed before the arrival of Anglo-Norman adventurers

---

196 *Alen's reg.*, p. 29. **197** See in general Paul Grosjean, 'Gloria postuma S. Martini tur-
onensis apud Scottos et Britannos', *Analecta Bollandiana*, 55 (1937), pp 300-48. **198** *Alen's
reg.*, p. 29. In 1785 a large quantity of bones and coffins was found by chance at Darby
Square (Bradley and King, 'Urban archaeology survey', ii, 117). **199** *Alen's reg.*, p. 29.
200 Aubrey Gwynn, 'The origins of St Mary's abbey, Dublin', *JRSAI*, 79 (1949), p. 119.
201 *Alen's reg.*, p. 3. The attribution to Bishop Dúnán in 1038 appears to be related to that
of the cathedral itself and the chapel of St Nicholas (*Register of wills and inventories of the
diocese of Dublin in the time of Archbishops Tregury and Walton 1457-1483 ...*, ed. and trans.
H.F. Berry (Dublin, 1898), p. 230). **202** Above, p. 35. **203** *Alen's reg.*, p. 7. The initial
references are to the cult figure John the Baptist. **204** Ibid., p. 29.

in 1170. Topographically there appear to have been three components. First, Christ Church cathedral, including a chapel dedicated to St Nicholas (that multifarious patron of dioceses, merchants, sailors and other interests), along with the bishop's palace and its chapel dedicated to St Michael, constituted a high-status quarter in the middle of the expanding town. This was the royal church, in which kings as well as bishops were presumably buried.[205] At some stage the cult of St Nicholas may have been refocused in a separate building due south of the cathedral. Secondly, there was a group of five churches situated in the eastern core of the town – those of SS John, Martin, Mary (del Dam), Olave and Werburgh. It is possible that some of these predated the cathedral; King Sitriuc may have been catering for an already existing Christian or part-Christian population when a diocese was re-established at Dublin *c.*1030. Thirdly, and in somewhat splendid isolation, stood the predecessor of St Audoen's, perhaps St Columba's, located in the western extension to the town that seems to have been settled from the early eleventh century onwards, as ancient Áth Cliath was recolonised with fashionable Hiberno-Norse houses.[206]

Outside the defences two further churches have yet to be brought into the picture. One was St Kevin's, a dedication that must represent an association with Glendalough. When this link originated is a matter of speculation. One possibility is the early part of the ninth century (before 841), when Uí Dúnlainge control was being asserted at Glendalough.[207] Another is that the cult was encouraged by Ua Briain overkings in the late eleventh and early twelfth centuries.[208] In the papal confirmation of *c.*1179 St Kevin's is described as a *villa*, that is, an estate that may have supported visitors from the monastery in the mountains.[209] Finally there was St Andrew's, standing across the Poddle from the east gate of the town and near which King Henry II would entertain Irish kings and chieftains in his temporary 'palace' during the winter of 1171-2.[210] This dedication could be a manifestation of Meic Ottair or Meic Torcaill patronage and of the ties of these families with Scotland.

Most of the post-1170 network of extramural parish churches was also in position, notably in the district between the Poddle and the Steine, and across the Liffey in Oxmantown. The proliferation of churches inside and outside

---

205 The tentative suggestion has been put forward that the first Irish underking of Dublin, Murchad of Uí Chennselaig, was buried on the left-hand side of the high altar (Seán Duffy, lecture delivered on 20 October 1998). 206 Hilary Murray, *Viking and early medieval buildings in Dublin* (British Archaeological Reports, British Series, vol. 119, Oxford, 1983), pp 43-6 and ill. 15. 207 MacShamhráin, *Church and polity*, p. 133. 208 Ibid., p. 212. 209 *Alen's reg.*, p. 7. Archbishop Alen equated it with the estate of St Sepulchre's, of which it formed a part, outside the liberty of the city (ibid., p. 8; Clarke, '*Urbs et suburbium*', p. 47, fig. 2). 210 *Chronica Magistri Rogeri de Houedene*, ed. William Stubbs (4 vols, Rolls Series, vol. 51, London, 1868-71), ii, 32: 'juxta ecclesiam sancti Andreae apostoli, extra civitatem Diveliniae, palatium regium ...'.

the twelfth-century walls would have necessitated at least a rudimentary level of parochial organisation by the bishops (as they were down to 1152). There are indications to this effect early in the Anglo-Norman period, at SS Audoen's (Columba's), Martin's, Nicholas' and Werburgh's inside the walls and at SS Brigid's and Patrick's outside them.[211] In rural parts of the diocese a parochial system could have been based on the ancient monastic sites, most of which appear to have been incorporated in a much enlarged episcopal estate in the course of the twelfth-century reform programme. It is a striking fact that some of the biggest parishes in the Anglo-Norman archdiocese were centred on Clondalkin, Lusk, Santry, Swords and Tallaght. In the initial stages of parochial development, these could have functioned rather like minster churches in late Anglo-Saxon England, which served large and diffuse rural communities.[212]

Prior to the change in status from episcopal to archiepiscopal, Dublin also acquired two monasteries belonging to continental reformed orders. One was St Mary's abbey, founded in 1139 as a Savigniac house and later (1147) joining the Cistercian affiliation.[213] St Mary's was not the only Savigniac establishment in Ireland, but the only one with a tradition going back to Abbot Geoffrey of Savigny (1122-39);[214] its foundation may reflect direct links with Normandy and it is interesting that Norman and other northern French pottery has come to light in late eleventh- and early twelfth-century levels of the Dublin excavations.[215] The second monastery was the Arroasian nunnery known as St Mary de Hogges and founded in c.1146. Its patron was Diarmait Mac Murchada who, perhaps with a nice sense of irony, located his nuns in close proximity to the former Viking assembly place, or Thingmount, and to the burial-mounds of erstwhile pagan warlords.[216]

---

211 Alen's reg., pp 3, 4, 29. Outside the walls, towards the west, early parishes seem to have been focused on two monastic houses, St John the Baptist's hospital and St Thomas' priory/abbey (ibid.).   212 John Blair, 'Secular minster churches in Domesday Book' in P. H. Sawyer (ed.), Domesday Book: a reassessment (London, 1985), pp 104-42; idem, 'Minster churches in the landscape' in Della Hooke (ed.), Anglo-Saxon settlements (Oxford, 1988), pp 35-58; idem, 'Anglo-Saxon minsters: a topographical review' and Sarah Foot, 'Anglo-Saxon minsters: a review of terminology' in Blair and Sharpe (eds), Pastoral care before the parish, pp 212-25, 226-66.   213 Gwynn, 'Origins of St Mary's abbey', pp 110-25.   214 Ibid., p. 111.   215 P.F. Wallace, 'Anglo-Norman Dublin: continuity and change' in Donncha[dh] Ó Corráin (ed.), Irish antiquity: essays and studies presented to Professor M.J. O'Kelly (Cork, 1981), p. 253; idem, 'A reappraisal of the archaeological significance of Wood Quay' in John Bradley (ed.), Viking Dublin exposed: the Wood Quay saga (Dublin, 1984), pp 124-5; idem, 'The archaeology of Anglo-Norman Dublin' in Clarke and Simms (eds), The comparative history of urban origins in non-Roman Europe ..., ii, 399.   216 P.J. Dunning, 'The Arroasian order in medieval Ireland', Irish Historical Studies, 4, no. 16 (Sept. 1945), pp 297-315; Gwynn and Hadcock, Medieval religious houses, pp 148-51 for the general background. The timing may have a political significance, reflecting Mac Murchada's

During the period from $c.$1030 to 1152, the reconstituted diocese of Dublin came to represent a powerful ecclesiastical force in the land. As early as 1074 the clergy resident in the town envisaged their church as the ecclesiastical capital of the island of Ireland (*Hiberniae insulae metropolis*).[217] Naturally enough, there were countervailing forces at work and the diocese of Dublin was subsumed into that of Glendalough in 1111.[218] Then came the challenge from Armagh ten years later. By that time the native Irish conception of Áth Cliath with its numerous churches was firmly established.[219] The mid-twelfth-century formulation of the *dún* of Duiblinn as one of the seven wonders of Ireland may have owed as much to the extraordinary array of churches as to the impressive stone defences.[220] With its centrally-placed cathedral, seven parish churches inside the walls and about the same number outside them, as well as two suburban monasteries belonging to continental reformed orders, Dublin contained the greatest single concentration of churches, not only in existence, but also that there had ever been in Ireland. Thus Bishop Gréne would have been in a strong position to promote the claims of his see to full and permanent metropolitan status before and during the synod of Kells-Mellifont.[221] As so often in human affairs, however, one problem solved is another problem created. With Gréne as archbishop of Dublin and with Gilla Meic Liac as primate of all Ireland, there was no longer any room for the church of Canterbury. There, malcontents began to advocate the idea of polit-ical intervention in Ireland,[222] with the result that the archdiocese of Dublin would take on a crucial pivotal role as it entered the brave new world of Jocelin of Furness and his opportunistic and rapacious compatriots.

assertion of authority as overking of Dublin following the death in battle of Ragnall mac Torcaill (*Ann. Tig.*, ii, 382; *Miscellaneous Irish annals (A.D. 1114-1437)*, ed. and trans. Séamus Ó hInnse (Dublin, 1947), pp 28-9; *Chron. Scot.*, pp 342-3; Duffy, 'Irishmen and Islesmen', p. 123 n. 152). **217** Ussher, *Whole works*, iv, 488. **218** Muirchertach Ua Briain's three-month stay in Dublin in the latter part of the year may have had some bearing on the matter (*Ann. Inisf.*, pp 270-1). An additional or alternative subject for nego-tiation may have been his nephew's annexation of the Scottish Isles (Duffy, 'Irishmen and Islesmen', p. 114). **219** *Lebor na Cert*, pp 118-19; *Bk Uí Maine*, 126 a 36. **220** *The Book of Leinster, formerly Lebar na Núachongbála*, ed. R.I. Best, Osborn Bergin, M.A. O'Brien and Anne O'Sullivan (6 vols, Dublin, 1954-83), i, 212, line 6362. **221** Aubrey Gwynn, 'The synod of Kells, 1152' in *The Irish Church in the eleventh and twelfth cen-turies*, reprinted, with revision, from *IER*, 5th ser., 77 (1952), pp 161-76, 250-64, here at pp 228-30. **222** Bethell, 'English monks and Irish reform', pp 129-35; F.X. Martin, 'Diarmait Mac Murchada and the coming of the Anglo-Normans' in Art Cosgrove (ed.), *A new history of Ireland*, ii, *Medieval Ireland 1169-1534* (Oxford, 1987), pp 56-7; Flanagan, *Irish society*, pp 38-55.

2

The emergence of the metropolitan see: Dublin, 1111-1216

Ailbhe MacShamhráin

Sound arguments can be advanced for viewing the twelfth to early thir-teenth centuries as an especially eventful period in the ecclesiastical his-tory of Ireland and Dublin. This timespan of little more than a hundred years witnessed the integration of Dublin into Ireland's emerging diocesan frame-work, its elevation to metropolitan status and its union with the earlier bish-opric of Glendalough. Parallel with this, Irish kings and Hiberno-Scandinavian lords struggled for control of the city-state which ultimately became the centre of the English lordship of Ireland. It was against this often stormy back-ground that the careers of such distinguished prelates as Samuel, Gréne, St Lorcán [Laurence] Ua Tuathail and John Cumin were played out.

I

From a modern perspective, the apparently ambivalent attitude of the medieval Irish Church towards the episcopacy of Dublin may seem strange. Yet there is no reference at all to Dublin in the surviving narrative of the synod of Ráith Bressail which, in 1111, provided Ireland for the first time with a permanent structure of territorial dioceses. Admittedly, there is no contemporary record of the proceedings of Ráith Bressail, but there is little reason to doubt the testimony of seventeenth-century historian Seathrún Céitinn (Geoffrey Keating) who supplies a list of sees approved at this synod. Aside from the fact that there is no mention of Dublin town, the parameters assigned to Glendalough appear to preclude the existence of another diocese in the Dublin region. It is expressly claimed that the limits of Glendalough extended: 'ó Grianóc go Becc Ériú ocus ó Nás go Reachru'.[1] The northern-

---

[1] John McErlean, 'The synod of Ráith Breasail', *Archivium Hibernicum*, 3 (1914), pp 11, 24; Pádraig de Barra (ed.), *Forus Feasa ar Éirinn le Seathrún Céitinn* (Dublin, 1982), ii, p. 160.

most point is now represented by Greenogue townland on the border of the modern counties of Dublin and Meath while, to the south, the site referred to as Becc Ériú is very likely the burial ground and well associated with St Íbar just south of Arklow.[2] The western and eastern extremities are easily identified as Naas and Lambay.

One could almost be forgiven for assuming that the bishopric of Dublin, the eleventh century foundation and development of which has been discussed above by Dr Clarke, had somehow been suppressed by the time of the synod. But there is ample evidence to demonstrate that this was not so. We know, for instance, that the cathedral of the Holy Trinity continued in being, having earlier been endowed with extensive lands.[3] Furthermore, an episcopal succession was maintained; indeed in 1111 the see was occupied by Bishop Samuel ua hAingliu.[4] The Irish prelates at Ráith Bressail, it seems, deliberately chose to ignore the existence of Dublin.

The defiant attitude of Bishop Samuel, in maintaining a dignity inconsistent with that of a suffragan, was cited by Aubrey Gwynn as a probable reason for the exclusion of the Hiberno-Scandinavian bishopric.[5] While Samuel's defiance may have been a factor, Gwynn underestimated the political considerations which so often lay at the heart of Church affairs in medieval Ireland. As is generally agreed, the Irish church reform movement of the twelfth century (in its earlier stages at least) was Munster-driven, with the Ua Briain kings of Dál Cais, claimants to the high kingship of Ireland, prominent as lay facilitators. Closer examination, however, reveals the extent to which the synod of Ráith Bressail was dominated by Muirchertach Ua Briain. The circumstances surrounding that council, not to mention some of the decisions reached, manifestly reflect the latter's dynastic interests. The location of Ráith Bressail was almost certainly in Munster – comfortably within the Ua Briain realm.[6] The presiding legate Gilbert [or Gille?] of Limerick was an Ua Briain nominee, as indeed was Bishop Máel Ísu [Malchus] of Waterford, who was promoted to the see of Cashel at the synod.[7] Furthermore, Ua Briain sought to fix the boundaries of several dioceses in

---

2 This site, otherwise Killapeckure (Cill Espuicc Íbair; the church of Bishop Íbar) is discussed by Liam Price, *Placenames of County Wicklow*, vii (Dublin, 1967), pp xciv, 488. 3 Archbp Alen's Reg., i, f. 148b; Charles McNeill (ed.), *Calendar of Archbishop Alen's register* (Dublin, 1950), p. 28. A number of the grants alluded to here are eleventh century. 4 For a full listing of bishops of Dublin and Glendalough see Francis John Byrne, 'Succession lists: bishops 1111-1534', in T.W. Moody, F.X. Martin and F.J. Byrne (eds), *A new history of Ireland*, ix, *Genealogies, succession lists, maps* (Oxford, 1984), pp 309-18. 5 Aubrey Gwynn, 'The twelfth century reform', in Patrick Corish (ed.), *A history of Irish Catholicism* (Dublin, 1968), II, i, p. 35. 6 Anthony Candon, 'Ráith Bressail: a suggested identification', *Peritia*, 3 (1984), pp 326-9. 7 Gwynn, 'Twelfth century reform', pp 7, 30, 36; Anthony Candon, 'Barefaced Effrontery: secular and ecclesiastical politics in early

a way that advantaged his dynasty. Hence, the Dál Cais overkingdom of Thomond and the realms of other dynasties loyal to Ua Briain feature as extensive, unified dioceses like Killaloe. In contrast, the lordships of less favoured dynasties in the midlands and north of the country were divided between adjacent bishoprics to deny the regional rulers the benefits of coordinating secular and ecclesiastical administration.

The claim implicit in Céitinn's account that the diocese of Glendalough included the bishopric of Dublin must be assessed in this context. The lordship exercised from the mid-eleventh century over the Hiberno-Scandinavian realm by Irish kings, especially by the Ua Briain rulers of Munster, has been explored by Candon and by Duffy – the latter particularly highlighting the close Irish Sea connections of Dublin and the extension of its ecclesiastical authority to Man and the Isles.[8] There is the additional consideration that, from the 1070s onwards, Ua Briain had promoted the Ua Lorcáin line of Uí Muiredaig to the key regional kingship of north Leinster, and its rulers loyally supported Dál Cais.[9] Given this convergence of political and ecclesiastical priorities, it seems reasonable that a unitary Glendalough-Dublin diocese was created to serve Ua Briain interests – combining, as it did, the Hiberno-Scandinavian kingdom and the Uí Muiredaig realm.

There is, however, another equally important factor to consider when one seeks to explain the omission of Dublin from the Ráith Bressail framework; that is, the position of the diocese in relation to Canterbury. It is clear that Muirchertach Ua Briain, like his father before him, had earlier supported the Canterbury initiative on Irish Church reform and received an advisory letter from Archbishop Anselm on this matter. As a subscriber to the reform movement, the aspiring high king was doubtless aware of difficulties concerning the validity of Irish episcopal orders. Presumably he understood that, according to canon law, the consecration of a new bishop required the offices of at least two canonically consecrated bishops. A shortage of prelates whose own orders would have qualified them to conduct consecrations probably explains why Muirchertach, as is clear from the English source *Historia Novum* of

twelfth century Ireland', *Seanchas Ard Mhacha*, 14 (1991), p. 6.   8 Anthony Candon, 'Muirchertach Ua Briain, Politics and Naval Activity in the Irish Sea 1075 to 1119' in G. MacNiocaill and P.F. Wallace (eds), *Keimelia: studies in medieval archaeology and history in memory of Tom Delaney* (Galway, 1988), pp 397-415; Seán Duffy, 'Irishmen and Islesmen in the kingdom of Dublin and Man, 1052-1171', *Ériu*, 43 (1992), pp 93-133; idem, 'Ostmen, Irish and Welsh in the eleventh century', *Peritia*, 9 (1995), pp 378-96. 9 Francis John Byrne, 'The trembling sod: Ireland in 1169' in Art Cosgrove (ed.), *A new history of Ireland*, ii (Oxford, 1987), pp 24-5; Ailbhe MacShamhráin, 'Uí Muiredaig and the Abbacy of Glendalough eleventh to thirteenth centuries', *Cambridge Medieval Celtic Studies*, 25 (1993), pp 55-75; idem, *Church and polity in pre-Norman Ireland: the case of Glendalough* (Maynooth, 1996), chapter 3.

Eadmar, lent his support in 1095-6 to the nomination of bishops Samuel of Dublin and Máel Ísu of Waterford and permitted them to proceed to Canterbury for consecration.[10] Each of these bishops-elect swore oaths of obedience to the primate of England; the text of Samuel's oath survives and is explicit in its acknowledgement of Canterbury's metropolitan authority.[11]

Although difficulties within the Irish Church prompted Muirchertach to accept Canterbury's paternalistic role prior to 1100 it can be surmised that, as he consolidated his position, he sought to extricate the Irish Church reform movement from external control. The appointment of Gilbert as bishop of Limerick in 1106 possibly marks a stage in this process; his election was (as Gwynn observed) announced to Canterbury, courteously but firmly conveying the message that Irish prelates could consecrate their own bishops without resort to foreign assistance.[12] The synod of Ráith Bressail may have brought this a step further; thus Máel Ísu of Waterford was, as noted earlier, translated to Cashel, and his former bishopric silently subjected to Lismore. Similarly, the synod's attempt to place Dublin under Glendalough may be interpreted as another step in disengagement from Canterbury. Quite possibly the expectation was that, on Samuel's death, the bishopric of Dublin would expire.

However, such plans as may have existed to absorb Dublin were put aside as the recurring illness of Muirchertach from 1114, and his death five years later, undermined the political dominance of the Ua Briain line. As the high king's power waned, the south Leinster dynasty of Uí Chennselaig re-emerged to flex its muscles in the Dublin area. Political supremacy ultimately passed to Connacht and, as leadership in ecclesiastical affairs was assumed by Armagh, the close connection between dynastic and diocesan interests was broken for a time. The youthful king of Connacht, Toirdelbach Ua Concho-

---

10 Martin Rule (ed.), *Eadmeri Historia Novum in Anglia* (London, 1884), pp 73-4, 76-7; Aubrey Gwynn, *The Irish Church in the eleventh and twelfth centuries*, ed. G. O'Brien (Dublin, 1992), pp 103, 105; David N. Dumville, *Councils and synods of the Gaelic early and central Middle Ages*, Quiggin Pamphlets no. 3 (Cambridge, 1997), pp 41-2. Emphasis on the consent of clergy and people in the selection of both Bishop Samuel of Dublin and Bishop Máel Ísu of Waterford implies that diocesan synods were convened. Muirchertach Ua Briain may have been especially conscious of local sensitivities in the case of Dublin, since he had reasserted control over the kingdom only a short time previously having expelled the intrusive Gofraid Crovan, king of Man and the Isles.   11 John Watt, *The Church and the two nations* (Cambridge, 1970), pp 7, 217; idem, *The Church in medieval Ireland* (Dublin, 1972), p. 3.   12 Gwynn, 'Twelfth century reform', pp 25-6. However, Gilbert subsequently features in a list of Canterbury suffragans party to the consecration of Bishop Bernard of St David's; *Eadmeri Historia*, p. 236; see Seán Duffy, in C. Harper-Bill (ed.), *Anglo-Norman studies*, 20, Proceedings of the Battle Conference 1997 (Woodbridge, 1998).

bair, staked his claim to the high kingship by marching on Dublin in 1118. As he consolidated his position, we find him acting as overlord of the city state. This enabled him to intervene when, on the death of Bishop Samuel in 1121, Armagh determined, as the Annals of Ulster attest, to appoint its archbishop Cellach to the Hiberno-Scandinavian see. On this occasion, Toirdelbach frustrated Armagh plans by approving the selection of Gréne [Gregorius] by the clergy and people of Dublin – presumably, as in the case of his predecessor, at a diocesan synod. Significantly, Gréne was sent to Canterbury for consecration – and Toirdelbach Ua Conchobair even appealed to King Henry I of England to secure this privilege for the young bishop-elect.[13] As there was no longer a canonical need for consecration by Canterbury, the decision of the Dublin electors in 1121 must be viewed as an assertion of ecclesiastical separateness. Politically the city-state had been dominated by Irish kings for seven decades; now it determined, through submission to a distant English primate, to avoid the absorption of its bishopric by either Munster or Armagh interests. However, this initiative on the part of the Hiberno-Scandinavian chapter was checked when Archbishop Cellach, backed by the power of Armagh and by some supporters within Dublin, denied the returning Gréne admission to the town. The Annals of Ulster indicate that the new Dublin bishop was obliged to acknowledge the supremacy of Armagh.[14] It appears that Gréne found it difficult to pursue an independent line to any great extent – at least until the death of Cellach in 1129.

During the 1120s, Dublin was dominated politically by Toirdelbach Ua Conchobair as he strove to assert his authority over Leth Moga (the southern half of Ireland). In 1126, the Uí Chennselaig king Énna Mac Murchada was appointed regent of the town by Toirdelbach. Following the premature death of Énna a year later, Toirdelbach designated his eighteen-year-old son Conchobar as ruler of Dublin, but he was soon expelled. This was the signal for the beginning of strong resistance to Toirdelbach, who faced widespread revolt against his overlordship of Leth Moga as well as Dublin from 1131. The 1130s also witnessed the emergence of the Meic Turcaill, who featured as regents of the city-state until the arrival of the Anglo-Normans.[15] Parallel with this, Diarmait Mac Murchada, younger brother of the deceased Énna, rose to become overking of Leinster. As early as 1134, *Chronicon Scotorum* attests, Mac Murchada had the support of the men of Dublin in resisting

13 *Annals of Ulster*, s.a. 1121; Watt, *Church in medieval Ireland*, p. 14; see Seán Duffy, *Ireland in the middle ages* (London and Dublin, 1997), pp 51, 53.   14 *Annals of Ulster*, s.a. 1129.   15 John Ryan, *Toirdelbach Ó Conchobair: king of Ireland, co freasabra*, O'Donnell Lecture no. 10 (Dublin, 1966), pp 14-15; Donncha Ó Corráin, *Ireland before the Normans* (Dublin, 1972), pp 155, 157.

Munster intervention in the town. However, insofar as the ambitious king of Leinster succeeded in restoring overlordship of the city-state, his authority was not destined to survive for long. A revolt against Mac Murchada's authority in northern Leinster, and renewed Munster aggression, facilitated the reassertion of Hebridean suzerainty over Dublin in 1142. It was not until the death of regent Ragnall Mac Turcaill in 1146 and that of the Hebridean king Ottar mac mic Ottir two years later that Mac Murchada regained dominance of the Hiberno-Scandinavian kingdom.[16]

Meanwhile, the initiative in relation to Church reform remained with Armagh. Máel Máedóc Ua Morgair, better known as St Malachy, held the archbishopric until 1137 and subsequently served as bishop of Down and papal legate. It was in this capacity that he visited Rome in 1139-40 to seek *pallia*[17] for the archbishoprics of Armagh and Cashel. It is not clear what Malachy's intentions were in regard to Dublin at this time, but it is clear that his continental travels resulted in the introduction to Ireland of the Cistercians and of the Augustinians. It is ironic that the introduction of both these orders into Dublin was due to the patronage of Diarmait Mac Murchada, whose confessor and friend Áed Ua Caellaide, bishop of Louth, was among the main protagonists of the Augustinians. Mac Murchada established the abbey of St Mary de Hogges (on the south side of Hoggen Green) for Augustinian nuns and was, as far as one can tell, behind the transfer of the Savigniac foundation of St Mary's (north of the Liffey, close to the Bradogue river) to the Cistercians.[18] Both of these developments may reasonably be dated to 1146-8, when Mac Murchada regained control of Dublin from the Hebrideans.

By the 1140s, Toirdelbach Ua Conchobair had regained much of his former authority and was still the foremost claimant to the elusive high-kingship. Striving to reassert his authority over Munster and the midlands he was, in theory at least, the overlord of Mac Murchada who in turn dominated Dublin. It is probable that these developments brought Dublin's growing importance in secular politics to the attention of St Malachy, who sought to reconsider the town's position within the diocesan framework. In 1148, Malachy convened a synod at Inis Pátraic (St Patrick's Island, Skerries) which, significantly, was situated within the bounds of the Hiberno-Scandinavian kingdom and bishopric. Following this, he again travelled to Rome in search of *pallia*.

---

16 Duffy, 'Irishmen and Islesmen', pp 120-22; for MacMurchada's career see F.X. Martin, *No hero in the house*, O'Donnell Lecture no. 19 (Dublin, 1975).   17 The *pallium* (plural *pallia*) was a short white cloak marked with a red cross – a symbol of archiepiscopal authority.   18 Watt, *Church in medieval Ireland*, pp 20-1; F.X. Martin, 'Diarmait Mac Murchada and the coming of the Anglo-Normans', in Art Cosgrove (ed.), *A new history of Ireland*, ii (Oxford, 1987), p. 49.

The subsequent death of Malachy en route to Rome interrupted the progress of diocesan reform. The years immediately following saw something of a political stalemate as the by now ageing Ua Conchobair strove to maintain his claims to the high-kingship against the rising Muirchertach Mac Lochlainn of the north. Notwithstanding his submission to the latter in 1150, it is clear that Ua Conchobair was still dominant in the southern half of Ireland. In 1151, he shattered the power of Ua Briain of Munster at the battle of Móin Mór near Fermoy, and continued to exercise some degree of authority in Meath. On that account it is scarcely surprising that when Cardinal John Paparo arrived towards the end of the same year to oversee the recasting of the diocesan framework, Ua Conchobair should have shared (with Mac Lochlainn) the role of secular patron at the synod of Kells that followed. Even more significant is the fact that Paparo, on this occasion, presented not two but four *pallia*, probably in answer to prior requests to Rome by both claimants to the high-kingship. The decision of the synod (which confirmed the existing archbishoprics of Armagh and Cashel) to provide for new ecclesiastical provinces centred on Tuam and Dublin was of great importance for both sees but, in view of later political developments, especially for Dublin.

Ryan was almost certainly correct in discerning Ua Conchobair's ambition behind the creation of Tuam.[19] The elevation of Dublin, however, is less easily explained. Diarmait Mac Murchada had submitted to Mac Lochlainn in 1149, but maintained a loyalty to Ua Conchobair and supported him at the important battle of Móin Mór. For strategic as well as dynastic reasons, therefore, neither of the would-be high kings had any reason to oppose the creation of an archbishopric for Dublin. Indeed, both would have welcomed the opportunity to detach it from the sphere of Cashel. Mac Murchada could be useful as a counterbalance to Ua Briain within Leth Moga, while the strategic importance of the Dublin fleet was increasingly recognised. In this context, it is scarcely accidental that the new ecclesiastical province, consisting of the dioceses of Ferns, Leighlin, Kildare, Ossory, Glendalough and Dublin itself, coincides with Mac Murchada's provincial kingdom plus the Hiberno-Scandinavian city state. One important consequence of this new arrangement was that it automatically severed the connection with Canterbury; the now ageing Gréne, consecrated by and having sworn obedience to the English primate, was now a metropolitan in his own right. Dr Flanagan has plausibly argued that Canterbury, incensed by the loss of what it viewed as its rightful jurisdiction in Ireland, was a prime instigator of the papal bull *Laudabiliter*, which authorised the king of England to intervene in Ireland for the purpose of furthering Church reform.[20]

19 Ryan, *Toirdelbach Ó Conchobair*, p. 21. **20** Marie-Therese Flanagan, *Irish society, Anglo-Norman settlers, Angevin kingship* (Oxford, 1988), chapter 1; cf. Candon, 'Barefaced

One striking feature of the Dublin province defined at the synod of Kells was the deliberate retention of the suffragan bishopric of Glendalough. This diocese included most of the modern County Wicklow and the south and east of County Kildare; the archdiocese broadly corresponded to the modern County Dublin, although there was clearly some overlap to the east between Shankill and Delgany. Geographically, the Glendalough diocese, as confirmed at Kells, closely corresponds to the Uí Muiredaig-dominated regional kingship of northern Leinster, where the Ua Tuathail ruling line was closely allied to Mac Murchada.[21] It so happens that the latter, having killed the reigning Ua Tuathail in his purge of 1141, had promoted to the kingship one Muirchertach, whose most illustrious son was Lorcán – the future St Laurence. It is clear from the saint's Latin Life (*Vita Sancti Laurencii*) that Mac Murchada distrusted his new sub-king; having taken the young Lorcán as hostage, he released him into the custody of the bishop of Glendalough only when Muirchertach Ua Tuathail threatened retaliation.[22]

However, by the time of the synod of Kells, a *modus vivendi* had been reached between the king of Leinster and his most senior lieutenant. Hence the diocese of Glendalough was not only retained, but was moulded more closely to the shape of the Uí Muiredaig overkingdom. The next year, Mac Murchada married Mór, daughter of Muirchertach Ua Tuathail. The promotion of Lorcán (now brother-in-law of the king of Leinster) to the prestigious abbacy of Glendalough in 1153 at the early age of twenty-five is viewed by most modern commentators in the context of these political manoeuvrings.[23] Four years later, on the death of the incumbent bishop of Glendalough,[24] Lorcán was offered the vacant see. He declined, on the grounds that he had not yet reached the canonical age of thirty; it is significant, nonetheless, that the offer should have been made to him at this stage.

II

The death in 1156 of Toirdelbach Ua Conchobair simplified the political situation by leaving Mac Lochlainn as the only credible candidate for the high kingship. Diarmait Mac Murchada retained the kingship of Leinster and Dublin under the lordship of the northern ruler. Having beaten off a Manx

effrontery', pp 17-18. **21** MacShamhráin, *Church and polity*, pp 104, 155, 212-13. **22** Charles Plummer (ed.), 'Vita Sancti Laurencii Archiepiscopi Dublinensis', *Analecta Bollandiana*, 33 (1914), cap. iii-iv. **23** See for instance Maurice F. Roche, 'The Latin Lives of St Laurence O'Toole' (Ph.D. thesis, University College Dublin, 1981), p. 8; Flanagan, *Irish society*, p. 101; MacShamhráin, *Church and polity*, pp 104, 155. **24** Probably a certain Ua Noídenáin (Byrne, 'Succession lists', p. 313, n.6).

attack on Dublin in 1162, Mac Murchada had Mac Lochlainn's support in taking tighter control of the Hiberno-Scandinavian town. This venture was facilitated by the death of the elderly Archbishop Gréne, which enabled Mac Murchada to engineer the elevation of Lorcán to the metropolitan see. The new archbishop was dutiful, if not indeed loyal, to his king. Certainly, he served as a witness to several of Mac Murchada's property transactions, including the foundation of a daughter house of the Augustinian priory of Louth (then under Mac Murchada's friend Bishop Áed Ua Caellaide) at All Hallows, Dublin, which was endowed with the lands of Baldoyle – heretofore property of the Mac Turcaill family.[25] Subsequently, Lorcán endorsed Mac Murchada's establishment of another house at Ferns. The eventual succession of Lorcán's nephew Thomas to the abbacy of Glendalough, and the confirmation of this by the king of Leinster, should also be viewed as a consequence of their political alignment.

The above acknowledgment of the dynastic considerations which underlay Lorcán's appointment, and the political dimension of his role, does not imply that he was either unsuitable for or undeserving of the archbishopric. Although he was the son of a regional king and brother-in-law of the overking of Leinster, there is little reason to doubt the testimony of his Latin 'Life' that he was a man of great personal charity, humility and spirituality. Details such as his abstention from meat, his wearing a hairshirt under fine robes where it would not be visible, and his drinking tinted water at banquets so that he appeared to be partaking of wine all have a ring of authenticity.[26] The anonymous canon of Eu, the compiler of the Latin 'Life', interviewed churchmen in Dublin and Glendalough who clearly regarded Lorcán as one who was humble before God, and who lived a life of private penance.

The consecration of Lorcán by Gilla Meic Liac (Gelasius), successor of St Patrick, reflects, as Professor Martin has pointed out, Mac Murchada's acknowledgement of the supremacy of Mac Lochlainn just as much as it symbolises Dublin's acceptance of the primacy of Armagh.[27] Archbishop Lorcán continued the reformist policies he had earlier pursued as abbot of Glendalough, when he had sought to reform the old ecclesiastical settlement through the establishment of an Augustinian community at Insula Sancti Salvatoris (St Saviour's) to the east of the valley. Now, as archbishop, he strove to improve standards of religious discipline at the cathedral of the Holy Trinity, Christ Church, by introducing a new chapter of Augustinian

25 The grant of Baldoyle to All Hallows is discussed by Marie-Therese Flanagan, 'St Mary's abbey, Louth, and the introduction of the Arroasian observance into Ireland', *Clogher Record*, 10, no. 2 (1980), pp 223-34.   26 'Vita Sancti Laurencii', cap. ix.   27 F.X. Martin, 'Ireland in the time of St Bernard, St Malachy, St Laurence O'Toole', *Seanchas Ard Mhacha*, 15 no. 1 (1992), p. 19.

canons regular, which followed the Arroasian rule.[28] According to the Black Book of Christ Church, Lorcán subsequently availed of Anglo-Norman patronage to reconstruct the cathedral, adding a choir, tower and side-chapels. However, it is doubtful that all this work can be attributed to him; there is a growing modern consensus that the architectural evidence indicates later refurbishment.[29]

The time of trial for Lorcán came not with the deposition of Mac Murchada from the provincial kingship in 1166, but with his retaking of that dignity more than three years later. In the summer of 1170, Mac Murchada presented himself before the walls of Dublin with the forces of Uí Chennselaig and those of his Anglo-Norman allies under the earl of Striguil, Richard de Clare, known as Strongbow. As both of the principals were related to Lorcán by marriage (his sister Mór was the wife of Mac Murchada and mother of the sixteen-year-old Aífe, now married to the middle-aged Strongbow), the archbishop was persuaded by the local authority to negotiate on their behalf.[30] While discussions were in progress, two impetuous young Anglo-Norman lords, Miles de Cogan and Reimund le Gros, stormed the walls and captured the town. This put Lorcán in an extremely difficult position, as it could easily have been construed that he had collaborated with the attackers because of his marriage connections. In the event, the archbishop was not subject to any such criticism, which freed him to concentrate on the pressing matter of tending to the victims of the sack, to which task he applied his personal energies.[31]

In the light of the political developments following the death of Diarmait Mac Murchada at the beginning of May 1171, which led to the establishment of the English lordship of Ireland, certain twentieth-century historians tended to assess Lorcán's motives according to the precepts of modern nationalism. By these criteria, there are several apparent contradictions in his actions. Following a failed attack on Dublin led by Askulv Mac Turcaill about a fortnight after Diarmait's death, a potentially more serious expedition was launched in September by Ruaidrí, son of Toirdelbach Ua Conchobair, claimant to the high-kingship. Despite the fact that Lorcán's brother Gilla Comgaill (now king of Uí Muiredaig) was party to this venture, there is noth-

---

28 G.J. Hand, 'Rivalry of the cathedral chapters in medieval Dublin', *Journal of the Royal Society of Antiquaries of Ireland* (hereafter *JRSAI*), 92 (1962), p. 193; Watt, *Church in medieval Ireland*, pp 22, 122.   29 Roger Stalley, *Architecture and sculpture in Ireland c.1150-1350* (Dublin, 1971), p. 584; idem, 'Corcomroe Abbey: some observations on its architectural history', *JRSAI*, pp 26-7; Harry Long, 'Three settlements of Gaelic Wicklow' in K. Hannigan and W. Nolan (eds), *Wicklow: history and society* (Dublin, 1994), p. 250. 30 Gerald of Wales [Giraldus Cambrensis] attests to this; see A.B. Scott and F.X. Martin (eds), *Expugnatio Hibernica by Giraldus Cambrensis* (Dublin, 1978), i, cap. xviii.   31 'Vita Sancti Laurencii', cap. xi.

ing to substantiate the claims of Gerald of Wales that the archbishop had instigated the siege. In fact, Lorcán negotiated on behalf of Strongbow that autumn. Subsequently, an ignominious rout of Ruaidrí's forces at Castleknock having broken the siege, the archbishop perhaps witnessed the submissions of Irish kings (including that of his own brother) to King Henry II over the winter of 1171-2. Moreover, a synod of the Irish Church at Cashel, which Lorcán attended, concluded in early 1172 by acknowledging the English king's lordship of Ireland. The indications are that the Irish hierarchy accepted the new political reality, and agreed to recognise the supremacy of the English crown insofar as its demands appeared reasonable. However, if the Church leaders had thought that English ambition in relation to Ireland was satisfied it soon became clear that this was not the case. Before the end of 1172, English crown authority was asserted over the local kingdom of Uí Fáeláin in north County Kildare, and by 1174 the conquerors were striving to extend their control beyond the boundaries of Leinster and Meath.

Although the political situation was rapidly deteriorating from the mid-1170s, one need not view the archbishop's increased commitment, about this time, to the cause of Ruaidrí Ua Conchobair as an awakening of national consciousness. It is true that Lorcán acted as Ruaidrí's envoy in the negotiations leading to the treaty of Windsor, when it was agreed that the king of Connacht should be recognised as high king of the Irish in those parts of the island (at this time about two-thirds) still under native control. However, while the treaty concerned the political division of Ireland as a whole, it had important implications at local level for the archbishop's dynasty. It served the goal of preserving the local kingdom of Uí Muiredaig, by curtailing the expansionist tendencies of the English settlers. Already Lorcán was striving, in association with his nephew Abbot Thomas, to preserve the properties of Glendalough which were by this time seen to be under threat. He success-fully prevailed upon the vice-regent Strongbow, his niece's husband, to con-firm the possessions of the abbacy as earlier granted by Diarmait Mac Murchada.[32]

Uí Muiredaig was weakened in 1176 not only by the death of Lorcán's brother Gilla Comgaill but by that of Strongbow, who seems to have adopted a sympathetic attitude towards the lineage of his wife's mother and uncles. Two years later, in 1178, Uí Muiredaig was overthrown when Dúnlaing, the last of Lorcán's brothers to rule, was slain by Robert Poer, custodian of Waterford on behalf of King Henry II. Price viewed these developments as the context for the archbishop's grants of land in south Dublin and in mid-Wicklow to augment the abbatial possessions of Glendalough, and further

32 Archbp. Alen's Reg., i, f. 21b; *Cal. Archbp. Alen's Reg.*, p. 2; MacShamhráin, *Church and polity*, pp 159, 238.

suggested that the displaced Uí Muiredaig dynasts and their retainers were settled on monastic lands.[33] Already fearing for his ecclesiastical possessions, Lorcán's anxiety was heightened the following year when, en route to the Lateran Council, he was sternly warned by King Henry II not to pursue any course of action contrary to the interests of the English crown. However, the fact that he returned from the council having secured two papal bulls to protect the interests of the archdiocese and of the diocese of Glendalough, and the fact that he was now papal legate, meant that Lorcán was in a stronger position than previously.[34] Moreover, because of the fall-out from the murder of Archbishop Thomas Becket, Henry II could not risk open confrontation with the pope. The king was, by all accounts, incensed. When, the following year, Lorcán set out once more on a diplomatic mission to Henry, this time bringing Ruaidrí Ua Conchobair's young son as a hostage, the English king refused to treat with him. Instead, Henry departed immediately for France. Lorcán followed, but it appears that the stresses of the previous decade caught up with him. He died prematurely, at the age of fifty-two, from fever, at Eu in Normandy on 14 November 1180.

III

The death of Lorcán inaugurated a new era of English crown intervention in the ecclesiastical affairs of Dublin. According to English law, licence to elect a new bishop had to be sought from the king, whose approval of the nomination was essential for appointment. Such legalities, new in an Irish context, provided an ideal opportunity for English crown interests to influence appointments to episcopal sees, particularly as the crown deemed it entirely appropriate, as Otway-Ruthven pointed out, to place those areas of the new Irish lordship closest to the centre of royal control under the jurisdiction of churchmen with whom it could work comfortably.[35] The crown's experience of Lorcán Ua Tuathail could hardly have been described as ideal, and his death enabled Henry II to secure the election of John Cumin, a royal clerk. Cumin certainly seemed to have the right credentials for a reliable supporter of crown interests; born in Somerset, he had a long track record of royal service and had already been singled out for royal favour.[36] In the event,

---

33 Archbp. Alen's Reg., i, f. 95b; *Cal. Archbp. Alen's Reg.*, p. 8; these lands were in Tír Meicei and Glenmalure (see Price, *Placenames*, i, p. 21; vii, p. xl); MacShamhráin, *Church and polity*, p. 161.   34 Maurice P. Sheehy (ed.), *Pontificia Hibernica: medieval papal chancery documents concerning Ireland 640 to 1241* (2 vols, Dublin, 1962), i, nos 9-10; M.F. Roche, 'Latin lives of St Laurence O'Toole', p. 18.   35 A.J. Otway-Ruthven, *A history of medieval Ireland* (London, 1968), p. 131.   36 John Cumin (or Comyn), an official at

Cumin was not imposed, but was formally elected by the canons. However, it seems that his election did not follow standard English practice; there is ample evidence to support Gwynn's contention that crown interests exploited divisions within the cathedral chapter.[37] It is almost certainly significant that the request for Henry to approve the selection of Cumin, preserved in the tract *Gesta Henrici*,[38] came from 'quorundam clericorum … Duvelinae'; this suggests that only a sector of the clergy was involved, most likely the Anglo-Norman party. The fact remains, however, that Cumin's election was confirmed by Pope Lucius III and the new archbishop was duly consecrated at Velletri.[39]

Quite apart from his pastoral responsibilities as archbishop, John Cumin was also a peer of the realm. The temporal possessions of the archdiocese confirmed to him under feudal law included the archiepiscopal manors of St Sepulchre, Swords, Finglas, Tallaght, Shankill, Ballymore and Castlekevin along with the land of Coillacht – an extensive wooded area extending from the upper Dodder to Tallaght.[40] The archbishop exercised jurisdiction in these manors through his seneschals and bailliffs, and also held licences for an annual eight-day fair in Swords and a Saturday market in Ballymore.[41] As expected, Cumin acted as a dedicated royal servant; following his consecration, he remained for some time at King Henry II's court, before travelling to Ireland in the autumn of 1184 to prepare for the visit of the young John, lord of Ireland.[42] Having spent four years attending to archiepiscopal duties, Cumin was called to serve in diplomatic and court duties from 1188. That summer, he was emissary to the king on behalf of Duke Richard; the following year, he was at the latter's coronation and attended the royal coun-

the royal chancery, was emissary for Henry II during the conflict with Archbishop Thomas Becket of Canterbury. He witnessed numerous royal charters and served as justice itinerant. His rewards included the archdeaconry of Bath in 1169 and, ten years later, appointment as judge of the northern division of England and warden of Glastonbury; see also below, chapter 3.   **37** See especially Aubrey Gwynn, 'Archbishop John Cumin', *Reportorium Novum*, 1, no. 2 (1956), pp 286, 293; Margaret Murphy, 'Balancing the concerns of Church and state: the archbishops of Dublin 1181 to 1228' in T. Barry, R. Frame and K. Simms (eds), *Colony and frontier in medieval Ireland: essays presented to J.F. Lydon* (London, 1995), p. 42, views Cumin's appointment as an 'undoubtedly political act'; M.V. Ronan, 'Anglo-Norman Dublin and diocese', *Irish Ecclesiastical Record*, 45 (1935), p. 149, went even further, describing Cumin's election as 'a farce'.   **38** W. Stubbs (ed.), *Gesta Henrici Secundi* (London, 1867), i, pp 280-1.   **39** *Pontificia Hibernica*, no. 11, p. 35.   **40** Archbp. Alen's Reg., i, f. 94b; *Cal. Archbp. Alen's Reg.*, p. 27; John T. Gilbert (ed.), *Crede Mihi* (Dublin, 1886), no. li; see James F. Lydon, 'Medieval Wicklow: a land of war' in K. Hannigan and W. Nolan (eds), *Wicklow: history and society* (Dublin, 1994), pp 154-5.   **41** For discussion of the possessions and privileges of the archbishopric, see Charles McNeill, 'The secular jurisdiction of the early archbishops of Dublin', *JRSAI*, 45 (1915), pp 81-108.   **42** *Expugnatio Hibernica*, §25; *Gesta Henrici Secundi*, i, 320, 339.

cils prior to the new king's departure on crusade. In 1199 and in 1201, Cumin assisted at the coronations of King John and of Queen Isabella.

Such service to the crown was quite in accordance with the archbishop's role as *de facto* palatine lord in Ireland, and there are ample indications that Cumin was himself conscious of his status in this regard. Shortly after his arrival in Ireland in 1184, he transferred his residence from the archiepiscopal palace on St Michael's Hill to the manor of St Sepulchre, where he was not subject to the civic jurisdiction of Dublin. His status was further augmented in 1190, with a confirmation of liberties and free customs by John, lord of Ireland, which gave the archbishop the right to hold courts in various parts of the Irish realm.[43] Cumin certainly used his authority and status to further the position of his extended family; he granted possessions in Holywood and Coillacht to his nephew Geoffrey de Marisco, and property in Domnach Imlech (Burgage, County Wicklow) to his nephew Gilbert Cumin. Another nephew, Walter Cumin, became parson of Swords while Helias Cumin, who held the manor of Kinsaley, may also have been related.

In the light of his position and his background, it is scarcely surprising that Cumin should feature as a strong defender of crown authority in Ireland. In this respect, it is significant that the provincial synod he convened during his early episcopacy, as well as standardising liturgical practice and combating abuses among the clergy, excommunicated armed men of Leinster who, by offering their services as mercenary or 'irregular' soldiers, threatened the *pax Normanica*.[44] It is also not surprising that Cumin should have been befriended by Gerald of Wales, nor that the latter should have approved of the archbishop's appointment. Both men shared broadly similar condescending views with regard to the Irish. Both also feared the capacity of the native rulers to strike at the colony, a factor which, in 1208, motivated Cumin to support the cause of erecting a royal castle at Dublin.

Cumin's devoted loyalty to the Crown did not prevent him from vigorously defending his archiepiscopal dignity and his possessions against competing authorities, be they ecclesiastical or secular. On the one hand, he laid foundations for later claims by Dublin for independence from Armagh when, shortly after assuming office, he obtained papal confirmation (13 April 1182) of his rights and privileges.[45] His stance in this regard prompted what became a protracted controversy over the primacy of Ireland. By the same token,

43 H.S. Sweetman (ed.), *Calendar of documents relating to Ireland 1171 to 1251* (London, 1877), nos 180, 1789.　44 Ronan, 'Anglo-Norman Dublin', p. 160; Aubrey Gwynn, 'Provincial and diocesan decrees of the diocese of Dublin during the Anglo-Norman period', *Archivium Hibernicum*, 11 (1944), p. 44; idem, 'Archbishop John Cumin', p. 306.
45 Archbp. Alen's Reg., i, f. 2; *Cal. Archbp. Alen's Reg.*, p. 9; *Crede Mihi*, no. ii; *Pontificia Hibernica*, i, no. 11; Ronan, 'Anglo-Norman Dublin', p. 154.

perceived threats to his temporalities from the civil government were opposed with equal resolve. In 1197, Cumin's clash over ecclesiastical properties with the justiciar, Hamo de Valognes, obliged him to flee to Normandy to escape repercussions. Unwilling to be bested, the archbishop secured a papal reprimand for both the justiciar and King Richard.[46] He showed equal determination in 1203 and again in 1205, when he resisted royal claims against his estates of Ballymore and Coillacht.[47] In short, while Cumin believed that Irish aspirations should yield to those of the crown, he likewise believed that the interests of the crown ought to be reconcilable to the dignities of his see.

Although not secured until after his death in 1212, and confirmed only in 1216, Cumin's most significant ecclesiastical achievement was the diocesan union of Dublin and Glendalough. A strong indication that this union was contemplated for some years before it was finally achieved lies in the absence of Glendalough from an 1182 list of Dublin's suffragan bishoprics, as noted by Dr Seán Duffy.[48] Further evidence is provided by the fact that John, lord of Ireland, 'by the advice of his barons', granted the bishopric of Glendalough to Cumin in 1185, and again seven years later.[49] The first of these grants proved stillborn, as an Irish cleric known as Macrobius was elected to the vacancy. The outcome of the grant following the death of Bishop Macrobius, seven years later, will be discussed presently.

For many historians, including Watt and Otway-Ruthven, the importance of this entire episode lay in the apparent support for the diocesan union on the part of Irish churchmen. Otway-Ruthven, seemingly anxious to present relationships between the Church *inter Anglicos* and the Church *inter Hibernicos* in a positive light, interpreted the union as an instance of Anglo-Norman and Gaelic Irish churchmen 'co-operating more or less happily'.[50] Certainly, the testimony which Archbishop Felix Ua Ruanada of Tuam presented to the Lateran Council of 1216 in support of this union appears to suggest Gaelic Irish and Anglo-Norman collaboration on the need for administrative restructuring in the interest of the Church. However, we cannot take Ua Ruanada's submission at face value. For instance, his statement that it was the original intention at the synod of Kells to make Dublin and Glendalough a single diocese, but that this had been blocked by 'the insolence of the Irish who then had power in that land', is not borne out by the

46 M. Murphy, 'Balancing the concerns of Church and state', pp 45-6.   47 Ronan, 'Anglo-Norman Dublin, pp 283-4.   48 Seán Duffy, 'The Bruce brothers and the Irish Sea world 1306-1329', *Cambridge Medieval Celtic Studies*, 21 (Summer 1991), p. 61, esp. n.9, argues convincingly that *Episcopatus Insularum* represents the bishopric of the Isles and not Glendalough.   49 Archbp. Alen's Reg., i, ff. 19, 21b; *Cal. Archbp. Alen's Reg.*, pp 11, 22; *Crede Mihi*, nos xxiv, xli.   50 Otway-Ruthven, *History of medieval Ireland*, p. 129.

surviving ordinances of Cardinal Paparo.[51] These contain no more than a general recommendation on the desirability of amalgamating small dioceses, and say nothing of uniting Glendalough with Dublin. It is also pertinent that, a mere five years after the synod of Kells, St Lorcán was considered for the vacant see of Glendalough and that, on his refusal, the see was administered successively by Cináed Ua Rónáin and Máel Calainn, for whom Lorcán sought papal confirmation of the diocesan temporalities in 1179. It may be added that, as McNeill observes, the testimony of Ua Ruanada was not forthcoming when John, lord of Ireland, issued his 1192 grant.[52]

Dublin could hardly have maintained a credible argument in support of its union with Glendalough based on economic need, since it was well endowed with ecclesiastical property, the greater part of it belonging to the archbishop. [53] Furthermore, the town was a thriving commercial port with far-reaching foreign connections, and so generated considerable wealth. It might understandably be argued that extension of the metropolitan boundaries would have strengthened Dublin's case, as conflict developed with Armagh regarding the primacy;[54] but while such considerations may well have fuelled a pre-existing commitment to absorb the lesser bishopric, they hardly explain why the project was first launched.

The extent to which an on-going process of Church reform could have drawn together Gaelic and Anglo-Norman clergy in common cause deserves some further consideration. The pro-reform party was committed to addressing what it viewed as abuses, and so sought to place the remaining 'traditional' Irish ecclesiastical centres under administrative structures which were more compatible with those of the universal Church. Glendalough was one of a handful of unreformed foundations which survived in the eastern and midland region; the remainder lay in the remote west and north-west of the country. These ecclesiastical settlements retained a quasi-monastic organisation of Early Christian insular origin and still had married (or at least noncelibate) clergy, senior office holders who were laymen (or at least men in minor orders) and, most significantly, hereditary ecclesiastical lineages. The survival of such practices, which were perceived as particularly Irish abuses, into the post-Norman period is attested to by the proceedings of a synod convened at Dublin in 1202 by the papal legate John de Monte Celio.[55]

51 Archbp. Alen's Reg., i, f. 52b; *Cal. Archbp. Alen's Reg.*, p. 40. 52 *Cal. Archbp. Alen's Reg.*, p. 41; see also A. Gwynn, *Irish Church in eleventh and twelfth centuries*, pp 268-9; Liam Price, 'St Kevin's Road', in John Ryan (ed.) *Féilsgríbhinn Eoin Mhic Néill* (Dublin, 1940; reprinted Dublin, 1995), p. 247. 53 A.J. Otway-Ruthven, 'The medieval church lands of County Dublin' in J.A. Watt et al. (eds), *Medieval studies presented to Aubrey Gwynn* (Dublin, 1961), pp 56-8. 54 Watt, *Church and two nations*, pp 112, 209. 55 *Annals of Ulster s.a.* 1201; Ronan, 'Anglo-Norman Dublin', pp 276-7.

At Glendalough, the Church families of Ua Rónáin and Ua Cathail continued to hold rank and to control ecclesiastical properties into the thirteenth century. In addition, as was the case at other large ecclesiastical settlements, the local ruling dynasty had an established interest; Uí Muiredaig maintained its dominance of Glendalough throughout Cumin's archiepiscopate in the person of Abbot Thomas, nephew of Lorcán Ua Tuathail.[56] There are indications that Thomas, whether or not he was an ordained priest, may have been a married man.[57] It is clear that the Glendalough community continued to view the abbot as the senior ecclesiastic and supported, or at least accepted, the continuation of hereditary office-holding; it may also have harboured some antipathy towards Anglo-Norman clergy.[58] In all probability, such unreformed Church organisation was deemed even less acceptable by the Romanised Anglo-Norman churchmen than by the native Irish reform party! However, it is difficult to explain the reduction, suppression or absorption of bishoprics and monastic foundations in marcher areas solely in terms of the implementation of Church reform. The persistence with which certain churchmen of the new order pursued such ends, with the active support of the civil administration, at times resorting to force and disregarding canon law, suggests that there was more at stake than mere ecclesiastical conformity.

While there is no explicit record of violence in the pursuit of union between Dublin and Glendalough, it would appear that possessions of the suffragan bishopric were seized by the metropolitan see and that strategies were adopted which, if not strictly uncanonical, were at least against accepted practice. Indeed, the situation is to some degree paralleled by that in other marcher areas, in which English-controlled dioceses pursued aggressive expansionist policies at the expense of their Irish neighbours.[59] When John, lord of Ireland, made his grant of Glendalough to Dublin in 1185, the incumbent bishop was still alive, which was certainly contrary to normal practice. It appears, indeed, that neither Lord John nor Archbishop Cumin had any great regard for Glendalough property rights; the former granted estates of the suffragan diocese for the augmentation of Dublin, the latter conveyed to his sub-tenants Church lands that were subject to Bishop Macrobius.[60] On the

---

56 MacShamhráin, *Church and polity*, pp 158-63.   57 Towards the close of the twelfth century, Alexander and Richard, apparently a son and grandson of Abbot Thomas, witnessed property transactions for the priory of St Mary's and St Thomas' abbey, Dublin; see John T. Gilbert (ed.), *Chartularies of St Mary's abbey, Dublin* (London, 1884), i, 32-3, ii, 3; idem (ed.), *The register of the abbey of St Thomas*, Dublin (London, 1889), no. 173.   58 See Katharine Simms, 'Frontiers in the Irish Church' in T. Barry et al. (eds), *Colony and frontier in medieval Ireland*, pp 196-7; MacShamhráin, *Church and polity*, p. 160.   59 Consider the case of Lismore, where the bishopric was taken over involving overt violence and uncanonical methods, or Clonmacnois where the diocese was reduced through aggressive expansion.   60 MacShamhráin, *Church and polity*, pp 161-2.

death of the latter in 1192 Cumin sought, with the support of the civil power, to bring Glendalough directly under his control.[61] Indeed, it seems reasonable, as Hand in fact has implied, to view the establishment of the new chapter of St Patrick's in this connection.[62] When the long-sought diocesan union was finally secured by Cumin's successor, Henry of London, it was confirmed by Rome on the basis of an individual testimony which advanced the dubious claim that such an arrangement was envisaged from the outset.

As argued above, the averment made in 1216 by Archbishop Ua Ruanada, that the union of Glendalough with Dublin was planned at the synod of Kells, cannot be accepted without serious reservation. It further emerges that, when the same submission is viewed in the context of the crown's support for the union and Ua Ruanada's personal circumstances, the prime motivation for the initiative was political. Ua Ruanada testified that the 'church in the mountains' had become 'so deserted and desolate for almost forty years that ... it has become a den of thieves and a pit of robbers' – a picture of decline which, as Gwynn has stressed, simply does not fit with the substantial evidence for cultural activity at Glendalough throughout this period.[63] The problem, quite clearly, was not the ecclesiastical centre *per se* but its political association with Uí Muiredaig; there are, after all, indications that remnants of Leinster dynasties had settled on monastic lands around Glendalough some forty years before the testimony was presented. Such resourcefulness would not only have shielded these Irish dynasts and their retainers from feudal dues,[64] but could well have left them sufficient scope to preserve elements of their royal dignity. Presumably their retainers figured, or were assumed to have figured, among the armed men excommunicated (for acts of rapine, as the record states) by Cumin at the provincial synod of 1186.

Clearly, Irish dynastic influence at Glendalough was equated with a breakdown of law and order, in which circumstances the incorporation of the suf-

---

61 *Crede Mihi*, §24, pp 31-2; Archbp. Alen's Reg., i, ff. 19, 21b; *Cal. Archbp. Alen's Reg.*, pp 11, 22; see Gearóid MacNiocaill (ed.), 'The charters of John, lord of Ireland, to the see of Dublin', *Reportorium Novum*, 3, no. 1 (1963-4), pp 285-8, 300-03; L. Price, *Placenames*, vii, pp xliii-xliv, maintains that the grant of the diocese while Bishop Máel Calainn was still alive was quite out of line with English ecclesiastical legislation, but that John was quite unscrupulous in dealing with the Irish Church.   62 Hand, 'Rivalry of the Cathedral chapters', p. 195; idem, 'The Church in the English lordship' in P.J. Corish (ed.), *The history of Irish Catholicism* (Dublin, 1968), II, iii, pp 10-11; see also below, chapter 3.   63 Archbp. Alen's Reg., i, f. 52b; *Cal. Archbp. Alen's Reg.*, p. 40; as indicated by Gwynn, *Irish Church in eleventh and twelfth centuries*, p. 267, this period witnessed on-going building, renovation, learning and scribal activity, co-inciding with the abbacies of the saintly Lorcán Ua Tuathail (1153-62) and his nephew Thomas (*c.*1166-1213), whom the author of *Vita Sancti Laurencii* clearly held in high esteem.   64 Price, *Placenames*, vii, introd. p. xxxii; MacShamhráin, *Church and polity*, p. 162.

fragan bishopric into an enlarged diocese of Dublin might seem justified. In assessing the validity of such an equation, however, account must be taken of Ua Ruanada's personal circumstances, which gave him reason to present fabricated evidence in support of Dublin's claim to Glendalough. An imposed candidate on the archbishopric of Tuam and a relentless campaigner for reform, he had made many enemies among the hereditary ecclesiastical lineages. Having suffered humiliation and expulsion he found a haven in Dublin at the expense, Warren reminds us, of King Henry's exchequer. Given Ua Ruanada's pro-reform sympathies, and more particularly his indebtedness to the crown, Gywnn's view of his testimony in relation to Glendalough as biased is persuasive.[65]

It remains to consider why Dublin opted for diocesan union, when Leinster-Irish aspirations might have been better accommodated by the expedient of bringing the suffragan bishopric directly under crown control. Perhaps this was Archbishop Cumin's plan when he secured the appointment of an Anglo-Norman candidate, William Peryn or Piro, to the vacant see in (or shortly after) 1192. Cumin received a grant in December of that year from John, lord of Ireland, authorising him to take charge of the temporalities of Glendalough at the next vacancy and to provide a bishop; presumably this is the arrangement sanctioned in the 1193 papal bull confirming to the archbishop the *capellania* of Glendalough. Based upon this, Gwynn concluded that Bishop William was little more than an archdeacon whose tenure of office merely represented a step towards diocesan union; this may be so, but the fact that Glendalough cathedral was remodelled about this time using Dundry limestone and that its episcopal possessions were augmented, albeit on a modest scale, suggests that matters were not so clear-cut.[66]

Alternatively, it is possible that Cumin intended William Peryn's appointment as suffragan bishop as a compromise arrangement short of diocesan union. It appears that the latter was successful in establishing his position at Glendalough (in view of the reconstruction of the cathedral), but persistent difficulties in dealing with the Irish Church establishment may well have frustrated such a compromise plan. To begin with, the possessions and sphere of authority of the abbot were almost inseparable from those of the bishop,

65 Gwynn, *Irish Church in eleventh and twelfth centuries*, pp 230-1, 267; Michael Dolley, *Anglo-Norman Ireland* (Dublin, 1972), pp 105, 116, presents a more sympathetic portrait of Felix; W.L. Warren, 'King John and Ireland', in James F. Lydon (ed.), *England and Ireland in the later Middle Ages: essays in honour of Jocelyn Otway-Ruthven* (Dublin, 1981), p. 38, discusses Felix's maintenance at the king's expense following his expulsion from Tuam as a possible motivating factor behind his testimony.   66 Gwynn, *Irish Church in eleventh and twelfth centuries*, p. 146; note that, in 1193, Cumin received papal confirmation of a grant of the chapelry of Glendalough; Archbp. Alen's Reg., i, f. 3; *Cal. Archbp. Alen's Reg.*, p. 23; *Pontificia Hibernica*, i, no. 27.

which undoubtedly made it difficult for the latter to function independently. Further complications must have arisen from the fact that the abbot, as noted above, was accepted within the unreformed ecclesiastical organisation of Glendalough as comarba Cóemgin, or successor of St Kevin. This, in effect, made him the senior ecclesiastic. In fact the tympanum of the 'Priests' House' in Glendalough, almost certainly a product of this same period, features a bishop and another cleric attending upon an enthroned abbot and so probably represents a deliberate statement on this very matter from Abbot Thomas.[67] It is also highly likely that Thomas was not without influence in his late uncle's chapter of Irish and Hiberno-Norse Augustinian canons at the Holy Trinity cathedral. Certainly, it is significant that Cumin's new chapter of St Patrick's (established, as already noted, in 1192) was formed of secular canons and was consciously modelled on English lines.[68] In the final analysis, difficulties in bringing the bishopric effectively under the control of Dublin and of the crown, especially in the light of contrary Uí Muiredaig interests, precipitated not only the diocesan union but the eventual dismantling of the Glendalough abbacy.

Although his strong support of crown interests (provided they did not conflict with his own) at times led him into conflict with the native Irish ecclesiastical establishment, there is nothing to suggest that Cumin was anti-Irish as such or was inclined towards bigotry. For instance, he maintained a good working relationship with 'politically safe' Irishmen, such as Bishop Ailbhe Ua Máelmuaid of Ferns – a man who was clearly acceptable to John, lord of Ireland. Neither was it the case that Cumin opposed all aspects of Irish culture; he was quite content to promote the cults of Irish saints, including Patrick, to whom he dedicated his new collegiate church. Furthermore, he supported the cause for canonisation of his predecessor Lorcán Ua Tuathail,[69] whose nephew Thomas so steadfastly opposed his designs in relation to Glendalough. By the same token, Cumin could take a strong stance against the Augustinians when his interests appeared to be threatened; he sidelined the Holy Trinity chapter, probably because they obstructed his plans for Glendalough, and asserted his authority over the Priory of All Hallows because claims by the bishop of Clogher infringed on the rights of the archiepiscopal see. At the same time, Cumin founded the new community of Augustinian canonesses at Grace Dieu and endowed it with tithes from several churches, including the new St Audoen's. Having augmented the community by transferring nuns from an older foundation at Swords, he charged them with educating daughters of the Anglo-Norman nobility.[70]

67 MacShamhráin, *Church and polity*, pp 163.   68 G.J. Hand, 'Rivalry of the cathedral chapters', pp 193-206; idem, 'The medieval chapter of St Patrick's, Dublin', *Reportorium Novum*, 3, no. 2 (1964), pp 229-48.   69 Ronan, 'Anglo-Norman Dublin', p. 284.   70

Archbishop John Cumin died, at an advanced age, on 25 October 1212. His passing, in many respects, marks a watershed in the history of the archdiocese of Dublin. The previous century had witnessed many changes, from the initial casting of a permanent diocesan framework which excluded Dublin, through elevation of the town to metropolitan status, to the intervention of the English crown. Cumin, while he owed his appointment to crown influence, had asserted his independence in ecclesiastical matters. He demonstrated a willingness to defend the rights of his see, even to the point of engaging in open confrontation with King John. At the same time, Cumin's pursuit of diocesan union with Glendalough, motivated as much by a desire for diocesan aggrandisement as by a commitment to Church reform, certainly served the political interests of the English Crown. Deprived of an ecclesiastical support network, the remnants of the Leinster Irish dynasties were all the more demoralised. In this way, Cumin bequeathed to his successor, Henry of London, an archdiocese which was considerably stronger than that which he had inherited; the extension of its boundaries was all but secured, and the strengthening of Crown authority thereby achieved would ensure relative political stability within the region for several generations.[71]

Ibid., p. 161.   71 I am grateful to Professor J.F. Lydon, Emeritus Lecky Professor of History, Dr Seán Duffy of the Department of Medieval History, Trinity College Dublin, and Dr Howard Clarke for reading drafts of this paper and generously offering advice on various points; any remaining errors are my own.

3

Archbishops and Anglicisation:
Dublin, 1181-1271

Margaret Murphy

During the episcopacies of the first four English-born archbishops of Dublin, which extended over ninety years from 1181 to 1271, the church of the diocese of Dublin was transformed as successive incumbents sought to anglicise ecclesiastical administration in personnel and in structure. New positions were created to fill the increasingly complex administrative machine that was put in place, and to support archbishops whose secular responsibilities frequently necessitated their presence outside the diocese and country and demanded a great deal of their attention and energy while *in situ*. New institutions were set up to provide the means of rewarding episcopal *familia* and to give effect to the particular enthusiasms and fashions of the newcomers. These changes had a distinct impact on the Church in the archdiocese, but they cannot be seen in local isolation because these years also witnessed the normalisation of the relationship between Church and state, with episcopal appointments, the establishment of jurisdictional areas of competence, and clerical privilege all conforming to 'that particular accommodation of ecclesiastical and lay interests which had already evolved in England'.[1] This was not accomplished without conflict, but then Dublin was no different from England and Europe, where similar changes were wrought during this crucial period of re-adjustment in Church-state relations.[2]

This chapter firstly considers the backgrounds of the four men who guided Dublin during this era and examines the factors which led to their appointment as archbishops of Dublin. The paucity of sources relating to the episcopates allows us no more than a glimpse into their spiritual life and actions, but their roles as pastors will be assessed as far as possible. There-

---

1 J.Watt, *The Church in medieval Ireland* (Dublin, 1972), p. 35.   2 See M. Murphy, 'Balancing the concerns of Church and state: the archbishops of Dublin, 1181-1228' in T.B. Barry, R. Frame and K. Simms (eds), *Colony and frontier in medieval Ireland: essays presented to J.F. Lydon* (London, 1995), pp 41-56.

after, the major elements in the process of anglicisation will be treated in more detail. This on-going process included the territorial reorganisation of the diocese, the foundation of the secular chapter of St Patrick's and the institution of the office of archdeacon. Actively pursued during the first three quarters of the thirteenth century, it can be said to have run out of momentum with the death in 1271 of Archbishop Fulk, because his episcopacy was followed by an eight-year interregnum during which the administrative machinery set in place over the previous decades had to bear the burden of governing the vacant see. This, inevitably, slowed down the impetus to reform and anglicise, and with the appointment of largely absentee archbishops in the latter part of the century it came to a virtual halt.

I

As the diocese of Dublin was, in many ways, the workshop where the principal elements of Angevin policy towards the Irish Church were forged, moulded and implemented, the appointment of the 'right' man to lead was of vital importance. The appointees had to be capable of establishing and maintaining administrative order in their diocese and of promoting similar activity in the Irish Church at large. Further, because the thirteenth-century archbishops were also the articulators of royal policy, frequently the dispensers of royal justice, and even, on occasion, the supervisors of royal military campaigns, they also had to possess political and military skills. This was a formidable list, and we can, in the first instance, establish the capacity of those who undertook the onerous task of governing the archdiocese by considering the background of the four men with whom we are concerned. As already stated, all were Englishmen.[3] John Cumin (1181-1212) probably

3 For more detailed biographical information on the four archbishops see M. Murphy, 'The archbishops and administration of the diocese and province of Dublin, 1181-1298' (Ph.D. thesis, Trinity College, Dublin, 1987). The careers of John Cumin and Henry of London are also covered in Murphy, 'Balancing the concerns of Church and state'. The early career of John Cumin was first traced by J.A. Robinson, 'The early career of John Cumin', *Somerset Historical Essays* (London, 1921), pp 90-9 and he and his successor have also been the subjects of articles by Aubrey Gwynn, 'Archbishop John Cumin', *Reportorium Novum*, 1 (1955-56), pp 285-310 and 'Henry of London, archbishop of Dublin: a study in Anglo-Norman statecraft', *Studies*, 38 (1949), pp 295-306, 389-402. See also the chapter on Henry of London in R.V. Turner, *Men raised from the dust: administrative service and upward mobility in Angevin England* (Pennsylvania, 1988), pp 91-106. John, Henry and Fulk have merited articles in *DNB* but Luke has been neglected by the historical biographers apart from a brief outline in G. Hand, 'The Church in the English lordship 1216-1307' in P.J. Corish (ed.), *A history of Irish Catholicism*, II, iii (Dublin, 1968), p. 38.

came from a minor family in Somerset where he spent his early years prior to entering into royal service at a young age. Henry of London (1213-28) was, as his toponym suggests, a Londoner, one of five sons of Bartholomew Blund, alderman of that city (d. 1201). Luke (1229-55) was also a Londoner, at least by adoption, since he held the important deanery of St Martin le Grand in the city from 1218. Fulk de Sandford (1256-71) was a member, albeit illegitimate, of the powerful Basset family. His uncle was Sir Philip Basset (d. 1271), royalist baron and English justiciar. He also had strong London connections, being either the nephew or perhaps the son of Fulk Basset, bishop of London (d. 1259). All were men of worldly experience whose early careers were spent in or close to metropolitan surroundings.

We have little contemporary description to add to these bare facts. Giraldus Cambrensis tells us that John Cumin was a learned and eloquent man with a profound love of justice.[4] Henry of London was sometimes called 'magister' in the records which suggests he had some university education, but it is not known where he earned this title. On his death he was described by the annalist of St Mary's as *vir sapiens et discretus*.[5] Luke also held the title of 'magister' but nothing is known of his education. The description which arguably holds most weight is that of Fulk de Sandford who was, according to Pope Alexander IV, 'a noble, lettered and honest man, circumspect in both spiritual and temporal affairs'.[6]

All four men were appointed to Dublin when in their 'middle years', probably between the ages of forty and fifty. One says 'probably' because the evidence for their age at the time of appointment can only be inferred. Thus John Cumin, on his death after holding the see for thirty-one years, was described as 'old and full of days'.[7] Henry of London was active in England for over twenty years before he was appointed to Dublin where he served for fifteen years. His successor Luke, who held the office for twenty-six years, was in poor health and blind when he died in 1255. It is possible that Fulk may have been appointed to the see of Dublin at an earlier age than the others, as he makes his first appearance in the English records just twelve years before his promotion to the episcopal see of Dublin. He too died in office after serving as archbishop sixteen years. The quartet was therefore old enough to have amassed considerable experience, but sufficiently young and, one must presume, sufficiently energetic to undertake the onerous duties required of them.

4 A.B. Scott, and F.X. Martin (eds), *Expugnatio Hibernica. The Conquest of Ireland by Giraldus Cambrensis* (Dublin, 1978), pp 198-9.   5 J.T. Gilbert (ed.), *Chartularies of St Mary's abbey*, Dublin (2 vols, London, 1884), ii, 280.   6 M.P. Sheehy (ed.), *Pontificia Hibernica: Medieval Papal Chancery documents concerning Ireland, 640-1261* (2 vols, Dublin, 1962-5), ii, no. 429.   7 *Chartularies St Mary's*, ii, 279.

All achieved eminence in their careers through a combination of hard work, talent and the support of a powerful patron. In John Cumin's case his patron was no less a person than Henry II whom he had served in an ambassadorial capacity.[8] Henry of London's early career was in the service of Hugh Nonant, bishop of Coventry, whose lead he had followed in supporting Count John in the conspiracy against his brother Richard. When John became king he found a loyal and able servant in Henry and his loyalty was rewarded with promotion in his ecclesiastical and secular careers. Luke's patron was the powerful English minister Hubert de Burgh, whose support allowed him to amass a considerable number of ecclesiastical preferments as well as to carve out a successful career in the Angevin administration. According to one chronicler, de Burgh was instrumental in securing Luke's election to Dublin in 1228.[9] Fulk de Sandford's prominent relative, the bishop of London, secured him the archdeaconry of Middlesex and was almost certainly instrumental in his appointment as treasurer of St Paul's. However, unlike the others, it was Fulk's influence at the papal curia which ensured his appointment to Dublin. He was in Rome in 1256 when Pope Alexander IV quashed the election of Ralph of Norwich, who had been chosen by the Dublin chapters, and he thereby became the first archbishop of Dublin provided by the Holy See.

On paper at least, each of the four appointed to the archdiocese had considerable experience of ecclesiastical administration in English dioceses prior to their election to Dublin. Three had held archdeaconries: John Cumin held Bath for close to twenty years; Henry of London was appointed to Stafford by Bishop Nonant, and Fulk held Middlesex. Given the busy careers pursued by John and Henry and their frequent absences abroad on the king's business it is unlikely that they performed many of the duties of their posts in person. Apart from Fulk, who appears to have limited himself to the treasurership of St Paul's, the other three also held multiple prebends in secular cathedrals.

John, Henry and Luke were royal appointees, and their years of service to the king were the main reason for their promotion. For the king, these men were tested and known quantities who were unlikely to succumb to the factionalism of colonial society. John Cumin served Henry II in the judiciary, the chamber and as a negotiator on a number of important diplomatic missions. Most crucially, he remained faithful to the king during the years of his dispute with Thomas Becket, even though his loyalty incurred the ecclesiastical censure of the archbishop of Canterbury.[10] Henry of London dis-

---

8 In 1163 Cumin represented the king's interests at the court of Frederick Babarossa, a task which would only have been entrusted to a skilled and proven servant. 9 H.R. Luard (ed.), *Matthew Paris, chronica majora* (7 vols, London 1872-83), v, 531. 10 J.C. Robertson

played an equal capacity to operate in different areas of government and he too proved his loyalty by standing staunchly by King John during the years 1208-14, when England and Wales lay under papal interdict. Luke was described by the chronicler of the Dunstable annals as one of the *maiores de curia regis*.[11] Most of the duties he performed for the king were financial in nature; he held the position of household treasurer and was periodically placed in charge of the wardrobe. By contrast, Fulk de Sandford was an unknown quantity. He does not seem to have held any position in the royal administration, although he would have been well informed about secular affairs in his capacity as treasurer of St Paul's since many of the canons of the cathedral were actively engaged in governmental business. At any rate, no objections to his appointment came from royal quarters and the temporalities of the diocese were speedily bestowed upon him.[12]

Only Henry of London is known to have had connections with Ireland prior to his appointment to Dublin. He visited the country at least twice and possibly four times.[13] It is not surprising, therefore, that Henry was prominent in the colonial government after his appointment. He served as chief governor on two occasions and was always among the chief advisers to the crown. This was clearly expected because, despite his lack of knowledge of Ireland and Irish affairs, John Cumin was required to make preparations for Prince John's visit to Ireland in 1185 shortly after his own arrival in the country. He also accompanied and advised John throughout this visit. For the remainder of Henry II's reign, those involved with the administration of the colony were frequently instructed to take the counsel of the archbishop of Dublin. Following Henry's death, Cumin lessened his ties with the royal court and ended up becoming embroiled in a serious dispute with the chief governor over the liberties of the diocese.[14] Luke did not hold an official position in the Irish administration, although he did perform a number of tasks on behalf of the king, most of them of a financial nature. He was, for example, asked on a number of occasions to audit the accounts of the treasurer and chief governor. By contrast, Fulk's relationship with the colonial government was characterised by conflict. From early on in his episcopacy his trenchant defence of ecclesiastical liberties set him at loggerheads with the secular authorities. It is surprising, therefore, to find that in 1265, during a period of crisis in Irish affairs following the capture of the chief governor Richard de la Rochelle, Fulk was requested by King Henry III to take over custody of Ireland.[15] He appears to have held the office of chief governor for

(ed.), *Materials for the history of Thomas Becket* (7 vols, London, 1875-85), vi, 602.   **11** H.R. Luard (ed.), *Annales Monastici, Rolls Series* (5 vols, London, 1864-9), iii, 118-19. **12** *Calendar of Patent Rolls, 1247-58*, p. 529.   **13** Murphy, 'Balancing the concerns of Church and state', p. 49.   **14** Ibid., pp 45-6.   **15** *Calendar of Patent Rolls, 1258-66*, p.

a short while – his only recorded service on behalf of the royal administration in Ireland.

II

The duties performed by the archbishops as representatives of government are relatively well-documented, as are the disputes with fellow ecclesiastics and royal and municipal officials. These inevitably tell us little about the spiritual concerns of the men or their impact as pastors on the diocese. In the normal course of events, one would turn to episcopal registers for such information, but the absence of records of this kind obliges one to look elsewhere.[16] The information that can be gathered thus is fragmentary but it does allow one to establish some perspective on the ways in which the activities of the four archbishops impinged upon the spiritual lives of religious and lay people in the diocese and province.

John Cumin appears to have addressed the matter of religious practices in the Dublin diocese shortly after his election, as the papal confirmation of his episcopal lands and dignities which was issued following his consecration included a detailed prohibition of abuses prevalent in the diocese. The prohibitions were almost exclusively concerned with the holding of benefices and chaplaincies, and stress the role of the archbishop in granting licences and assenting to appointments.[17] Abuses such as the assertion of hereditary rights to benefices and cemeteries and the holding of chaplaincies by regular clergy are explicitly forbidden. As this indicates, the prohibitions are of a fairly general nature and are not case specific. At the same time, they do show that from an early stage in his episcopacy the new archbishop was concerned to redress some of the abuses which were central to the concerns of the native reform movement in Ireland.[18]

407   16 One of the most important sources is the *Liber Niger Alani*, a compilation of diocesan records made for Archbishop John Alen in the early sixteenth century calendared by C. Mc Neill, *Calendar of Archbishop Alen's register, c.1172-1534* (Dublin, 1950). Many of the early documents reproduced in Alen's register as well as some others can be found in the late thirteenth-century compilation known as *Crede Mihi*, a collection of early to mid-thirteenth-century ecclesiastical grants, charters and letters: see J.T. Gilbert (ed.), *Crede Mihi: the most ancient register book of the Archbishops of Dublin before the Reformation* (Dublin, 1897). The deeds and chartularies of the Dublin religious houses contain much useful information on the activities and patronage of the archbishops and the papal correspondence found in collections such as Pontificia Hibernica is also invaluable.   17 *Pontificia Hibernica*, i, no. 11.   18 For an excellent summary of the pre-invasion reform movement see J.A. Watt, *The Church and the two nations in medieval Ireland* (Cambridge, 1970), chap. 1.

This willingness of Archbishop Cumin to address the particular problems of the Irish Church is manifest in the canons approved by the provincial council he summoned to meet in Dublin early in 1186. These canons, preserved in a confirmation of Pope Urban III, are believed to be largely the work of Cumin himself and, while reflecting the main topics of English statutes of the period, they are in the tradition of the native Irish reforming synods.[19] They display a particular concern with the proper administering of the sacraments, which was also the subject of the opening sermon of the council given by the archbishop.[20] Other topics covered by the canons include the freeing of benefices from lay control, the regularisation of marriage practices and the specification of those goods on which tithe was to be paid. The archbishop's efforts to enforce clerical celibacy are manifest in the canon forbidding a priest or deacon from having any woman in his house apart from his mother, his sister or a woman of advanced age. Cumin is known to have imposed sanctions on priests, both Irish and English, arising out of their contumacy.[21]

As this suggests, Cumin sought at the outset of his episcopacy to combine his involvement with the royal court with an active ministry. His activities in this latter respect were interrupted by his exile for nine years after 1197, and the combination of poor health and advanced years which prevented him from living up to this early promise thereafter.[22] It was his wish to bring the Church in Dublin into line with its English counterpart, but there is no evidence to suggest that he rode rough-shod over existing structures. He was responsible for the foundation of St Patrick's cathedral, but never ceased to treat Christ Church with the respect it deserved as the cathedral church of his diocese. He also displayed a willingness to co-operate with native churchmen, for while he was reluctant to allow any member of the Irish episcopate to perform spiritual functions in his diocese he pursued this policy by compromise rather than by prohibition.[23] Cumin was also gener-

---

19 *Pontificia Hibernica*, i, no. 16. See also A. Gwynn, 'Provincial and diocesan decrees of Dublin during the Anglo-Norman period', *Archivium Hibernicum*, 11 (1944), pp 39-44 and C.R. Cheney, 'The earliest English diocesan statutes', *English Historical Review*, 75 (1960), pp 1-29. A full English translation of the statutes can be found in M.P. Sheehy, *When the Normans came to Ireland* (Dublin, 1975), pp 40-4.   20 J.S. Brewer (ed.), *Giraldi Cambrensis opera* (8 vols, London, 1861-91) i, 65-6.   21 *Ibid.*, 66; *Pontificia Hibernica*, i, no. 19.   22 For details of the dispute leading to Cumin's exile see M. Murphy, 'Ecclesiastical censures: an aspect of their use in thirteenth-century Dublin', *Archivium Hibernicum*, 44 (1989), pp 91-2.   23 He was successful in negotiating an end to the jurisdictional claims of the bishop of Clogher over the Augustinian house of All Hallows, Dublin and by moving the Convent of Grace Dieu to a new residence in Lusk he effectively removed it from the control of its one-time mother house of Clonard in the diocese of Meath (*Alen's Register*, p. 35; M.T. Flanagan, 'St Mary's Abbey, Louth and the

ous with gifts of lands and tithes and, in his benefactions, showed a particular favour for houses of nuns, endowing both the convent of Grace Dieu in
Lusk and the nuns of Timolin in Kildare.[24]

Compared to Cumin, his successor Henry of London was more noted for
his administrative expertise than for his pastoral care. Yet there is evidence
that even this consummate 'civil servant' did not entirely neglect his spiritual responsibilities. While churchmen who held high offices of state were
able to delegate a great proportion of their religious work, there were some
duties which required personal attention. Thus, Henry attended the Fourth
Lateran Council in Rome in 1215, accompanied by two of his suffragan bishops and other representatives of the Irish Church.[25] No information survives
on the part he played in its affairs, but he was held in sufficiently high standing to be appointed papal legate on his return to Ireland in 1217. He held
this post for three years until he was removed by Pope Honorius III amid
suggestions that he was too closely involved in discriminatory royal mandates
relating to the exclusion of Irish clerks from ecclesiastical office.[26]

As legate, Henry presided over a general synod of Irish clergy that,
according to one contemporary source, passed much beneficial legislation for
the Irish Church.[27] Unfortunately the decrees of this synod have not survived. We do have evidence for one of Henry's spiritual concerns. While at
Rome in 1215 he informed the pope about his dissatisfaction with those religious men in his diocese who, not observing religious discipline, lived in scat-
tered cells and wandered around in search of alms.[28] As a result, he received
papal authorisation to compel such men to gather together in a suitable place,
which he later used to justify his political decision to grant the Irish abbey
of St Saviour's of Glendalough to All Hallows Priory in Dublin.[29]

Henry displayed a practical piety through his generous benefactions to
religious houses in and around Dublin. He followed the example of several
English bishops with similar backgrounds in the royal service by favouring
institutions which cared for the sick and the poor. He made gifts to St
Thomas' abbey to help with the care of paupers and to the hospital of St
John the Baptist.[30] He also founded a new hospital, St James at the Steyne,

introduction of the Arroasian observance into Ireland', *Clogher Record*, 10 (1980), pp 224-
7). **24** *Alen's Register*, pp 19, 31, 32, 34. **25** P.J. Dunning, 'Irish representatives and
Irish ecclesiastical affairs at the fourth Lateran Council' in J.A. Watt, J.B. Morrall and
F.X. Martin (eds), *Medieval studies presented to Aubrey Gwynn SJ* (Dublin, 1961), pp 90-
113. **26** *Pontificia Hibernica*, i, nos 135-6. **27** *Chartularies St Mary's*, ii, 280. **28**
Pontificia Hibernica, i, no. 101. **29** R. Butler (ed.), *Registrum Prioratus Omnium Sanctorum
juxta Dublin* (Dublin, 1845), p. 100. **30** J.T. Gilbert (ed.), *Register of the abbey of St
Thomas* (London, 1889), no. 341; E. St John Brooks (ed.), *Register of the hospital of St
John the Baptist, Dublin* (Dublin, 1936), no. 338.

which was intended to cater specifically for the needs of poor pilgrims who planned to visit the shrine of St James at Compostella.[31] He also continued the ongoing building work at St Patrick's and at Christ Church. During his episcopacy most of the nave at Christ Church was completed with stone and sculptors brought over from England.[32] In 1220 Henry granted rents to the prior and convent for the construction of a new entrance, in return for which they undertook to celebrate his obit forever.[33] It was appropriate, therefore, when he died in 1228, that he was laid to rest in Christ Church.

The early days of Luke's tenure of office were taken up with raising funds to defray the considerable debts he accrued in having his election to Dublin accepted at the papal court, and it seems that the special attention he devoted to the regulation and extension of tithes was linked to his financial necessity. Apart from one or two short visits to England, Luke does not appear to have been absent from his diocese for any long periods, neither did he hold any secular office which necessitated travel outside his province. He therefore had plenty of time to devote to spiritual concerns, yet very little evidence survives that provides any insight into his role as pastor of souls. In many respects Luke is the most shadowy Dublin archbishop of the thirteenth century. He appears to have taken a special interest in St Patrick's because he passed legislation further bringing it into line with the English secular cathedrals on which it was modelled. He also concerned himself with the problem of illegitimacy among churchmen in his diocese, arising out of which he received special papal permission to dispense priests and other religious of 'defective birth'.[34] Luke himself was of illegitimate birth, which had prevented his elevation to the bishopric of Durham two years prior to his nomination to serve in Dublin.[35] Unlike his predecessor, he was not a great benefactor. Some years before his death he granted lands to the hospital of St John the Baptist for which the prior and brethren agreed to offer special prayers. Each sick person in the hospital and each attendant was thereby committed to say five paternosters daily at stated hours for the soul of the archbishop. It appears that Luke's aptitude for accountancy extended even to the provision he made for salvation.[36]

The episcopacy of Fulk de Sandford proved more controversial than those of his three predecessors because of his reformist energy and his concern for

31 *Alen's Register*, p. 55. The foundation was apparently encouraged by Pope Innocent III who made it a condition of his confirmation of the union of the diocese of Glendalough with Dublin.   32 R. Stalley, 'Three Irish buildings with West Country Origins' in *Medieval art and architecture at Wells and Glastonbury* (Oxford, 1981), pp 62-80.   33 M.P. Sheehy (ed.), 'The Registrum Novum of Holy Trinity, the medieval charters', *Reportorium Novum*, 3 (1961-4), pp 270, 273.   34 *Pontificia Hibernica*, ii, no. 263.   35 *Calendar of Patent Rolls, 1226-32*, p. 191.   36 *Alen's Register*, p. 83.

spiritual affairs. One of his first actions on arriving in Dublin in the winter of 1256-7 was to embark upon a provincial visitation. Judging by the litigation that ensued it is likely that this was the first such visitation of the Dublin province. This conclusion is reinforced by the fact that some of the complaints relate to the level of procurations levied by the archbishop and the size of his accompanying retinue. Thus, the bishop of Ferns sent a petition to Rome complaining that when the archbishop of Dublin had made his visitation of the city and diocese of Ferns he brought such a huge number of attendants with him that the church of Ferns could not support them all, and that the procurations he had sought were too large. Significantly, this is contradicted by the experience of the bishop and clergy of Leighlin who found Fulk more accommodating.[37] He replied to their request that he take into consideration the poverty of their diocese by limiting the procurations taken from each of the five deaneries to ten pounds.[38]

Fulk was less than satisfied with the conditions he found in many religious houses in the province. He informed the pope that religious observance had been all but abandoned in some Benedictine and Augustinian houses, and received permission for four houses to be united and three to be transferred to more suitable places.[39] The archbishop was well aware that such actions would provoke hostility, as he requested the pope in the summer of 1257 to allow him to choose a confessor who could, if necessary, absolve him from sentences of excommunication.[40]

The readiness demonstrated on his appointment to confront problems head-on became a feature of Fulk's episcopacy. As a result, he spent a great deal of time embroiled in various disputes not only with fellow churchmen but also with royal and municipal officials, and the first decade of his episcopacy was the most turbulent in the history of the archdiocese in the thirteenth century. The most serious disputes were jurisdictional and appertained to the use of secular power against clerics and the obstruction of spiritual punishments. In addition, the archbishop inveighed with particular bitterness against attempts by the mayor and citizens of Dublin to limit customary offerings to the Church. These conflicts reached crisis-point in 1265-6 when Fulk excommunicated the mayor and some of the citizens and laid an interdict on the city of Dublin.[41] Through his influence with the papal legate in London,

---

37 *Crede Mihi*, p. 104.   38 *Alen's Register*, p. 88.   39 *Pontificia Hibernica*, ii, no. 443. These religious houses are not named and cannot be definitely identified. Archbishop Alen claimed that the convent of Holmpatrick was transferred from St Patrick's Island as a result of this indult: (*Alen's Register*, p. 87). It is likely that the Augustinian abbey of Kells in Ossory was one of the houses under threat as the prior and convent at this time obtained a papal indult that they were not to be molested in any way or their property injured or diminished.   40 *Pontificia Hibernica*, ii, no. 445.   41 Murphy, 'Ecclesiastical

he eventually obtained a settlement of his grievances. However, there is no evidence that his determined struggle to protect his ecclesiastical liberties resulted in any long-term improvement in the position of the Dublin Church.[42]

Fulk's term of office ended on a calmer note, possibly because the archbishop was in poor health. In April 1267 letters of protection were issued to him for a pilgrimage to the tomb of St James at Compostella.[43] During his absence, the affairs of the diocese were administered by his brother John de Sandford who acted for him until late in 1270. Fulk died early in 1271 and is thought to have been buried in St Patrick's, where a late thirteenth-century tomb effigy has been identified as belonging to him or possibly to his brother, who became archbishop of Dublin in 1285.[44]

In view of Fulk's evident energy and eagerness to enhance the Church in the province of Dublin, it is reasonable to surmise that undated synodal canons transcribed into the *Crede Mihi* date from his episcopacy.[45] The 'core' of the canons, amounting to some one-third of the total, may have been brought by him to Ireland and promulgated during his 1256-57 provincial visitation. From what one can tell, these canons are derived from those of the diocese of York and are devoted, in the main, to providing elementary instruction for the parochial clergy. In this they resemble most surviving English thirteenth-century diocesan statutes which, according to Christopher Cheney, 'represent the most practical and most conscientious attempt by the ecclesiastical authorities of the time to acquaint an ignorant parochial clergy with the rudiments of the Christian faith and the obligations which attached to the cure of souls'.[46] The remaining two-thirds of the collection cannot with equal conviction be ascribed to the episcopacy of Archbishop Fulk, though the case for such an attribution is strong. Taken together, they represent a most important source for religious practice in the Dublin diocese and province in the thirteenth century and provide tangible evidence of Fulk's determination to raise the religious standards of the lower clergy.

III

This examination of the episcopacies of the first four English-born archbishops of Dublin reveals that for all the similarity of their backgrounds and,

censures', pp 91-93.   **42** *Alen's Register*, p. 130; *Calendar Patent Rolls, 1266-72*, p. 54. **43** *Calendar Patent Rolls, 1266-72*, p. 53.   **44** See J. Hunt, *Irish Medieval figure sculpture, 1200-1600* (2 vols, Dublin, 1974), i, 140; ii, plate 73   **45** Gwynn, 'Provincial and diocesan decrees', pp 44-55. The dating of these canons has gone through a range of possibilities, see C.R. Cheney, 'A group of related synodal statutes of the thirteenth century' in Watt et al (eds), *Medieval studies Gwynn*, pp 114-32.   **46** C.R. Cheney, 'The legislation of the English Church', *English Historical Review*, 50 (1935), p. 197.

to a lesser extent, their education and training, their pastoral concerns as diocesans took different forms and achieved varying degrees of success. They were at one, however, in their desire to introduce the structures and practices with which they had become familiar in the English dioceses where they had served time as ecclesiastical administrators. It is now intended to look in more detail at some aspects of this anglicisation process, which commenced with the diocesan reconstruction implemented during the first four decades of English control. This was the union of the diocese of Glendalough with Dublin. Traditionally, this has been presented as an unprincipled take-over by the English of an historic Irish diocese.[47] While it is true that the absorption of Glendalough into Dublin dovetailed with the political agenda of the colonists, it can also be argued that the union represented an extension of the process of diocesan reorganisation arising out of the reforming councils of the twelfth century.

The council of Kells in 1152 had raised Dublin to metropolitan status, and named Glendalough as one of its suffragan dioceses. It was at this council also that Cardinal Paparo had ruled that small and impoverished dioceses should be incorporated into larger dioceses on the death of their present bishops.[48] Whether Glendalough fitted into the category of 'small and impoverished' at that time is not known, but it is suggestive that Archbishop Cumin received a grant from Prince John of the bishopric of Glendalough in order to increase the size and wealth of the Dublin Church shortly after his arrival in 1185.[49] The lands already held by the archbishop of Dublin were considerable by most standards. It has been estimated that the archbishop held 53,200 statute acres – about a quarter of the total area of County Dublin – though most of these lands were already in Church possession before the conquest.[50]

The grant to Dublin of Glendalough was reaffirmed in 1192 when it was stated that the union of the two dioceses would come into effect when Glendalough next became vacant.[51] In this same year William Peryn or Piro, an Anglo-Norman clerk, became bishop of Glendalough. The see became vacant at his death some time before July 1213 when the newly-appointed Henry of London received a further grant of the diocese of Glendalough

47 M.V. Ronan, 'The union of the dioceses of Glendalough and Dublin', *Journal Royal Society Antiquaries Ireland* (henceforth *JRSAI*), 60 (1930), pp 56-62.   48 This ruling was referred to at the diocesan synod held by the bishop of Meath in 1216 (D.Wilkins, *Concilia Magnae Britanniae et Hiberniae* (4 vols, London, 1737), i, 547).   49 G. Mac Niocaill, 'The charters of John, lord of Ireland, to the see of Dublin', *Reportorium Novum*, 3 (1961-4), p. 285.   50 A.J. Otway-Ruthven, 'The medieval Church lands of County Dublin' in Watt et al. (eds), *Medieval studies Gwynn*, pp 56-8.   51 Mac Niocaill, 'Charters of John', p. 300.

from King John.[52] While he was attending the fourth Lateran Council in 1215-16, Henry ensured that the royal grants were placed before Pope Innocent III, and in February 1216, he received confirmation from him of the unification of the two dioceses.[53] The unification received the support of other Irish prelates then in Rome, who testified that it was indeed intended by Cardinal Paparo that Glendalough should be incorporated into Dublin on the death of its incumbent.[54] This was significant, since there had been previous resistance to such a suggestion. From 1216 however, the unification was a *fait accompli* whose legality could not be doubted; the union was not challenged and there was no further mention of a bishop of Glendalough in the thirteenth century.

Arguably, the most important element of the diocesan re-organisation that was implemented during the episcopacies of the first two English archbishops was the foundation of St Patrick's cathedral.[55] St Patrick's was set up as a secular cathedral, based on the Norman model, where each canon was allowed his own prebend as a source of income. This type of cathedral organisation was introduced into England from Normandy because monks and clerics living a semi-monastic life were unable to meet the increased demands made of them by bishops and monarchs.[56] Well-educated clerks with independent sources of income, mobile, and capable of working flexible and often long hours were needed, and secular chapters provided, in the form of individual prebends, the ideal method of rewarding these ecclesiastical 'civil servants'. The need for administrators supplied from secular chapters was particularly acute in newly conquered lands where monastic chapters were the norm. They emerged in England in the years following the Norman invasion, and similar factors ensured the foundation a century later of secular chapters in Ireland.[57]

---

52 T.D. Hardy (ed.), *Rotuli Chartorum, 1199-1216* (London, 1835) p. 194.   **53** *Pontificia Hibernica*, i, no. 93.   **54** Doubt has been cast on the motives of some of the Irish prelates who testified in favour of the union: see A. Gwynn, *The Irish Church in the eleventh and twelfth centuries*, ed. G. O'Brien (Dublin, 1993), pp 267-8.   **55** Still unsurpassed for the history of Dublin's secular cathedral is William Monck Mason, *The history and antiquities of the collegiate and cathedral church of St Patrick near Dublin* (Dublin, 1820). It is described as 'incomparable' by Geoffrey Hand whose own articles are indispensable: see 'The medieval chapter of St Patrick's cathedral, Dublin, I: the early period *c*.1219-*c*.1279', *Reportorium Novum*, 3 (1961-4), pp 229-48 and 'The rivalry of the cathedral chapters in medieval Dublin', *JRSAI*, 92 (1962), pp 193-206.   **56** On the organisation of secular chapters in England the major work remains K. Edwards, *The English secular cathedrals* (rev. ed., Manchester, 1967). See also A.T. Bannister, 'The origin and growth of the cathedral system', *Church Quarterly Review* (1927), pp 86-96 and J.H. Strawley, 'The origin and growth of cathedral foundations as illustrated by the Cathedral Church of Lincoln', *Lincoln Minster Pamphlets*, i (1951).   **57** See K.W. Nicholls, 'Medieval Irish

All four archbishops played an important role in the early organisation of St Patrick's, thereby ensuring that it resembled the secular cathedrals of their homeland in most major respects by the middle of the thirteenth century. It was John Cumin who commenced the process in 1191 when he raised the parish church of St Patrick's to collegiate status and instituted a group of thirteen clerks 'of approved life and learning' with the stated aim that they should provide, by their example and learning, education for the less learned Irish people.[58] A year or so later, he granted to the canons the same liberties and privileges enjoyed by the secular canons of Salisbury cathedral, but he made no provision for the governing of the body of canons and appointed no officials or dignitaries.[59] It fell to his successor, Henry, to complete the internal organisation of the cathedral when he decreed in 1220-1 that the cathedral should possess the dignitaries of dean, chancellor, precentor and treasurer.[60] Additional legislation during Henry's episcopacy, extending the jurisdictional freedom of the canons in their prebends, brought St Patrick's even closer into line with the English secular cathedrals in general and with Salisbury in particular.[61]

With the cathedral on a sound administrative footing, the primary task faced by Archbishops Luke and Fulk was to correct abuses such as the non-residence of canons. The efforts made to address this problem bear comparison with those adopted in England, where non-residence plagued the secular cathedrals. The object was not to force residence on all the canons but to ensure that those canons that did reside were financially rewarded, usually at the expense of non-residents. As a former dean of St Martin le Grand, Archbishop Luke was familiar with the problems caused and resentments generated by non-resident canons who used their prebends to finance their administrative or academic careers and who contributed nothing in return. Anxious to put an end to this practice, he passed legislation instructing newly-appointed canons to appear in person at St Patrick's within a year of appointment and to fulfil any obligations, pecuniary or otherwise, connected with their succession to a prebend.[62] He also directed that each canon should provide a vicar to sing in the cathedral and to take his place if he was absent for any reason; and, at the request of one of the canons, gave the vicars a plot of ground on which to build a common hall of residence.[63]

Throughout the thirteenth century, the deans of St Patrick's were closely connected with successive archbishops. While, as in most English cathedrals, the chapter had the privilege of conducting a free election for the position

cathedral chapters', *Archivium Hibernicum*, 31 (1973), pp 102-11.   **58** N.B. White (ed.), '*Dignitas Decani*' *of St Patrick's cathedral, Dublin* (Dublin, 1957) pp 1-3.   **59** Ibid., p. 41. **60** *Pontificia Hibernica*, i, no. 143.   **61** *Dignitas Decani*, pp 6-7.   **62** Ibid., p. 34.   **63** *Alen's Register*, p. 71; *Dignitas Decani*, p. 164-5.

of dean, St Patrick's differed in that the archbishop of Dublin reserved and exercised the right, as a prebend-holder, to share in the election.[64] It is not surprising, therefore, to find that the first two deans, William Fitz Guido and Richard de Gardino, were nephews of Archbishops Henry and Luke respectively, that Richard of St Martin, who became dean c.1259, was for a long time a clerk of Archbishop Luke's, and that he was succeeded in 1275 by John de Sandford, brother of Archbishop Fulk. Though the potential for abuses was high, this exercise of patronage on behalf of the archbishops was not injurious to the chapter, as all four deans appear to have been able administrators and to have been largely resident. They were also prepared to conduct themselves independently of episcopal control when the needs of the chapter warranted it.[65]

The influence of the archbishop percolated through the chapter into the composition of the prebendaries in general. Most of the men who are described in contemporary documents as 'clerks of the archbishop' were prebendaries in St Patrick's, but it is impossible in most cases to say whether these men owed their prebends to the fact that they were members of the archbishop's *familia* or whether they became clerks by virtue of holding prebends. It has been found in most English chapters that the bishop's council was normally composed of canons and that the bishop picked his official staff from their ranks.[66] The identification of such a group of canons within the medieval chapter of St Patrick's is rendered impossible by the poor survival of episcopal *acta* from the thirteenth century. However, what evidence there is suggests that the canons that most frequently witnessed the archbishop's charters were not chosen randomly, but rather formed a distinct group from which the archbishop chose his spiritual and secular staff.

The foundation of a secular cathedral reflected a political as well as an ecclesiastical agenda and it is no surprise, therefore, to find the personnel of St Patrick's played an important role in secular administration.[67] This was particularly marked during the episcopacies of bishops who were themselves heavily involved in such administration. Like their masters, these canons demonstrated their ability to move easily from one employment into another, as is well illustrated by the case of Master Thomas de Chedworth (d. 1311). He held the chancellorship and the deanship of St Patrick's and was also chancellor and deputy treasurer in the Irish exchequer. As an official of Fulk

---

64 Edwards, *English secular cathedrals*, p. 105. Salisbury was the only exception to this rule. *Dignitas Decani*, p. 5; *Alen's Register*, pp 273, 290.   65 See for example the dean and chapter's complaint against Archbishop Fulk's attempts to limit the payment of some tithes on episcopal lands (*Pontificia Hibernica* ii, nos 479 & 496).   66 C.R. Cheney, *English Bishops' chanceries 1000-1250* (Manchester, 1950).   67 H.G. Richardson and G.O. Sayles, *The administration of Ireland 1172-1377* (Dublin, 1963), pp 2-4.

de Sandford, he presided over the ecclesiastical court of Dublin, while simultaneously serving as itinerant justice of the crown and a justice of the common bench. The similarity of the interests shared by the canons and archbishops goes some way to explaining the cordial relations they enjoyed during the thirteenth century. Episcopal visitations, for example, which were a source of so much conflict between the English chapters and their bishops during this period, were not a cause of discord in Dublin.

The foundation of St Patrick's did, of course, mean that there were two cathedrals a mere few hundred yards apart. This inevitably produced complications, most notably over the right to participate in archiepiscopal elections.[68] Difficulties first arose in 1228 when both chapters claimed and were given royal licence to elect. Representatives of the secular chapter proceeded to elect Luke under strong royal influence, to the dissatisfaction of the chapter of Holy Trinity (Christ Church) which complained bitterly but unsuccessfully. Luke attempted to broker an agreement during his episcopacy but the problem had not been resolved by the time it came to elect his successor. Indeed, matters were to worsen following Fulk's death in 1271 when the chapters elected rival candidates and their refusal to compromise resulted in an eight-year vacancy in the see. The end result of the conflict between the chapters was that they had virtually no say in the elections of any of the thirteenth-century archbishops and, in the latter part of the century, their inability to agree resulted in the accession of non-resident or largely absentee prelates. As a result, while it can be shown that the foundation of St Patrick's played a major part in the anglicisation of the Dublin Church in the late twelfth and early thirteenth centuries, it was also responsible to a large extent for the slowing down of that process that took place in the latter part of the thirteenth century.

Another significant innovation in ecclesiastical administration brought about in the post-conquest Dublin Church was the introduction of the office of archdeacon.[69] In England, while the title archdeacon pre-dates the Norman Conquest, the office itself only emerged after 1066.[70] Thereafter it spread quickly and virtually every diocese had at least one archdeacon by 1100. This most important member of the bishop's *familia*, in fact his chief officer in the diocese, first appears in the Dublin sources in 1185 when 'Macrobius, Archdeacon of Dublin' witnessed the ratification of Archbishop Cumin.[71]

---

68 See Hand, 'Rivalry of the cathedral chapters'.   69 The introduction of the office of archdeacon into the Irish Church is generally seen as an innovation of the Anglo-Normans. There is no mention of the office in the early letters of the archbishops of Canterbury concerning the Irish Church or in the *Liber de Statu Ecclesiae* of Bishop Gilbert of Limerick written *c.*1100.   70 C. Brooke, 'The archdeacon and the Norman Conquest' in D. Greenway, C. Holdsworth & J. Sayers (eds), *Tradition and change: essays in honour of Marjorie Chibnall* (Cambridge, 1985), pp 1-20.   71 *Chartularies of St Mary's*, i, 173.

Little is known of this first archdeacon, although it seems probable that Macrobius was chosen from John Cumin's household clergy, and he went on to become bishop of Glendalough.[72] His successor, William, appears to have held the office for about thirty years but he too has left little trace in the records beyond his appearance in witness lists. Archbishop Alen notes in his register that '... before the position was created in St Patrick's the archdeacon of Dublin had a stall in Holy Trinity'.[73] It is not clear if he means by this that the office became annexed to St Patrick's in 1191 when the collegiate church was founded, or later in 1220 when the four cathedral officials were instituted. William appears in records from at least the 1190s in association with a group of prebend holders of St Patrick's. He held the prebend of Lusk in the cathedral, although later in the century the prebend of Taney was assigned to the archdeaconry.[74] One of the houses in the cathedral close was also in the possession of the archdeacon.[75] Relations between St Patrick's and the archdeacon were good, in contrast to many English dioceses where friction frequently developed between the archdeacons and cathedral chapters over such matters as prebendal exemption from jurisdiction and procurations. As St Patrick's had been clearly granted such exemptions from its very foundation, the archdeacon had no precedence on which to base any claims and thus disputes were avoided.[76] Christ Church claimed privileges similar to St Patrick's with regard to exemption from archidiaconal visitation and procurations but with less success. Disputes between the parties continued well into the fourteenth century, with the archdeacon insisting on rights to visit and collect proxies from the churches which pertained to the common fund of the regular cathedral.[77]

No archidiaconal registers survive for pre-reformation Dublin. However, information about the duties and functions of the office can be found in other ecclesiastical sources. There is evidence, for example, of the archdeacon performing such tasks as conducting enquiries into vacant benefices, inducting clergy appointed by the archbishop and formally handing over churches granted to religious houses.[78] From as early as 1181 (the provincial synod of John Cumin) there is reference to the occasions when an archdeacon might act as a substitute for the bishop, while the synodal canons which can be dated to the episcopacy of Archbishop Fulk outline not only episcopal duties which could equally be performed by the archdeacon but also some functions which specifically pertained to the archdeacon's office.[79] In particular,

---

72 *Register of St Thomas'*, pp 291-2.   73 *Alen's Register*, p. 157.   74 Ibid., p. 87.   75 Ibid., p. 76.   76 *Dignitas Decani*, pp 1-3.   77 The dispute was finally settled in 1339 when the archdeacon's claim was upheld by Archbishop Alexander de Bicknor who then fixed the amount of proxies to be paid (*Alen's Register*, p. 86).   78 See for example *Alen's Register*, pp 198-200; *Register of St John's*, pp 210-11.   79 Gwynn, 'Provincial and dio-

the role of the archdeacon as overseer of the morals and behaviour of both the lower clergy and laity emerges clearly. The canons provide no information about how these duties were performed, but it is known that each year the archdeacon held a number of chapters which the lower clergy were obliged to attend.[80] Presumably the archdeacon carried out most of his activities at these chapters, which occasions could also have been availed of to acquaint the lower clergy with episcopal mandates and other matters of general importance. The archdeacon was also expected to carry out corrections while on visitation. Little evidence and no records of archidiaconal visitation survive for the diocese of Dublin in the thirteenth century. However, exemption from archidiaconal visitation was a sought-after privilege, which indicates that the visitation itself was real.

Archdeacons became so indispensable to diocesan administration that they were given the title of 'oculus episcopi' – the bishop's eye. During some episcopacies they undertook the greater part of the bishop's duties. If the archbishop was often absent or taken up with secular affairs, business would be conducted by the archdeacon either in his own court or, as the archbishop's representative, in the Court of Christianity. While the archdeacon exercised jurisdiction on behalf of the archbishop he also exercised jurisdiction in his own right, in his own court. In general the archdeacon's court dealt with lesser cases – particularly those concerning the moral conduct of the lower clergy and laity. He was responsible, for example, for examining witnesses in matrimonial cases.[81]

From the available evidence, it appears that the thirteenth–century archdeacons of Dublin were generally practical men of affairs, skilled in legal and financial matters. They frequently served the archbishop in more than one capacity, while holding positions in the secular administration of the colony.[82] Geoffrey de Turville, who held the archdeaconry from c.1227 to 1244, also functioned as a royal justice, chamberlain of the exchequer, deputy chancellor and treasurer of Ireland (1234-50). His service to king and archbishop was rewarded in 1244 when he was appointed bishop of Ossory. Hugh de Mapilton (archdeacon, 1244-51) simultaneously exercised the spiritual functions of the archdeacon's office and the secular functions of the office of seneschal, providing a good example both of the versatility of episcopal staff and of the way in which the archbishop (in this case Luke) made full use of the abilities of his officials. He also became treasurer of Ireland

cesan decrees', pp 39-55.   80 A further privilege granted to the canons of St Patrick's at the church's foundation was that the priests in their prebends were obliged to attend only two of the archdeacon's general chapters – that after Easter and that after Michaelmas (*Dignitas Decani*, pp 2-3).   81 Gwynn, 'Provincial and diocesan decrees', p. 51.   82 For more details and references see Murphy, 'Archbishops and administration', pp 223-32.

in 1251, the same year in which he succeeded Geoffrey de Turville in Ossory. William de Northfield (archdeacon 1255-74) does not appear to have been active in the secular administration. After his death in 1274, the office was held by a succession of royal appointees who were heavily involved in the king's business.

Such archdeacons spent little time engaged in purely pastoral activity. With so many and such varied duties, an archdeacon required skilled assistance and inevitably, once the archdeacon had established his right to perform certain functions and receive certain fees, he delegated the work to an official whom he paid with a portion of the fee. By the early thirteenth-century, all English dioceses had an archdeacon's official and it was not long before this individual was encountered in the Dublin diocese.[83] The existence of this office is confirmed in mid-thirteenth-century synodal canons, where it is stated that the duties assigned to the archdeacon can equally be carried out by his official.[84] Given what is known of the careers of the thirteenth-century Dublin archdeacons it is probably to this largely anonymous official that the title 'oculus episcopi' more accurately belongs.

IV

The era covered by this chapter was one of enormous change for the Church in Dublin as it was for the Irish Church in general. Indeed, it is difficult to disagree with the view that the English invasion of the twelfth century was the single most important event in the Irish Church between the fifth and the sixteenth centuries.[85] Yet, if one overstates the importance of the conquest in initiating ecclesiastical change one runs the risk of 'subscribing to the conqueror's view of the significance of his victory'.[86] Did the election of John Cumin in 1181 begin a period of profound change during which the progressive introduction of English usage brought a backward and uncivilised Dublin Church into line with European norms? This was certainly his personal view, as he asserted on a number of occasions that the Church he was sent to govern was un-reformed and that its people were in dire need of instruction and civilising. Writing almost a century later, Thomas de Chedworth, the English dean of St Patrick's, echoed Cumin's words when

---

83 A royal mandate of September 1231 to the bishop of Lismore refers to a James de St Martin, archdeacon of Dublin. As Geoffrey de Turville held the archdeaconry of Dublin at this time, it is likely that James was functioning as his official, (*Calendar of Close Rolls 1227-31*, p. 557).   84 Gwynn, 'Provincial and diocesan decrees', p. 41.   85 Watt, *Church in medieval Ireland*, p. 119.   86 R.R. Davies, *Domination and conquest: the experience of Ireland, Scotland and Wales 1100-1300* (Cambridge, 1990), p. 2.

he claimed that his Church had been founded 'in a land almost desert and hostile'.[87]

The words of men like Cumin and de Chedworth arose out of a rhetoric which portrayed the English invasion as a campaign of ecclesiastical reform and religious regeneration. This rhetoric almost totally disregarded the vigorous programme of reform which was well under way in the pre-Conquest Irish Church, though it is clear that John Cumin was not only aware of the Irish reform movement, but his activities in Dublin 'often corresponded with the highest aims of the native reform party'.[88] In truth, it is impossible to say which of the developments characterised as part of the 'anglicisation process' would have occurred without English intervention as the Irish Church drew ever closer to mainstream European practices. It is almost certainly true, however, that the introduction of English churchmen, veterans of both ecclesiastical and secular administration, accelerated the pace of change in the Irish Church even if it did not necessarily alter its direction.

The archbishops whose episcopacies have been examined here were certainly of a type new to the Irish and the Dublin Church – Englishmen of worldly experience, royal servants, diplomats and deans from a metropolitan milieu. Yet however important their common backgrounds were in securing them the appointment to Dublin, once in office their individual personalities and preoccupations, factors which arguably transcend nationality, determined the direction taken by their episcopacies.

87 *Dignitas Decani*, p. 12.   88 Sheehy, *When the Normans came to Ireland*, p. 39.

4

The diocese of Dublin in the sixteenth century: clerical opposition and the failure of the Reformation

James Murray

HISTORIOGRAPHY

Most modern studies of sixteenth-century Ireland's religious history have as their starting point the important, but inconclusive, historiographical debate on the failure of the Reformation that took place in the 1970s. Until then, the bulk of the work on the subject upheld the view that the Tudor state failed immediately and irrevocably to win support for its religious dictates, because of the inherently conservative character of Ireland's inhabitants. Sharing a deterministic vision, and an undisguised partisanship in their approach, the only major differences between such studies were their opposing, confessional glosses. For Catholic writers, the conservatism of the Irish implied an ancient and praiseworthy attachment to the religion of their forefathers, which ensured that they battled courageously to preserve the true faith. Protestant writers, in contrast, represented such conservatism as a defect in the native character – an obstinate force built upon ignorance, which the Church of Ireland and Protestantism generally were unable to overcome.[1]

---

1 J. Murray, 'The Church of Ireland: a critical bibliography, 1536-1992. Part I: 1536-1603', *Irish Historical Studies* (henceforth *IHS*), 28 (1993), pp 345-6; A. Ford, '"Standing one's ground": religion, polemic and Irish history since the Reformation' in A. Ford, J. McGuire and K. Milne (eds), *As by law established: the Church of Ireland since the Reformation* (Dublin, 1995), pp 1-10. For some nineteenth and early twentieth century examples of these confessional histories see, on the Catholic side, M.J. Brennan, *An ecclesiastical history of Ireland, from the introduction of Christianity ... to the year MDCCCXXIX* (2 vols, Dublin, 1840), ii, 86-163; and M.V. Ronan, *The Reformation in Dublin, 1536-58* (London, 1926); *The Reformation in Ireland under Elizabeth, 1558-1580* (London, 1930); 'The Reformation in Ireland' in E. Eyre (ed.), *European civilisation: its origin and development* (7 vols, Oxford, 1934-9), iv, 561-629. On the Protestant side see R. Mant, *History*

This cycle of deterministic writing was broken by Brendan Bradshaw, whose pioneering work employed what was, in Irish terms, a fresh series of intellectual templates for the exploration of the Reformation. Earlier attempts to do so – by practitioners of the modern 'scientific' school of historical writing – were unsuccessful, largely because the perspectives that were used then were still heavily coloured by the confessional mode of writing, or because the authors themselves were unable to break free from the habits of thought associated with such writing, even though their own source-based researches were beginning to point them in new directions.[2] Bradshaw removed the subject out of this inward-looking, controversial and necessarily constrictive setting by treating the Reformation initiative seriously and by placing the movement firmly within its contemporary political and social contexts.[3]

The overall and most valuable effect of the Bradshaw oeuvre was to challenge the traditional assumption that the Irish people resisted the Reformation from its inception. Indeed, his work seemed to demonstrate that the political community of English Ireland willingly accepted many of the alterations in religious practice introduced by Henry VIII, especially the royal supremacy. The main reason for this was the linkage of the Reformation with the conciliatory programme of political reform, the 'constitutional revolution', advanced by the crown during the viceroyalties of Sir Anthony St Leger; a feature which ensured that the Reformation also secured some adherents in

of the Church of Ireland (2 vols, London, 1840), i, 1-106; W.D. Killen, The ecclesiastical history of Ireland from the earliest period to the present times (2 vols, London, 1875). 2 The classic examples of this are Robin Dudley Edwards' Church and state in Tudor Ireland: a history of the penal laws against Irish Catholics, 1534-1603 (Dublin, 1935); and G.V. Jourdan's contributions on the Reformation in W.A. Phillips (ed.), History of the Church of Ireland from the earliest times to the present day (3 vols, Oxford, 1933-4), ii, 169-524; see also J. Murray, 'Historical revisit: R. Dudley Edwards, Church and state in Tudor Ireland (1935)', IHS, 30 (1996), pp 233-41; idem, 'Critical bibliography', p. 346; Ford, 'Standing one's ground', p. 9. 3 The key Bradshaw works are: 'George Browne, first Reformation bishop of Dublin' (M.A. thesis, University College Dublin, 1966); 'The opposition to the ecclesiastical legislation in the Irish Reformation parliament', IHS, 16 (1969), pp 285-303; 'George Browne, first Reformation archbishop of Dublin, 1536-1554', Journal of Ecclesiastical History (henceforth Jn Ecc Hist), 21 (1970), pp 301-26; 'The beginnings of modern Ireland' in B. Farrell (ed.), The Irish parliamentary tradition (Dublin, 1973), pp 68-97; The dissolution of the religious orders in Ireland under Henry VIII (Cambridge, 1974); 'The Edwardian Reformation in Ireland, 1547-53', Archivium Hibernicum, 24 (1976-7), pp 83-99; The Irish constitutional revolution of the sixteenth century (Cambridge, 1979); 'The Reformation in the cities: Cork, Limerick and Galway, 1534-1603' in J. Bradley (ed.), Settlement and society in medieval Ireland (Kilkenny, 1988), pp 445-76; 'The Tudor Reformation and revolution in Wales and Ireland: the origins of the British problem' in B. Bradshaw and J. Morrill (eds), The British problem, c.1534-1707: state formation in the Atlantic archipelago (London, 1996), pp 39-65.

Gaelic Ireland. Thus, even by the end of Edward VI's reign, although Edwardian Protestantism had been greeted with little enthusiasm, there appeared to be no definitive response to state-sponsored religious reform in Ireland, whether in the English Pale or in the Gaelic heartlands of the north and west of Ireland.

This situation changed, according to Bradshaw, during the reign of Mary Tudor when Catholicism was officially restored. One result of this was that the Counter-Reformation secured an early foothold in the important battleground of the English Pale, much of which lay in the diocese of Dublin. This nascent attachment of the Englishry to the Counter-Reformation soon hardened into a convinced recusancy – a development encouraged by the simultaneous political alienation of the community that followed from the Tudor regime's abandonment of the conciliatory reform programme of St Leger, in favour of the coercive policies advocated by a new generation of hardline English Protestant officials.

Bradshaw's revision of the traditional assumptions that were held about the Irish Reformation was immensely stimulating. Yet it did not win universal approval. His pronouncements on the Elizabethan Reformation, for example, lacking the same force as his views on the more deeply-researched Henrician period, were the subject of some trenchant criticism by Nicholas Canny. Professor Canny's most important contribution was to identify the need for further research into the meaning and significance of the Pale community's attachment to conservative religious practices. Unlike Bradshaw, Canny characterised the latter not as an attachment to Counter-Reformation norms of religious behaviour but as the maintenance of traditional medieval Catholic forms within the context of the established Church. The existence of this survivalist Catholicism or church-papism was very significant. Given that the same phenomenon also occurred in England and is known to have been transformed gradually into an overt allegiance to the Church of England, its continuance in the English Pale suggests that the same opportunity for conversion was available to the Church of Ireland throughout much of the second half of the sixteenth century.[4]

Overall, then, the Bradshaw-Canny debate has given rise to a more intellectually mature version of Ireland's Reformation story. As a result, the sixteenth century is now generally recognised as a period of blurred and ambiguous religious allegiances, until Queen Mary's reign or until the 1590s, depending on whether one accepts Bradshaw or Canny. Yet the revisionist conclusions of these historians have not been easily absorbed, nor have they encouraged many scholars to undertake further and more systematic research

4 N. Canny, 'Why the Reformation failed in Ireland: *une question mal posée*', *Jn Ecc Hist*, 30 (1979), pp 423-50.

to test and develop their ideas in greater detail and depth. Although significant new work has appeared on such areas as the provision of pastoral care in the Church in early Tudor Ireland;[5] on the structural deficiencies of the Church of Ireland;[6] on the creation of an ideological attachment to the Counter-Reformation amongst the Englishry in the late sixteenth and early seventeenth centuries;[7] and on the influence of Gaelic culture in the development of Irish Catholicism in the early modern period,[8] the fundamental question raised by Canny and Bradshaw – the nature of the response of the English Irish community to the Reformation throughout the duration of the sixteenth century – has still to be answered definitively.

CLERICAL OPPOSITION IN DUBLIN: THE EVIDENCE AND ITS SIGNIFICANCE

It is in this historiographical context that the importance of studying the diocese of Dublin becomes apparent, and recent developments in the historiography of the English Reformation underline the value of adopting a regional focus. At the same time that Brendan Bradshaw was reinvigorating the study of the Irish Reformation, a new generation of historians began to explore the practical implications of the Reformation at grassroots level in English society. Conducted, generally, at diocesan or county level, and having recourse to previously ignored or under-used records such as visitation act books, consistory cause papers and churchwardens' accounts, these studies revealed that the rate of religious change in the localities, and the speed with which the Reformation was enforced and accepted, varied considerably from region to

---

5 H.A. Jefferies, *Priests and prelates of Armagh in the age of reformations, 1518-58* (Dublin, 1997).   6 A. Clarke, 'Varieties of uniformity: the first century of the Church of Ireland' in W.J. Sheils and D. Wood (eds), *The Churches, Ireland and the Irish* (Oxford, 1989), pp 105-22; H. Coburn Walshe, 'Enforcing the Elizabethan settlement: the vicissitudes of Hugh Brady, bishop of Meath, 1563-84', *IHS*, 26 (1989), pp 352-76; S.G. Ellis, 'Economic problems of the Church: why the Reformation failed in Ireland', *Jn Ecc Hist*, 41 (1990), pp 239-65.   7 C. Brady, 'Conservative subversives: the community of the Pale and the Dublin administration, 1556-86' in P.J. Corish (ed.), *Radicals, rebels and establishments* (Belfast, 1985), pp 11-32; C. Lennon, 'Recusancy and the Dublin Stanihursts', *Archivium Hibernicum*, 33 (1975), pp 101-10; idem, *Richard Stanihurst the Dubliner, 1547-1618* (Dublin, 1981); idem, *The lords of Dublin in the age of Reformation* (Dublin, 1989); idem, 'The rise of recusancy among the Dublin patricians, 1580-1613' in Sheils and Wood (eds), *The Churches, Ireland and the Irish*, pp 123-32; idem, 'The chantries in the Irish Reformation: the case of St Anne's Guild, Dublin, 1550-1630' in R.V. Comerford et al. (eds), *Religion, conflict and coexistence in Ireland* (Dublin, 1990), pp 8-25.   8 S. Meigs, *The Reformations in Ireland: tradition and confessionalism, 1400-1690* (Dublin, 1997).

region. The overall effect of this work was to undermine the traditional view of the English Reformation as a process in which crown policy, Lollardy, an emerging Lutheranism and popular anti-clericalism combined to create a successful protestant Reformation.[9] For Irish historians, however, they created the natural and reasonable assumption that the application of the same methodological approach might provide comparable insight into the problems and questions raised by the Bradshaw-Canny debate on the Irish Reformation.

In practice, however, the application of this regional approach has proved difficult. Although there are sufficient sources extant to reconstruct the basic structure and workings of the diocese of Dublin during the sixteenth century,[10] the documentation available to English historians to plot the rate of religious change in the localities is almost wholly lacking. Churchwardens' accounts, for example, exist for only one parish in the diocese – St Werburgh's

---

9 The most scholarly exposition of the traditional view is A.G. Dickens, *The English Reformation* (London, 1964); its early development is surveyed by R. O'Day in *The debate on the English Reformation* (London, 1986). The development of the revisionist review of the English Reformation, and the part played in it by diocesan and local histories, is best approached through the series of essays edited by C. Haigh, *The English Reformation revised* (Cambridge, 1987). For some examples of these diocesan and local studies see R.B. Manning, *Religion and society in Elizabethan Sussex* (Leicester, 1969); C. Haigh, *Reformation and resistance in Tudor Lancashire* (Cambridge, 1975); R.A. Houlbrooke, *Church courts and the people during the English Reformation, 1520-70* (Oxford, 1979); M. Bowker, *The Henrician Reformation in the diocese of Lincoln under John Longland, 1521-47* (Cambridge, 1981); D. MacCulloch, *Suffolk and the Tudors* (Oxford, 1986); S. Brigden, *London and the Reformation* (Oxford, 1989); R. Whiting, *The blind devotion of the people: popular religion and the English Reformation* (Cambridge, 1989).   10 C. MacNeill (ed.), *Calendar of Archbishop Alen's register, c.1172-1534* (Dublin, 1950); H. Wood (ed.), *Court book of the Liberty of St Sepulchre within the jurisdiction of the archbishop of Dublin 1586-90* (Dublin, 1930); N.B. White (ed.), *The 'Dignitas decani' of St Patrick's cathedral, Dublin* (Dublin, 1957); idem (ed.), 'The *reportorium viride* of John Alen, archbishop of Dublin, 1533', *Analecta Hibernica*, 10 (1941) pp 180-217; idem (ed.), *'Registrum Diocesis Dublinensis': a sixteenth century Dublin Precedent Book* (Dublin, 1959); idem (ed.), *Extents of Irish monastic possessions, 1540-1, from manuscripts in the Public Record Office, London* (Dublin, 1941); H.F. Berry (ed.), *Register of wills and inventories of the diocese of Dublin in the time of Archbishops Tregury and Walton* (Dublin, 1898); M.J. McEnery (ed.), 'Calendar to Christ Church Deeds, 1174-1684' in *Report of the Keeper of Public Record Office of Ireland*, 20 (1888), 23 (1891), 24 (1892), 27 (1895); J.C. Crosthwaite (ed.), *The book of obits and martyrology of the cathedral church of Holy Trinity* (Dublin, 1844); Survey of the possessions of St Patrick's cathedral, 1547 (St Patrick's cathedral, Muniments, no. 112, printed in W. Monck Mason, *The history and antiquities of the collegiate and cathedral church of St Patrick near Dublin* [Dublin, 1820] pp 28-99 passim); Chapter Act Book of Christ Church 1574-1634 (Representative Church Body, Dublin (henceforth RCB) Christ Church Muniments, C.B., C.6.1.7 no. 1).

in the city of Dublin – and even then the series is very incomplete. Crucially, there are no extant records for the period of most intensive religious change, 1534-69, the period in which the surviving English churchwardens' accounts detail the alterations that were made (or not made as the case may be) to the fabric, fittings and decoration of parish churches consequent upon the introduction of the various Tudor religious settlements.[11] The same is true of visitation records and the records of the church courts. Apart from one very unusual document from the episcopate of Archbishop Browne,[12] and some *acta* from an archiepiscopal visitation of St Patrick's cathedral dating from 1569-70,[13] visitation records from the diocese are entirely lacking for the duration of the Tudor Reformation. Church court proceedings likewise are represented only by the surviving portion of a single act book from the archbishop's consistory, which covers the period 1596-9. Moreover, the bulk of the cases recorded in this act book are party *versus* party actions, and throw precious little light on the enforcement and progress of the Reformation under the Elizabethan archbishop of Dublin, Adam Loftus.[14]

The absence of the requisite documentation precludes then the possibility of undertaking the kind of close regional analysis of the progress of the Reformation in Dublin or elsewhere in Ireland that has been undertaken in England.[15] An awareness of the impracticability of this approach does, however, prompt an alternative line of enquiry. Although the paucity of the sources is in part an historical accident, the extraordinary poverty of material that has survived is in itself symptomatic of a deeper problem.[16] The very preservation of documentation in England attests strongly to the fact that the

---

11 Churchwardens' Accounts of St Werburgh's, 1481-1627 (RCB, P 326/27/1/1-21); J. Robinson, 'Churchwardens' Accounts, 1484-1600, St Werburgh's Church, Dublin', *Journal of the Royal Society of Antiquaries of Ireland*, 6th series, 4 (1914), pp 132-42; R. Hutton, 'The local impact of the Tudor Reformations' in Haigh (ed.), *English Reformation revised*, pp 114-138. 12 J.P. Collier (ed.), *The Egerton papers* (Camden Society, London, 1840), pp 7-10; J. Murray, 'The Tudor diocese of Dublin: episcopal government, ecclesiastical politics and the enforcement of the Reformation, *c*.1534-1590' (Ph.D. thesis, University of Dublin, 1997), pp 126-7. 13 '*Registrum Diocesis Dublinensis*', pp 40-52; Murray, 'Tudor diocese of Dublin', pp 233-41. 14 Act book of the Dublin consistory court, Michaelmas 1596 to Michaelmas 1599 (Marsh's Library, Ms Z4.2.19, pp 1-126 passim). 15 One might exclude Armagh from this generalisation, although its series of episcopal registers does not extend beyond the reign of Mary Tudor (Jefferies, *Priest and prelates of Armagh*, p. 13). 16 The same historical accident has led to considerable variation – from diocese to diocese and from jurisdiction to jurisdiction – in the rate of survival of manuscripts in the English Church. On this point see R. O'Day and F. Heal (eds), *Continuity and change: personnel and administration of the Church in England 1500-1642* (Leicester, 1976), pp 17-8; D.M. Owen, *The records of the established Church in England* (Cambridge, 1970); idem, 'Handlist of ecclesiastical records: a supplement to records of the established Church', *Archives*, 10 (1971-2), pp 53-6.

enforcement of the Reformation – an administrative process engaged in jointly by the agencies of the Church and state – was systematically undertaken, however uneven the outcome. By the same token, the pronounced absence of analogous documentation in Dublin and other Irish dioceses suggests strongly that routine collaboration, which was necessary for the survival of such a continuous record, never occurred there.

This contention is borne out by other evidence. It has long been recognised that the local clergy were reluctant to lend their support to the Reformation cause. Not only did they resist the imposition of Reformation legislation in the Irish parliament of 1536-7, they actively subverted the efforts of reformers like Archbishop Browne of Dublin to enforce the provisions of this legislation amongst the local community thereafter.[17] What has not been generally appreciated, however, is the extent and significance of this clerical opposition. It is apparent from the most rudimentary exploration of the structures of the diocese of Dublin that clerical opposition was both extremely powerful and highly motivated, because it possessed its own unique ethos and identity, and because it controlled the institutional fabric of the local church. The implications of this for the study of the Irish Reformation are striking. Because the Tudors chose to enforce their Reformations through the pre-existing ecclesiastical structures, through the bishops, their officials and the traditional courts Christian – a feature which distinguished them markedly from their continental equivalents[18] – it is apparent that Dublin's clerical opposition was ideally placed to negate the best efforts of the reformers to secure indigenous allegiance to the Tudors' religious settlements, because they, and they alone, controlled those structures through which this process was supposed to be effected.

This leads to one other inescapable conclusion. The nature of the English Irish community's response to the Reformation will not be found by charting the impact of a reform-led diocesan administration's efforts to enforce it in the parishes of the diocese of Dublin. Rather, it is to be found in the battle conducted within that administration itself, between reforming archbishops enjoined to use the conventional ecclesiastical structures for reformist purposes, and conservative clergymen who were equally determined to maintain their traditional stranglehold over those same structures and to use them for their own, essentially Catholic, ideological ends. It is this struggle for power and control over local Church structures, a struggle won by the conservative

17 Edwards, *Church and state*, pp 9-10, 47-64; Bradshaw, 'George Browne', p. 310.   18 O'Day and Heal (eds), *Continuity and change*, p. 15; D. MacCulloch, *The later Reformation in England 1547-1603* (London, 1990), pp 32-3. On the construction of new institutional structures in the continental reformed churches during the sixteenth century see E. Cameron, *The European Reformation* (Oxford, 1991), pp 257-61.

clerical opposition during the decisive years of change 1536–1569, which forms the essential drama in Dublin's Reformation story.

THE MEDIEVAL LEGACY AND THE ORIGINS OF CLERICAL OPPOSITION

It was the diocese of Dublin's medieval inheritance that created the unique set of circumstances out of which local clerical opposition to the Reformation emerged, and from which it drew its strength and effectiveness. The most important aspect of this inheritance was the cultural ethos of the diocese's clerical élite – the senior clergy of the cathedral and monastic chapters – who through their appropriation of the vast majority of parochial livings in the diocese (c.84 per cent in the early 1530s), their greater access to higher education, formal and informal, and their monopolising of ecclesiastical judgeships and other senior posts associated with the administration of the canon law, effectively controlled the local Church. Individually and collectively, the senior corporate clergy were proud upholders of the Anglo-Norman ecclesiastical tradition, a tradition intimately associated with the original English conquest of Ireland.

The grant of lordship over Ireland to the English crown had been sanctioned by Pope Adrian VII in his bull *Laudabiliter* in 1179 on the understanding that the English would make the Irish people obedient to the canon law of the Western Church. In practice, the establishment of canonical standards in Ireland was achieved through the introduction of ecclesiastical structures and practices modelled directly on the uses and customs of the medieval English Church. And it was on this basis that many of the ecclesiastical corporations of Dublin and the English Pale, including cathedrals like St Patrick's and monasteries like St Mary's abbey, were founded. By the early sixteenth century, the clergy of these corporations were still very conscious of their original *raison d'être*. Born of 'English blood', and deeply proud of it, they believed that the Englishry's presence in Ireland was justified both on the grounds of Adrian VII's grant of lordship over Ireland to Henry II, and their concomitant responsibility to civilise Gaelic Irish society according to the standards of behaviour enshrined in medieval canon law. On the eve of the Reformation, then, what made the corporate clergy's attachment to Catholicism stand out was its politico-cultural dimension. To be of English blood in Ireland was to be an adherent of medieval, canonically orthodox Catholicism, because it was for the promotion of this very adherence that their own community, and their own corporate bodies, had been brought into being.[19]

19 Murray, 'Tudor diocese of Dublin', chapter 2 passim.

This was hugely significant. Because the traditional reforming mission of the clergy was papally sanctioned, bound up with their English identity, and dedicated to extending Roman canon law and to preserving English medieval ecclesiological norms, the corporate clergy were predisposed to side with the old religion. By implication, they were no less predisposed to resist the Reformation, as this was a movement which, through its attack on papal authority, on the legitimacy of canon law, on clerical privilege and on traditional Church structures, threatened to destroy their venerable ethos. For the cathedral and monastic clergy of Dublin and elsewhere in the English Pale, the Tudors' breach with Rome and all that came in its wake was not simply an attempt to rid the realm of a foreign and interfering jurisdiction, or an effort to curb the worst excesses of traditional medieval religion; it was nothing less than an attack on the English, canonically-based identity of their own community. They, as governors of the local Church and the direct descendants of those Anglo-Norman clergy who had originally established the ecclesiological and canonical norms which comprised the *Laudabiliter* settlement – the very essence of English cultural identity in Ireland – were thus impelled to assume the role of guardians of this settlement and to reject and resist the Reformation.

But that was not all. The corporate clergy were also well-versed in the practice of this role of guardianship. Indeed, their entire history, right up to the very eve of the Reformation, had been about defending the *Laudabiliter* settlement against erosion by the Gaelic Irish. As they saw it, the English Pale – the last bastion of English cultural identity following centuries of corrosive Gaelic resurgence, of the 'degeneration' and Gaelicisation of areas formerly under English rule, and of neglect by the medieval English monarchy – was under siege; it seemed to them to be threatened with extinction, if not physically, then at least culturally, whether directly through the encroachment of marauding Irish lords, or, more insidiously, through the replacement of English husbandmen by Gaelic peasants on the lands of the English Irish magnates like the earl of Kildare. The latter phenomenon, in particular, raised the terrible spectre that social and cultural degeneration, on a scale similar to that which had occurred in the outlying areas of the English lordship, was about to become an everyday reality in the hitherto undefiled Pale Maghery. In these circumstances, the English Irish corporate clerical elite was less concerned than their Anglo-Norman forebears had been with their traditional reforming role; their aim was simply to defend and preserve intact its most tangible remnant, the ecclesiastical inheritance of the English Pale.[20]

They did this in practice by excluding those of Gaelic Irish extraction from all ecclesiastical offices and bodies over which they exercised control.

20 Ibid.

In the 1494-5 parliament, for example, the Knight's Hospitallers at Kilmainham secured the passage of an act which stipulated that no person should be made prior of their house 'but of the English blood'.[21] Similarly, in 1505, Dean Aleyn of St Patrick's cathedral established an almshouse in St Kevin's Street in Dublin. For him, the poor to be received and preferred in his almshouse were not to be 'any poor whatsoever, but faithful Catholics of good repute, honest conversation and of the English nation'.[22] And, in 1515, his successor Dean Rochfort and the chapter of St Patrick's cathedral entered into an agreement with Archbishop William Rokeby which formally renewed the dean's ancient jurisdictional rights over the chapter of St Patrick's. Significantly, the new cathedral statute also confirmed the ancient custom, which denied membership of St Patrick's to anyone of the Irish nation, manners and blood, and was later approved by Pope Leo X.[23]

The reason that the corporate clergy maintained this exclusionist policy derived from their perception that Gaelic Irish society had proven itself, in the past as well as the present, to be resistant to Anglo-Norman reform, or, as they saw it, English civility; for here was a polity whose social and cultural mores still contravened many of the most basic principles associated with canon law and, by extension, their English identity. The flouted principles, to which the senior clergy in Dublin were particularly sensitive because they often suffered directly the consequences of their contravention, included the notion of the rule of law itself; the sacrosanct nature of ecclesiastical property (many ecclesiastical properties in the marches and Gaelic enclaves of the see of Dublin were forcibly withheld from the ecclesiastical establishment); and the iniquity of 'nicolaitism', or sexual aberrance among the clergy, which was particularly evident in the widespread clerical concubinage practised in the north and west of Ireland.[24] By excluding the Irishry from the upper echelons of the local Church, and controlling their entry at the lower levels, the ruling corporate clergy of Dublin reaffirmed their ongoing commitment to maintain their own ethos, by preventing what they believed to be the worst excesses of the Irish clergy's canonical deviancy taking a hold in, and corrupting, their own diocese. Thus, this ideology lay at the heart of the Dublin provincial council's enactment in 1518 that priests from Ulster and Connacht were not to be admitted in the province unless, in the judgement of the ordi-

---

21 D.B. Quinn (ed.), 'The bills and statutes of the Irish parliaments of Henry VII and Henry VIII', *Analecta Hibernica*, 10 (1941), p. 92; A. Conway, *Henry VII's relations with Scotland and Ireland, 1485-98* (Cambridge, 1932), p. 210. 22 'Non tamen quoscunque pauperes, sed fideles catholicos, bone fame, honeste conversacionis et Anglice nationis' (Mason, *History of St Patrick's*, app. XII, p. xv). 23 *Alen's Reg.*, pp 262-3; Mason, *History of St Patrick's*, pp 143-4; *Dignitas decani*, pp 56-64. 24 Murray, 'Tudor diocese of Dublin', pp 77-82.

nary, they were found to be fit pastors; a stipulation that demanded the unquestioned acceptance of the principle of priestly celibacy and the other canonical requirements enshrined in the *Laudabiliter* settlement.[25]

At the outset of the 1530s, then, the corporate clergy of Dublin and the English Pale believed that the main danger to the survival of their anglocentric, *Laudabiliter*-based, communal identity was the nefarious influence of the deviant Irishry. Yet a new and potentially more damaging enemy emerged during this decade to threaten the existence of the culture they and their predecessors had done so much to sustain throughout the medieval period. Most disturbingly, this new enemy was one of the foundation stones upon which their culture was built and to which they traditionally looked for sustenance, the English monarchy. The harbinger of this new and threatening state of affairs was George Browne, the diocese of Dublin's first Reformation archbishop, a man who witnessed up close the willingness and capacity of the senior clergy to fight on behalf of their traditional religico-cultural beliefs.

ARCHBISHOP BROWNE AND CLERICAL RESISTANCE

George Browne was archbishop of Dublin for eighteen years following his appointment in 1536. The duration of his confrontation with his senior clergy was much shorter, and lasted for just about three years between 1537 and 1540 during what was effectively the introductory phase of the Henrician Reformation in Ireland.[26] Yet, if it was relatively short-lived, the experience was still deeply exasperating for the archbishop and ultimately self-defeating. Throughout these years he faced opposition at every turn in his efforts to advance the Henrician settlement, both from the senior clergy within his cathedrals and from the senior religious. One of the major areas of contention was the unwillingness of his clergy to participate in any preaching campaign on behalf of the new religious dispensation. 'Neither by gentle exhortation, evangelical instruction', he wrote in frustration to Thomas Cromwell in January 1538, 'neither by oaths of them solemnly taken, nor yet by threats of sharp correction, can I persuade or induce any, either religious or secular

25 'Presbyteri Conactenses et Ultoniensis non admittantur, nisi judicio ordinarii inveniantur idonei' in D. Wilkins (ed.), *Concilia Magnae Britaniae et Hiberniae* [4 vols, London, 1737], iii, 660, calendared in H.J. Lawlor (ed.), 'Calendar of the Liber Ruber of the diocese of Ossory', in *Proceedings of the Royal Irish Academy*, 27C [1908-9], p. 165.   26 Browne's fraught relationship with his clergy is treated in detail in J. Murray, 'Ecclesiastical justice and the enforcement of the Reformation: the case of Archbishop Browne and the clergy of Dublin, 1536-1554' in Ford, McGuire and Milne (eds), *As by law established*, pp 33-51.

... once to preach the word of God, or the just title of our most illustrious prince'. This was in sharp contrast to the situation which had prevailed prior to the declaration of Henry VIII as Supreme Head of the Irish Church, for 'they that then could and would, very often until the right Christians were very weary of them, preach after the old sort and fashion'.[27]

This refusal to preach was only the thin end of the wedge. From within the same group of cathedral clergy and religious as he sought his preachers, the archbishop was also supposed to find ecclesiastical ordinaries and administrators who, according to the logic of the Henrician Reformation, were responsible for enforcing the new religious precepts outside the periods of the archbishop's own triennial visitations. Browne had little or no confidence that his officials would discharge this responsibility. Indeed, the lack of cooperation that he received prompted him to request Cromwell to grant the Irish treasurer, the chief justice and the master of the rolls a 'straight commandment' over all ecclesiastical persons, in the belief that this would help him 'prick other forthwards that been underneath me' to execute their offices. In effect, Browne believed that he would only secure the help of his clergy to enforce the Reformation if they were compelled to do so by the secular authorities.[28]

Browne had no illusions, then, about where his clergy's loyalties lay. They were committed to the old religion and had no intention of supporting the new order. Worse, led by men like James Humphrey, the prebendary of St Audoen in St Patrick's cathedral,[29] they were determined to subvert all Browne's efforts to promote the Reformation in his diocese, whether overtly or covertly. According to the archbishop, 'in corners and [amongst] such company as them liketh', the senior clergy of his diocese 'hindereth and plucketh back amongst the people the labour that I do take in that behalf'. It was they, the 'Spiritualty', he concluded, who 'seduceth the rest'.[30]

The archbishop enjoyed little or no success in tackling the problem of clerical resistance. To a large extent, this was because the secular authorities, otherwise engaged in the task of winning local support for their political reform initiatives, were generally unwilling to back the archbishop's efforts to confront clerical malcontents and coerce them into full acceptance of the Henrician settlement. Such reluctance was particularly evident in the summer of 1538 when Lord Deputy Grey summarily released Prebendary Humphrey from the episcopal gaol, following his incarceration there by Browne, without any reference or deference to the archbishop's authority. Browne had imprisoned Humphrey for openly disobeying an episcopal injunction, communicated to all his clergy, to read the pro-reform bidding prayers (The

27 *State Papers, Hen VIII*, ii, p. 539.   28 Ibid., p. 540.   29 On Humphrey see Murray, 'Tudor diocese of Dublin', pp 138-41.   30 *State Papers, Hen VIII*, ii, pp 539-40.

Form of the Beads) during Mass, and it was his intention to bring the recalcitrant cleric to trial on the grounds that his omission was in contravention of the recently enacted statute against the authority of the bishop of Rome. By failing to back the archbishop, the lord deputy greatly undermined his authority in full view of an already unco-operative clergy. As Browne himself bitterly complained to Cromwell, 'the simplest holy water clerk is better esteemed than I am'.[31]

The Humphrey incident offered a very strong signal that the archbishop was fighting a losing battle against his clergy. Over the next two years, following his exposure to the gathering storm of the conservative clerical reaction in England – ushered in by the notorious act of six articles in 1539 and confirmed by the fall of his patron Cromwell in 1540 – his humiliation was completed. While no equivalent act was introduced in Ireland, the fact that Browne was a married man – contrary to one of the main provisions of the act of six articles – placed him in an acutely embarrassing and potentially dangerous situation. His response, which provides an indicator of how formidable he thought his clerical opponents were, was to solicit the support of his erstwhile enemies to extricate himself from his predicament. Prebendary Humphrey, ironically, emerged as one of a group of local clergymen and gentlemen who helped him cast off his wife Elizabeth Miagh, and who were entrusted with the upkeep of his children. As part of the bargain, Humphrey secured a promotion to the precentorship of St Patrick's cathedral from the archbishop. More importantly, he and his clerical allies forced Browne to abandon his career as a reformer. For the remainder of Henry VIII's reign, and throughout much of Edward VI's, the archbishop was a largely anonymous figure. His battle with his clergy ceased, as did his active involvement in the enforcement and promotion of the Reformation. Indeed, if we are to believe the Protestant reformer, John Bale, Browne reinvented himself in the image of those conservative clerics whom he had once sought to destroy. Where in the past he had prayed for Ireland's Reformation, according to Bale he now 'commandeth her to go a whoring again, and to follow the same devil that she followed before'.[32]

In a very real sense, then, Dublin's clerical elite defeated the diocese's first reformist archbishop and, in the process, did much to stifle the progress of the early Reformation. In truth, however, it was a Pyrrhic victory. While Browne fought with his clergy, and following his departure thereafter into the shadows, secular-minded officials like the lord deputy, Sir Anthony St Leger, took over the leadership of the Reformation campaign. Although St Leger and his like were unwilling to challenge the clergy on matters of conscience in the same

---

31 Murray, 'Tudor diocese of Dublin', pp 138-41; *State Papers, Hen. VIII*, iii, pp 8-9.
32 Murray, 'Tudor diocese of Dublin', pp 142-5; P. Happé and J.N. King (eds), *The vocacyon of Johan Bale* (Binghamton, New York, 1990), p. 68.

direct and confrontational manner as Browne had done, their actions were in practice more damaging to the clergy's interests. It was under the auspices of such officials that corporate religious life, arguably the most fundamental expression of the Anglo-Norman ecclesiastical tradition, was virtually destroyed, as first the monasteries, and later St Patrick's cathedral, were suppressed during Henry VIII's reign. By the end of Edward VI's reign the corporate, canonical culture that the English Irish clergy had maintained for centuries, and which was so much a part of the cultural life of their community, was heading towards extinction. Indeed it was only through the accession in 1553 of the Catholic queen, Mary Tudor, that it secured an unexpected reprieve.

THE MARIAN REVIVAL OF THE ANGLO-NORMAN ECCLESIASTICAL TRADITION

The accession of Queen Mary provided the context for the revival of the corporate clergy's fortunes. The actual process of revival was driven by the local clergy themselves, under the leadership of the newly-reinstated archbishop of Armagh, George Dowdall – a loyal Palesman, former religious and long-time canon lawyer – who was a product and strong adherent of the Anglo-Norman ecclesiastical tradition, with its inherent corporate, anglocentric, canonical culture. Under Dowdall, the protestant reforms of Edward VI were swept away, and much of the old religion restored, in the metropolitan province of Armagh through the enactment of traditional synodal legislation. The use of provincial canonical legislation as a medium for formally restoring Catholicism was possible because Edwardian Protestantism had never received parliamentary sanction in Ireland. Rather, it had been enjoined upon the crown's subjects through royal proclamation and royal injunctions, and thus did not require repealing legislation in the Dublin parliament. However, Dowdall's action was not merely a clever legal manoeuvre. It was part and parcel of a much more ambitious project: the revival of the full panoply of medieval, English Irish clerical values throughout the English Pale at large.[33]

Dowdall's plans came to fruition in early 1555, following a period of negotiation between a group of English privy councillors and a Dowdall-backed party of former prebendaries from the dissolved cathedral of St Patrick, when Queen Mary and Cardinal Pole sanctioned three related measures. The first of these, approved in February 1555, was the restoration of St Patrick's cathedral, which not only re-established the richest and most powerful symbol of corporate religious life in the Pale, but also re-established the canonical and

---

33 On Dowdall's role in the Marian restoration of Catholicism see Murray, 'Tudor diocese of Dublin', chapter 4 passim.

judicial centre of the diocese of Dublin, following the disruption caused by the Henrician dissolution. Thus the diocese was provided once again with its pre-Reformation administrative structure and the capacity, like Dowdall's administration in Armagh, to engineer a restoration of the old religion through the enactment and enforcement of local canon law.[34]

The second measure – the appointment of a canonically sound and canonically inclined successor to the married, and thus canonically illegitimate, archbishop of Dublin, George Browne – completed this *desideratum*. Hugh Curwen, an English doctor of laws who was selected because he met the canonical credentials which Dowdall and his cohorts had specified for the job, was appointed in place of the deprived Browne in February 1555. With Curwen in place and St Patrick's restored, the see of Dublin was once again fully qualified to take responsibility for the revival of canon law and the restoration of the old religion within its own domain. The process began in earnest in the winter of 1555-6 when Curwen and his clergy, following the Dowdall paradigm, passed the requisite synodal legislation in a provincial council that lasted forty-two days.[35]

The final measure sought by Dowdall – in essence a restatement of the papal bull *Laudabiliter* and made necessary by Henry VIII's parliamentary assumption of the kingly title to Ireland in 1541 – was to secure renewed papal backing for English rule in Ireland, and, by extension, for all the English Irish politico-cultural activities which derived therefrom, including the now restored and reinvigorated English Irish ecclesiastical culture. This was duly achieved in June 1555 when Pope Paul IV confirmed the kingly title to Queen Mary and King Philip, following a request made to his predecessor Julius III by Cardinal Pole the previous March. The grant of this new papal bull effectively restored the medieval constitutional context in which the old religion had functioned in the English Pale prior to the innovations of Henry VIII and Edward VI.[36]

The period of the Marian restoration of Catholicism and the episcopacy of Hugh Curwen (1555-67) was to prove hugely significant to the future of Catholicism in the diocese of Dublin. Not only did it witness a full restoration of the old religion, a process which encompassed a full and self-conscious revival of traditional English-Irish clerical values orchestrated by the Pale clergy under the leadership of Archbishop Dowdall of Armagh; but, under the protective eye of Archbishop Curwen – who with many of his administrative officials and cathedral clergy remained *in situ* following the parliamentary enactment of the Elizabethan settlement in 1560 – also saw the continued reinvigoration of the spirit, and the preservation of many of the

34 Ibid., pp 174-5, 179-81, 183-4.   35 Ibid., pp 182-3 and chapter 5 passim.   36 Ibid., pp 167-71, 185-6.

practices, of Catholicism in the opening decade of Elizabeth's reign. Thus Elizabethan Protestantism made virtually no progress in this crucial opening phase of its existence. Worse, even when Curwen departed Ireland in the winter of 1567, following his translation to the bishopric of Oxford, he left behind him a clerical body willing to battle once again for the continued survival of the old religion. The man charged with the task of overcoming this Dowdall-Curwen legacy of clerical conservatism was Adam Loftus, Curwen's successor as archbishop of Dublin.

ARCHBISHOP LOFTUS AND CLERICAL RESISTANCE

Unlike his reformist predecessor, George Browne, Adam Loftus was fully aware at the time of his accession of the difficulties that the conservative clergy of Dublin were likely to pose the progress of the Reformation in the diocese for which he was responsible. As a member of the commission for ecclesiastical causes appointed in 1564, he had seen at close hand how the conscious neglect of Curwen and his clergy had allowed Catholic practice to flourish unchecked even after it had been proscribed by ecclesiastical legislation ratified by the 1560 parliament. Similarly, as the successor to Archbishop Dowdall in Armagh, and as dean of St Patrick's cathedral for two years prior to his promotion to the see of Dublin, he had encountered up close the lingering and, for Protestantism, harmful effects of the canonical restoration of Catholicism which Dowdall, Curwen and the prebendaries of St Patrick's cathedral had instituted during the reign of Mary Tudor.[37]

It also seemed clear how the new archbishop would proceed to deal with the problem of clerical resistance. For three years between 1563-6, Loftus had been one of the most vocal proponents of a government-sponsored scheme to dissolve St Patrick's cathedral, and to use its resources and revenues to establish a university in its place. For Loftus, this scheme not only had the virtue of creating a seminary for the education of ministers to serve the Church of Ireland, it would also destroy the nerve centre of the conservative canonical culture that sustained the old religion.[38] Given his particular insights into the problem of clerical resistance, then, and his previously and passionately expressed beliefs that a solution to the problem would be found by suppressing St Patrick's, it seemed inevitable that an attack on the cathedral and its clergy, resulting in outright dissolution, would form the centrepiece of Loftus' episcopal strategy to advance Protestantism.

37 Ibid., pp 224-6. 38 J. Murray, 'St Patrick's cathedral and the university question in Ireland c.1547-1585' in H. Robinson-Hammerstein (ed.), *European universities in the age of Reformation and Counter-Reformation* (Dublin, 1998), pp 11-21.

When the attack came it was less direct than either Loftus or his clerical enemies may have imagined at the outset of his episcopacy. The main reason for this was the intervention of the new lord chancellor of Ireland, Sir Robert Weston, who, as part of his remuneration from the government, received the deanery of St Patrick's cathedral as a sinecure. Weston did not treat it as such, however. As a pious and devout Protestant, and a very experienced ecclesiastical lawyer to boot, he viewed his responsibilities as dean, and the future progress of the Protestant Reformation in Ireland, as matters of great moral seriousness, to which he devoted much time and energy. In particular, he helped Loftus institute a carefully modulated programme of ecclesiastical discipline in his diocese aimed at investing the Elizabethan settlement and its advocates with the same kind of legitimating canonical credentials that were possessed, in the eyes of the local community, by the old religion and the conservative clergy.[39]

There were two elements to this strategy. The first endeavoured to nullify the influence of the conservative clergy by reducing their power and influence in St Patrick's cathedral, and ultimately by marginalising them. In practice, this was done by a concerted policy of legal harassment. Thus, for example, in a visitation of the cathedral undertaken in 1569-70, a significant number of Marian and Curwen appointees to the chapter – most of whom were Palesmen like Edmund Barnewall, Leonard Fitzsimon, Thomas Fleming and John Dillon – were deprived of their livings by the diocesan authorities for, ironically, a variety of canonical offences and impediments. For Weston and the now converted Loftus, this was a better approach to the problem of clerical resistance than the radical option of suppressing the cathedral, because it could not be gainsaid in terms of its legitimacy and because it also had the advantage of preserving a valuable resource for the use of the newly emerging Protestant establishment in Dublin.[40]

The second strand of the Loftus-Weston strategy was to build up trust and allegiance amongst the local community for their own Protestant ecclesiastical establishment, and to ensure that that establishment was imbued with the same veneer of canonical legitimacy as previous diocesan regimes had been. The way in which Loftus and Weston tried to secure popular support for their regime was by adopting a relatively lenient approach to the laity, when it came to pursuing offences against the ecclesiastical law. It was a markedly different approach from that taken against the conservative clergy. One man who appreciated this contrast was Christopher Browne, the conservative prebendary of Wicklow, who had witnessed the visitorial rigour employed in St Patrick's cathedral in 1569-70. Following a metropolitan vis-

---

39 Murray, 'Tudor diocese of Dublin', pp 229-33.   40 On the 1569-70 visitation see ibid., pp 233-42.

itation of the diocese and province of Dublin in 1570, he complained bitterly to the English privy council that the archbishop's vicar general, 'having any rich man of the country in the censures of the Church for fornication, adultery or any like offence', would absolve them 'for money ... with the Pope's absolution, *Absolvo te* ... and hath been seen and heard of credible persons giving that absolution on horseback in the fields, the penitent kneeling before him ...'[41] Yet while the Loftus-Weston regime was lenient in dispensing ecclesiastical justice, it also made every effort to ensure that the bodies responsible for this task looked and acted like their medieval predecessors, in order to invest their regime with the same authority, and to ensure it was accorded the same respect. Hence their efforts to domesticate the Reformation by turning its legislative aspects, via the Dublin provincial council, into local ecclesiastical law, and by giving new and innovatory bodies like the High Commission the formal appearance of conventional Church courts.[42]

Initially, at any rate, there were signs that the Loftus-Weston programme might work, especially in the willingness of a younger generation of aspiring ecclesiastical lawyers to attach themselves to the new régime. However, the gradualist nature of the strategy itself, the loss of momentum that it suffered in the wake of Weston's untimely death in 1573, and, above all, the continuing subversiveness of the indigenous clergy – now realised in a series of overtly political plots, straddling Dublin and the English court in London and designed to destabilise the Loftus-Weston régime – combined to ensure that more tangible and impressive results were not obtained in the short term. This proved fatal for the archbishop's plans. Other officials with an interest in reform, notably Lord Deputy Sidney, viewed Loftus' goals with impatience or disdain and his strategy was finally deconstructed and abandoned at the deputy's behest in 1577. Thereafter, the archbishop was forced to adopt the more coercive programme of enforcement favoured by Sidney and the government in London. It was the rigorous implementation of this programme in the late 1570s and early 1580s which finally and irrevocably alienated the Pale community from the established Church. However, the seeds of this alienation had been planted and nourished by the indigenous clergy over many decades.[43]

CONCLUSION

The opposition of the indigenous clergy, then, worked on a number of different levels. Not only was it instrumental in preserving the spirit and prac-

41 'Articles objected against Sir John Bale, clerk, commissary unto the archbishop of Dublin' (Public Record Office, SP 63/71, no. 10).   42 Murray, 'Tudor diocese of Dublin', pp 241-4, 247-53.   43 Ibid., pp 253-94.

tices of the old religion in the opening decade of Elizabeth's reign, but thereafter it was consciously enmeshed within a web of ecclesiastical political
intrigue that contributed to the destruction of those very measures that were
instituted to combat it. Yet the strength and power of the indigenous clergy
and their ethos also operated on a level far deeper than the direct actions
they took during the episcopacies of Archbishops Browne, Curwen and
Loftus. The very structures of the diocese of Dublin embodied the essentially medieval values of the indigenous clergy and, even after the generation
who had fought the Reformation had passed away or had become involved
in the nascent Counter-Reformation movement in the Pale, continued to
haunt the reformers.

One of these structures was the medieval system for financing the
parochial clergy. Through the device of appropriation, the overwhelming
bulk of parochial income in the diocese of Dublin had been diverted towards
the support of the ecclesiastical corporations of the medieval English Pale.
This system was inherited in a largely unreformed condition by the established Church, and was one of the key factors that prevented it from trans-
forming the largely stipendiary and inadequately educated clergy of the diocese into a learned, expository ministry capable of evangelising the local
community.[44]

In contrast to the parochial system that was left unreformed largely by
default, the cathedral of St Patrick was the focus of great attention from the
reformers. As the nerve-centre of clerical conservatism in the English Pale,
the cathedral earned the opprobrium of the most committed reformers in
Tudor Ireland, many of whom wished to see it abolished permanently. Yet,
as the holder of the most valuable livings in the diocese of Dublin, it was
also perceived as a resource that could be exploited for a whole host of 'godly'
reasons, from supplementing the incomes of Protestant bishops to supporting Protestant graduate preachers. This ambivalent attitude to the institution
was seen at its greatest and, as far as Protestantism was concerned, most damaging effect, in the debate that raged between the reformers over the issue
of converting it into the much-needed university. Their inability to resolve
this issue delayed the foundation of a university in Dublin for nearly half a
century, a period in which the practice of educating the youth of the Pale in
continental Catholic universities grew apace.[45]

The final institution which embodied the medieval values of the corporate clergy, and which haunted the reformers, was Christ Church cathedral.
A regular institution at the outset of the Reformation, whose primary and
popular function was to act as a large chantry foundation, the cathedral never
found a new role after the enactment of the Elizabethan settlement. Although

44 Ibid., chapter 7 passim.   45 Ibid., chapter 8 passim.

it continued, as the only major religious foundation within the old city walls, to host state officials for divine service on a regular basis, its major preoccupation throughout the reign of Elizabeth was to shore up the creaking fabric that collapsed in 1562. To the clergy and officials who worshipped within its walls, this creaking fabric must have appeared as a very striking, but depressing, metaphor for the ailing Church of Ireland, which had been brought to its knees by the old corporate clergy who had once served therein.[46]

After this, then, what can be said about the crucial issues raised by the Bradshaw-Canny debate is clear but hardly definitive. In relation to the primary dispute over chronology, there are very good grounds for arguing that by the time Adam Loftus – a man who was far more responsive to the religious sensibilities of the local community than he has sometimes been given credit for – took up the episcopacy, the Reformation had failed. The fact that Loftus identified the basis of conservative religious resistance in his diocese, developed a plausible strategy to overcome it, but still failed to dislodge it, suggests very strongly that the revival of the old religion in the mid-Tudor period created an ideological force which was impervious to the theology, worship and ideas espoused by the reformers. Of this religious conservatism itself, its roots and strength were to be found not in the heroic spirit of the Irish nation, nor in the ideology of post-Tridentine Catholicism, but in the values and reflexes of the corporate clergy, who had long sustained the identity of the old colonial community in a hostile world.

46 Ibid., chapter 9 passim.

5

Mass in the manor house: the Counter-Reformation in Dublin, 1560-1630

Colm Lennon

Every gent ... hath a prist or a frier for theire domesticke chaplen, and maintaines and abbets them, ... who doo celebrate Mass, and execute their function in his mansion howse ..., frequented by neighbouring townes publiquely.[1]

The Counter-Reformation, beginning in the period of the Council of Trent (1545-63), was a movement for the revival of the Roman Catholic Church. Its advent in a diocese was normally marked by the pastorate of a reforming, resident bishop who implemented the decrees of the Council in his see. The principal mechanism was a synod of clergy who were, ideally, imbued with zeal for bringing higher standards of Catholic practice to the localities. The bishop was charged with close supervision of the parishes and religious institutions within his diocese (and other dioceses if he were a metropolitan) mainly through regular visitation. The focus of change at local level was the parish church, ideally staffed by a seminary-trained parish priest who had the task of introducing reforms on the ground. These included proper and regular administration of the sacraments, preaching on the subject of the Tridentine norms, channelling of pious practices and confraternal activities through the parochial system, and arranging for the catechising of youth in parish schools. In most areas where such programmes were introduced, transition was slow, even painful, as new ecclesiastical standards frequently came into conflict with social mores and traditions, in relation, for example, to baptismal, marriage or funeral customs.[2]

---

1 Cited in Myles V. Ronan (ed.), 'Archbishop Bulkeley's visitation of Dublin, 1630', *Archivium Hibernicum*, 8 (1941), p. 82. 2 For a recent survey of the Counter-Reformation, see R. Po-Chia Hsia, *The world of Catholic renewal, 1540-1770* (Cambridge, 1998); see also John Bossy, *Christianity in the west* (Oxford, 1985), ch. 7; idem, 'The Counter-Reformation

In the diocese of Dublin the formal introduction of the Counter-Reformation was delayed by the absence of a Roman-appointed archbishop for several decades after 1560. The prevailing political conditions made it impossible for a resident Catholic episcopate to function effectively. Yet during the hiatus, before the Catholic ecclesiastical leadership necessary to initiate the Tridentine reforms was in place, at least two generations of laymen and women continued to practise the older faith. Technically they were recusants in the eyes of the state, refusing to conform to the terms of the Reformation statutes of 1560. The role of the socially ascendant patricians – the gentry in the countryside and the mercantile *élite* in the city – was very significant for the emergence of a Catholic system of worship, shadowing that of the state Church. Long accustomed to participating actively in the management and patronage of religious institutions such as parish confraternities, the leading families had been boosted by grants of abbey lands and properties after the dissolution of the religious orders in the region of Dublin. These benefits brought with them perquisites such as church income and rights to appoint clergy. For much of the period from 1560 to 1630 the men and women of these lay *élites* played an important part in preserving traditional devotions and practices. At first, this response may have been merely atavistic, but as the issue of conformity to the state religion became crystallised from about 1580 onwards the contribution of the patricians became more self-consciously recusant.[3]

By the time a resident Catholic archbishop of Dublin began the work of reorganising the diocesan administration in the 1620s, a network of places of worship had been established, mostly under the auspices of the gentry and merchant families. Appointments to Catholic benefices and schools lay in the gift of these laypeople. This article will examine how an alternative system of Catholic practice came into being in the absence of archiepiscopal leadership. An assessment of the position in the parishes in the 1560s and 1570s as the state Church failed to establish a significant presence will be followed by an examination of the pattern of domestication of religious activities in the homes of the laity. The turbulent period of the late 1570s and 1580s will

---

and the people of Catholic Ireland, 1596-1641' in T.D. Williams (ed.), *Historical Studies*, viii (1971), pp 155-69; P.J. Corish, *The Catholic community in the seventeenth and eighteenth centuries* (Dublin, 1981), pp 32-42.   3 See Colm Lennon, 'The Counter-Reformation in Ireland, 1542-1641' in Ciaran Brady and Raymond Gillespie (eds), *Natives and newcomers: essays on the making of Irish colonial society, 1534-1641* (Dublin, 1986), pp 75-93 and 'The chantries in the Irish Reformation: the case of St Anne's guild, Dublin, 1550-1630' in R.V. Comerford, Mary Cullen, J.R. Hill and Colm Lennon (eds), *Religion, conflict and coexistence: essays presented to Patrick J. Corish* (Dublin, 1991), pp 7-12; see also Eamon Duffy, *The stripping of the altars* (New Haven, 1992), pp 131-54.

be seen as galvanising the members of the Catholic community into more confessional certitude and decisiveness. Thereafter the deployment of Church perquisites, especially the right of appointment of priests which came with grants of monastic property, will be assessed in an effort to establish the mechanism whereby Catholic practice in the archdiocese came to centre upon the mansions of the leading gentlefolk. When the regular and secular clergy began their work of ecclesiastical reorganisation in the early 1600s, they aspired to the Tridentine norm of religious activity revolving around the parish churches, and it may be instructive to conclude this study by asking to what extent the interface between the Counter-Reformation missioners and the lay patrons was a smooth one.

I

With the acceptance by Archbishop Hugh Curwen of Dublin of the oath of supremacy of Queen Elizabeth in 1560, the diocese was thereafter ruled by an apostate in the eyes of Rome.[4] As Curwen strove to bring his clergy and lay flock within the Reformation fold, the Vatican was faced with a dilemma. On Curwen's early retirement and replacement by Adam Loftus, translated from the primatial see of Armagh, it was obvious that control of the archiepis-copate was firmly in the hands of the state. Yet given the diplomatic impli-cations of any attempt to appoint a rival claimant to such an important posi-tion, the Curial authorities preferred to temporise, and there is no clear evidence of a Roman nominee to the archdiocese until Matthew de Oviedo was preferred in 1600.[5] The first actual presence of a papally-appointed arch-bishop among his flock is not recorded until after May 1611, although two vicars-general were appointed in Dublin during the previous decade. The fates of Primate Richard Creagh in Armagh and Archbishop Dermot O'Hurley in Cashel signalled the dangers which Roman-nominated arch-bishops faced in actively pressing their claims. The alternative was to depute either priests or bishops *in situ* in other parts of the country to take charge of Dublin administrative matters, without necessarily establishing an episco-pal presence in the archdiocese. Dislocation of the normal means rendered appointments at lesser levels impossible and impractical. Another approach was to delegate special agents such as Thady Newman, empowered by papal emissary David Wolfe in 1563 to ensure Catholic worship in Dublin and the

---

4 Myles V. Ronan, *The Reformation in Ireland under Elizabeth, 1558-80 (from original sources)* (London, 1930), p. 33; R.D. Edwards, *Church and state in Tudor Ireland* (Dublin, 1935), pp 187-90, 208-11.   5 Patrick F. Moran, *History of the Catholic archbishops of Dublin since the Reformation* (Dublin, 1864), pp 217-18.

greater Leinster region and to absolve those who had lapsed into heresy or schism.[6] Details of Newman's subsequent career are sketchy: he appears to have been operating in the Wicklow region about 1580 and was questioned about his connections with the Baltinglass revolt.[7] Later Newman, described as a 'preeste', was commended for his 'good and faithful service' to Queen Elizabeth in the matter of dealing with survivors of the Spanish Armada who landed in the north of Ireland.[8] Apart from fleetingly-glimpsed members of religious orders, the only other 'official' representation of Catholicism within the diocese for most of the earlier Elizabethan period was through the unreconstructed beneficed clergy who dressed up old liturgical practices in vestments of the new order, aptly described by Loftus as being nothing better than 'new wine in old bottles'.[9] That the more ceremonial side of Catholic devotion was left completely unattended is attested by the evidence of those who told Father Henry Fitzsimon SJ, about 1597 that High Mass had not been celebrated in Dublin for forty years.[10]

Apart from the deprivation of prominent beneficed priests who did not publicly conform to the Elizabethan settlement, the Reformation statutes made little difference to the disposition of Church properties and patronage within the Dublin archdiocese. The lay leaders of the community clung to their gains of the previous decades, having been granted lands and buildings in return for their acquiescence in the early Reformation.[11] These possessions in town and countryside throughout the diocesan area, which greatly consolidated the social and economic status of the gentry and mercantile *élites*, yielded considerable resources of wealth and patronage within the ecclesiastical sphere. Besides profiting from the income of tithes from these benefices, the lay possessors won the rights of appointment of rectors or vicars which had formerly been vested in the monastic proprietors. Potentially the greater number of parishes within the archdiocese were thus effectively under lay and not episcopal control from the mid-sixteenth century onwards.[12] As long as the lay impropriators adopted a position of benign neutrality towards the

6 Public Records Office (henceforth PRO), S.P. 63/93/80.   7 PRO, S.P. 63/93/80.   8 *Analecta Hibernica*, 1 (1930), p. 96.   9 E.P. Shirley, *Original letters and papers illustrative of the history of the church of Ireland during the reigns of Edward VI, Mary and Elizabeth* (London, 1851), pp 158, 160, 275; Colm Lennon, *The lords of Dublin in the age of Reformation* (Dublin, 1989), p. 142; see also James Murray, 'The Tudor diocese of Dublin: episcopal government, ecclesiastical politics and the enforcement of the reformation, *c.*1534-1590', (Ph.D. thesis, University of Dublin, 1997), chapter five.   10 Edmund Hogan (ed.), *Ibernia Ignatiana: seu Ibernorum Societatis Jesu patrum monumenta collecta*, i (Dublin, 1880), p. 41.   11 Brendan Bradshaw, *The dissolution of the religious orders in Ireland under Henry VIII* (Cambridge, 1974), appendices 1-2.   12 Alan Ford, 'The Protestant Reformation' in Brady and Gillespie (eds), *Natives and newcomers*, pp 52-3; idem, *The Protestant Reformation in Ireland, 1590-1641* (Dublin, 1997), pp 86-7.

state Church, eschewing matters of theological controversy, the use of these resources of profit and patronage within the established Church was feasible and ultimately more than likely.

Such lay involvement in the sphere of ecclesiastical management within the archdiocese had a long history. Gentry and merchant families were accustomed to building and ornamenting their local parish churches.[13] In some cases, gentlefolk built churches or chapels on their manorial estates, retaining rights of advowson or clerical appointment.[14] In addition, colleges for small numbers of chantry priests were constructed with lay sponsorship, as in the case of the St Lawrence family at Howth.[15] Chantries were provided for by pious lay people in their local parish churches, the Portlester chapel of the Eustace family in St Audoen's, Dublin, being among the best endowed. As well as adding to the beauty of their churches by donating funds for new chapels, altars and aisles, the wealthy gentry and merchant families were patrons of priests, supernumerary to diocesan clerics. Among this group were guild or confraternity chaplains who were maintained by the patrons of religious corporations established for the provision of services in perpetuity for the souls of members and their families.[16] The territorial proprietorship of gentry families often entailed cultivation and protection of private devotions and shrines such as wayside crosses and holy wells. Those of Mulhuddard and St Doulagh's were patronised by the Luttrell and Fagan gentry families respectively, for example.[17] Thus the lay *élites* were accustomed to disposing of a large amount of patronage, largely independent of diocesan jurisdiction, and may not have been acutely affected by the absence of episcopal oversight after the Elizabethan settlement. The integration of Church life within the bailiwicks of the lords of the soil was a feature of the pre-Reformation period and could in theory form the basis of an alternative system to the parish network of the established Church, were the latter to fail to satisfy their devotional and pastoral needs.

It would be understandable if the lay families should decline to abandon their parish and manorial churches and chapels to the protagonists of the new religious regime. These buildings after all housed much of the communal pious investment in the sacred, in the form of favoured shrines, statues,

13 Henry F. Berry (ed.), *Register of the wills and inventories of the diocese of Dublin, 1457-83* (Dublin, 1898), pp 13-15, 58-60, 66-8, 109-11, 112-13, 118-20, 148-9. 14 H.G. Leask, *Irish churches and monastic buildings: iii medieval Gothic, the last phases* (Dundalk, 1960), pp 11-40. 15 Lennon, 'Chantries in the Irish Reformation', pp 10-11. 16 Ibid.; Raymond Refaussé and Mary Clark, *Directory of historic Dublin guilds* (Dublin, 1993), pp 32-40. 17 Myles V. Ronan (ed.), 'Royal visitation of Dublin, 1615', *Archivium Hibernicum*, 8 (1941), pp 32-3; Caoimhín Ó Dahachair, 'The holy wells of County Dublin', *Reportorium Novum*, 2, no. 1 (1958), pp 68-87; 2, no. 2 (1960), pp 233-5.

pews, funeral monuments and wall plaques.[18] There is evidence that Church buildings down to the 1560s were maintained to a high standard of adornment.[19] But the spirit in which at least some of the gentry families approached their parish churches may have been changing, perhaps not least in response to changes in architecture and furnishing. The earl of Sussex reported in 1562: 'The people, without discipline and utterly void of religion, come to divine service as to a May-game'.[20] Top gentleman-officials within the Dublin region were compliant with the state Church in their public careers while maintaining private Catholic devotions. Sir John Plunkett of Dunsoghly, chief justice of the queen's bench for many years until his death in 1582, was fulsomely praised by state and Church officials for his service and loyalty. Yet an examination of his private chapel with its funerary sculpture in Dunsoghly Castle reveals many of the features of Catholic iconography of the late sixteenth century.[21] James Stanihurst of Corduff, sometime speaker of the House of Commons and a trusted administrator until his death in 1573, was, according to his son, Richard, 'very Catholic' and refused the lord chancellorship on that account.[22] The position of James Bathe of Drumcondra, chief baron of the exchequer until he died in 1570, was equally ambiguous.[23] Such signs of Church papistry were not unusual among public figures of that generation in England and Ireland. But while their sons and daughters were conformable for the most part in the former country, in the latter dissent became entrenched, as separation from the established Church was manifested through a withdrawal to worship in private dwellings.

The rôle of women in fostering this alternative system of worship was significant. Their withdrawal from services in the parish churches of the established religion preceded that of the men, and their controlling influence in the domestic sphere facilitated the maintaining of Catholic worship.[24] The case of Margaret Ball, widow of Alderman Bartholomew of Dublin, is the best known. She maintained a school of Christian doctrine for the instruction of girls and boys, and employed a domestic chaplain who was arrested with her on the occasion of her first imprisonment in the late 1570s.[25] The displaced clergy of the Marian period may have served in the capacity of chaplain-schoolteachers in the houses of the city merchant patricians and

---

18 Rolf Loeber, 'Sculptured memorials to the dead in early seventeenth century Ireland: a survey from "Monumenta Eblanae" and other sources', *Royal Irish Academy Proceedings*, 81C (1981), pp 267-95.   19 Raymond Gillespie, *The sacred in the secular: religious change in Catholic Ireland, 1500-1700* (Vermont, 1993), p. 4.   20 Shirley (ed.), *Original letters*, p. 17.   21 David McNally, 'Sir John Plunkett of Dunsoghly' (B.A. thesis, NUI, Maynooth (1987), pp 99-107.   22 Colm Lennon, *Richard Stanihurst the Dubliner* (Dublin, 1981), p. 22.   23 Sean Ó Mathúna, *An tAth. William Bathe, C.I.: ceannrodaí sa teangeolaíocht* (Dublin, 1980), pp 39-41.   24 Lennon, *Lords of Dublin*, pp 212-13.   25 Ibid., pp 213.

county gentry. In the 1570s a list of the men of learning in Ireland included the names of many schoolmasters in Dublin, most of whom must have worked as tutors in private establishments. That some or most of these were priests is a reasonable conjecture. Among the names mentioned on the list are those of Patrick Cusack, Michael Fitzsimon, Matthew Talbot, and two whose surnames alone are given: Travers and Magrane.[26] Youngsters who enrolled at the continental seminaries of Douai and Salamanca stated that their early schooling was provided by Catholic schoolmasters in their homes.[27] Among these was William Bathe, the future Jesuit scholar and linguist, who was of the Drumcondra gentry family.[28] The priest-schoolmaster Michael Fitzsimon of Dublin was among those executed for their part in the uprising of James Eustace, Viscount Baltinglass, in 1580.[29]

The events surrounding this revolt were decisive in forging certitude among the hitherto uncommitted laity of the archdiocese (in the southern reaches of which some of the fighting occurred). Among the agents of Baltinglass' conspiracy were Catholic priests who operated in a freelance way, travelling from house to house under the protection of men and women of the gentry. They included Robert Rochford, Edmund Tanner and Nicholas Eustace, who liaised between lay families involved with the viscount. Old, retired priests were maintained by the viscount at his home in Monkstown, County Dublin.[30] The shock of witnessing open rebellion so close to the heart of the diocese and the subsequent arrests, interrogations and executions of leading gentry figures galvanised the rest of the community into decisiveness. Thereafter the option of Church papistry was not open. From the mid-1580s the majority of the leaders of the community forged a recusant identity, choosing not to attend state Church services, sending their offspring for education to continental colleges, forming marital alliances with clans whose religious convictions were close to their own, and eschewing the small Dublin native Protestant coterie.[31] Among clerical scholars abroad such as John Howlin SJ, and also among the educated lay *élites* at home, a martyrological version of the events of the late 1570s and early 1580s emerged.[32] On the

26 Liam Miller and Ellen Power (eds), *Holinshed's Irish chronicle* (New York, 1979), pp 95-112.   27 Helga Hammerstein, 'Aspects of the continental education of Irish students in the reign of Elizabeth I' in Williams (ed.), *Historical studies*, 8, pp 143-53.   28 Ó Mathúna, *An tAth William Bathe*, pp 38-42.   29 'Ware's annals' (Oxford, Bodleian Lib., Ms Rawlinson B 479, f. 103r).   30 Elizabeth Ann O'Connor, 'The rebellion of James Eustace, Viscount Baltinglass' (M.A. thesis, NUI, Maynooth, 1989), pp 68-105.   31 Ciaran Brady, '"Conservative subversives": the community of the Pale and the Dublin administration, 1556-86' in P.J. Corish (ed.), *Radicals, rebels and establishments* (Belfast, 1985), pp 11-32; Lennon, *Lords of Dublin*, pp 151-65.   32 'Perbreve compendium' of John Howlin, *c.*1590 (Maynooth, College Library, Salamanca MSS, legajo xi, no. 4); 'Magna supplicia a persecutoribus aliquot in Ibernia sumpta' of Christopher Hollywood, early seventeenth

strength of this committed Catholicism they began to deploy the ecclesiastical resources to hand against the state Church and in favour of an alternative, Catholic model. The subject of control of the profits and patronage of the Dublin archdiocese in the later sixteenth and early seventeenth century may now be addressed more closely.

II

In at least 60 (that is, 40 per cent) of the approximately 150 parishes within the diocese in the early seventeenth century the tithes were impropriate.[33] This meant that tithe income was not under the direct control of the Church of Ireland authorities, and in most of these instances the farmers of tithes were Catholics. Impropriations had arisen from the dissolution of the monasteries in the region in the late 1530s. The religious houses had the right to income from ecclesiastical lands on which churches stood, and were in most cases entitled to nominate clergy to serve the parishes. When the properties of the religious orders were granted by the crown to lay people in the years after 1540, the rights, privileges and responsibilities associated with these were transferred also. An examination of the monastic extents for the Dublin area in 1540 reveals that local gentry, merchants and farmers already had a considerable stake in the possessions of the monks and nuns, not just in the renting of lands but also in the leasing of tithes.[34] Thus, for example, in the case of the rectory of Balmedon, a parcel of the nunnery of Grace Dieu, the tithes of 23 couples, worth $1\frac{3}{4}d.$ each, were held by Thomas Fitzsimon from the prioress on a term lease for £15 3s. 4d.[35] In many cases, the pattern of leasing in the pre-dissolution period may have influenced the favourable consideration of lessees in the granting of property. In the deanery of Taney, almost all of the lands in the parishes of Mulhuddard and Clonsilla, including the parish church at Coolmine, a total of almost 1,000 acres, had been held by the abbey of St Mary. The local gentleman, Thomas Luttrell, had extensive leases of lands and tithes in the parishes, and was the major grantee of the properties on the dissolution.[36] The number of advowsons in the diocese of Dublin which had been carried over from the monastic era was approximately 58, not all of these being parish churches. The nominating patrons included many lay people as well as corporations such as that of the Dublin municipality.[37]

century (Brussels, Bibliothèque Royale, Ms 2158-67).   **33** 'Archbishop Bulkeley's visitation', pp 56-7.   **34** Newport B. White (ed.), *Extents of Irish monastic possessions* (Dublin, 1943), pp 1-90.   **35** Ibid., p. 76.   **36** Ibid., p. 16; Colmcille Ó Conbhuí, 'The lands of St Mary's abbey, Dublin', *Royal Irish Academy Proceedings* 62C (1961-3), pp 34-6.   **37** James F. Ferguson, *Remarks on the limitation of actions bill intended for Ireland together*

An analysis of the pattern of lay impropriation which emerges from the visitation by Archbishop Bulkeley of the archdiocese in 1630 reveals that members of the county gentry continued to hold extensive ecclesiastical property. To the north, south and west of the metropolitan centre of Dublin, substantial gentlemen were farmers of tithes of parishes. Of these, at least 60 per cent can be identified as Catholics or recusants.[38] Among the prominent families associated with church livings in the northern deaneries of Swords, Garristown and Lusk were at least two branches of the Barnewalls, the Fagans of Feltrim, the Fitzsimons and Plunkets of the Grange (Baldoyle), the Talbots of Malahide and the Usshers of Cromlin (Santry).[39] The western and southern deaneries in the county area contained parishes in which the Luttrells of Luttrellstown, the Fitzwilliams of Merrion, the Allens of St Wolstan's and the Wolverstons of Stillorgan were impropriators.[40] In the Wicklow and Kildare deaneries of Bray, Wicklow and Arklow, Castledermot and Athy and Leixlip, such gentry families as the Aylmers, Cheevers, Fagans, Archbolds, Whites, Peppards, Eustaces and Sarsfields were in receipt of tithes.[41] Apart from this group of Old English gentry, New and Old English state officials and widows of servitors made up about 27 per cent of the impropriators. These included Viscount Moore (Hollywood, Grallagh and the Naul), Sir Barnaby Bryan (Holmpatrick), Justice Mayward (Delgany), Sir William Parsons (Ballintemple and Bealan) and Thomas Hovendon (Tanckardstown).[42] The corporation of Dublin leased or subleased the tithes of parishes formerly impropriate to the priory of All Saints within the diocese, including Cloghran-Hiddert and Rathdrum.[43] Of the tithe income of £4,753 gathered in the archdiocese, £1,461 was allocated to stipends of clergy serving the cures. The highest proportion of tithe income assigned to clerical livings was produced by the deaneries of Swords, and Arklow and Wicklow (39 per cent and 38 per cent respectively), and the lowest in Garristown (11 per cent). The average figure for the diocese (excluding the intra-mural and suburban Dublin parishes where 84 per cent of tithe income went for stipends) was 24 per cent. Thus in the rural parts of the archdiocese about three-quarters of the income from ecclesiastical property was not available to provide the salaries of clergy serving the cures.[44]

with short extracts from ancient records relating to advowsons of churches in Ireland (Dublin, 1843), pp 33-41. I am grateful to Dr Christopher J. Woods for bringing this pamphlet, which is in the Haliday collection (1860/4) in the Royal Irish Academy, to my attention. **38** Lennon, *Lords of Dublin*, appendix ii, 'Prosopography of the aldermen of Dublin', pp 224-276; see also John Kingston, 'The Catholic families of the Pale', *Reportorium Novum*, 1, nos 1-2 (1955-6), pp 76-90; 2, nos 1-2 (1957-60), pp 88-108, 236-56. **39** 'Archbishop Bulkeley's visitation', pp 63-71. **40** Ibid., pp 71-7. **41** Ibid., pp 77-98. **42** Ibid., pp 69,70, 83, 93, 94, 95. **43** Ibid., pp 77, 89-90. **44** Ibid., p. 57.

The alternative system of worship set up by the Catholic priests is very evident in the returns of Archbishop Bulkeley's visitation of 1630. Almost every parish had the service of a 'Mass-priest' who, in quite a number of cases, served more than one church. A key feature is the 'Mass-house' in town and countryside, which could be a permanent, purpose-built edifice, a derelict premises taken over for the purpose (as in Garristown), a dwelling converted into a Mass-house as in Mounctowne (Monkstown), or an area made available in the residence of a patrician or gentry family as occurred in Hollywood, Grallagh and the Naul, where the houses of Mr Caddle and Mr Cruise alternated as places of Catholic worship.[45] In a number of instances the impropriators provided the location for the celebration of Mass: the Fitzsimons and Plunketts of Baldoyle and Portmarnock, the Talbots of Malahide and the Cheevers of Mounctowne opened their mansion-houses to congregations.[46] Over fifty gentlemen and women were identified as 'abettors and harbourers' of priests and friars, offering facilities for the saying of Mass and the carrying out of their ministries. Among these were principal aristocratic personages such as the Lady Dowager of Howth in Westpalstown, Sir Christopher Plunkett of Dunsoghly, Theobald Walshe of Carrickmines and Robert Barnewall of Shankill, each of whom opened their mansions or castles to worshippers from their own and neighbouring parishes.[47] The homes of the gentry were nodal points not just in the social and economic life of their districts but also in sustaining a working system of Catholic worship which covered all parts of the archdiocese. The rôle of the leading families went beyond merely supporting clergy and providing Mass-centres: it also encompassed fostering religious careers as priests and nuns for their own and their neighbours' offspring, and sustaining the pedagogical activities of Catholic schoolmasters.[48]

The direct relationship between gentry families, whether impropriators or not, and Mass-priests is evidenced in the returns of the 1630 visitation. In the vast majority of cases the reference is to the provision of facilities for the celebration of Mass in the manor house or castle of gentry folk. Some of the priests may have lived permanently at these venues but others were itinerant. The size of livings granted to priests by patrons is not stated but in one case, that of Father John Begg in the extra-mural Dublin parish of St Kevin and St Bride, the eight shillings per annum provided by the sixty recusant households gave him an income of £24.[49] This is very close to the aver-

---

45 For a list of Mass-houses in Dublin city in the 1610s, see Myles V. Ronan, 'Religious life in old Dublin', *Dublin Historical Record*, 2 (1939-40), pp 106-7; see also 'Archbishop Bulkeley's visitation', pp 57-8, 68, 69, 86.   46 'Archbishop Bulkeley's visitation', pp 65, 66, 68, 86.   47 Ibid., pp 69, 76, 82.   48 Ibid., pp 64, 70, 74, 77, 82, 85; 87; Lennon, *Lords of Dublin*, pp 213-14.   49 'Archbishop Bulkeley's visitation', p. 62.

age sum per parish of undisposed-of tithe income (£23) gathered by impropriators who did not spend a significant amount on the maintenance of churches or chancels, to judge by the reported state of disrepair of most of them. In some cases, definite family connections can be drawn between named Mass-priests and patrons. Stephen Browne, a member of the order of Discalced Carmelites, who resided at the house of his mother, Mary Sedgrave, in Cook Street, Dublin, is mentioned as being the celebrant of Mass in St Michan's parish.[50] Marcus Barnewall, possibly a member of the nearby Turvey branch of that family, was referred to as the Mass-priest at Cloghran-Swords, and members of the Begg, Fitzgerald and Sutton gentry and merchant patrician families were listed as serving in parishes in the diocese as priests.[51] Mr Robert Barnewall of Shankill provided shelter for his sister, Mary, a nun.[52] Henry Cusack SJ was living with his sister, Cecilia, and her third husband, John Finglas, in their house at Westpalston.[53] The names of some Gaelic priests show up particularly in relation to the Kildare and Wicklow parts of the archdiocese: in the parish of Wicklow itself, for example, the names of the Mass-priests given are Edmond Quyn, Cale O'Conly, James O'Trenor and Patrick O'Connell.[54]

In the case of at least thirty-five of the impropriated parishes throughout the diocese in 1630, the right of advowson or appointment of clergy to serve the cure remained in lay possession. The perquisite had been granted along with the property of the abbeys and monasteries of St Mary, St Thomas, All Saints near Dublin, Grace Dieu in Swords, Graney in County Kildare and the Knights Hospitallers of Kilmainham. In some cases, these rights had been held continuously by the same families for a century since the dissolution. Clonsillagh, a grange of the late abbey of St Mary, Dublin, remained in the possession of the Luttrells throughout the period, the family retaining their rights of advowson.[55] Baldoyle, a parcel of the priory of All Saints, came into the hands of the Fitzsimon family of the Grange after the dissolution by way of a lease from Dublin Corporation, the grantee of the property. In 1630, the great-grandson of the original lessee, Thomas Fitzsimon, opened his house to Catholics on Sundays and holydays for the celebration of Mass.[56] The Church of Ireland parish church was 'altogether ruinous' and there were reported to be no Protestants in the parish of Baldoyle. The rectory of the

50 Lennon, *Lords of Dublin*, p. 214.   51 'Archbishop Bulkeley's visitation', pp 63, 77, 78, 79, 80.   52 Ibid., p. 82.   53 Lennon, *Lords of Dublin*, p. 214.   54 'Archbishop Bulkeley's visitation', pp 88-9.   55 White (ed.), *Extents of Irish monastic possessions*, p. 16; O Conbhui, 'The lands of St Mary's abbey, Dublin', pp 34-6; Ferguson, *Remarks on ... actions bill*, pp 33-41; 'Archbishop Bulkeley's visitation', p. 77.   56 John Gilbert (ed.), *Calendar of ancient records of Dublin*, ii (Dublin, 1898), pp 4, 143; Ferguson, *Remarks on ... actions bill*, pp 33-41; 'Archbishop Bulkeley's visitation', p. 65.

parish church of Donabate had been impropriate to the abbey of Graney in County Kildare. When Graney was secularised it fell to Sir Anthony St Leger who in turn leased the Donabate holdings to James Luttrell who in his will of 1557 directed that the presentation to the parish of Donabate should be forever in the gift of the house of Luttrell. His wish was honoured down to 1638 when the guardian of Simon Luttrell presented to the cure.[57] Among the other impropriated churches to which recusant gentry had the right of advowson were Ballyboghill, Kiltiernan, Garristown and Westpalston.[58] In all of these parishes the Church of Ireland vicars or curates were in receipt of low stipends.

The picture which emerges from the report of 1630 is of an organised Catholic network, operating parallel to the Church of Ireland parochial system. Modifications had been made to take account of the concentration of population in the manorialised countryside, the natural foci being the houses of the gentry in the rural areas, and strategically-placed dwellings in key streets in the city. Much of this pattern was in accordance with the guidelines laid down by the first of the post-Tridentine provincial synods, held under the supervision of the recently-installed Archbishop Matthews in 1614.[59] At this assembly provision was made for coverage of the country in a practical and economical way. The results of such a rationalisation can be seen to a great extent by 1630.

The funding of the Counter-Reformation system of ministry was underpinned by the gentry's ecclesiastically-generated revenues through their control of impropriations. As we have seen, it was possible in most parishes for Mass-priests to earn up to £24 per annum, in some cases up to ten times more than their Church of Ireland counterparts (who admittedly had much smaller congregations). In addition, as I have shown elsewhere, a not inconsiderable sum may have been generated by religious guilds and chantries which continued to operate as property-leasing concerns, almost exclusively among Catholics, down to the 1630s.[60] These institutions also had residual patronage rights attached to them which enabled and accustomed lay people to appointing priests and chaplains. For at least four generations since the initial disruption of diocesan parochial patterns, the engagement of lay people with Church patronage and property had intensified in the absence of any

57 Ferguson, *Remarks on ... actions bill*, pp 33-41; 'Archbishop Bulkeley's visitation', p. 63. 58 Ferguson, *Remarks on ... actions bill*, pp 33-41; 'Archbishop Bulkeley's visitation', pp 68-9, 71, 85. 59 Alison Forrestal, *Catholic synods in Ireland, 1600-1690* (Dublin, 1998), pp 47-51; M. Comerford (ed.), *Collections relating to the dioceses of Kildare and Leighlin* (3 vols, Dublin and London, 1886), i, 245-52. 60 Colm Lennon, 'The survival of the confraternities in post-Reformation Dublin', *Confraternitas*, 6 (1995), pp 5-12; 'Archbishop Bulkeley's visitation', p. 59.

controlling or restraining authority. The domestication of the system of Catholic worship throughout the archdiocese of Dublin began in earnest in the 1580s and the culmination can be seen in the report of the 1630 visitation. By that time, a newly-established Counter-Reformation hierarchy was coming to terms with a confident and assertive lay leadership.

III

The tentative rooting of a clerical Counter-Reformation campaign began about 1597 with the establishment of a new Jesuit residency in Dublin. The flamboyant and dynamic Henry Fitzsimon SJ was the principal figure in the Catholic Church's efforts to circumvent the burgeoning evangelism of the Church of Ireland.[61] Both he and Christopher Hollywood SJ, the head of the mission, belonged to prominent Dublin families, the former to a municipal patrician clan and the latter to the gentry-proprietors of the Artane estate in the north county.[62] They returned to their network of kinsfolk which they used effectively in their missionary activity. Among Fitzsimon's benefactors were Thomas Fagan of Feltrim and Michael Taylor of Swords, both of whose families are listed as prominent protectors of priests in 1630.[63] Fitzsimon immediately began an active pastorate of preaching, hearing confessions, converting apostates, distributing alms and settling disputes. The crowds who gathered to hear Mass were so large that he appointed a chapel in a nobleman's house, having it carpeted and adorned with tapestries. High Mass was celebrated with an orchestra to hand, giving Henry Fitzsimon an ideal platform for publicising the Sodality of the Blessed Virgin, which grew rapidly. Fitzsimon attested that 'the joy of all was unbounded as that High Mass was the first solemn Mass celebrated for the last forty years'.[64] Fitzsimon's activities were so open and popular as to be provocative. A fellow-Jesuit wrote:

> Crowds flock to hear him and are converted; his Sodality is spreading the practices of solid piety; he collects money for the support of the Irish college at Douay; he leads rather an open, demonstrative life, never dines without six or eight guests and when he goes through the country, he rides with three or four gentlemen who serve as companions.[65]

61 Edmund Hogan (ed.), *Words of comfort to persecuted Catholics by Father Henry Fitzsimon* (Dublin, 1881), pp 200–84. 62 Lennon, *Lords of Dublin*, pp 155, 159, 174–5. 63 *Words of comfort*, p. 251; 'Archbishop Bulkeley's visitation', pp 64, 65. The Taylors of Swords also produced Alderman Francis Taylor who died in prison in Dublin in 1621 for his Catholic beliefs and who has recently been beatified by the Catholic church. 64 *Words of comfort*, pp 206–8. 65 Ibid., p. 209.

Not surprisingly, Fitzsimon was arrested and held in Dublin Castle for four years. Despite this, fellow-Jesuits such as Hollywood, Richard Field, Patrick Lennon and Henry Cusack, as well as members of other orders and secular priests, increased in numbers in the early years of the seventeenth century in defiance of proclamations ordering their banishment issued under James I.[66]

The tenuousness of the position of Catholic clergy was illustrated by the arrest and imprisonment of Dr Robert Lalor, the vicar-general of the arch-diocese, in 1606.[67] This was, as a contemporary wrote, despite his 'confidence in the favour and secrecie of his friends in Dublin, as that he presumed often to harbour there a month or two together'.[68] Security was the watchword for some of the lay protectors: Richard Netterville, an elderly gentleman of County Dublin, confined to his residence under house arrest because of his dissidence, was reported to have had a curtain hung between his domestic altar and the rest of his chapel so that he could swear to the authorities that he saw no priest celebrating Mass.[69] Despite the edict forbidding the har-bouring of priests, Henry Fitzsimon reported that he was received with great hospitality wherever he went.[70] The relationship between the newly-ensconced Counter-Reformation clergy and the lay leadership in Dublin city and com-munity was mutually supportive. The priests were in receipt of 'great con-tributions' from the Catholic community and open house treatment from those who were their kinsfolk.

The impact of the presence of seminary-trained clerics among the pious but 'poorly instructed' laypeople was inspiriting and encouraging. Instead of shaping and fashioning 'their faith according to their temporal interests and convenience', the laity were confirmed in their beliefs and schooled in the politico-religious issues of the day by the priests.[71] When the aldermen of Dublin were put to the test in 1604-6 by the attempt by the authorities to compel them to conform to Anglicanism, the head of the Jesuit mission, Hollywood, was at hand to explain the issues at stake and to urge them to withstand the 'fury of the wolves'. He also sent to the leading citizens copies of answers that could be given to questions which were likely to be put by the commissioners. Expressing satisfaction at the recusants' 'sticking to this instruction', he remained vigilant throughout the months of the conflict, responding to queries sent, sometimes dispelling doubts and at other times praising their 'constancy'.[72]

By the second and third decades of the seventeenth century the Catholic lay leadership had become more assured in the profession of their faith. The period down to 1630 witnessed the harmonising of the mission of the priests

66 Corish, *Catholic community*, pp 21-36.   67 Moran, *History of the Catholic archbishops*, pp 217-18.   68 Lennon, *Lords of Dublin*, pp 214-15.   69 Ibid., pp 212, 322 n.   70 *Words of comfort*, p. 211.   71 Ibid., pp 140, 149-51.   72 *Ibernia Ignatiana*, pp 194-202.

with the nexus of the social *élite*. The provincial synod of 1614 held at Kilkenny decreed that unprovided parishes were to be assigned to pastors in neighbouring ones until a full complement of priests became available. Various measures were to be taken to ensure that Mass was celebrated with due solemnity and reverence even though the places of worship were not always consecrated. Open-air and derelict sites were to be protected in order to prevent desecration to the host.[73] When Henry Fitzsimon wrote in *The justification and exposition of the divine sacrifice of the Masse and of al rites and ceremonies*[74] concerning the ideal venue for the celebration of the eucharist, he could experience at first hand the baroque splendour of the Counter-Reformation in the Spanish Netherlands. His prescription for the dedicated church on a hill, clean and lightsome, with its altar centrally positioned, could not be applied to a region in which the Catholic faith was not only not the official state religion but was also subject to sporadic harassment. But, at the very least, the domiciles of the patrician families offered both comfort and decorousness which were conducive to the saying of Mass. Fitzsimon himself designed a chapel in the home of a nobleman, lining a hall with tapestry and covering it with carpets. The altar which he had made was 'as handsome and as elegantly furnished as any altar in Ireland'.[75]

Despite the strenuous efforts by the Counter-Reformation clergy to regulate baptisms, marriages and burials and to promote clerically-controlled confraternities, the Catholic community 'forming itself around the Mass'[76] in the early seventeenth century was essentially outside the bounds of parochial organisation. In seeking to impose a pattern of parishes upon that community, the priests were engaged in a drive towards socio-religious ascendancy, the maintenance of which by their lay kinsfolk in the transitional phase from Reformation to Counter-Reformation had ensured the very survival of their religion in the diocese of Dublin.

---

73 Comerford (ed.), *Collections relating to Kildare and Leighlin*, i, 245-52.   74 Published at Douai in 1611.   75 *Words of comfort*, p. 207.   76 Corish, *Catholic community*, pp 33-4.

6

Catholic religious cultures in the diocese of Dublin, 1614-97

Raymond Gillespie

It is self-evident that 'any proper assessment of a body whose stated purpose is spiritual should place first the devotional life of its faithful', yet applying such a principle to the study of the Catholic Church in the diocese of Dublin in the seventeenth century is a difficult task.[1] Those who have considered the subject have been preoccupied either with the doings of bishops and clergy or with the political implications of living in a country where the European norm of '*cuius regio, eius religio*' failed to apply. Less attention has been paid to the question of what it meant to be a Catholic in that world. To put it anthropologically, almost nothing is known of the system of Catholic symbols that generated long-lasting moods and motivations in people which enabled them to formulate conceptions of the order of existence and which made those conceptions real in everyday life.[2]

The reasons why historians have rarely tried to describe the Catholic system of the sacred are not hard to identify. The main one is the lack of significant bodies of evidence. Much of the documentation emanating from the Catholic Church in the seventeenth century is concerned with the administration of a Church that was only beginning to establish itself in an organisational sense. It was not until the appointment of Eugene Mathews in 1611 that the diocese of Dublin had a resident bishop for the first time since the mid-sixteenth century. The provincial synod held at Kilkenny in 1614 marked a further stage in the internal reform that was needed to bring the workings of the diocese of Dublin into line with the norms of the Council of Trent.

1 Donal Kerr, 'Under the Union flag: the Catholic Church in Ireland, 1800-70' in *Ireland after the Union* (Oxford, 1989), p. 23. For an extended treatment on a national level, see Raymond Gillespie, *Devoted people: belief and religion in early modern Ireland* (Manchester, 1997). 2 The definition is drawn from Clifford Geertz, 'Religion as a cultural system' in Michael Banton (ed.), *Anthropological approaches to the study of religion* (London, 1966), p. 4.

The process of religious change that took place within seventeenth-century Irish Catholicism creates problems of interpretation, not just because it occurred in an era of poor record-keeping but also because the religious culture that evolved does not fit a single schematic model. There were a number of sub-cultures within Catholicism. At the simplest level these may be reduced to two. First, there was a culture of traditional religion in which the sacraments, especially the Mass, were seen as part of a 'social miracle' whereby the local community was continually re-formed around a sacred mystery.[3] Communities inherited from the middle ages a social parallel to their own world in a world of saints whose heavenly community mirrored their earthly one. This gave rise to communal devotions addressed to these holy men and women based on rituals performed at particular places validated by a hagiographic tradition. To reformers, both Tridentine Catholics and Protestants, this world of traditional religion was regarded with suspicion because it bore close comparison with superstition, and relied on rituals rather than a genuine interiorised spirituality. A more individualistic piety, underpinned by greater detailed knowledge of faith in a catechetical tradition, in which the communal element was less prominent, shaped the second Catholic sub-culture which was becoming well-established in the diocese by the end of the seventeenth century. These two sub-cultures were not totally distinct, either conceptually or geographically. Despite differences in emphasis between urban and rural areas, traditional religion was not confined to the rural world nor the reformed spirituality to the towns. Nor was there a clear social division within the diocese of Dublin between the sub-cultures; indeed the two often interacted. The continuity of the sacramental tradition meant that at Mass, for instance, a form of spirituality which blended the localism of traditional religion with the more universal reform movement emerged. This essay attempts to describe the main features of the two dominant sub-cultures within Catholicism in the diocese of Dublin during the seventeenth century and, also, to identify the changes that occurred in the course of the century.

I

One of the main characteristics of traditional Catholic religious life in the diocese of Dublin in the seventeenth century was its localism. The manifestation of the holiness of God, that lay at the centre of religious belief and experience, was something that happened in particular places and at particular times. These gateways to the holy were validated not by the Church or

3 John Bossy, *Christianity in the West* (Oxford, 1985).

by individual clergy but by a hagiographical tradition that was in a continual state of flux. This was stabilised by associating the power of the saints
with particular places. This might be done by localising a saint through bodily
relics or statues that linked a saint to a particular place and that made his or
her power manifest there. Certainly the provincial synod held in 1614 claimed
that the laity in the diocese used relics to cure cattle.[4] A further example of
the desire to localise the power of saints is provided by the use of parochial
dedications.

The most important way in which the power of the saints was made manifest to the inhabitants of the seventeenth-century diocese was the association of particular features in the landscape with the activities of saints. The
most common natural feature utilised in this way was the holy well, each
of which was dedicated to a saint and was usually associated with the activities of that saint. Wells with curative powers were common features in the
diocese of Dublin.[5] According to the late seventeenth-century antiquarian,
Robert Ware, the main wells around the city had

> attributes ascribed to them by the Roman Catholics of wonders and
> miracles which they say have been wrought there; in which as sancti-
> fied places (as they say) the blind are made to see, the lame are made
> to walk and all diseases whatsoever, never so strange, never so invet-
> erate are to be cured.[6]

Such wells were located in both the city and the surrounding countryside.
Perhaps the most famous lay in the immediate environs of the city. St
Patrick's well, lying near the cathedral of St Patrick, was, according to Ware,
most frequented on St Patrick's day; St James' well at St James' Gate was
visited on 25 July, the feast of St James. Trinity well was frequented, as
might be expected, on Trinity Sunday with people coming from both the
city and the surrounding countryside to perform their devotions.[7] Indeed,
according to one Carmelite in Dublin, the riot that followed the attempts to
close the Catholic churches in the city in late 1629 erupted because the town
was full of people from the surrounding countryside who had come 'to go
to St Stephen's well by way of pilgrimage to drink of that water'.[8]

4 *Constitutiones provinciales et synodales ecclesiae metropolitanae et primatialis Dubliniensis*
([Dublin], 1770), pp 22-3.   5 Caoimhín Ó Danachair, 'The holy wells of County Dublin',
Reportorium Novum, 2, no. 1 (1957-8), pp 68-87; 'The holy wells of County Dublin – a
supplementary list', *Reportorium Novum*, 2, no. 2 (1959-60), pp 233-5.   6 Ware's History
and antiquities of Dublin, 1678 (Armagh Public Library, p. 160).   7 Ibid., pp 161, 162;
Barnaby Rich, *A new description of Ireland* (London, 1610), pp 52-3.   8 Nicholas Archbold,
'Evangelicall fruict of the Seraphicall Franciscan Order, 1628' (British Library (hereafter

The effectiveness of holy wells depended on the performance of certain rituals that were sanctioned not by clerical participation but rather by tradition, and that were specific to the well site. Robert Ware described the rituals at St James' well as 'the ceremonies anciently performed'. This involved 'casting the water backward and forward on the right side and on the left and over their heads' after the water was drunk.[9] This is an unusual custom, since most of the descriptions of activities at holy wells from seventeenth-century Ireland refer to the making of 'rounds' of the well and the reciting of prayers such as the Our Father or the Ave Maria.[10] The origin of these rituals is obscure but some at least may be imitative of clerical rituals as, in the case of St James' well, the aspersion of holy water or the ritualised re-enactment of baptism. It was the customary validation of such events which made the clergy of the reorganising Catholic Church suspicious. The lack of clear meaning in the ritualised practices of the holy well, together with the inability of the clergy to reshape them, led to their condemnation as '*super-stitiones*' by the provincial synod of 1614. The synod did allow that if there were healing effects of wells arising out of natural properties or the patronage of saints, access should not be denied, but 'superstitious usages' were proscribed.[11] In practice, however, such prohibitions had little practical effect.

Such events as the pattern at the holy well helped to define the nature of Catholicism. While some Protestants may have visited holy wells, few did so on patron days. The events at the holy well were thus rituals of denominational exclusion for them. However, for Catholics they were rituals of inclusion because they were occasions when the various elements of the Catholic community bonded together. Wells, for instance, bridged the urban-rural divide in that they were frequented by urban as well as rural dwellers. No less consequently, they bridged the social divide, since those who frequented them came from a wide range of social groups, from the 'country clowns' described by a Dublin Carmelite in 1629 to Sir John Talbot of Malahide who returned from Connacht in the 1650s to visit the well at Malahide.[12] Certain wells were also under lay protection such as that of St Doulagh near Baldoyle which was cared for by the local landowners, the Fagan family of Feltrim. In the 1660s, Patrick Fagan decorated the well with frescoes depicting SS Patrick, Brigid and Columcille and the local patron Duileach and a representation of the descent of the Holy Spirit

BL), Harley Ms 3888, f.110).   9 Ware's *History and antiquities of Dublin*, 1678 (Armagh Public Library, pp 162).   10 This custom is certainly documented for later periods, see Ó Danachair, 'Holy wells', pp 68–9 and below pp 165–6.   11 *Constitutiones*, pp 23-4.   12 Nicholas Archbold, *Evangelicall fruict of the Seraphicall Franciscan Order*, 1628 (BL, Harley Ms 3888, f.110); Joseph Byrne, 'A rhapsody on the carved oak chimney piece … at Malahide Castle', *Archivium Hibernicum*, 52 (1998), p. 25.

on the apostles. In 1678, Robert Ware described it as 'beautiful with an arch erected over it, painted in the concave thereof with the scheme of heaven representing the sun and moon amongst the stars of that celestial fabric'.[13]

The nature of the social and confessional cohesion generated by patterns at holy wells did more than merely create a common religious community between the ordinary and the elite and the urban and rural. The holy well ritual was the primary bonding force within the world of traditional Catholicism. The holy well experience can be divided into three parts.[14] From Ware's description of events at Dublin holy wells it seems clear that, in many cases, they involved a journey that removed the pilgrims from their normal social world and created a sense of community among the travellers. Secondly, the rituals of the holy place, sanctioned by tradition, elided the normal social divisions within the larger community so that landlord and tenant were bonded together in a form of spiritual equality, all performing the same ritual actions and saying the same prayers. Thirdly, social bonds were recreated in the secular celebrations that followed the sacred acts. This was facilitated by the fact that many patterns were held on the same day as fairs. Ware, for example, noted of the pattern at St James' well that the pilgrims 'having drank of the water ... gravely proceeded to the fair and then installing themselves in some booth they sat and drank all the day after'.[15] A similar description of the pattern day activities in the parish of Lusk in the 1690s emphasises the social conviviality that accompanied the religious event.[16] The experience of a visit to a holy well on the saint's day associated with that well served to cement a community, irrespective of social division, around ideas of traditional Catholicism.

The holy well may, therefore, be seen as a paradigm of traditional Catholicism. It was based on a religious community which by tradition held particular times and specific places as sacred. The nature of that shared experience came from accessing the power of God through a saintly intermediary, one of the friends of God. The historicity of many of those figures is questionable, but what validated their position in the eyes of the traditional community was not ecclesiastical decree or clerical authority but rather the experience of the miraculous, revealed in cures and other wonders identified with specific places.

13 M.V. Ronan (ed.), 'Royal visitation of Dublin, 1615', *Archivium Hibernicum*, 8 (1941), p. 21, n 58; Ware's History and antiquities of Dublin, 1678 (Armagh Public Library, p. 163). 14 The model here is drawn from Victor Turner, *The ritual process: structure and anti-structure* (London, 1993), ch. 3 and Victor Turner and E.L.B. Turner, *Image and pilgrimage in Christian culture* (New York, 1978), ch. 1. 15 As note 9. 16 The Fingallian Travesty (BL, Sloan Ms 900, ff 36-7).

II

While the religious belief of the traditional community focused on a world of wonders, a second model of belief emerged in the seventeenth-century diocese of Dublin under the influence of Tridentine reform. There is one piece of evidence which brings this religious culture into clear focus. In 1688, as the Jacobite revanche moved towards its zenith, the Dublin bookseller William Weston issued a reprint of *A short and plain way to the faith and Church* by the English Benedictine, Richard Huddleston, who had been credited with Charles II's conversion. That event in itself was not exceptional. In the same year there were three reprints of the work in London and one in Edinburgh. What was unusual was that Weston used the last page of the tract to advertise the other titles which were available in his High Street shop. The seventeen titles described were all works of Catholic theology. Although they were described as 'printed and sold' by Weston, it is unlikely that he printed any of them, and most can be identified as works that had been published in London in the previous year or at Douai, Paris or Ghent over the previous five years. It is likely that they represent a consignment of books brought to Dublin by Weston in 1688. That Catholic works should have been openly available in Dublin was not unexpected. There was a thriving smuggling trade which ensured that, at least in the city, Catholic books were fairly freely available. One Dublin student at Lincoln's Inn, for instance, deposed that his travelling companion to Ireland in 1609 carried Catholic catechisms in his luggage. In 1639 when the goods of John Gilpin in the city were valued, they included 'six popish books' valued at four shillings.[17] Indeed the frequency with which some Catholic books are referred to suggests continued popularity. The fact that a Jesuit work entitled *Mariana* which was sought from Dublin booksellers in 1641 was attacked in a Church of Ireland visitation sermon in 1679 suggests it was both popular and available.[18]

There are considerable difficulties associated with interpreting lists of books, such as that of William Weston. It is not clear, for example, whether such works were available in rural parts of the diocese or indeed whether those who had access to Dublin bookshops were able to read what they found there. Some light is cast on the latter problem by the bail books from the Tholsel court for 1693-4 which indicate that some 81 per cent of bailsmen

---

17 Examination of William Dongan, 8 Apr., 1609 (Chester City Archives, Chester Quarter sessions examinations, QSE/8/12); Dublin Praisements, 1635-7 (BL, Add. Ms 11,687, f. 127v). More generally, Raymond Gillespie, 'The circulation of print in seventeenth-century Ireland', *Studia Hibernica*, 29 (1995-7), pp 48-9.   18 Trinity College, Dublin (hereafter TCD), Ms 820, f. 266v; Richard Tenison, *A sermon preached at the primary visitation of ... archbishop of Armagh* (Dublin, 1679), pp 29, 66.

could sign their names, although this ranged from a high of 100 per cent among the professions to about 70 per cent among craft workers to a low of 20 per cent among yeomen.[19] Given that writing was a skill learned after reading and, therefore, that more people could read than write, it seems a high proportion of the city's population could read Weston's stock.

Weston's inventory of seventeen Catholic works may thus provide a window into the ideas in circulation that shaped the spiritual lives of Catholics in the Dublin diocese. It is worth remembering that Weston was engaged in a commercial activity. His stock was intended to be sold and, as such, represents at least one man's judgement of what Dublin Catholics, both lay and clerical, wanted to read. Categorisation is problematic but, in broad terms, three of the titles on the list can be described as doctrinal, one as confutational, and the remaining thirteen as devotional works. Of these thirteen, three were concerned with what might be described as public devotion, in particular commentaries on the Mass, while the remaining ten were prayerbooks for private use. There is some overlap between these two groups, as prayerbooks often contained commentaries on the Mass or prayers for use before or after Mass. Even allowing for this overlap there is still a pronounced orientation towards books of private devotion.

The books which Weston offered were, increasingly, the sort of books which the clergy read and wished the laity to read. Some are to be found in the libraries of clergy. Bishop Daton of Ossory, for example, possessed a copy of Dominique Bouhours' *Christian thoughts for every day in the month* which was on Weston's list, while Bishop Luke Wadding of Ferns owned Henry Turberville's *Abridgement of Christian doctrine* and W.C., *A little manual of the poor man's daily devotion*.[20] One of Weston's offerings, C.J.'s *A net for the fishers of men* (n.p., 1687), was so appreciated by one cleric, Father Cormac Mac Pharlane, that he copied the entire text into his commonplace book.[21] Other clergy expressed their approbation for Weston's stock by distributing copies of the same books to their flock in an effort to educate them. Luke Wadding handed out 144 copies of Henry Turberville's *Abridgement of Christian doctrine*, 1,200 copies of Pedro de Ledesma's *Christian doctrine*, at least three dozen copies of Dominique Bouhours' *Christian thoughts for every*

19 I am grateful to Dr T.C. Barnard for these figures which will be more fully analysed in his forthcoming book.   20 Hugh Fenning (ed.), 'The library of Bishop William Daton of Ossory, 1698', *Collectanea Hibernica*, 20 (1978), p. 41; P.J. Corish (ed.), 'Bishop Wadding's notebook', *Archivium Hibernicum*, 29 (1970), pp 63, 65.   21 TCD, Ms 1375. McPharlane seems to have left Ireland for Spain in the 1690s, possibly after the Bishop's Banishment Act: see Cuthbert Mhag Craith (ed.), *Dán na mbrathar mionúr* (2 vols, Dublin, 1967-80), i, pp 260-1, ii, pp 244-5. He also owned another theological miscellany now BL, Egerton Ms 136.

day in the month and various copies of *The most devout prayers of St Brigit* as well as 'little books of the Mass' which may correspond to Weston's *The mysteries of the holy Mass.*[22]

These books provide some leads to the sort of weighting that can be accorded to the books listed by Weston and, hence, to the sort of Catholics that the proponents of reformed Catholicism wished to produce. Works such as Turberville on doctrine, usually known as the Douai catechism since it had been composed there in the late sixteenth century, or that of Ledesma, were intended to ensure that there was a knowledge of faith. Turberville's work, for instance, expounded the creed, the commandments, the precepts of the Church, the sacraments, the four last things and the works of mercy. It also promoted a rather different attitude to Mass from that previously advanced by including a commentary on the actions of the priest. W.C.'s *A little manual of the poor man's daily devotion* likewise contained a detailed commentary on the Mass, including an explanation of the ornaments and ceremonies used at Mass and a commentary on the actions of the priest from his entrance on to the altar. It also included prayers for use before and after but not during Mass, as had traditionally been customary. Now the world of print guided the reader through the actions of the Mass and they were expected to follow and understand the symbolism of the priest's actions rather than to perform their own devotions by reciting traditional prayers.

To comprehend the role which books played in the Reformation of Catholicism it is necessary to understand not only the texts but also the social context in which they operated. Some insight is provided by the works themselves. One of the works on Weston's list, *Christian thoughts for every day of the month*, carried a preface which explained how it was to be used. It was a work, the preface explained, for the laity that contained 'plain thoughts, short and easy which may be understood without difficulty and read with less than a minute's expense'. It was to be resorted to after prayers in the morning when the owner should 'read the thoughts of that day but read them leisurely that you may understand them thoroughly'. One was not to be content with a simple comprehension of the truth contained in the work but also to consider how it might be applied.[23] Clearly this was a text to be read privately in a meditative mood, in the context of prayer, and it was to be absorbed slowly and fully. There were others of a similar nature. The *Devout prayers of St Brigitte*, which was sold by Weston and given away by others, are based on the fifteen traditional prayers of St Brigitte of Sweden to be said in honour of the wounds of Christ, and was meant for personal meditative prayer rather than for communal recital. This was an interiorised form of devotion that

---

22 Corish (ed.), 'Bishop Wadding's notebook', pp 88, 89, 90.   23 *Christian thoughts for every day of the month* (n.p., 1698), sig A2-A3v.

relied on the response of the individual to the written word for its effect
rather than on communal assent to the meaning of the work.

The sense of interiorised devotion which characterised this world is
revealed most clearly in the institution which was most identified with the
Catholic Reformation, the sodality. The sodality rules reprinted in Dublin
in 1703 emphasise the importance of reading pious books and meditating
upon them frequently.[24] Sodalities with their emphasis on this style of devotional reading were not new features of Dublin diocesan life. The first Dublin
Jesuit sodality was founded in 1598, although it was only formally aggregated
in 1628, and a Carmelite sodality of the brown scapular existed in the city
by 1627. Neither of these can be regarded as truly popular organisations,
since their membership was small, but they remained the spiritual *élite* of the
diocese and were intended, through frequent reception of the sacraments,
works of piety and devotional reading, to spearhead the acceptance of the
new ideas of Trent.

William Weston's list of books for sale may serve as a paradigm for the
world of reformed Catholicism in the seventeenth-century Dublin diocese.
This was a world of faith which concentrated on an individualised devotion
inspired by meditation on the mysteries of Catholicism and active, informed
participation in the sacraments rather than on the performance of communal rituals. It demanded knowledge not that one was a Catholic but rather
why one adopted that confessional position. Thus the catechism became a
key text in the world of reformed Catholicism. This was a literate world of
books as well as of prayer which required skills and training to enter.

III

The worlds of traditional and Tridentine Catholicism were not separate. They
had many features in common. The devotional life of both was based around
the Mass and their self-definition came from a common conviction that they
were not Protestants. The Mass and its setting provides a way of understanding the linkages between traditional and Tridentine Catholicism. It is
possible to distinguish two experiences of the Mass within the diocese of
Dublin in the early seventeenth century. The first derived from a domestic
setting. This world is most vividly portrayed in the 1630 visitation of the
diocese by the Church of Ireland archbishop, Lancelot Bulkeley.[25] Within

---

24 *Rules and instructions for the sodality of the Immaculate conception of the most glorious and
ever Virgin Mary, mother of God* ([Dublin], 1703). The text is clearly drawn from an
English exemplar but is assigned to Dublin by the Eighteenth Century STC on the basis
of the typography.   **25** Myles Ronan (ed.), 'Archbishop Bulkeley's visitation of Dublin,

the city Bulkeley detected a growth of the number of places at which Mass
was said, over and above the five locations identified in a 1610 list. He specifically mentioned a new 'priest's chamber' that was recently built in the parish
of St Katherine and St James. Into such buildings large numbers could
gather. According to some witnesses, one Mass celebrated at St Audoen's
Arch in 1663 had over 300 in the congregation, 'most of whom were women
and but a few men'.[26] More typical settings for Mass were private houses
belonging to middle sized Catholic landowners. At Baldoyle, for instance,
where the main landowner was Thomas Fitzsimons, it was noted that 'Mass
[is] commonly said upon Sundays and holy days in the said Mr Fitzsimon's
house, where the parishioners commonly resort'. Moreover in the cases of
Finglas and Tempelogue parishes it is clear from Bulkeley's visitation not
only that Mass was said in the houses of the gentry but that priests were
maintained by them.

The implications of this for the experience of Mass were considerable.
First, the priest was maintained not by the parish but by a single individual.
This collided with the Tridentine view of Church order, which saw the parish
as the basic unit of ecclesiastical organisation and the priest as the central
figure within that parish. The fact that the priest was brought under the control of lay individuals reduced ecclesiastical power and strengthened the secular order. Secondly, presence at Mass was permitted not as a parochial right
but at the discretion of the person in whose house it was held. The result
was that gathering to hear Mass came to have the flavour of secular community assemblies, the criterion for membership of which was one's
Catholicism. Hints of this equation of the community and religion are provided in the comments made by Protestants following the outbreak of the
rising of 1641. In Wicklow, for instance, one man claimed that his goods
would be restored if he and his wife would go to Mass while another testified that he was pressed to go to Mass or be hanged. In County Dublin,
Peter Fletcher, when describing the password necessary to get through the
Irish lines, declared that 'although he had the word yet it should not be safe
without he would turn and go to Mass'.[27] Significantly, in each of these contexts, the Mass seems to be understood as a liturgical admission rite into the
community for those previously outside it; in other words, to go to Mass was
not merely to make a religious declaration but also to indicate that one had
aligned oneself to the social group that did likewise. Thus a rather traditional

1630', *Archivium Hibernicum*, 8 (1941), pp 56-98. See also Colm Lennon's essay, above
pp 121-2.   **26** TCD, Ms 567, f. 42; Depositions on suprisal of Mass in Dublin, 1663
(Bodleian Library, Carte Ms 32, ff 218, 220, 222).   **27** Deposition of Thomas Reynolds
(TCD, Ms 811, f. 88); Deposition of John Fenn (TCD, Ms 811, f, 97); Deposition of
Peter Fletcher (TCD, Ms 809, f. 210).

experience of Mass was articulated as part of the pre-Tridentine idea of the Mass as a manifestation of the local community. In this case, the domestication of the experience, under the control of a local landowner, only served to enhance that understanding.

The second type of experience of the Mass was that envisioned by the decrees of Trent, which saw the ritual of the Mass as a parochial celebration led by the parish priest in an environment of splendour appropriate to the sacrament. Such a celebration emphasised the position of the clergy who, though weak in worldly terms, were supremely powerful in a liturgical context which itself contributed to the dissolution of social boundaries. This was the understanding of the Mass that the provincial synod for Dublin of 1614, which began the implementation of the decrees of Trent, attempted to enforce. Rules were set down to enhance the splendour of the celebration, though it was conceded that this might not always be possible. Ideally, however, it was directed that only silver chalices should be consecrated and that older pewter chalices should be broken up; wax lights were deemed essential for the altar and a silver pyx, not a wooden one, was to be provided for reservation of the sacrament. These directions were reiterated throughout the century. For instance, in 1685 the requirement for gold or silver chalices was restated and open air Masses prohibited.[28]

Significantly, one of the first acts of missionary religious orders was to create a suitable setting for the celebration of Mass. Thus the Jesuit Henry Fitzsimon in 1598 persuaded one Dublin gentleman to allow him to establish a chapel in his house which was fitted out to the appropriate standard.[29] By 1630, the Dublin Jesuits had acquired a church in Back Lane which they fitted out in the latest European style with confessionals, a pulpit adorned with pictures and a railed-off high altar.[30] The Carmelites contrived to do likewise. Their house in 1629 was open to all for sermons, Mass was celebrated and 'processions are also made with due ecclesiastical ornaments and sacred vessels and sometime too the blessed sacrament is borne in procession'.[31] Churches under the control of the secular clergy were less well organised in so far as we can tell, due to their temporary nature, but within the city great efforts were made to improve the conditions under which Mass was celebrated. According to the 1637 will of Edmund Doyle, who was vicar general of Swords in 1630 and parish priest of St Audoen's from 1631 until his death, he had a chapel on lease from James Bellew in the Cornmarket in

28 *Constitutiones*, pp 19-26, 84-5.   29 Edmund Hogan (ed.), *Ibernia Ignatiana* (Dublin 1880), p. 41.   30 Edward Hawkins (ed.), *Travels in Holland, the United Provinces, England, Scotland and Ireland by Sir William Brereton* (London, 1844), pp 141-2, *Cal. State Papers Ire., 1625-32*, p. 510.   31 Superior of Carmelites to Propaganda Fide, Mar. 1629 in P.F. Moran, *History of the Catholic archbishops of Dublin* (Dublin, 1864), pp 313-4.

which there were vestments of cloth of silver, altar cloths with lace and around the altar and chapel six pictures of various saints.[32]

It can confidently be asserted that the conditions for the saying of Mass improved dramatically in the later seventeenth century. By the 1670s, four settled convents of religious could be listed, with five permanent Mass houses being identified in the city.[33] However, it is not clear to what extent these improvements extended into the countryside. Certainly, by the time of the Catholic revival that took place in Dublin in the late 1680s it was possible to experience a wide range of liturgical events in Dublin city, including the solemn procession of the Blessed Sacrament through the streets, and ritual scourging.[34] This level of public liturgical celebration had to be scaled down after the Williamite victory, but the impression provided by the 1697 listing of the priests of the diocese is of a settled parochial structure with fixed chapels in the city at least; the impression also is that the rural parts of the diocese were rather more loosely organised.[35]

However one experienced Mass, whether in the domesticated setting of a landlord's house as part of a traditional community or as part of the drama for a parish grouping as envisioned by Tridentine legislation, one element joined the two perceptions. Both had in common the miracle of transubstantiation whereby the bread and wine became body and blood. This does not mean that everyone present understood the orthodox theology of the experience. Capuchin priests ministering in Wicklow in the 1660s were told by some local residents that the host was the grace of God, by others that it was a picture of God, while still others simply described it as good.[36] However the eucharist was conceived, it was an object held in devotion by Catholics of all shades of opinion in the diocese.

To profane the host was a sign that one was not a Catholic and therefore liable to the judgement of God. In 1663, for instance, the government had recourse to a Dublin newspaper to challenge a rumour circulating around the city that the body of a soldier found floating in the river Liffey was that of a man who, the previous Christmas at a raid on a Mass, 'did take the chalice and drink saying that he would put their God into his belly and that night as a just judgement of God did drown himself'.[37] The Catholic clergy, for their part, had ready recourse to a number of miraculous stories centring on

32 Will of Edmund Doyle, 25 Apr. 1637 (National Library of Ireland, G.O. Ms 290, p. 140).   33 List of the popish chapels and convents in Dublin, 1679 (Bodleian Library, Oxford, Carte Ms 38, f.695).   34 *The sad estate and condition of Ireland* (London, 1689), p. 5; *Ireland's lamentation* (London, 1689), p. 12.   35 William O'Riordan (ed.), 'A list of the priests, secular and regular, of the diocese of Dublin in the year 1697', *Reportorium Novum*, 1, no. 1 (1955), pp 140-53.   36 Gillespie, *Devoted people*, pp 66-7.   37 *Mercurius Hibernicus or Ireland's Intelligencier*, no. 2, 20-27 Jan. 1663, p. 12.

the host. Thus it was reported in the 1630s that the Discalced Carmelite priest Stephen Brown performed an exorcism at the gates of Dublin Castle by placing a finger which had touched a consecrated host in the mouth of a possessed girl, while in 1626 a girl attending Mass with the Capuchins at Dublin was, it was reported, unable to receive the sacrament because she was possessed.[38]

However one experienced the Mass, it seems clear that something which may be termed a 'sacramental community' transcended the various sub-cultures of seventeenth-century Catholicism in the diocese of Dublin. Perhaps more than the holy well or the world of books, it was the experience of the sacramental community that made one a Catholic in the everyday world.

IV

To make a reality of the ideas of reformed Catholicism within the context of the seventeenth-century diocese of Dublin was a task which fell mainly to the clergy. These men had the responsibility of communicating the ideas formulated at Trent and shaping them to meet the experience of the laity in the diocese. It is possible at one level to measure the progress of this enterprise by charting estimates of the number of clergy in the diocese. A list made for the government in 1613 named seventeen priests, of which seven were in religious orders. However, this was confined to the city. This may, in fact, be a relatively accurate list for it recorded six Jesuits at a time when there were nine in Dublin.[39] Some indication of progress over the next twenty years is provided by two statements of the number of Catholic clergy in Dublin at the height of the disputes between the secular and regular clergy in 1633, since these provide some measure of the numbers of clergy in the diocese as the early seventeenth-century restructuring of the diocese neared its apogee. The first estimated that there were forty-six religious persons in Dublin, of which twelve were secular clergy and the remainder regulars. Of the thirty-four members of religious orders Franciscans, Carmelites and Capuchins accounted for over 70 per cent. Of these, eight were lay members of the orders and the remainder were priests. A second account, from about the same date, puts the number of religious at ninety-one, of which ten were

38 Marcellus Glynn and F.X. Martin (eds), 'The "Brevis relatio" of the Irish Discalced Carmelites', *Archivium Hibernicum*, 25 (1962), pp 150-1; Nicholas Archbold, Evangelicall fruict of the Seraphicall Franciscan Order, 1628 (BL, Harley Ms 3888, f. 128). **39** 'List of priests and friars, Nov. 1613 (TCD, Ms 567, f. 35v); Fergus O'Donoghue, 'The Jesuit mission in Ireland, 1598-1651' (Ph.D. thesis, Catholic University of America, 1981), p. 76.

secular clergy and the remainder in religious orders.[40] It is difficult to say which of these two accounts is the more accurate but, based on the estimates of the size of the Jesuit community – five in the first list and twenty-one in the second – the latter is more likely since the real size of the Jesuit community in Dublin in 1629 was nineteen. This conclusion is strengthened by the fact that the Carmelite community, listed as having fifteen members in the second list, actually had sixteen in 1628.[41]

It is clear that clerical numbers, together with the Church structure they supported, took a heavy battering in the 1650s. By 1657, it was claimed that there was only one secular cleric left in the diocese of Dublin and only a few Jesuits, Dominicans, Discalced Carmelites and Franciscans in the city. How many is not clear, but the number must have been small since as early as 1649 there were only two Jesuits in the city.[42] In the 1660s the structures of reformed Catholicism had to be rebuilt in the diocese. This was a slow process and it failed to equal the level of manpower or organisation achieved earlier until the end of the century. When Archbishop Edmund O'Reilly recorded clerical numbers in the diocese of Dublin in 1662, he found only ten men and no resident bishop. [43] A 1688 list records that thirty-seven clergy attended the diocesan synod held that year, although this clearly does not include members of religious orders. Other clergy that are known to have been in the diocese are not included on the list.[44] By 1697 there were almost 140 named clergy in the diocese.[45]

At the forefront of the movement to make the decrees of the Council of Trent a reality in Ireland were the religious orders whose members were, in the main, trained in continental Europe. Within Ireland it was the diocese of Dublin, with its large urban population and network of Old English patrons, that saw the greatest activity by these orders. In the 1630s the regular clergy outnumbered their secular counterparts by nine to one with the Franciscans contributing the largest grouping.[46] Recruitment to the seculars ranks grew in the decades that followed till by 1697, according to a digest made that year of the Catholic clergy in each Revenue district, the national

40 State of the Romish ecclesiastics in Dublin, Sept. 1633 (Sheffield City Library, Wentworth Woodhouse Muniments, Strafford letters books, vol. 20, no. 175).   41 O'Donoghue, 'Jesuit mission' p. 203; S.C. O'Mahony, 'The Irish Discalced Carmelites, 1625-53' (Ph.D. thesis, Trinity College, Dublin, 1977), p. 31.   42 Richard O'Ferrall and Robert O'Connell, *Commentarius Rinuccinianus de sedis apostolicae legatione as foederatos Hiberniae Catholicos per annos 1645-9*, ed. Stanislaus Kavanagh (6 vols, Dublin, 1932-49), v, 403-5; O'Donoghue, 'Jesuit mission', p. 341.   43 Benignus Millett (ed.), 'Archbishop Edmund O'Reilly's report on the state of the Church in Ireland', *Collectanea Hibernica*, 2 (1959), p. 109.   44 The list is printed in William O'Riordan (ed.), 'Two documents in the *Liber Decanatus I* in the Dublin diocesan archives', *Reportorium Novum*, 1, no. 1 (1956), p. 370.   45. O'Riordan (ed.), 'A list of the priests'.   46. As note 40.

ratio of regular to secular clergy was about one to two; five to one in Dublin city and about equal in County Dublin. Only in the rural Wicklow district did it approach the national average.[47] The secular clergy seem to have been less well-equipped for the Irish mission in the early part of the seventeenth century, although less is known of their backgrounds. By the 1680s, however, the situation had improved. Of the thirty-seven secular clergy that attended the diocesan synod of 1688, about 40 per cent had been ordained on the continent, suggesting some European training, while a quarter had been ordained at home. Nothing is known about the educational background of the remaining third.[48] This situation continued to improve so that in Dublin city and county by 1704 the division between those ordained in Ireland and abroad was almost equal although within the city, European-trained clergy outnumbered those trained at home by two to one while the situation was almost reversed in the county.[49]

The effect on the diocese of a high concentration of regular clergy educated in the ways of missionary activity in continental Europe was dramatic. Their techniques for spreading the devotional enthusiasm of Trent were often spectacular. Dramatic preaching and ritual were directed not primarily at Protestants but at awakening a new devotional sense among traditional Catholics. The techniques used were similar to those employed by missioners in continental Europe. The most important element in their armoury was forceful and dramatic preaching. In this, the sermon was more of a performance than a strategy for conveying information or a call for repentance. Thus the Franciscan Thomas Strong, preaching in Dublin in the early seventeenth century, was described as 'incomparable for instructing, delighting and captivating the ear of his auditor with his variety and multiplicity of doctrinal matter. He was of a prodigious memory'.[50] Gesture and intonation were all-important in creating an atmosphere in which emotional barriers could be broken down and a way created through which both traditional Catholics and Protestants could pass into a world of reformed Catholicism. The Capuchin Luke Bathe offers a good illustration of how those conducting preaching missions in the diocese of Dublin operated in the early part of the seventeenth century. Bathe as a preacher was described as a man who to his hearers 'inflamed their coldness and melted their hardness' and thereby

47. W.P. Burke, *The Irish priests in the penal times* (Waterford, 1914), pp 127-8. 48. O'Riordan (ed.), 'Two documents', p. 370. Biographical material on the clergy of the diocese can be found in William O'Riordan, 'A list of seventeenth-century Dublin diocesan priests', *Reportorium Novum*, 2, no. 1 (1957-8), pp 109-19; 2, no. 2 (1959-60), pp 257-68; 3, no. 1 (1961-2), pp 137-52. 49. *A list of the names of the popish parish priests throughout the several counties of the kingdom of Ireland* (Dublin, 1704). 50 Nicholas Archbold, Evangelicall fruict of the Seraphicall Franciscan Order, 1628 (BL, Harley Ms 3888, f.110).

provided them with an emotional solvent for conversion.[51] The way this was achieved was by powerful emotional preaching. His sermons were described as

> rare and incomparable in moving. He cared not for curiosities but kept a mean strain. His talent for moving was such that he never preached but the tears rolled down continually from his auditor's eye. Some said that the Holy Ghost himself spake by that man. Others that his very countenance did preach ...

Some sense of the impact of this sort of preaching is provided by a description of the reaction to Bathe's preaching at Lusk in 1635:

> the people were so ravished in his speech and transversed in spirit with compunction and tears that for a quarter of an hour they ceased not to howl, to cry, to clap hands, to lament, not regarding the preacher's dissuading them in manner howsoever. A thing not unusual in Italy as they say but in these cold countries rare and unheard of.

Such emotional solvents paved the way for individuals to leave traditional communities of Catholicism or Protestantism and to embrace the new ideas of Trent.

Accomplished regular missioners, such as Bathe, were prone to look down on their less well-educated or poorly trained secular counterparts in the early seventeenth century. The Capuchins, for example, disparaged the preaching of one Dublin secular priest, Paul Harris:

> this man so exceeded in delighting that he became rather histrionical than evangelical. He moved his auditors not to compunction or tears but to laughter and tearing at the eyes for laughing from which himself also could hardly and then refrain. He so compleased himself in odd conceits, quirks, composed phrases, verses, exotical proverbs and the like as who of a grammarian schoolmaster suddenly became a preacher. This manner of delighting I comprehend not in the divine gift of evangelically delighting.[52]

Harris' preaching was a parody of the true gift of awakening emotional power. Not surprisingly, given the quality of the regular clergy and the shortage of secular clergy in the diocese in the early part of the seventeenth century, some regulars found themselves with a considerable following meaning that

51 For Bathe, see ibid., ff 105-5v, 106v.   52 Ibid., f. 106v.

both the support and income of their secular equivalents fell. The tensions this generated came to a head in the 1630s in a dispute in which two Dublin clergy, Paul Harris and Peter Caddel, attacked the growing power of the regular clergy.[53] This dispute rumbled on to 1640 but the strengthened position of the secular clergy in the later seventeenth century meant that in contrast to other parts of the country, secular-regular tensions did not resurface in Dublin in any serious way.

V

The Catholic diocese of Dublin in the seventeenth century was a complex organisation. It contained within its geographical bounds a number of sub-cultures, all of which can legitimately be regarded as Catholic. On the one hand there were a set of symbols and experiences, such as the holy well and the domesticated Mass, which looked to a traditional world of Catholicism founded on local communities and validated by tradition. On the other hand a much more modern world, embracing the ideas of reform promulgated at the Council of Trent, was being brought into existence. This was a world of interiorised piety fed by the printed word, with the sacraments celebrated by a spiritually powerful priest in as splendid a way as political conditions would allow. What held these two sub-cultures together was a wider sense of a sacramental community, based on the experience of the miraculous power of the eucharist, which helped to define the nature of Catholicism in a rapidly changing world. The nature of that change, and the speed at which it took place, was determined by the supply of suitably trained clergy able to use the missionary techniques of continental Europe in the Irish situation. These men could produce emotional solvents through dramatic preaching to enable individuals to move from the world of traditional Catholicism to its reformed counterpart. By the end of the seventeenth century that process was well under way in the diocese of Dublin, after a false start before 1650. However, the process was still far from complete by 1700. If by the end of the seventeenth century, the Reformation had decidedly failed in the diocese of Dublin, the Counter-Reformation had not yet succeeded.

---

53 For the bones of the dispute see Moran, *Archbishops*, pp 369-80.

7

The impact of the penal laws

James Kelly

The improvement that took place in the fabric and fortunes of the Catholic Church in the diocese of Dublin in the final years of the reign of Charles II (1647-85) and during James II's brief reign (1685-8) was brought to a precipitate conclusion with the military defeat of the Irish Jacobites in 1690-1.[1] The treaty of Limerick, which signalled the end of formal hostilities, provided that Catholics should 'enjoy such privileges in the exercise of their religion as are consistent with the laws of Ireland; or as they did enjoy in the reign of Charles the II',[2] but this was never the promise of toleration many Catholic and nationalist historians have claimed. Experience during the 1680s affirmed and strengthened the convictions of Protestants in Britain as well as Ireland that Catholicism was ineluctably repressive and Irish Catholics 'perfidious', and that Protestants would, 'on the first opportunity', experience a repeat of the difficulties and the despair they had endured under Lord Tyrconnell if they did not take appropriate steps to secure the 'Protestant interest' against Catholic revanchism.[3]

The implementation of legal bulwarks proved less straightforward than enthusiasts deemed either politic or necessary. But persistent reports throughout the early and mid-1690s that the French were planning an invasion combined with the ill-concealed Jacobitism of many Catholic clergy to enable Protestant hardliners who advocated repression to progress from simple harassment in the early 1690s to the introduction, from 1695, of a series of statutory restrictions and prohibitions aimed at enfeebling Catholics and

---

1 Nicholas Donnelly, *A short history of some Dublin parishes* (17 parts, Dublin, 1904-17) (henceforth Donnelly, *Parishes*), part 1, pp 11-2; part 3, p. 100; part 6 (i), pp 33-4; part 10, p. 12. 2 J.G.Simms, *The treaty of Limerick* (Dundalk, 1965), p. 19. 3 Reginald Walsh, 'Glimpses of the penal times, part 9', *Irish Ecclesiastical Record* (henceforth *IER*), 27 (1910), p. 611; C.I McGrath, 'Securing the Protestant interest: the origins and purpose of the penal laws of 1695', *Irish Historical Studies* (henceforth *IHS*), 30 (1996), pp 25-46.

Catholicism. Inevitably, given its prominence in the Catholic polity, the Catholic Church was a prime target, and the repressive measures sanctioned by the Irish parliament between 1695 and 1710 not only limited its freedom to minister in the short term, but left a legacy of institutional poverty and attitudinal deference that ensured that the Church in the diocese still bore the scars of repression a century later.

I

The negative consequences for the Catholic Church of the military deficiencies of the Jacobite armies were manifested earlier in Dublin than in most of the country. According to one Catholic account, the imminent arrival of the Williamite army in Dublin following their victory at the Boyne on 1 July 1690 prompted the wholesale 'pillaging and plundering' of vacant and unguarded Catholic property by the Protestant 'rabble'. Given their prominence in the Catholic community, clergy, inevitably, were a prime target. Many secular priests felt obliged to go into hiding or to flee the country to avoid being taken up for failing to profess allegiance to the Protestant succession, though the authorities' priorities were regulars and those exercising ecclesiastical jurisdiction. A small number were arrested and imprisoned. Two were Jesuits; Nicholas Netterville and Edward Chamberlain, who was threatened with 'great torments' in order to compel him to 'discover where and in whose hands the money and goods of the Jesuits lay', were incarcerated for a year.[4]

The imprisonment of Archbishop Patrick Russell, who had been an energetic pastor during the 1680s, was more consequential. He was arrested and taken into detention on two occasions and died in custody in 1692.[5] Russell's loss was compounded by the fact that his appointed successor, Peter Creagh (1693-1705), chose not to return from Europe. The diocese was not left leaderless, as Father Fenning points out,[6] but the combined impact of the pursuit of priests and the closure of churches in the early 1690s seriously compromised the capacity to minister. This is vividly revealed for country parts of the diocese by the decision of Father Laurence O'Toole, who ministered

---

4 Rivers to Eustace, 1692 in Donnelly, *Parishes*, part 9, pp 215-7; Linegar to [ ], 1692 in idem, part 12, p. 82; Francis Finnegan, 'The Jesuits in Dublin, 1660-1760', *Reportorium Novum*, 4, no. 1 (1971), pp 60-63.   5 John D'Alton, *Memoirs of the archbishops of Dublin* (Dublin, 1838), pp 446-57; Nicholas Donnelly, 'The diocese of Dublin in the eighteenth century, part 7', *IER*, 10 (1889), pp 731-2; Donnelly, *Parishes*, part 16, pp 94-5; part 6 (i), pp 32-4.   6 Fenning, below, p. 176; Donnelly, *Parishes*, part 6 (i), pp 34-5; part 10, p. 14.

in the Glen of Imaal in west Wicklow, to place his vestments and altar furniture in safekeeping in the spring of 1692; and, for the metropolis, by the
decisions of the Augustinians to withdraw from their house and chapel on
Arran Quay, of the Jesuits to close their premises on Lucy Lane, and of the
Benedictine nuns to leave Channel Row for Yprès.[7]

Though the fact that parish churches in the city (and one must presume
elsewhere) were open in 1693 indicates that conditions improved following
the surrender at Limerick, the parlous financial circumstances of many priests
posed a further obstacle to religious regeneration. More seriously, the capacity of the Church as a whole to fund its mission had been seriously set back
by military defeat in 1690-91 because the Catholic gentry, who had traditionally provided rural priests with accommodation as well as financial support, were much reduced numerically and economically as a consequence of
their Jacobitism.[8]

Priests obliged by financial need to live with relatives, and by the apprehension of incarceration or exile to keep a low profile, were hardly ideally
placed to perform their sacramental duties. Yet the situation was not totally
gloomy. In Dublin city, where the fear of arrest caused the Jesuits to close
their chapels and to forsake their distinctive mission for parish work, the
order sustained a successful sodality of the Blessed Virgin.[9] The fact that
twenty-three men and forty-four women participated in this sodality in 1696
cautions one against exaggerating the impact of repression in the years
immediately following the conclusion of the Williamite wars. This conclusion is reinforced by the fact that the diocese also possessed a sufficiency
of clergy. The accuracy of contemporary returns cannot be assumed, but
an official list made in 1697, which indicates that there were over one hundred priests (thirty-eight parish priests, thirty curates and approximately
thirty-eight regulars) ministering in the Dublin diocese, demonstrates that
the Church had the manpower to satisfy the sacramental needs of the
Catholic population when it was not precluded from doing so by state
repression.[10]

7 Edward O'Toole, 'The primitive churches of Rathvilly parish, County Carlow', *Journal
of the Kildare Archaeological Society*, 11 (1929-33), pp 99-100; Donnelly, *Parishes*, part 11,
p. 50.   8 J.Redmond, 'Notes on the parish of S.S. Mary and Michael, Rathdrum',
Reportorium Novum, 3, no. 1 (1961-2) p. 193; Donnelly, *Parishes*, part 5, pp 201-3.   9
Among those arrested and imprisoned was James Gibbons SJ (Donnelly, *Parishes*, part
10, p. 15); Finnegan, 'The Jesuits in Dublin', pp 62-3; M.V. Ronan, 'Religious life in
Old Dublin', *Dublin Historical Record*, 2 (1939-40), p. 107; Louis McRedmond, *To the
greater glory: a history of the Irish Jesuits* (Dublin, 1991), pp 104-5.   10 N[icholas]
D[onnelly] (ed.), 'The diocese of Dublin in the year 1697', *IER*, third series, 9 (1888),
pp 407-13, 511-19; N. D[onnelly], 'The diocese of Dublin in the eighteenth century, part

The presence of such a substantial number of Catholic clergy in the archdiocese strengthened the hand of those Protestants who contended that it was incumbent on the legislature to curb the activities of the Catholic Church. In an attempt to prevent Catholics (particularly seminarians) travelling to Europe for training, the Irish parliament approved legislation interdicting foreign education in 1695. Two years later, it struck a more direct and injurious blow when 'An act for banishing all papists exercising any ecclesiastical jurisdiction, and all regulars of the popish clergy out of the kingdom' was approved. Because the diocese of Dublin did not possess a resident bishop, this provision of the act did not pose an immediate threat, but the directive that the regulars, who constituted more than one-third of the diocese's clergy, should leave the kingdom was profoundly disruptive. The communities of Augustinians (at St Audoen's Arch), Dominicans (Cook Street and Arklow), Franciscans (Cook Street), Carmelites (Cornmarket) dispersed, as they, and the small numbers of Capuchins and Jesuits, then in the diocese considered what they should do. Most concluded they had little choice but to leave the country, and the regular presence in the diocese was reduced to a fraction of its former complement as a result. One cannot say for certain how many of the regulars who lived and worked in the Dublin diocese during the mid-1690s were obliged to accept involuntary exile, but it can confidently be assumed that they constituted a significant proportion of the 153 priests transported via Dublin port. This, certainly, is the implication of the return made for the Irish privy council in April 1698 which indicates that there were only twenty-six secular clergy and one regular in County Dublin at that date. Significantly, the situation was better in neighbouring counties, but the fall in clerical numbers overall was sharp and consequential.[11]

Life for those that remained and for those that defied imprisonment and transportation by returning from the continent was more arduous and more dangerous in the years immediately following the ratification of the banishment provision than it had been at any point since James II's overthrow. Because the number of priests apprehended was small, it has been argued that the act was not systematically enforced; but the enforced departure of

1', *IER*, 9 (1888), pp 840-2.   11 McGrath, 'Securing the Protestant interest', pp 42-3; Donnelly, 'Diocese of Dublin, part 1', p. 842; Ignatius Fennessy, 'Franciscan guardians in County Kildare 1629-1872', *Journal of the Kildare Archaeological Society*, 18 (1992-3), p. 153; Dermot Walsh, 'The Dominicans of Arklow', *Reportorium Novum*, 3, no. 2 (1963-4), pp 310-11; Hugh Fenning, *The Irish Dominican province 1698-1797* (Dublin, 1990), pp 14-5, 19-23; Finnegan, 'The Jesuits in Dublin', pp 63-7; An account of the Romish clergy in Ireland, Apr. 1698 (Gilbert Library, Privy Council Papers 1640-1707, Ms 205 no. 15). According to the latter, six of the twenty-one clergy in County Wicklow, nine of the twenty-five in County Kildare, twelve of the fourteen in County Louth and nineteen of the twenty-three then in County Meath were regulars.

so many regulars in 1697-8, the periodic promulgation of its provisions against regulars thereafter, the apprehension and lengthy incarceration of two Dominicans (Dominic MacEgan and Felix Dowell), three Franciscans (George Antony Martin, Philip Brady and John Kelly *alias* Purcell, who was transported) and one Jesuit (Edward Chamberlain) in Dublin between 1699 and 1706, along with the arrest of two 'ffryers' in County Kildare in 1702, suggests that it was a potent short-term tool.[12]

Moreover, the secular clergy were also significantly constrained by official repression at this time. This was exemplified at the beginning of the eighteenth century by the refusal of local officials in Wicklow town to allow the Catholic community to use 'a new Mass house' as a place of worship. Rome was certainly in no doubt that the shortage of priests was the root cause of the fact that 'the faithful are not sufficiently attended to'.[13] To make matters worse, the Irish parliament introduced a registration procedure in 1704 that permitted only one secular cleric per parish. Had this enactment defined the Catholic parish as its administrative unit, the Church in Dublin would have suffered a reverse as consequential as that inflicted in 1697, since there were only thirty-eight functioning Catholic parishes in the diocese. Instead, because the more numerous civil parishes were deemed the appropriate administrative unit, a grand total of ninety-one priests were enabled to register.[14] This was more than the diocese could easily maintain, with the result that some priests who registered for Dublin parishes may have ministered elsewhere.

If the diocese was able to negotiate the 1704 registration legislation without undue difficulty, the fact that the authorities directed in the same act that none of the registered clergy should be replaced emphasised their continuing eagerness to disable the Catholic Church. This disposition was repeatedly demonstrated over the following decade, when clergy and others engaged in Catholic ministry were targeted by the authorities for arrest. It is not possible to measure the impact of their actions, but the fact that the Church of Ireland archbishop of Dublin, William King, 'banished a Mass house from a church at Finglas by presenting it as a disturbance' in 1707; that William Dalton, parish priest of St Paul's in Dublin city, began a lengthy spell in prison in 1705; that Robert Robinson (alias Brady), a Franciscan who main-

12 C.Giblin (ed.), 'Catalogue of Nunziatura di Fiandra, part 2, *Collectanea Hibernica*, 4 (1961), p. 84; Donnelly, 'Diocese of Dublin, part 1', pp 842; Walsh, 'Glimpses, part 2', *IER*, 20 (1906), pp 346-7; parts 3 and 4, 22 (1917), pp 76-7, 79-80, 260-2, 267; part 7, 25 (1909), pp 615-6; Finnegan 'The Jesuits in Dublin', pp 67-8; W.P. Burke, *Irish priests in the penal times 1660-1760* (Waterford, 1914), p. 155.   13 Burke, *Irish priests*, p. 309; Giblin (ed.), 'Catalogue of Nunziatura di Fiandra, part 9', *Collectanea Hibernica*, 13 (1970), pp 74-5.   14 Donnelly, 'Diocese of Dublin, part 1', pp 846-9; Donnelly, *Parishes*, part 6, pp 38-9; W.J. W[alsh], 'An act for registering the popish clergy', *IER*, 12 (1876) pp 381-91, 426-31, 546-9.

tained a classical school, and printers and vendors of Catholic prayerbooks were taken into custody in 1708, indicates that it was more than merely inconvenient. In most instances, persons apprehended for infringing anti-Catholic regulations were detained indefinitely rather than transported as the law provided. This may have influenced Rome's decision in 1708 to authorise the despatch of 'as many priests as can live there in hiding and help the Catholics without being subject to the vexations which those ... known to the government have to endure'.[15] If so, it was the wrong time to undertake such an initiative, as increased Jacobite activity in the late 1700s and 1710s ensured that the authorities showed no inclination to relax their anti-Catholic activities.

The fear of Irish Protestants that they might be plunged at any moment into a renewed struggle for survival by a Jacobite invasion, as well as disappointment that the 1697 and 1704 acts had failed either to curb clerical activity or to hasten the decline of Catholicism, prompted a number of intense repressive outbursts from the late 1700s to the mid-1710s making these among the most difficult years the Catholic Church experienced during the penal era. They commenced in March 1708 when reports that England was to be invaded prompted a proclamation for the apprehension of 'the pretended Prince of Wales and all his traitorous confederates and adherents' including 'popish priests'. Following this, the lord mayor of Dublin decreed that thirty-one named priests should dispel any doubts about their loyalty by subscribing to the oath of abjuration. However, instead of coming forward, most of the clergy of the diocese, its County Kildare parishes excepted, went into hiding.[16] The Irish parliament was not prepared to be circumvented so easily and it responded by approving legislation in 1709 which, as well as stipulating that all registered priests should swear an oath by 25 March 1710 to abjure the Stuarts and uphold the Protestant succession, provided for increased rewards for the discovery of regulars and those exercising ecclesiastical jurisdiction. A small number of priests responded by taking the oath as the law decreed, but once Rome pronounced that it was neither 'lawful nor binding', few were prepared to come forward. Indeed, following the example of their archbishop, Edmund Byrne (1707-23), most closed their Mass houses and went into hiding. It is unclear how long churches were closed and priests unavailable as a result, but there is convincing evidence that the institutional Church did not function at all in Dublin city during the summer of 1710, when the oath crisis was at its height.[17]

15 King to Foy, 10 May 1707 (Trinity College Dublin (henceforth TCD), King Papers, Ms 730/3/2 f. 115); Walsh, 'Glimpses, part 3', *IER*, 22 (1907), p. 79; part 11, 29 (1911), pp 140-1; Burke, *Irish priests*, p. 212; Giblin (ed.), 'Fiandra, part 2', p. 103; John Brady (ed.), *Catholics and Catholicism in the eighteenth-century press* (Maynooth, 1966), p. 10. 16 Brady (ed.), *Catholics in the press*, pp 9-10; Burke, *Irish priests*, pp 309, 327. 17 Giblin

By October, as conditions ameliorated, priests throughout the city began to reopen the doors to their places of worship. However, the least infraction of the penal laws that was brought to the authorities' notice was prosecuted, and several priests found themselves in difficulty in the years that followed. In 1711, for example, prosecutions were inaugurated against two priests in Dublin city for saying Mass in parishes other than those for which they were registered, whilst the emergence of 'priest catchers', like the disreputable Edward Tyrell, posed a new and unpredictable threat.[18] The impact of 'priest catchers' has been exaggerated, but the information they passed on to the authorities helped fuel the strongly anti-Catholic disposition of Protestant officialdom in the 1710s. It was not surprising then that the premature attempt to introduce Poor Clare nuns into the city from Galway in 1712 produced a proclamation for their apprehension, as well as for the apprehension of the Franciscan provincial who authorised their translation to Dublin, for 'divers' other 'Popish regulars' and for Archbishop Byrne and Father Cornelius Nary for 'exercis[ing] ecclesiastical jurisdiction contrary to the laws'. Ironically, attempts to prosecute the nuns, whose 'imprudence' precipitated this 'raging storm', failed because the penal laws were deemed not to apply to female religious, but many of their male counterparts were once again obliged to take steps to avoid being ordered for transportation. As far as one can tell, none was brought to trial, though some were arrested. However, most priests concluded that it was opportune to lock their chapels and to go into 'close hiding' until the storm blew over. This did not take very long, for though Archbishop Byrne was pursued with especial zeal by Edward Tyrell, he evaded apprehension until conditions allowed him to resume his work.[19]

Despite his success in evading capture, repression such as that resorted to in 1710 and 1712 greatly inhibited Archbishop Byrne's attempts to reform the Church in the archdiocese. He had demonstrated by his decision, shortly after his consecration, to divide the unwieldy parish of St Michan, and by his revival of the 'long defunct' parish of St Andrew's in 1709, that he believed administrative changes were needed.[20] However, most of the major

(ed.), 'Fiandra, part 2', pp 111, 115-21; idem, 'Catalogue of ... Nunziatura di Fiandra, part 4', *Collectanea Hibernica*, 5 (1962), pp 8-9, 11, 21; Walsh, 'Glimpses, part 5', *IER*, 25 (1909), pp 406-07; part 8, *IER*, 26 (1909), p. 293; N. Donnelly, 'Diocese of Dublin in the eighteenth century, part 8', *IER*, 11 (1890), p. 928.   **18** Giblin (ed.), 'Fiandra, part 4', p. 30; Walsh, 'Glimpses, part 11', *IER*, 29 (1911), p. 131; parts 13 and 15, *IER*, 30 (1911), pp 378, 578; Burke, *Irish priests*, pp 150-1; Brady, ed., *Catholics in the press*, pp 15, 21.   **19** Brady (ed.), *Catholics in the press*, pp 18-9; Burke, *Irish priests*, pp 297-100, 327-8; Finnegan, 'The Jesuits in Dublin', pp 73-4; John Kingston, 'The Carmelite nuns in Dublin 1644-1829', *Reportorium Novum*, 3, no. 2 (1963-4), p. 343; Donnelly, *Parishes*, part 10, pp 16-17; King to Ossory, 18 Sept. 1712 (TCD, King Papers, Ms 2532 f. 48).   **20** Donnelly,

problems he and the diocese faced defied easy resolution. In particular, the accelerating flight of Catholic landed families towards Protestantism, the shortage of and deplorable state of many churches (four people were killed and many seriously injured when 'two of the lofts in one of the Popish chapels in Cook Street fell' in 1716) and the riotous antagonism of the Catholic populace towards the officers of the state as well as towards 'priest catchers' were beyond his capacity to redress.[21] He was not so powerless when the problem at issue was an internal Church matter. Disturbed by the growing tension between seculars and regulars over the latter's practice of celebrating Mass in private houses, he introduced a set of six rules in 1712 which, inter alia, provided his priests with guidance on this sensitive subject. The other matters on which he offered instruction included avoiding attracting hostile official attention and parish administration. It was, as this suggests, a modest document when compared with later diocesan statutes, but this is less significant than the fact that it was prepared.[22]

As well as his own drive, Archbishop Byrne was encouraged to take steps to improve the operation of the Church in the diocese by the hunger of the Catholic population for spiritual nourishment. This was manifested by the attendance of an estimated 10,000 people at the annual St John's well pattern in Kilmainham in 1710; by the continuing willingness of young men to join the priesthood; and, most saliently, by the enhanced availability of Mass (and, one may presume, of other sacraments). Indeed, a contributory factor to the authorities' decision to enforce the penal laws strictly in 1712 was the open celebration in the city of Dublin of Mass by non-registered and non-juring priests.[23] Another, which grew in consequence as the end of the Stuart dynasty approached, was concern about the security of the Protestant succession.

In the summer of 1714, as Queen Anne's life ebbed away, the authorities set about compiling a statement of the number and status of Catholic priests and teachers living and working in the diocese of Dublin. Arising out of this, warrants were issued for the apprehension of a number of non-registered priests and teachers, but most were able 'find shelter and protection' with, among others, sympathetic justices of the peace. Following the death of Anne in early August, and the uncertainty caused by intensified Jacobite activity,

Parishes, part 10, pp 1, 15-16; part 6, pp 37-8; Walsh, 'Glimpses, part 4', IER, 22 (1907), p. 249; Donnelly, 'Diocese of Dublin, part 8', pp 922-3. **21** Donnelly, Parishes, part 1, pp 13-4; Neal Garnham, Crime and the courts (Dublin, 1996), p. 268; Walsh, 'Glimpses, part 14', IER, 30 (1911), p. 512; Brady (ed.), Catholics in the press, pp 15-6, 25; John Ainsworth (ed.), The Inchiquin mss (Dublin, 1961), p. 103. **22** Giblin (ed.), 'Fiandra, part 2', pp 113-4; idem, 'Fiandra, part 9', p. 81; 'Diocesan regulations', 1712, P.F. Moran (ed.), Spicilegium Ossoriense (3 vols, Dublin, 1874-84), iii, 128-9. **23** Burke, Irish priests, p. 329; Donnelly, Parishes, part 16, p. 104; Brady, Catholics in the press, p. 22.

the authorities issued six proclamations between August 1714 and October 1716 authorising magistrates and justices of the peace to disarm 'papists', to enforce the laws against non-jurors and to apprehend 'popish priests, rebels and disaffected persons'. Despite this, the impact of repression in Dublin and environs in the mid-1710s was less than this catalogue of directives would imply, which suggests that official commitment to the enforcement of the laws against Catholicism had diminished since 1712. This conclusion is reinforced by the increasing disinclination of the authorities to pursue non-registered and non-juring priests, or to give effect to the sentences of transportation imposed on the small number who lay in jails in Dublin and Wicklow. In fact, the most overtly anti-Catholic act at this time was not directed at religious personnel, but against the annual pilgrimage to Glendalough which was forcefully 'dispersed' in June 1714 by a *posse comitatus* of local Protestants raised by the high sheriff of Wicklow.[24]

Once the Hanoverian succession was safely in place, the authorities in Dublin displayed a diminishing interest in strictly enforcing the laws against Catholic religious. This was welcomed by clergy like the Dominican bishop of Elphin, Ambrose MacDermott, who deemed Dublin a safer place to live than his own diocese in 1717.[25] At the same time, Catholic clergy could not afford to relax because of the continued activity of 'priest catchers', of whom John Garzia was the most infamous and the most successful. Garzia took up priest catching as a livelihood, and he well demonstrated what a talent for deceit could achieve by securing guilty verdicts in 1718 against six priests (five regulars and one non-registered secular) brought for trial for infringing the 1697 banishment and the 1704 registration legislation. More critically, his claim that Edmund Byrne 'exercised ecclesiastical jurisdiction contrary to the laws of the realm' led to the archbishop's arrest and would, Byrne admitted, have resulted in his 'exile for life' except that Garzia did not present himself to give evidence when the case came to trial in November 1719.[26]

---

24 Burke, *Irish priests*, pp 195, 300-2, 309-10, 327-8; Donnelly, *Parishes*, part 14, pp 19-21; Walsh, 'Glimpses, part 13', *IER*, 30 (1911), p. 381; Brady (ed.), *Catholics in the press*, pp 23-4, 25, 27. It can also be suggested that the escape of Bryan McHugh of the diocese of Ardagh from Newgate in 1716 also reflected a decline in official eagerness to enforce the penal laws (J. Kelly, 'The Catholic Church in the diocese of Ardagh 1650-1870' in R. Gillespie and G. Moran (eds), *Longford: essays in county history* (Dublin, 1991), p. 72). 25 Giblin (ed.), 'Fiandra, part 4', p. 73. 26 Brady, *Catholics in the press*, pp 29, 34; Bossnett [Byrne] to Santini, 8 July 1718 in Giblin (ed.), 'Fiandra, part 4', p. 83; John Meagher, 'Edmund Byrne (1656-1723) archbishop of Dublin', *Reportorium Novum*, 3, no. 2 (1963-4), pp 385-6; Kevin McGrath, 'John Garzia, a noted priest catcher and his activities 1717-23', *IER*, 72 (1949), pp 494-504; Burke, *Irish priests*, pp 220-23; Moran (ed.), *Spicilegium Ossoriense*, iii, 131-2; H. Fenning (ed.), 'Some eighteenth century broadsides', *Collectanea Hibernica*, 12 (1969), pp 48-52.

While Garzia's failure to testify against Archbishop Byrne defies conclusive explanation, the refusal of the authorities subsequently to provide him with the moral and financial support he believed was his entitlement confirms that the moderation in official antipathy towards the Catholic Church that took place in the mid-1710s was unlikely to be reversed. There was, at the same time, no question of the authorities acknowledging the legitimacy of the Church's mission or message. But, as the evidence given during the 'Garzia trials' of regular and secular clerics attired in priestly 'robes' openly celebrating Mass in Dublin chapels attests, the Church felt sufficiently secure to minister more openly than at any time since 1690.[27] This also explains the accelerated return from exile of female and male religious that followed.[28] To be sure, the Church was not free of the threat or of the experience of repression. In May 1720 when '6 or 7 popish priests were taken up' for promoting an attack on the Quaker meeting house in Meath Street, only one city chapel opened the following Sunday. Regulars were even more vulnerable.[29]

Even so, the Church had already negotiated the worst of the penal era, and it had emerged in a better condition than it could have anticipated when repression was at its height. The state of the regular clergy in the diocese did, of course, leave much to be desired; the fabric and aspect of many churches were shabby, and the authority of the archbishop diminished, but this was counterbalanced by the fact that the diocese possessed committed clergy (approximately forty of whom were located in the capital)[30] and a largely loyal laity. Most importantly of all, it once again possessed the opportunity to embark on the task of putting in place a Church that functioned according to the spiritual and administrative ideals laid down by the Council of Trent.

II

Though caution continued to be its preeminent characteristic, the decision of Edward Murphy, following his elevation to the archbishopric in 1724, to request a pallium (which had not been granted to his immediate predeces-

---

27 MacGrath, 'John Garzia', pp 504-14; Fenning, 'Eighteenth- century broadsides', pp 48-52.   28 As well as the Poor Clares (Franciscans), the female religious who took up residence were Dominicans, Augustinians and Carmelites (Donnelly, *Parishes*, part 10, pp 17-18; part 11 p. 52; part 9, p. 223; Kingston, 'Carmelite nuns in Dublin', pp 339-41). For male religious see Maureen Wall, 'The penal laws' in Gerard O'Brien (ed.), *Catholic Ireland in the eighteenth century: collected essays of Maureen Wall* (Dublin, 1989), p. 52; Donnelly, *Parishes*, part 10, p. 18.   29 Brady (ed.), *Catholics in the press*, p. 34; Peter O'Dwyer, *The Irish Carmelites* (Dublin, 1988), pp 128-9.   30 Lista de ... sacerdotes Papistas ... de Dublin, 1721 (Public Record Office, S.P., 63/380).

sors) provided a clear signal that the Church in the Dublin diocese perceived that the worst of the repression identified with the 'penal era' was over by the mid-1720s. Rome was not convinced, however, and since only seven years had elapsed since Archbishop Byrne had declined to promulgate *Unigenitus*, the papal bull against Jansenism, on the grounds that it would be 'very dangerous' to do so, it denied the request.[31] Though the reason offered was the fear of attracting adverse official notice, it seems likely that Rome also possessed doctrinal concerns. Archbishop Byrne and his suffragan bishops had condemned Jansenism in 1718. But the facts that a number of priests had been ordained for the Jansenist Church of Utrecht in Dublin in 1715 by Luke Fagan, the bishop of Meath, and that Byrne supported the publication in 1718 of Father Cornelius Nary's disputed New Testament and recommended Sylvester Lloyd's controversial translation of the doctrinally dubious Montpellier Catechism were all causes of concern to the Roman authorities.[32]

Nary's and Lloyd's forays into the world of religious publication had been encouraged by Byrne, and welcomed by many priests in the archdiocese of Dublin, because of the acute shortage of Catholic literature. Ironically, instead of aiding the mission of the Church, doctrinal doubts about the propriety of Lloyd's endeavour served to excite 'serious divisions and scandals' between those who favoured Lloyd's version and those who took their guidance on such matters from Rome.[33] These differences, following rapidly upon the 'Rivers controversy' which blighted Archbishop Byrne's final years,[34] and factional manoeuvring over the episcopal succession,[35] diminished the capacity of the Church to take full advantage of the ameliorating atmosphere of the 1720s, for though Archbishop Murphy had a calming impact, several problems which were left unattended during his episcopate did not go away and

---

31 Giblin (ed.),'Fiandra, part 4', pp 80-4, 114; C. Giblin (ed.), 'Catalogue of Nunziatura di Fiandra, part 7', *Collectanea Hibernica*, 11 (1968), pp 78-9; idem, 'Catalogue of Nunziatura di Fiandra, part 10', *Collectanea Hibernica*, 14 (1971), p. 39; idem, 'Fiandra, part 9', p. 97. **32** Giblin (ed.), 'Fiandra, part 4', pp 83-4; C.Giblin (ed.), 'Catalogue of Nunziatura di Fiandra, part 11', *Collectanea Hibernica*, 15 (1972), p. 31; Donnelly, *Parishes*, part 11, p. 52; Patrick Fagan, 'Luke Fagan – eighteenth-century prelate', *Riocht na Midhe*, 8 (1992-3), pp 96-7; idem, Cornelius Nary (Dublin, 1991); idem, *An Irish bishop in penal times: the chequered career of Sylvester Lloyd* (Dublin, 1993). **33** Raymond Gillespie, 'The cultivation of print in seventeenth-century Ireland', *Studia Hibernica*, 29 (1996-8); Giblin (ed.), 'Fiandra, part 7', pp 77-8; idem, 'Fiandra, part 4', pp 106-09; idem, 'Catalogue of Nunziatura di Fiandra, part 10', *Collectanea Hibernica*, 14 (1971), p. 39; Brady (ed.), *Catholics in the press*, p. 42. **34** Fenning, below, pp 179-82; Donnelly, *Parishes*, part 9, pp 218-22; part 8, pp 192-3; Giblin (ed.), 'Fiandra, part 9', p. 98; idem, 'Fiandra, part 11', p. 31. **35** Fenning, below, p. 183; Donnelly, *Parishes*, part 11, pp 52-3; part 16, pp 104-5; Giblin (ed.), 'Fiandra, part 7', pp 76-7; Patrick Fagan (ed.), *Ireland in the Stuart papers* (2 vols, Dublin, 1995), ii, 41-4.

reemerged after his death. Indeed, they were added to and exacerbated by mounting tensions between the regular clergy, whose numbers recovered rapidly from their early century low, and the secular clergy, who resented competition for alms in the exceptionally difficult economic climate of the late 1720s. There were, as this suggests, important jurisdictional disputes which Archbishop Murphy did little to defuse by siding with the seculars. However, such problems did not become serious until one of the Canons Regular of the Lateran (Thomas O'Kelly) secured papal support in 1729 for the restoration of parishes attached to monasteries held by his order before the Reformation, and claimed the city parishes of St Catherine's, St Thomas' and St James' on behalf of his order.[36] With the emergence of this complex issue and a split in the diocesan chapter following the death of Archbishop Murphy in December 1728,[37] it appeared that the diocese was about to embark on a long period of debilitating internal division. In fact, though Murphy's successor, the elderly but impressive bishop of Meath, Luke Fagan (1729-33), was no less a caretaker appointment, the diocese he took charge of was in a sounder condition than a narrow focus on the behaviour of quarrelsome clerics might suggest.

Luke Fagan's most striking contribution to the administration of the diocese of Dublin was the preparation of a new and enhanced set of diocesan statutes. Comprising 47 in all, they represented the most comprehensive guide to their duties and responsibilities the secular and regular clergy in the diocese had yet received. Some of the doctrinal and organisational objectives laid down were, it can be assumed, long-term aspirations rather than immediately realisable goals, but the statutes represented a clear statement of the spiritual and organisational ambitions of the Church's leadership.[38]

If the preparation of new statutes was, in part, a response to current administrative and jurisdictional problems, it also attested to the need for a tighter definition of Church procedures and clerical responsibilities as their number grew rapidly in the improving atmosphere of the 1720s. This was highlighted by an unexpected source, the parliamentary *Report on the state of popery*, which maintained in 1730 that there were between 163 and 178 priests ministering to the estimated 115,000 Catholics resident in the diocese. The

36 James Kelly, 'Harvests and hardship: famine and scarcity in Ireland in the late 1720s', *Studia Hibernica*, 26 (1991-2); Fenning, below, pp 184-5; Fagan (ed.), *Stuart papers*, ii, 99; Donnelly, *Parishes*, part 15, pp 58, 81; Fagan, 'Luke Fagan', pp 104-6; C. Giblin (ed.), 'Catalogue of Nunziatura di Fiandra, part 5', *Collectanea Hibernica*, 9 (1966), pp 60-1, 64-5.   37 Donnelly, *Parishes*, part 11, p. 52; part 16, pp 106-07; Fagan (ed.), *Stuart papers*, ii, 140-1, 150-1; Fagan, 'Luke Fagan', pp 101-2; Giblin (ed.), 'Fiandra, part 5', pp 8-11.   38 Diocesan statutes, 1730 in Moran (ed.), *Spicilegium Ossoriense*, iii, 139-48; Fagan, 'Luke Fagan', p. 104.

priest to people ratio of between 1:646 and 1:706 these figures represent indicates that the Church now possessed sufficient personnel to offer a comprehensive religious service, but the combined impact of statutory restrictions and internal problems ensured that the effective ratio was significantly less advantageous. At the same time, the fact that there were over seventy chapels or Mass houses (approximately 40 per cent of which had either been built anew or refurbished since 1714) and a slightly greater number of schools provided the Church with an infrastructure on which it could develop and expand.[39] However, they were unevenly distributed, with the result that there were rural parishes with too few or, in some instances, no churches or schools. Fagan sought to ease this problem in north County Dublin by dividing the sprawling parish of Lusk into three – Lusk, Rush and Skerries – in 1730 but, as the continuing poor condition of so many of the diocese's churches attests, there were distinct fiscal limits as to what the Church could achieve. Indeed, as many as 60 per cent of functioning churches in the diocese at this time were decrepit, inconsequential and, in some instances, unsafe buildings that were unsuited to the religious purposes to which they were being put. One can obtain an insight into their condition from the fact that, compared with them, the 'small, dark and badly ventilated' edifice erected by the Dominicans on Bridge Street in 1719 was comfortable.[40]

The priests of the archdiocese constructed and worked in such buildings because, while there were fewer incidents of repression in the 1720s and 1730s, the political environment remained tangibly unadvantageous. This was vividly highlighted by the reaction Irish Protestants afforded the *Report on the state of popery*. During the late 1720s, many among them had expressed disquiet with what they termed the 'insolence' of the increasing numbers of Catholic clergy on the streets of the capital. Mavericks like the Carmelite, Francis Lehy, whose assertive evangelising antagonised Protestants, and the unstable Father Allen, who assaulted and insulted 'heretics' on the street, were easily silenced.[41] The more efficient and discreet were a larger problem, and the publication of the *Report on the state of popery* prompted calls in the House of Commons and a recommendation by the Lords 'that mag-

39 'Report on the state of popery in Ireland, 1731: Diocese of Dublin', *Archivium Hibernicum*, 4 (1915), pp 131-6; Fagan, 'Luke Fagan', pp 102-3; idem, 'The population of Dublin in the eighteenth century with particular reference to the proportion of Protestants and Catholics', *Eighteenth-Century Ireland*, 6 (1991), pp 135-7.   40 Donnelly, *Parishes*, part 16, pp 108, 114; part 12, p. 83; part 9, pp 235-6; part 8, pp 178-9, 192; part 17, pp 137, 139, 154; part 7, pp 140-42; part 11, pp 48-9; part 4, p. 145; part 2, p. 52. 41 TCD, King Papers, Ms 750/8-10 passim; Brady (ed.), *Catholics in the press*, pp 43, 47, 48, 49-50, 51; O'Dwyer, *Irish Carmelites*, pp 129-30. The comments of Archbishop Hoadley (Fagan, 'Luke Fagan', p. 102) are particularly pertinent.

istrates ... do immediately enter upon a more steady and vigorous execution of the laws against popery, especially those against all regulars, and persons exercising ecclesiastical jurisdiction contrary to the laws of this kingdom'.[42] Following this, there was a short, sharp burst of official repression during the mid-1730s which resulted in the temporary closure of churches,[43] but its subsequent cessation suggests that the state, if not all of Protestant opinion, had concluded that the laws against Catholics, so far as they concerned the clergy and religious services, should only be appealed to during emergencies.

This conclusion is supported by the fact that the last significant phase of repressive anti-Catholic activity spanned the difficult years 1739-45. It was precipitated by the seizure in Derry in June 1739 of what Sylvester Lloyd described as 'some stupid missioner's letters'. Apprehending an 'insurrection', the authorities in Dublin arrested those clergy they could locate and ordered that convents be searched for arms.[44] None were found, but the outbreak of war between Britain and Spain in October initiated a further spate of anti-Catholic initiatives. As well as ordering the by now customary search for arms, the aldermen of Dublin Corporation undertook to make regular returns to the grand jury of 'all popish schoolmasters and nunneries, or friars' in their wards so they could be 'prosecuted and suppressed'. No prosecutions ensued, so far as one can tell, but 'great numbers of Irish Catholics' fled to Flanders in the winter of 1739-40 'to avoid the persecution ... threatening' at home. They were over-reacting, but this impulse remained strong for, two years later, Catholic clerics contemplated flight when the privy council directed that those exercising ecclesiastical jurisdiction and all regulars (male and female) should be apprehended and monasteries and nunneries 'extirpate[d]'.[45]

Once more, the threat was not delivered upon. Indeed, excepting the dispersal of some Carmelite nuns in 1743, it took until the winter of 1743-44, when the perennial fear of a Jacobite invasion seemed about to become reality, for the authorities to back up their word with deeds. As in 1739, the anti-Catholic initiatives included a directive to gather information on the state of the Church, but since it came accompanied with an order to arrest clergy

42 Brady (ed.), *Catholics in the press*, pp 41-2; Giblin (ed.), 'Fiandra, part 7', p. 87; *A report ... from the Lords Committee appointed to enquire into the present state of popery* (Dublin, 1731) reprinted in *Catholic Directory*, 1842, pp 375-6.   43 Burke, *Irish priests*, p. 304; Fenning, below p. 188.   44 Lloyd to Edgar, 27 Aug. [1739] in Fagan (ed.), *Stuart papers*, ii, 292; J.Kelly, 'The formation of the modern Catholic Church in the diocese of Kilmore 1580-1880' in R. Gillespie (ed.), *Cavan: essays in county history* (Dublin, 1995), pp 126-7.   45 Brady (ed.), *Catholics in the press*, p. 61; Giblin (ed.), 'Catalogue of Nunziatura di Fiandra, part 6', *Collectanea Hibernica*, 10 (1967), pp 81-2; R.M. Gilbert (ed.), *Calendar of ancient records of Dublin*, viii (Dublin, 1901), p. 359.

and to close Mass houses, it was no mere intelligence-gathering exercise. Despite this, and the widespread disruption caused by clergy going to ground, repression was measurably less intense than it had been on many occasions between 1692 and 1720. Indeed, following the death of ten people on 27 February 1744, when an 'old house' in Pill Lane in which they were hearing Mass collapsed, the lord lieutenant, Lord Chesterfield, ordered that the pursuit of clergy and the closure of Mass houses be suspended. Churches were reopened on 17 March and the events of the winter of 1743-4 had already been consigned to memory by the following January, when Rome expressed itself 'pleased with the latest news from Ireland'.[46]

It was broadly satisfied too with the leadership provided the Church by John Linegar (1734-57) who succeeded Luke Fagan. Though the environment in which he operated demanded circumspection, Linegar defused several long-running factional and jurisdictional disputes. Unfortunately, there always seemed to be new ones, among the most intractable of which were those caused by Rome's appointments to parishes without proper prior consultation.[47] He was less able to mount effective opposition to the Charter Schools, the first of which opened virtually synchronously with his appointment, but he managed (with some papal support) to augment the educational provision for Catholics without ever neutralising the 'danger being done daily in Ireland' by the existence and operation of such proselytising bodies.[48]

As a pastor and administrator, Linegar was facilitated in the exercise of power by the goodwill he generated among his clergy.[49] But if he was sensitive in his dealings with others, he also held firm views on the need to exercise greater control over the admission of young men to the priesthood. From the early 1730s, claims that there were 'near three priests for every parish in the kingdom and as many friars' and that this facilitated 'loose behaviour', 'public quarrels' and the proliferation of 'couple beggars' fuelled a demand for the imposition of strict limits on the number of young men admitted to

---

46 Kingston, 'Carmelite nuns', pp 343-4; Burke, *Irish priests*, pp 305-6, 310, 328; Brady (ed.), *Catholics in the press*, p. 65; Donnelly, *Parishes*, part 10, pp 20-1; M.B. Buckley, *The life and writings of the Rev Arthur O'Leary* (Dublin, 1868), p. 47; C. Giblin, ed., 'Fiandra, part 6', pp 98, 103.   47 For which see Fenning, below, pp 189-90; Giblin (ed.), 'Fiandra, part 10', pp 73-4; H. Fenning (ed.), 'Documents of Irish interest in the Fondo missioni', *Archivium Hibernicum*, 49 (1995), p. 13. One of Linegar's difficult disputes is well-chronicled in C. Giblin (ed.), 'Ten documents relating to Irish diocesan affairs 1749-84', *Collectanea Hibernica*, 20 (1978), pp 61-72.   48 Kenneth Milne, *The Irish charter schools 1730-1830* (Dublin, 1997), chapter 1; H. Fenning, *The undoing of the friars of Ireland: a study of the novitiate question in the eighteenth century* (Louvain, 1972), pp 135-96 passim; R.E. Ward, *An encyclopaedia of Irish schools 1500-1800* (Lampeter, 1995), p. 105; C. Giblin (ed.), 'Catalogue of Nunziatura di Fiandra, part 10', *Collectanea Hibernica*, 14 (1971), p. 72.   49 Giblin (ed.), 'Fiandra, part 5', p. 42; idem, 'Fiandra, part 6', pp 99-100.

the priesthood.[50] Archbishop Linegar and his two vicars general were enthusiastic *zelanti*, as the reformers were known, but they were neither consulted by Pope Benedict XIV nor pleased with his decision of May 1741 to limit the number of priests each bishop ordained *titulo missionis* to twelve. As a result, the archbishop joined with others in seeking to have the terms of the decision relaxed in 1748. Concessions were generally allowed to bishops who maintained they needed to ordain above the permitted quota, but they did not prevent a fall in the number of clergy in the country. This did not cause any problems in Dublin in the short term if the report, dating from 1745, that the city was 'encumbered with a superfluous number of regular and secular clergy' is to be believed. The capital certainly attracted a disproportionate number of footloose, discredited and disobedient regulars to whom clandestine marriage and 'other illegal and shameful practices' were reflexively attributed.[51] Eager to put an end to such abuses and to assert his authority over the regulars, Archbishop Linegar had to wait until 1750 when Benedict XIV ratified a series of decrees, many of them originating with the *zelanti*, forbidding the reception by religious orders of novices in Ireland and placing regulars under the authority of the ordinary.[52]

If, in retrospect, it appears that the combined impact of the extension of episcopal authority, the capping of clerical numbers and Lord Chesterfield's decision to suspend repression prematurely in 1744 paved the way for the Catholic Church in the diocese of Dublin finally to put the penal laws behind it, both Archbishop Linegar and his priests knew that they could not afford to conduct themselves less than discreetly. Indeed, the second half of the 1740s saw the publication of a number of fiercely anti-Catholic diatribes warning Protestants that 'popery [is] always the same',[53] and the repulse of Catholic clerics who trespassed upon areas regarded by Protestants as their preserve.[54] Despite this, the Church possessed more freedom to conduct its mission than it had at any point since the 1680s, and the opportunities this allowed and the limitations it imposed as the mid-point of the century approached are well reflected in the state of its churches.

50 Burke to [ ], 6 Dec. 1733 in H. Fenning (ed.), 'Some problems on the Irish mission 1733-74', *Collectanea Hibernica*, 8 (1965), pp 60, 62-3.   51 Fagan (ed.), *Stuart Papers*, ii, 26-8.
52 Fenning, *The undoing of the friars*, pp 92-207 passim; Moran (ed.), *Spicilegium Ossoriense*, iii, 161; Fenning (ed.), 'Some problems on the Irish mission', p. 79; Fenning (ed.), 'Fondo missioni', pp 9-11.   53 *The sufferings of John Custos for free masonry and for his refusing to turn Roman Catholic in the Inquisition at Lisbon* ... (Dublin 1746); *Popery always the same: exemplified in an authentic account of the persecution now carrying on against the Protestants in the south of France* (Dublin, 1746) (This tract was sold in bulk to enable gentlemen 'give to those who cannot afford them': *Dublin Courant*, 20 Dec. 1746); Samuel Delap, *The deliverance of Great Britain and Ireland from popery, slavery and the pretender* (Dublin, 1746).   54 Brady (ed.), *Catholics in the press*, pp 91-2; Burke, *Irish priests*, pp 193, 306.

Viewed from without, one could portray the Catholic Church in Dublin in the early eighteenth century as an apprehensive, retiring, decrepit institution. This is certainly the impression created by the converted stable which served as a church on Hawkins Street in which there were fatal accidents in 1738 and 1750.[55] It was not representative, but it is equally true that none of the diocese's churches were buildings of architectural significance, and that none was to be found in a prestigious or prominent location because Catholics, one of their number pointed out in 1746, 'never dared erect or establish a public chapel but always chose the most private, the least offensive place for their divine service'.[56] Thus in Dublin city, their chapels tended to be located on side streets or alleyways; while the positioning of the church for the County Wicklow parish of Ballymore Eustace outside the town, probably as a result of the unwillingness of local Protestant landowners to provide a more suitable location, indicates that reserve was also necessary elsewhere in the diocese. This reserve was particularly manifest in the contour and composition of Church buildings. Most were T-shaped rather than cruciform; their walls constructed of rubble finished, as in the case of St Nicholas' Church on Francis Street, with pebbledash rather than cut-stone; and – as illustrated by churches in Howth, Celbridge and Rathdrum – possessed of low, thatched roofs rather than high, slated roofs capped with spires or steeples.[57]

The chapel interiors, by contrast, offer a quite different impression. According to a report on the 'state and condition' of Roman Catholic chapels in the city of Dublin made in 1749, most contained seating aligned in galleries, reserved pews for the principal parishioners, confessionals and pulpits. It was the sanctuaries, and the altars particularly, that most vividly demonstrate how misleading it is to generalise about the state of Catholicism from the external architecture of its churches. Altars were constructed of materials ranging from wainscotted wood to polished Kilkenny marble and, as well as elaborate tabernacles, usually carried gilt candlesticks and large paintings portraying key events such as the crucifixion, annunciation and ascension. In

---

55 Brady (ed.), *Catholics in the press*, pp 58, 79; Donnelly, *Parishes*, part 7 pp 143-4; Arthur Flynn, *History of Bray* (Cork, 1968), pp 110-11. As a result of such accidents, doubts about the stability of Catholic churches led to scenes of panic and confusion (Brady, op. cit., p. 79).   56 *Address from the Catholics of Ireland ... to ... E[ar]l of Ch[este]r[fiel]d* (Dublin 1746) cited in K. Whelan, 'Catholics, politicisation and the 1798 rebellion' in R. O Muirí (ed.), *Irish Church history today* (Armagh, [1991]), p. 64.   57 William Hawkes, 'Parish of Ballymore Eustace, 1791' *Reportorium Novum*, 2, no. 1 (1957-8), p. 122; Donnelly, 'Diocese of Dublin, part 3', p. 1006; Donnelly, *Parishes*, part 9, p. 230; part 15, p. 60; part 16 p. 114; Tony Doohan, *A history of Celbridge* (privately printed, 1985), pp 74-5; O'Toole, 'Rathvilly parish', pp 68-9; Redmond, 'Notes on ... Rathdrum', pp 193-4.

addition, some chapels displayed portraits of apostles or saints in the sanctuary, on or near side altars or at other locations such as the nave or sacristy.[58] Such decorative features were manifestly not the achievement of a clergy or laity utterly lacking in self-belief or wanting in confidence for the future. On the contrary; they present an image of a *quietly* dynamic and increasingly assured institution.

Unfortunately, because the 1749 report confines itself to the nineteen chapels located in Dublin city, it is not possible to comment with equal confidence on the state of the chapels and Mass houses in the rest of the diocese. However, given the range of furnishings in the city's churches, it is reasonable to assume that they also contained a range of church furniture, but that they were, in the main, less ornately decorated and structurally less impressive buildings than their city equivalents. If the surviving registers are an accurate guide, the differential speed at which parish registers were inaugurated certainly suggests that the Catholic Church was developing at a faster pace in the city than elsewhere. Eight out of the nine parishes in the diocese for whom registers exist prior to 1750 were located in the metropolis; Wicklow town (1747) is the only exception.[59]

III

The presence of paintings and other decorative features in chapels suggests that the devotional enthusiasm of Catholic church-goers remained strong during the early and mid-eighteenth century, and this is borne out by other evidence. Peter O'Dwyer has shown how Tadhg Ó Neachtáin expressed his devotion to Mary in poetry, while, as well as the healthy congregations at Sunday Mass, evening services which featured singing as well as preaching and praying were held in Dublin chapels until they were suspended in 1739.[60] It is not possible to calculate what percentage of Catholics attended church regularly, or how frequently Mass was celebrated. Some priests, we know,

---

58 N.K. Donnelly, *State and condition of R.C. chapels in Dublin, both secular and regular, A.D. 1749* (Dublin, 1904), pp 11-21; Ronan, 'Religious life in Old Dublin', pp 110-11; Nuala Burke, 'A hidden Church? The structure of Catholic Dublin in the mid-eighteenth century', *Archivium Hibernicum*, 32 (1974), pp 88-91. For an illustration of one of these altar pieces and other artifacts see Joseph MacDonnell, *Ecclesiastical art of the penal era* (Maynooth, 1995). **59** Brian Mitchell, *A guide to Irish parish registers* (Baltimore, 1988), pp 38-44, 58-62, 132-4. The parishes were St Michan's (1726), St Paul's (1731), St Mary's (1734), St Catherine's (1740), St Nicholas Without (1742), St Andrew's (1742), St Michael and John's (1743), St Audoen's (1747) and Wicklow (1747). **60** Peter O'Dwyer, *Mary: a history of devotion in Ireland* (Dublin, 1988), pp 233-4; Brady (ed.), *Catholics in the press*, p. 60.

said more than one Mass daily, but the substantial number of priests (regulars as well as seculars) attached to the city chapels at this time ought to have ensured that individual clergy were not unfairly imposed upon. The situation was more difficult in rural parishes, with the result that it is likely that many Catholics in such locations did not satisfy the Sunday obligation described in Andrew Donleavy's bilingual catechism published for the Irish Catholic market in Paris in 1742.[61] At the same time, it appears that the greater freedom priests now possessed enabled them to seek to win back many who had strayed from the fold in more difficult times. James Lyons, a young ordinand recently returned from the continent, reported in 1764 that he 'encounter[ed] many who have not approached the Holy Sacraments these three, four, eleven, sixteen and twenty years', and that he sought to redress this by giving instruction and by hearing confessions.[62]

The alertness of many priests to the material as well as spiritual needs of their parishioners contributed to the esteem in which figures like Father John Murphy of St Catherine's were held by the Catholic laity.[63] If, as this suggests, relations between priests and people were broadly harmonious, the general standard of catechesis left much room for improvement, as Archbishop Lincoln (1757-62) conceded when he availed of a papal jubilee in 1759 to promote the sacrament of confession, and to direct his priests to redouble their efforts to instruct 'their penitents ... in the necessary points of the Christian Doctrine' and to tailor their sermons to the understanding of their parishioners. Further evidence, dating from the same year, of the Church's eagerness to improve the devotional commitment of the laity at this time is provided by the award of a novena to St Joseph to the parish of St James, as well as by the ever greater availability of devotional aids such as rosaries and the publication of an impressive list of religious literature.[64]

As the Church contrived to improve the delivery of its doctrine and the standard of devotional practice, it could not afford to ignore old problems like clandestine marriages and couple beggars. Governmental sensitivities on both subjects were emphasised in 1725 when it was made a capital offence

61 Brady (ed.), *Catholics in the press*, p. 60; Ronan, 'Religious life in old Dublin', p. 109; Michael Maher, 'Sunday in the Irish Church', *Irish Theological Quarterly*, 60 (1994), pp 176-7.   62 Hugh Fenning, 'The journey of James Lyons from Rome to Sligo 1763-65', *Collectanea Hibernica*, 11 (1968), p. 106.   63 Brady (ed.), *Catholics in the press*, pp 83, 84, 86, 92; see also pp 217-8; Donnelly, *Parishes*, part 9, p. 222.   64 Fenning, *The undoing of the friars*, pp 198, 200, 206; Pastoral address to the clergy of Dublin, 1759 in Moran (ed.), *Spicilegium Ossoriense*, iii, 267-71; Hugh Fenning, 'The Udienze series in the Roman archives', *Archivium Hibernicum*, 48 (1994), p. 104; Brady (ed.), *Catholics in the press*, pp 113-4, 137; Thomas Wall, *The sign of Dr Hay's head* (Dublin, 1958), chapter 5 passim; Hugh Fenning, 'Dublin imprints of Catholic interest 1701-1739', *Collectanea Hibernica*, 39 & 40 (1997-8), pp 106-54.

for a priest to officiate at a marriage involving a member of the Church of Ireland. Further enactments followed in 1735 and in the late 1740s when it was decreed that clandestine marriages involving Protestants were invalid and the penalties against couple beggars were reaffirmed.[65]

As a consequence, the Church had little option but to be seen to take action also, and six priests 'were declared excommunicated for solemnising clandestine marriages ... in all [the] Popish chapels' in Dublin on 24 April 1748. This was an unambiguous statement of the Church's eagerness to ensure all clergy adhered to its rules and observed its lines of authority, but both couple beggars and clandestine marriages were too firmly entrenched to be eradicated easily. Indeed, one of those excommunicated in 1748 was subsequently arrested 'for marrying several soldiers and other persons and apprentices to Roman Catholicks' and sent for transportation in 1753. There were plenty to take his place, but the fall in ordinations following Benedict XIV's decrees of 1741 and 1750 meant it was a diminishing problem.[66]

The very existence of couple beggars attested both to the weakness of clerical discipline and, the heavy expenditure on church furniture in the 1740s notwithstanding, to the continuing poverty of the Church and the bulk of the laity to which it ministered. The clergy depended for their income on voluntary offerings. Most of this came from church door collections, but additional 'emoluments' could also be earned by the performance of marriages and baptisms. Combined, these provided Patrick Fitzsimmons, parish priest of St Michan's, with an income of £50 to £60 in 1751. This was substantial enough to allow a parish priest a comfortable lifestyle or, if he was so motivated, to pay for some church renovation. The fact that substantial sums were allocated to church improvement may partly explain why few priests or bishops left substantial assets and why curates had to get by on very modest stipends, but the Church also sought to do what it could to relieve the poor.

From the mid-eighteenth century, chapels became a favourite resort of alms seekers, so much so that the collection for 'the relief of the industrious poor' organised by the Church in the difficult conditions of 1767 raised £682 10s. At the same time, there can be no doubt but that money was tight, because when James Lyons returned to Ireland in 1763, he was provided with clothes becoming a priest by the brother of a curate he befriended, rather than by clerical colleagues.[67] Given this background, it is hardly surprising

---

65 James Kelly, 'The abduction of women of fortune in eighteenth-century Ireland', *Eighteenth-century Ireland*, 9 (1994), p. 24. 66 Brady (ed.), *Catholics in the press*, pp 76, 81-2, 109. 67 Burke, *Irish priests*, p. 308; Donnelly, *Parishes*, part 11, p. 56; part 6, pp 50-1; Brady (ed.), *Catholics in the press*, pp 128, 318; Fenning (ed.), 'Journey of James Lyons', pp 103, 105-6.

that some priests were tempted by the prospect of a regular income of £30 or £40 to desert Catholicism for the Established Church. It is not clear precisely how many priests of the Dublin diocese chose this controversial option, since the capital was the primary national location for converts to make a declaration of their new-found convictions, but, as with the laity, the number of clerical converts in Dublin rose during the third quarter of the eighteenth century.[68]

The number of conversions that took place was never large enough to be a major worry, though it was perceived in some quarters as the concomitant of the 'religious indifference' that was making 'large and hasty strides' by 1770.[69] Like greater religious zeal this is frequently difficult to demonstrate. But the facts that 'riotous behaviour' due to drunkenness caused the suspension of the Christmas midnight Mass in 1755, that pickpockets and thieves habitually targeted churches, and that priests were robbed, assaulted and, in a number of cases, killed by criminals suggest that a substantial section of the city's lower classes possessed few religious sensibilities.[70] Such behaviour offended the devout who, when opportunity allowed, expressed their disapproval of pickpockets and thieves by inflicting public beatings or by ducking them in the Liffey.[71]

A problem that proved more resistant to eradication was factionalism within the clergy. One 'dissension' that caused scandal during the mid-eighteenth century arose out of the refusal of a section of the Franciscan community to recognise their 'lawfully appointed guardian'.[72] This might have been settled quickly had Archbishop Linegar not been obliged, as a consequence of his declining faculties, to rely on others with the result that animosities intensified.[73] These were 'calmed ... by the zeal and prudence' of his successor, Richard Lincoln (1757-62), though he in turn became embroiled in a dispute with the regulars over confraternities. His successor, Patrick Fitzsimons (1763-9), calmed things down and there were fewer problems with the regular clergy thereafter. Despite this, and the sharp decline in the number of regular clergy, regular-secular tensions persisted.[74]

---

68 Giblin (ed.), 'Ten documents relating to Irish diocesan affairs 1749-84' p. 60; Brady (ed.), *Catholics in the press*, pp 47-8, 58, 61-2, 84, 86, 114, 128, 153; T.P. Power, 'Converts' in idem and K. Whelan (eds), *Endurance and emergence: Catholics in Ireland in the eighteenth century* (Dublin, 1990), pp 101, 122-3.   69 O'Conor to Carpenter, 25 Oct. 1768, 10 Sept 1770 in Moran (ed.), *Spicilegium Ossoriense*, iii, 284, 286.   70 Brady (ed.), *Catholics in the press*, pp 88, 318, 76, 79, 81, 84, 86-7, 93-5, 112, 127, 136-7, 139, 144-5, 151, 184, 188-9, 193, 230, 231.   71 Brady (ed.), *Catholics in the press*, pp 81, 86, 93, 95, 193.   72 Giblin (ed.), 'Nunziatura di Fiandra part 6', *Collectanea Hibernica*, 10 (1967), pp 112-4; idem, part 10, *Collectanea Hibernica*, 14 (1971), p. 79.   73 Donnelly, *Parishes*, part 11, pp 56-8; part 1, p. 16; Fagan (ed.), *Stuart Papers*, ii, 170-71.   74 Fagan (ed.), *Stuart papers*, ii, 257; Donnelly, *Parishes*, part 7, p. 145; part 12, p. 85; Fenning, 'Some problems of the

Continuing intra-clerical tension combined with a disimproving priest-to-people ratio to prevent the Church extending its ministry at a pace necessary to enable it to provide adequately for the rising Catholic population in the diocese. This undoubtedly contributed to the continuing strength of 'popular' religion. The account provided by Thomas Monk in 1682 suggests that the religious world view of the peasantry towards the end of the seventeenth century wove Christianity and superstition in a close and powerful synergy. They believed, for example, in the concept of an 'evell eye' and the transmigration of souls between species; were 'much given to credit charms, spells, incantacons, devinacions … [and] witchcraft', and 'worship[ped] the new moone'. At the same time, they believed that holy water was a protective against evil and possessed a strong sense of an afterlife.[75] It is not clear how strongly such beliefs were held in the eighteenth century, but it is noteworthy that when the grave of the English Jesuit Thomas Tasburgh, who came to Dublin in the 1720s, became identified with miracles 'his remains were almost carried away by the people'.[76]

Holy wells, which were by a large margin the most visible and the most important manifestation of popular religion in the eighteenth century, were also commonly identified with miracles. There were over two hundred such sites in counties Dublin and Wicklow, and while many were frequented for their curative qualities, their predominant ethos was Christian. This is highlighted by the dedication of so many wells to major figures in Irish and Christian religious history – Mary, St John, St James, St Patrick, St Brigid, St Kevin, St Colmcille – as well as to a bewildering variety of local saints. Furthermore, the religious rites performed at the patterns held at these venues during the summer months routinely involved extensive prayer. As this suggests, holy wells were an important feature of the religious calendar of many Catholics in the eighteenth century. This was especially true in rural parts where access to Church-based religion was less easy than it was in the capital, and they offer, therefore, a useful illustration as to how Christian conviction, the superstitious acceptance of the curative power of well water, and prayer delivered in a particular sequence on a designated occasion could combine to create a powerful emotional and religious sensibility.[77]

Irish mission', pp 86, 91, 100, 103-4, 105-7; Fenning, *The Irish Dominican province*, p. 373; O'Dwyer, *Irish Carmelites*, pp 149-51, 154. **75** Thomas Monk, 'A descriptive account of the county of Kildare in 1682', *Journal of the Kildare Archaeological Society*, 6 (1909-11), pp 345-6. **76** Finnegan, 'The Jesuits in Dublin', p. 75. **77** Geraldine Lynch, 'The holy wells of County Wicklow: tradition and legend' in Ken Hannigan and W. Nolan (eds), *Wicklow: history and society* (Dublin, 1994), pp 627-8; C. Ó Danachair, 'Holy wells of County Dublin', *Reportorium Novum*, 2, no. 1 (1957-8), pp 68, 70-1, 76, 80; O'Dwyer, Mary, p. 248; Donnelly, *Parishes*, part 14, p. 16.

Of course, patterns were not simply religious events. They were also occasions of ethnic and communal celebration and release. Music, singing, dancing and drinking were as central to these occasions as praying, and since it was not always possible to suspend human resentments, they led, on occasions, to drunken brawls and violent exchanges between local factions. There were also occasional clashes between revellers and the authorities, which heightened official dislike of these events.[78] In the main, Protestants perceived patterns as manifestations of religious superstition incompatible with true faith, but they also viewed them with politico-religious animus because they were distinctly Catholic occasions. Pilgrimages to holy wells were defined as 'riots and unlawful assemblies' in 1704, though there was little enthusiasm for the strict enforcement of the law on this point. Indeed, with the infamous exception of Glendalough in 1714, most patterns and pilgrimages proceeded without interference until the second half of the century when the Protestant authorities and Catholic clergy agreed that 'the enormities and scandalous excesses' associated with these events were occasions of public scandal. This led to a number of localised attempts by both to prevent the erection of beer tents and stalls, and to Sir Edward Newenham's aggressive attempt to prohibit all assembly at St Doulagh's Well near Baldoyle in 1764.[79] Though Newenham won clerical support for his efforts to clean up the St Doulagh pattern, most such festivals were too well-established to be easily eradicated. They reflected both the strength and importance of popular religion to a population which had either not yet been properly inculcated in orthodox institutional Catholicism or which found it wanting, though it was gaining ground.

IV

As befitted an archbishop who, as a curate, argued for better treatment for clergy of that rank, John Carpenter (1770-86) was an energetic pastor. One of his first decisions was to direct that church door collections should 'be divided equally' among the secular clergy to ensure all were supported with 'that decency which their character requires'. In return, he demanded a high standard of personal conduct and attention to duty from his priests:

> Those duties principally consist in breaking the bread of life to the little ones; in relieving as much as in them lies the distresses of the

---

78 Lynch, 'Holy wells of Wicklow', pp 63-31; Omurethi, 'Customs peculiar to ... County Kildare', *Journal of the Kildare Archaeological Society*, 3 (1899-1902), p. 453.   79 Above, p. 152; Brady (ed.), *Catholics in the press*, pp 85, 178-9; A.S. Mag Shamhráin, *Sir Edward Newenham* (Belcamp, 1984), p. 4.

indigent, in reclaiming after the example of our heavenly master with temper, with gentleness, and with meekness the stubborn and refractory manners; and in a word, in edifying the faithful by a decency of behaviour, sobriety of life and purity of morals.[80]

The problem for Carpenter was that not all priests shared his definition of what was proper conduct, but as the refractory parish priest of Castledermot, Randolph Byrne, and the intemperate parish priest of St Margaret's, William Fletcher, soon learned, he was unwilling to allow transgression pass unpunished. He demonstrated an equally firm hand in his dealings with the Jesuits on the suppression of that order in 1773, and with the Capuchins, whose internal dissensions caused him continuing problems. High standards were also demanded of the laity; Carpenter exhorted them to join with their priests in redressing 'scandals' and in shunning 'like a leper all those who obstinately stop their ears against the voice of God and his holy Church', and sought to give effect to his admonitions through regular visitation.[81] It is a measure of his impact and of the continuing improvement that was taking place in diocesan organisation that, following on the eight Dublin parishes that inaugurated parish registers in the diocese in the two decades before he became archbishop, those remaining in County Dublin, most of those in County Kildare and a number in Wicklow all introduced registers during his episcopate.[82]

Parallel with this, Carpenter sought actively to promote good Catholic practice. During the 1770s, when he was at his most vigorous, he admitted 42,317 people to confirmation.[83] He secured permission from Rome to grant plenary indulgences, and continued the process commenced by Dr Linegar

---

80 M.J. Curran, 'Instructions, admonitions etc of Archbishop Carpenter 1770-86', *Reportorium Novum*, 2, no. 1 (1957-8), pp 150-2.   81 Curran (ed.), 'Carpenter's instructions', pp 154-5, 158, 161-2, 168; M.J. Curran (ed.), 'Archbishop Carpenter's epistolae 1770-80, part 1', *Reportorium Novum*, 1, no. 1 (1955), pp 158, 160, 162-3; idem, 'Carpenter's epistolae 1770-80, part 2', *Reportorium Novum*, 1, no. 2 (1956), pp 384, 386-7; McRedmond, *The Irish Jesuits*, pp 121-5; O'Conor to Carpenter, 1 Sept. 1776 in Moran (ed.), *Spicilegium Ossoriense*, iii, 302.   82 The parishes that introduced registers between 1751 and 1770 were Skerries, Booterstown and Dundrum, Swords, Dun Laoghaire, Donabate and Portrane, Finglas, Lusk and St James (all Dublin). The parishes that commenced registers between 1771 and 1786 were Clondalkin and Lucan and Palmerston, Artane, Baldoyle and Howth and Kinsaley and Kilbarrack, Blanchardstown, Rathfarnham, Clontarf, Rush (County Dublin), Athy, Newbridge, Ballyna, Clane, Kilcock, Kilcullan (County Kildare) and Tomacork and Ballymore Eustace (County Wicklow).   83 However, the annual number confirmed between 1780 and 1785 was less than half that (43 per cent) confirmed in the 1770s ('Confirmations by Dr Carpenter and Dr Troy 1770-1812', *Reportorium Novum*, 1, no. 2 (1956), p. 492).

of transferring holyday obligations to alternative, less contentious days in the liturgical year.[84] More famously, he prepared 'a form of instruction, exhortation and prayer suitable for use before the Sunday parochial Mass' and, conscious of the need to provide both his priests and people with suitable devotional literature, published a missal, a catechism, diocesan statutes and other religious works.[85]

On the evidence of the 'crowded' congregations that assembled during the six-month jubilee celebrated in 1776, Carpenter's efforts can be seen to have borne fruit, but he was acutely conscious that much remained to be done. There were, as he acknowledged at the close of the jubilee, 'many in this city, who have not yet thought seriously of their conversion nor are resolved to partake of the spiritual treasures ... so abundantly offered to them'.[86] He also knew that if they were to be brought into the Church, the diocese needed more priests. Carpenter ordained over seventy priests during his episcopate, but the continuing restrictions on recruitment by the regulars combined with the growth in the Catholic population to ensure the priest-to-people ratio disimproved further.[87] Moreover, there is some evidence to suggest that the Church was not held in high regard by the poor. They certainly harboured resentment towards the practice of reserving pews for the well-off while the congregation at large was obliged to worship in crowded galleries.[88] The impact of the ill-feeling this engendered was alleviated by the increasing preparedness of the Church to encourage almsgiving, to relax the Lenten fast when famine or scarcity threatened and, on its establishment in 1773, to support the Dublin House of Industry. However, the support the priests of St Michael's parish gave the efforts of municipal and House of Industry officials to clear the streets of the indigent in 1774, and ongoing problems with beggars at chapel doors and with crime directed at priests and churches suggest that relations with the poor remained ambivalent at best.[89]

---

84 Fenning, below, p. 192; Curran (ed.), 'Carpenter's epistolae, part 1', pp 159, 160; M.J. Curran (ed.), 'Correspondence of Archbishop Carpenter with Bishop Sweetman of Ferns', *Reportorium Novum*, 1, no. 2 (1956), p. 403.   85 William Hawkes, 'Irish form of preparation for Sunday Mass in the eighteenth century', *Reportorium Novum*, 1, no. 1 (1955), pp 183-5; Fenning, below, p. 209; Curran (ed.), 'Carpenter-Sweetman corres', *Reportorium Novum*, 1, no. 2 (1956), p. 403.   86 Curran (ed.), 'Carpenter's instructions', pp 160-1; see also pp 169-70.   87 'Ordinations 1769-1785' and 'Priests returned home from studies 1770-98', *Reportorium Novum*, 1, no. 2 (1956), pp 485, 488-90. The quota of twelve laid down in 1741 was clearly not observed in Carpenter's case.   88 Brady (ed.), *Catholics in the press*, p. 145.   89 Curran (ed.), 'Carpenter's instructions', p. 153; Brady (ed.), *Catholics in the press*, pp 155, 193, 211, 223, 225-6, 230-31, 271, 275-6 234; James Kelly, 'Scarcity and poor relief: the subsistence crisis of 1782-84', *IHS*, 28 (1990); Donnelly, *Parishes*, part 8, p. 194.

It is more than a little ironic that this should be so, since Archbishop Carpenter cited poverty as the reason for his rejection of a request from the Dominicans at Louvain for permission to make a collection in the archdiocese in 1772.[90] Indeed, the irony is reinforced by the fact that though the Church was now better circumstanced financially than it had been during the reign of George I, the amount of church building that took place in the 1770s and early 1780s was less. Part of the reason for this was that the Church did not yet feel secure enough to replace its existing retiring chapels and Mass houses with more commodious churches.[91] At the same time, the construction of chapels in rural parishes such as Finglas, Balbriggan and Oldtown improved access to the sacraments in parts of the diocese hitherto poorly provided for.[92] Parallel with this, access to Catholic education improved. There was a small number of religious schools – exclusive boarding schools for girls run by Dominican, Carmelite and Augustinian nuns, and charity schools for boys run by Carmelite friars – in being for some time by 1765. They were augmented by the commencement by Teresa Mulally of her educational endeavours in 1766, and by a burgeoning in education at parish level in the 1770s and 1780s, as a result of which forty-seven parish schools provided 1700 pupils with Catholic education by 1787-8.[93]

One of the main reasons for the rapid growth in Catholic schooling was the repeal in 1782 of the 1695 and 1709 provisions against Catholic education. The fact that this took place was due in large part to the identifiable thaw in anti-Catholicism that took place among an influential section of Irish Protestant opinion in the 1770s and early 1780s. Recent writing on the repeal of the penal laws has emphasised the military and strategic concerns of the British government in ensuring their repeal,[94] but the diminution in domestic sectarian antipathy was probably of greater consequence to priests and teachers. It is in this context also that the impact of the increasing willingness of the Church to encourage the Catholic population to conduct itself with greater decorum must also be assessed.

90 Curran (ed.), 'Carpenter's epistolae, part 1', p. 158; see also Mark Tierney (ed.), 'Butler Papers', *Collectanea Hibernica*, 18 & 19 (1976-7), p. 116.   91 It is noteworthy that the Dominicans of Bridge Street rebuilt their chapel completely in 1771. I wish to thank Father Hugh Fenning for this information.   92 Donnelly, *Parishes*, part 9, p. 224; part 15, p. 76; part 16, pp 125-6; part 17, pp 155-6, 170; *Journal of the Kildare Archaeological Society* 7 (1912-14), p. 330.   93 Patrick Fagan, *The second city: Dublin 1700-60* (Dublin, 1986), p. 30; O'Dwyer, *Irish Carmelites*, p. 161; Rosemary Raughter, 'Female charity as an aspect of Catholic resurgence 1750-1800', *Pages*, 1 (1994), pp 30-35; Ward, *Encyclopaedia of Irish education*, p. 182; J. Brady, 'Catholic schools in Dublin in 1787-8', *Reportorium Novum*, 1 (1955), pp 193-6.   94 Thomas Bartlett, *The fall and rise of the Irish nation: the Catholic question 1690-1830* (Dublin, 1992), pp 72-5, 82-6; R.Kent Donovan, 'The military origins of the Roman Catholic relief programme of 1778', *Historical Journal*, 28 (1985), pp 79-102.

Though they had called publicly on Catholics not to engage 'in any riot or tumult' as early as 1729, it was not until the 1750s (during the episcopacy of John Linegar) that the Catholic clergy of Dublin intervened routinely to exhort 'those of our communion from joyning in riots'. It is difficult to assess what impact, if any, appeals of this kind made in 1748, 1750, 1752, 1754, 1755, 1759, 1760, 1762, 1764, 1772, 1775, 1779 and 1780 had on the behaviour of the Catholic populace, but the clergy maintained that their 'instructions ... always made a just impression'.[95] What is less problematic is that the reiteration of the message contained in the instruction of Archbishop Lincoln in 1762 that 'the law of God and your religion command you, in the strongest and most explicit terms, to be faithful, dutiful and obedient to the powers and governors, His vicegerents, which the Omnipotent has placed before you' contributed to the improvement in the way in which the Catholic Church was perceived.[96] Arising out of this, there were a number of contacts between the vice-regal court and the archbishop of Dublin in the 1760s, but both Archbishop Fitzsimons and Archbishop Carpenter's doctrinal unease with the oath of allegiance demanded of Catholics ensured that they were not continued.[97]

Carpenter's disinclination to deal with the state ensured that he was eclipsed politically by James Butler the second, the gallican-minded archbishop of Cashel, though illness may account for the fact that he played no part in the events that resulted in 1782 in the ratification of two Catholic relief acts that effectively freed the Church from all but a handful of the sanctions and restrictions introduced in the 1690s and 1700s.[98] By these acts, secular clergy were afforded legal recognition provided they took the 1774 oath (which most priests in the diocese of Dublin had already done),[99] while regulars were permitted to minister without penalty so long as they registered with the state. This was not liked, but in common with the retention of sanctions against the conversion of Protestants, and bans on the addition of steeples or bells to

95 Brady (ed.), *Catholics in the press*, pp 49, 67-8, 76, 78, 80, 87, 88, 89, 103-4, 109-10, 143-4, 172, 204-5; *Universal Advertiser*, 15 Sept. 1759, 1 Mar. 1760; Sean Murphy, 'The Dublin anti-union riot of December 1759 in Gerard O'Brien (ed.), *Parliament, politics and people* (Dublin, 1989), pp 57-8; *Public Gazetteer*, 26 Jan. 1762.   96 *Public Gazetteer*, 20 Feb. 1762.   97 Curran (ed.), 'Carpenter-Sweetman correspondence', pp 403-04; idem (ed.), 'Carpenter's epistolae, part 2', pp 401, 381-4; Giblin (ed.), 'Fiandra, part 7', pp 66-7; Giblin (ed.), 'Fiandra, part 6', pp 129-30; Fenning, below, pp 212-13.   98 E. O'Flaherty, 'Ecclesiastical politics and the dismantling of the penal laws in Ireland 1774-82', *IHS*, 26 (1988), pp 33-50; Maureen Wall, 'The making of Gardiner's relief act, 1781-2' in G. O'Brien (ed.), *Collected essays of Maureen Wall*, pp 135-45; Bartlett, *Fall and rise of the Irish nation*, pp 98-101.   99 Carpenter and eighty-two priests of the diocese took the oath in 1778 ('A list of ecclesiastics who took the oath of allegiance', *Archivium Hibernicum*, 1 (1912), pp 54-65).

Catholic churches and chapels, on Catholic priests officiating at funerals, on the public wearing of vestments and the assumption of ecclesiastical ranks and titles, it proved more of an inconvenience than a hindrance. The stipulation that Catholics could only establish schools under license from the Protestant ordinary was unwelcome, but since it also represented an improvement on the existing situation, Catholics were prepared to work with the regulation.[100]

The repeal of the bulk of the penal legislation against the Catholic religion in 1782 meant that the penal era neared its end as far as the clergy were concerned. Further concessions in respect of education were granted in 1792, but, in practice, neither these changes nor those sanctioned in 1782 made a decisive difference to the work of the Church. Symbolically, the most significant development of these years was the decision to appoint John Thomas Troy (1786-1823), a Dominican, to succeed Carpenter on his death in 1786, since prior to 1782 regulars had had no legal right even to be in the country. Troy's appointment did not pass unnoticed in Protestant circles, but though the mid-1780s witnessed a conservative Protestant revival of some consequence, those Protestants who favoured the reimposition of the penal laws were in a small minority.[101] They were not entirely without influence, but they were more than counterbalanced by the readiness of some Church of Ireland clergy and laity to attend charity sermons in Catholic churches in the 1780s and 1790s, and by the financial support provided to some hard-pressed Catholic parishes by 'enlightened' Protestants.[102]

As befitted a skilled politician and pastor, Troy took advantage of the improved denominational atmosphere and the dilution of the penal laws to reclaim the leadership of the Catholic Church for the diocese of Dublin, as well as to develop the Church in the diocese.[103] At the same time, he was as anxious as his predecessors to do nothing that would provide Protestants with cause to contemplate either enforcing the existing penal laws or introducing new ones. In this context, it is instructive that he justified his appeal to Catholics not to attend the annual pattern to St John's Well, Kilmainham in 1787 on the grounds that it would 'scandalise their holy religion and disturb public peace'. He also supported a request to the Holy See in 1788 to revoke

---

100 Wall, 'Gardiner's relief act', pp 141-3; 22 George III, c. 62. 101 H.E. Peel, 'The appointment of Dr Troy to the see of Dublin', *Reportorium Novum*, 4, no. 1 (1971), pp 5-17; James Kelly, 'The genesis of "protestant ascendancy": the Rightboy disturbances of the 1780s and their impact upon protestant opinion' in O'Brien (ed.), *Parliament, politics and people*, pp 93-127. 102 Brady (ed.), *Catholics in the press*, pp 231, 249, 278, 279, 280-2, 293-4. 103 Fenning (ed.), 'Fondo missioni', pp 44, 45; V.J. MacNally, *Reform, revolution and reaction: Archbishop John Thomas Troy and the Catholic Church in Ireland 1787-1817* (Lanham, 1995); Dáire Keogh, *'The French disease': the Catholic Church and radicalism in Ireland 1790-1800* (Dublin, 1993).

its 'censure of excommunication against freemasons' on the grounds that its implementation would oblige the Church to condemn politicians and officials whose goodwill they wanted.[104] Troy's pragmatism was further demonstrated the following year when, following consultation with his priests, he declined to promulgate the relevant 'decree of Trent' on marriage, though the number of clandestine, mixed and precipitous marriages being performed in the diocese was a cause of concern, because it was likely to provoke difficulties with the state as well as resistance from the poor and marginalised whose lax practices were the main source of clerical anxiety. Instead, he took the softer option of directing that 'contracting parties should be married by their pastor only' and that 'couple beggars' should be automatically excommunicated.[105]

Troy's acceptance of the advice of his senior clergy not to promulgate Tridentine law on marriage indicates that a culture of caution continued to pervade the Church as the end of the eighteenth century approached. This was a direct consequence of operating for nearly a century with the penal laws. At the same time, as his critical response to the oaths formulated for English Catholics in the early 1790s attests, Troy refused to compromise on matters of doctrine or in his loyalty to Rome.[106] This might have caused a less politically adroit pastor problems, but as the attendance in April 1789 of several peers and gentlemen (including the duke of Leinster, the earl of Tyrone, Henry Grattan and David Latouche) at the 'solemn thanksgiving' held in the Francis Street chapel in honour of the recovery from illness of George III indicates, Troy was a shrewd judge of the temper of the times.[107]

Of greater consequence for the near 400,000 Catholics Troy estimated in 1802 were in the archdiocese of Dublin was the improvement of the Church. Progress continued to be made. This is well demonstrated by reference to the introduction of parish registers in the outstanding rural parishes, the break-up in 1787 of the unwieldy south Dublin parish of Donnybrook, Booterstown and Dundrum, the construction or refurbishment of chapels in towns like Arklow and Stratford-on-Slaney in County Wicklow and Skerries in County Dublin, and churches and parochial residences in other areas in need.[108] It is further indicated by the increased availability of religious publications, the activities of the Confraternity of Christian

104 Brady (ed.), *Catholics in the press*, p. 256; M. Tierney (ed.), 'Papers of James Butler, part 2', *Collectanea Hibernica* 20 (1976), p. 93.   105 Clandestine Marriage enquiry, 1788 (Dublin Diocesan Archives (hencefort DDA), Troy Papers); 'Archbishop Troy's pastoral on clandestine marriages, 1789', *Reportorium Novum*, 1, no. 2 (1956), pp 481-5.   106 Tierney (ed.), 'Butler papers, part 2', p. 97; Moran (ed.), *Spicilegium Ossoriense*, iii, 425-32.   107 Brady (ed.), *Catholics in the press*, pp 266-7.   108 Brady (ed.), *Catholics in the press*, pp 234, 278, 293-4; Donnelly, *Parishes*, part 6 (iii), pp 78-9; part 3, pp 105-7; part 1, pp 19-22; part 16 p. 120.

Doctrine, the availability of Benediction and the greater recourse to choirs and organ music in church services.[109]

Parallel with this, the Church in the archdiocese became visibly more active providing aid and welfare to those on the margins of society. At a basic level this took the well-established form of donations to the Society for the relief and release of poor confined debtors, or charity sermons to raise funds for schools or the House of Industry.[110] But the Church also displayed a disposition to engage in the direct provision of care. Prior to 1780, its efforts in this respect were primarily aimed at providing for orphans (the Patrician Orphan Society (*c.*1750) and the Virgo Maria Orphan Society (1769) operated in Dublin and North Wicklow respectively). This remained a key challenge, as the foundation of the Denmark St Orphan and Daily school in 1785 and the Josephinian Orphan Society in 1797 attests, but the establishment of a Widow's House (1792) and two Magdalene Asylums in 1780 and 1791 indicated that the Church was eager to expand into other areas as well.[111]

If this suggests that the Church was fast leaving the difficulties of the penal era behind it, there was another less reassuring dimension to its mission. In a number of city centre and rural parishes, the combination of an impoverished laity and a shortage of chapels and curates, which obliged priests in areas like Loughlinstown and Dundrum in Dublin and Rathdrum in County Wicklow to attempt ministries beyond the capacity of an individual to sustain, meant that there was a section of the Catholic population that continued to have little contact with and which only gave conditional allegiance to the Church. This was highlighted by the reports on clandestine marriage conveyed to Archbishop Troy in 1788 which reveal that there was a substantial body of people who did not feel bound by the law of the Church if it was personally inconvenient.[112]

One cannot say that this situation would not have existed had the penal laws not been enacted. What is certain is that both the condition of the Church in the diocese of Dublin and the circumstances in which it operated were dramatically different as the end of the eighteenth century approached from what they had been a century earlier. This is highlighted by the fact

109 Wall, *Dr Hay's head*, passim; O'Dwyer, *Mary*, pp 247-8; Fenning (ed.), 'The Udienze series', p. 104; Brady, *Catholics in the press*, pp 261, 284, 286-7. 110 Brady (ed.), *Catholics in the press*, pp 234, 256-7, 285, 291, 295. 111 O'Dwyer, *Mary*, p. 248; 'The Catholic Directory for 1821', *Reportorium Novum*, 2, no. 2 (1959-60), pp 341, 348, 333-4; *The Catholic Directory for 1845* (Dublin, 1845), pp 234-5; Raughter, 'Female charity', pp 26-8. 112 W.M. O'R[iordan], 'Curates in the archdiocese of Dublin 1797-1824', *Reportorium Novum*, 4, no. 1 (1971), p. 161; Redmond, 'Notes on ... Rathdrum', p. 195; Donnelly, *Parishes*, part 8, p. 180; part 5, pp 205, 207-9; part 3, p. 109; part 4, pp 151-2; Clandestine marriage enquiry, 1788 (DDA, Troy Papers).

that in 1795 the religious highlight of the year was a 'solemn High Mass' attended by most of the Catholic hierarchy of the country; such an event could simply not have been held in the capital in 1695 or at most points in between.[113] At the same time, the fact that the 1795 ceremony was held in a chapel rather than in a cathedral, and that it was in honour of the state's decision to allow the Catholic Church to establish a domestic seminary, indicates that the Church had still some way to go before it put behind it the experience of repression and legacy of deference produced by the penal laws.

V

In the light of this conclusion, the two dominant historiographical views of the penal laws – the Catholic and secular interpretations – are both in need of modification. The Catholic view is eminently represented in the case of the diocese of Dublin by Nicholas Donnelly, Reginald Walsh and Myles Ronan.[114] They portray the laws as a draconian and systematic initiative to undermine the Church, and maintain that they failed in this object because of the zealous attachment of the population to their religion and the determination of their priests and bishops both to withstand persecution and to endure privation in the name of their faith. This has been criticised for exaggerating the capacity of the state to undermine, and the vigour of the Church. However, the depiction of the penal laws as an *ad hoc* political response to Protestant fears and the claim that their anti-Catholicism is overstated is also open to objection, because it does not fully acknowledge their anti-Catholic intent or the extent and duration of their impact.[115] Certainly, the experience of the Catholic Church in the diocese of Dublin during the eighteenth century reveals a complex and variegated picture of toleration as well as disruptive repression; of self-inflicted as well as state-generated difficulties. It is hardly surprising then that the Church did not minister confidently or comprehensively throughout the diocese during what is problematically termed the 'penal era'; but it is also true that this was not an era of extreme or sustained repression.[116]

---

113 Brady (ed.), *Catholics in the press*, p. 296.   114 For Donnelly and Walsh see notes above; Myles Ronan, *An apostle of Catholic Dublin: Father Henry Young* (Dublin, 1944). 115 This viewpoint has received its firmest exposition in S.J. Connolly, *Religion, law and power: the making of Protestant Ireland 1660-1760* (Oxford, 1992), pp 263-78.   116 I would like to thank Father Hugh Fenning for his comments on an earlier draft of this paper.

8

The archbishops of Dublin, 1693-1786

Hugh Fenning

When writing in 1838 on the archbishops of Dublin, John D'Alton devoted only forty rather insubstantial pages to the eighteenth century. Although some of the eight prelates who ruled the see of Dublin during that time have since found better biographers, three of the more important – Linegar, Lincoln and Fitzsimons – are still hardly more than passing shadows on the printed page. What follows is a short account of each of the eight archbishops in turn. The emphasis here will be on their family background, so far as that is known, their education, characters and careers. If, in the process, a little light is thrown on broader themes, so much the better, but that will only be incidentally.[1]

For the Catholics of Dublin, this period began ominously with 'the breach of the Boyne' in 1690. King William's victory immediately overturned their modest political and social standing in the capital. From having been, ironically, the loyalists of their time, they were left practically outcasts in their own land by the successful 'Glorious Revolution' against James II. John Linegar, a clerical student of the diocese, wrote from his college at Lisbon to a friend in Rome describing the disastrous situation in Ireland as he had witnessed it in February 1691.[2] The letter has particular interest, for the young writer would end his days as archbishop of Dublin. Shortly after Linegar wrote to Rome, Archbishop Patrick Russell, worn out by his trials as a fugitive and occasional prisoner, died 'in a filthy undergound prison cell'[3] in the late summer of 1692 and was buried at Lusk.[4]

---

1 The basic and best history of the diocese is that by C. Mooney, 'Dublin', in *Dictionnaire d'Histoire et de Géographie Ecclésiastiques*, xiv (1960), cc 830-936. This article, in effect a book, is enriched by several excellent bibliographies. Even Mooney, however has little to say (cc 880-83) about the archbishops discussed here. 2 Linegar to Thomas Eustace, 19 Mar. 1692 in N. Donnelly, *A short history of some Dublin parishes, 17 parts* (Dublin, 1904-17) (henceforth, Donnelly, *Parishes*), part 12, pp 81-2. 3 James Lynch, archbishop of Tuam, to Propaganda, 28 Oct. 1692, quoted by O.J. Burke, *History of the Catholic archbishops of Tuam* (Dublin, 1882), p. 186. 4 D. McCarthy (ed.), *Collections on Irish Church*

From the safety of Paris, James II exercised one of his few remaining pre-
rogatives by nominating a new archbishop of Dublin. His choice fell on Peter
Creagh, bishop of Cork and Cloyne, who happened to be in Paris at the time.[5]
Creagh was accordingly translated to the see of Dublin in March 1693, but
never in fact returned to Ireland. By 1694, he was auxiliary bishop in the
diocese of Strasbourg in Alsace and there ended his days in 1705. No one
could doubt his distinguished birth as one of the Creaghs of Carrigeen,
County Limerick, nor his long experience at Limerick, at Rome and for thirteen years as bishop of Cork and Cloyne. He had even spent two years in
prison and narrowly escaped joining St Oliver Plunkett on the scaffold. Yet
it was either unrealistic or unduly optimistic in 1693 to expect a prelate of
fifty-three to leave the safety and comfort of the continent to settle down in
Dublin, where his predecessor had died in prison six months before and the
political clouds grew darker all the time.

Nonetheless Archbishop Creagh did take possession of his see and ruled
it *in absentia* through John Dempsey, his procurator general. Dempsey, only
a few years younger than Creagh, was also of noble birth, being one of the
Dempseys of Clanmalier. After studies at Paris, he became parish priest of
St Michan about 1670 and precentor of Christ Church by 1688. Although
promoted in 1694 to the diocese of Kildare and Leighlin, he retained the
parish of St Michan and stayed in the city. By 1697 he was living in Church
Street with the widow of Maximilian O'Dempsey, last lord viscount of
Clanmalier. From a Protestant clergy-list, also of 1697, one can see that his
real status was not quite unsuspected: 'John Dempsey ... said to be a titular
bishop.'[6] It is reasonable to suppose that he had been made a bishop not so
much for the sake of Kildare as for the sake of the capital. When all the bishops, Church dignitaries and friars of Ireland were ordered to leave the country, as most of them did, in 1698, John Dempsey stayed where he was, ostensibly parish priest of St Michan's, but bishop (of Kildare) and ruler of the
archdiocese. When all parish priests were required to register in 1704,
Dempsey allowed Cornelius Nary to register for St Michan's. He himself
registered as parish priest of Kilraney, County Kildare, and died soon after
in the summer of 1706.[7]

history from the mss of ... L.F. Renehan (Dublin, 1861), pp 233-4.   5 The best account
of Peter Creagh is by E. Bolster, *A history of the diocese of Cork from the Reformation to
the penal era* (Cork, 1982), pp 265-86. This refers to and improves on the earlier work of
C. Mooney.   6 Donnelly, *Parishes*, part 6, p. 35; part 11, pp 49-50. Also Donnelly, 'The
diocese of Dublin in the year 1697', *Irish Ecclesiastical Record* (henceforth *IER*), third
series, 9 (1888), p. 412. Dempsey's status emerges much more clearly from a long and
later letter (3 Feb. 1729/30) from Cornelius Nary to Benedict XIII, now in the archives
of San Clemente, Rome (hereafter SCAR), Codex I, vol. 2, ff 249-50.   7 Word of
Dempsey's death had reached Paris by 3 Sept. 1706 (SCAR, Codex I, vol. 3, f. 543). His

There was therefore, from 1694 to 1704, a resident bishop in Dublin with delegated authority over people and clergy. There was also a vicar general, Edmund Murphy, to whom Archbishop Creagh in 1699 gave full authority in matters spiritual.[8] Murphy, whom we shall meet again as archbishop, was of course subject to Dempsey the procurator. Living as they did in constant danger of transportation or imprisonment, both bishop and vicar general were extremely careful not to be discovered exercising 'popish jurisdiction', and managed the archdiocese between them in the worst of times. No doubt, they sometimes visited the many friars and priests then lying in the filthy prisons of Dublin. By 1706, Edmund Murphy alone manned the helm as vicar general, awaiting the appointment of an archbishop. A curious protest of this time, made by the 'pastors of Dublin', shows that the friars had begun to return from exile and that secular priests from other parts had come unbidden to the city:

> These libertines ... do gather great congregations in stables, yards and waste houses ... having some sordid lucre in view ... whereby they bring the indignation of the government upon the whole body of the Catholics, who take a handle at our own indiscretion to execute the laws against us.[9]

At this time, Dublin was by modern standards quite a small city of some 90,000 people, of whom about 30,000 were Catholics, cramped into narrow lanes and alleys well inside the area enclosed by the present North and South Circular Roads. Whatever happened 'in stables, yards and waste houses' was quickly known to all, but the natural ties of blood, friendship and commerce between Catholic and Protestant played some part in softening the application of penal laws.

Having heard towards the end of 1706 that the aged archbishop of Cashel was 'perhaps' the only bishop in the whole of Ireland, the Roman authorities began at once to restore the hierarchy by naming several new bishops in 1707.[10] Among them was a new archbishop of Dublin: not, strangely enough,

---

will (12 July 1703) has been published by Carrigan in *Archivium Hibernicum*, 4 (1915), pp 80-2. Dempsey was still procurator of the absent archbishop Creagh in 1704, but surely lost that status on Creagh's death on 20 June 1705.   8 According to J. Meagher, writing in *Reportorium Novum*, 3, no. 2 (1964), p. 386, the original of Murphy's appointment was then in Dublin Diocesan Archives (hereafter DDA). It is not there now.   9 Quoted by P. Fagan, *Dublin's turbulent priest: Cornelius Nary, 1658-1738* (Dublin, 1991), p. 39. The original, known as 'Dr Byrne's Constitutions, 1712', is in DDA, 116/1 (71).   10 H. Fenning, 'The three kingdoms: England, Ireland and Scotland' in J. Metzler (ed.), *Sacrae Congregationis de Propaganda Fide Memoria Rerum* (Freiburg, 1973), 2, pp 605-6.

the vicar general Edmund Murphy, who would have to wait his turn, but Edmund Byrne, parish priest of St Nicholas in Francis Street. The ceremony of consecration, in some locked chapel or private room within the city, was performed by the bishop of Dromore who providentially had just emerged from prison in Dublin itself. His accusers had failed to prove in court that he was in fact a bishop.[11]

Archbishop Byrne, born about 1655 in Ballybrack, a townland in the present parish of Borris, County Carlow, was of respectable and once wealthy Wicklow stock.[12] At least some of his immediate family, however, moved to Dublin within his own lifetime. In 1672 he sailed for Spain to study at the Irish college in Seville where he was ordained in 1679 and stayed on for a short while to teach.[13] After taking his doctorate in 1681, he returned to Dublin where the archbishop, Peter Talbot, had recently died in the Castle, a victim of calculated neglect. Things could only improve, and for a short while they did. By 1688, Edmund Byrne was a member of the chapter and parish priest in Francis Street, a position he was to occupy until his consecration.

Throughout his episcopate, from 1707 to 1723, Edmund Byrne was harassed by government proclamations, priest-catchers and informers eager for reward. Since it has become fashionable to say that the penal laws against the clergy were seldom enforced, it may be as well to explain why the archbishop was chiefly concerned 'in rendering himself invisible'.[14] In March 1708, when fears of a French invasion led to the proclamation of thirty-one priests in Dublin, Seán Ó Neachtain wrote a poem in Irish on six who were then prisoners in the Black Dog.[15] The year 1709 brought an act of parliament offering handsome rewards for the discovery of friars and persons (like Edmund Byrne) exercising ecclesiastical jurisdiction. Fifty pounds was the sum offered for a bishop. Worse still, all priests, whether registered or not, had to take an oath of abjuration declaring that the son of James II had no right or title to the throne. Only thirty-three priests in the entire country

---

11 Archives of Propaganda Fide, Rome (hereafter APF), Acta 77 (1707), f. 162; *Scritture originali riferite nelle congregazioni generali* (hereafter SOCG) 559, ff 13-16.   12 J. Meagher, 'Edmond Byrne (1656-1723), archbishop of Dublin: part 1', *Reportorium Novum*, 3, no. 2 (1964), pp 378-86. The second part of this article was never published. There is an excellent account of Archbishop Byrne by J. H., 'The one before', *Catholic Bulletin*, 11, no. 10 (Oct. 1921), pp 603-15.   13 His portrait, long preserved in the college, has unfortunately been lost.   14 The phrase is that of Donnelly, *Parishes*, part 6, p. 39. There are many other interesting details here (pp 38-48) on Archbishop Byrne's career.   15 T. Ó Fiaich, 'Dán ar an Chléir i bpríosúin i mBaile Atha Cliath, 1708', *Reportorium Novum*, 2, no. 1 (1958), pp 172-84. The poet Ó Neachtain was related by marriage to Archbishop Byrne. See Nessa Ní Sheaghdha, 'Irish scholars and scribes in eighteenth-century Dublin', *Eighteenth-Century Ireland*, 4 (1989), pp 41-54.

took this oath; all the rest, even the registered priests of 1704, lost whatever legal standing they had. In practice, however, the registered priests did retain a certain local acceptance denied to others newly come to the country or 'of no fixed abode'.

Archbishop Byrne went into hiding in 1709, on hearing that an informer threatened to have him and forty other priests arrested. The chapels in Dublin shut their doors from March to July 1710. Sixteen priests in Newgate awaited transportation in May but were released on bail on 28 July. The chapels opened again, but only between four and five in the morning.[16] There was another bout of persecution between September and December 1712 occasioned by the arrival in Dublin of Franciscan nuns from Galway. A proclamation for Dr Byrne's arrest encouraged him to withdraw to his native Borris in Carlow, while the priest-hunter Edward Tyrrell galloped about searching for him in Kildare, Wicklow and Drogheda.[17] Tyrrell also combed the house of 'one Byrne, a cooper, in Francis Street' but found 'only some old accounts of hoops and barrels'.[18] The Jesuit superior of the time wrote to the continent:

> All chapels have been closed, the pastors put to flight and laymen in some places brought to the courts to swear what priest's Mass they have heard in six months, in what place and who was present; part of their goods is to be confiscated if they refuse to answer ... I have asked that none of ours be sent [from abroad] until this raging storm calms.[19]

During another 'storm' in 1714, the chapels had to close again and the pilgrimage at Glendalough was broken up by a mounted group of officials and local gentry.[20] In October 1716, the collapse of two galleries in Cook Street chapel occasioned a proclamation by the lords justices and the brief imprisonment of both Dr Byrne and the bishop of Ossory, Malachy Dulany.[21] The archbishop's final brush with the law came in 1718 when he and seven

16 G. O'Brien (ed.), *Catholic Ireland in the eighteenth century: collected essays of Maureen Wall* (Dublin 1989), pp 15-16, 18; P. Moran (ed.), *Spicilegium Ossoriense* (3 vols, Dublin, 1874-84), ii, 413; R. Walsh, 'Glimpses of the penal times – part 10', *IER*, 28 (Oct. 1910), pp 377-78; also 'Glimpses of the penal times – part 13', ibid., 30 (Oct. 1911), pp 369-87 passim.   17 S.J. Connolly, *Religion, law and power: the making of Protestant Ireland* (Oxford, 1992), p. 278; W.P. Burke, *Irish priests in the penal times: 1660-1760* (Waterford 1914), pp 298-99.   18 DDA, 116/1 (72). Quoted by J. Meagher, 'Edmund Byrne', pp 385-86.   19 F. Finegan, 'The Jesuits in Dublin, 1660-1760', *Reportorium Novum*, 4, no. 1 (1965-71), p. 73.   20 Wall, *Catholic Ireland*, p. 52.   21 Santini at Brussels to Propaganda, 17 Dec. 1716 (APF, Scritture riferite nei congressi (hereafter SC), Anglia 2, ff 157-58). Dublin newspapers carried an account of the chapel accident and the full text of the proclamation (J. Brady, *Catholics and catholicism in the eighteenth-century press* (Maynooth 1965), pp 25-7).

priests were arrested on the information of a Portuguese Jew, John Garcia, who posed as a priest to collect his evidence. Dr Byrne was released on bail but when he finally appeared in court, Garcia was unaccountably absent. The authorities had, it seems, detained their chief and only witness to avoid awkward political consequences. The archbishop walked out of court a free man and had no further trouble with the law, even though again identified by Garcia in a report of 1722: 'In a chapel in Francis Street, Doctor Burn papist archbishop and primate of Ireland.'[22]

This was the unhelpful setting in which Edmund Byrne took care of the diocese and kept an eye on some broader issues affecting the Irish Church. In 1707 he established two new parishes north of the Liffey where for centuries there had been only one. The old parish of St Michan's was now divided into three by the creation of St Paul's to the west and St Mary's to the east. There was still, however, only the one chapel of St Michan's in Mary's Lane which the three parish priests shared until 1729. Among the assistant priests of that chapel, from as early as 1713, were two or three Jesuits who conducted a classical school. Once the students became proficient in Latin, they were directed to the 'seminary' of Father John Harold who taught philosophy and theology in the city.

A brief but revealing set of diocesan regulations appeared in 1712; the text is undated and prudently unsigned.[23] They open with a declaration of intent: to prevent imprudent or over-zealous priests from attracting the attention of magistrates. Nowhere is the archbishop's existence implied; each of the six rules depends simply on the consent of one or more parish priests. Their permission is required for the celebration of Mass in a disused chapel, for the employment of an assistant priest, and whenever more than two priests are to say Mass on the one day in the same house or private room. Pastors are warned not to baptise or marry outside their own parishes. Those who are not pastors are forbidden to hear confessions or administer the sacraments without permission. Since the laws of the state render it impossible to implement Church constitutions and canons, there has been 'a relaxation and total neglect of ecclesiastical discipline'. Finally, any priest transgressing these rules is hereby declared unfit for priestly duties.

A few accidental references show that Archbishop Byrne carried out visitation of the diocese. In 1709 he strayed beyond it, to consecrate a chapel

---

22 The list, compiled for Archbishop William King, is given in full by K. McGrath, 'John Garzia, a noted priest-catcher and his activities, 1717-23', *IER*, 72 (1949), pp 494-514; also in Spanish by J. Brady, 'John Garzia's report on the Catholic clergy of Dublin in 1722', *Reportorium Novum*, 2, no. 1 (1958), pp 217-19. There would have been more 'priest-catchers' had it not been such a dangerous occupation. See P. Fagan, 'The Dublin Catholic mob (1700-1750)', *Eighteenth-Century Ireland*, 4 (1989), pp 133-42.   23 Latin text from DDA in Moran (ed.), *Spicilegium Ossoriense*, iii, 128-9.

for Captain Edmund Byrne in his native Borris where a stone marking the occasion displays the family coat of arms.[24] When troubled by Garcia in 1718, the archbishop was 'forced to break off his visitation in country parts'.[25] Even in 1723, the last year of Dr Byrne's long life, a Protestant pamphleteer complained that he was 'going constantly and publicly his visitations with his chaise and retinue without any question or interruption'.[26] Naturally, he also administered the sacrament of confirmation, on one occasion to a boy named Thomas Burke who later became bishop of Ossory and mentioned the detail in his book *Hibernia Dominicana*.[27] Dr Byrne also encouraged the religious orders within the city. The friars and Jesuits drifted back of their own accord, as they were entitled to do, from as early as 1707, but it was the archbishop who invited the Franciscan nuns in 1712 and the Dominican nuns in 1717; both groups came from Galway. They supported themselves by running boarding-schools for the daughters of the landed gentry.

The archbishop took a natural interest in the appointment of bishops within the province of Leinster, recommending likely candidates to Rome and sometimes consecrating the bishops-elect in Dublin itself. In February 1714 he consecrated Malachy Dulany as bishop of Ossory.[28] He also consecrated his own vicar general Edward Murphy as bishop of Kildare and Leighlin in December 1715; Dr Byrne had recommended Murphy at least twice for that diocese.[29] Two western bishops were later consecrated at Dublin: Edmund Kelly of Clonfert in May 1718 and Francis Burke of Kilmacduagh in May 1720. The latter, certainly, was consecrated by Archbishop Byrne.[30]

The fact that the archbishop had no legal status, and was liable to transportation on discovery, made it dangerous for him to sign any document and correspondingly difficult to resolve clerical disputes. Appointment to a particular parish, for instance, could not be given in writing, and this factor alone proved enough to ignite a long and serious controversy. In 1719 a priest named Valentine Rivers, then merely administrator of St Catherine's parish in Meath Street, claimed to be its parish priest. When Dr Byrne rejected the claim, Rivers appealed to Hugh MacMahon, archbishop of Armagh, who was only too happy to accept the appeal in order to demonstrate his jurisdiction over Dublin.[31] MacMahon went so far as to send some of his own northern

---

24 Meagher, 'Edmund Byrne', p. 380, with illustration on opposite page.   25 Moran (ed.), *Spicilegium Ossoriense*, iii, 132.   26 Fagan, *Cornelius Nary*, pp 114, 139.   27 T. de Burgo, *Supplementum Hiberniae Dominicanae* (n. p., 1772), p. 818, n. (e).   28 APF, Congregazioni Particolari (hereafter CP) 34B, f. 176. In 1713, Dr Byrne had recommended Bernard Dunne for Ossory (APF, SOCG 589, ff 277-78).   29 APF, SC Irlanda 7, f. 498. For the recommendations see APF, CP 34b, ff 214-15; SOCG 589, ff 277-78.   30 APF, SC Irlanda 9, ff 3-4; 8, ff 37-38.   31 There is a full discussion of the 'Rivers Controversy'

priests to help Rivers in the capital. On the other hand, Dr Byrne felt obliged to excommunicate Rivers. This sorry and most complicated story brings two aspects of Edmund Byrne's character into strong relief: his absolute resolve to defend the primatial rights of the see of Dublin, and the meekness with which he made peace with Rivers after four years of painful dispute. On 4 May 1723, the archbishop wrote feelingly to Rome:

> In this case I have laid aside all semblance of episcopal authority, and have arranged all peacefully, accepting laws and conditions from him [Rivers] who had promised obedience to me ... One thing I ask the Sacred Congregation to grant, that it impose silence on the pretensions of Armagh, and command that it shall not presume to busy itself about this diocese by entertaining appeals therefrom.

There is only one instance of Archbishop Byrne's concern for problems outside Ireland. For the training of priests, the mission depended on foreign colleges, among them the Irish College at Bordeaux which in 1721 was being monopolised by the clergy of Munster. Edmund Byrne signed a protest, with the archbishops of Armagh and Tuam, explaining to Cardinal Imperiali that while the Irish Church was being 'attacked right and left at home', it now had to suffer at the hands of the officials of the college at Bordeaux who 'seek what is their own and not what is of Jesus Christ.'[32]

Other troubles and disappointments clouded the archbishop's last few years. He was closely concerned with the publication of Nary's *New Testament* in 1718, and disappointed in 1720 when the book was withdrawn at the request of the papal nuncio at Brussels. Two years later, he applied with some other bishops for definitive approval of Nary's work, insisting that the Rhemish version was so old as to be incomprehensible, and that people were using Protestant bibles for want of better.[33] Nary himself, on Archbishop Byrne's advice, asked Rome whether he might not publish the Rhemes version and his own in parallel columns.[34] The archbishop also recommended in 1722 Sylvester Lloyd's translation of the unorthodox Montpellier catechism which aroused intense controversy among the clergy of Dublin until it was banned by the Holy Office in 1725.[35]

in Donnelly, *Parishes*, part 9, pp 218-21. For a more recent account, see Laurence J. Flynn, 'Hugh MacMahon ... archbishop of Armagh, 1715-37', *Seanchas Ard Mhacha*, 7, no. 1 (1973), pp 153-57.   **32** Signed also by Kildare, Ossory, Achonry and Meath on 28 Apr. 1721 (APF, SC Irlanda 8, ff 616-17). The quotation is from St Paul, Phil. 2:21.   **33** 14 Aug. 1722, APF, SC Irlanda 8, ff 142-43.   **34** Nary to Spinelli, 30 Apr. 1723 (APF, SC Irlanda 8, f. 146). The whole question of Nary's translation is fully discussed by Fagan, *Cornelius Nary*, pp 79-91.   **35** The controversy is discussed at length by P. Fagan, *An*

According to the register of the Irish College at Seville, Archbishop Byrne died on 27 December 1723 at the age of sixty-nine.[36] At least two Gaelic poets resident in Dublin wrote elegies on his death.[37] Some of his immediate family are mentioned in his will: his brothers Henry and Richard, his brother-in-law Richard Barry and a nephew, Edmund Barry, doctor of physick. His library he bequeathed to 'Thomas Power of the City of Dublin, Esq.'[38] As to Dr Byrne's place of burial, there are two opinions: he was laid to rest either, as tradition claims, at Kiltennel, County Carlow, or in the grave of Sir Toby Butler in St James' graveyard, Dublin.

Differences among the clergy, particularly within the chapter, delayed and to some extent influenced the translation of Edward Murphy, bishop of Kildare, to the see of Dublin in September 1724. Being already in poor health and about seventy-four years old at the time, he had evidently been chosen as a caretaker. As for his career, we know that he was born in Balrothery, north of Lusk, about 1651, studied at Salamanca, was ordained in the Escorial at Madrid in 1677, and in 1685 acted as secretary to a provincial synod in Dublin.[39] In 1687, he became parish priest of St Audoen's by papal provision; ten years later he transferred the parochial chapel from Audoen's Arch to the chapel in Cook Street vacated by the Dominicans on their transportation in 1698. Since the older parochial records of Dublin no longer exist, it is interesting to note that in 1708 Edward Murphy was able to issue a baptismal certificate from St Audoen's parochial register of 1677.[40] He was a member of the chapter from 1688 and vicar general under two archbishops from at least as early as 1697 until his promotion to the diocese of Kildare in 1715.

One wonders whether Dr Murphy as bishop of Kildare up to 1724 continued to live in Dublin. The city was to prove a safer haven for many bishops than any to be found in their own dioceses. He left money in his will 'to the poor of the parish of St Audoen's where I lived the most part of my life'. In May 1720, he acted as assistant bishop at the consecration in Dublin of

Irish bishop in penal times: the chequered career of Sylvester Lloyd OFM, 1680-1747 (Dublin, 1993), pp 20-32.   **36** *Historia de el Collegio Irlandes de Sevilla*, f. 27r. This entry mentions that there was a portrait (now lost) of the archbishop in the college and refers also to a student who had seen the inscription on Dr Byrne's grave. The original register is now National Library of Ireland, MS 16236.   **37** Seán Ó Neachtáin and Aodh Buidhe Mac Cruitín. The full texts are in J. H., 'The one before', *Catholic Bulletin*, xi, no. 10 (Oct. 1921), pp 614-15.   **38** Found and published by Donnelly, *Parishes*, part 6 (ii), pp 47-8.   **39** The complicated disputes of 1724 before Dr Murphy's appointment are discussed by Fagan, *Cornelius Nary*, pp 143-4. The basic details for Murphy's early career are given by W.M. O'Riordan, 'A list of 17th-century Dublin priests', *Reportorium Novum*, 3, no. 1 (1962), p. 138. For Dr Murphy's episcopate see Donnelly, *Parishes*, part 8, p. 174; part 16, pp 104-7.   **40** M. Walsh, 'A baptismal certificate from St Audoen's, 1677', *Reportorium Novum*, 2, no. 1 (1958), p. 207.

the bishop of Kilmacduagh.[41] Wherever he lived, the clergy of Kildare and Leighlin were content under his government. On some attempt being made in 1722 to appoint a bishop of Leighlin alone, sixteen priests of Leighlin declared that 'some years before' they had obtained permission for Edmund Murphy, bishop of Kildare, to administer the diocese of Leighlin, and they were perfectly happy with that arrangement; under Bishop Murphy, they had 'enjoyed concord, fraternal charity and regular discipline.'[42]

Like his predecessor, Dr Murphy had no mensal parish in Dublin, but lived in Cook Street close to his old parish chapel of St Audoen. From about 1726, Bernard Dunne, now bishop of Kildare, assisted the aged archbishop who had in fact asked Rome for a coadjutor bishop but never received one. While Dr Murphy was indeed old and sick, he was a prelate of long experience closely acquainted with the clergy of the capital. There was peace while he lived, save for some wrangling in 1728 about a new chapel erected by Francis Lehy, a somewhat unruly Carmelite, in the Coombe.[43] The archbishop was not inclined to encourage the regular clergy, now competing in increasing numbers with the parochial clergy for the pennies of the poor, and was actually accused in print of trying to starve them out:

> The archbishop had been very careful in his visitation of his diocese to forbid his diocesan gentlemen not to entertain or give aid or assistance, directly or indirectly, to any poor clergyman [i.e. a friar] without his positive order ... I am surprised to hear his Lordship so careful of their purses about extending their charity, and neglect at the same time their idle and unnecessary expenses in gaming and drinking ... I am sure his Lordship would not like to be served so himself. No, no, he will have the best of meat and drink.[44]

This gibe must have been all the more hurtful because of conditions in the late 1720s which caused the poor of Dublin to wander starving about the streets 'like living spectres'.[45]

One may pass on to what in hindsight seems an error of judgement on Archbishop Murphy's part. In 1725, and more urgently on 25 November 1728, he wrote to Rome asking for the appointment of Joseph Walsh as coad-

41 APF, SC Irlanda 8, ff. 37-38.   42 C. Giblin (ed.), 'Catalogue of material ... *Nunziatura di Fiandra*', *Collectanea Hibernica*, 5 (1962), p. 105.   43 Fagan, *Cornelius Nary*, pp 106-11.   44 S. J., *A sermon in vindication of Mr Francis Lehy* (Dublin, 1728). Quotation from Fagan, *Cornelius Nary*, pp 106-07. The writer also remarked that the archbishop had written a 'letter on the jubilee a year past'; and that, of eighty priests in the city, only six ever preached.   45 I. Ehrenpreis, *Swift: the man, his works, the age* (3 vols, London, 1983), iii, 544, 571, 627.

jutor with right of succession. Walsh was chancellor of the diocese and had been a pastor for more than forty years. However, he was also almost as old as the archbishop himself, 'nearly eighty' some people claimed, with the result that six canons immediately objected to the proposal, old wounds opened again, and Dr Murphy left to his successor a legacy of discord worse than that he had himself inherited in 1724.[46] Less than a month later, in December 1728, he died 'of an incurable malady' at the age of seventy-seven and was buried, it is supposed, in St James' graveyard.[47]

Archbishop Murphy's will is that of a relatively poor man. There is no mention of a library, nor even of a house, for he left to his cousin Mrs Mary Morphy 'now living in Dublin' all his 'household stuff' and the furniture of his 'room'. The closest relatives mentioned are two nephews, Michael Morphy and a Richard Morphy 'of Leixlip'. What little money the archbishop had he doled out in small sums to his only servant and a host of friends, lay and clerical, among them John Linegar, parish priest of St Mary's and later archbishop.[48]

Such was the disarray of the chapter that some canons refused to recognise the dean and the chapter failed even to elect a vicar capitular. Soon there were two vicars general, representatives of opposing factions within the chapter which busily recommended rival candidates to Rome.[49] As usual in such cases, the Holy See waited almost a year for passions to die down, ignored all the capitular candidates, and brought in an outsider, Bishop Luke Fagan of Meath, who in view of his advanced age could scarcely be more than a caretaker as Dr Murphy had been before him.

The new archbishop, Luke Fagan, was born about 1656 into a gentry family at Lick Bla in the parish of Castlepollard, County Westmeath.[50] Where he received ordination is unknown, but he was already a priest before begin-

---

46 C. Giblin (ed.), 'Catalogue of material ... Nunziatura di Fiandra', Collectanea Hibernica, 9 (1966), pp 9-10. The archbishop claimed in this letter that he proposed Walsh, 'having obtained the advice and consent of the chapter'. Yet, on 23 Nov. 1728, six members of the chapter objected to Walsh's promotion. The Stuart court was informed by James Dunne (an ecclesiastic in Paris) as early as Oct. 1725, that the archbishop of Dublin 'and his adherents' had applied for a coadjutor directly to the pope without consulting James III (Windsor Castle, Stuart Papers, vol. 87, no. 9). This may not have been true. 47 W.M. O'Riordan, 'The tombs, monuments and epitaphs of the bishops and archbishops of Dublin', IER, 72 (Aug. 1949), p. 159. 48 W. Carrigan, 'Catholic episcopal wills ... province of Dublin', Archivium Hibernicum, 4 (1915), pp 69-71. This will establishes his birthplace, his long residence in St Audoen's, his address in Cooke Street and his death before 26 Dec. 1728 when probate was granted. The same article contains also the wills of all subsequent archbishops of Dublin to 1786. 49 The subject is sufficiently treated by Fagan, Cornelius Nary, pp 109, 149-52. 50 For this and most other details on Dr Fagan, see P. Fagan, 'Luke Fagan: eighteenth-century prelate', Riocht na Midhe, 8, no. 4 (1992-93), pp 94-111.

ning his ecclesiastical studies at Seville in 1682. There, as a student of the Irish College, he ably defended two *'conclusiones generales'* in 1688, and one year later left Spain 'for the mission'.[51] One is inclined to suspect that he went rather to Paris, where his brother James, also a priest, was resident in 1690. At all events, after a hidden life of eighteen years, he reached Dublin from abroad only in 1707. When James Fagan, then in Rome as agent for some Irish bishops, refused to accept the diocese of Meath, it was bestowed in 1713 on his brother Luke, then pastor of Howth and Baldoyle.

Dr Fagan's consecration as bishop of Meath on 7 February 1714 was performed by the bishops of Elphin and Achonry. While he may have gone to Connacht for the ceremony, it is likely that he lived habitually in Dublin, from which he could attend more conveniently and in greater safety to the needs of his diocese. Between 1715 and 1716 he was persuaded to ordain twelve priests for the schismatical Church of Utrecht, and it is for this indiscretion that he is best remembered. Much later, in 1729, he had a brush with the law which might have led to his transportation, but he escaped on a legal technicality thanks to William Shiel, a deputy clerk of the crown. Somewhat earlier, in 1727, Bishop Fagan wrote from Dublin to the Pretender in Rome, expressing his wish to retire from active service: 'Now being seventy years old, infirm and daily decaying, I am disabled to undergo the fatigue necessary for the administration of so large a district.' His request for a successor was ignored until 24 September 1729 when, rather than being allowed to withdraw from Meath and prepare for death, he was appointed archbishop of Dublin. Bishop Dunne of Kildare undertook to serve as his coadjutor, as he had already done for Archbishop Murphy before him.

Despite advanced age and frailty, Archbishop Fagan did rather more for Dublin than he has been given credit for. Above all else, he brought peace to the clergy, regular and secular. In 1730 he introduced the Carmelite nuns to Dublin from Loughrea and also revised the seventeenth-century statutes of the diocese.[52] The population of Dublin city was now about 110,000, of whom almost half were Catholics.[53] By 1731 there were fifteen 'Mass-houses' in the city served by a hundred priests, and no fewer than forty-five Catholic schools. Throughout the rest of the diocese, Catholics numbered 65,000 or 75 per cent of the population. There were, of course, occasional threats from on high: in 1730 the Protestant primate said he would 'prosecute with the utmost rigour several of the principal popish clergy', and in 1731 parliament

51 Ms. *Historia* of the college, cited above in note 36, ff. 27v, 31v; J.J. Silke, 'The Irish College, Seville', *Archivium Hibernicum*, 24 (1961), p. 131.   52 The text of the 1730 statutes is in Moran (ed.), *Spicilegium Ossoriense*, iii, 139-48.   53 P. Fagan, *Catholics in a Protestant country: the papist constituency in eighteenth-century Dublin* (Dublin, 1998), pp 44-5, 51.

planned to 'hang on the gallows' such priests as would not take the oath of abjuration. During this latter crisis, Dr Fagan called a meeting of the bishops at Dublin and arranged the diplomatic intervention of some foreign governments to prevent the confirmation of the act at London.[54] On this level, 'the principal popish clergy' had more real power than the Protestant archbishop of Dublin.

Irish business at Rome was handled by the bureau for missionary countries called Propaganda Fide, which proved its worth by choosing bishops and settling disputes. There was, however, the drawback that a contentious priest in Dublin, for instance, having opposed the archbishop and appealed to Rome, enjoyed immunity from interference for six months or more until his case was heard. Another Roman bureau, the Datary, caused far greater trouble by granting benefices and titles in Ireland to practically anyone who asked and paid for them. In 1732 a priest named James Andrews turned up in Dublin with a papal bull for the parish of Saggart, to the amazement of the parish priest and people there; and in the same year Archbishop Fagan was commanded to confer at least the *title* of abbot of St Thomas on Henry O'Kelly, the canon regular.[55] Dr Fagan wrote at once to Cardinal Imperiali on 'the obtuse and reckless' attitude of James Andrews and complained of the Roman warning, backed by 'tremendous censures', which obliged him to admit Andrews to the parish. All this, protested the archbishop, was due to 'the ignorance or malice of some of our busybodies at Rome. No Roman tribunal save that of Propaganda should handle our affairs'.[56]

On 30 August 1733, considering his own 'infirmities and old age', Dr Fagan asked the Pretender to name John Clinch, his vicar general, as coadjutor with right of succession. Shortly after, on 15 November, he died in Phrapper-Lane, now Beresford Street, and was buried in St Michan's churchyard.[57] Dr Fagan made two wills, one for his considerable French assets (about £200,000 in modern currency) and another for his Irish estate. His French funds were to be used to establish four burses, two each for Meath and Dublin, at one of the seminaries in Paris depending on St Sulpice. Interestingly, he made special provisions lest the time should come when there might be *no* bishops in Ireland. In his Irish will, Dr Fagan left various sums to his three servants, to imprisoned debtors, and to the sick of the Charitable Infirmary.[58]

54 F. Finegan, 'The Jesuits in Dublin, 1660-1760', *Reportorium Novum*, 4 (1965-71), p. 77. 55 SCAR, Codex I, vol. 2, ff. 253-7, 264-5, 281-2. 56 SCAR, Codex I, vol. 2, ff. 281-2. 57 The date of death, 15 November, is given with the election of a vicar-capitular on the same day (APF, SC Irlanda 9, ff 316-17). The correct date was probably 10 November, as given by L. Swords, 'Calendar of Irish material in the files of Jean Fromont, notary at Paris', *Collectanea Hibernica*, 36 and 37 (1994-95), p. 135. I owe this second reference to P. Fagan. 58 Founded in Cook Street in 1718 by six surgeons, Catholic and

The succession of Archbishop John Linegar (1734-57) marked a welcome return to normality. An unhappy decade of capitular disputes and caretaker archbishops drew mercifully to a close. Oddly enough, though Linegar was archbishop of Dublin for twenty-three years, no one seems to have written even an article about him. He was, at all events, a Dubliner whose family lived at Broadstone ten years before his birth in 1671.[59] After early studies with the Jesuits of Chancery Place he went in 1691 to the Irish College at Lisbon where he was ordained in 1694 and remained until his return to Ireland in 1697. At once he became a curate in St Michan's, resident 'at widow Linegar's in Church Street'.[60] In practice he served St Michan's until 1729, although registered in 1704 as parish priest of 'St Mary's' and collated to St Mary's in 1707 on the creation of that parish. There was no parochial chapel in St Mary's, and it took John Linegar twenty-two years to find a site, collect the money and build one.[61] Pending that happy day, he said public Masses and gave instruction in a room in Mary Street. All baptisms and marriages, then celebrated in private or even public houses, were entered in the registers of St Michan's. Finally, in 1729 he opened his chapel, dedicated to the Conception of the Blessed Virgin, in Liffey Street. Linegar became a member of the chapter before 1718 and vicar general by 1733.

After the death of Archbishop Fagan in November 1733, Linegar was elected vicar capitular; chapter and clergy soon postulated him as archbishop, and he was provided to the see of Dublin in March 1734. He was also permitted to retain St Mary's as a mensal parish.[62] From the outset, his vicar general was Patrick Fitzsimons, a man who for twenty years would be Linegar's shadow and *alter ego*. One hears no more of 'priest-catchers', but there was another sharp outburst of persecution between December 1733 and April 1734: 'the most terrible and shocking which has been since Oliver [Cromwell]'s days', according to the bishop of Ferns.[63] At Dublin the chapels closed for several weeks, but the clergy seem not to have been molested.

Protestant. In 1738 Laurence Richardson O.P got leave to publish a sermon 'on behalf of the Charitable Infirmary on Inns Quay' (H. Fenning, 'Laurence Richardson, O.P., bishop of Kilmore, 1747-53', *IER*, 109, no. 3 (March 1968), p. 144). The Infirmary was the forerunner of Jervis Street Hospital.   59 He was perhaps related to William Linegar, an alderman of Dublin, 1656-84 (M. Clark, 'List of the principal inhabitants of the city of Dublin, 1684', *Irish Genealogist*, 8, no. 1 (1990), p. 51).   60 Donnelly, *Parishes*, part 12, pp 81-2; W. M. O'Riordan, 'A list of the priests ... 1697', *Reportorium Novum*, 1, no. 1 (1955), p. 142. For an account of Linegar's early life, see H. Fenning, *The undoing of the friars of Ireland* (Louvain, 1972), pp 136-7.   61 SCAR, Codex I, vol. 2, ff. 249-50. On his collation see an interesting affidavit of 11 Oct. 1729 in Moran (ed.), *Spicilegium Ossoriense*, iii, 138.   62 Donnelly, *Parishes*, part 6, p. 5; part 11, p. 56. The postulation and date of appointment are in APF, SC Irlanda 9, ff 316-17, 690-3. There is a full and recent account of Linegar's contested election in Fagan, *Cornelius Nary*, pp 153-8. On 31 July 1734, Dr Linegar was named not merely administrator but bishop of Glendalough.   63 H. Fenning,

During his first ten years, Dr Linegar attended to ordinary business, some of it the sequel to or recurrence of earlier problems. With other prelates he complained forcibly in 1736 that the Munstermen had again taken control of the college at Bordeaux through the rigged election of Robert Lacy as rector. The problem, he remarked, resurfaced every twenty years, despite 'our letters' to important figures in France.[64] Also in 1736, and again with the support of several bishops, he begged the Holy See to put an end to the pretensions of Henry O'Kelly, a Canon Regular, abbot of St Thomas, St Catherine and St James, who laid claim to the pastoral care 'of a great part of this city'.[65] Bishops in Ireland had already become accustomed to act in concert. Appeals to Rome often bore the signatures of several bishops actually in Dublin and of others in the country whose names were added 'by commission'. Such an appeal was made in 1737 when the superiors of the Irish College in Paris wished to exclude students already ordained in favour of younger and more pliable candidates. Dr Linegar, for whom Paris was 'the mother and nurse of the parish priests of Ireland', protested with six other bishops that these superiors were destroying the Irish College; they were a greater danger and more harmful to the mission than the magistrates themselves.[66] In the event, Bordeaux did become a Munster enclave, but the Canons Regular withdrew from Dublin and the Collège des Lombards at Paris continued to train student-priests already ordained in Ireland.

Between 1736 and 1742 there was considerable to-do and earnest correspondence with Rome concerning the parish of St Nicholas in Francis Street. On the one hand a Roman bull, issued in August 1737, united the parish to the deanery of Dublin; on the other, there was some concern about the future successor of the ailing parish priest, Thomas Austin, who complicated matters by delaying his death until 1741. Linegar, as early as 1738, wanted Rome to appoint George Byrne parish priest on Austin's death: 'to prevent a struggle between candidates in which I might be forced to show my jurisdiction and be betrayed to the Protestant relatives of some candidates'.[67] When the papal provision for Byrne duly arrived, it was rejected out of hand by three assistant priests of the parish who defied the archbishop, the vicar general and the dean for issuing the bull 'without the consent of the people'. This

The Irish Dominican province, 1698-1797 (Dublin, 1990), p. 143.	**64** Dublin, Armagh, Tuam and others to Cardinal Imperiali, 27 Mar. 1736 (SCAR, Codex II, vol. 2, ff 620-1).	**65** Linegar and others to the pope, 9 June 1736, in Moran, *Spicilegium Ossoriense*, iii, 148-50. Fenning, *The undoing of the friars of Ireland*, pp 118-20. The death in 1737 of Cardinal Imperiali, long a supporter of the Canons Regular, brought this dispute effectively to an end.	**66** Linegar and others to Cardinal Imperiali, 18 June 1737 (SCAR, Codex II, vol. 2, ff 501-2). On the whole dispute, see Fenning, *The undoing of the friars*, pp 109-16.	**67** Linegar to Clement XII, 4 May 1738 (SCAR, Codex I, vol. 2, f. 298; see also ff 294-5).

democratic flourish offers a rare example of Gallican influence in Dublin. The rebel leader, Christopher Bermingham, had 'an apostate brother' who availed of a penal law to take possession of the chapel, thus preventing the celebration of Mass there for quite a while.[68]

The Roman Datary, that ancient fount of discord, again disturbed the diocese in 1741 when Thomas Austin died, for he had been archdeacon as well as parish priest. Although Dr Linegar, on Austin's death, named Patrick Fitzsimons to the vacant archdeaconry, a few months later Richard Reynolds received a papal bull appointing *him* archdeacon. The archbishop, writing to the pope, declared himself 'stupified that ancient custom should have been set aside ... Your Holiness, I suspect, has been deceived ... Please preserve for the bishops of Ireland the rights and customs granted by the Roman pontiffs, your predecessors ... and please revoke the bull given to Richard Reynolds.'[69] Three months later, Linegar returned to the charge in a letter to the cardinal protector. Most disorders and scandals on the mission, he wrote, arose from benefices granted by the Datary without so much as a word to the bishops concerned. This practice had been forbidden by Roman decrees in 1633, 1683, 1693 and 1714, but still the Datary proceeded as before. Dr Linegar had suffered at its hands, not only in the case of the archdeaconry, but also with respect to the parish of Castledermot. There a priest of Longford, armed with papal provision, had been installed as pastor by the bishop of Ferns without a word to the archbishop, although another priest had been in peaceful possession of the parish for thirty years.[70]

The year 1742 marks a watershed in Dr Linegar's long episcopate. Now, for the first time, there is talk of his advanced age, his need of a coadjutor, opposition from some of the chapter and from three suffragan bishops, all coloured by the rumour that it was Patrick Fitzsimons, the vicar general, who effectively ruled the diocese in Linegar's name. On the other hand, thanks to appeals from anonymous *zelanti* in Dublin, Rome had finally decided to reorganise the mission. Benedict XIV, the pope to whom Dr Linegar appealed against the Datary, began this reform by calling for an accurate account of the situation. John Kent of Louvain, the man chosen to survey the Irish scene on Rome's behalf, visited Dublin in the summer of 1742 and was duly impressed by Archbishop Linegar: His report leaves no doubt that Linegar himself was among the *zelanti*:[71]

---

68 There are various contemporary notes on this affair in SCAR, Codex I, vol. 2, ff 327-8.   69 Linegar to Benedict XIV, 25 June 1741 (SCAR, Codex I, vol. 2, f. 316). Reynolds appears to have remained archdeacon until his death in 1781.   70 Linegar to Cardinal Corsini, 10 Sept. 1741 (SCAR, Codex I, vol. 2, ff 317-18).   71 H. Fenning, 'John Kent's report on the state of the Irish mission, 1742', *Archivium Hibernicum*, 28 (1966), pp 93-4. The whole question of Benedict XIV's reform is discussed by Fenning, *The undoing of*

The archbishop of Dublin, John Linegar, a venerable man of advanced years, is held in the highest esteem by his subjects. Since completing his studies at Lisbon in the College of St Patrick, he has worked to good effect for forty-six years in the vineyard of the Lord, first as assistant pastor, then as pastor of the large city parish [St Mary's] he still holds. It is easy therefore to believe that he is well-known throughout the kingdom for his administrative ability and zeal in maintaining ecclesiastical discipline. Although he thinks of retirement, and has asked the Holy See for a coadjutor, those who spread the word that he does nothing, but leaves everything to be done by his vicar [Patrick Fitzsimons], are wrong. It is however true that he no longer accepts commissions outside his diocese, because he cannot ride a horse. Although he rules his subjects with the greatest mildness, he has often been vexed by three of his suffragans who reject or refuse to recognise his court.

Dr Linegar certainly asked for a coadjutor in 1742, but since Rome would not appoint his only candidate, Patrick Fitzsimons, the archbishop never asked for anyone else. Ten members of the chapter also petitioned for a coadjutor in 1742, alleging that the archbishop 'because of age and infirmity feels unequal to the task'. They proposed four candidates, each of whom solemnly signed the petition in favour of the other three.[72] The early opposition to Fitzsimons came from three suffragan bishops who refused to recognise the metropolitan court of Dublin. All three, in Ferns, Ossory and Kildare, had granted parishes to friars, their secular clergy had then appealed to Dublin, and Fitzsimons upheld these appeals. The fact that two of the protesting bishops were friars themselves did nothing to douse the fire.[73] In the event, the question of a coadjutor did not surface again until 1755.

In February 1744, when there were fears that the Pretender would invade the country, the government closed all the Mass-houses of Dublin and gave orders for the arrest of the clergy. One priest was taken from the altar and brought to jail in his vestments, others too were arrested, but when the collapse of a makeshift chapel killed both the priest and several of his congregation the viceroy intervened. The chapels of Dublin opened again on St

---

the friars, pp 123-227.   **72** Ten canons to Propaganda, 1 Oct. 1742 (SCAR, Codex I, vol. 2, f. 327). Among the signatories were Valentine Rivers, who had formerly appealed from the decision of his own archbishop to Armagh, and Richard Reynolds, recently named archdeacon by the Datary without reference to Dr Linegar.   **73** Kildare and Ferns at Enniscorthy to Propaganda, 2 June 1742 (APF, SOCG 712, f. 87). This is the basic and most detailed accusation that Fitzsimons was in complete control of the the diocese and upheld the appeals of every dissolute and troublesome priest in the whole province.

Patrick's day 1744 after what proved to be the last 'general' persecution of the clergy.[74] Ironically, the persecution of 1744 caused priests to flood *into* Dublin, where they were safer than in the countryside. The same point was made in March 1746 by the bishops of Ferns and Waterford. Having been appointed commissaries apostolic in a case between the archbishop of Armagh and three of his priests, they delivered their sentence at Dublin in the house of the printer Ignatius Kelly. They had undertaken the long and dangerous journey to the capital 'not merely because Dublin is a safer place, but because in the present circumstances it is the *only* safe place'.[75] This goes far to explain why Dublin took the lead in the elaborate decoration of chapels (minutely described in a report of 1749), the development of confraternities, and the printing of religious literature.[76]

From 1742, a Roman decree limited each Irish bishop to the ordination of only twelve priests during his lifetime, irrespective of the size or needs of his diocese. Archbishop Linegar tried without success in 1749 to have the decree withdrawn.[77] No similar embargo stopped him from consecrating several bishops, among them the bishops of Ossory in 1736, of Down and Connor in 1740, of Kilmacduagh in 1744 and of Ferns in 1745. These ceremonies took place in Dublin itself, often in the chapel of the Dominican nuns in Channel Row. Dr Linegar also commissioned Thomas Burke OP to prepare the necessary texts for the liturgical celebration of the feasts of Irish saints, a book eventually published in 1751.[78] On the other hand, Dr Linegar was anxious to reduce the large number of holydays of obligation, a constant source of annoyance to landowners and economists.[79] Thanks to his efforts, the clergy of Dublin were able to announce from the altars in 1756 that nineteen feastdays had been abolished.[80]

All this while, the authorities at Rome had been working fitfully on their plans to reorganise the Church in Ireland. In 1750 they were jolted into unwonted decision by Canon John Murphy who arrived from Dublin with

---

74 Thomas de Burgo, *Hibernia Dominicana* (Cologne, 1762), pp 175-6.   75 Ferns and Waterford to nuncio, 12 Mar. 1746 (SCAR, Codex I, vol. 1, ff. 119, 131).   76 N. Donnelly (ed.), *State and condition of the R.C. chapels in Dublin ... 1749* (Dublin, 1904); N. Burke, 'A hidden Church? The structure of Catholic Dublin in the mid eighteenth-century', *Archivium Hibernicum*, 32 (1974), pp. 81-92; H. Fenning, 'Letters from a Jesuit in Dublin on the confraternity of the Holy Name, 1747-48', *Archivium Hibernicum*, 39 (1970), pp 133-54.   77 H. Fenning, 'Michael MacDonogh OP, bishop of Kilmore, 1728-46', *IER*, 106 (1966), p. 143.   78 Thomas de Burgo, *Hibernia Dominicana*, p. 553. The book was called *Officia propria sanctorum Hiberniae* (Dublin, Ignatius Kelly, 1751). Note that Rome had authorised the feasts of several Irish saints as early as 1741 (H. Fenning, 'Michael MacDonogh, bishop of Kilmore', *IER*, 106 (1966), p. 149).   79 Linegar, probably to James Purcell in Rome, 21 Oct. 1749 (APF, SC Irlanda 10, ff 288-9).   80 Brady, *Catholics in the eighteenth-century press,* pp 89-90.

a commission bearing the seals, if not the personal signatures, of all four archbishops. Overjoyed by Murphy's success, Dr Linegar thanked Propaganda for 'the wonderful decrees' his agent had obtained.[81] There were in fact two sets of decrees, one each for the secular and regular clergy, which were to have important consequences for the whole country, quite apart from the decimation of the friars, who might no longer receive novices in Ireland, and their increased subjection to the bishops. All told, the year 1751 marked the peak of Dr Linegar's achievement, for it witnessed the publication of the decrees and was followed by swift physical decline. Quite fittingly he sat for his portrait in the same year.[82] Although then eighty-three – according to the painted inscription – he looks closer to sixty-five. The keen eyes, intelligent and somehow apprehensive, invite the viewer to notice the pallium and double-barred crozier, lying on an altar nearby, and the coat of arms painted in the top right-hand corner.[83] It would be interesting to know whether Dr Linegar, or the other Irish archbishops of his time, had in point of fact a pallium to wear.

By 1753, Archbishop Linegar greatly depended on two vicars general, for John Clinch had by now joined Patrick Fitzsimons, and relied also on Richard Lincoln, parish priest of St Nicholas. He had begun to enter his dotage. One writer unkindly remarked that 'the old doctor is entirely a child, nay he does not even remember that he is a bishop.'[84] Two years later, the archbishop of Armagh explained the situation with northern bluntness in a letter to his Roman agent. Dr Linegar urgently needed a coadjutor, for he had become merely a 'baby' managed by an old priest named Francis Archbold, and his two vicars general had resigned in disgust.[85] Yet the old archbishop still had moments of complete lucidity, evidenced by some letters to Rome about Catholic schools and the hostile intentions of parliament, but most clearly

---

81 Fenning, *The undoing of the friars*, p. 209.   82 The date is painted on the portrait as part of the inscription, yet the artist is said to have been James Latham who died in 1747 ([J. McDonnell], *Maynooth College bicentenary art exhibitions* (Maynooth 1995), p. 17, where the portrait is reproduced with notes).   83 The portrait is in Holy Cross College, Clonliffe, and two duller versions (probably copies) at Sienna Convent, Drogheda, and in the archbishop's house at Thurles (where it is believed to represent Archbishop Christopher Butler of Cashel). It is reproduced in *Reportorium Novum*, 2, no. 1 (1958), facing p.129, but apparently from the duller Sienna copy, since neither the inscription nor the coat of arms is visible. Dr Linegar's age, as given on the portrait, contradicts his own statement of 21 Feb. 1745 that he was then in his 75th year. In the same letter Linegar mentioned that he had dislocated his shoulder and was too weak to visit 'the remote parts' of the diocese (Linegar to James III, 21 Feb. 1745 (Windsor Castle, Stuart Papers, vol. 262, no. 185)).   84 H. Fenning, 'Clerical recruitment, 1735-83: documents from Windsor and Rome', *Archivium Hibernicum*, 30 (1972), p.14.   85 Armagh to John Purcell, summer 1755 (referred to in APF, SC Irlanda 10, ff 479-85, 499-505).

shown after a dispute in 1756 with his newly consecrated coadjutor Richard Lincoln. 'How necessary it is', Dr Linegar protested, 'how necessary for the good of the whole kingdom, that the archbishop of Dublin should be *a man of peace.*'[86]

Archbishop John Linegar died in Abbey Street on 21 June 1757 at the age of eighty-six and was laid to rest in St Michan's churchyard. He made no will, nor does any inscription mark his grave.

While Richard Lincoln's father was an alderman of Dublin during the reign of James II, there were unfortunately two aldermen of that name, Nicholas and Michael Lincoln. The archbishop appears to have been born in Dublin about 1706, for he was said to be 'under fifty' when proposed as coadjutor in 1755. His father was, perhaps, Nicholas Lincoln 'merchant of Capel Street' who stood surety for Cornelius Nary and another priest in 1704. The young Richard Lincoln studied with distinction at Salamanca from which he returned to the mission in 1730.[87] During his early years as a priest in Dublin he was assistant in the parish of St James where he was 'very comfortably fixed' and enjoyed 'perfect peace and tranquillity'.[88] He was also honoured in 1736 by admission to the chapter as archdeacon of Glendalough.[89]

Early in 1741, Lincoln was collated to the parish of St Nicholas in Francis Street which he held for the rest of his life. That was the worst year of the famine, brought on by severe frost, which killed about 300,000, was long remembered in country parts as 'the year of the slaughter', and which brought death by starvation and fever to thousands in Dublin itself.[90] Perhaps the resultant poverty of the clergy lay behind the two-year struggle (1741-43) between three of the assistant priests of St Nicholas and Lincoln, the incoming parish priest. Lincoln described the situation himself in a letter of 1743.[91]

> Upon my first appearance to them tho in the mildest manner I was most injuriously treated by the principal of the three, Christopher Bermingham, and that in the presence of three other priests ... The collectors that I appointed at the chapple door to receive the oblations of the faithful as usual and which is for the support of the assistant

86 Linegar to nuncio, 13 Sept. 1756 (APF, SC Irlanda 10, ff 550-1).   87 D.J. O'Doherty, 'Students of the Irish College, Salamanca', *Archivium Hibernicum*, 4 (1915), p. 26.   88 C. Giblin, 'Ten documents relating to Irish diocesan affairs, 1740-84', *Collectanea Hibernica*, 20 (1978), p. 62.   89 Moran (ed.), *Spicilegium Ossoriense*, iii, 149. Assistant priests were often appointed canons, but Lincoln's appointment as archdeacon suggests either that he was over thirty, or that he was well connected. He was not archdeacon of Dublin, which would have required greater age and experience.   90 M. Drake, 'The Irish demographic crisis of 1740-41', T.W. Moody (ed.), *Historical Studies: papers read before the Irish conference of historians*, 6 (London, 1968), pp. 101-24.   91 Lincoln to Peter MacCormick, 9 Feb. 1742-3 in C. Giblin, 'Ten documents', pp 61-6.

priests, were turned off by Bermingham and Dowdall with threats and menaces, and the same day they publicly affronted me in the face of my congregation, refusing me admittance to say Mass at my own parish chapple. This kind of violence and usurpation they continued for about six months and engrossed all the collections to themselves ... and I was obliged out of my own pocket to pay the assisting priests of the parish and to say Mass for them [i.e. those] six months at the Carmelite chapple which is in this parish.

The next one hears of Richard Lincoln is in an anonymous and highly partisan letter sent from Dublin in 1753 to the Pretender in Rome. The main thrust of the letter was to warn James III that the leading clergy in Dublin were undermining his right to nominate bishops for Irish sees.[92]

It was reported here some years ago by Mr [John] Murphy that Cardinal Corsini assured him that after your death, the royal family would meddle no more in the Irish Church affairs ... This has alarmed very much all the ancient families of Ireland ... Two common plow-men's children, viz. [Patrick] Fitzsimons and [John] Clynch, a Protestant mean chandler's son John Murphy, and [Richard] Lincoln parish priest of Francis Street whose uncles are coal porters, he him-self a silly ignorant man and of the meanest extraction, tho a sorte of an alderman's son – Your Majesty knows that any tradesman may be invested with that quality – are the authors of this fine history. If they can be believed they receive daily accounts to that purpose from their agent [James] Purcel in Rome. The rector of the Irish Jesuits or community in Rome [Stephen Ussher] is related to Lincoln and assures him that he will, in default of Fitzsimons or [John] Clynch, make him archbishop of Dublin, which would really destroy both reli-gion and the attachment we have for the royal family, since they are all mean ignorant men.

Father Lincoln was certainly neither ignorant nor silly. Even his family background was moderately respectable. What is more interesting to note here is the resentment felt by 'ancient' families, presumably aristocratic and Jacobite, because representatives of a lower class not only controlled the dio-cese of Dublin, but could scarcely wait to be rid of the Stuarts for ever. The

92 H. Fenning, 'Clerical recruitment, 1735-1783', *Archivium Hibernicum*, 30 (1972), pp 13-14. Lincoln's 'coal-porter' uncles may have been the brothers either of his mother or step-mother; a suggestion made to me by Patrick Fagan who also tried to identify Lincoln's alderman father.

writer's chief purpose was to hinder the promotion of Murphy, Clinch, Fitzsimons or Lincoln, now that Archbishop Linegar was 'entirely a child'. John Murphy, as it happened, died in July 1753, thus removing one candidate, but Richard Lincoln was named coadjutor with right of succession on 21 November 1755.[93] His consecration took place 'in the greatest secrecy' on 11 January 1756, in the presence of several bishops.[94]

By pure coincidence, Dr Lincoln's term of office as coadjutor (during which he was effectively in charge) and archbishop, began and ended with the Seven Years War between England and France (1756-63). Lincoln's promotion also coincided with the furtive beginnings of the Catholic Association, whose work was discouraged even after Lincoln's death because both the aristocracy and Catholic clergy steadily shunned public notice. Besides, if the clergy opposed the Association on the score of discretion alone, the aristocrats also despised its members as tradesmen and merchants.[95] The impression that Dr Lincoln shrank from public notice is offset a little by his energetic protest in 1757 against the admission of Catholic children to the Charter Schools. When a paper from him to this effect was read at a meeting of the Charter School board, they threatened to put the law on him should he attempt to interfere.[96]

On 21 June 1757, Richard Lincoln automatically became archbishop on Dr Linegar's death. Patrick Fitzsimons and Richard Campbell served as his vicars general. Almost immediately he had to attend to what was known as the 'Tremblestown Pastoral', a letter composed by the archbishop of Armagh and others at the request of Lord Trimleston. This document, intended only for private circulation among the bishops, denied that the pope might depose kings, exercise even indirect power over the temporal jurisdiction of princes, or permit the taking of false oaths. While Dr Lincoln firmly rejected the Pastoral, another letter, which had much in common with it, was read in all the chapels of Dublin on 4 October. After expressing thanks to God and to

93 M. J. C. 'The archbishop Linegar-Lincoln succession', *Reportorium Novum*, 2, no. 1 (1958), pp 211-12. This somewhat inaccurate article is based on notes from APF, SC *Irlanda* 10.   94 Kildare to Propaganda, 22 Jan. 1756 (APF, SC Irlanda 10, ff 519-20). 95 There is a recent and full account of the Association in T. Bartlett, *The fall and rise of the Irish nation: the Catholic question, 1690-1830* (Dublin, 1992), pp 57, 60-5.   96 Brady, *Catholics in the eighteenth-century press*, pp 91-2. On the subject of schools, there are two interesting letters (both dated 29 Nov. 1759) addressed by Dr Lincoln to Cardinal Spinelli and James Purcell. Propaganda's subsidy, intended to offset the Charter Schools, would not pay one teacher for a year. All Catholic schoolmasters are liable to transportation. The parish priests do what they can with the help of lay teachers. Pupils are taught reading, writing and arithmetic, and especially Christian doctrine. There are 60 teachers in 30 rural parishes. The problem is getting worse because of an increasing number of children in the schools of the city (APF, SOCG 792, ff 125-6).

those rulers and magistrates who had saved thousands in the recent famine, this Dublin pastoral urged 'a peaceful submissive bearing', declared that 'no power on earth' could dispense from false oaths, and ended with an appeal for prayers for the king and the royal family 'that they might continue to show clemency and moderation towards their Catholic subjects'. This, be it noted, was almost nine years before the death of the Pretender, James III. Soon after, in January 1758, a parliamentary bill, the brain-child of James Hamilton, which envisaged the registration of the secular clergy in return for their explicit allegiance to George II, coupled with the exclusion of all other clergy, narrowly failed to pass the Irish Privy Council. Since June 1757, Dr Lincoln had been writing to Rome, Madrid and London in a bid to prevent its ratification.[97] Once the bill failed, the bishops immediately ordered exposition of the Blessed Sacrament as an act of thanksgiving.[98] Another exhortation was read in all the Dublin chapels in March 1762 for the king's success in war and 'for the spiritual and temporal happiness of the present royal family'.[99] Archbishop Lincoln had certainly said good-bye to the Stuarts.

So far as his suffragan dioceses were concerned, Dr Lincoln became involved only in the affairs of Ossory. James Dunne, named bishop of Ossory in 1749, came late to Ireland in 1751, fell foul of the Protestant bishop at Kilkenny and had to leave the country in 1753 for his own safety.[100] Although the bishop soon returned to administer his diocese with greater security from Dublin, poverty and declining health forced him to leave Ireland forever in 1757. There was no helping hand or word of sympathy for him in the capital, partly because Dr Dunne, unlike the archbishop, was a loyal Jacobite. On the contrary, Dr Lincoln wrongly accused him of having incurred vast debts and proposed that the administration of Ossory be given to the bishop of Kildare.[101] Later he urged the appointment of James Purcell, his Roman agent, to redress 'the woeful state' of the diocese,[102] but had the mortification in 1759 of witnessing the promotion to Ossory of Thomas Burke, who was not merely a strong Jacobite, but a Dominican friar as well. Bishop Burke

---

97 Lincoln to Corsini, 13 Dec. 1757 (APF, SC Irlanda 10, f. 596).   98 The Trembleston pastoral and Hamilton's bill (1755-58) are discussed at length in Fenning, *The Irish Dominican province*, pp 267-75; also, more recently and more fully, by P. Fagan, *Divided loyalties: the question of the oath for Irish Catholics in the eighteenth century* (Dublin, 1997), pp 87-124.   99 Brady, *Catholics and Catholicism*, p. 103.   100 Dunne, 'on board ship near Wexford', to Lady Lismore, 18 Oct. 1753 (Windsor Castle, Stuart Papers, vol. 344, no. 34). I am indebted to Patrick Fagan for a full transcript of this important letter.   101 Lincoln to Corsini, 20 Aug. 1757 (APF, Udienze 8, ff 362, 384). Incidentally, this autograph letter shows that Lincoln could write French extremely well. In the same volume (ff 370-1) there is a letter written at Paris by Bishop Dunne to the nuncio at Brussels, in which he denies having any debts he cannot pay.   102 Linegar to Corsini, 13 Dec. 1757 (APF, SC Irlanda 10, f. 596).

almost at once, and with some reason, challenged the right of a priest named Patrick Molloy to hold the parish of St Mary's in Kilkenny. In July 1759, Dr Lincoln, with the bishops of Kildare and Ferns, sided with Molloy against his own bishop. When Propaganda in August 1762 gave a decision in favour of Bishop Burke, it warned the archbishop to agree, and to make Father Molloy agree. Nonetheless, Dr Lincoln ignored the warning and sent two commissaries secretly to Kilkenny, only to be rebuked by Propaganda in 1763 for interference.[103] One should mention, in all fairness, that Molloy had appealed to Archbishop Lincoln as his metropolitan.

From incidental references, we know that the archbishop held visitation throughout his own diocese at least in 1757 and 1762. In 1759, he issued an interesting pastoral letter on the jubilee, perhaps the only religious text in English known to have come from his hand.[104] Several exhortations 'to be read in all the chapels' appeared during his time, especially after the accession of George III in 1760, expressing complete submission to the throne and asking Catholics to pray both for an end to war and for the welfare of the royal family. He is also said to have promoted devotion to the Sacred Heart.[105] What little else is known about Dr Lincoln's work for the diocese is unhappily contentious, either because our archival sources bear largely on disputes, or more likely because the archbishop never shrank from a quarrel. Far from being 'a man of peace', he was rather a man of war. Even Charles O Conor, a founding member of the Catholic Association, usually referred to the archbishop as the 'hyper-doctor', overbearing and slow to forgive.[106] He disagreed even with the aged Viscount Nicholas Taaffe, Count of the Holy Roman Empire, who came from Austria to Dublin in 1762, helped the Discalced Carmelites to set up a convent in Stephen Street, and intervened to calm the dispute at Kilkenny. Dr Lincoln treated Taaffe roughly, telling him to mind his own business and to stop meddling in Church affairs. 'I find there is no calming him', said Taaffe, even when he had offered to ask the archbishop's pardon on his knees if that were necessary to restore peace.[107] Cardinal Corsini at Rome, when approached on this affair, confessed that even he would not be acceptable to Dr Lincoln because of the Molloy case in Kilkenny, although, as he wrote: 'I alone was the one who caused him, a parish priest, to be nominated to the primatial see of Dublin.'[108]

---

103 W. Carrigan, *The history and antiquities of the diocese of Ossory*, i (Dublin, 1905), pp 163-7. There is at Propaganda Fide a vast amount of material on the 'Molloy Case' which was not finally closed until 1765.   104 Moran (ed.), *Spicilegium Ossoriense*, iii, 267-71. 105 I have failed to find supporting evidence for this statement. Dr Lincoln was, however, well disposed towards the Jesuits and subscribed to *The Life of St Francis Xavier*, printed by Ignatius Kelly at Dublin in 1743.   106 Quoted by Bartlett, *The fall and rise of the Irish nation*, p. 62.   107 Fenning, *The Irish Dominican province*, pp 310-11.   108 Undated note

Archbishop Lincoln's two great contests were with the regular clergy of Dublin, first on the question of approval for faculties, and then about confraternities and religious processions. In February 1759, withdrawing all faculties granted by himself or his predecessors, he summoned all the clergy save parish priests to a general examination. The archbishop then issued faculties to all, to some for only a few months, but to none for more than a year. There was, accordingly, another general examination in February 1760, conducted by Dr Lincoln himself. Many senior friars – provincials, guardians, priors – had the mortification of being approved for a short period while others far junior to themselves were given unlimited faculties. What the archbishop wanted was the abolition in Ireland of the 'privileges' of the regular clergy, in short their complete subjection to the bishops, and so he pressed on to challenge their traditional forms of public devotion, already practised at Dublin from the 1720s. A certain financial interest, as one can see, lay not too deep below the surface.

> There are many other crying abuses among them that loudly call for a reformation, such as pecuniary sodalities, expositions of the Blessed Sacrament perhaps twice a week *ad nauseam populi* to swell their collections at the door, processions of three or four score lubberly fellows with scapulars about their shoulders, the same of the Belt with wax tapers in their hands, and the *Venerabile* at the rear of these monthly processions to the great scandal of the heretics who constantly attend these as spectators to turn our holy religion into ridicule. Yet if when I shall attempt to reform these abuses and scandals they will roar out their privileges which, if they have any such, should never be practised in this country.[109]

Warming to his task, Dr Lincoln laid down seven rules for the friars of Dublin in April 1761, saying when precisely exposition and processions of the Blessed Sacrament might be held, and going so far as to declare that 'no indulgences may be gained save those expressly recognised by ourselves or our predecessors'. When Rome decided matters a few months later, not simply for Dublin but for Ireland as a whole, Dr Lincoln was overruled with regard to indulgences, to faculties (once they had been granted indefinitely) and to processions held indoors without the Blessed Sacrament. Otherwise, these Roman decrees went far towards meeting the archbishop's wishes, and he was pleased.

of 1762 from Corsini to Charles O'Kelly OP (SCAR, Codex II, vol. 3, f. 754). **109** Quotation taken from a full discussion of these disputes in Fenning, *The Irish Dominican province*, pp 277-88.

Dr Lincoln, 'after a short but fatal illness', died at his house in Smithfield on 21 June 1763, his anniversary as archbishop, and was buried four days later in the family plot in St James' churchyard.[110] His will reveals nothing about his family or circumstances, beyond the fact that he left £200 to Richard Campbell, presumably the vicar general of that name, and everything else to his step-mother and executrix, Mary Lincoln. Archbishop Lincoln's successor proved to be Patrick Fitzsimons whom Dr Linegar so very much wanted to have as coadjutor twenty years before.

Patrick Fitzsimons too was a Dubliner, born at Clonsilla about 1695, the son of Richard Fitzsimons who may well have been 'a common plowman' as was alleged in later years.[111] For his ecclesiastical studies he went to Spain where, for some time at least, he lived in the English College at Seville, was ordained about 1718 and took his doctorate.[112] From about 1722 he spent seven years at London serving the chapel of the Spanish ambassador and came briefly to Ireland in 1729 to take possession of the parish of St Paul's, Arran Quay, to which he was provided by Giuseppe Spinelli, internuncio at Brussels. For reasons unknown, Fitzsimons then returned to London and by January 1730 was at the nunciature in Brussels itself, wondering whether he should appoint an administrator for St Paul's and accept the invitation of the Spanish ambassador at London, who needed help with some negotiations.[113] Towards the end of 1731, when a new rector was being sought for the Irish College at Louvain, the internuncio recommended Fitzsimons as 'a man of the greatest modesty and integrity, very well known to me'. The post went to John Kent, later famous for his 'Report on the Irish mission', and Patrick Fitzsimons remained at Dublin where one finds him already a canon in 1733 and vicar general under Dr Linegar from 1734. Donnelly describes his work for the parish of St Paul's:[114]

110 The newspaper death-notice styled him 'titular archbishop of Dublin, a gentleman of great piety and learning' (Brady, *Catholics in the eighteenth century press*, pp 107-8). No monument survives. The date of burial, curiously delayed, is given in the parish register of St James (1742-95), p. 91, for 'Father Lincoln, Smithfield'. The register is with the Church Representative Body at Braemor Park. Looking through it for other Lincolns buried at St James between 1742 and 1765, I found Mary of Francis Street (8 Oct. 1754), Francis, no address given (23 Aug. 1760), and John of Francis Street (11 July 1764). 111 There is a good account of Fitzsimons' early years by T. Ó Fiaich, 'Dán ar Phádraig Mac Siomóin', *Reportorium Novum*, 2 no. 2 (1960), pp 288-97. 112 There were four students named Patrick Fitzsimons at Seville between 1718 and 1742. Our archbishop must have been one of the first two, and therefore of the English college, ordained either in 1718 or 1722. The earlier date is the more likely, *pace* J. Silke, 'The Irish College, Seville', *Archivium Hibernicum*, 24 (1961), pp 132-3. 113 Fenning, *The undoing of the friars*, pp 138-9. 114 Donnelly, *Parishes*, part 10, p. 19.

His great work was the building of the first chapel which may be dated from 1730. Hitherto the old warehouse at the rere of 'Arran's Key', which had already killed three people and wounded several others, had been doing duty as parish chapel. Dr Fitzsimons thought that it was high time that this dangerous structure should come to an end. He acquired a lease of the site, and, organising a subscription, he erected thereon a seemly chapel, described in the manuscript of 1749 as 'having a good gallery, convenient sacristy, near to which an additional building is made, where the priests lodge'.

Dr Linegar thought so highly of Father Fitzsimons that he appointed him archdeacon in 1741, all unknown to the Holy See which some months later conferred the same dignity on Richard Reynolds. While challenging this curious procedure, the archbishop described Patrick Fitzsimons as a man 'who for many years has laboured and suffered much to establish ecclesiastical discipline in this archdiocese'. A much greater disappointment lay in store, because priests throughout Leinster who were at odds with their own bishops often appealed to the metropolitan in Dublin, and it fell to Patrick Fitzsimons as vicar general to hear and advise on each case. This drew upon him the annoyance of the bishops of Ferns, Ossory and Kildare who carried their complaints in no uncertain terms to Rome. In consequence, when Dr Linegar proposed Fitzsimons as his own coadjutor in 1742, Cardinal Corsini warned Propaganda that his promotion would cause 'disorders and uneasiness'. Again in 1744, when Linegar proposed Fitzsimons for the vacant see of Ferns, Corsini gave positive orders to the secretary of Propaganda to search for any damaging reports on Fitzsimons that he could find.[115] Dr Linegar even wrote twice to James III, in 1742 and 1745, asking that Fitzsimons, as a man loyal to the Stuart cause, be given 'a lease in reversion of this place', but to no avail.[116] All one can rescue from the wreckage of this plan is Linegar's description of Fitzsimons in 1744: 'learned, exemplary, wise, prudent, impartial, incapable of acting unjustly, experienced in Church affairs and worthy of the highest praise'. In the same year, the year of persecution, when a priest was arrested in his vestments during Mass in the chapel of Arran Quay itself, Father Fitzsimons was moved to the parish of St Michan's and became dean of the diocese.

115 Corsini to Propaganda, 5 Dec. 1744 (APF, SC Irlanda 10, f. 167). It has been surmised that Fitzsimons' Spanish connections prevented his promotion on political grounds, but the opposition of three suffragans is a sufficient and documented explanation of the difficulty. See Donnelly, *Parishes*, part II, pp 56-7.   116 Fenning, *The undoing of the friars*, p. 139. The 'lease in reversion' was the coadjutorship with right of succession to the diocese of Dublin.

In November 1751, when Dr Sweetman of Ferns was arrested and brought to Dublin, a committee of the Privy Council thought it would be a good idea to question Patrick Fitzsimons as well. The answers of both show that they corresponded with each other, and that Sweetman had recently performed ordinations at Dublin for old Dr Linegar. It is from this document we learn that Patrick Fitzsimons was seven years a priest at London and came to Dublin in 1727. He spoke of collections made in Dublin to employ lawyers 'before the Council' at London, presumably to hinder legislation. Another interesting point is that 'if required, the archbishop would employ him to write', which explains why so many of Dr Linegar's letters are in the same neat round hand, quite different from his tall heavy signature. In one paragraph Fitzsimons speaks of his own parish of St Michan's:

> Has six or seven priests to assist him. There are about a hundred in Dublin. The collections at the door provided for them. A share of that collection and some emoluments make up about fifty pounds or sixty pounds a year which is his provision, and has some exceedings [sic] upon the Chapel Rent. Michans his parish is numerous but small. Nicholas Without is the best parish ... Linegar never visits. Has little power over his suffragans.[117]

When James Hamilton, earl of Clanbrassil, was preparing his parliamentary bill to register the clergy in 1755, he held discussions with the two vicars general and archdeacon of Dublin: Clinch, Fitzsimons and Lincoln. Hamilton insisted that Catholics would have to take an oath of loyalty if they were to be helped by parliament. Fathers Clinch and Fitzsimons circularised the bishops on the subject, but nothing came of the matter except that it gave the friars an opportunity to complain that the secular clergy were inspiring the laws being prepared against them. That, at least, is what the bishop of Kildare had to say on the subject in 1756.[118]

Father Fitzsimons served again as vicar general under Archbishop Lincoln from 1757, was elected vicar capitular on his death in 1763, and led the poll when the chapter voted for Dr Lincoln's successor. On the very day of the archbishop's funeral, the regular clergy of the capital, still nursing their recent wounds, appealed to Rome for a new archbishop who would be 'a lover of peace, and an enemy to the accursed distinctions between regular and secu-

---

117 Both interrogations are in Burke, *Irish priests in the penal times*, pp 307-9, 316-19.
118 James O'Keeffe, bishop of Kildare, to Cardinal Corsini, 22 Jan. 1756 (APF, SC Irlanda 10, ff 519-20). The matter is fully explained by Bartlett, *The fall and rise of the Irish nation*, pp 55-7.

lar'.[119] Dr Fitzsimons was duly elected archbishop in September but had not as yet been consecrated on 8 January 1764.[120] Maurice O'Gorman, a Gaelic scribe of the capital, wrote a long poem in his honour, crediting him rather surprisingly with a knowledge of classical Irish, praising him for innumerable virtues, but including the more plausible and relevant tribute that he was 'benevolent, liberal and pleasant'.[121] There was to be no trouble with the regular clergy during his time, and only a few minor tiffs with Bishop Burke of Ossory who was in fact his friend. Dr Fitzsimons received the parish of St Nicholas, the richest in the city, for his support and left Arran Quay for Francis Street. Richard Reynolds and Christopher Bermingham, both stormy petrels in their youth, must have mellowed with time, for the archbishop appointed them his vicars general. Dr Fitzsimons, in fact, held Bermingham in particularly high regard.

Dublin itself, with a population of 145,000 in 1766, was by now a larger and growing city in which Catholics – a majority since about 1750 – outnumbered Protestants by three to two, exactly the reverse of their relative proportions in 1733.[122] Politically, of course, Protestants still had the field entirely to themselves, but the cession of French Canada to Britain in 1763 involved a treaty which guaranteed the religious rights of England's new Catholic subjects. That treaty, although not accepted by the British parliament until 1774, did help to create a climate favourable to emancipation in Ireland. In this respect an even more important event was the death of James III at Rome in 1766 and the refusal of the pope to recognise his successor. Catholics were free at last from the constant accusation, true or false, that they gave their allegiance to the Stuarts and not to the House of Hanover. For a decade before his death, James III had played little part in the choice of Irish bishops, but that was not something the Protestants of Ireland were to know.

One could say of Archbishop Fitzsimons that his great work for the diocese was done as vicar general over a period of thirty years. He was sixty-

---

119 Regular superiors to a cardinal, 25 June 1753 (SCAR, Codex IV, doc. 155). There seem to be no papers on this election at Propaganda Fide. Fitzsimons was recommended by two suffragan bishops, including Burke of Ossory (SCAR, Codex I, vol. 2, f. 440). But there was a hostile note (16 Aug. 1763) from Bartholomeo Soffredini, administrator of the nunciature at Brussels, claiming that Fitzsimons 'lacked esteem and general veneration', that his postulation had been arranged by 'friendly friars', that he was 'thought to be the author of the famous Oath of Allegiance', and that Dr Lincoln 'had hoped to be succeeded by his vicar general Richard Campbell, whom he greatly esteemed' (Vatican Archives, Fondo Missioni, pacco 57). 120 McCarthy, *Collections on Irish Church history ... Renehan*, p. 323, note. 121 Edited by T. Ó Fiaich. See note 111. 122 P. Fagan, 'The population of Dublin in the eighteenth century with particular reference to the proportions of Protestants and Catholics', *Eighteenth-Century Ireland*, 6 (1991), pp 140-3, with graph on p. 156.

nine on becoming archbishop and ruled for only six years. In the circumstances it is not surprising that his episcopate was uneventful, which in a way is a tribute to the man himself, for he brought peace where there had been war and was more encouraging than Dr Lincoln had been to those who sought to come to terms with the civil authorities.

So far as Dublin diocese was concerned, the archbishop had to answer a protest (1763-4) from twenty-seven assistant priests of the capital who alleged that most parish priests gave them only a derisory part of the collections made specially for the assistants at the chapel doors. The term 'curate' was not then used, because illegal. In his calm, secretarial way, Dr Fitzsimons recalled that there had been a dispute of this kind in 1729, and another in the parish of St Nicholas Without in 1743. The usual Mass-stipend was a shilling, and the parish priests gave each assistant three shillings a week from their own total income. Whenever the assistants preached at Vespers on Sundays and feast-days, they got abundant alms collected entirely for themselves at the church doors. In fact the archbishop was rather puzzled by the complaint. Never had he seen an assistant priest who was not well dressed and well fed. Why was it, he asked, that he could not easily find assistants for country parishes, or that these protestors vied for the few *rich* parishes of the city?[123]

On the political front, Dr Fitzsimons was in contact with Dublin Castle even before he became archbishop. He was called there in 1762 and given a lenten address to be read in every chapel in the country, imploring God's aid for King George 'in dangerous times.[124] Five years later, the archbishop was evidently in touch with Dublin Castle again concerning the Whiteboy disturbances in Munster. He could regret in September 1767 that the aged archbishop of Cashel had not followed the advice of the Lord Lieutenant's secretary given privately to Fitzsimons to be communicated to the other bishops. Had Cashel followed this advice as the others did, he added darkly, 'it would have put a stop to evils without number, and certainly some of those who perished miserably on the scaffold would not have come to such a sorry end'.[125] Lord Bristol, the viceroy in question, never actually visited Ireland. He did, however, obtain for his brother, Frederick Augustus Hervey, the bishopric of Cloyne. Bishop Hervey at once set his mind to the formulation of an oath of allegiance and discussed the matter with Dr Fitzsimons. What passed between them was rather a mystery, even to contemporaries. The leading secular clergy of Dublin, writing in 1770 after the archbishop's death, offered a reasonable summary of events:[126]

---

123 There are at least four letters on this dispute in APF, SOCG 805, ff 164-93, 201-2. Propaganda took the part of the archbishop. 124 Limerick Diocesan Archives, Father White Ms., p. 176. 125 Fitzsimons to nuncio at Brussels, 10 Sept. 1767 (APF, SC Irlanda 11, ff 352, 354). The nature of this advice is not disclosed. 126 Eight canons to

What happened in 1767 under Archbishop Fitzsimons? Bishop Hervey was brother of the Viceroy. The Viceroy was well disposed, but required an oath of allegiance. We consulted with the regular clergy. The archbishop framed an oath in consequence, but we never saw it. Bishop Hervey and the Internuncio were in correspondence about the four Gallican Articles, but what happened we do not know.

What happened in fact was that Hervey, having agreed with Dr Fitzsimons on a particular formula, then included the four Gallican Articles, generally unacceptable to Catholics even in France, and gradually succeeded in his real intention which was to split the Catholic body. Dr Fitzsimons acted cautiously in these transactions, for while favouring the idea in principle, he kept both the nuncio Ghilini and Cardinal Corsini fully informed of devopments during 1768 and 1769.[127] Most of the bishops of Munster, with whom Ghilini and Dr Fitzsimons had also been in contact, received the nuncio's letter of 14 October 1768 condemning the oath, and utterly rejected the oath itself in May 1769.[128] One must therefore dismiss the often-repeated story that Dr Fitzsimons, when instructed by the nuncio to send copies of his condemnatory letter to the other metropolitans, 'prudently kept that letter to himself'.[129]

By March 1769, Archbishop Patrick Fitzsimons was already in poor health. Parliament was not expected to discuss the oath for the first time until October, but on 25 November the archbishop died in Francis Street at the age of seventy-four. He was laid to rest in his native Clonsilla where a tombstone was placed above his grave.[130] From his will it appears that he had at least one brother and six married sisters, all of whom save Catherine Flanagan predeceased him. To his vicar general and 'dear friend' Christopher Birmingham, he left his 'gold cross, chain and mitre etc.', and all his plate to a nephew in the male line 'with an obligation of engraving my coat of arms on them'.

nuncio at Brussels, 3 Mar. 1770 (APF, SC Irlanda 12, ff 513-14). **127** Fitzsimons to Corsini, Dec. 1768, in Moran (ed.), *Spicilegium Ossoriense*, iii, 315-17. The editor gives the correct year, but wrongly attributes this important letter to John Carpenter. Tommaso Ghilini, nuncio, to Cardinal Castelli, 21 Mar. 1769 (Vatican Archives, Fondo Missioni, pacco 129). **128** James Butler I to Ghilini, 21 May 1769 (Vatican Archives, Fondo Missioni, pacco 130). Butler had received copies of the formula both from Dr Fitzsimons and from Brussels. **129** John Ward at Dublin to John King, 15 Mar. 1768 (Galway Diocesan Archives, box 13); Bartlett, *The fall and rise of the Irish nation*, pp 78-81. Also J.R. Walsh, *Frederick Augustus Hervey, 1730-1803: fourth earl of Bristol, bishop of Derry* (Maynooth, 1972), pp 17-22. The best and most recent account is by Fagan, *Divided loyalties*, pp 125-56. **130** The informative inscription is given by McCarthy, *Collections on Irish Church history*, p. xi.

Dr Fitzsimons was succeeded, not by his 'dear friend' Christopher Bermingham as the chapter wished, nor by a less intimate friend, Thomas Burke, bishop of Ossory, as the chapter greatly feared, but by 'a poor tailor's son, an unbeneficed, inservient and indigent priest', John Carpenter.[131] This surprising choice was due to a veto lodged by the regular clergy against Bermingham and others, to the active lobbying at Rome of Bishop Burke of Ossory, and to the desire of the Roman authorities to have an archbishop of Dublin who would be both cautious and soundly orthodox with respect to the oath of allegiance. Whether by accident or design, the archbishop-elect was also a man in the prime of life, being little more than forty years of age. That in itself was a blessing. Of all the archbishops considered here, Dr Carpenter is the only one now generally remembered, partly for his love of the Irish language and the Gaelic past, but chiefly because his fine diocesan records are the earliest of their kind which now survive. Besides, the old days of real danger had passed, the clergy ventured out of the shadows into the light of day, and the movement towards Catholic emancipation gathered momentum. These factors gave Dr Carpenter a prominence his predecessors were rightly careful to avoid.

John Carpenter, we are told, was born in a large house in Chancery Lane, Dublin, in 1729, the son of 'a respectable merchant tailor'.[132] Certainly Chancery Lane, linking Bride Street and Golden Lane in the civil parish of St Bride, could then boast some substantial houses in a heavily Protestant part of the city, but unfortunately we do not know the names, status or origin of his parents.[133] The archbishop himself used the forms Mac an tSaor and Maca tSaoir which, if equivalent to MacAteer, would indicate a south-Ulster background. Dalton records the curious tradition that the boy was dumb until the age of seven when, frightened on being lost among a crowd, he blurted out his father's name and address.[134] Between 1744 and 1747 he seems to have been the pupil of Seán Ó Neachtain, under whose influence he compiled an Irish grammar, a miscellany of prose and poetry – enlivened by several drawings of the same bespectacled gentleman, thought to have been Ó Neachtain himself – and a book of devotion for his personal use which

---

131 The story of this election is discussed by Fenning, *The Irish Dominican province*, pp 371-5, where the above quotation from Burke of Ossory is on p. 374.   132 Born, perhaps, on 5 December, the date of a birthday ode written in his honour in 1777: see *Reportorium Novum*, 1 no. 2 (1956), p. 387.   133 Dr Wall's suggestion that the archbishop was related to the Gaelic poet Henri Mac an tSaoir cannot easily be sustained, for the latter (as Mr P. Fagan tells me) anglicised his name as Wright (T. Wall, 'Archbishop John Carpenter and the Catholic revival', *Reportorium Novum*, 1, no. 1 (1955), p. 182).   134 D'Alton, *Memoirs of the archbishops of Dublin*, pp 472-3. My own theory is that Irish was the language of Carpenter's home, and that the boy was speechless until the age of seven only in English!

included part of the *Imitation of Christ* in Ulster Irish.[135] Nor can the boy have been short of pocket-money, for in 1745 he bought a Gaelic manuscript written in Westmeath and inscribed it in Latin, evidence that he was already learning that language.[136]

In 1747, John Carpenter sailed to Lisbon where he spent seven years at the Irish College, was ordained a priest in 1752 and took the local equivalent of the doctorate before returning to Dublin in August 1754.[137] For several years he worked as an assistant in St Mary's chapel, Liffey Street, and in 1763 put his name to the complaint that many parish priests were defrauding their assistants.[138] That did not cost him the esteem of Archbishop Fitzsimons, for in 1764 he was admitted to the chapter as prebendary of Cullen. Besides, when problems arose concerning the Irish college at Lisbon, he was the one chosen to approach the king of Portugal on behalf of the Irish bishops.[139] In the aftermath of the catastrophic earthquake which destroyed most of Lisbon in 1755, and the suppression of the Jesuits of Portugal in 1759, the energetic prime minister Pombal was then confiscating Jesuit property, including the Irish College of which they were directors. Carpenter travelled to Lisbon in March 1764 to treat with the Portuguese government on the question. While not an immediate success, his mission staved off confiscation of the property and laid the basis for the eventual recovery of St Patrick's. Although the archbishop wrote to Pombal himself in January 1766, thanking him for the restoration of the college,[140] it was not to function properly again for twenty years.

---

135 B. MacGiolla Phadraig, 'Dr John Carpenter, archbishop of Dublin, 1770-1786', *Dublin Historical Record*, 30, no. 1 (Dec. 1976), pp 2-17; C.G. Buttimer, 'Gaelic literature and contemporary life in Cork, 1700-1840', in P. O'Flanagan and C.G. Buttimer (eds), *Cork: history and society* (Dublin, 1993), pp 634-5, 652.   136 P. Fagan, *Éigse na hIarmhí* (Dublin, 1985), p. 149. I am indebted to Mr Fagan not only for this reference, but for the details on Chancery Lane given above.   137 Attestation by Francis Ribeiro SJ, rector of the Irish College, 8 Aug. 1754, that John Carpenter, now going to Ireland, has studied philosophy and theology at the college (APF, CP 137, f. 305). For his reception of orders, beginning in Jan. 1751, see H. Fenning, 'Irishmen ordained at Lisbon, 1740-1850', *Collectanea Hibernica*, 36 and 37 (1994-5), p. 144. The statement that he had spent seven years in Lisbon and taken his doctorate there was made on 5 June 1769 by two Irish priests at London (APF, CP 137, ff 310-11).   138 The leaders of the regular clergy, when warmly recommending Carpenter for the vacant see, mentioned that he had built three schools for the poor and orphaned; that he was not a party-man; and that he was both an elegant preacher and zealous catechist (Regular superiors to Propaganda, 28 Nov. 1769 (APF, CP137, ff 260-6)).   139 Autograph original, 28 Mar. 1764, signed by Dr Fitzsimons (APF, CP 137, f. 304).   140 M.J. Curran, 'Archbishop Carpenter's Epistolae', *Reportorium Novum* 1, no. 1 (1955), p. 155. Michael Daly at Lisbon to Troy, 1 June 1780. Daly explains that after the earthquake, the students were sent to Evora; Daly himself returned to Lisbon in 1758 to recover the property and was named rector in 1778 (DDA, 117/7, under date).

Others too, particularly the members of the Catholic Committee, appreciated his talents, and sent him to London in the winter of 1767-8 to serve as secretary to Lord Nicholas Taaffe. Taaffe, at the age of eighty-six, had travelled from Vienna to London to play what part he could in the emancipation of his fellow Irishmen. Clearly, John Carpenter was already on terms of close friendship with Dr John Curry and Charles O Conor of Belanagare, leaders of the Committee, whose views he shared.[141] He also still enjoyed the confidence of Archbishop Fitzsimons who on this occasion gave him some other work to do at London, probably in connection with the Irish colleges in Spain. Not being able to meet his expenses, Carpenter had to appeal twice to Curry for a weekly subsidy: 'Let only a reasonable estimate be made of a proper allowance for a plain honest man, who can go a-foot and drink porter.'[142]

While Taaffe and Carpenter reached Dublin in February 1768, and Taaffe returned soon after to Silesia, their brief partnership had a curious echo in June 1769 when two priests at London warmly recommended Carpenter in a letter to Propaganda 'on the directions of Lord Taaffe'. Such letters invariably had in mind promotion to the episcopate, yet this was written five months before Archbishop Fitzsimons' death; more curiously still, the writers did not recommend him as John 'Carpenter', but as John 'Mac an tSaor'.[143] Probably Dr Fitzsimons was already in poor health and Taaffe was thinking of a likely successor. A letter from France in mid-September described the archbishop rather unkindly as 'old, blind, *hors de combat*, and perhaps already dead'.[144]

The appointment of John Carpenter as archbishop of Dublin on 16 April 1770 owed little to the 'warm support of the secular clergy of Dublin' traditionally mentioned by historians. Similarly, his consecration on 3 June 1770 in a private house somewhat dilutes the 'prevailing spirit of tolerance' one reads about so often.[145] In an Irish inscription on several of his books he supplied the date of his consecration and styled himself, characteristically, as 'coarb of St Lorcan'.[146] From the outset he held the parish of St

---

141 D'Alton, *Memoirs of the archbishops of Dublin*, pp 473-8.   142 Moran (ed.), *Spicilegium Ossoriense*, iii, p. 279. In the same volume there are many letters from O' Conor to Carpenter covering the years 1768-83 (pp 285-315).   143 Gerard Shaw and Gerard Robinson, Irish priests at London, to Propaganda Fide, at the request of Viscount Taaffe, 5 June 1769 (APF, CP 137, ff 310-11). This is the letter which speaks of his 'seven years' in Lisbon and his taking of the doctorate there.   144 William Fitzharris Giffard at Corbeil sur Seine to cardinal prefect, 15 Sept. 1769 (Vatican Archives, Fondo Missioni, pacco 58). Giffard was proposing himself as Dr Fitzsimons' coadjutor or successor.   145 The official document is published by M. J. C., 'Consecration of Archbishop Carpenter', *Reportorium Novum*, i, no. 1 (1955), pp 237-8.   146 For example, *The earl of Castlehaven's memoirs* (Waterford, 1753). Copy in the Irish Folklore Commission, bearing also his book-

Nicholas as mensal, and though living in a large house on Usher's Island, went to Francis Street every Sunday to say Mass and preach at eight o'clock. The clergy, with the exception of the disappointed candidate Christopher Bermingham, gave him their loyal support once he had taken possession of the see, while he found social acceptance in 1773 on becoming a corresponding member of the Royal Dublin Society. Charles O Conor describes the occasion:

> I lately sat with the Committee of Antiquarians and introduced Dr Carpenter to them. He was received with great respect: a revolution in our moral and civil affairs the more extraordinary, as in my own days such a man would only be spoken to through the medium of a warrant and constable.[147]

On his first appearance before priests and people at Francis Street chapel, after asking for their help and prayers in his ministry, the archbishop declared that in future the chapel-door collection was to be divided equally among the assistant priests. Clearly Dr Fitzsimons had done nothing to settle what his successor keenly felt to be a case of fraud. From the very outset Dr Carpenter kept exact administrative records: an inventory of the few mitres, rings, croziers and other poor 'ornaments' of the diocese; an annual record of the number he confirmed; a notebook of instructions and admonitions, lists of those he ordained, of priests returning from their studies abroad, and also of the appointment of priests to parishes. Similarly, he kept copies of letters received and of many letters written by himself. As early as 1770 he published his first book, a set of the provincial and synodal constitutions of the archdiocese of Dublin.[148] From these records one first hears in any detail of diocesan events outside the capital – at Castledermot, Ballymore Eustace and Blessington – even if these parishes are mentioned usually because of local disputes. Not only was the archbishop always resident, but he went annually on at least partial visitation of the diocese. If he kept a visitation register, as he very likely did, it is not known to have survived.

The most personally revealing of these various records is the volume of 'Instructions and Admonitions', intended for the most part to be read from the altars.[149] Not only was the archbishop highly conscious of his responsi-

plate, with a rather grandiose coat-of-arms, dated 1770. It has been possible to trace about 28 of his books and manuscripts, invariably with his bookplate and similarly inscribed. **147** Quoted by Diarmuid Ó Catháin, 'Charles O'Conor of Belanagare: antiquary and Irish scholar', *Journal of the Royal Society of Antiquaries of Ireland*, 119 (1989), p. 154.   **148** *Constitutiones provinciales et synodales ecclesiae ... Dubliniensis anno 1770* ([Dublin], 1770), p. 122. His administrative records have been edited by M.J. Curran and W.M. O'Riordan in all four volumes of *Reportorium Novum*.   **149** M.J. Curran, 'Instructions, admonitions,

bilities, and of the many virtues needed to carry them out, but there is evidence enough here that if he was not quite another Gregory or Leo, it was not for want of effort. What Dr Carpenter wrote on the duties of pastors or on the care of the poor could hardly be bettered today. He had a particular aversion to the abuse of 'spirituous liquors', especially by priests, whom he was shocked to hear in 1780 were in the habit of 'frequenting public taprooms in this city and its liberties'. Another practice often condemned was the 'combination' of workers, early trade-unionists who not only went on oath-bound strike but were inclined to maim soldiers detailed to protect 'other hands' called in to prevent the 'total stagnation of trade'. Dr Carpenter also denounced rioters and destroyers of property; sometimes he even excommunicated public sinners, yet one feels it was his nature to persuade rather than condemn. Towards the close of the Jubilee in 1776, he remarked: 'we had the satisfaction of seeing our confessionals these five months past, and the chapels where the stations are performed, daily crowded with pious and edifying souls.' The same tone of pastoral concern colours his advice in 1780 on how his flock should behave at a delicate moment in the advance towards Catholic emancipation: .

> Most signal favours have been lately conferred on this kingdom and a very special benefit is daily expected ... We trust ... that no branch of our friendly Government will have reason to reproach any of you with mixing in tumultuous meetings to annoy the highest tribunals; or in disordering wanderings at irregular hours to distract the tranquillity of peaceable subjects; or in wicked cabals to disturb trade and manufacturers ... A steady concurrence with these admonitions will entitle you to singular graces from the supreme majesty of heaven and we trust move our gracious legislature to give you additional marks of their favour and protection.[150]

Looking through Dr Carpenter's correspondence, one notices that as early as 1771 he was concerned about the liturgical celebration of the feasts of Irish saints.[151] Catholic education, still illegal, depended precariously on the offerings of the people. One city school in 1772 had sixty pupils, but 'the influx

---

etc. of archbishop Carpenter, 1770-1786', *Reportorium Novum*, 2, no. 1 (1958), pp 148-71. This valuable record has been missing since Monsignor Curran's death, after which his papers were dispersed.   **150** Dated 13 Feb. 1780, in preparation for Lent (Ibid., p. 167).   **151** M.J. Curran, 'Archbishop Carpenter's Epistolae: part 1 (1770-75)', *Reportorium Novum*, 1, no. 1 (1955), pp 154-72; 'part 2 (1776-80)', ibid., 1, no. 2 (1956), pp 381-98. This is a calendar of Dr Carpenter's Latin letters from copies in his own hand. He may not have kept copies after 1780.

of poor widows into Dublin' gave rise to the danger that their children would be 'handed over to Protestants'. Clandestine marriages posed an insoluble problem because the decree of Trent declaring such marriages invalid had never been promulgated in the diocese. Even if it had, the state still recognised as valid all marriages between Catholics contracted before an ordained minister, even a reprobate couple beggar or 'Father Tack-'em'. This problem, dragging so many other pastoral difficulties in its wake, was not definitively solved until 1827.

In 1780, Dr Carpenter submitted a formal report on the diocese to Rome, being the first eighteenth-century archbishop of Dublin to comply with this requirement. The chapter then consisted of six dignitaries and twenty-two canons. Nine of the forty-five parishes were in the city. Each of the city chapels had between six and eight assistant priests who celebrated Mass daily, heard confessions and took it in turn to preach. Among these curates there was an interesting distinction, because only four at most in each parish were entrusted with 'pastoral' duties, meaning that only they might marry, baptise or give the last sacraments.[152] What Dr Carpenter had to say of the friars, who had six chapels in Dublin, was less than flattering, for they neither lived the common life nor kept a common table. Worse still, they insisted on appointing superiors to 'blind convents' which existed only on paper, and even accepted novices for such convents, with the result that Dublin was plagued by unemployed religious who became couple beggars or turned Protestant in order to eat. Be that as it may, Dr Carpenter had taken rather a high hand with the Capuchins in 1772, and on the suppression of the Jesuits – there were eleven of them at Dublin in 1773 – expressed in no uncertain terms his belief that by joining the secular clergy these former Jesuits had stepped onto a higher spiritual plane:

> The members of the suppressed Society have now become members of the most perfect and illustrious body of men that ever was or will be on the face of the earth, and one that never has suffered, nor ever will suffer either dissolution or suppression.[153]

If the range of Archbishop Carpenter's interests, whether within Ireland or abroad, was far greater than that of his predecessors, it was partly because Propaganda Fide consulted him more often and gave him various commissions, treating him in effect as a national figure as it was later to do more obviously with his successor Archbishop Troy. With respect to the foreign

152 *Reportorium Novum*, 1, no. 2 (1956), p. 394.   153 Carpenter to Sweetman, 23 Feb. 1774, summarised in M.J. Curran, 'Correspondence of Abp. Carpenter with Bp. Sweetman of Ferns', *Reportorium Novum*, 1, no. 2 (1956), p. 400.

colleges, he intervened in the affairs not only of Lisbon, but also of Louvain, Bordeaux, Nantes, Salamanca and Rome. In 1774 he urged the appointment of Irish rectors both at Rome and Salamanca in view of the danger that these positions, formerly held by Jesuits, would pass to foreign nationals. Propaganda frequently asked Dr Carpenter's opinion on episcopal candidates from every corner of the country: for Armagh, Derry, Tuam, Clonfert, Kildare, Cloyne and probably for other dioceses too. Whenever the archbishop knew nothing about a particular candidate, he had the engaging trait of being honest enough to say so. The sad state of the province of Ulster brought two commissions to Dr Carpenter. First, in 1772, he became administrator of the diocese of Dromore and helped to persuade the local bishop, a man unsuited to the task, to withdraw to the continent. A second northern problem brought him twice, in 1774 and 1775, to Dundalk within the diocese of Armagh itself where two priests contended for the parish.[154] Archbishop Hugh MacMahon, author in 1728 of *Jus Primatiale Armacanum*, can hardly have imagined such a future intrusion into his primatial see.

The dismantling of the penal code, begun in 1771 and maintained up to 1782 thanks largely to the American Revolution and the economic needs of Ireland, enabled Catholics to take longer and better leases, disposed of the gavel-act and gave legal recognition to the clergy once they were duly registered. Catholic schoolteachers too were freed from earlier penalties.[155] All this surely consoled the archbishop and gave him greater freedom of action, but the path to freedom also brought him sorrow and distress. The whole process depended on a test-oath or oath of allegiance, successfully devised by the Protestant Bishop Hervey in such a way as to divide Catholic opinion, or in Charles O'Conor's phrase: 'to destroy popery by popery itself.' The stumbling block was a denial of the pope's temporal power, refused by Archbishop Carpenter, but accepted and promoted even in the streets of Dublin by James Butler, archbishop of Cashel. Many took the oath in 1775, but Dr Carpenter prudently delayed until quite certain that the Holy See had no objection to the most recent formula. Only then, in November 1778, was he ready to take

154 The episode is fully documented by B. Hoban, 'Dominick Bellew, 1745-1812, parish priest of Dundalk and bishop of Killala', *Seanchas Ard Mhacha*, 6, no. 2 (1972), pp 342-4.   155 J. Brady, 'Catholic Schools in Dublin in 1787-8', *Reportorium Novum* 1, no. 1 (1955), pp 193-6. This is an edition of highly detailed parliamentary returns.   156 For the political background see Bartlett, *The fall and rise of the Irish nation*, pp 75-102; E. O'Flaherty, 'Ecclesiastical politics and the dismantling of the penal laws in Ireland, 1774-82', *Irish Historical Studies*, 26, no. 101 (May 1988), pp 33-52. The ecclesiastical setting is better explored by Walsh, *Frederick Augustus Hervey*, pp 21-6. On Troy and the relief act of 1782 see Fenning, *The Irish Dominican province*, pp 455-69. The search for a suitable 'test-oath' while Carpenter was archbishop has been more recently and fully discussed by Fagan, *Divided loyalties*, pp 138-69.

the oath of allegiance with seventy of his priests and several hundred laymen.[156] This slow testing of the ground may have made the archbishop unpopular with the prelates of Munster, but it preserved the unity of the Church in Ireland and its doctrinal bond with Rome.

The ideas of the Enlightenment, which played some role in emancipation, also weakened religious faith and encouraged atheism. The answer lay in the proper teaching of Christian doctrine, but there was no Catholic school system, none of the great teaching orders, no trained teachers and hardly any suitable textbooks. Dr Carpenter had to work through the pulpit and the printing press. His edition of the *Ritual* in 1776 included an appendix of his own 'Instructions and Exhortations', translated into 'common' Irish by Charles O Conor at the archbishop's request.[157] The same year saw the publication of his altar-missal, the first, he claimed, 'that was ever printed in these kingdoms'. Despite his differences with Dr Butler of Cashel, he immediately saw the value of Butler's new catechism and had it printed anonymously at Dublin in 1777 under the title *A Catechism for the instruction of children.*[158] In 1780 he produced the second and fuller edition of Alban Butler's *Lives of the Saints* in which, as in the *Missal*, he gave the saints of Ireland a prominence previously unknown.

After a short bout of serious illness in 1771, the archbishop's doctors offered the opinion that he was 'not destined for longevity' and time was to prove them right. Whatever the reason, Dr Carpenter seems to have rested on his oars after 1780. Most of the episcopal lobbying at Dublin in connection with the relief act of 1782, was done, not by Dr Carpenter, but by the younger bishop of Ossory, John Thomas Troy. Yet he still wrote occasionally to Rome, complaining that the bishops of Cashel, Waterford and Meath, influenced by Bishop Hervey, were working on a new Gallican mode of electing bishops in Ireland with little if any reference to Rome.[159] During 1783 Dr Carpenter went on visitation to Arklow, but one hears little more of his activities until his unexpected death on 29 October 1786 at the age of fifty-eight. He was buried at St Michan's in a grave owned by his brother-in-law Thomas Lee, husband of Christian Carpenter and merchant in Pill Lane

157 This paragraph is based on T. Wall, 'Archbishop John Carpenter and the Catholic revival, 1770-1786', *Reportorium Novum*, i, no. 1 (1955), pp 173-82. Carpenter's 'formula of preparation for Mass' has been reproduced and studied by W. Hawkes, 'Irish form of preparation for Mass in the eighteenth century', ibid., pp 183-92.   **158** McCarthy (ed.), *Collections on Irish Church history*, p. 355.   **159** Carpenter to Propaganda, 13 June 1781 and 26 March 1782 (APF, SC Irlanda 15, ff 65, 134); Troy to Antonelli, 25 Nov. 1786 (Vatican Archives, Fondo Missioni, pacco 117). There is a later letter, commenting on candidates for Clonfert: Carpenter to Propaganda, 29 Sept. 1784 (APF, SC Irlanda 13, ff 453-54).

nearby. On the sale of his furniture and effects, the proceeds went to Teresa Mulally for the benefit of the school she had established as far back as 1766.[160] The archbishop's impressive library of 4,000 books was auctioned off. A plaster bust of Dr Carpenter was advertised for sale at Dublin and London. But neither a catalogue of the books nor a copy of his bust appears to have survived.

160 R. Burke Savage, *A valiant Dublin woman* (Dublin, 1940), p. 129.

9

'The pattern of the flock':
John Thomas Troy, 1786-1823

Dáire Keogh

By the time of his death in 1823 John Thomas Troy had been a bishop for almost half a century. Enormous changes had been wrought in the life of the Catholic Church and the reticence of the penal era had given way to the bold confidence which became the hallmark of nineteenth-century Catholicism. Throughout this long period the fortunes of the Catholic Church in Ireland were directed by Troy, who gave Irish Catholicism its distinctive character. The most able ecclesiastic of his generation, and possessed of boundless energy, he displayed constant enthusiasm for his pastoral duties and an eagerness to impose Roman discipline and practice on the Irish mission. Indeed, immediately prior to Troy's appointment to Ossory in 1776, Cardinal Stefano Borgia, secretary of Propaganda Fide, expressed the desirability of such an able cleric in Ireland to 'execute the commands of the Sacred Congregation at all times'.[1] Troy, however, was far more than an efficient functionary, a mere bureaucrat or 'Roman hack'. He was, above all, a conscientious pastor hailed by a suffragan as 'the pattern of the flock and all things to all men'.[2]

I

Curiously, a satisfactory biography of the archbishop remains to be written. Perhaps the span of his life has intimidated most would-be biographers, but surely such considerations would not have deterred the indomitable William James FitzPatrick? John D'Alton's *Memoirs of the archbishops of Dublin* devotes a mere eight pages to Troy; the *Irish Ecclesiastical Record* carried a brief sketch in 1898. Henry Peel published studies in the 1950s and 1960s; Patrick

---

1 Valentine Bodkin to James Butler, 24 June 1789 (Cashel Diocesan Archives).   2 Caulfield to Propaganda, December 1786 in H. Peel, 'The appointment of Dr Troy to the See of Dublin', *Reportorium Novum* 4 no. 1 (1965), p. 14.

O'Donoghue published a piece as part of the Dublin Millennium celebrations and the *Dublin Historical Record* carried a reflective article by Mary Purcell based on her unequalled familiarity with the archbishop's papers.[3] However, the only attempt at a complete study of Troy is Vincent McNally's doctoral thesis, submitted to Trinity College, Dublin, in 1976 and published twenty years later under the revealing title of 'Reform, revolution and reaction: Archbishop John Thomas Troy and the Catholic Church in Ireland 1787-1817'.[4] This study, is broad in scope but it is essentially a political study of Troy's episcopate rather than an integrated work which takes account of his pastoral impact.

Yet in this focus lies the key to Troy's neglected memory, since the perception of the archbishop as a reactionary 'steady loyalist' inhibited his accommodation within the nationalist historiography of the nineteenth century.[5] There is, too, a tendency to present Troy as a remote figure, not merely at odds with the ambitions of his flock, but actively conspiring to undermine their realisation. Such analysis is reflected in McNally's assertion that 'Troy and his colleagues regarded the Catholic layman as an alien'.[6] Certainly the archbishop was convinced that the Catholic laity entertained hopes and aspirations different from his own, but there is no evidence of differences warranting appeal to the term 'alien'. Without doubt, Troy's concern was for the welfare of the Catholic Church in Ireland, but there is no indication that he did not share the wishes of the laity for a full repeal of the penal laws. At the Catholic Convention in December 1792 he boldly announced his determination to rise or fall with the people of Ireland, declaring that the bishops and clergy were 'second to no description of Catholics [in the demand for] their emancipation'.[7] While the focus of this paper is the life of the Catholic community in Dublin, it is essential to consider Troy's political perspective, since a great deal of his pastoral energy was directed towards the political objectives of elevating the legal status of the Catholic Church and preserving peace within the diocese.

---

3 J. D'Alton, *The memoirs of the archbishops of Dublin* (Dublin, 1838) pp 480-7; N. Murphy, 'Archbishop Troy', *IER* (1898), pp 232-43; H. Peel, 'Some aspects of the life of Doctor John Thomas Troy, O.P. 1739-1823', *Iris Hibernia* (1957), pp 52-9; idem, 'The appointment of Dr Troy to the see of Dublin', *Reportorium Novum* 4 no. 1 (1965) pp 5-16; P. O'Donoghue, 'John Thomas Troy, archbishop of Dublin, 1786-1823: a man of his times' in J. Kelly and U. MacGearailt (eds), *Dublin and Dubliners* (Dublin, 1990), pp 25-35; M. Purcell, 'Archbishop John Thomas Troy (1739-1823)', *Dublin Historical Record* (1977), pp 42-52. 4 Vincent McNally, 'Archbishop John Thomas Troy and the Catholic Church in Ireland 1787-1817' (Ph.D., University of Dublin, 1976), published as *Reform, revolution and reaction; Archbishop John Thomas Troy and the Catholic Church in Ireland 1787-1817* (Lanham, 1995). 5 D'Alton, *Memoirs of the archbishops of Dublin*, p. 486. 6 McNally, 'Troy', p. 565. 7 Troy to Bray, 8 December 1792 (Cashel Diocesan Archives).

Troy's reputation had suffered greatly as a result of his decision to side with Lord Kenmare and the aristocratic faction when the Catholic Committee divided in 1791. Wolfe Tone described him as a 'great scoundrel' and a recent commentator has included the archbishop amongst the 'supreme practitioners of the traditional, and ineffectual, strategy of supplication' for repeal of the penal laws.[8] On every occasion Troy opposed the spread of revolutionary principles in Ireland. He excommunicated the Defenders and later the United Irishmen as he had done the Rightboys ten years earlier. For this he became a target of the radical press, which launched an assault on his 'pious alliance' with Dublin Castle.[9] Throughout the 1790s his pastorals repeated the need for deference and obedience to the Crown and the authorities. Behind this lay his deep-rooted fear that, just as the various concessions made to Catholics in 1778 and 1782 had resulted from a combination of expediency and the benevolence of the administration, they could be repealed with equal ease.[10]

It was for this reason that he counselled loyalty and gratitude, the most frequent theme of his political pastorals. In many respects, however, Troy's differences with the radical laity were based on the grounds of prudence rather than the content of their demands. From the mid-1770s he increasingly enjoyed the confidence of the administration; Troy's views on relief had been sounded by the Castle in 1778 and in the following year Luke Gardiner assured him that no further bill would be forwarded without consultation with the hierarchy.[11] In 1791, when bitter divisions manifested themselves within the Catholic Committee, Troy outlined for Major Hobart at the Castle the genuine grievances of the Catholics. In a reflection of his subtle but determined diplomacy he declared that 'the most loyal and conscientious Catholics wish the right to suffrage at the country elections to be communicated to respectable freeholders of their persuasion'.[12] On other occasions Troy relayed similar complaints from country bishops to the Castle and in his private correspondence he attributed the disturbed state of Armagh to 'the supine neglect of the magistrates and prejudice of the gentry'.[13]

Again, in 1795 Troy shared the despondency of his flock at the withdrawal of Fitzwilliam and the subsequent failure of the relief bill. While he

---

8 J. Smyth, *The men of no property* (London, 1992), p. 54; M. Burke, account of a conversation with Tone and Teeling in France, n.d. [1798] (Nat. Archives, Rebellion Papers, 620/52/123). 9 *Irish Magazine*, March 1815. 10 See T. Bartlett, *The fall and rise of the Irish nation: the Catholic question 1690-1830* (Dublin, 1992). 11 Troy to M.P. MacMahon, 27 November 1779 (Dublin Diocesan Archives (henceforth DDA), Troy Papers). 12 Troy to Hobart, 29 November 1791 (PRO, HO 100/34/33). 13 Troy to J. Carroll, 13 August 1796 (Baltimore Diocesan Archives, cited in P. O'Donoghue 'The Catholic Church and Ireland in an age of imperialism and rebellion 1782-1803' (Ph.D. thesis, University College, Dublin, 1975) p. 299).

enthusiastically welcomed the passage of the Catholic education bill establishing Maynooth, which was bitterly dismissed by the radical laity as a mere sop for the failure of emancipation, Troy made every effort to ensure that the relief bill and the education question were not confused in case bitter reaction to one endangered the passage of the other. Condemnation of the 1798 Rebellion, too, and the excommunication of the United Irishmen brought further criticism. Threats were made upon his life, but amongst the radicals his opposition was generally ridiculed. In 1797, the racy *Dublin Morning Post* mocked his pastoral address, declaring that 'it is rightly termed a pastoral as there is sufficient wool gathering in it to show that the Doctor considered his flock to be sheep'.[14] The United Irishman Watty Cox later condemned the archbishop for sending a man 'to the devil for loving his country'.[15] The archbishop firmly believed that the rebellion had weakened the hand of the Catholics in their quest for emancipation. For twenty years he had striven to assert Catholic loyalty, but thereafter it fell to him to rescue the Catholic position from the ashes of 1798 and the bitter anti-Catholic polemic that followed.

Despite the fact that he had in the past assured Castlereagh that no arrangements to pacify Ireland could succeed so long as 'the Catholic body was excluded from the benefits of the constitution', the bishops were in no position to offer sustained opposition to the Union.[16] Bishop Young of Limerick expressed the most bitter sentiments, arguing that he would never 'accept a bribe to acquiesce in the annihilation of the independence' of the country.[17] Troy echoed Pitt's view that the Union would open the way for emancipation, but that emancipation first would jeopardise its passage. In the end Troy accepted the Union, on the grounds that it contained no bar to future Catholic hopes, but he was forced to concede a limited Crown veto on episcopal appointments. Confiding in his Roman agent, Luke Concanen, he explained his action:

> we all wish to remain as we are, and we would so, were it not that too many of the clergy were active in the wicked rebellion or did not oppose it ... If we had rejected the proposal in toto, we would be considered here as rebels ... if we agreed to it without reference to Rome we would be branded schismatics. We were between Scylla and Charybdis.[18]

There is little justification, then, for the assertion that 'Archbishop Troy ... conspired with the murderous viceroy [*sic*] Castlereagh for the Act of Union'.[19]

14 *Morning Post*, 18 March 1797.   15 *Irish Magazine*, March 1815.   16 Troy to Castlereagh, 15 December 1795 (Public Record Office of Northern Ireland (henceforth PRONI), Castlereagh Papers, D3030/412).   17 Young to T. Bray, 30 Dec. 1798 (Cashel Diocesan Archive).   18 Troy to L. Concanen, Spring 1800 (DDA, Troy Papers).   19 D. Kelleher,

The veto question reemerged to dog the last years of Troy's life. Yet in this episode we have a perfect insight into the archbishop, one which reflects his shrewd political nature. Troy was no sycophant seeking to ingratiate himself in Castle circles; rather his actions show his astute handling of embarrasing circumstances. Near contemporary commentators, however, were not so kind and Watty Cox's *Irish Magazine* of 1808 gave a classic interpretation of Troy's actions. Commenting on the appointment of Bishop Patrick Ryan, a loyal Dublin priest of '98, to the see of Ferns, Cox asks 'since Dr Troy makes such bishops they might as well be appointed by the King'.[20]

It is this interpretation of Troy which has largely survived. But examination of the evidence suggests that on the contrary Troy sought to protect the interests and the independence of the Irish Church. The bulk of his correspondence with the Castle is in direct response to specific needs, particularly in the run-up to the establishment of Maynooth, and in the aftermath of the rebellion of 1798 when he sought to secure compensation from Cornwallis for the damage to Catholic chapels in Wicklow and Wexford. After 1801 communications were never so frequent, perhaps due to the disappearance of an immediate need; gone too was Troy's anxiety to stress Catholic loyalty. The bitterness of the post-Union period may also have been a factor, while the Catholic cause never again met with the sympathy it had received from Cornwallis, or Crop-wallis as he was dubbed by his loyalist critics.[21]

In any event, Troy cared little for adulation or criticism. On many occasions he declared his indifference to popularity; in December 1793, referring to radical criticism of his actions, he declared that we are 'equally indifferent to their praise or censure. We are neither aristocrats or democrats ... We have spoken as bishops, without taking notice of any party'.[22] Troy's concern remained what it had always been, the interests of the Irish Church. As John Milner observed in 1807 'he is for getting what ever can be gotten for the good of religion, let it come in whatever shape it may.'[23]

II

It could also be argued that the failure to recognise Troy's contribution results from a tradition amongst historians to exaggerate the duration of the penal era. This emphasis on the impact of the penal laws has obscured the reality and spawned the images contained in Daniel Corkery's emotive *Hidden*

'Republicanism ...', *Irish Times*, 2 September 1997.   **20** *Irish Magazine*, March 1808.   **21** Bartlett, *Fall and rise*, p. 236.   **22** Troy to L. Concanen, 24 December 1793 (Archives of Propaganda Fide (henceforth APF) *Scrittino originali riferite nelle congregazioni generali*, vol. 899 f 289).   **23** Milner to Gibson, 23 February 1807, cited in McNally 'Troy', p. 333.

Ireland.[24] Recent scholarship has re-examined the impact of the laws, and the work of Bartlett, Cullen and Connolly offers a more realistic assessment of the effects of the code.[25] Their research indicates that, rather than a period of blanket repression, the penal era was a time of 'endurance and emergence' for Ireland's Catholics. A similar conclusion is reflected in Kelly's study of the Dublin diocese in this volume.

Where the practice of religion is concerned it can be argued that the Catholic revival was well under way by 1760. By that date, the Hanoverian dynasty was secure on the throne and the Holy See's failure to recognise Charles Edward, on the death of the Old Pretender in 1766, removed a great deal of suspicion of Catholic loyalty. Rogers, in his history of Catholic emancipation, traced the rise of the Irish Church 'from the catacombs' to the 1760s; more recently, Whelan has placed the 'Tridentine surge' in the following decade.[26] Certainly contemporary travellers, such as Arthur Young and Thomas Campbell, were struck by the vitality of the Catholic Church in the 1770s. This revival, however, was uneven in geographical and chronological terms. Broadly speaking it began in mid-Munster/south Leinster and percolated only slowly into Ulster/north Connacht. Contrary to the received image, Catholicism as an institutional force was more firmly established in richer areas, the upper social classes and the towns.

Following his return to Ireland in 1776, 'freighted with the prerogative doctrines of the Court of Rome', Troy spearheaded the renewal of the Church in Ireland.[27] In Ossory his priority was the improvement of clerical discipline and practice; these objectives remained constant following his translation to Dublin in 1786. Indeed the circumstances of Troy's installation in the primatial see reflect the extent of the Catholic revival. John Carpenter, his immediate predecessor, had been consecrated in a private house in June 1770; one of the two assisting clergy was not a bishop, but the dean of the chapter. By contrast, Troy was installed with 'unusual solemnity' in the presence of the archbishops of Cashel and Armagh, two suffragans and the diocesan chapter.[28]

Yet, while the political climate had improved, Troy faced an onerous task. Dublin was a city of great contrasts, as Lecky remarks:

24 Daniel Corkery, *The hidden Ireland; a study of Gaelic Munster in the eighteenth century* (Dublin, 1925).   **25** L.M. Cullen, 'Catholics under the penal laws' in *Eighteenth-Century Ireland* (1986), pp 23-36; Thomas Bartlett, *Fall and rise* (Dublin, 1992), pp 17-29; S.J. Connolly, 'Religion and history', *Irish Economic and Social History* (1983), pp 66-80.   **26** P. Rogers, *The Irish Volunteers and Catholic emancipation, 1778-93* (London, 1934), p. 2; K. Whelan, 'The regional impact of Irish Catholicism 1700-1850' in W. Smyth and K. Whelan (eds), *Common ground: essays on the historical geography of Ireland* (Cork, 1988), p. 254.   **27** Troy to Fallon, 15 May 1778 (DDA, Troy Papers).   **28** T. Wall, 'Archbishop John Carpenter and the Catholic revival, 1770-1786', *Reportorium Novum*, 1, no. 1 (1955), p. 171; Troy to Antonelli, 10 March 1787 (APF, Irlanda, 16: 241).

strangers were equally struck with the crowds of beggars, the inferiority of the Inns, the squalid wretchedness of the streets of the old town, and with the noble proportions of the new quarter and the brilliant hospitable society that inhabited it.[29]

Of the diocese's forty-five parishes, nine were located within the city, which Troy mistakenly believed to contain 200,000 Catholics, and a further thirty-six in counties Dublin, Wicklow, Kildare, Carlow, Wexford and Queen's County. In these rural parishes the archbishop estimated the faithful to number another 200,000.[30] The city was served by one hundred priests, while a further fifty-four ministered in the rural areas of the diocese. These numbers included upwards of forty regulars dispersed between seven religious houses or employed as assistants to the diocesan clergy.

The discipline and welfare of the clergy were of paramount importance to the archbishop. In 1788 Dublin he undertook a full visitation of the diocese; each year after that, except for the period of rebellion, he visited several parishes and met the clergy of each deanery successively.[31] In addition to these visits, the pastors of the diocese were obliged to submit regular reports in reply to the Archbishop's queries. These responses were principally statistical and focused on the extent of the parish, the numbers of Catholic and Protestant families, estimates of communicants and converts, recorded baptisms and marriages and other information regarding education.[32]

The dislocation caused by the penal laws contributed to the weakness of institutional structures within the Church. Many abuses did exist and it is not unreasonable to assume that the conditions which Troy discovered in some rural parishes in the diocese were similar to those recorded by Bishop Patrick Plunket in his visitation of the neighbouring diocese of Meath. At Kilskeer (Kilskryne), in the barony of Upper Kells, on 29 June 1780 Plunket remarked:

> 1. The altar step and the place about the altar, by no means clean or orderly. The crucifix too bad. A cruet or small phial for wine absolutely wanting. The chapel not closed and therefore exposed to dirt and profanation. A clerk absolutely necessary to keep up some little decency in the house of God.

---

29 W.E.H. Lecky, *A history of Ireland in the eighteenth century*, i (London, 1902), p. 319.
30 J. Troy, *Relatio Status*, 1802 (DDA). These figures are clearly exaggerated; in 1798 Whitelaw estimated the population of the city to be 172,091 (James Whitelaw, *An essay on the population of Dublin ...* (Dublin, 1805), p. 25). 31 J. Troy, *Relatio Status*, 1802 (DDA). 32 See William Hawkes, 'Parish of Ballymore Eustace, 1791', *Reportorium Novum*, 2, no. 1 (1958), p. 121.

2. One of the chalices not to be used until the screw be mended; the chalice should at the same time be cleaned, being at present black.

3. A register of births, marriages and deaths wanting, and to be made out immediately. A missal wanting.

4. The children in general ignorant of the essential parts of the Christian doctrine, and not understanding what they say ...

5. Ordered, in the strictest manner, that on every Sunday of the year and on the principal festivals, the Gospel or epistle of the day be read and expounded to the faithful ...

6. The pastor must be sure that the midwives know how to administer validly the sacrament of baptism.[33]

Troy's consciousness of such failings was reflected in his *Relatio Status* of 1802, but the picture he offers is significantly better than that in Meath two decades earlier. In it he commented that the 'vestments were not splendid, but decent' while records of baptism and marriage were now kept in every parish. He was confident, too, that priests preached on Sundays and feasts and taught 'the rudiments of faith, obedience to God [and] assisted school teachers and other pious people'.

Troy took radical steps to reinforce discipline and order amongst his clergy. While Carpenter had pursued vigorous reform, under his successor this process took on a systematic and institutional character. In November 1787 Troy issued comprehensive pastoral instructions to his clergy in which he sought to order religious practice and clerical behaviour. Times of worship were regulated, midnight Masses were forbidden, while acts of faith, hope, charity and contrition were to be read before each Mass. In addition, priests were to catechise, promote the Easter duty and encourage the various indulgences granted to the diocese and the requirements necessary for their reception, i.e. confession, communion prayers and almsgiving.[34]

The priests of the diocese were forbidden from frequenting hunts, races or public concerts, but more significantly they were required to attend regular meetings of the clergy. As bishop of Ossory, Troy had initiated diocesan conferences, through which he attempted to renew the clergy. One-day seminars were held between the months of April and October and it appears that fines were imposed on those absent without reason. In Dublin, Troy continued this practice but the urban clergy were obliged to attend monthly meetings through the winter. Troy chose a theme for each year, and the surviving Dublin plan for 1790 reflects his meticulous approach:

---

33 P. Plunket, Visitation diary, Kilskeer, 29 June 1780 in A. Cogan, *The diocese of Meath*, iii (Dublin, 1870), p. 27.   34 D'Alton, *Memoirs of the archbishops of Dublin*, p. 483-4.

January	Paschal communion can it be deferred?
February	Viaticum for children and Mass stipends.
March	Why hear Mass, the altar and vestments.
April	The ceremony of the Mass, its language, can it be said in the vernacular?
June	Penance, what is it? Is it necessary, is it a true sacrament of the New Law?
July	Matter for penance and contrition.
August	Sacramental confession.
September	Is contrition necessary only for mortal sins?
October	The minister of penance.
November	Reserved cases, who has faculties to absolve them?
December	The sign of confession.[35]

Few such schemes survive, and while commentators have inferred the theological ignorance of the clergy from this 1790 plan, it would appear that Troy adopted a developmental approach.[36] The surviving scheme of the 1786 conference in Ossory, for example, the sixth in the diocese, discussed critical philosophical aspects of the Natural Law, the nature of civil society and the 'perverse opinions of Cumberland, Hobbes and Collins [which were] destructive of government and religion'.[37] These gatherings formed a vital part of the archbishop's pastoral plan; the priority he placed on them may be inferred from the fact that he continued to plan and direct the conferences until 1820.

It appears that Troy was satisfied with the conduct of the clergy. In 1802 he informed the Holy See that the morals of the secular clergy were excellent and there is little in his correspondence to equal Archbishop Carpenter's preoccupation with clerical drunkenness.[38] There was, nevertheless, no complacency on Troy's part and his vigilance is reflected in his immediate response to discipline cases and his willingness to meet with delegations of the faithful.[39] There was also the celebrated case in which the archbishop excommunicated Robert McEvoy, a priest of the diocese who had married a widow to himself according to the Protestant rite. Troy published a pastoral on the occasion in 1792; that address was subsequently reprinted in the aftermath of the rebellion of 1798. Of particular concern to the archbishop was McEvoy's attempt to justify his actions by an appeal to the decrees of the French National Assembly; Troy was determined to prevent such novelty in

35 J. Troy, Schema for 1790 diocesan conference (DDA).   36 D. Keogh, 'The French disease'; the Catholic Church and Irish radicalism, 1790-1800 (Dublin, 1993), p. 9.   37 D'Alton, Memoirs of the archbishops, p. 482.   38 J. Troy, Relatio Status, 1802 (DDA). 39 Parishoners of St Andrew's to Troy, 28 November 1796; Troy to Michael Hughes, 30 November 1796 (DDA, Troy Papers).

Ireland and to send a clear warning to the Catholic Convention about to assemble in Dublin.[40] A similar determination is reflected in the archbishop's decision, in 1814, to fight the Dublin grand jury in the courts in an effort to overturn its appointment of an incompetent priest to the chaplaincy of Newgate prison.[41]

The financial support of the clergy remained a sensitive issue throughout Troy's long episcopate; indeed it was a key political question, since as early as 1782 the government contemplated a series of measures intended to break the dependence of the clergy on the people.[42] The fullest record of clerical incomes for Ireland is contained in the returns made to Lord Castlereagh by the bishops in 1800.[43] The figures distinguish between 'voluntary oblations' – offerings on occasions of Christenings, burials and marriages – and what were described as 'stated contributions' or Christmas and Easter dues.[44] Clerical incomes varied through the country, but within dioceses there were significant differences. In 1800 the national average income for a parish priest was £65; in the diocese of Dublin it was £121, but these figures excluded the cost of keeping a curate, which amounted to £10. The latter expense made an important difference in urban parishes; the parish priest of St James', for example, employed two curates from an annual income of £100. Liffey Street, the archbishop's mensal church with an income of £250, was the wealthiest parish in the diocese, while at the bottom of the scale the parish priest of Irishtown and Donnybrook depended upon £60.[45] These incomes compared favourably with the monetary earnings of the more prominent lay members of the parish, as large farmers with around 150 acres had a cash income of only £50. Added to this, the clergy enjoyed many gifts, while their ministry involved receiving extensive hospitality; the 1800 returns declared that 'in general, they dine nearly half the year in private families'.[46] That said, Troy was conscious of the poverty of many of his priests and immediately on his appointment to Dublin he established a fund for the needy, which was administered by 'the Clerical Society'.[47] There were also instances where the clergy benefited from the charity of the Established Church; in 1792, for example, Rev. James Whitelaw made provision for Catholic curates from the estates of St Catherine's parish.[48]

40 J.T. Troy, *The excommunication of the Rev Robert M'Evoy, priest of the archdiocese of Dublin for promulgating and upholding principles established by the French Revolution* (London, 1798). 41 D'Alton, *Memoirs of the archbishops of Dublin*, p. 486. 42 J.A. Murphy, 'The support of the Catholic clergy in Ireland, 1750-1850' in *Historical Studies*, V (1965), pp 103-21. 43 Charles Vane (ed.), *Memoirs and correspondence of Viscount Castlereagh* (4 vols, London, 1850), iv, pp 133-8. 44 Keogh, *'French disease'*, p. 10. 45 *Castlereagh correspondence*, iv, pp 133-8. 46 Ibid., p. 154. 47 J. Troy, *Relatio Status*, 1802 (DDA). 48 *National Evening Star*, 7 April 1792.

III

The neglect of Troy's memory might also be the attributed to the concept of a 'Devotional Revolution' which raises serious questions about the nature of pre-Famine Catholicism in Ireland.[49] Yet, while this concept has been revised, there was certainly a recognition at the time of Daniel Murray's death that religious practice had been brought to a new level. Certainly the oration delivered at his month's mind Mass drew stark contrasts with the past:

> The poorest Metropolis in Christendom – as far as the goods of this world are concerned – in spiritual riches, 'tis not unlikely the most opulent ... Dublin is teeming with faith, exuberant in works of Godliness, crowded with saints. It was not always so ... When the holy man, over whom our tears have fallen, was called to take a leading part in its eternal concerns, very different indeed was the nature of its prosperity. It was very wealthy and very wicked very gay and very dissolute.[50]

The achievements of 'the archbishop of the reconstruction', as Murray has been called, were indeed immense, but it would be mistaken to suggest that Troy's Church lacked religious vitality. One account, published in 1821, presented an image of a thriving community:

> In each of the parish chapels and friaries there is a regular succession of Masses, generally from 6 o'cl[ock], in the morning until 11 o'cl[ock] in the day of Sundays and Holidays; and from 7 until 11 o'cl[ock], and in some chapels, until 12 o'cl[ock] on every other day. On the Sundays and Holidays all these Masses are attended by crowded congregations. In the parish chapels and friaries, sermons are preached on the evenings of every Sunday and Holiday during the winter season, and immediately after last Mass in the summer and autumn months; and generally in the evenings of every day during the penitential times of lent and advent. On these occasions the chapels are crowded to excess.[51]

49 E. Larkin, 'The Devotional Revolution in Ireland, 1850-1875', *American Historical Review*, 87 (1972), pp 625-52; T.G. McGrath, 'The Tridentine evolution of modern Irish Catholicism, 1563-1962; a re-examination of the "Devotional Revolution" thesis' in R. Ó Muiri (ed.), *Irish Church history today* (Armagh, [1991]), pp 84-99. 50 W. Meaghar, *Notes on the life and character of ... Daniel Murray* (Dublin, 1853), p. 8. 51 John McGregor, *New picture of Dublin ...* (Dublin, 1821), p. 148.

Once more, however, a distinction must be drawn between the rural and urban portions of the diocese. Clearly, there were great local variations in a diocese which spanned six counties, and conditions in the rural parishes in 1821 were closer to Plunket's observations in Kilkskeer, forty years earlier, than McGregor's description of the city churches.

Such differences were reflected in the contrasting architecture of the rural and urban churches. The city chapels were on a grander scale. Taking one of their number, Liffey Street, it is possible to gain an insight into the devotional life of the period. The chapel, built in 1729 by John Linegar, was described in the famous 1749 report on the state of Catholic chapels of Dublin:

> This chapel, though small, is neat, altar railed in, steps ascending to it in oak; fore part of the altar covered with gilt leather, and name of Jesus in glory in the midst. On the altar is a gilt tabernacle, with six large gilt candlesticks, and as many nosegays of artificial flowers. The altar piece carved and embellished with four pillars, cornices and decorations gilt and painted. The picture of the Conception of B.V.M., to whom the chapel is dedicated, fills the altar piece; and on each side are paintings of the apostles Peter and Paul. Opposite the altar hangs a handsome brass branch for tapers, near it a neat oak pulpit, on the sounding board of which is the figure of a gilt dove, representing the descent of the Holy Ghost. In said chapel is a small sacristy, four decent confessionals, two galleries, several pews for the better sort, and two sprinkling pots of black marble in the chapel yard.[52]

The chapel had been Dr Linegar's mensal parish until he conferred it on his nephew, William Clarke, in 1757. Upon his death, in 1797, Troy petitioned Rome and it was subsequently restored to the archbishop.[53] By this time, however, the chapel had become inadequate for the needs of the parish and on Troy's initiative a site was purchased for a new cathedral. Yet, a continuity with the past is reflected in the decision to form the side altars in the Pro-Cathedral from the pillars and cornices from Liffey Street. The altar piece, the painting of the Blessed Virgin, hung above the new high altar until the 1860s when it was transferred to the presbytery on 83 Marlborough Street.[54] Curiously the oak pulpit has disappeared; perhaps more than any other item it symbolically linked the penal age and the revival, since it was

52 N. Donnelly, *Roman Catholics; state and condition of Roman Catholic chapels in Dublin both secular and regular A.D. 1749* (Dublin, 1904), p. 12.   53 McNally, 'Troy', p. 28.   54 I am grateful to Father John Delaney for assistance in identifying these items.

constructed by James McGauley, father of Catherine McAuley, foundress of the Sisters of Mercy.[55] Yet, while the Pro-Cathedral is certainly the finest church built during Troy's episcopate, it was but one of many significant buildings which included St Michan's, Halston Street (1817) and the graceful SS Michael and John's (1815), now regrettably transformed into the Dublin Viking Museum.[56]

In the country many churches retained the characteristics of penal chapels; they were small, mud-walled, thatched, clay-floored buildings which were devoid of external decoration. In the late eighteenth and early nineteenth century many of these gave way to the so-called 'barn chapels', sturdy churches, commonly built according to a cruciform plan with flagged floors, galleries and improved sanctuaries.[57] While such developments bore physical witness to the revival of the Catholic Church, it is one of the great ironies of the period that the rebellion of 1798, dubbed a popish plot by loyalists, facilitated this emergence. As many as sixty-nine chapels destroyed in the aftermath of the rising were replaced at government expense following the intervention of Archbishop Troy.[58] It is inaccurate, then, to assert as McNally does that 'Troy built only one church during his lenghty term as archbishop'.[59]

The Mass was the central act of worship in the Church, but Counter-Reformationary devotions were well-developed, particularly in urban areas. Exposition of the Blessed Sacrament had been common in the order churches from about 1720, while many chapels performed benediction and sung vespers on Sunday afternoons. There is evidence, too, that the solemn liturgies of the city were of the highest quality. From 1779, Francis Street chapel employed a Neapolitan musical director; Tommaso Giordani's most celebrated composition was a grand *Te Deum*, first performed on the occasion of the thanksgiving for the King's recovery in May 1789. That, indeed, was the most spectacular liturgy witnessed in the city for centuries. Troy, assisted by three of his suffragans, presided at the altar before a congregation of three thousand which included the duke of Leinster, Lord Kenmare, the earl of Tyrone, Lord and Lady Arran, Henry Grattan and David Latouche.[60] Less auspicious occasions were marked with similar formality. Charity sermons were often the prelude for orchestral recitals; in November 1791, for exam-

55 R. Burke Savage, *Catherine McAuley: the first Sister of Mercy* (Dublin, 1949), p. 15. **56** See 'Blessings of foundation stones, churches etc., by Dr Troy', *Reportorium Novum*, 1, no. 2 (1956), pp 497-98. **57** K. Whelan, 'The Catholic parish, the Catholic chapel and village development in Ireland', *Irish Geography*, 14 (1983), pp 1-16. **58** O'Donoghue, 'The Catholic Church in Ireland in an age of revolution and rebellion', p. 371 ff. **59** McNally, *Reform, revolution and reaction: Archbishop John Thomas Troy* (Lanham, 1995), p. 27. **60** *Faulkner's Dublin Journal*, 7 May 1789.

ple, a sermon by Father John Connolly OFM in Townsend Street chapel was followed by an organ performance and an orchestra consisting of forty violins, twenty basses and a proportionate number of wind instruments.[61]

Each of the order churches had their particular devotions. The Dominicans of Denmark Street had a confraternity of the Rosary; the Carmelites had a confraternity of the Scapulari, in John's Lane there was a confraternity of the sacred Cincture, while both branches of the Franciscans had a confraternity of the Sacred Cord. Sodalities of the Sacred Heart met in the various convents of the city, while in many parishes there was common recitation of the rosary, stations of the cross and Purgatorian societies. Clearly, by the end of Troy's episcopate the beginnings of the characteristics attributed to the 'devotional revolution' were already in place.[62]

Evidence suggests that services were well attended; if there was cause for concern, it was on account of the passivity of the congregations, who said their prayers and let the priest get on with his business at the altar.[63] Archbishop Troy's principal concern was the difficulty in getting people to receive the sacraments and to fulfill the essential Easter duty. This he attributed to a shortage of priests.[64] Dublin, in fact, with one priest for every 2,000 people was comparatively well served at a time when the national average was one to every 2,676. Yet it is clear that these ratios had deteriorated; ironically in 1731, at the height of the 'penal era', the national average was one priest for every 1,587 Catholics.[65]

The situation became more critical as the French Revolution closed the continental colleges which had accommodated 400 students for the Irish mission.[66] Maynooth, Troy's own creation, could cater for no more that 200 students, and this shortfall resulted in a continuous decline in the clergy-to-people ratios. Even allowing for the removal of the limitation on ordinations secured by Troy from Rome in 1816, by 1843 the national figure was one to 2,996.[67] These difficulties, Troy believed, 'made the piety of the people grow cold'.[68] The situation was compounded by the fact that the Sunday Mass was the principal occasion for instruction by the priest. While the diocese possessed many fine preachers, it was difficult to facilitate preaching because so many Masses had to be provided. As late as 1820, for example, the celebrated Father Henry Young would walk from Harold's Cross through the fields to

61 *Dublin Chronicle*, 29 November 1791.   62 W. Hawkes, 'The Catholic Directory for 1821', *Reportorium Novum*, 2, no. 2 (1960), pp 324-63.   63 P. Corish, *The Irish Catholic experience: a historical survey* (Dublin, 1985), p. 134.   64 J. Troy, *Relatio Status*, 1802 (DDA).   65 S.J. Connolly, *Priests and people in pre-Famine Ireland 1780-1845* (Dublin, 1982), pp 32-3.   66 P. Corish, *Maynooth College 1795-1995* (Dublin, 1995).   67 J. Troy, *Relatio Status*, 1816 (DDA); Cardinal Litta to Troy, 5 September 1816, (DDA, Troy-Murray Papers).   68 J. Troy, *Relatio Status*, 1802 (DDA).

Milltown to say a second Mass in the converted barn which served as a chapel of ease.[69]

Yet, while evidence reflects the religious enthusiasm of the people, many of the Irish bishops were concerned at its heterodox expression. A source of perennial anxiety was the popular celebration of festivals and patterns, since the religious observances were generally a prelude to more secular celebrations. In Ossory, Troy had attempted to halt the celebration of 'patrons' and May balls, and one of his first acts in Dublin was a renewal of his predecessor's condemnation of the mid-summer festival at Kilmainham where, under the pretext of devotion, Carpenter claimed, 'many scandalous enormities ... disgraceful to religion [and] civil society' had been committed.[70] Troy published a pastoral condemning the excesses associated with the occasion, drunkenness, riot and 'transgressions of every duty', but significantly he urged the faithful to express their devotions in a 'becoming manner', in the chapels of the city.[71] While this injunction reflected his attempt to Christianise, or indeed Romanise, traditional religious expression, it could equally be interpreted as a sign of the increasing social control exercised by the clergy in the period. It is clear, however, that Troy's attempts to stem the celebrations failed since the pattern at Kilmainham continued to be celebrated, if in a more ordered fashion, until the 1830s.

The absence of effective catechesis was a cause of great concern for the Irish bishops, many of whom refused confirmations on account of poor preparation. Indeed, the priority of catechesis is emphasised in almost every episcopal report to Rome in the period 1782-1803. In the absence of an adequate educational system, the bishops increasingly relied on the Confraternity of Christine Doctrine to assist in their task of evangelisation.[72] Its members gave instruction to the children of the parish for one hour after the last Mass each Sunday. The sexes were educated separately; the boys were instructed in the aisles, while the girls were taken to the balconies.[73] The societies were governed by a priest and he was assisted by a president, vice-president and treasurer who were elected annually by the predominantly female membership. Each member of the confraternity contributed 6½d. per month; from this, catechisms, prayer-books and candles were purchased. A surviving register of the Confraternity of the Blessed Sacrament and Christian Doctrine, which was established in Mary's Lane in November 1798, illustrates the institu-

69 M.V. Ronan, *An apostle of Catholic Dublin: Father Henry Young* (Dublin, 1944), p. 99.
70 John Carpenter, before St John's Day, 1786, in M.J. Curran, 'Instructions, admonitions etc of Archbishop Carpenter 1770-86', *Reportorium Novum*, 2, no. 1 (1957-58), p. 171.   71 Pastoral address of J. Troy, *Dublin Chronicle*, 23 June 1787.   72 M. Brennan, 'The Confraternity of Christian Doctrine in Ireland', *IER* (1934), pp 560-77.   73 W. Hawkes, 'The Catholic Directory for 1821', p. 358

tionalised nature and character of the society.[74] Two of the nineteen rules extant are of particular interest:

> 11. The children be divided into different classes according to the following order: 1st Class, Prayers including the Acts of Faith, Hope and Charity. 2nd Class – Small Catechisms. 3rd Class – Abridgement of the General Catechism. 4th Class – General Catechism. 5th Class – Fleury's Historical Catechism. But to this last no one is to be admitted but such as shall be declared fit by some priest of the Chapel ...
>
> 15. That the Members do recite each day some one of the following devotions, viz:- the Office of the Blessed Sacrament, or the Pange Lingua ... [75]

From his arrival in Dublin Troy promoted the confraternity. In 1788 he secured indulgences from the Holy See for its members on completion of prescribed conditions which included the reception of Holy Communion on the third Sunday of each month. By the time of his death, in 1823, there was a confraternity in every parish of the diocese.[76]

In a similar way, the archbishop sought to regulate the celebration of marriage in his diocese, which, as Kelly has observed, often reflected a tendency amongst the laity to ignore inconvenient Church rules.[77] Clandestine marriages presented particular difficulties, since Ireland's civil law made no regulations for Catholic marriages. In England the situation was more complex, since practice was governed by the Hardwicke Act of 1753 which required marriages to be celebrated in the parish church. The Irish bishops feared the extension of this legislation to Ireland, since it would have obliged Catholics to marry in the Protestant Church, but they were equally reluctant to enforce the Tridentine Tamesti decree of 1563. This was not usually published in non-Catholic countries and, while it was gradually applied in Ireland, it was only in 1827 that it was enforced in the diocese of Meath, the wardenship of Galway and the province of Dublin. In these difficult circumstances, as Corish remarks, the couple beggar, the irregular cleric or degraded minister, remained a feature of Irish life, but Troy took action to limit his effectiveness.[78] Following consultation with his clergy, the archbishop published a pastoral in March 1789 in which he formally renewed the excommunication of couple beggars and the contracting parties in illicit marriages.[79]

---

74 Ronan, *An apostle of Catholic Dublin*.   75 Ibid.   76 *Ex audientia*, 10 August 1788 (DDA, Troy Papers).   77 Kelly, above, p. 172.   78 Corish, *The Irish Catholic experience*, p. 135.   79 Clandestine marriages enquiry 1788 (DDA, Troy Papers); John Brady, 'Archbishop Troy's pastoral on clandestine marriages, 1789', *Reportorium Novum*, 1, no. 2 (1956), pp 266-7.

Two points, however, may be made at this point. On one level, Troy's choice of the 'softer option', rather than publishing the *Tamesti* decree, may reflect what Kelly has called the 'culture of caution which pervaded the Church', but it might also be a measure of the practical difficulties faced by Catholic bishops in a Protestant state. Certainly his Relatio status of 1802 made several references to his reliance on 'persuasion rather than authority' since the 'Catholic religion is simply tolerated, not backed by force'.[80] It is important, too, to note Troy's pastoral sensitivity expressed in his 1788 decree. While the address was undoubtedly a salutary warning, it contains a palpable sense of the archbishop's sympathy for the plight of women, 'outcasts of society, reduced to the sad necessity of prolonging a wretched existence by the wages of prostitution'.[81] Significantly, too, Troy gave every support to the establishment of institutions along the lines of the General Magdalen Asylum (est. 1798), Townsend Street, which cared for thirty-seven women.[82]

IV

By the turn of the nineteenth century the archdiocese of Dublin had been brought firmly into line with Roman practice. Troy, assisted by his vicar general, Thomas Betagh SJ, and a diocesan chapter, had presided over the transformation of a mission to a church. The second half of his episcopate witnessed a more sophisticated development, reflected in increased institutionalisation and a flowering of religious life. This period is perhaps the more difficult to assess, since in these years Troy was assisted by a coadjutor, described by one commentator as the greatest Irish bishop of the last century and probably since Oliver Plunkett.[83]

In 1808 Troy was unable to administer Confirmation in the diocese due to 'disability from illness' (see appendix). Clearly the burden of responsibility had begun to take its toll on the archbishop, now in his seventieth year and alarmed at the increasing controversy over the veto and the anti-Catholic tendencies of the Richmond viceroyalty (1807-13).[84] Accordingly, he applied to Rome for a coadjutor, naming Daniel Murray, 'a doctor of theology ... a canon of Dublin, and a most celebrated preacher ... held in high regard by both the clergy and people' as his preferred successor.[85] Within months this

---

80 Kelly, above p. 172: J. Troy, *Relatio Status*, 1802 (DDA).   81 John Brady, 'Archbishop Troy's pastoral on clandestine marriages, 1789' *Reportorium Novum*, 1, no. 2 (1956), p. 267.   82 J. Troy, *Relatio Status*, 1802 (DDA); W. Hawkes, 'The Catholic Directory for 1821', p. 333.   83 Desmond Keenan, *The Catholic Church in nineteenth century Ireland* (Dublin, 1983), p. 2.   84 See Bartlett, *The fall and rise of the Irish nation*, pp 268-303. 85 J. Troy to Pius VII, 28 November 1808 (APF, SC Irlanda 18 f. 481).

request received a positive response and Murray was duly consecrated in St Mary's chapel, Liffey Street, on 30 November 1809. Once more, the solemnity of the occasion reflected the progress of the Church in Dublin: Troy was assisted at the altar by the archbishop of Armagh (Richard O'Reilly), together with the bishops of Ferns (Patrick Ryan) and Kildare and Leighlin (Daniel Delaney). Significantly, given the political temper of the period, Troy authorised the publication of an English translation of the rite of consecration, not for the benefit of the congregation alone, but their 'fellow Christians, who, though estranged from the Roman Catholic communion, might, however, desire to inspect ... [its] ceremonies'.[86]

The Troy-Murray partnership was a winning combination; the archbishop's vision remained as ever, but what he now lacked in vigour was amply compensated for by the trojan efforts of his coadjutor. Murray, while temperamentally moderate, enthusiastically advanced the achievements of his predecessor; through his efforts the institutions were put in place which gave nineteenth-century Catholicism its self-confident character. Under Murray's direction the chapel building commenced by Troy was greatly extended, but perhaps the greatest achievements of their partnership were in the fields of education and religious life.

It is not my intention to treat of these advances here, since they are developed by Enright and Kerr below. Suffice it to say that in education the 'hedge schools', or private schools like Betagh's celebrated academy at Saul's Court, which characterised eighteenth-century Catholic instruction, gradually gave way to parish and religious schools which in time formed the basis of the National School system.[87] The religious life, too, witnessed unprecedented growth; by the time of Troy's death the Christian Brothers were in Dublin, the Sisters of Charity in William Street, the Loreto nuns in Rathfarnham, the Presentation Sisters in George's Hill, the Sisters of Charity in Harold's Cross, the Carmelites in Ranelagh, while the restored Jesuits had opened a school at Castle Browne, Clane, County Kildare.[88]

It is clear that Troy, little by little, handed responsibility to Murray, his 'excellent coadjutor', but he remained active to the end. He remained Rome's most trusted advisor in Ireland, a confidence which is reflected in the fact that his opinion carried sway in the selection of bishops, not only for Ireland, but for England and North America. Troy continued to preside at episcopal

86 *The order of the Latin rite for the ordination of bishops in the Roman Catholic Church, translated and published with the approbation of the Most Reverend John Thomas Troy* (Dublin, 1809) in McNally, 'Troy', p. 377.   87 Mary Daly, 'The development of the National School system, 1831-40' in A. Cosgrove and D. McCartney (eds), *Studies in Irish history presented to R. Dudley Edwards* (Dublin, 1979), pp 150-63.   88 Purcell, 'John Troy', p. 52.

consecrations until 1820, by which time he had ordained eighteen archbishops and bishops.[89] Indeed, he had been vital to the formation of a corporate identity amongst the Irish hierarchy. The creation of a national synod
had long been his hope and one year after his appointment to Dublin, the
first steps were taken towards its realisation. At his invitation, the four archbishops assembled in Dublin and in a letter to Rome, written by Troy, they
expressed the purpose of their meeting 'as the preservation of unity of the
Spirit in the bond of peace, and the fostering of uniformity in enforcing ecclesiastical laws'.[90] The metropolitans met again in the following year and their
renewed confidence is reflected in their successful petition to Rome for a
restoration of pallia.[91] The process was completed in 1795 with the foundation of the Royal College at Maynooth, which signalled not only the emergence of a national episcopal conference but the establishment of a *modus
operandi* between the Catholic Church and the protestant state.

Within the diocese, Troy's priority remained the realisation of his planned
cathedral. While the Marlborough Street site was purchased at a cost of
£5,100 in 1803, progress was frustratingly slow. Difficulties were principally
financial; the archbishop laid the foundation stone in April 1815, but six years
later the building committee expressed its deep regret that 'a national feeling' had not 'been found ... in the public' to supply the funds necessary for
its completion.[92] Troy chaired this committee and, despite his advanced years,
each week he joined the Westland Row collectors in their effort to see its
completion.[93] It was, then, fitting that the archbishop's obsequies should take
place within the walls of his unfinished cathedral.

V

Death came to the Troy on 11 May 1823 – like so much in his life it passed
with little notice. Writing to his wife at Tours, Daniel O'Connell broke the
news of the archbishop's demise:

> You have I suppose seen by the newspapers that Dr Troy is dead. He
> arrived at a fine old age and died in sentiments of the purest religion.
> May the great and good God be merciful to his soul ... Dr Troy died
> without a guinea. He was a most charitable man and never known to

89 'Episcopal consecrations by Archbishop Troy', *Reportorium Novum*, 1, no. 1 (1956), pp
492-3.   90 H. Peel, 'Some aspects' p. 57.   91 O'Donoghue, 'The Catholic Church and
Ireland in an age of imperialism and rebellion', p. 42.   92 McNally, 'Troy', p. 29; Report
of the committee for building the Roman Catholic metropolitan chapel ... held in the new
building on 11 June 1821 (DDA, Pro-Cathedral Papers).   93 Purcell, 'John Troy', p. 52.

refuse giving what he could to a person in distress. He governed the Catholic Church in Ireland in a stormy period and was very much loved by his own clergy.

Tellingly, however, the Liberator continued: 'Darling, I mean to take a bath on my way to O'Meara's'.[94]

Time had moved on; Troy was from another generation and his passing created little stir in a city preoccupied with the Catholic Association founded the month before. The papers carried a brief announcement of the death of 'the venerable, learned and pious Doctor John Thomas Troy' and for days following plans were developed for his funeral.[95] An outline of the proceedings is extant, but curiously no copy of the funeral oration appears to survive. The following was the order of procession

> The Conductor, riding
> Six Mutes: Mr J. Esmonde, Mr Fitzsimmons, Mr R. Coyne, Mr Daniels,
> Mr Foley and Mr T. Daniel
> The Hearse having white plumes bore the coffin, which
> was draped in black with full gilt mounting
> Stewards on each side of the Hearse carried white wands
> The Deceased's carriage
> A mourning coach with the Chief Mourners, Walter Troy Esq and the Most Rev. Dr Murray
> Another Coach with Dr Lee and Mourners
> Two coaches with the Reverend Gentlemen of Liffey Street Chapel
> A sixth coach with the servants of the deceased
> The Roman Catholic Clergy of the Archdiocese walking four abreast with scarves and hat bands
> Private gentlemen with scarves and hat bands, four a breast
> The Trade Societies, two a breast with scarves and hat bands
> Private gentlemen and other carriages
> The Committee that superintended the proceedings[Chaired by Sir John Brown], four a breast with white wands, scarfs and hat bands
> Private Gentlemen and other carriages
> During the day the shipping had their colours raised half mast high.[96]

94 D. O'Connell to Mary O'Connell, 25 May 1823 in M.R. O'Connell (ed.), *The Correspondence of Daniel O'Connell* (Dublin, 1973) vol. 2, p. 447. 95 *Freeman's Journal*, 12 May 1823. 96 Ibid., 16 May 1823.

The procession moved to the incomplete Metropolitan Chapel where the office of the dead was led by the primate, Dr Curtis, assisted by five bishops and the clergy of Dublin. The funeral oration was delivered extempore by Bishop James Doyle, who stepped from the congregation to replace the celebrated Michael Bernard Keogh, Capuchin parish priest of Baldoyle, who was unable to give the panegyric.[97] Following the High Mass, Dr Troy's remains were carried to the vaults of George's Hill convent, where they remained until their translation to the Pro-Cathedral in May 1824. This was, indeed, a symbolic last journey for the pastor who had led his diocese from the twilight of the penal age to the dawn of a new age.[98]

APPENDIX:
DR TROY'S CONFIRMATIONS

Year	Men	Women	Total
1788	2,128	2,615	4,743
1789	586	610	1,196
1790	610	715	1,405
1791	770	635	1,405
1792	604	522	1,126
1793	393	415	808
1794	550	559	1,079
1795	217	304	521
1796	2,051	2,183	4,234
1797	86	98	184
1798	*	*	*
1799	*	*	*
1800	*	*	*
1801	256	290	546
1802	2,375	2,565	4,940
1803	634	871	1,505
1804	3,342	3,243	6,585
1805	631	718	1,349
1806	2,967	2,832	5,799

* No Confirmations on account of the disturbed state of the country

97 Ibid., 16 May 1823; T. McGrath, *Religious renewal and reform in the pastoral ministry of Bishop James Doyle of Kildare and Leighlin, 1786-1834* (Dublin, 1998), p. 76.   98 I am very grateful to Dr Hugh Fenning OP for his assistance in the preparation of this paper.

Year	Men	Women	Total
1807	2,112	2,508	4,620
1808	**	**	**
1809	***	***	***
1810	901	989	1,890
1811	530	600	1,130
1812	413	502	914
TOTAL	22,156	23,773	45,929

** No Confirmation except in Dublin, Dr Troy being disabled by illness
*** No Confirmation

Source: Regestum, I: 18, DDA; *Rep. Nov.*, 1, no. 2 (1956), p. 492

10

Dublin's Greek Pro-Cathedral

Michael McCarthy

The background to the creation of the Pro-Cathedral of Dublin has been sketched above in Daire Keogh's outline of the accomplishments of Archbishop Troy.[1] It is a most surprising building in the grandeur of its severe and assertive portico of six baseless, fluted Doric columns supporting a full architrave, pediment and statuary (fig. 7).

For the art-historian the entrance portico is the first of several surprises. On entering the building we find that all the internal columns are also baseless, fluted Doric columns (fig. 8). There is nothing here of the hierarchical progression of the orders common in Irish and the other architecture of the period, from Doric at the entrance to Ionic in the nave to Corinthian in the chancel. Whoever conceived the design was unaffected by contemporary usage and the uniform use of the baseless, fluted Doric externally and internally marks him as pedantic or dogmatic. The only parallel that comes to mind in this respect is the cathedral at Syracuse, which is an adaptation to Christian worship of a Greek temple of the fifth century BC.

But then there is the dome. There was never a dome on a classical Greek building. Domes entered the vocabulary of modern western architecture with the completion of Brunelleschi's dome of the cathedral in Florence and proliferated throughout the Renaissance, finding definitive sanction in Michaelangelo's dome of St Peter's in Rome. They spread to Paris and London and Dublin, most recently in the great works of James Gandon, the Four Courts and the Custom House. The dome is an anomalous addition to the architecture of the Pro-Cathedral, absent from the original model.

Beyond the dome is another un-Greek feature, the semi-circular apse, from which springs a semi-dome framed by an arch that responds to the barrel-roof of the nave. Glazed arched openings to left and right give the illusion of a crossing with transepts. Spandrels connect the arches to rise to

---

1 Above, p. 233; see also Dáire Keogh, 'Archbishop John Thomas Troy (1739-1823)', *Archivium Hibernicum* 49 (1995), pp 105-10.

the coffered ring from which the dome springs, decorated with a pattern of receding coffers to give it an illusion of depth quite foreign to its external appearance, which is of a shallow saucer dome resting on an octagonal base. This illusion of height in the dome may be justified by the relief sculpture of the Ascension of Christ modelled in stucco in the half-dome of the apse, but it is contrary to the finish of the nave as a barrel-vault. That is also anachronistic to the Greek system, which would require a flat ceiling. Unlike the dome, however, the vaulting of the nave and the semi-circle of the apse are original to the conception of the building, as the model and the earliest drawings demonstrate (fig. 9) and (fig. 10).

The Pro-Cathedral therefore was a hybrid of the Greek temple with the Roman basilica from its conception, and at some point its Roman aspect was accentuated with the addition of the dome. The difference externally may be demonstrated by comparing two drawings, fig. 11 and fig. 12. The earlier is faithful to the architecture seen in the model, and it supplies the statuary intended for the portico of the south front. It is by an unknown artist and is from the collection of the archdiocese. The second is from the collection of the Royal Irish Academy and is by George Petrie. It imposes the dome on the structure, but with fictive lighting; and the south portico is also invented, since it is untrue to both the model and to the portico as constructed. Both side elevations were to have featured a recessed entrance between pavilions, seen in the model, but this was omitted on the right hand side in execution (fig. 13). The omission argues strongly in favour of the supposition that the building was originally conceived with a larger site in view.

There is a regrettable lack of documentation for the planning and execution of the building prior to 1834, and its completion with the erection of the portico under the direction of the architect J.B. Keane by the firm of Henry and Mullins of Talbot Street.[2] Explanation of the architectural character of the Pro-Cathedral must therefore be sought in contemporary scholarship and fashion in ecclesiastical architecture in Dublin and other capital cities. Account must also be taken of the personal architectural leanings of the patron of the building, Archbishop Troy, and its unidentified architect. The identification of the architect is particularly problematic. The design chosen at the public competition was marked 'P', and I offer here an extension of an argument I made previously for interpreting this as 'Pontifex' and identifying the conception of the building with Archbishop Troy. The argument still rests on circumstantial evidence and cannot be proven in the absence of documentation. The only argument in its favour to be made from the documents is a negative one. There is no record of the award of the £50

2 These are published in Mary Purcell (ed.), 'Dublin Diocesan Archives: Hamilton papers', *Archivium Hibernicum*, 46-51 (1991-6).

premium allotted to the winning design and this would be an understandable omission if Archbishop Troy had entered a design of his own conception under the letter 'P'. This is not to argue that the Archbishop was an architect or even an amateur architect or architectural draughtsman. His conception would have been explained to professional architects and draughtsmen and handed over to them for realisation in visual terms.

THE GREEK REVIVAL IN IRELAND

Francis Johnston was the pioneer of Greek Revival architecture in Ireland, using the baseless Doric order at Townley Hall in County Louth, Slane Castle in County Meath, and in the colonnades of the Cornmarket at Drogheda, all in the early 1790s.[3] At the courthouse in Dundalk, County Louth, the Greek Revival found its first and most prominent expression in secular public architecture, with a portico taken directly from the print of the Temple of Theseus at Athens in the third volume of James Stuart and Nicholas Revett's *The Antiquities of Athens* (1796). This was designed by the Dublin architects James Bowden and Edward Park under the patronage of John Leslie Foster from 1813, and, by fortunate coincidence, there survives a model of the portico in the Irish Architectural Archive and a remarkable set of water-colour drawings for the building by Owen Fahy (fig. 14).[4]

In the year following the design of the Dundalk Courthouse, a committee was appointed to advise on an appropriate monument to the duke of Wellington. Stanford has recorded the firmly Greek Revival character of the recommendations of members of the committee, who protested against 'Italian writers, who professed to revive the architecture of the Greeks at a time when the state of Europe denied all access to every surviving production of this art.'[5] A very strong lobby for the Greek Revival existed in Dublin, therefore, by the time of the commencement of work on the new Pro-Cathedral, described in the printed notice as 'a handsome, commodious and Metropolitan Chapel'.[6]

The Wellington Monument was to be Egyptian in style rather than Greek, but Dublin's most recent monument was a baseless fluted Doric column designed by William Wilkins, author of *The Antiquities of Magna Graecia* (1807). Its construction was supervised by Francis Johnston from 1808 (fig. 15).

3 Edward McParland, 'Francis Johnston, Architect, 1760-1829', *Irish Georgian Society Bulletin*, 12, nos 3 and 4 (July-Dec. 1969), pp 61-139. 4 Christine Casey, 'The Greek Revival courthouse, Dundalk, Co. Louth', *Irish Arts Review*, 3, no. 2 (Summer 1986), pp 16-20. 5 W.B. Stanford, *Ireland and the classical tradition* (Dublin 1984), p. 117. 6 Dublin Diocesan Archives (henceforth DDA), Papers of John Thomas Troy, AB2/30. 4-6 Correspondence (1818-1823), no. 30/4/13.

Nelson's Pillar was the centrepiece and focal point of the city's principal thoroughfare, Sackville (later O'Connell) Street, till its destruction in 1966. Directly across from the Pillar stood the new General Post Office. Begun in 1802 to the designs of Francis Johnston, this was completed with a noble portico of the Greek Ionic order in 1814. The architectural character of this newly developed area of the city was firmly settled as Greek Revival by these buildings.[7]

This may have a closer than generic relevance to the architecture of the Pro-Cathedral, or Metropolitan Church as it was first called. The site of the General Post Office is the site that was originally intended for the Pro-Cathedral, apparently.[8] The order of Nelson's Pillar may therefore have determined the choice of the baseless fluted Doric as the order of the building to stand across from it. This site was thought too central for any Catholic metropolitan chapel in the years before the passing of the Catholic Emancipation Act in 1829, however, and it was erected one block east of Sackville Street, fronting on the much narrower Marlborough Street, to which it has always been out of proportion. In these circumstances the retention of the grandeur of the portico must have seemed as superfluous as the relentlessly dogmatic character of the order throughout the building.

A printed notice records the purchase of the site, on which Lord Annesley's town house stood, for £5,100 and the demolition of the house in 1814.[9] At the same time a notice in the newspapers invited designs for the new Metropolitan Church and of these the one marked 'P' was chosen. The foundation stone was laid in 1815 and the building is described as 'now roofing' by Archbishop Troy at the end of 1819.[10] The accounts mention payments to the architects John Taylor, George Papworth and John B. Keane and a payment to Bryan Bolger for measuring. He was frequently associated with the Morrisons and £1 7s. 8d. was paid on 12 July 1817 for 'coach hire on a deputation to Mr Morrison at Bray'. On the same date £307 0s. 3d. was recorded as payment 'to expenses of model and account furnished by Mr J. Sweetman' (fig. 16).[11]

John Sweetman and John Thomas Troy had had a lifelong acquaintance, if we make the reasonable assumption that Mr Henry Sweetman, first mentioned in Troy's diary of his journey to Rome in 1755, was brother to John.[12] Any reference to John Sweetman in Troy's correspondence is indirect and occurs in the letters from the Irish College in Paris of late 1819, by which time John Sweetman had been back in Paris for a year. Dr Long wrote from Paris on 2 October: 'Poor Mr John Sweetman has passed a most painful winter. He

7 For the design of Nelson's Pillar see Ruari Liscombe, *William Wilkins, 1778-1839* (Cambridge, 1980), pp 57-8 and for the General Post Office, see McParland at note 3 above.   8 Peter Costello, *Dublin churches* (Dublin, 1989), p. 23.   9 As note 6 above.   10 Irish College Papers, 1718-1853 (DDA/Coll.1, no. 239).   11 Books of Accounts (DDA). 12 Diary of John Thomas Troy, ff 11, 14-16 (DDA, Troy Papers).

has been confined for eleven months and has only lately begun to go out. If some friend come not over, I fear for him during his intended journey, which can scarcely take place before the end of this month.'[13] On 20 December, Archbishop Troy asked Dr Long to present 'best compliments to Mr and Mrs Wm. Sweetman and tell him that his brothers gave me £300 from him. I presume it is for the building of the Chapel in Marlboro' Street, which is now roofing.'[14] John Sweetman had therefore returned from Paris by this date, if we assume that his return journey to Dublin was the journey referred to in the earlier letter. He does not appear as a member of the Building Committee, however, till 18 September 1822, and his name does not occur as a member of that committee after 2 April 1823, a period of just over six months, when the Pro-Cathedral was already completed except for the portico added to it under the direction of John B. Keane from 1834.[15] The only recorded involvement of John Sweetman was in connection with the contract for the model, the accounts for which begin on 12 September 1816 and end with the account of the deputation to Mr Morrison at Bray on 12 July 1817.[16] Any inference that he was the designer of the Pro-Cathedral cannot be proven from the documents that have survived, though in view of the generosity of the Sweetman contribution to the building fund, the family's enthusiastic support of the project is well-substantiated. It should also be noted that the architects' proposals for the new Pro-Cathedral were to be addressed to Mr William Sweetman, 3 Temple Street.[17] There is no record of payment of the £50 premium promised for the winning design. It would be perfectly understandable that had John Sweetman presented it he would have declined the premium: but that could be true of each of the several professional architects involved and, *a fortiori*, of the archbishop, if his was the defining conception.

JOHN THOMAS TROY AND ARCHITECTURE

The reader of the future archbishop of Dublin's travel diaries will not find any reason to attribute to him specialised knowledge or particular interest in architecture, nor does his correspondence provide further illumination on the subject.[18] Born in Porterstown near Dublin in 1738, he went to Rome in 1756 and

---

13 Irish College Papers, 1718-1853 (DDA/Coll.1, no. 227). 14 As note 10. 15 As note 11. 16 Ibid; for Morrison see *The architecture of Richard Morrison and William Vitruvius Morrison* (Dublin, 1989). Their connections with Owen Fahy and John B. Keane are the subject of the Appendix, p.187. 17 Mary Purcell, *Dublin's Pro-Cathedral* (Dublin, 1975), p. 9; Dermod McCarthy, *Saint Mary's Pro-Cathedral, Dublin* (Dublin, 1988). 18 Journal etc. 1777, ff 4, 6 (DDA, Troy Papers) for examples of his few comments on architecture. The first is of the cathedral in Siena, 'which, tho' a Gothic structure, is a prodigy of magnificence and art'. The

spent his formative years and early life as a Dominican priest at the basilica of San Clemente in Rome, of which he was prior, before returning to Ireland to become bishop of Ossory in 1777 and from 1786 till his death in 1823, archbishop of Dublin (fig. 17). His period at San Clemente, an early Christian basilica, suffices to explain the attraction he would have had for the basilican plan of the new metropolitan chapel he was to commission for the archdiocese. The same period provides the most likely explanation for a predisposition on his part to favour the most dogmatic form of the Greek Revival, the baseless, fluted Doric order so insistently used throughout the building he commissioned.

The baseless, fluted Doric column as a defining feature of the Greek Revival came to the attention of architects and scholars in printed form between the years 1764 and 1778, when no fewer than six illustrated treatises were published on the temples of the city of Paestum, the principal site to feature the use of that column (fig. 17).[19] The same period saw unsuccessful attempts to publish treatises on the site, and we are particularly well-informed about the unpublished treatise prepared by James Bruce of Kinnaird, thanks to the survival of his correspondence with Andrew Lumisden, whose brother-in-law, Robert Strange, was the engraver of the plates for it.[20] The closeness of Troy's friendship with Lumisden is shown by the frequency with which they met in Paris, where Troy stayed for a week in the course of his return journey from Rome to Ireland in 1777. The entry for 14 May of that year – 'Went to Mr Lumisden with whom and Mr Strange I dined at the Chevalier McMahon's' – confirms that this Mr Lumisden was Andrew Lumisden, who had been secretary to the Old and the Young Pretenders in Rome from 1750 to 1768.[21]

In Rome, Lumisden had taken a particular interest in the archaeology of the city and was to publish in 1797 *Remarks on the Antiquities of Rome and its Environs*. In the course of it he gives the text of an inscription found in a vineyard belonging to the Irish Dominicans near Porta Maggiore and states: 'With pleasure I mention the place, since it recalls to memory the hospitable manner in which I was there entertained by the good and worthy fathers to whom it belonged'.[22] His continuing closeness to the Dominican community at St Clemente during the years of Father Troy's residence there is evidenced further by a letter he addressed to them on the history of the Dominican order in Scotland.[23]

---

second is of the Annunziata in Florence, 'built and ornamented in the modern stile rich in marble and silver ornaments'. 19 Joselita Raspi Serra (ed.), *La Fortuna di Paestum e la memoria moderna del Dorico* (2 vols, Florence 1986), for the most complete account of the publication of the temples at Paestum. 20 Michael McCarthy, 'Una nuova interpretazione del "Paestum" di Thomas Major e di altri disegni inglesi di epoca successiva' in Serra (ed.), *La Fortuna*, pp 39-57; idem, 'Paestum e l'Irlanda', in ibid., ii, 290-5. 21 Michael McCarthy, 'Andrew Lumisden and Piranesi', forthcoming from the British School in Rome. 22 James Dennistoun, *Memoirs of Sir Robert Strange and Andrew Lumisden* (2 vols, London, 1855), i, 149-51.

It should be mentioned also that the architect Robert Mylne, who also projected a treatise on the temples at Paestum, was a very close friend of the Lumisden family, as the letters of Elizabeth Lumisden to her brother Andrew witness.[24] Finally the closeness of Andrew Lumisden's friendship with Giovanni Battista Piranesi, whose final masterpiece of engraving was devoted to the temples at Paestum, is apparent from Lumisden's book and serves to underscore the extent to which Lumisden and his friends, including Father Troy, were alert to the significance of the baseless, fluted Doric column to the contemporary Greek Revival in architecture (fig. 18).[25]

NEW CHURCHES IN PARIS AND LONDON

There is no indication in Troy's diary of his visit to Paris in 1777 that he paid any attention to contemporary church building, of which the most prominent examples were Saint-Geneviève, subsequently renamed the Pantheon, by Jacques-Gabriel Soufflot, and St Philippe du Roule by Jean François Thérèse Chalgrin, both commissioned by the Marquis de Marigny. The former was nearing completion in that year and was more Roman than Greek in inspiration. But the architect Soufflot had accompanied the Marquis de Marigny to Italy in 1750 and had visited the temples of Pacstum with Gabriel Dumont, the first architect to publish measured engravings of the site.[26] Soufflot's own drawings were used also in preparing the English account of Paestum in 1768 and these studies of the baseless, fluted Doric order may well have been familiar to Troy through his friendship with Andrew Lumisden, whose correspondence shows intimate acquaintance with these publications.[27]

Soufflot had indeed proposed Paestum-like columns in drawings for the crypt of the new church, begun twenty years earlier. It is unlikely that Troy would have known this, however and if Sainte-Geneviève had any relevance for the design of the new Pro-Cathedral in Dublin it can only have been in its combination of a porticoed church with a dome as an example of the fusion of the Greek with the Roman systems.

St Philippe du Roule's plan dates from 1774 and has greater relevance in being the first of the basilican churches in its layout. It was the most fashionable new area of the city, parallel to the Champs-Elysées which was eventually to be dominated by the Arc de Triomphe, also designed by Chalgrin, though not completed till thirty years after his death in 1806. Indeed, correspondence in the papers of Archdeacon Hamilton from 28 August 1835 shows that Dr Hamilton, then administrator of the Pro-Cathedral, had sent

23 Ibid., i, 149-51. 24 Ibid., p. 307. 25 As note 21. 26 Joselita Raspi Serra (ed.), *Paestum: idea e immagine* (Modena, 1990), pp 25-8. 27 As note 22.

to Paris for copies of the original drawings for St Philippe du Roule, which strongly indicates that Chalgrin's church was a formative influence on the design of the Pro-Cathedral then nearing completion in Dublin.[28]

Daire Keogh has emphasised above the turbulence of the period, politically, militarily and economically, in Ireland as much as in France, that witnessed the conception and realisation of these architectural metropolitan improvements. The invasion of Ireland by French troops under General Humbert in support of the rebellion of 1798 underscored an *entente cordiale* between Catholic Ireland and Revolutionary France with which Archbishop Troy, who opposed the rebellion, did not feel comfortable. Old friendships survived political differences, however, notably the friendship between himself and the Sweetman family. John Sweetman had been intimately associated with Wolfe Tone and was obliged to flee to exile in Paris on the collapse of the rebellion. Since he was later responsible for the making of the model for the Pro-Cathedral, it is reasonable to suppose that he was the channel through which the designs of Chalgrin's church were transmitted to Dublin. But the Pro-Cathedral owes nothing to Parisian examples in its adoption of the baseless, fluted Doric order within and without, its most exceptional feature.

Nor can that be found in metropolitan improvements in London in the period. The two major areas under development were Regent Street and St Pancras and each had a Greek Revival church as a focal point. The earlier church was the new St Pancras, erected between 1819 and 1822 to the designs of the father and son team of William and Henry William Inwood, the latter having travelled to Greece with this specific commission in mind. It was the most expensive church of the age at £70,000 and Sir John Summerson has characterised it as 'the queen of early nineteenth – century churches; its architecture earns it the title as much as its size and cost'.[29] Its portico is of the Ionic order of the Erectheum, its tower is based on the Tower of the Winds and the flanking chambers at the east end are recognisable but hardly convincing replicas of the Caryatid Porch of the Erectheum. The plan owes a great deal to Gibb's St Martin-in-the-Fields at the entrance, but the columned hall within is closed by a semi-circular apse and can therefore be characterised as basilican.

The church on Regent Street was built from 1823 to 1825 and was known as the Hanover Chapel till its demolition in 1896. Charles Robert Cockerell was the architect and his church, located on an awkward site, looked to the designs of Wren and Hawksmoor in plan, which is based on a square lit by a dome of glass and iron that may have provided some justification for the probably earlier addition of a dome to the Dublin Pro-Cathedral. Sir Howard

28 As note 2, 46 (1991), 129, no. 164; André Déveche, *L'Eglise Saint Philippe du Roule de Paris* (Paris, 1975). 29 John Summerson, *Georgian London* (London, 1988), pp 210-12.

Colvin has characterised Cockerell as 'at once the most fastidious and the least pedantic of English neo-classical architects' and at the Hanover Chapel he married the English Baroque plan with a beautiful Greek Ionic portico with architrave and pediment between two towers on the entrance facade.[30]

The most notable Catholic church built in London in this period was St Mary's in Moorfields, begun in 1817 and completed in 1820 to the designs of John Newman. The architect disowned responsibility for the Corinthian facade by an unknown hand, but the interior was remarkable for the drama of the apse, lit by concealed lighting behind an open colonnade of paired Corinthian columns with a theatrical scene of the Crucifixion providing a setting for the celebration of the Eucharist at the raised high altar. The effect was considerably heightened by the simplicity of the ordering of the nave, with unadorned square piers from which arches rose to a cornice below the elliptical coffered ceiling.[31] Archbishop Troy's papers contain a printed notice relating to burials in St Mary's Moorfields, dated 28 September 1820. He was therefore aware of this church rising in London at the same time as his own Metropolitan Church was in construction. It can hardly have affected the design of the Pro-Cathedral, however, in the most prominent features of the Dublin church.

CONCLUSION

The above brief review of the main new churches in London and Paris reveals that the principal features of the Pro-Cathedral in its plan and lighting are to be found in both cities; but current fashion in major ecclesiastical architecture fails to account for the most surprising feature of the Pro-Cathedral, the use of the baseless, fluted Doric column internally and externally (fig. 18). This relentless deployment of the most primitive version of the Greek Orders makes an architectural manifesto of the new building. Certainly the climate of advanced architectural opinion in Dublin for the Greek Revival had been prepared in the decades immediately preceding, principally in the work of Francis Johnston. And the original site, fronting the new Nelson's pillar on Sackville Street, affords a possible explanation of the choice of the order. Archbishop Troy's own predilection for the order chosen, argued here by inference from his close association with Andrew Lumisden, who was at the centre of the circle involved in publications of the temples at Paestum, is a further factor to be taken into consideration.

30 Howard Colvin, *A biographical dictionary of British architects, 1660-1840* (London 1995), pp 256-62. See also David Watkin, *The life and work of C.R. Cockerell* (London, 1974), ch. 9.   31 Summerson, pp 222-3.

Political strategy may also have played a part in the choice of the most doctrinaire of the Greek orders. Ireland's most recent instance of modern ecclesiastical architecture was the Royal Chapel at Dublin Castle, built to the designs of Francis Johnston from 1807 to 1814. It is also Ireland's finest example of Gothic Revival architecture.[32] The use of that style by the Protestant establishment might have provided a precedent for its use in the new Pro-Cathedral, but the architecture of the latter is diametrically opposed to that of the Chapel Royal in style. Perhaps the Archbishop was using the language of architecture to distance himself from the Castle authorities, to whom, because of his opposition to the rebellion of 1798, he was seen by many of his flock to be too closely allied.[33]

Whatever the reason or complex of reasons that gave form to the new Pro-Cathedral, it gave Dublin a monument unique in the architecture of Neo-Classicism and one to be prized and preserved in the interests of European cultural history. Nor is there any doubting the clarity of intention of the design, since the fittings were also Greek Revival in style, most notably in the beautiful pulpit based on the Tower of the Winds in Athens.

It gave a lead also to the church buildings of Dublin erected in the years immediately following Catholic Emancipation: St Francis Xavier in Gardiner Street, St Andrew's, Westland Row (baseless, fluted Doric portico in antis) and the great churches of the quays of the Liffey, and St Nicholas of Myra. A facile association of the Roman Catholic faith with architectural style most often leads to this architectural reshaping of the city being characterised as modelled on Roman church architecture. The characteristic Roman church of the Renaissance and Baroque periods however, with few exceptions, never sports a portico: its columnar order is always engaged to the wall. The free-standing church portico so prominent in the cityscape of Dublin is a manifestation of the Greek Revival. There can be little doubt that its adoption at the Pro-Cathedral in so uncompromising a manner was a defining factor in this most attractive feature of the Dublin cityscape.[34]

32 As note 3.   33 Keogh as note 1.   34 ACKNOWLEDGMENTS Mr David Sheehy at the Dublin Diocesan Archives has been most helpful in guiding me to the relevant documents and I have profited greatly from his advice and that of Mr David Griffin, Director of the Irish Architectural Archive, Dr Freddy O'Dwyer of the Office of Public Works and my colleagues in University College Dublin, Dr Eileen Kane and Dr Christine Casey kindly read the first draft of the text and discussed the issues in detail with me. Illustrations are courtesy of the Irish Architectural Archive, to whom we are deeply indebted.

Fig. 7: View of the Pro-Cathedral, Dublin (Irish Architectural Archive).

Fig. 8: 'View of the interior of the Pro-Cathedral, Dublin'
(Collection of the archdiocese of Dublin).

Fig. 9: Section of the Pro-Cathedral, Dublin (National Library of Ireland).

Fig. 10: Plan of the Pro-Cathedral, Dublin (National Library of Ireland).

Fig. 11: 'View of the Pro-Cathedral, Dublin'
(Collection of the archdiocese of Dublin).

Fig. 12: George Petrie, 'View of the Pro-Cathedral, Dublin'
(Royal Irish Academy).

Fig. 13: A. Rosborough, 'Model of the Pro-Cathedral, Dublin', 1817
(Photo, Irish Architectural Archive).

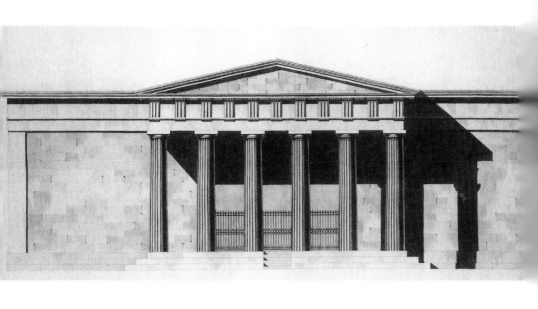

Fig. 14: Owen Fahy, Elevation of the Courthouse, Dundalk, Co. Louth
(Old Dundalk Society).

Fig. 15: Nelson's Pillar, O'Connell Street, Dublin
(Photo, Irish Architectural Archive).

Fig. 16: A. Rosborough, 'Model of the Pro-Cathedral, Dublin', 1817
(Photo, Irish Architectural Archive).

Fig. 17: G.B. Piranesi, 'View of the Temples at Paestum', 1777
(Sir John Soane's Musuem, London).

Fig. 18: Interior of the Pro-Cathedral, Dublin (Irish Architectural Archive).

11

Dublin's forgotten archbishop: Daniel Murray, 1768-1852

Donal Kerr

O f the Irish bishops in the first eighty years of the nineteenth century only two stand out in popular memory – John MacHale and Paul Cullen. Each has been the subject of a number of studies. MacHale is a folk-hero, symbol of resistance to England and protector of Ireland's cultural heritage. Cullen is regarded as the anti-nationalist, who excommunicated the Fenians and romanised the Irish Catholic Church. Although both assessments are far from accurate, at least the two archbishops are remembered. It is not so for Daniel Murray, one-time opponent of both MacHale and Cullen. On a pop-ular level he could be said to be almost invisible in the ranks of Dublin Catholic bishops and very little serious study has been done on him.[1] The vague image that remains of him is of one who had taken anti-national atti-tudes and was perceived in his own day as a 'government bishop'.

The achievement of a bishop – the chief pastor of his diocese – is measured not only by his Christian witness and his preaching the gospel but also by his ability to create the right pastoral structures for his people. On this last and

1 The principal writings on Murray upon which this paper is based are: William Meagher, *Notice on the life and character of His Grace Most Rev. Daniel Murray, late archbishop of Dublin ... with historical and biographical notes* (Dublin, 1853); Myles Ronan, 'Archbishop Murray of Dublin (1768-1852)', *Irish Ecclesiastical Record*, 5th series, 77 (Apr. 1952), pp 241-9; Kevin B. Nowlan, *New Catholic Encyclopaedia*, x (New York, 1967), p. 68; M. Lysaght, 'Daniel Murray, archbishop of Dublin, 1823-1852', *Dublin Historical Record*, 27 (1974), pp 101-8; P.J. Murray, 'Daniel Murray, archbishop of Dublin, 1823-1852', *Arklow Historical Society Journal* (1984), pp 12-20; David C. Sheehy, 'Archbishop Murray of Dublin and the Great Famine in Mayo', *Cathair na Mart*, 11 (1991) 118-28; 'Archbishop Murray and the response of the Catholic Church to the Great Famine in Ireland', *Linkup* (Dec. 1995), pp 38-42; Donal A. Kerr, *Peel, priests, and politics: Sir Robert Peel's admin-istration and the Roman Catholic Church in Ireland, 1841-1846* (Oxford, 1982); *'A Nation of Beggars'? Priests, people, and politics in Famine Ireland 1846-1852* (Oxford, 1994); these two volumes deal mainly with the controversies in which Murray became involved from

most easily verifiable count Daniel Murray scores high. While still archbishop of Hierapolis and coadjutor to the archbishop of Dublin, his pastoral achievements in pre-Emancipation Ireland were impressive. He was fortunate in that he was able to build on the many achievements of his mentor, Archbishop Thomas Troy, who gave him a free hand in the diocese. Murray identified the much-neglected education of the people as a major need and, as a first step, he set about finding religious men and women who would undertake that work.

There was only one convent of sisters when Murray began his episcopate; when he died there were twenty-nine. In 1812, he asked Mary Aikenhead to begin the Sisters of Charity, to set up schools and to do charitable work for the poor. A few years later he asked Frances Ball to start a congregation to provide education for the better-off girls and, with his help, she started the Irish branch of Mary Ward's congregation – the Loreto Sisters. He provided for the training of both women, sending them to the Bar Convent in York. In 1812 he persuaded Edmund Rice to send Christian Brothers to Dublin to provide free or inexpensive Catholic education for poorer boys and gave them a site in Hanover Street for a school. At the same time, he encouraged and supported Father Peter Kenney, the re-founder of the Jesuits in Ireland, who established Clongowes Wood College in 1814 for the sons of the better-off. To all 'charismatic founders', Murray proved a constant support and counsellor. In 1824, encouraged by Murray, Catherine McAuley began what was later to become the largest congregation ever established in the English-speaking world – the Sisters of Mercy. They soon had schools, orphanages and hospitals in Ireland and abroad. Murray was there to help in the difficult early stages, providing counsel and help. The three congregations of sisters gave a new impetus to religious life in Dublin. Of all Murray's achievements, his involvement in the launching of the sisters of Charity, of Mercy and of Loreto is rightly regarded as his greatest.

In 1813, his fellow-bishops thought so highly of him that they asked him to become president of Maynooth College, which was experiencing a stormy period in its history. The one condition he made was that he could have as his vice-president Peter Kenney, on whom the greater part of the work devolved. Murray, however, spent most of the week in the college, driving to the city to preach on Sunday to his parishioners in St Andrew's church, Westland Row and returning to Maynooth on Monday having dealt with diocesan business. He and Kenney were in office together for a year and a

1838 until his death; Donal Kerr, *The Catholic Church and the Famine* (Dublin 1996). See, too, Seán Cannon, *Irish episcopal meetings, 1788-1882; a juridico-historical study* (Rome, 1979). Murray's episcopal papers are in the Dublin Diocesan Archives: I am grateful to David Sheehy for permission to consult them and to Mr Danny Parkinson for allowing me to copy some valuable Murray letters.

half and had a steadying effect. It was Murray who introduced the sodality of the Sacred Heart to the college. He promoted that devotion too in Dublin, as well as devotion to the Virgin Mary and other practices associated with the 'Devotional Revolution'. Again at the request of his fellow-bishops, Murray, in 1815, undertook the difficult task of representing their views on the Veto controversy to Pope Pius VII and to a Roman curia which did not understand Irish attitudes on the matter.

When, in 1823, Murray succeeded Troy as archbishop of probably the most important diocese in Ireland, his field of operations broadened to include the whole country. Troy had persuaded the Irish bishops to meet on a national basis but these meetings often had to do solely with Maynooth College and not all bishops attended. After the critical meeting of 1808 when Bishop Coppinger of Cloyne and Ross insisted that the metropolitans had no power to act for the suffragans, the bishops met more regularly, but it was during Murray's time that full meetings of the bishops became an annual event. These meetings were quite significant for although the decisions taken were not binding on individual bishops, a co-ordinated policy emerged which increased their authority with their clergy and faithful and strengthened their bargaining power with the government.

In 1828, a committee of bishops was set up to examine and co-ordinate the discipline of the Church throughout the country. Murray, with the aid of his friend, the bishop of Kildare and Leighlin, James Warren Doyle – who probably drafted the decrees – led the way. All four bishops of the province of Dublin, after preliminary meetings among themselves, held synods in 1831 which enacted reforms for their dioceses. The Dublin reforms served as a model for others. Murray followed up this reforming policy by making a visitation of his parishes every few years, in preparation for which the parish priest and curate had to furnish reports on the state of the parish. This made for constant revision and renewal. His own edifying life endeared him to clergy and laity alike. The new pope, Leo XII, anxious to renew the Church, enthusiastically proclaimed the only jubilee of the nineteenth century for 1825-6 and made it a call to conversion. It brought many Catholics back to a more active practice of their faith, not least because Pope Leo urged confessors to abandon the older rigorist approach for the gentler theology of Alphonsus Liguori. In Dublin, Murray promoted the jubilee vigorously. His biographer and friend, Father William Meagher, claims that during his reign as archbishop the vice-ridden city of Dublin was transformed. By the 1840s, it is clear that it was sharing in the Catholic revival throughout Europe that followed the French Revolution.

In 1832, a group of four young priests and Father Philip Dowley, a dean at Maynooth College, came together to found what was to become the Irish Vincentians. Murray encouraged them and gave them a copy of the rule of

St Vincent de Paul. On his advice, they started the day-school at Ussher's Quay which he hoped would provide students for the priesthood. In the 1830s, too, when Pope Gregory XVI was promoting the foreign missions, Murray introduced into Dublin Pauline Jaricot's Society for the Propagation of the Faith, which involved the laity in the work of the missions. Before long the diocese was to have one of the Society's most generous branches in all Europe. Murray helped John Hand to set up the College of All Hallows to train priests for the Irish abroad. With the provision of priests, religious and sisters that the development of All Hallows, the Sisters of Mercy, Sisters of Charity and Loreto Sisters represented, Catholic Ireland was poised to take on the astounding missionary role in the Americas and the British Empire that is one of the Church's distinguishing contributions in the nineteenth and twentieth centuries. Murray also welcomed to Dublin Father Matthew's temperance movement and the Society of Saint Vincent de Paul.

What is striking about these ventures is the enabling role Murray played. His was the unusual ability to involve others in his work for the Church. As often as not, as with Mary Aikenhead and Frances Ball, he gave the initial push and helped them through their difficult moments. With Peter Kenney, Catherine McAuley, the Vincentians, John Hand and others, his role was one of encouragement and support. A rich Catholic bourgeoisie had developed during the penal period that was only too pleased to show their pride in their Church, while O'Connell's successful movement for Emancipation served to make them more conscious of their religion. Murray, by his vision and encouragement, was able to win the co-operation of well-to-do Catholic families like the O'Briens, the Balls and the Corballises. They endowed the new religious congregations and provided funds for schools, orphanages, churches and hospitals such as St Vincent's. Undoubtedly, the great increase in churches, convents, schools and religious foundations owed most to the initiative of the priests, religious and laity who promoted them, but these initiatives might not have taken place or prospered were it not for Murray. It is not unusual for bishops to raise difficulties when confronted with new untried initiatives but Murray, prudent and cautious though he was, welcomed anyone who had something useful to do for the diocese and people of Dublin. Always willing to help and advise, he was reluctant to interfere. Meagher put it well when he said of him:

> If apprised of any undertaking for God, he hearkened, he aided, he advised – but there his part terminated ... he did not overwhelm with a load of patronage; he did not confound by the frequency of his interference; he left the matter in the hands to which providence had entrusted it – to the guidance of the minds that had been inspired to originate it.

The education of the people was a priority for him. Shortly after becoming archbishop, he engaged in dialogue with Goulburn, the hostile chief secretary, to persuade the government to provide for the whole country 'some general system of education in the advantages of which our Roman Catholic poor could freely participate'. After unsuccessful negotiations he set up his own Catholic Education Society. Then, with Anthony Blake, an influential Catholic in Anglesey's private cabinet, he worked towards producing the National System of Education which Stanley, the chief secretary, introduced in 1832. He accepted being a commissioner of the National Schools and was highly regarded by his fellow-commissioners, all of whom, except Blake, were Protestant. As a result of his policies Dublin diocese which, when he became archbishop, had but one school for girls and one or two schools for boys, had by his death some 220 schools suitable for Catholics. With all these measures in place by the late 1830s, Murray, a venerable prelate of advanced age, had accomplished as much as any bishop could do in a lifetime. There was one further service which Murray, in the final years of his long life, rendered to the Irish people at its most critical hour. During the Great Famine, his name, position, and the trust people of all persuasions placed in him meant that money poured into him from all over the world and enabled him to organise an extensive relief work which he kept going while the Famine lasted.

Such an extensive list of achievements suggests the need for a full-scale biography. The scope of this article, however, is more modest; it seeks to explain why, after such a long and successful career, Murray has been largely forgotten. It will look at his experiences during his decisive formative years as a young cleric, at the changes that took place during his long life, and finally, since temperament influences attitude, it will endeavour to throw some light on the man behind the mitre.

REBELLION AND REPRESSION – THE YOUNG PRIEST AND
REVOLUTIONARY IRELAND

Daniel Murray was born into a family of farmers, tenants of Lord Wicklow in County Wicklow, on 18 April 1768. The family had risen in the world, for Lord Wicklow had promoted them from a previous less productive holding to a substantial farm at Sheepwalk not far from Arklow where Daniel was born. He had four brothers and one sister. At the age of eight, his parents brought him to Dublin to the school for Catholics run by Dr Thomas Betagh, where he learned Latin, Greek, French and the humanities. At the Irish College at Salamanca where, from 1784 to 1792, he trained for the priesthood, he was the outstanding student and the president, Patrick Curtis, later archbishop of Armagh, reported of him:

> This youth manifests a true ecclesiastical vocation, with wonderful talent, application and edifying conduct, and has made such rapid progress in all he has hitherto undertaken that he far surpasses all his companions and causes us to entertain the highest hopes of him.

Three years after his return to Ireland, Troy sent Murray as a curate to Arklow. 1795 was a momentous year in Irish history. It was the year of the Fitzwilliam débâcle and of the trial of the Reverend William Jackson, the French agent, who committed suicide in the dock. It was the year, too, of the foundation of Maynooth College which mollified the hierarchy but antagonised still further militant lay Catholics. It was the year of Burke's *Letters on a Regicide Peace*, in which he raged against the revolutionaries in France and the blindness of the Protestant 'junta' in Dublin for driving the Catholics into the arms of revolution. These were not groundless fears, for in that summer the United Irishmen became a secret revolutionary society attracting many disaffected Catholics, while in Armagh, the Orange order was founded. In Murray's own county of Wicklow, to which he now was posted, his two brothers, Tom and Peter, joined the United Irishmen. The active sympathy of members of Murray's family towards the Revolution's ideals – the abolition of privilege, the achievement of equality and freedom for all – may not have left him untouched. In Dublin, in the years from 1795 to 1798, over thirty Dublin priests joined the United Irishmen.

When, after the imposition of the Oath to the Civil Constitution on the clergy, the revolution in France became anti-religions, Archbishop Troy warned Catholics against the 'French disease'. Strongly influenced by events in France and under pressure from the government to prove their loyalty, many of the Irish clergy swore allegiance to the crown and attempted to persuade their people to surrender arms. Daniel Murray took an oath of allegiance and swore in the presence of the Reverend Bailey, the unsympathetic local magistrate who was also the Protestant rector, that he gave no countenance to the United Irishmen. His life was threatened. On a pastoral visit in Arklow town, an officer of the militia saw him and shouted to his men: 'Shoot that papist priest!' Quickly, Murray turned into a shop and escaped through the rear. One midnight early in June 1798, the Antrim militia returning from Vinegar Hill burst in on Father William Ryan, parish priest of Arklow, ill in bed at a relative's house at Johnstown, and shot him where he lay. What happened next was related many years later by Mary Johnson, Murray's niece:

> The soldiers proceeded to the chapel, the morning after the parish priest's death, for the purpose of taking the Revd Daniel Murray's life. He had just finished Mass, when the people shouted in great

excitement: "The soldiers are coming on us!" They had just time to raise the priest on their shoulders to a window at the back of [the] Altar ...

On a horse borrowed from the Reverend Bailey, Murray crossed the river at Shelton Abbey. The soldiers, incensed at his escape, pursued him to Sheepwalk but by the time they arrived, he had changed horses and fled. They set fire to the outhouses, burning four horses and the cattle and destroying the hay and corn in the haggard. One soldier, rushing through the house to shoot any male members of the family, came to a bedroom where Daniel's nephew lay sick of a high fever, but on being told the infectious nature of the disease, he instantly fled, warning his fellow-soldiers not to risk their lives. Daniel, meanwhile, was already on his way to Dublin. To evade patrols, he avoided main roads, and rode via Glenealy along a track known only to locals.

The loyalist terror following the rebellion took on a decidedly anti-Catholic tenor. Sixty Catholic chapels were burned in the south-east, most of them long after the battle of Vinegar Hill and the recapture of Wexford in June 1798. A horrified Lord Cornwallis, now both commander-in-chief and viceroy, reported of conservative protestant circles that 'if a priest has been put to death the greatest joy is expressed by the whole company'. As late as August 1799, Archbishop Troy complained to Dublin Castle that no 'priest can appear in the N.E. parts of that distracted county [Wexford] nor in the neighbourhood of Arklow'. Prudently, he did not send Murray back to his parish.

This, then, was young Daniel Murray's experience – a hunted priest whose parish priest was murdered and whose family was terrorised and home torched. He had personal experience of a period when more people died violent deaths than in any other comparable period in Irish history. The horror of what he saw and heard at this time, and the stories retailed in his own family, remained indelibly etched on his mind and permanently marked his attitude towards rebellion.

THRONE AND ALTAR – THE YOUNG BISHOP AND THE ROYAL VETO

Murray's early experiences of ecclesiastical politics also influenced his outlook. Just at the time he became bishop, the 'veto' became a major issue. At the root of the controversy lay the broader question of how the Church should be governed and what role, if any, should be accorded the crown. In 1799 the British government offered a package of measures in return for

Catholic emancipation. It proposed that it obtain a veto in the nomination of bishops, pay the clergy, and subsidise and retain some control over Maynooth College; it sought, in effect, to make a type of subordinate establishment of the Catholic Church. In the aftermath of 1798, Archbishop Troy and some senior bishops met and accepted the measure, though with reservations. Since George III blocked emancipation and Rome did not approve of the payment of the clergy, the matter was dropped and when it came up again in 1808, it centred around the one element – a veto on the appointment of bishops. The bishops, now in full session, rejected it. Troy was dismayed for he felt that the veto, in better circumstances, might still be an option.

His defeat, after playing the leading role in the Church for decades, may have influenced him to seek a coadjutor. He had a high regard for the young Daniel Murray, whom he had placed first in Saint Andrew's chapel in Hawkins Street, then in St Mary's chapel in Upper Liffey Street. Shortly after the 1808 meeting he proposed him to the Holy See as his coadjutor with the right of succession. Murray was consecrated coadjutor to Troy and archbishop of Hierapolis in 1809. Almost immediately he found himself at the centre of ecclesiastical high politics in Ireland, for the debate over the veto intensified as the crown, the lower clergy, the laity, Rome and the bishops all put forward their own claims. As a promising young bishop, Murray was chosen by his fellow-bishops to represent them in Rome. Twice he travelled there to put their case. Troy, his friend, mentor and archbishop, could accept the veto. Murray, preaching on Good Friday 1815 on the passion of Christ, said:

> To this bound and suffering victim I would now implore the attention of those misguided Catholics who seem willing to impose new and disgraceful bonds, not indeed on his sacred person, but on his mystical body, that is, his Church, which was ever more dear to him than his personal liberty – more dear to him than even his life ... And what virtuous Catholic would consent to purchase the chance of temporal advantages at the price of such a real spiritual calamity?

These remarks, on such a solemn occasion, from a man whose sermons were normally sweet reasonableness, caused a minor sensation and delighted the hearts of O'Connell and the anti-vetoists.

The negotiations with Rome were protracted and fruitless at first, but the final settlement in 1828 represented something of a triumph for Murray. The form of domestic nomination arrived at excluded royal intervention and accorded well enough with the bishops' wishes. The arrangement arrived at determined the structure of the Church, externally as regards relations with the government and internally as between bishops, priests and laity, for a hundred years. Although further research is needed, it appears that Murray's role in negotiating this settlement was significant. Yet the views expressed during the controversy are a reminder that during these early years of Murray's episcopate, his own admired archbishop, many leading Catholics in Britain and Ireland and the saintly Pope Pius VII would have accepted as normal that the government, as elsewhere in Europe, could be involved in the affairs of the Church in Ireland.

THE CONTROVERSIES

By the 1830s Murray was at the height of his influence. He was the leading bishop of a Catholic people that had recently gained full emancipation, was embarking on an ambitious church building programme, and, due to his determined efforts in the face of fierce opposition, was benefiting greatly from the National School system. Murray was favourably viewed both by O'Connell and by the Whig government. Dublin Castle and, in particular, the well-disposed under-secretary, Thomas Drummond, did not hesitate to contact Murray on matters concerning the Church. In 1838, however, the first of a series of controversies arose and these offer some explanation as to why Murray's reputation has suffered an eclipse.

The first controversy concerned the National School system. John MacHale, archbishop of Tuam, a fearless and formidable adversary, attacked the system as dangerous to Catholic children, since the schools did not fully measure up to the ideal of Catholic education, and almost succeeded in having them condemned by Rome. Murray, whose kindness and consideration for others concealed a strength of character, felt obliged to fight to save the schools. Most of the bishops sided with him. The reason he gave to Paul Cullen, rector of the Irish College in Rome, was a considered one:

> We were long struggling to obtain public aid, which could be safely applied towards the education of our poor; and, when obtained he [Archbishop MacHale] seems desirous to wrest it from us, and throw it back into the hands of those who would employ it against us. For as for his pretended hope of procuring a separate grant for the education of the Catholic poor, it is so utterly visionary that no rational person could entertain it for a moment.

As so often, Murray's approach was a pragmatic one and more in tune with the political reality of the day. He and others before him had struggled to get for the poor an acceptable, non-proselytising system of education and, although the National Schools did not meet all their wishes, they went far in that direction and were the best that could be obtained from a state that was officially Protestant. He fought his case hard and Rome's decision in 1841 to leave the matter to individual bishops represented a successful settlement for Murray. The schools were saved and the poor guaranteed an elementary education.

Although Murray had won, the quarrel left bitter roots. Episcopal unity was the main casualty of the dispute. Prudently steered by Murray, the bishops had hitherto worked harmoniously together. From now on they were divided. In later historiography, when the denationalising effects of the National Schools were recognised and repudiated, MacHale was perceived as the champion of an education that was not merely more Catholic but more Irish, and Murray was seen as supine in the face of a malign government intent on anglicising the nation.

REPEAL AND THE ARCHBISHOP

The next major problem was more political than religious. Shortly after the Relief Act of 1829 became law, Murray, feeling that the full emancipation of Catholics had been achieved, was instrumental in having all the bishops issue a call to their clergy not to get involved in politics. In the 1840s Daniel O'Connell, who had become the national hero, built up a massive popular movement for Repeal, holding monster meetings throughout the country, while in Dublin, the highly articulate Young Irelanders trumpeted forth a strident nationalism in the pages of the *Nation*. Priests and bishops, such as MacHale, played an essential role in O'Connell's repeal movement and, at the monster meeting at Mullingar, Bishop William Higgins of Ardagh categorically declared:

> I have reason to believe, I may add, I know, that every Catholic bishop in Ireland, without exception, is an ardent Repealer ... I have now again formally to announce to you that they [the bishops of Ireland] all declared themselves as such.

Shocked at such an unfounded claim, Murray took the unusual step of writing to the *Dublin Evening Post* to dissociate himself totally from the remark. This did not endear him to O'Connell or the nationalist bishops and priests. Yet, with a prescience that others lacked, he believed that 'England' would resist with force the attempts for the repeal of the Union and in 1843, at the height of the repeal fervour, he wrote to his trusted *factotum*, Archdeacon John Hamilton:

It appears to me as certain as that the sun is now in the firmament the Repeal can never be carried without such a convulsion as the great majority of its present supporters could not contemplate without horror.

His efforts to rein in his own clergy were not successful. Some of his priests attended the monster meeting at Tara where Bishops McLaughlin of Derry and Cantwell of Meath, with harpers strumming and green flags flying, advanced through applauding thousands to take their places on the platform with O'Connell. When the great meeting was planned for Clontarf for 8 October 1843, no less than twenty-four priests of Fingal (North Dublin) sign-ed the necessary requisition despite his remonstrances. One of them, Father Peter Tyrell, parish priest of Lusk, was later indicted with O'Connell. The government proclaimed the meeting, poured troops into Dublin and trained artillery from the Pidgeon House on Clontarf. O'Connell wisely abandoned the meeting. On the evening of the aborted meeting, Murray elaborated his views to Hamilton at some length:

The array of military force that paraded so ostentatiously before our church on Sunday evening, seems to have been intended as an indica-tion that our clergy are objects of peculiar suspicion (can we wonder at it?) and that in case of an outbreak, they would be amongst the first victims to be aimed at. I long foresaw, and it required no spirit of prophecy to do so, that if the agitation were persisted in the whole power of England would as far as necessary be employed to crush it, but I was ridiculed as over-timorous (or something worse) and the dream of moral influence as able to accomplish everything was clung to, in opposition to the plainest dictates of common-sense. I was quite as much alive as any of the agitators to the benefits which a domestic Legislature would be capable, if peacefully obtained, of conferring on the country; but I trembled to think on the effects of a struggle to obtain it by means of physical force. All doubt on the subject has now van-ished. England has announced its determination to encounter all the calamities of civil war rather than submit to the monster evil of a repeal of the Union. But for the prudence evinced by our poor people...the shores of Clontarf would be again steeped in torrents of blood...

Murray's assessment of the Repeal movement was shrewd. Unlike most other Irishmen, he had seen the real limits of moral force as a weapon: its effectiveness was strictly related to English limits of political tolerance. These latter had now unequivocally been reached. Murray was clear-sighted, too, in measuring government resolve, for Peel and Wellington had determined to crush the Clontarf meeting with cannon and cavalry. The terrible events of 1798 were still vivid memories for Murray. He feared, too, the social upheaval that a revolution would create; he was, he claimed, 'quite as much alive as anyone to the benefits which Repeal would bring' but violence would cause the mayhem of 1798 all over again.

The next controversy, and one of the fiercest in which Murray became involved, concerned Peel's offer, in 1844, of a Charitable Bequests Act to replace the older discriminatory act which prevented Catholics from leaving bequests to the Catholic Church. O'Connell and MacHale opposed the act but Murray, courageously noting its benefits, accepted it and agreed to become a Commissioner on the Charitable Bequests Board. False rumours of a concordat exacerbated the debate. An advertisement in the nationalist paper *The Pilot*, protesting against Murray's support for the Charitable Bequests Act, put him in the same category as clerics who, it alleged, had abetted the Norman invasion of the twelfth century. A priest from St Audoen's church in Dublin, reported that the people were crying out that 'their *archbishop* ... [was] betraying them to the enemies of their creed and country.' O'Connell, speaking to a Dublin crowd a few hundred yards from Murray's church, reminded them that in the great question of the Veto, thirty years before, the people had cried out 'we will have no Soggart Sassenagh, we will have no Bishops made by an English pope!' Then to the roar of the approving crowd, the great Irish leader, called out: 'People of Ireland, you have the same remedy now!' Despite this pressure and the accusation that he was supine in his attitude to the government, Murray remained firm. His stand was vindicated a half-century later. Archbishop William Walsh, who was a lawyer by training and a committed nationalist, wrote a lengthy commentary in which he demonstrated how highly beneficial to Irish Catholics the act was and how Murray had been right.

THE REBELLION OF 1848

Revolution broke out in France in February 1848 and all Europe caught the contagion. Some revolutionaries saw this as the 'Springtide of the Nations' and, in a year of panic, many governments at first gave way. In Ireland, John Mitchell began preaching armed revolt and the Young Irelanders sent a delegation to Paris to plead for support from the new French republic. A rebellion seemed possible, indeed likely. The pragmatic Murray was thoroughly alarmed. Fearing that the horrors of the 1790s could come again, he took the unusual step of writing to the papers to appeal directly to the people in the public press to have no part in a rebellion. He spoke movingly of his own experience of 1798:

Fifty years ago I witnessed the miseries which a convulsion – such a scene like this might give birth to – inflicted on the political, social and moral condition of this unhappy country. Can any one be surprised that a thrill of horror should rush through my soul at the thought of the recurrence of such a calamity. May God in his mercy avert it!

Not content with exhorting, he took action. At the end of June 1848, knowing that some of the clergy were involved in the revolutionary clubs, he republished earlier decrees issued by the whole hierarchy warning the clergy to avoid politics. The more nationalist clergy were again angry. Murray's move was publicly disowned by some bishops and attacked by some of the clergy, one of whom contrasted his action unfavourably with that of his predecessor, 'the great Lawrence O'Toole [who] encouraged ... King Roderick and other Irish princes to unite for the total expulsion of the English marauders'. Murray stood firm. Unlike Bishop Kennedy of Killaloe who dealt severely with rebel priests like John Kenyon, Murray was never harsh towards his clergy even when they took radical political stands. When Father John Miley explained away the inflammatory language he had used, Murray graciously accepted. 'Your kind explanation gives me sincere pleasure,' he wrote, 'it has particularly gratified me by putting me in a position to prove authentically that "the whetting of the scimitar" had no reference whatever to the preparation for the threatened insurrection.' Undoubtedly, Murray's action played a part in limiting the scope of the rebellion. After the rebellion the leader, Smith O'Brien, in what he believed would be his final statement before his execution, placed the blame for the failure on certain bishops. Although he did not name him, Murray would have topped his list. Smith O'Brien blandly ignored other factors, in particular the incompetence he and his colleagues had shown as leaders of a revolution.

THE QUEEN'S COLLEGES

The last controversy that Murray became involved in was the acceptability of the Queen's Colleges. Other issues, such as the Famine and the government's denunciation of Irish clergy to Rome, sharpened the controversy. The primate and archbishop of Armagh, William Crolly, appeared to change his mind on the matter but died in 1849. Murray, who felt that the government's modifications made the bill acceptable, was left alone to face the three other archbishops, now led by the dynamic new primate and apostolic delegate, Paul Cullen. Accepting that the bill, like the other government concessions, was far from perfect, he justified his decision to take a less confrontational approach by his 'conscientious convictions ... drawn from long experience of our position, living, as we are, under a Protestant government'. He clung to his opinion even after the synod of Thurles pronounced against the colleges with Rome's approval. This obstinacy infuriated his opponents. Archbishop Michael Slattery of Cashel wrote a severely critical letter to Pope Pius IX, asking rhetorically: 'who are those who now are commonly known as *Government Bishops?*' The answer was Murray and his supporters. From a nationalist point of view, no more serious charge could be made. When Murray stubbornly held out on the issue, Paul Cullen angrily asked who was to govern the Church in Ireland – the pope through the bishops or the English viceroy through Archbishop Murray? Murray, for his part, declared:

> Some of our ardent Prelates may wish me to join secular agitation but that I can never do because I think it unworthy of a bishop and injurious to the interests of religion ... My continuing to act like this may be imputed to worldly motives, but I look to my heart and find no such motive there, and consoled by the recollection that our ever Blessed Saviour himself was reviled as an imposter, I have only to take advantage of it for my spiritual benefit by forgiving as I do so from my heart, this injurious and unfounded imputation ...

His refusal, as unworthy of his office, to mix politics with religion is admirable, even if from MacHale's point of view this was tantamount to supporting the government position. The 'injurious imputations' cast a shadow over his declining years – he was eighty-three when he wrote the above – and are no doubt a reason why Murray has been largely eclipsed in Irish history. In the controversies from 1844, he had been perceived by nationalists as succumbing to government pressure, too compliant and too ready to accept interference.

MURRAY'S CHARACTER

Murray was a mild-tempered-man according to many contemporaries. During his life-time he was often compared to St Francis de Sales – whom he regarded as his patron – and like him he believed that more could be won by a spoonful of honey than by a barrel-full of vinegar. The very able Bishop Doyle called him 'the most holy and prudent man I know.' J.P. Kennedy, who resigned from the Board of National Education because of differences with other commissioners, excepted Murray, for with him, he said, 'I could go on forever.' The young Count Charles de Montalembert, visiting Ireland in 1831, felt honoured to sit at table in Maynooth College, next 'to the celebrated and venerable Dr Murray, the real head of the Irish Church ... I was charmed by his manners, his tone, his opinions ...'. A later visitor, Edward Bouverie Pusey, the Tractarian leader, told Newman in 1841 that he found Murray 'apologetic and conciliatory'.

During the Famine, many of the priests who benefited from his benevolence referred to him as 'an angel of a man'. Even when he disagreed he did so in a quiet way. When Cullen asked him to agree with him for the sake of unity, Murray, conciliatory but firm, pointed out that in the early Church Peter and Paul had a difference of opinion: 'We differ', he told Cullen, 'as ever has been the case in the Church on matters of mere prudence.' Prudence, as Doyle mentioned, was another notable characteristic. Sir Dominic Corrigan, one of Dublin's leading physicians, described an important interview he had with some bishops: Crolly of Armagh and Denvir of Down and Connor took an active part but 'Dr Murray with his characteristic caution said little'. The Jesuit, John Lynch, described him as 'a most cautious man who never gave a direct answer when he could possibly avoid it.' He was also slow to reprimand. His perceptive friend, Bishop Doyle, thought him too gentle with people but the wisest of all. When he remonstrated with him for not taking sterner action, Murray gave him the disarming reply that 'it was difficult to know the exact point where clemency should cease and severity begin'.

His mildness predisposed him to cooperate with others. The Dublin bishops, because of their location in the capital city, were those with whom the government normally negotiated. Troy, whom Murray admired, had done so and Murray made no secret of co-operating with a whole line of viceroys from Anglesey in the 1820s to Clarendon in the late 1840s. For him, this contact presented an opportunity to represent the views and needs of the Church at the centre of political power in Ireland. Yet if this relationship became too cosy, it could generate suspicion of collusion from those who could not have the same influence. Angry for once, Murray complained of those 'fools who became quite suspicious of every kind of mischief, if we come at all into contact with people in power'. Lord Stanley, Lord John Russell, Sir James Graham and many other British statesmen praised his moderation while Clarendon, no friend of Catholicism, described him as a model of a bishop.

This winning gentleness came across in his sermons. When he preached, in his early years particularly, his congregation found him charmingly simple at a time when sermons were long, proclaimed in stentorian voice and with many rhetorical flourishes. His voice was low but distinct. He could electrify his audience, as in his Good Friday sermon when he compared the Church bound by the Veto to Jesus bound at the pillar by his false friends. In his sermons for charity he raised hundreds of thousands of pounds in today's money for the needs of the diocese. Daniel O'Connell had this to say of his sermons:

Others amazed the parliament and the nation by their profound eru-
dition, by their overwhelming eloquence, by their perfect acquaintance
with all the social and moral intricacies of our strange condition, but
for the good archbishop of Dublin it was reserved to lead not only the
intellects of his auditors captive, but their hearts also, showing up the
dogmas of faith, not only as irrefragably true, but divinely amiable and
beneficent.

In the words 'amiable and beneficent', O'Connell identified two of Murray's
principal characteristics.

His amiable manner is revealed in his relations with his friends. Writing
to Hamilton, he gently corrected the spelling: 'draw your pen over the i in
... *grievous*. I mean the abominable second i with which our friend Meagher
used to annoy us so grieviously'. With tongue-in-cheek he cautioned Hamilton
against fighting with the women who looked after St Mary's chapel for it
was a battle he could not win. Stay clear, he warned him, from getting
involved with 'the pious ladies who have made a Holy Hobby of the Statues.
Depend on it, with all their "holy indifference" they are a sturdy race, and
when the interests of piety appear to them to be concerned, it is not safe to
come into collision with them.' Welcoming Hamilton, who had just returned
from Paris to a meal in his house, he gently poked fun at him. 'We shall not
be so churlish as not to give you a share of it, provided the grandeur of Paris
will allow you to sit down with humble people at such very humble fare as
we can offer.' A number of the Corballis family – generous benefactors of
the Catholic Church and of the National Schools – were good friends of the
archbishop. John Richard Corballis appears to have been particularly close
and Murray's letters to him reveal his easy manner with his friends. An invitation to John Richard Corballis to dine with him is delightful:

> Come here on Wednesday evening next the 23rd inst at six o'clock
> and we can have our chat enliven'd by an occasional recourse, in spite
> of Father Mathew, to a drop of the fruit of the vine. In other words,
> come and dine with Yrs etc, D Murray.

The reference to Father Mathew's teetotal movement was playful not deroga-
tory, for Murray, unlike some of the bishops, was a friend of the temperance
leader, and had welcomed him warmly to his diocese. A birthday invitation
to Corballis is also gently humorous:

> If I live until Thursday next, the 18th inst. I shall enter on the 77th
> year of my earthly pilgrimage and if you wish to ascertain how an old
> stomach (not a teetotaller one) can do its duty, come on that day at

six o'clock ... and partake of that very plain kind of fare which you prefer.

Such warm friendship is engaging but it had pitfalls, too, as Father Peter Cooper told Cullen. Cooper, a curate in Murray's church in Marlborough Street and one of Murray's fiercest critics, complained that once Murray had given his friendship he could see no wrong in those friends. 'Years and years ago I perceived this amiable weakness in Dr Murray, that once he comes to form a friendship for a man – particularly a layman – he can see in him but perfection.' Cooper's concerns were about the charitable bequests bill where he feared that Anthony Blake got Murray to agree to plans which 'if left to himself ... Dr Murray would as soon put hand in the fire as approve it'. The result, he complained, was that one layman appeared to have more influence than all the rest of the bishops and priests.

To John Corballis one is indebted for an unusually intimate picture of the archbishop in his old age. Recounting to Anthony Blake how attentive Murray was when his father died, he described the touching scenes at the family house at Roebuck:

> myself and my two sisters on our knees at his bedside and his attached and steady friend – and such a friend – of fifty years standing, the Archbishop, under the roof, who gave his parting Benediction to him the night before; slept here that night, immediately after his decease on Monday morning, said Mass for the repose of his Soul – and with what fervour and sincerity he prayed by my poor father's bed after! To see this venerated and venerable old Archbishop, the [glory?] of the Church, in his cassock, on his knees at the bed side where his deceased friend of near 80 years of age lay – and in the same house where for near fifty years they had so often met together, was truly a touching, an interesting scene to the greatest stranger ... for two successive mornings after, did this good man rise out at seven o'clock to celebrate Mass in the house for him – professing all these duties with more humility and less parade, than the youngest and rawest curate in his Archdiocese.

'Less parade' again catches something of the goodness that Murray communicated. 'Parade' or show was alien to Murray. His way of acting reflected an unassuming, unostentatious manner. The same applied to his writing and preaching.

In a non-ecumenical age he had good relations with Protestants. Pusey was not the only leading Protestant to find him moderate. He worked well with Richard Whately, the archbishop of Dublin, and the other Protestant members of the National Education Board. In 1835 he wrote to his clergy of the grief he felt at 'the attempt to sow dissensions between our separated brethren' and claimed that the whole tendency of [my] life has been directed to soften the asperity of those religious dissensions which distract, and weaken, and dishonour us'. At a time when the Repeal movement was emphasising Irish nationality and Lord Lyndhurst dismissed the Irish as aliens in religion, language and blood, Murray played down the differences. One of his finest letters was an appeal to British Protestants. In a preaching tour of England, two Irish evangelical preachers had unfairly misrepresented the Catholic Church and attempted to stir up anti-Catholic feeling. Murray, too, was misrepresented. After a long silence, he decided to appeal to the Englishman's sense of fair play. He wrote publicly 'To The Protestants of Great Britain' in the warmest tones and said:

> Beloved Fellow-Christians, ...You are lovers of justice; you are slow to decide on partial statements ... Generous Britons! You whose honourable reverence for truth forms such a prominent feature in your character ... Let us, as our blessed Saviour commands, have love for one another ... not in word and in tongue, but in deed and truth; and let us give glory to God, not by the intemperance of our zeal, [but] by the sincerity of our efforts to promote peace among men.

Again when, in 1850, all Catholic Ireland united to condemn the virulent 'no-popery' outcry throughout England and the Prime Minister Russell's pledge to introduce the penal ecclesiastical titles bill, Murray remained conciliatory:

> We can readily make allowances for the inconsiderate expressions of unkindness towards us which the advocates of intolerance were enabled to evoke from many a humane, and generous and upright heart... but...the good sense of England will check that spirit of intolerance, so hostile to Religious and to Social Improvement.

When Russell persevered with the bill, Murray was dismayed and protested strongly. Sir James Graham read the protest in parliament, praising Murray's goodness and moderation. Some modifications were made as a result. Yet as Cullen and Murray were not slow to point out, Russell's bill and the insultingly anti-Catholic tenor of the debates in parliament destroyed the case Murray had pleaded for decades – the goodwill of the British government to Irish Catholics. The deeply-rooted 'no-popery' which the episode revealed, discredited Murray's efforts to persuade the bishops and Rome itself to trust the government. Paradoxically, however, neither Cullen nor Russell but Murray was proved right, in the long term. The penal nature of the Eccle-

siastical Titles Act proved unacceptable in modern England for the very reasons Murray had given and the act was quietly repealed by Gladstone twenty
years later.

PASSIVITY OR TURBULENCE?

The question must be asked whether Murray's willingness to work with the
government went too far. Murray and many of the well-to-do Catholics with
whom he associated – Bellew, Corballis and others – believed that they should
not antagonise the government but take whatever was of benefit to Irish
Catholics. From the Emancipation Act of 1829 on, the governments of Melbourne, Peel and Russell had offered a number of relief measures: tithes,
national education, the Charitable Bequests Board, Maynooth grant, Queen's
Colleges. The problem for the Church leaders was that while these concessions contained much that was useful to the Church, they also contained,
deliberately or not, some negative elements. MacHale and his party, in calling attention to these, played a role in alerting Catholics to possible pitfalls.
Murray's assessment, however, underlined the positive side of the concessions and his display of trust often succeeded in winning further concessions
from the government.

   At the height of the row over the Charitable Bequests Act, a not
unfriendly observer gave an interesting assessment of the question and may
have put his finger on the problem. Writing from Maynooth to Cullen in
Rome, Father Edmund O'Reilly, later a Jesuit and founder of Milltown Park,
described the ongoing dispute between Murray and MacHale:

> Dr MacHale's party whatever be *their cause, whether good or bad,*
> appear to act in a factious spirit at times ... those who wish to pro-
> mote the interests of this house and ... of religion, have considered
> themselves called on to stand together with Dr Murray. ... There are
> two *scopuli* to be avoided – passiveness and turbulence. There may be
> too much of the former on the one side, too much of the latter on the
> other side.

O'Reilly's considered and balanced remarks may contain a key to the negative reactions towards Murray. When, in 1849, Queen Victoria's visit to
Ireland was announced, he prepared a memorial to her from the bishops.
The other two archbishops, MacHale and Slattery (the see of Armagh was
vacant) rejected the memorial because it did not call the Queen's attention
to the mass mortality that 'has in several parts of Ireland diminished your
Majesty's subjects by a fourth, and in some by a half', the 'cruel evictions'

and suffering from famine. Murray amended the memorial to contain a reference to the 'many woes of our suffering poor'. Slattery and MacHale still thought it too milk and water and refused to sign or to meet the Queen. Murray saw their stance as mere trouble-making. He forwarded MacHale's reply to Clarendon, with the pained comment: 'Your Excellency will perceive by the accompanying what I have to endure from some of my Brethren'. MacHale and Slattery were not lone voices, however, for Lord Monteagle and Lord Fitzgerald, Father John Spratt, the relief organiser, and Father John Miley, O'Connell's friend, felt that the whole costly exercise of lavishly entertaining the Queen and shielding her from the suffering of the people was like 'fireworks in Glasnevin' and 'a great lie'. It is difficult not to conclude that Murray, on this occasion, was too passive and too anxious to please the lord lieutenant who had organised the visit. He had too great a regard for the person of the sovereign and was convinced, as he told MacHale, that Queen Victoria had done much for famine relief. Yet the devastation of the Famine was so acute that, in hindsight, he could be accused of not pressing for more active government intervention. The situation in Dublin, however, looked different from that in Connaught and Munster where the devastation of famine, disease and eviction was far more horrendous.

If Murray's attitude on this issue can be interpreted as 'passivity', on other issues he showed moral courage in swimming against the tide. Unwilling to cause pain, forgiving of those who hurt him, he was, when necessary, able to take a stand. The controversy over the National Schools showed him fighting courageously for what he believed was the good of the country's children. He again showed his courage when, on the question of his attitude towards Repeal, he openly challenged Bishop Higgins' claim that all bishops were repealers. Similarly, he showed his mettle in supporting the Bequests Act in the teeth of opposition from nationalists and clergy in his own city. Despite the fact that he was tired of controversy, he still held by his views on the Queen's Colleges. Though some like Cullen saw it as the stubbornness of old age, Murray had the courage to stand by his convictions. Nor, despite his co-operation with the government, could he be called a 'Castle Catholic'. He was a patriot who felt deeply for the suffering of his country, as he exclaimed publicly in the Pro-Cathedral in Dublin on one occasion. What he wanted was a working relationship that would both benefit his church and maintain social stability.

A NEW WORLD?

Perhaps the most important consideration in understanding the criticism Murray encountered in the 1840s, is the realisation of how things had changed since he was consecrated archbishop in 1809. Father Peter Cooper, complained that Murray's actions reflected 'the timid, crouching policy of the last century'. Despite his lack of understanding of what was possible in the eighteenth century, Cooper's remark identified the importance of the change in the position of Catholics. By 1850, the Ireland Murray knew as a student in Salamanca, as a curate or even as a coadjutor-archbishop in Dublin had disappeared. As for most people, his habitual modes of perception and response had been formed in young and early manhood when his thinking was taking shape. His attitude to violent political agitation was moulded in the furnace of the mayhem of 1798; his views on the connection between Church and state had been formed when co-operation with the government, as in Europe generally, was still a respectable position. By the 1840s, Murray's world had disappeared. The Young Irelanders and many young clerics were sufficiently distant from the horrors of rebellion and repression that they no longer feared to speak of '98, and Meagher's romantic 'sword speech' found an echo in many young patriotic hearts. A new generation of Catholics had emerged, grown confident in the wake of O'Connell's great campaigns and no longer willing to accept all that eighteenth-century Catholics had accepted. They could, and did, contemplate more forceful means to remedy their griev-ances. With this attitude the ever-prudent, ageing Murray could have no sympathy. It was not in his nature to wage war on the might of England as Smith O'Brien attempted, nor even to excoriate viceroys and prime minis-ters as the 'Lion of the West', John MacHale, so often did. Even without the generation gap, Murray's was a different temperament.

The future of the Irish Church in the nineteenth century lay neither with Murray nor MacHale but with Cullen, who completed Murray's reorganisa-tion of the Dublin diocese and reshaped the Irish Church along Roman lines. For the success of his work, Murray's diocesan and pastoral care had paved the way. Such, however, was the lustre of Cullen's episcopate and its mould-ing influence on generations of Irish Catholics that they have obscured Murray's achievement in laying the foundations. It was reliably reported that when, in February 1852, Clarendon, the viceroy, learned of Murray's death, he wept. Many others mourned his passing because he was a good man who had accomplished much for the archdiocese of Dublin.

12

Women and Catholic life in Dublin, 1766-1852

Séamus Enright

Women and women's initiatives emerged as a central feature of Catholic life in Dublin during the late eighteenth and early-nineteenth centuries, as women engaged for the first time, in a simultaneous and modern way, in a wide range of evangelical and social activities. This chapter examines some aspects of this response, focusing on the contribution of particular women from 1766, when Teresa Mulally opened a school for poor girls, to the death of the friend of many of those endeavours, Archbishop Daniel Murray, in 1852.

Women's evangelical and philanthropic activity, and the female religious communities which emerged out of and around this endeavour, were not an isolated Catholic response to the religious and social needs of late eighteenth and early-nineteenth century Ireland. Rather, they were part of a broader movement of reform and modernisation in which women were significant agents of change. Acting alone or in partnership with sympathetic priests, they were supported by wealthy Catholic families and enjoyed the confidence of successive archbishops.

The women who made up this movement were evangelists and catechists first and philanthropists second. They were, like their clerical counterparts, agents of a Tridentine-style, Counter-Reformation catholicism, developed in late sixteenth and early seventeenth-century France, where its proponents believed that 'the conquest of souls required the formation of minds.'[1] They were part of a movement, with both Catholic and Protestant roots and parallels, that sought 'to develop a programme for elementary instruction that would include the masses and acquaint them with true religion.'[2] The women also preserved an older tradition in which the poor were seen as an *alter Christus*. Service of the poor was a direct service of Christ.

1 Henri-Jean Martin, *The history and power of writing* (Chicago, 1994), p. 337.   2 Ibid., p. 338.

I

Teresa Mulally (1728-1803), a milliner and businesswoman, was a pioneer of the Catholic revival in Dublin.[3] She devoted her limited wealth and considerable business acumen to the establishment of a school for poor girls in St Michan's parish. She was supported in this by James Philip Mulcaile (1727-1801), a Jesuit priest, and was backed financially by a number wealthy Catholics. Mulally's decision to provide free education for poor girls was inspired by the work of Thomas Betagh SJ (1738-1811), on behalf of poor boys. Mulally was also influenced by Nano Nagle (1718-84), an early activist in the cause of Catholic education and a pioneer of new forms of religious life for women in Ireland.[4] Nagle began her schools for the poor in Cork in 1751 or 1752, introduced the Ursulines from Paris to Cork in 1771 and, when it became clear that the Ursulines were unwilling to co-operate fully with her plans, founded the Society of Charitable Instruction of the Sacred Heart of Jesus in 1775. The members of Nagle's new society, who were known as Presentation Sisters from 1791, devoted themselves exclusively to the education of poor children and the visitation of the sick poor. Significantly, Nagle and Mulally corresponded for some years and Mulally visited Nagle in Cork in 1778 and 1779.[5]

Mulally's school began in rented rooms in Mary's Lane in 1766. She purchased land at George's Hill in 1787, on which she built a school, an orphanage and a convent. Mulally entrusted the enterprise to the Presentation Sisters in 1794. She had planned this for many years, having previously sent four of her followers to Cork to be trained as Presentation Sisters.

Mulally articulated her understanding of the purpose of her school in *An address to the charitable of St Michan's parish*, which was published in 1766. The pupils were to be instructed in 'prayers and catechism, in reading and writing' and in the practical skills necessary to earn 'honest bread' and to become useful members of society. The girls who attended the school in Mary's Lane knew the 'hardship of extreme poverty,' but their 'chief mis-

3 Roland Burke Savage, *A valiant Dublin woman* (Dublin, 1940).   4 T.J. Walsh, *Nano Nagle and the Presentation Sisters* (Dublin, 1959); Mary Pius O'Farrell, *Nano Nagle: woman of the gospel* (Monasterevin, 1996); William Coppinger, *The life of Nano Nagle* (Cork, 1794); Dominic Murphy, *Memoirs of Miss Nano Nagle and the Presentation and Ursuline orders in Ireland* (Cork, 1845); William Hutch, *Nano Nagle: her life, her labour and their fruits* (Dublin, 1875); see also L.M. Cullen, 'The Blackwater catholics and County Cork society and politics in the eighteenth century' in Patrick O'Flanagan and Cornelius G. Buttimer (eds), *Cork: history and society* (Dublin, 1993), pp 535-84.   5 Eight of Nano Nagle's letters to Teresa Mulally and a transcript of another are preserved in the Presentation Convent, George's Hill, Dublin.

fortune', Mulally argued, was 'to be without any means of instruction', because without instruction, they acquired 'habits of ignorance, idleness and vice' which made them a danger to themselves and to society.[6]

The ultimate purpose of instruction, as in every other activity undertaken by Catholic women activists of this ilk, was evangelical. Nagle and Mulally were among the early advocates of 'the ideology of the school' in Ireland. They embraced its core principle that childhood instruction was 'the only way by which vice could be destroyed and virtue established.'[7] This is borne out by the opening sentences of the Annals of the Presentation Convent in James' Street, founded by two of Mulally's followers in 1807, which highlight Nano Nagle's concern for the spiritual wellbeing of the poor:

> During her stay in Ireland, she was deeply afflicted at seeing the total ignorance of the lower classes of its inhabitants, their consequent immorality and the ruin of their souls ... Their miserable condition was ever present to her imagination – no company, no employment, no pleasure, no pain could mitigate her anxiety for the poor people ... Tracing their vices to their source, viz. the ignorance of religion among them, she conceived the most earnest desire at striking at the root of all their evils, by providing them with the proper means of Instruction.[8]

Nagle's approval of a 'very fine sermon' preached by Father Nicholas Barron (1719-84) to the members of her society on the feast of the Presentation of the Blessed Virgin Mary, 1782, provides further insight into her thinking and of the significance she, Mulally and her followers, attached to their work.[9] Barron made a strong link between such women and Christ, whom he described as 'a walking missioner.' The women were his 'Copartners ... in completing the redemption of mankind, by instructing the ignorant in the paths of life.' However, because not everyone approved of their efforts, he urged the sisters to be patient with those who did not appreciate or understand the purpose of those whom they labelled pejoratively as 'Walking' and 'Galloping' nuns.[10]

6 Burke Savage, *A valiant Dublin woman*, pp 58-60.   7 Elizabeth Rappley, *The dévotes: women and Church in seventeenth-century France* (Montreal, 1990), p. 119; Rappley's book is essential reading for anybody wanting to understand the development of the modern religious life movement among women.   8 Annals of the Presentation Convent, Terenure (Presentation Convent, Terenure, Dublin).   9 Nano Nagle to Teresa Mulally, 31 Jan. 1783 (Presentation Convent, George's Hill, Dublin).   10 Ms sermon of Nicholas Barron (South Presentation Convent, Cork); I am grateful to Sister Pius O'Farrell PBVM for sharing her identification of Nicholas Barron as the author of the sermon with me.

The transition of George's Hill from secular *ad hoc* project into an organised religious community was not without difficulty. Mulally objected to the pattern of life prescribed in the Presentation constitutions. Differences centred on the conflicting needs of the school and religious life. Mulally observed that some of the community's exercises interfered with the efficient running of the school. She was opposed to the fact that the sisters were expected to make their annual retreat and to follow this with their summer vacation. She wanted the retreat and the vacation staggered so that the school would never close for a long period of time. Sister Francis Tobin (1764-1826), the mistress of novices in Cork, took a contrary perspective; she defended the way of life provided for in the constitutions and supported the exact observance of the rules:

> You wished to have a religious establishment as the only means of rendering your schools permanent, and you now enjoy it but sure, my dear friend, you could never have proposed to yourself to get Religious who would be content to devote themselves to the instruction of others and neglect their own perfection, which would be the case were they deprived of their regular times of prayer and Retreat.[11]

The sisters in George's Hill forsook some of Nano Nagle's original inspiration in 1806 when they opted to make solemn vows and adopted enclosure. Despite this, George's Hill contributed, in a small way, to the remarkable expansion of the order that took place after 1806. Sisters from George's Hill established communities in James' Street, Dublin (1807), Drogheda (1813) and Rahan, County Offaly (1817). The James' Street community moved to Fairview in 1820 and sent colonies to Maynooth (1823) and Mullingar (1825).[12] The Rahan and Maynooth communities combined to send sisters to Madras in India in 1842.

The change in their canonical status did not diminish the Presentation sisters' commitment to the education of the poor which remained at the heart of their mission. Thus, the nuns described themselves as 'the adopted Mothers of the poor' and understood their care as 'part of the self-sacrifice [they] made to God.'[13] Indeed, they insisted that they could only be true to their vocation by 'constant, close attendance' on the poor.[14] Poor children, in particular, were accorded special mention; they were, one member of the order maintained, 'the favourites of Heaven' and the 'beloved portion' of the order. Without them it would have no reason for existing.[15]

---

11 Tobin to Mulally, 28 Feb. 1795 (Presentation Convent, George's Hill, Dublin).   12 The community moved to Terenure in 1867.   13 di Pazzi Leahy, Considerations adapted to the Presentation religious in a spiritual retreat, p. 331 (South Presentation Convent, Cork).   14 Ibid., p. 305.   15 Mary Joseph McLoughlin, A memorial of friendship from

Such commitment won the Presentation nuns enormous respect and admiration among the reform-minded Catholic laity. The attitude of James Hardiman (1782-1855) was not untypical. There were four communities of nuns in Galway when Hardiman published his *History of Galway* in 1820. While the Poor Clares, Dominicans and Augustinians had been in the city since the seventeenth century, Hardiman chose to praise the Presentation nuns who had arrived as recently as 1815:

> From the charitable labours of these exemplary ladies many benefits have already accrued, and are thereafter likely to accrue, to society by the moral, religious and usefully domestic education of so many of its most helpless and most generally neglected members. At present thirty female orphan children are dieted, lodged, clothed and educated; and upwards of three hundred female day scholars are instructed in useful needlework, reading, writing, the common rules of arithmetic, and the principles of religion

Indeed, Hardiman was so impressed by the sisters, he gently chides the other orders for not 'adopt[ing], even on a limited scale, this humane plan'.[16] The need to be useful in a time of overwhelming need slowly changed the face of the old orders.

II

There were five communities of nuns in Dublin when Teresa Mulally began her poor school in 1766. There were Poor Clares in North King Street[17] and Dorset Street, Dominicans in Channel Row, Carmelites in Fisher's Lane and Augustinians at Mullinahack.[18] There is, however, no evidence to suggest that any of them directed their activities towards the welfare of the poor, though this issue increasingly occupied the minds and imaginations of reform-minded Catholics. Indeed, in 1750, Father John Murphy (1710-53) complained to Rome that the nuns of Dublin were not teaching catechism and domestic economy to poor girls.[19] The convents, with the single exception

Sister Mary Joseph McLoughlin to her beloved sisters of the Presentation Convent, Kilkenny, p. 221 (Presentation Convent, Kilkenny). **16** James Hardiman, *The history of the town and county of Galway* (Galway, 1926), p. 287. **17** This community moved to Kingstown in 1826 and disbanded in 1836. **18** This community was extinct by 1770; see Nicholas Donnelly, *A short history of some Dublin parishes* (3 vols, Dublin, [*c.*1905-12]), ii, 223. **19** Hugh Fenning, *The undoing of the friars of Ireland* (Louvain, 1972), p. 198.

of the Poor Clares of Dorset Street, devoted themselves to the education of the daughters of wealthy Catholic families and to keeping lady boarders. They were generally in decline by the 1760s.

The Poor Clares of Dorset Street were the first of the old religious communities to respond to the needs of the poor and, in the process, re-invented themselves as a religious community.[20] Their decision to re-orientate their activities towards caring for the poor was not a spontaneous action, but was the price they had to pay for survival. Facing financial collapse the community was saved by, among others, Denis Thomas O'Brien and his daughter, Maria, whose support was dependent on the nuns undertaking the care of orphans. Maria O'Brien (1765-1827) managed an orphanage in Hendrick Street and was anxious to transfer it to the care of a religious community. Persuaded that 'Christ's little ones were hungering and perishing for instruction', the nuns agreed to care for them and to move to Harold's Cross on condition that some traditional Poor Clare observances were modified.[21] The Holy See agreed to their request in 1804 provided that the nuns devoted themselves to the instruction of poor girls 'in Catholic Doctrine and the practice of religion.'[22] This was not an obstacle; the sisters moved to Harold's Cross in 1804 and were followed by the orphans, two years later. G.N. Wright, noted that the Harold's Cross 'nunnery ... [is] more conspicuous than the others for the magnitude of its charities' and that the 'benevolent sisters' currently educated, clothed and supported one-hundred female children.[23] The Harold's Cross sisters, established a foundation at Dundrum in 1827. This community moved briefly to North William Street, where they replaced the Sisters of Charity, before finally settling in Newry in 1830.

There is a parallel between the development of the respective institutions established at George's Hill and Harold's Cross. The decisive initiative was undertaken by lay people in response to the needs of poor, at-risk Catholics and, in both instances, the institutions were eventually entrusted to the care of religious communities which guaranteed commitment, stability and permanence. We can see this pattern in the case of the Henderick Street orphanage. It was founded in 1801 by three working men, Patrick Quarterman, James Auger and George Poland. They entrusted its management to Maria O'Brien and she in turn transferred it to the care of the Poor Clares of Harolds Cross. The inaugural appeal of Quarterman, Auger and Poland in 1801 echoes Teresa Mulally's appeal of 1766.

20 [Francis Clare Cusack], *St Clare, St Colette and the Poor Clares* (Dublin, 1864), pp 355-68; Mrs Thomas [Helena] Concannon, *The Poor Clares in Ireland* (Dublin, 1929). 21 [Francis Clare Cusack], *In memoriam Mary O'Hagan, abbess and foundress of the convent of the Poor Clares, Kenmare* (London, 1876), p. 16.   22 Brief, 13 June 1804 (Dublin Diocesan Archives (henceforth DDA), Troy Papers, 29/10, 21).   23 G.N. Wright, *A historical guide to the city of Dublin* (London, 1825), p. 96.

At a time when vice and impurity prevail in this city, where numbers of poor destitute female orphans are left prey to infamy and immorality, at an early period not having the fostering aid of parental care to cherish their youthful days in the paths of virtue – a few elderly men, from motives of charity, and to stop the torrent of such growing vice and wickedness, as much as in them lie, propose with God's help and the assistance of a charitable and generous public, to establish a Female Orphan Institution in this city, under the title of the MARIA FEMALE ORPHANS.[24]

Prior to his involvement with the Henderick Street orphanage, Patrick Quarterman, had already founded the General Magdalen Asylum in Townsend Street in 1798. This was supported by penny collections among the poor and the work of the residents,[25] and aimed to provide a refuge for women who were 'anxious to quit the paths of prostitution, [and] prefer Repentance and Virtue to Infamy and Guilt'.[26] This was a goal upon which there was widespread agreement and the asylum provides a fine illustration of the alliance between working-class and middle-class Catholics, between women and men, as well as between reform-minded, socially-aware Catholics and the emerging women's religious communities that such causes helped forge. For present purposes, the movements of most direct pertinence are the latter because they had most influence both on each other and on the emergence of an infrastructure of caring Catholic agencies. Initially, during the late eighteenth and early nineteenth centuries, the lay Catholic activist movement was stronger, but as the nineteenth century progressed, it was subsumed over time into the religious life movement. This can be seen in the case of the Magdalen Asylum by the fact that following the foundation by working-class Catholics, control passed initially to wealthy members of the Catholic business community and then to the Sisters of Charity. Denis Thomas O'Brien was treasurer from the asylum's foundation until his death in 1814, while John Ball (1728-1803), whose daughters were to play such pivotal roles in the Catholic revival, was an early vice-president. However, with the emergence of religious communities it was deemed appropriate that control of the institution should pass into their hands and Mary Aikenhead's Sisters of Charity assumed responsibility for the asylum in 1833 and transferred it to Donnybrook in 1837.

24 Concannon, *Poor Clares*, p. 124.   25 Matthew Davenport Hill, *Our exemplars, poor and rich; or biographical sketches of men and women who have by an extraordinary use of their opportunities, benefited their fellow creatures* (London, 1861), pp 95-109.   26 John Watson Stewart, *The gentleman's and citizen's almanack, for the year of our Lord 1802* (Dublin, 1802), p. 135.

A similar process of adaptation and re-invention was occurring among the Carmelite and Dominican communities. A Carmelite convent was founded at Warrenmount in 1813 'for the object of uniting perpetually the Teresian Observance with the charitable Instruction of destitute Female Children'.[27] Its founder was Mother Clare Lyons (1785-1855), who had become prioress of the Carmelites at Ranelagh in 1811, just six months after her profession. Eager to improve the order, she set about reforming the community along traditional Carmelite lines, but her reforming efforts, which included the introduction of the habit, met with such resistance from the older nuns that she withdrew and founded a new convent at Warrenmount. Prior to her departure, Lyons consulted Daniel Murray and Father Peter Kenney (1779-1841) who both encouraged her to leave Ranelagh. Kenney, an extraordinary Jesuit, was friendly with many of the prominent Catholic women of his day and was close to most of the women's communities.[28]

The Presentation influence was strongly evident in the establishment of Warrenmount, which is hardly surprising since Clare Lyons deeply admired the Presentation system for their 'fourth Vow of instructing poor females.'[29] Moreover, prior to her admission to the Carmelites, she made three unsuccessful attempts at entering the Presentation convent in Kilkenny. Two of her sisters were members of the South Presentation convent in Cork.[30] In 1814 Archbishop John Thomas Troy petitioned the Holy See to allow the Warrenmount community devote itself to the free instruction of poor children and to grant it the same relaxations that the Poor Clares of Harold's Cross enjoyed.[31] The request was immediately granted.[32] In 1815 there were 200 children in the poor school and thirty 'of the most comfortless' were cared for in the convent itself.[33]

Colonies of sisters were sent from Warrenmount to found communities in Blackrock (1823), North William Street (1830) and Tallow, County Waterford (1836).[34] The Ranelagh community recovered, meanwhile, from the departure of Clare Lyons and established convents in New Ross (1817), Clondalkin (1824) and Blanchardstown (1828).[35] These foundations resulted

27 Clare Lyons to Cardinal Lorenzo Litta, 23 Nov. 1815 (DDA, Troy Papers, 30/2, 96); Sister Teresa O'Shea, Annales Moniales Ordinis Carmelitorum Discalceatorum Dubliensis (Carmel, Malahide, County Dublin); Patrick of St Joseph, Carmel in Ireland (London, 1897), pp 268-283.   28 Thomas Morrissey, As one sent: Peter Kenney SJ, 1779-1841 (Dublin, 1996).   29 Lyons to Litta, as note 27.   30 Maureen Hegarty, Isabella and Catherine and the Presentation Sisters of Kilkenny (Kilkenny, 1995), p. 5.   31 Archbishop Troy to the Holy See, 27 June 1814 (DDA, Troy Papers, 30/2, 2).   32 Brief (DDA, Troy Papers, 30/2, 3).   33 Lyons to Litta, as note 27.   34 The North William Street community moved to Lakelands, Sandymount in 1857 and to Roebuck in 1876, having transferred the care of the orphanage at Lakelands to the Sisters of Charity.   35 The Clondalkin community moved to Firhouse in 1827 and the Blanchardstown community

from tensions within the Ranelagh community as much as from apostolic zeal and some of the partings were acrimonious.[36] The Ranelagh community and its foundations, following the earlier example of Warrenmount, eventually severed their canonical connection with the Carmelite Order and placed themselves under the jurisdiction of the archbishop of Dublin. Subsequently, a number of dissidents, anxious to be canonically reunited with the Carmelite friars, established the Tranquilla community in Dublin in 1833.

Troubled by reports of lax religious observance, the Holy See requested that Archbishop Daniel Murray should investigate the affairs of the Ranelagh Carmel in 1824. It had been reported to Rome that the nuns were not keeping their rule and admitted outsiders to the convent.[37] Murray replied that there was little or no foundation to these reports, since the nuns lived piously and had little contact with the outside world. Some contact was necessary, he observed, to enable the nuns to run their two schools – a free school for the poor which they maintained out of the income raised in their fee-paying school for the daughters of well-to-do parents, since without the poor school the girls would attend Protestant schools.[38] Indeed, according to Wright, the Ranelagh nuns also contributed 'munificently' to the support of two orphanages, one in Paradise-row, where twenty orphans were 'admitted at the age of three years, and supported and instructed until sufficiently qualified to be apprenticed' and another orphanage, where sixty boys and girls were 'clothed, fed and supported.'[39]

Like the Carmelites who had been based in the city before their move to Ranelagh, the Dominicans of Cabra had originally been city-based. Located in Channel Row (now North Brunswick Street) since 1717, they moved to Clontarf in 1808 and to Cabra in 1819. They began the process of adaptation and modernisation when they opened a poor school in 1820 and reestablished their boarding school in 1836.[40] Magdalen Butler (1798-1856) and Ann Columba Maher (1777-1855) were the guiding lights in this small, struggling, community.

Maher, a former lay sister, negotiated the community's future with the Holy See which involved a canonical separation from the Dominican Order. Regarded by some of her contemporaries as 'quite uneducated, very silent and rather dry', the collapse of her relationship with Magdalen Butler led to

transferred to Hampton, Drumcondra, in 1858.   36 O'Shea, Annales ... Dubliensis.   37 Cardinal Somaglia to Murray, 1824 (DDA, Murray Papers, 30/8, 107).   38 Murray to Somaglia, 11 Nov. 1825 (DDA, Murray Papers, 30/9).   39 Wright, An historical guide to the city of Dublin, p. 96.   40 Cécile Diamond and Rose O'Neill, 'Here begins the chronicle of the Cabra Dominican Congregation' in Dominique Horgan (ed.), Weavings: celebrating Dominican women (Dublin, 1988), pp 4-18.

a split in the community. Butler departed, in acrimonious circumstances, in 1836, to found a new community at Mount Street, which moved to Sion Hill four years later.[41] This community might never have got off the ground but for Pope Gregory XVI's decision that the Cabra house should provide Butler and her companions with £800.[42] She served as prioress at Sion Hill for three terms until 1846, when, 'wanting to be united to the order', she transferred to Siena in Drogheda, which had maintained a juridic relationship with the friars.[43] Despite this upheaval, the struggling community at Cabra developed into a flourishing centre from which four Irish and three overseas convents were established. This community's most innovative departure was the establishment of a school for deaf and dumb children in 1846.

As a consequence of the success with which the Harold's Cross, Warrenmount and Cabra communities negotiated the transition from a semi-contemplative to an active lifestyle, they effectively re-invented themselves as religious communities. In the process, the nuns discarded practices, such as the divine office and fasting, essential in traditional monastic communities, and embraced features of the semi-monastic teaching institutes that emerged in seventeenth-century France which were already represented in Ireland by the Ursulines, and from 1806, by the Presentation Nuns. They thereby succeeded in establishing an apostolic model of religious life within the old orders that went some way towards meeting the pressing needs of the time and that attracted enough members to allow for a limited expansion.

As part of their survival strategies, these female religious communities severed their connections with the male branches of their orders and accepted the jurisdiction of the archbishop of Dublin. The nuns, especially at leadership level, shared the prejudice of reform-minded Catholics toward the friars. Mother Magdalen Butler, one-time prioress of Cabra and founder of the Sion Hill community, was typical. She had an 'almost unbounded' respect for secular priests in contrast to the Dominicans whom she considered 'boorish and uncouth.'

III

The struggles of the communities like the Carmelites, Poor Clares and Dominicans took place, to some extent, on the margins of the Catholic revival. While they were attempting to negotiate a way into the future, new convents

41 Annals of the Monastery of St Catherine of Siena, Drogheda, commencing from the date of its foundation by Ven. Mother Catherine Plunkett, AD 1722, p. 141 (Siena Convent, Drogheda). 42 Book of Annals (Dominican Convent, Sion Hill). 43 Ms Life of Magdalen Butler, pp 9-11 (Siena Convent, Drogheda).

and new institutions were being established in Dublin. These developments were driven and underwritten by the faith, wealth and increased confidence of the Catholic middle-class highlighted by Maureen Wall, as long ago as 1958.[44]

Two families, O'Brien and Ball, in particular, stand out for their involvement in almost every aspect of the Catholic revival that took place in the late eighteenth and early nineteenth centuries. Denis Thomas O'Brien, described by Lord Hardwicke, the lord lieutenant in 1805, as 'a merchant of considerable weight and responsibility', was active in social and political as well as religious spheres.[45] A generous supporter of Catholic causes, a trustee of the Lay College at Maynooth and treasurer of the General Magdalen Asylum in Townsend Street, he was a longtime member of the Catholic Committee and a signatory of the Catholic petition in 1805.[46] In common with most of the Catholic merchant class, O'Brien was 'very impatient for Emancipation' and, like them, possessed of 'much influence with the clergy to whom they are very hospitable.'[47]

When Denis Thomas O'Brien died in 1814, he left a 4,000-acre estate in Rahan, County Offaly and £50,000 to his daughter, Maria. She was an even more generous supporter of Catholic causes than her father. As we have seen above, Maria O'Brien, managed an orphanage in Hendrick Street until this responsibility was entrusted to the care of the Poor Clares in 1806. She had an abiding interest in the welfare of orphans and sent children from Dublin to lodge with families in the vicinity of Tullow, County Carlow, on the understanding that they would attend the Brigidine convent schools. When O'Brien discovered that some of the children were being exploited by the families with whom they were sent to stay, she asked the Brigidines to manage the scheme for her. Maria O'Brien entered the Presentation convent in Rahan, which she had earlier endowed, in 1822 and died there in 1827.

Maria's brother, John O'Brien, married Anna Maria Ball (1785-1871) in 1805.[48] She was one of the most significant and influential lay Catholics of

44 Maureen Wall, 'The rise of a catholic middle class in eighteenth-century Ireland' in Gerard O'Brien (ed.), *Catholic Ireland in the eighteenth century: the collected essays of Maureen Wall* (Dublin, 1989), pp 73-84; see also David Dickson, 'Catholics and trade in eighteenth-century Ireland: an old debate revisited' in T.P. Power and Kevin Whelan (eds), *Endurance and emergence: Catholics in Ireland in the eighteenth century* (Dublin, 1990), pp 85-100.   45 Hardwicke to Hawkesbury, 28 Jan. 1805 in Brian MacDermott (ed.), *The Irish Catholic petition of 1805: the diary of Denys Scully* (Dublin, 1992), p. 47; O'Brien was a founding member of the Dublin Chamber of Commerce in 1783: cf. P. Fagan, *Catholics in a Protestant country; the Protestant constituency in eighteenth century Dublin* (Dublin, 1998), pp 168-71.   46 Ibid.   47 'Robert Marshall's Notes on the Irish Catholics' in ibid., p. 157.   48 Beatrice Bayley Butler and Kathleen Butler, 'Mrs John O'Brien: her life, her work and her friends', *Dublin Historical Record*, 33 (1979/80), pp 141-56.

her day, and Sarah Atkinson (1823-93) captures something of Ball's spirit, and that of the resurgent Catholicism she represented, in her biography of Mary Aikenhead:

> [She] had very decided notions concerning the duties of Catholics at this particular time; they should not any longer continue, she thought, to hide in back streets, to wear that cowering expression which distinguished them in public from their Protestant fellow-countrymen, to allow themselves be jostled off a path which they had as much a right as any of their countrymen to tread ... Mary Aikenhead was not long ... in finding out what interests were dearest of all to her friend. These were the interests of the Catholic community, and everything connected with the poor, the helpless, the afflicted.[49]

Anna Maria was one of five children of John Ball and his second wife, Mabel Clare Bennet. Cecilia (Mother Regis, 1784-1854) was educated by the Ursulines in Cork where she later became superior; Anna Maria, Isabella (Mrs Sherlock) and Frances (Mother Teresa) went to the Bar Convent in York. Nicholas (1791-1865), who enjoyed a successful political and legal career, went to Stonyhurst before studying at Trinity College. Anna Maria O'Brien and Mother Teresa Ball (1794-1861) worked closely with Archbishop Daniel Murray (1768-1852) in developing services for the poor and in promoting Catholic education in Dublin. Contemporaries were impressed by the qualities they noticed in these women. Mother Angela Browne (1796-1874), a Dublin-born member of the Bar Convent and lifelong friend of Teresa Ball, knew the family from childhood. She commented on 'the heroic charity' of Mrs O'Brien and 'the unobtrusive virtues' of Mrs Sherlock in a letter to Mother Scholastica Somers (1805-85).[50] The annalist of the Cork Ursulines noted the 'great kindness of heart, gentleness, consideration and amiability' of Mother Regis.[51]

Mrs O'Brien's life and that of Mary Aikenhead (1787-1858) were intimately connected from 1808, when they met at Regis Ball's profession as an Ursuline. Mary Aikenhead had become a Catholic in 1803, having been inspired by a sermon of Bishop Florence McCarthy (1761-1810), coadjutor bishop of Cork, on the parable of Dives and Lazarus. She was so moved by McCarthy's exposition of the parable 'that she made up her mind to cast

49 Sarah Atkinson, *Mary Aikenhead: her life, her work, and her friends* (Dublin, 1879), pp 116-17. 50 Browne to Somers, 27 Nov. 1866 in [Evangeline McDonald], *Joyful mother of children: Mother Frances Mary Teresa Ball* (Dublin, 1961), pp 34-5. 51 Annals, i, pp 156-7 (Ursuline Convent, Blackrock, Cork).

in her lot with the lowly and despised whom Jesus loved and called to his heavenly kingdom.'[52] Aikenhead visited O'Brien in Dublin in 1809 when O'Brien and her friends were fund-raising for their recently-established refuge for Catholic girls in Ash Street. The refuge was transferred to Stanhope Street in 1814 and entrusted to the Sisters of Charity in 1819. The appeal of O'Brien and her companions, reminiscent of Mulally's 1766 appeal and the Quarterman, Auger and Poland appeal of 1801, well illustrates the spirit and ambition of such reform-minded Catholic women:

> A more interesting object cannot be presented to the commiseration of the charitable than a virtuous and unprotected female struggling with distress, and unable to extricate herself from it. Amongst the numerous victims comprehended in this extensive class of misery, a prominent place belongs to those destitute orphans, who have been saved by charity from early ruin, but who are afterwards, when depending for subsistence on their own industry, deprived from employment and consequently of support ... To afford shelter to industrious and unprotected females, when reduced to distress, the House of Refuge has been opened in Ash Street. On producing unquestionable vouchers for the propriety of their conduct, they are received under its protection, and employed in washing, mangling, plainwork, and other branches of female industry, until suitable circumstances are provided for them. In the mean time, much care is taken to enlighten their minds, and to impress the duties of religion more deeply on their hearts; so that during their temporary residence in the House of Refuge, they are not only rescued from the hardships which they were suffering, and the dangers of vice to which they were exposed, but they are improved in those beliefs of virtue and honesty, which will render them more certainly useful to those who shall hereafter employ them.[53]

Aikenhead's lifelong engagement with the poor began in O'Brien's company. Atkinson describes how they would

> wrap themselves in their cloaks and take their way through miserable lanes and up crazy stairs, bringing to the sick and poor food for the body and comfort for the soul.[54]

---

[52] Atkinson, *Mary Aikenhead*, p. 87.   [53] Leaflet, House of Refuge, Ash Street, c.1809 in Maria Luddy, *Women in Ireland, 1800-1918: a documentary history* (Cork, 1995), pp 55-6.   [54] Atkinson, *Mary Aikenhead*, p. 117.

Mary Aikenhead met Daniel Murray for the first time in John and Anna Maria O'Brien's house on Mountjoy Square. They became lifelong friends and worked together to improve the plight of Dublin's Catholic poor. Murray persuaded Aikenhead to found the Sisters of Charity and arranged for her to make a novitiate at the Bar Convent, York, which she and Catherine Walsh (1773-1854) entered in 1812. The history of the Sisters of Charity begins when they returned to Dublin in 1815.[55] Significantly, Luddy and Murphy include the foundation of the congregation on their 'list of significant events and dates' for Irish women.[56] Mary Aikenhead described the wide-ranging purpose of the congregation in a letter written during the cholera epidemic of 1833:

> The object of our Institution is to attend to the comforts of the poor, both spiritual and temporal; to visit them at their dwellings and in hospitals, to attend them in sickness, to administer consolation in their afflictions, and to reconcile them to the dispensations of an all-wise Providence in the many trials to which they are subject. The education and relief of orphans, and the religious instruction of the lower orders, is part of our duty.[57]

When Catherine Walsh described Mary Aikenhead as being 'full of charity and zeal for souls' she also identified the philanthropic and evangelical focus of the community's efforts.[58]

Aikenhead and Walsh took charge of the Trinitarian orphanage on North William Street on their return to Dublin. The sisters began teaching in the local poor school and visiting the sick in the neighbourhood. The North William Street community, under the leadership of Catherine Walsh, transferred to Summer Hill in 1828 and to Gardiner Street in 1830. Walsh spent her life among the poorest of the poor and became, in Sarah Atkinson's phrase, 'the *beau ideal* of a Sister of Charity'.[59] She gave living witness to her own observation that 'there is *plenty* of work in Ireland for those whose life and time is devoted to the service of the poor'.[60] In 1819, the Sisters of Charity assumed responsibility for the House of Refuge in Stanhope Street.

55 Atkinson, *Mary Aikenhead*; [Mary Padua O'Flanagan], *The life and work of Mary Aikenhead* (London, 1925). 56 Maria Luddy and Cliona Murphy, '"Cherchez la Femme:" the elusive woman in Irish history' in Maria Luddy and Cliona Murphy (eds), *Women surviving: studies in Irish women's history in the 19th and 20th centuries* (Dublin, 1990), p. 4. 57 Mary Aikenhead to the Commissioners of Inquiry, 30 Dec. 1833 quoted in Donnelly, *Some Dublin parishes*, i, p. 38. 58 Catherine Walsh to Xaviera Fitzgerald, 3 Oct. [1843?] (Bar Convent, York). 59 Atkinson, *Mary Aikenhead*, p. 392. 60 Walsh to Fitzgerald.

Mary Aikenhead had begun her apostolic work in this refuge when it was still in Ash Street during her first visit to Dublin. Three young women, who were working as assistants in the House of Refuge, entered the Sisters of Charity as lay sisters. Their decision illustrates how the appeal of religious life transcended class boundaries, but their status bears witness to the introduction of a two-tier, class-based system into the community.

From 1819, the Sisters of Charity also provided religious instruction in the Abbey Street parochial schools, where they started a Sunday school. They inagurated visitation to Jervis Street Infirmary, and Aikenhead and Walsh began visiting prisoners in Kilmainham Gaol in 1821, when they were asked to visit two young women who had been sentenced to death. They prepared these women for death and remained with them until the time for their execution. This was not Walsh's first experience of prison visitation. Atkinson recounts how she went 'from prison to prison' following the rebellion of 1798 'to carry messages from friends, or to console the inmates who were the source of her deepest sympathy'.[61]

Anna Maria O'Brien actively participated in the work of the community. She managed the Abbey Street schools, where the sisters gave religious instruction and accompanied them on visitation in Jervis Street Infirmary and in Kilmainham Gaol. O'Brien was also involved in Aikenhead's plans to establish a Catholic hospital in Dublin. The Sisters of Charity gained practical nursing experience during the cholera epidemics of 1832 and 1833. Grangegorman Penitentiary was converted into a temporary hospital in 1832 and sisters, under the indefatigable leadership of Catherine Walsh, nursed there at the request of the public authorities. The recently founded Sisters of Mercy nursed in another temporary hospital in Townsend Street on the south-side of the city.

There was another particularly virulent outbreak of cholera in the villages of Ringsend and Irishtown in 1833. Sisters of Charity from the Sandymount convent worked in these villages. The Sandymount convent had been established in 1831 with the assistance of Mrs Barbara Verschoyle. The sisters, with the assistance of Richard More O'Ferrall (1797-1880), then a member of parliament and later governor of Malta, solicited funds and opened a temporary twelve-bed hospital and a dispensary. O'Ferrall's sister, Sister Francis Teresa, who was a member of the Sandymount community, was a noted catechist, specialising in the instruction of adults. She worked with the sailors and fishermen of Irishtown, teaching them the catechism and preparing them for the sacraments.[62]

61 Atkinson, *Mary Aikenhead*, p. 136; Mrs Thomas [Helena] Concannon, *Women of 'Ninety-Eight* (Dublin, 1922), pp 260-3.   62 Atkinson, *Mary Aikenhead*, p. 221.

The planning of a major Catholic hospital, to be called St Vincent's, was accelerated after these experiences. In 1833 sisters, accompanied by Archbishop Murray and John and Anna Maria O'Brien, travelled to Paris to study nursing with the Hospitallers of St Thomas of Villanova. Following this, a prospectus, explaining the community's decision to establish a hospital, was published in 1834. Sisters, it explained, had been attending 'a class of sick person' for nineteen years

> who will not go to the common Hospitals; and they have constantly had the painful trial of witnessing their best exertions ... defeated by the unpropitious circumstances of their patients, the want of wholesome air, and of those comforts and accommodations which are strangers to the abodes of the poor.[63]

Funded by Sister Francis Teresa O'Ferrall, who provided £3,000 to purchase the earl of Meath's town-house on Stephen's Green, the hospital admitted its first patients in April 1835. The establishment of St Vincent's Hospital represents an important moment in the revival and modernisation of Irish Catholicism. Corish hails it as 'the beginning of a new era.'[64] It was also the first hospital in Dublin to be founded, owned and managed by women.

A crisis of leadership and purpose developed in the congregation as the final preparations for the establishment of St Vincent's Hospital were being made.[65] Aikenhead moved from Stanhope Street, where she had lived since 1819, to Sandymount in 1834. Her health was deteriorating and the burden of leadership was becoming greater. When William Ullathorne visited her in 1837 'she sat in bed, with a little low table over the bed on which she wrote and had her working materials.'[66] Aikenhead appointed Sister Ignatius Bodenham to replace herself as superior of the Stanhope Street community and as mistress of novices. Bodenham came to question both Aikenhead's authority and the congregation's exclusive commitment to the service of the poor. She secretly planned a foundation in England and proposed to take some of the more intellectually-gifted novices with her. There was a certain justification for Bodenham's questioning of Aikenhead's authority, although she seems to have been motivated more by ambition than by concern for correct procedures, since Aikenhead was remiss in not organising an election for the position of superior-general once the Holy See approved the

63 [Mary Aikenhead], *Prospectus of an institution to be established in Stephens-Green, Dublin, by the Sisters of Charity* (Dublin, 1834), p. 4. 64 Patrick Corish, *The Irish Catholic experience: a historical study* (Dublin, 1985), p. 171. 65 Morrissey, *As one sent*, pp 365-71. 66 William Bernard Ullathorne, *From cabin-boy to archbishop: the autobiography of Archbishop Ullathorne* (London, 1941), p. 102.

congregation's constitutions in 1833. There was no legal basis to her author-ity from May 1833 to July 1835, when the Holy See took special measures to confirm her in office.

Aikenhead, somewhat isolated in Sandymount and preoccupied with the plans for the new hospital, did not become aware of what was happening until 1835. She removed Bodenham from office and transferred her to Sandymount. Bodenham continued to plot against Aikenhead and won over some of the Sandymount community. The affair dragged on until Bodenham was expelled from the congregation in 1837. Thirteen novices and two pro-fessed sisters left with her. Francis Teresa O'Ferrall was one of the professed; Margaret Aylward (1810-89), who would become active in Catholic circles in Dublin from 1848, was one of the novices who left.[67]

The congregation survived the crisis and the loss of some supporters, including the influential O'Ferrall family. It survived and flourished, accord-ing to Aikenhead, because of its efforts at promoting 'the divine honour and the spiritual and corporal good of our Lord's poor members.'[68] Aikenhead founded ten convents in Ireland, of which six were located in Dublin. She also sent sisters to Paramatta, New South Wales in 1838, the first women religious to work in Australia.

There were no Catholic boarding schools for girls in Dublin in Murray's early years as a bishop. Wealthy Catholic families sent their daughters to the Ursulines in Cork and, to a lesser extent, to Thurles and Waterford, to the Bar Convent in York and to the Canonesses Regular of the Holy Sepulchre at New Hall, near Chelmsford, in England or to convents on the continent. Irish Benedictines maintained a school at Yprès which was mostly frequented by the daughters of the Catholic gentry.[69]

Eager to make good this deficit, Murray invited the Institute of the Blessed Virgin Mary at the Bar Convent to make a foundation in Dublin. The Institute had been founded by Mary Ward (1585-1645) in 1609 at Saint-Omer and the Bar Convent was established by some of her followers in 1686.[70] The sisters declined this invitation, whereupon Murray persuaded Teresa Ball to go to York and join the institute with a view to establishing a house in Dublin.[71] Murray had been Ball's spiritual guide for some years and knew of

67 Jacinta Prunty, 'Margaret Louisa Aylward' in M. Cullen and M. Luddy (eds), *Women, power and consciousness in nineteenth-century Ireland* (Dublin, 1995), pp 55-88; idem, *Margaret Aylward 1810-1889; Lady of Charity, sister of faith* (Dublin, 1999); Margaret Gibbons, *Life of Margaret Aylward* (London, 1928).   68 Mary Aikenhead to Mary de Chantal Coleman, 21 June 1837 in [Padua O'Flanagan] (ed.), *The letters of Mary Aikenhead* (Dublin, 1914), pp 78-80.   69 Patrick Nolan, *The Irish dames of Yprès* (Dublin, 1908). 70 Henriette Peters, *Mary Ward: a world in contemplation* (Leominster, 1994); [Hilda Haigh], James Henry Coleridge (ed.), *St Mary's Convent, Micklegate Bar, York, 1686-1887* (London, 1887).   71 Desmond Forristal, *The first Loreto sister: Mother Teresa Ball,*

her strong desire to enter a religious community. The community agreed to accept Ball, a former pupil of theirs, and to prepare her for a foundation in Dublin. The Bar Convent had strong Irish connections and there were six Irish members of the community when Teresa Ball joined in 1814. Mary Aikenhead and Catherine Walsh were still in the novitiate at this time.

Seven years after her entry to the Bar Convent, Teresa Ball, Ignatia Arthur (1792-1842) and Baptist Therry (1796-1827)[72] returned to Dublin to establish the Loreto Sisters, as the Institute of the Blessed Virgin Mary came to be known in Ireland. They lived with the Sisters of Charity in Stanhope Street and in rented accommodation in Harold's Cross while Rathfarnham House was being prepared as a convent and school. Archbishop Murray paid £2,300, on Teresa Ball's behalf, for the house and forty acres in 1821.

The sisters took possession of Rathfarnham House in 1822. The first person to enter the community there was a former pupil of the Bar Convent in York. Catherine Corballis (1800-35) entered the community shortly after it moved into its new home.[73] Gonzaga Corballis (1801-39), her sister and another former pupil of the Bar Convent, entered in 1825.[74] A third sister, Anna Maria, attempted to become a Cistercian at Stapehill in England and a Carmelite at North William Street, Dublin, before entering the Presentation Convent in Bagnalstown in 1850. As Mother Charles, she founded the Presentation community in Mountmellick in 1854. She inherited £1,000 and an annual income of £400 on her father's death in 1833 and she used this to fund the Mountmellick foundation. Their father, Richard, was one of Archbishop Murray's principal advisors and it was Murray who suggested that he send his daughters to school in York. He was one of Mother Teresa Ball's advisors and financial supporters and was a benefactor of the Harold's Cross orphanage from its foundation.[75] Teresa Ball was one of the great founding women of the nineteenth-century Irish Church. Following on the establishment of the abbey at Rathfarnham, she was responsible for nine suc-

---

1794-1861 (Dublin, 1994); [McDonald], *Joyful mother of children*; William Hutch, *Mrs Ball, a biography* (Dublin, 1879); Henry James Coleridge, *The life of Mother Frances Mary Teresa Ball* (Dublin, 1881).   **72** [Teresa Ball?], 'A sketch of the life of Anne Therry, eldest daughter of John Therry, Esq., county of Cork, late one of the Chief Commissioners of His Majesty's Excises', (Loreto Convent, Navan).   **73** Anon, *Memories of Loreto* (Dublin, 1927), pp 105-15.   **74** Ibid., pp 151-76; [Teresa Ball], 'The life of Mother Mary Euphrasia [Gibbons] of the Institute of the Blessed Virgin Mary and the life of Mother M. Gonzaga Corballis, religious of the Institute of the Blessed Virgin Mary, copied exactly, from the sketch, transcribed by our first Revd. Mother' (Loreto Abbey, Rathfarnham).   **75** Annals, Presentation Convent, Mountmellick (Presentation Convent, Mountmellick, County Laois); Danny Parkinson, 'The Corballis-Corbally families in County Dublin', *Dublin Historical Record*, 45 (1992), pp 91-100.

cessful foundations in Ireland and sent sisters to India (1841), Gibraltar (1845), Mauritius (1845), Canada (1847), England (1851) and Spain (1851).

IV

Catherine McAuley (1778-1841) did not intend founding a new religious community when she established the House of Mercy on Baggot Street in 1827.[76] McAuley had been engaged in 'works of piety and charity' for many years, first in Coolock village and then in St Mary's parish, Abbey Street, where she helped instruct girls in schools for the poor.[77] Her apostolic activity was paralleled by a life of intense piety. She was

> very regular in the performance of every duty of religion, fasted rigorously, and during Lent never touched wine. She rose early, prayed much and was most assiduous in her attendance at Sermons and the public offices of the Church.

McAuley decided to use a substantial inheritance to realise a dream 'of offering shelter to unprotected young women.'[78] She leased property in Baggot Street in 1824, where she commenced construction of the House of Mercy. She studied the teaching methods of the proselytising Kildare Street Society and went to France in 1825 to examine Catholic approaches to the education of the poor. The House of Mercy opened in 1827 and McAuley joined the embryonic community in 1828. The centre, she wrote to Father Francis L'Estrange, was designed for women who, because of existing obligations, could not enter religious communities. They were soon engaged in educating 'hundreds of poor female children and the instruction of young women who sleep in the house.'[79] Mother Clare Moore (1814-74) described how they 'visited and relieved' the sick poor in the neighbourhood and in Sir Patrick Dun's Hospital. McAuley, who spent much of her time in the poor schools, had, in Moore's estimation, 'an admirable method of conveying religious instruction.'[80]

---

76 [Mary Vincent Harnett], *The life of Rev. Mother Catherine M'Auley, foundress of the Order of Mercy*, ed. Richard Baptist O'Brien (Dublin, 1864); [Mary Austin Carroll], *Life of Catherine McAuley, foundress of the institute of Religious Sisters of Mercy* (New York, 1866); Roland Burke Savage, *Catherine McAuley, the first Sister of Mercy* (Dublin, 1949); Mary Bertrand Degnan, *Mercy unto thousands: life of Catherine McAuley* (Westminster, 1957); Mary C. Sullivan, *Catherine McAuley and the tradition of mercy* (Dublin, 1995). 77 [Mary Ann Doyle], 'Notes on the life of Mother Catherine McAuley by one of the first Sisters of Mercy' in Sullivan, *Catherine McAuley*, p. 45. 78 Ibid. 79 Catherine McAuley to Francis L'Estrange, 10 Sept. 1828 in M. Angela Bolster (ed.), *The correspondence of Catherine McAuley, 1827-1841* (Cork, 1989), p. 2. 80 [Mary Clare Moore], Excerpts from

In 1830 McAuley described the centre as 'a Pious House, after the manner of a Convent' and outlined the activities of the women who lived there:

> 1. They employ themselves in striving as much as they possibly can to give a Christian and truly Roman Catholic education to poor wretched girls who could not otherwise procure or obtain it. 2. They bring together and lodge poor servant girls who, owing to the prejudices of heretical employers or other misfortunes, find themselves deprived of employment; as well as others who, though they have some trade or profession, are unfortunately not able to find work and therefore stand in need of food and help. 3. They visit the Hospitals and there serve and assist the sick; performing for them the most necessary and useful services. All of which works of charity they exercise in the true spirit of religion and obedience.[81]

Eighteen thirty-four proved to be a difficult year for McAuley and her companions. Mother Vincent Harnett (1811-65), McAuley's first biographer, describes how 'the existence of the little community' and its work for the poor was threatened. There had been 'whispered' criticism for some time, but her critics became more outspoken in 1830.[82] Some of the opposition originated with Mary Aikenhead's supporters. These were fearful that the new community, which was already assuming some of the features of religious life, would undermine what Mary Aikenhead and her companions were attempting to achieve. They did not believe that Dublin was capable, either financially or demographically, of supporting two similar congregations of women. There is no evidence that Aikenhead was party to the sniping that resulted, but there are hints that some of the criticism found an echo among the Sisters of Charity. Writing to de Chantal Coleman early in 1833, Aikenhead mentioned recent professions in Baggot Street and warned against 'false zeal or false love' for one's own community.[83]

Opposition to McAuley also derived from the conviction that her behaviour was inappropriate for a woman. Mother Austin Carroll, the first Mercy historian, records how a priest, believing that McAuley's behaviour had somehow 'unsexed' her, wrote to her 'in the most contemptuous style, addressing the letter to "C. McAuley, Esq."'[84] Of greater consequence, Archbishop

'The Annals of the Convent of Our Lady of Mercy, Bermondsey' in Sullivan, *Catherine McAuley*, p. 104.   81 From the petition of Catherine McAuley requesting the approval of the Holy See for the House of Mercy in Bolster, *Correspondence*, p. 3.   82 Harnett, *Catherine M'Auley*, pp 53-54.   83 Aikenhead to de Chantal Coleman, 25 Jan. 1833 in O'Flanagan, *The letters of Mary Aikenhead*, p. 19.   84 [Austin Carroll], *The life of Catherine McAuley*, pp 154-155.

Murray was ill at ease with the idea of a secular religious-type community. His 'manner was cold' when, in view of the mounting opposition, she sought his advice. He objected to their adoption of the title 'Sisters of Mercy' and maintained that he had never expected to see 'a convent rising up of itself in such a manner.'[85] Following Michael Blake's intervention, the community was given a choice. They could either live as 'secular ladies or become religious.'[86] McAuley and her companions decided, against her earlier judgement, to transform the secular community of the House of Mercy into a religious congregation dedicated to the service of the poor. Harnett argued that the decision guaranteed the future of their undertakings. Religious life was 'the means of securing to them permanent successors for their holy mission.'[87]

McAuley and two of her companions made religious profession in 1831, on completing their novitiate with the Presentation Nuns in George's Hill. Ten others were received into the congregation on two occasions in 1832. These formed the nucleus of a congregation which grew rapidly in Ireland and throughout the English-speaking world. There are a number of reasons for this expansion but perhaps the most significant are McAuley's development of a model of religious life that enabled women to respond to a range of evangelical and social needs, the changing climate in the Church regarding the role and lifestyle of women religious and the presence in the new community of women of outstanding ability. Catherine McAuley's genius lay, not in her capacity to pioneer new responses to existing needs, but in her ability to devise a form of religious life that suited the needs of the Irish Church. The constitutions of the new congregation were an adaptation and development of the Presentation constitutions, which were, in turn, based on those of the Cork Ursulines.[88]

The autonomy of the local community and its close relationship with the diocese lay at the heart of the Ursuline and Presentation systems of government. Authority resided in the community which normally elected its own superiors and, subject to episcopal approval, made important decisions as a body. McAuley maintained this structure. She valued flexibility and adaptability. 'Every place has its own particular ideas and feelings which must be yielded to when possible'.[89] This was unusual in the nineteenth century where most con-

---

85 Harnett, *Catherine M'Auley*, p. 59.   86 Ibid., p. 60.   87 Ibid., p. 53.   88 *Constitutions of the Ursuline religious of the Congregation of Paris* (Dublin, 1812); *Rules and constitutions of the Religious Sisterhood of the Presentation of the ever-blessed Virgin Mary* (Cork, 1829), *Rules and constitutions of the religious Sisters of Mercy* (Birmingham, 1844); Mary C. Sullivan's edition of the manuscript version of McAuley's original constitutions, as revised by Daniel Murray, in Sullivan, *Catherine McAuley*, pp. 294, 328.   89 McAuley to Warde, 17 Nov. 1838 in Bolster, *Correspondence*, p. 74.

gregations opted for a highly centralised system of government.[90] Mary Aiken-head's Sisters of Charity and, in an incomplete way, Teresa Ball's Loreto Sisters were more typical of nineteenth-century developments in this respect. Where McAuley departed from the Ursuline and Presentation model was in her, initially reluctant, acceptance of simple vows and the freedom to minister outside the confines of the convent it offered. Mary Aikenhead had already, with equal reluctance, reached a similar conclusion. Women in simple vows were not considered as real religious until the beginning of the twentieth century.

The changing climate in the Church also facilitated the emergence of both the Sisters of Charity and the Sisters of Mercy. Nineteenth-century women religious, unlike their predecessors, 'could make space in a widening world to develop their own visions.'[91] This is evident from the Holy See's reactions to the requests of the Society of Charitable Instruction, the Sisters of Charity and the Sisters of Mercy for approval. Nano Nagle's Society of Charitable Instruction included the visitation of the sick poor among its activities. When it was granted approval in 1791, however, Pius VI restricted members of the society to the visitation of poor women in hospitals.[92] No such restriction was imposed on the Sisters of Charity or the Sisters of Mercy when Gregory XVI granted them approval in 1833 and 1835 respectively. Gregory XVI, whose tenure as prefect of the Congregation for the Propagation of the Faith from 1826 to 1831 gave him some understanding of conditions in Ireland, praised 'the great heroism' and 'the total disregard of every danger of death' of the Sisters of Charity during the cholera epidemic of 1832.[93] The *decretum laudis*, granted to the Sisters of Mercy in 1835, praised the congregation's commitment to 'helping the poor and relieving the sick in every way.'[94]

This need to receive ecclesiastical approval and the possibility of their decisions being unilaterally modified illustrates the extent to which women religious were 'subordinate to men and subject to male authority in decisions about their lives.'[95] There is no evidence to suggest that any of the women who are the subject of this study ever questioned that reality. They accepted the situation and proceeded to carve out powerful and meaningful roles within it.

Both because of her untimely death and the structure of government she put in place, Catherine McAuley never dominated the Sisters of Mercy in

90 Claude Langlois, *Le Catholisme au féminin: les congrégations françaises à superieure générale au XIXe siécle* (Paris, 1989); Mary Ewens, *The role of the nun in nineteenth-century America: variations on an international theme* (Salem, N.H., 1984).   **91** Jo Ann Kay McNamara, *Sisters in arms: Catholic nuns through two millennia* (Cambridge, Mass, 1996), p. 606.   **92** Walsh, *Nano Nagle*, p. 136.   **93** Confirmation Brief, in O'Flanagan, *Mary Aikenhead*, 137.   **94** *Decretum Laudis*, Rome, 24 March 1835 in Bolster, *Correspondence*, p. 17.   **95** Cullen and Luddy (eds), *Women, power and consciousness*, p. 15.

the way that Mary Aikenhead did the Sisters of Charity. The superior of each new Mercy foundation could, with the support of her community, become a founder herself. Fanny Taylor compared each new foundation to 'a swarm of bees' leaving the parent house to 'find honey for themselves.'[96] This structure, which facilitated speedy decision-making in response to urgent need, also required women of considerable calibre to lead new communities and in Clare Moore, Frances Warde, Elizabeth Moore, Ursula Freyne and Vincent Harnett, the Sisters of Mercy possessed some of the ablest and most skilled. Each played a significant role in the expansion and development of the congregation.

Clare Moore was one of McAuley's first companions. She entered the community in 1828 when it was still in its secular phase.[97] McAuley sent her to Cork as superior in 1837, and she went from there to London in 1839 to become superior of the first English foundation at Bermondsey. She was responsible for nine other foundations in England over the next thirty-five years. She became friendly with Florence Nightingale while nursing during the Crimean War. Nightingale came to admire both her 'worldly talent of administration' and her 'spiritual qualifications.'[98] Frances Warde (1810-84) also entered the community in 1828.[99] McAuley sent her to Carlow as superior in 1837, when she was only twenty-seven. Warde quickly exhibited her leadership qualities by establishing three communities in Ireland before departing for Pittsburgh in 1843. In the United States she founded a network of convents in Pennsylvania, Illinois, Rhode Island, Connecticut, New York, New Hampshire, Maine, Vermont, New Jersey, Nebraska and California. Elizabeth Moore (1806-68), entered the Sisters of Mercy in 1832, having already spent some time with the Sisters of Charity.[100] She was the first superior of St Mary's, Limerick, in 1838. Moore made twelve foundations, including two in Scotland, between 1844 and 1862. Vincent Harnett, who entered the community in Baggot Street in 1837 and was professed in Limerick in 1838, was Moore's assistant for twelve years.[101] She was a noted educator and was one of the earliest Mercy writers. She published a bible catechism in 1852[102] and the first biography of McAuley. Harnett left Limerick in 1853 to establish a Mercy community in Roscommon.

96 Fanny Taylor, *Irish homes and Irish hearts* (London, 1867), p. 43.   97 Sullivan, *Catherine McAuley*, pp 77-84; see also Evelyn Bolster, *The Sisters of Mercy in the Crimean War* (Cork, 1964).   98 Ibid., p. 78.   99 Kathleen Healy, *Frances Warde: foundress of the American Sisters of Mercy* (New York, 1973).   100 [Mary Austen Carroll], *Leaves from the annals of the Sisters of Mercy*, i (New York, 1881), pp 274-324.   101 [de Chantal Meagher], Memoir of Mother Mary Vincent Harnett (St Mary's Convent of Mercy, Limerick); de Chantal Meagher (1816-1898) was a founding member of the Roscommon community in 1853 and the first superior in Athlone in 1857.   102 [Vincent

Ursula Freyne (1816-85), who entered the community in 1834, never served as a superior in McAuley's lifetime.[103] She spent some time in Carlow and Booterstown, County Dublin, before returning to Baggot Street in time to nurse McAuley during her final illness. Freyne went to Newfoundland in 1842, returned to Dublin in 1843 and departed for Perth in Western Australia in 1845. She remained in Perth, in difficult and oppressive circumstances, until 1857 when she left to establish a community in Melbourne, where she died in 1885.

Largely as a result of the drive and selflessness of such women, the Sisters of Mercy gradually replaced the Presentation Order in the popular imagination. People came to admire their dedication in visiting the poor with the result that the phrase 'Walking nun' came to be used affectionately rather than in the pejorative sense it had been applied to Nano Nagle's companions, the first women religious to visit the sick. A contemporary commentator described how

> [The Sisters of Mercy] are bound each day to visit the sick and poor in their own houses, and give them such charitable relief as they may stand in need of for their bodily wants; and what is yet more precious, and yet more rarely administered, the kind sympathy and merciful consolation which the poor sufferer, as he tosses to and fro in the agony of his pain, is so seldom fortunate enough to find.[104]

The sisters themselves were no less committed to the education and training of women. McAuley believed that nothing was 'more productive of good to society, or more conducive to the happiness of the poor than the careful instruction of women.' She was convinced that women possessed great influence and that 'where ever a religious woman presides, peace and good order are generally to be found.'[105] The sisters went to great lengths to find suitable employment for the women in their care and 'to place them in situations for which they are adapted.' They were instructed 'in the principal mysteries of Religion, and required to comply with their religious obligations.'[106] Everything the Sisters of Mercy did was shaped by their own religious faith and evangelical purpose. 'The Sisters shall always have spiritual good most in view.'[107]

Harnett], *A catechism of bible history* (London, 1852).   **103** Geraldine Byrne, *Valiant women: letters from the foundation Sisters of Mercy in Western Australia, 1845-1849* (Melbourne, 1981).   **104** Anonymous review of *La regula e le costitituzioni della religiose nominate Sorelle della Misericordia* in *Dublin Review*, March 1847, p. 19.   **105** [Catherine McAuley], Rule and constitutions of the Religious Sisters of Mercy, Sullivan, *McAuley*, p. 296.   **106** Ibid., p. 299.   **107** Ibid., p. 298.

A similar concern for the spiritual and material wellbeing of the poor gave rise to other women's initiatives. Frances Clarke (1803-87) and some friends began visiting the sick poor about 1831 and nursed the sick in their homes during the cholera epidemic of 1832. They acquired property in North Ann Street, established a community there and opened a day school for the daughters of middle-class Catholic families. A year later, the women emigrated to the United States, where they settled first in Philadelphia and then moved to Dubuque in Iowa. This community developed as the Sisters of Charity of the Blessed Virgin Mary.[108] The last major women's initiative to take place during Archbishop Murray's episcopate was the introduction into Ireland of the Ladies Association of Charity of St Vincent de Paul for the Spiritual and Temporal Relief of the Sick Poor. The first Irish branch of the association, which was founded by St Vincent de Paul in France in 1617, was established in Kingstown by Margaret Kelly in 1843. Margaret Aylward, who had been working with Kelly since 1848, founded a metropolitan branch in 1851. Parrallel with this, the Association for the Propagation of the Faith was established in Dublin in 1838.[109] The first Dublin branch of the Children of Mary was established at Loreto Abbey, Rathfarnham, in 1849.[110]

By the time Archbishop Murray died in 1852, there were twenty-eight women's communities in the archdiocese. Every one of them was engaged in the provision of services to the Catholic community, especially to the poorer members of that community. James Godkin, writing fifteen years after Murray's death, described a city full of

> magnificent hospitals ... numerous orphanages, several widow's houses, and other refuges for virtuous women; ragged and industrial schools, night asylums, penitentiaries, reformatories, institutions for the blind and deaf and dumb; institutions for relieving the poor in their own houses, and Christian doctrine fraternities almost innumerable.[111]

He marvelled that 'the daughters of some of the most respectable and best connected Roman Catholic families leave their happy homes and take the veil' and devote themselves and their often 'ample fortunes' to the education and relief of the poor.[112] William Meagher made a similar observation at Murray's funeral when he reminded the congregation of the 'high rank and

108 In the early days: pages from the Annals of the Sisters of Charity of the Blessed Virgin Mary, 1833-1887 (St Louis, 1925). 109 Edmund M. Hogan, The Irish missionary movement (Dublin, 1990), pp 62-8. 110 Katherine Tynan, A nun, her friends and her order (London, 1901), pp 171-2 for an account of a meeting of an adult branch of the Children of Mary. 111 James Godkin, Ireland and its churches (London, 1867), pp 94-5. 112 Ibid., p. 95.

ample fortunes' of some of the women who entered convents under Murray's spiritual direction.[113]

V

Archbishop Murray's death marked the end of an era in the history of the Catholic Church in Dublin. Mary Aikenhead, Teresa Ball and Anna Maria O'Brien survived him, but women were not generally involved thereafter in the life of the Church in as public, proactive and innovative a way as they had been during his time as a priest and bishop. The exception was Margaret Aylward. Otherwise, women were progressively disempowered and marginalised as the Church became more structured and better organised. Joan Thirsk's observation 'that whenever new openings have appeared ... women have usually been prominent alongside the men, sometimes even outnumbering them' is true of the history of the Catholic Church in Dublin in the late eighteenth and early nineteenth centuries. Her continued observation about how this changes once 'the venture has been satisfactorily and firmly established' is equally valid. Both the 'direction' and the 'style' passed into the hands of men once the venture became 'institutionalised, formalised, and organised.'[114] Women were disempowered and their contribution marginalised in the very Church that they had helped reform and modernise.

113 William Meagher, *Notices of the life and character of His Grace Most Rev. Daniel Murray, late archbishop of Dublin* (Dublin, 1853), p. 38.   114 Joan Thirsk, 'The History Woman' in Mary O'Dowd and Sabine Wichert (eds), *Chattel, servant or citizen: women's status in Church, state and society* (Belfast, 1995), pp 1-2.

13

The pastoral politics of Paul Cullen

Ciaran O'Carroll

The successor to Daniel Murray was the remarkable Paul Cullen, the most influential and powerful Irish ecclesiastical figure of the nineteenth century.[1] Following two years as archbishop of Armagh, Cullen was the popular choice of the suffragans and priests of Dublin when he took up office as archbishop, primate and apostolic delegate on the feast of SS Peter and Paul, 29 June 1852.

Paul Cullen was born into a farming family of nationalist political aspirations in Ballitore, County Kildare in 1803.[2] He attended the local Quaker school before entering Carlow College at the age of fourteen. One of the main influences on the students at the time was Father James Doyle OSA. Later to become a noted nationalist bishop of Kildare and Leighlin, Doyle had witnessed the excesses of the 1798 rising and was firmly opposed to revolution. He strongly supported constitutional reform as advocated by Daniel O'Connell.

In November 1820, Cullen commenced his studies in Propaganda Fide College, Rome with a scholarship from the recently consecrated Bishop Doyle.[3] A placement in Maynooth for their son was unacceptable to the strongly nationalist Cullens because all Maynooth students were required to take an oath of allegiance to the sovereign. Cullen's academic achievements in Rome were impressive. While still in minor orders, the excellence of his theological disputation attracted the notice of Pope Leo XII and other senior

---

1 See D. Bowen, *Paul Cardinal Cullen and the shaping of modern Irish Catholicism* (Dublin 1983). 2 In Cullen's academic records the date given is 27 April 1803. See Archives of Propaganda Fide (henceforth APF), Scritture riferite nei Congressi (henceforth SC), *Collegio Urbano*, vol. 15, f. 56 (v); P. MacSuibhne, *Paul Cullen and his contemporaries* (5 vols, Naas, 1961) and Bowen, op. cit. p. 2 both give the date as 29 Apr. 1803. However Cullen himself was later to maintain that he was born sometime in 1804. See Cullen to Kirby, 29 Dec. 1876 (Irish College Archives Rome (henceforth ICAR), NC, III, 3, 5, no. 64). 3 APF, *SC, Collegio Urbano*, vol. 13, f. 280 (285); Bowen, op. cit., p. 5, maintains that Cullen came to Rome in 1821.

Church figures, with the result that he was appointed a professor in Propaganda Fide immediately following his ordination in 1829.[4] Two years later he became rector of the Irish College in the city, a position he held until he was consecrated archbishop of Armagh nineteen years later. As rector of the Irish College and with his connections at Propaganda he was seen as a man of status and influence, and was occasionally consulted by the pope on matters relating to the Irish Church. This gave him a unique insight into the machinations of the Irish Church and in particular the disputes among the bishops.

Cullen's status as an outstanding Church figure in Rome was widely acknowledged, and predictably in 1830 his name was proposed as a candidate for the position of coadjutor bishop for Philadelphia.[5] Subsequently he was proposed on two occasions for a posting in New York and a new diocese in Pittsburgh.[6] In August 1834 he was actually nominated as titular bishop of Orien and coadjutor bishop of Charleston. Cullen declined the nomination and his refusal was accepted.[7] In a remarkable recognition of his merits he was given charge of the College of Propaganda when it was under serious threat from the insurgents in Rome in 1848. At this time the pope and the curia had fled Rome and sought refuge in Gaeta.

As rector of the Irish College, Cullen's dedicated guidance of the students under his direction further substantiated his credentials for appointment to high office. During his time as rector in Rome his advice was respected and his help sought by many members of the Irish hierarchy as well as various Vatican congregations. Most Irish bishops, with few exceptions, invited him to act as their agent in Rome. Arising out of this Cullen became increasingly aware that bitter divisions existed in the Irish Church and that its leadership was deficient in a number of ways. This was accentuated by the fact that by the mid-nineteenth century the long regime of discrimination against Catholics in Ireland had given way to a climate of grudging tolerance. When,

---

4 APF, *SC, Collegio Urbano*, vol. 15, ff 56v, 101-22   5 Kenrick to Prop., 5 May, 11 June, 27 July 1830 (APF, *SC, America Centrale*, vol. 10, ff 369v, 388v); Prop. to Kenrick, 27 July 1830 (APF, *LDB*, vol. 311, ff 644-5).   6 England to Cullen, 13-15 May 1834 (ICAR, *American Papers, 1828-49*, no. 22); Kenrick to Prop., 6 Feb., 12 Sept. 1837 (APF, *SC, America Centrale*, vol. 12, ff 30, 189).   7 England to Cullen 1/2 Aug. 1834 (ICAR *American Papers, 1828-49*, no. 28); O'Connor to Cullen, 2 Aug. 1834 (ICAR, *O'Connor Papers, 1834-47*, no. 4); Memo. n.d. [Aug 1834] (APF, Congressi, *America-Antille*, vol. 5, ff. 836-1); Sec. of Cong. of Extraordinary Ecc. Affairs to Prop., 22 Aug. 1834 (APF, SC, *America-Antille*, vol. 5, f. 834); Prop. Fide to Sec. of Briefs, 22 Aug. 1834 (APF, *LDB*, vol 315, f. 469); O'Connor to Cullen, 2 Sept. 1834 (ICAR, *O'Connor Papers, 1834-47*, no. 5); Cullen to O'Connor [Aug. 1834] (APF, *SC, Irlanda*, vol 25, ff 808-9); Cullen to Mai, 4 Sept. 1834 (APF, *SC, Irlanda*, vol. 25, ff 820-1); Cullen to Prop., 4 Sept. 1834 (APF, *SC, Irlanda*, vol. 25, f. 822).

in 1849, he was appointed archbishop of Armagh he immediately set about reforming the infrastructure of the Irish Church, unifying the hierarchy and reinforcing the authority of Rome. The office of apostolic delegate, conferred on Cullen in February 1850, gave him the authority and the responsibility to undertake, in consultation with the Irish bishops, a thorough examination of the Church in Ireland. To this end Cullen, with his authority as arch-bishop – and from February 1850 apostolic delegate – summoned a synod of the Irish hierarchy to meet in Thurles, County Tipperary, in August 1850.

The synod of Thurles opened on 22 August 1850. Cullen had chosen the venue, pointedly by-passing Maynooth, which was financially supported by the Westminster government. For Cullen the synod proved to be a traumatic experience, the first in a series of events that were to leave him at times phys-ically exhausted and emotionally drained. The provisions of the synod dealt with a wide range of both organisational and doctrinal issues. Many of the conclusions of Thurles – which were duly adopted in Rome as statutes in 1851 – related to organisational matters and were designed to bring Irish Church practice into line with Rome and to compensate for arrears accu-mulated since the penal times. These included rules for the celebration of Mass and the sacraments and the maintenance of registers and archives. Measures to counter proselyting were recommended: missions were to be advocated and sodalities established. The circulation of approved books was proposed and proselytising tracts prohibited; the spread of freemasonry was to be watched. Elements which later proved contentious included the con-demnation of secret societies, the ban on political denunciations by priests from the altar, restrictions on denominationally mixed marriages and a rec-ommendation to abolish station Masses in private houses.

Education also proved a divisive issue. In relation to national schools, individual bishops had taken independent decisions as to whether to support them or not. Although Archbishop MacHale of Tuam, amongst others, had rejected the National School system outright and attempted to provide an inferior service through religious orders, other members of the hierarchy con-tinued to support the National School system. Cullen supported state fund-ing and proposed implementing reforms through the Board of Education in order to adapt the existing system to meet the requirements of Catholic chil-dren. This proved to be a slow process and became a source of conflict within the hierarchy; Archbishop MacHale of Tuam remained trenchant in his oppo-sition to Cullen's stance on the National School issue.

In relation to secondary education Cullen promoted the introduction of religious orders into the country. In addition he fostered Irish foundations such as the Christian Brothers to provide second level education for Catholic children. In an address accompanying the formal conclusions of the synod, Cullen outlined his commitment to the preservation and reinforcement of the Catholic faith in Ireland. He emphasised the responsibility of parents with respect to the education of their children and he highlighted the dangers of 'evil literature' and proselytism. Particular emphasis was placed on the negative influence of the new Irish universities established by the British government, popularly referred to as the 'Queen's Colleges'. These had been condemned in Rome as 'godless' and Cullen was determined to provide an alternative Catholic university education. A minority of the bishops, led by Archbishop Murray of Dublin, pointed out that the Queen's Colleges provided the only third-level education for Catholics apart from Trinity College, which was avowedly Protestant. To Cullen's dismay his proposal for condemnation of the Queen's Colleges was barely carried despite the papal rescripts that were invoked in the discussion. Cullen's ambition to found an Irish Catholic university in Dublin reflected his commitment to denominational third-level education. This proved to be a contentious, expensive and controversial project ultimately doomed to failure. It was also a project to which Cullen personally dedicated enormous time, effort and energy.

At Thurles the clergy were urged to pay particular attention to those living in poverty who had been subjected to both temporal and spiritual persecution. The poor, however, were advised to bear their afflictions with patience and to avoid secret societies as a means for redress. In a veiled reference to the Westminster parliament, oppressors were reminded of the obligation to remove injustices.

Both in the statutes passed at Thurles and in his concluding address to the synod, Cullen attested to his ambition to preserve and strengthen the Catholic faith throughout his episcopacy. However some of his episcopal colleagues resisted what they viewed as Roman 'interference' in the affairs of the Irish Church. Daniel Murray, who was amongst the minority who dissented at Thurles, expressed serious reservations in relation to some of the decrees even after Rome approved them.[8] Murray's stance contrasted starkly with that of Cullen, whose unquestioning acceptance of papal authority was the guiding star of his episcopacy; in time, it was to see him play a major part in the drafting of the text of infallibility at the Vatican Council of 1870.

During his two years as archbishop, Cullen found conditions in Armagh most unsatisfactory. He was shocked to find that, because of a legal complication, the house occupied by his predecessor was not available to him and he had to live in Dundalk. Under his predecessor, administration had been neglected; there were no archives; there was not a single convent in the town;

8 See John Ahern, 'The plenary synod of Thurles', *Irish Ecclesiastical Record*, 75 (May 1951), pp 385-403; D.C. Barry, 'The legislation of the synod of Thurles, 1850', *Irish Theological Quarterly*, 26 (1959), pp 131-66; *Acta Sacrae Congregationis* (A), vol. 213 (1851), ff 147-238.

the cathedral was in an unfinished state and Cullen found the approach to the liturgy unacceptably informal. More pressing issues were the differences he found among members of the clergy. In addition, divisions among the Irish bishops remained rife. With the deaths of members of the hierarchy opposed to his policies, most significantly in February 1852 of Murray himself, Cullen's influence over the Irish Church and his power within the hierarchy increased appreciably. The inevitable appointment by Rome of episcopal candidates recommended by Cullen reinforced his influence within the Irish hierarchy. Such appointments also indicated the continuing high esteem with which Cullen was held by the Holy See. In addition to playing a pivotal role in relation to episcopal appointments to vacant sees, Cullen established a policy of appointing coadjutor bishops with the right of succession where incumbents were elderly or infirm. In this way he gradually gained further support for his mission to establish a more united Irish Church, obedient to Rome. By 1860 some twenty new bishops had been appointed, all approved by Cullen. His recommendations also resulted in the appointment of Irish bishops abroad, especially in the United States of America and Australia.

In 1852 Cullen was appointed to succeed Murray as archbishop of Dublin. During his two years in Armagh (1850-2) and subsequent twenty-six years in Dublin (1852-78), Cullen sought to ensure compliance with the edicts of Thurles. To this end he presided at numerous meetings of the hierarchy at provincial and national level. Before leaving Armagh, Cullen reported progress to Rome on the observance of the statutes of the synod of Thurles, despite continuing episcopal disunity. It was a measure of his standing that, by way of response, the pope wrote personally on 25 March 1852 to all the Irish bishops urging unity especially in regard to the third-level education issue.[9]

Cullen's prolific output of pastoral letters was indicative of his commitment. Despite the extent of his responsibilities as apostolic delegate, Cullen did not neglect his local diocesan duties as archbishop in both Dublin and Armagh. He participated with enthusiasm in a full diocesan programme of parish visitations and personally examined candidates for Confirmation prior to its administration. In addition to his regular pastoral duties, he also made himself available for charity sermons, visits to hospitals, schools, convents, orphanages and other institutions. Callers to his house at Eccles Street, Dublin, were seen personally if at all possible. His lifestyle was essentially frugal and he allowed himself little time for leisure.

Cullen's programme of visitation heightened his awareness of the plight of the poor. From the very outset of his episcopacy he had demonstrated a keen appreciation of the distress of so many because of poverty. In his very

9 Pius IX to the Irish Bishops, 25 March 1852 (APF, *SC, Irlanda*, vol. 31, ff 132-9).

first pastoral letter, penned in Rome on the day of his episcopal ordination, he wrote to the people of his archdiocese: 'I know that your sufferings are exceedingly great and I cannot but weep for your privations and afflictions'.[10] This theme permeates his pastorals and personal correspondence. Letters written in his early years in Dublin refer with emotion to poor harvests, famine, persecution, poverty, oppression, distress, misery and disease as well as to the high level of emigration.[11] To this poverty and distress Cullen attributed the extremely unsettled state of the country. In the face of such deprivation, Cullen regarded the response of the authorities as utterly inadequate, bordering on irresponsible. He was frustrated by the fact that the condition of the Irish people fell well short of that in other regions of the United Kingdom, despite the promises of material improvement given by the proponents of the Act of Union half a century earlier. Cullen argued that by their continuing failure in this respect, Westminster provoked resentment which led inevitably to unrest and violence. He repeatedly expressed his frustration that successive Westminster governments failed to see the consequences of their ineptitude.[12]

In an attempt to alleviate the plight of poor Catholics, Cullen embarked on a policy of social, educational and medical relief. His submissions to various government commissions were numerous. In the absence of adequate government assistance, after a series of disastrous harvests in early 1860s, Cullen joined with the lord mayor of Dublin in forming the Mansion House Relief Committee in 1862.[13] His dedication to the poor is acknowledged in the engraving on his monument in the Pro-Cathedral. He realised that the suffering of the people facilitated their easy recruitment into secret societies. In a succession of pastorals throughout his episcopacy he actively discouraged people from joining such societies.[14] Rather than inciting revolution, Cullen urged the poor to suffer their privations pending the arrival of relief. His advice was that pressure to remedy their plight must be directed exclusively through parliamentary channels, though his exhortations in this respect lacked credibility because of the inactivity of elected parliamentary representatives.

As a prelate, Cullen repeatedly expressed concern that proselytisers were taking advantage of the Catholic poor, and adopted a combative stance against

10 See P.F. Moran (ed.), *The pastoral letters and other writings of Cardinal Cullen* (3 vols, Dublin, 1882), i, 13.   11 See for example Cullen to Prop., 7 June 1850 (APF, *SC, Irlanda,* vol. 30, f. 430); Cullen to Kirby, 18 Nov 1853 (ICAR, *NC III,* 1, 3, no. 109); Cullen to Smith, 7 Oct. 1851 (Benedictine Archives, Rome (henceforth BAR), *Smith Papers*).   12 See for example Cullen to Kirby, 5 Feb 1863 (ICAR, New Collection (henceforth *NC*), *III,* 3, 1, no. 73); Cullen to Prop., 13 Mar 1863 (APF, *SC, Irlanda,* vol. 34, f. 909v), Cullen to Prop., 12 Jan 1866 (APF, *SC, Irlanda,* vol. 35, f. 629).   13 See E. Larkin, *The consolidation of the Roman Catholic Church in Ireland, 1860–1870* (Dublin, 1987), p. 83.   14 For examples see Moran, op. cit., i, 576, 839, 869; ii, 143; iii, 89, 260-9.

the agents of proselytism. For thirty years before Cullen came to Dublin there had been an active campaign to convert the Irish people to Protestantism, directed by the evangelical movement in the Anglican Church and financed from England. The poverty of the Famine years added a critical dimension to the campaign, which attracted distressed Catholics to Protestantism. In an effort to counter their influence, he supported the foundation of institutions to cater for the medical, social and educational requirements of Catholics. Cullen dedicated much time and energy to the building of institutions throughout the diocese which cared for the spiritual, educational and medical welfare of the people. He oversaw the building of numerous hospitals administered by a variety of religious orders. These included the Mater Hospital in 1852 run by the Sisters of Mercy; St Joseph's Children's Hospital in 1872 run by the Irish Sisters of Charity; St Vincent's Hospital, Fairview in 1875 run by the Daughters of Charity; St Michael's Hospital, Dun Laoghaire in 1876 run by the Sisters of Mercy and St John of God Hospital, Stillorgan in 1877 run by the Brothers of Saint John of God. Secondary schools providing for the educational needs of Catholics under the auspices of various religious congregations opened during the time of Cullen's reign as archbishop, included Blackrock College (CSSp) in 1860, Terenure College (OCarm) 1860; St Joseph's College (CM) in 1873 and St Patrick's College (CM), Drumcondra in 1875.

No fewer than thirty-nine religious foundations were opened during Cullen's time in Dublin. These included St Michael's Convent of Mercy, Athy in 1852; the Sisters of Our Lady of Refuge, High Park and the Sacred Heart convent in Mount Anville in 1853; the Dominican St Mary's of the Rosary, Tallaght in 1855; and the Sisters of the Holy Faith, Eccles Street in 1856. Also in 1856, the Passionist Fathers established Mount Argus, the Oblates of Mary Immaculate opened in Inchicore and the Daughters of the Heart of Mary opened St Joseph's in Dun Laoghaire. The Daughters of Charity opened St Vincent's, North William Street, in 1857, the same year as the Loreto Convent in Balbriggan was built and the Presentation Sisters established themselves in Kinclondal. The Society of Jesus opened Milltown Park the following year, the same year as the Carmelite Sisters established the Convent of the Incarnation and the Irish Sisters of Charity, St Mary's, Merrion. The contemplative Redemptorist Sisters established Mount St Alphonsus in 1859 and, in 1861, as the Bon Secours Sisters established Mount Street, the Sisters of Mercy established St Joseph's, Cork Street and the Daughters of the Heart of Mary St Joseph's Orphanage, Dun Laoghaire. Belmount House was established by the Oblates of Mary Immaculate in 1863 and the following year the Sisters of Mercy established St Vincent's Goldenbrige, Inchicore, the Irish Sisters of Charity Linden Home, Blackrock, and the Sisters of St Joseph of Cluny, Mount Sackville, Chapelizod. The

Sisters of the Holy Faith came to Glasnevin in 1865, the Presentation Sisters to St. Joseph's in Terenure, the Irish Sisters of Charity to St Joseph's in Mountjoy Square and the Sisters of Mercy to Rathdrum, all in 1866. The Catholic University School, Lower Leeson Street, was established by the Marist Fathers in 1867, as was St Joseph's by the Presentation Sisters in Lucan. The Convent of the Visitation was founded by the Irish Sisters of Charity in Baldoyle, in 1869 and St Mary's Dominican convent in Wicklow the following year. The Augustinian Fathers came to Templeogue in 1872 and the Sisters of the Holy Faith to Skerries in 1875. The Holy Faith Convent in Clarendon Street was established in 1876, as was the Sisters of Mercy Convent in Arklow. The Carmelite Sisters' Immaculate Conception Convent of the Nativity, Sandymount and Our Lady of Refuge and Magdalen Asylum were opened in 1877, and the following year the Sisters of the Cross and Passion established St Sebastian's, Kilcullen, and the Sisters of the Holy Faith a foundation in Celbridge.

The years of Cullen's episcopacy also witnessed the construction of many churches throughout the archdioceses of both Armagh and Dublin. Some of the building projects in Dublin included the construction of Mary Immaculate, Refuge of Sinners, Rathmines (1855); Catholic University Church, St Stephen's Green (1856); Church of the Assumption, Ballyboughal (1858); St Patrick's, Celbridge (1859); St Saviour's, Dublin (OP) (1861); SS Mary and Peter, Arklow (1861); Our Lady of Mercy, Blessington (1861); Chapel of the Mater Hospital (1861); SS Patrick, Brigid and Colmcille, Rathgar (1862); Immaculate Heart of Mary, City Quay (1863); St Assan's, Raheny (1864); St Peter's (CM), Phibsboro (1872); St Kevin's, Dublin (1872); St Laurence O' Toole's, Roundwood, Co Wicklow (1872), St Joseph's, Ballymedan (1876); Holy Cross Church, Clonliffe (1876); The Annunciation, Rathfarnham (1877); Mary Immaculate, Inchicore (1877); St Paul of the Cross (1878) and St Mary of the Angel's, Church Street (1882). Cullen also oversaw the building of the Dublin diocesan seminary, Holy Cross College, whose foundation stone he blessed in October 1860. This was a project to which he devoted considerable attention and where his remains now lie.[15]

In addition to the building of an educational and ecclesiastical infrastructure, Cullen was also responsible for the introduction of new devotional practices to Ireland.[16] During his time in Rome he had been captivated by the diversity of liturgical celebrations he experienced. These included the Forty Hours of Eucharistic Adoration which he inaugurated on 24 September 1852. Within months of Cullen's arrival in the capital, this devotion was established

15 See for details *Irish Catholic Directory* (henceforth *ICD*) 1853-1879.   16 See E. Larkin, 'The devotional revolution in Ireland, 1850-75', *American Historical Review*, 77 (1972), pp 626-52

in all the city churches. The devotions proved to be very popular with the people. Sodalities, often segregated on grounds of gender, were widely established in parishes throughout the diocese. As well as introducing and promoting new devotions, Cullen also encouraged his priests to don a Roman mode of clerical dress and to decorate their churches in the Roman style by installing statutes in the fashion of contemporaneous Roman basilicas.

On the political front, at the time of Cullen's return to Ireland a leadership vacuum had opened up in the country. Following the death of Daniel O'Connell, no successor of equal calibre had emerged. In the absence of a strong political leader, Cullen involved himself in the realm of public affairs bordering on politics. A feature of O'Connell's high profile campaigns for Catholic emancipation and Repeal of the Union was the strong support forthcoming from the Catholic people, led by their clergy. Both the British government and the Roman ecclesiastical authorities were uneasy about the active public involvement of priests in Irish political affairs. Cullen perceived that political issues were divisive for both clergy and people. He encouraged the people to proceed by way of parliamentary democracy as opposed to violent revolution.

This issue, addressed by him as early as the synod of Thurles, was to remain a source of serious concern throughout his episcopacy. The task confronting the new archbishop was formidable. The difficulty lay in attaining improved living conditions for the people without political agitation on the part of the clergy. The people were distressed and impoverished after the Famine.[17] Morale was low amongst young people who emigrated in tens of thousands. In response to the prevailing feeling of agrarian discontent and the rising tide of eviction, local tenant protection societies were formed to agitate for the protection of tenants.[18] Clerical participation was prominent. At a meeting in Dublin on 6 August 1850 these societies came together to form the Tenant League, with the objective of campaigning through parliament for fixity of tenure, lower rents and for the protection of tenants facing eviction.[19] Cullen supported the objectives of the League, but was concerned by the aggressive stance of activists within it, amongst whom were some clergy. Consequently Cullen's support for the League was guarded.[20] His support was more wholehearted for the Catholic Defence Association, founded in August 1851 following the re-establishment of the Catholic hierarchy in

17 See S.G. Osborne, *Gleanings in the West of Ireland* (London, 1850).   18 See, for example B. Kennedy (ed.), 'Sharman Crawford on Ulster tenant right, 1846', *Irish Historical Studies*, 8 (1963), pp 246-53; E. Lucas, *Life of Frederick Lucas* (2 vols, London, 1886), ii, 217-18.   19 J.H. Whyte, *The Independent Irish Party 1850-9* (Oxford, 1958), p. 6; *Freeman's Journal* (henceforth *FJ*), 7, 8, 9, 10 Aug. 1850.   20 Cullen to Girdwood, 24 Jan 1851 (*Tablet*, 1 Feb. 1851); Cullen to Keappock, 11 July 1851 (*Tablet*, 19 July 1851).

England and the implementation of the Ecclesiastical Titles Act.[21] The role of the Catholic Defence Association was pivotal in the evolution of a new political organisation known as the Independent Irish Party, nicknamed the 'Pope's Brass Band'. This party was also supported by the Tenant League and a number of Irish members of parliament. The Independent Irish Party represented the interests of the Catholic Defence Association and the Tenant League, demanding both religious freedom and improved conditions for tenant farmers. They pledged themselves to a policy known as 'independent opposition', promising to support government administration only if their demands were satisfied.[22]

In the 1852 general election, some forty-eight Irish members out of a total of one hundred and five pledged themselves to remain independent of government unless substantive legislative reforms were guaranteed. However, the opportunity to become a significant political force was lost when two party members, Sadleir and Keogh, defected to join the newly-formed government without seeking a guarantee of tenant or religious reform in Ireland. These defections undermined the party and led to further withdrawals. They led to general public disillusionment amongst those who had looked forward to a new parliamentary strategy. Cullen's refusal to condemn Sadleir and Keogh publicly heightened disillusionment amongst both people and clergy. The continuing conflict between Cullen and MacHale of Tuam was highlighted by their dispute in relation to, firstly, the issue of an appointment in the Catholic Defence Association and, subsequently, the question of the involvement of priests in politics. This disagreement underscored the estrangement of these two prelates, which caused difficulties for many years.

Cullen's unwillingness to condemn Sadleir and Keogh was based on his belief that co-operation with the government in Westminster would benefit the people of Ireland. Unconvinced of the long-term benefits of maintaining a policy of 'independent opposition', he was not prepared to condemn individual politicians nor parliamentary political parties as long as they did not pass legislation directly in conflict with Church edicts.[23] MacHale dissented. He publicly favoured the continuation of the 'independent opposition' party to which candidates had been elected with his overt support. He was therefore scathing in his condemnation of Sadleir and Keogh and all those, including Cullen, who failed to condemn them publicly for what he viewed as their betrayal of the Irish people.[24]

---

21 *FJ*, 20 Aug. 1851.   22 See Sir C.G. Duffy, *My life in two hemispheres* (2 vols, London, 1898), i, 249.   23 Cullen to Kirby, n.d. [Jan 1853] (ICAR, *NC, III*, 1, 3, no. 57); Cullen to Prop., 8 May 1855 (APF, *CP*, vol. 158, ff 81v-2).   24 MacHale to Moore, 15 Jan. 1853 in *FJ*, 18 Jan. 1853; B. O'Reilly, *John MacHale, archbishop of Tuam, his life, times and correspondence* (2 vols, N.Y. and Cincinnati, 1890), ii, 340-1; *FJ*, 2 Feb 12 Apr 1853.

This break with MacHale was followed by another unhappy personal experience for Cullen. Frederick Lucas, editor of the Dublin-based *Tablet* magazine, was a prominent leader of the Independent Party. While Lucas maintained that a party seeking to advance the interests of Irish Catholics required the active and energetic support of the clergy if it was to achieve its aims of religious and agricultural improvement, Cullen was increasingly disillusioned with the whole idea of 'independent opposition'. Acrimonious public, as well as private, exchanges on the merits of the active participation of clerics in the field of politics took place throughout early 1854.[25] The issue came to a head at a national synod in May 1854. The hierarchy reiterated the restriction on priests in politics, despite minority opposition from MacHale and his supporters.[26] Two priests in Callan, County Kilkenny, amongst the founders of the Tenant League, were disciplined by their bishop because of their persistent political activity.[27] Lucas responded by means of a formal protest to the pope, [28] and various separate petitions to the pope were drafted both by the aggrieved clergy and by Lucas himself.[29]

This campaign provoked a strong reaction in Rome. It coincided with the proclamation of the dogma of the Immaculate Conception by Pope Pius IX. Cullen played a key role in the drafting of this dogmatic decree. He was therefore, along with other members of the hierarchy, including MacHale, present in Rome when Lucas arrived there to present the petitions. A remarkable series of exchanges culminated in the pope meeting both Cullen and Lucas. Lucas levelled serious allegations against Cullen with respect to his condemnation of active political involvement on the part of the clergy, accusing Cullen of excessive partiality to the government.[30] MacHale supported this contention, pleading that the public type of political activity in which his own priests engaged was consistent with obedience to the Holy See.[31] Cullen was clearly disturbed by such criticism and remained in Rome to defend his position on this and other issues. After several months of deliberation, during which both sides of the argument were considered, the Vatican predictably directed in favour of Cullen.[32]

25 Lucas to Newman, 1 Jan 1854 cited in F. McGrath, *Newman's University: idea and reality* (Dublin 1951), p. 231.   26 *Acta e decreta conventus Archiepiscoporum et episcoporum hiberniae ....* *Cum duabus litteris encyclicis D.N. Pii Papae IX* (Rome, 1855): Cullen to Kirby, 21 May 1854 (ICAR, *NC, III*, 2, 1, no. 17).   27 *FJ*, 31 Oct. 1854; see also Walsh to Cullen, 20 Nov. 1854 (Dublin Diocesan Archive (henceforth DDA), Cullen Papers, 332/1, no. 207).   28 *Tablet*, 4 Nov. 1854.   29 'To His Holiness Pope Pius IX. The Memorial of the undersigned Catholic priests of Ireland', 'The Memorial of the undermentioned Irish Members of Parliament' (National Library of Ireland (henceforth NLI), Ms 1587); 'Statement of Frederick Lucas' in Lucas, op. cit, ii, 139-442; Archivo Segreto Vaticano, ASV *Pio IX, Oggetti Vari*, no. 1212.   30 Lucas to Anon., 9 Jan 1855 (NLI, Ms 3738); Lucas op. cit., ii, 118; see also Diary of Bernard Smith, 11 Jan. 1855 (BAR, *Smith Papers*).   31 MacHale to Prop., 29 Jan 1855 (APF, *CP*, vol. 158, ff 86-7).   32 APF, *CP*, vol. 158, ff 48-50.

Despite Vatican endorsement for his position, Cullen remained shaken by the controversy following his return to Ireland. He continued to justify his refusal to condemn the leaders of the Independent Irish Party who had defected to the government, by suggesting that the pre-election promises they had made were rash and not binding. In place of unreserved commitment by Irish Catholics to what Cullen viewed as a suicidal policy of 'independent opposition', he proposed the active promotion of Catholics to positions of influence. He viewed this as the most beneficial strategy for the Irish people.[33] Others disagreed. The Archdeacon of Limerick publicly criticised Cullen and was censured by Rome. In defiance of Cullen, a number of clerics continued to participate actively in bye-elections as well as the general elections in 1857 and 1859, which were marked by divisive activity by both priests and bishops.[34] After the 1857 election Cullen reported MacHale to Rome for violation of the rules in relation to active political clerical involvement.[35] At the same time, two Mayo priests were prosecuted in the civil courts for election offences. Continuing conflict within the clergy posed an enormous burden upon Cullen, who suffered from bouts of depression throughout his life. Indeed, he became so depressed at this time that, he contemplated resignation.[36]

The collapse of the Irish Independent Party in the late 1850s was accompanied by growing disillusionment with constitutional parliamentary politics. The failure of constitutional politics was repeatedly cited by those who supported the use of physical force to obtain political objectives over the following decade. Appealing to Irish mythology, they bound themselves into a secret oath-bound organisation, officially known as the Irish Republican Brotherhood but more popularly termed 'the Fenians'. They were officially founded in Dublin on St Patrick's Day, 17 March 1858.[37] Their object was an independent, democratic republic achieved through military force. The people, disillusioned by political impotence, were receptive to the Fenian message. In an ironical coincidence of timing, on the day of their inauguration a pastoral letter from Cullen was circulated in the Dublin churches, warning of the dangers of secret societies.[38] The battle lines drawn that day between advocates of physical force and the archbishop of Dublin were to absorb much of Cullen's time, effort and energy over the years ahead.

Cullen's repeated and forthright opposition to the Fenians as a military force recieved its first major challenge in 1860, as a result of his prominent

33 Cullen to Kirby, 23 Oct. 1855 (ICAR, NC, III, 2, 1, no. 82). 34 FJ, 26, 27, 28 Mar. 1857; Daily Express (henceforth DE), 1 Apr. 1857. 35 Cullen to Prop., 21 July, 21 Aug. 1857 (APF, SC, Irlanda, vol. 33, ff 383, 408v). 36 [Cullen] to Kirby, 27 June 1858 (ICAR, NC, III, 2, 2, no. 80). 37 J. O'Leary, Recollections of Fenians and Fenianism (2 vols, London, 1896), ii, 81; Joseph Denieffe, op. cit., 22. 38 Moran, op. cit., i, 576.

role in the organisation of an armed force of over one thousand Irishmen to fight for the defence of the papal states. The so-called 'Brigade of Saint Patrick' was dispatched in response to an appeal by Pope Pius IX for volunteers to defend his territorial patrimony. The brigade, though officially outlawed by the British authorities in Ireland, was dispatched in 1860 and participated in a number of military conflicts in Italy before it was defeated by nationalist forces fighting for Italian unification.

The episode was significant in that Cullen, a strong advocate of constitutional politics at home and an outspoken opponent of the Fenians' physical force strategy, was prepared to sanction physical force abroad in defence of the legitimate cause of the papal states. This papal brigade was to be quoted in due course by the Fenians in justification of what they contended was their legitimate right – the independence of Ireland.[39]

The friction arising from the Fenian issue between Cullen on the one hand and the IRB and Archbishop MacHale on the other increased in 1861. The funeral and burial of Terence Bellew McManus in 1861 fuelled this conflict. A prominent nationalist, McManus had participated in the 1848 Rising. He was then deported to Australia to serve his sentence and later settled in the United States of America, where he died in early 1861. Several months after McManus' death the Brotherhood of St Patrick – an organisation representing the civil arm of the IRB – had his body exhumed and returned to Dublin. Cullen refused both a request for Requiem Mass and a funeral service in the Pro-Cathedral.[40] While Cullen's instructions to his own clergy to avoid the funeral were obeyed, the service was attended by several clerics, of whom Patrick Lavelle of Tuam archdiocese was the most notable. At the burial Lavelle openly criticised Cullen's approach both to the Fenians and to politics.[41] This public condemnation amounted to a direct challenge to Cullen, since earlier that year a joint pastoral, warning the people against secret societies, had been issued by Cullen and his fellow bishops, MacHale excepted. The bishops had also hinted at serious consequences, including possible excommunication, for those who ignored their instruction.[42]

Despite these warnings, Patrick Lavelle actively and publicly promoted the Fenian cause. He persistently ignored censure from Cullen, several Irish bishops and Rome itself.[43] In his cause Lavelle claimed the support of

39 See *FJ*, 9 Feb. 1860; *Irish People* (henceforth *IP*), 6 Feb. 1864. 40 MacManus to Cullen, 15 Oct. 1861 (DDA, Cullen Papers 340/2, no. 122); Ryan to Cullen 16 Oct. 1861 (DDA, Cullen Papers, 340/2, no. 122); Cullen to Prop., 16 Nov. 1861 (APF, *SC, Irlanda*, vol. 34, f. 191). 41 *FJ*, 11 Nov. 1861; Cullen to Kirby, 12 Nov. 1861 (ICAR, *NC, III*, 2, 3, no. 174). 42 Moran, op. cit., 830-56; *FJ*, 24 Apr. 1862. 43 Cullen to Kirby, 17 Jan 1862 (ICAR, *NC, III*, 3, 1, no. 2); [Kirby] to Prop., [Apr. 1862] (APF, *SC, Irlanda*, vol. 34, f. 362); Cullen to Moran, 4 Apr. 1862 (ICAR, *NC, III*, 3, 1, no. 22); *FJ*, 27 May 1862; *ICD*, 1863, pp 268-

Archbishop MacHale. This undermined Cullen's efforts to discourage young men from joining the Fenian movement and its membership increased steadily throughout the decade. In response, Cullen renewed his efforts to alleviate the distress of the poor and oversaw the formation of the central relief committee in 1862. In anticipation of imminent insurrection, Cullen began to stress the futility of a civilian-armed attack on the well-armed government forces.[44] Despite Cullen's efforts, the Church ban on secret societies was largely disregarded by those sympathetic to the revolutionary, republican, nationalist cause.

By August 1863, the Fenian movement was openly dismissive of Cullen's exhortations to abandon armed insurrection. Later that year a Fenian newspaper, the *Irish People*, was established, and it openly attacked Church involvement in political affairs. One of its main contributors, Charles Kickham, declared that the withdrawal of priests from politics was essential for the success of the Fenian movement.[45]

To counter the militant tendencies of the Fenians in the early 1860s, Cullen sought to revive a parliamentary alternative. The vehicle was a new organisation called the National Association, whose objectives were the disestablishment of the Church of Ireland and the promotion of tenant rights and denominationally equal education.[46] Cullen canvassed his episcopal colleagues and the majority, with the exception of MacHale, agreed to support the new Association. Because of the disastrous experience with 'independent opposition', the supporters of the Association declined to form a political party, and sought instead to persuade individual parliamentary candidates to work for their cause.

The Association, established in late 1864, was supported by all the bishops in their Lenten Pastorals with the exception of MacHale and Nulty of Meath, who sought to revive the 'independent opposition' political pledge. The Association competed with the Fenian cause for public support, and, actively supported by Cullen, continued to develop policies on land, Church and education questions. Some twenty-two Irish MPs were persuaded to promote the Association's policies on the basis of a working arrangement with the Whigs, who later assumed office as a result of the 1865 general election.[47]

9; Murray to Cullen, 27 May 1862 (DDA, Cullen papers 340/3 (iii), nos 5, 7, 8); *Catholic Telegraph* (henceforth *CT*), 20 June, 25 July 1863; *San Francisco Irish News*, 6 June 1863; Pius IX to MacHale, 24 Sept. 1863 (ICAR, *NC, III*, 3, 1, no. 84); Barnabo to Prop., 12 Nov. 1863 (APF, *SC, Irlanda*, vol. 34, f. 968); Lavelle to Pius IX, 25 Jan 1864 (APF, *SC, Irlanda*, vol. 35, f. 74); Cullen to Prop. 18 Mar 1864 (APF, *SC, Irlanda*, vol. 34, f. 1245).   **44** Cullen to Prop., 28 June 1863 (APF, *SC, Irlanda*, vol. 35, f. 136v).   **45** *IP*, 28 Nov. 1863, 27 Feb., 14, 21 May, 4, 14 June, 16 Sept., 5, 19 Nov., 17 Dec. 1864, 6 May, 16 Sept. 1865.   **46** *FJ*, 30 Dec. 1864.   **47** Whyte to Cullen, 25 Apr. 1865 (DDA, Cullen Papers 327/3, no. 62); *FJ*,

The emergence of Gladstone as leader of the Liberal party brought about a change in the attitude of the Westminster government to the Church of Ireland, and a general change of heart in Britain towards Irish demands. It is difficult to estimate the degree to which the persuasiveness and political astuteness of the National Association played a role in this change of direction.

The Fenian press continued to promote their cause for several years until the government finally acted on 14 September 1865 and the police raided the offices of the *Irish People*. The arrested leaders were tried and received lengthy jail sentences. Cullen used the occasion to issue his strongest condemnation of the Fenian leadership. At the same time, he castigated the government for their failure to address the conditions of the people.[48] As social and political tension increased, Cullen was elevated to the status of cardinal by Pope Pius IX in 1866. He was the first Irish prelate to hold such an honour.

Meanwhile, living conditions in the country worsened, with a cholera outbreak leading to a massive increase in emigration in the second half of 1866. The Westminster government, aware of the increased possibility of unrest, strengthened military installations. The discovery of arms led to the arrest of Fenian leaders. Cullen expressed mixed feeling about these moves in the light of the increased social problems in the country. He displayed an understanding and concern for the safety of the volunteers who had joined the Fenian movement, but refused to deny that government intervention was the only means to prevent self-destruction by the people.[49]

In 1866 Cullen issued a pastoral proposing parliamentary reforms as a means of resolving the people's grievances on such issues as tenant right, education and disendowment of the established Church.[50] Cullen's proposals predictably found little support amongst Fenians. Committed to a revolutionary strategy, the Fenians' abortive attempt at insurrection took place in March 1867. The Royal Irish Constabulary crushed this with ease. Cullen condemned the attempted revolution, but also reiterated that government failures had contributed to the rise of Fenianism.[51]

Numerous arrests and prison sentences ensued, culminating in the issuing of two death sentences. One was commuted to life imprisonment but the other was confirmed. Cullen actively participated in the campaign for the convicted man's reprieve, personally visiting the lord lieutenant on his behalf. The campaign was successful and Cullen was generally credited with the outcome.[52] His popularity in Fenian circles was short-lived, however. Neither the post-rising repression by the authorities, nor further condemnations of the

20 June 1865.   48 Moran, op cit., ii, 388-404.   49 Cullen to Prop., 12 Jan 1866 (APF, *SC, Irlanda*, vol. 35, f. 630).   50 Moran, op. cit., iii, 15-25.   51 FJ, 15 Mar. 186; see also Cullen to Prop., 15 Mar. 1867 (APF, *SC, Irlanda*, vol. 35, f. 992).   52 *FJ*, 28 May 1867; see also [Kirby] to Prop., [June 1867] (APF, *SC, Irlanda*, vol. 35, f. 1106(v)).

movement by the hierarchy, halted the rise of Fenianism; the execution of the 'Manchester Martyrs' caused a dramatic increase in public favour for them. Cullen refused to plead for the reprieve of these men prior to their execution, realising that such a plea had no realistic hope of success. His failure to campaign on behalf of the so-called 'martyrs', coupled with his ban on the celebration of public Masses in their memory, meant that the months following the executions of the Manchester Martyrs were difficult.[53] Some priests, anxious to show that their disapproval of the rising did not mean support for British rule, met in Limerick in January 1868 and signed a declaration calling for legislative independence for Ireland.[54] While Cullen did not support their case, he issued a pastoral highlighting the distressed state of the country and calling for government action to alleviate the plight of the poor. He reiterated that such action should take place within the confines of what was deemed legally permissible, in a ritualistic condemnation of Fenianism.[55]

Ignoring the popular groundswell of support for Fenianism, he continued to condemn the movement, issuing two further pastorals before the end of 1869.[56] The British government appealed to the Vatican for the movement to be proscribed. At the same time an ecclesiastical crisis with respect to the movement took place in January 1870 in Rome, the Irish bishops were assembled for the First Vatican Council and the group, with the exception of MacHale of Tuam and Derry of Clonfert sought a ruling on the status of the Fenians. In reply, the Holy See proclaimed that 'the society known as the Fenians is forbidden and condemned and declared to be subject to an "excommunication latae sententiae" reserved to the Roman Pontiff ...'.[57]

The excommunication of the Fenian organisation, more than any of his other hard-fought achievements, overshadowed Cullen's legacy amongst the nationalist Catholic community. He was recognised both during his episcopacy and after his death on 24 October 1878 as the most significant ecclesiastical figure of nineteenth-century Ireland, and a visible legacy of his episcopacy still remains in Dublin in many churches, schools, hospitals, religious houses, including Holy Cross College where he was buried. The rituals and religious practices which Cullen brought from Rome flourished in Ireland for a hundred years until modified by the Second Vatican Council. However the brilliance of Cullen's religious achievements was not matched by his record in the political arena. Compelled by the plight of the people to seek to improve their living conditions and to secure religious freedom, the only means acceptable to Cullen to attain these goals was the parliamentary vehicle. However, the absence of a strong political leader greatly limited the effec-

53 Cullen to Prop., 16 Dec. 1867 (APF, SC, Irlanda, vol. 35, ff 1331v-2).   54 Times, 23 Jan 1868; see also FJ, 3, 21 Jan. 1868.   55 FJ, 27 Jan. 1868.   56 FJ, 13 Mar. 1869; Moran, op. cit., iii, 260-9.   57 ASS, 5, 369-70.

tiveness of this mechanism. He opposed completely the active participation of clergy in political issues. Unfortunately the constitutional lobby failed to realise the strenght of those who supported physical force.

Cullen's first priority was the Church and religious affairs; hence his concerted campaigns to oppose legislation such as the ecclesiastical titles bill in 1851 and to obtain the disestablishment of the Church of Ireland in the following twenty-year period. With respect to both the 'Independent Party' and the Tenant League, he failed to disclose his reservations and less than wholehearted support for these movements until after their demise. In restraining priests in politics Cullen found himself in a most difficult situation. The opposition was formidable: it included nationalist churchmen like MacHale and Lavelle and members of the Independent Party. His allies were an extraordinary combination and included the British government. Ironically, the group to which he was most opposed – the Fenians – campaigned with him for the withdrawal of priests from the field of politics!

In his public campaign against the Fenians Cullen never hid the most powerful practical reason for condemning them. This was that in any encounter with the British forces they had no chance whatever of success. He was proven correct in 1867. Cullen, however, did not appear to appreciate fully the powerful emotions which produced revolutionary nationalism, and Fenianism in particular, and which ensured so much support for the separatist idea. The grievances of the Irish Catholic people were deeply felt. In particular, the fierce anti-British resentment of post-Famine emigrants resulted in their resolution to rectify the wrongs of their people. Their justification lay in the fact that the constitutional alternative was failing to produce solutions. Cullen mistakenly judged the Fenian movement to be, in some way, a threat to the Catholic Church. It is true that a number of prominent Fenians turned against the Church later in protest against what they regarded as unfair treatment. At no time, however, did the Fenians threaten to kidnap priests, burn churches or confiscate Church property. On the contrary, they united their cause with that of a Church which was itself at loggerheads with the British government.

The extent to which Cullen allowed himself to become obsessed by the Fenian menace is striking. Even while he was reporting to Rome on declining support for the movement, he was preparing yet another pastoral condemning Fenianism and visiting all kinds of punishments on its members. This obsession led to requests, both by Cullen's supporters in the hierarchy and by the British government, to have the Fenians excommunicated. If Cullen had allied his cause with that of Irish constitutionalists against the Fenians, this might have been tolerated, even excused, whereas his ostensible collaboration with the British government against the Fenians was unforgivable in the eyes of the people.

Cullen's policies undoubtedly antagonised those who did not support them. His loyalty to the Holy See, though not fully reciprocated, also had the unfortunate consequence of giving credence to the 'Home Rule is Rome rule' slogan of Tory-led Protestants who opposed self-government for Ireland in later decades. Cullen lacked political training and thus did not possess the armoury which would have enabled him to defend himself from attack and adapt to a variety of ever-changing situations. In addition, there existed no newspaper or journal to espouse his cause or explain his message. The *Irish Catholic*, which sought to fulfil this role in later times, was not founded until after his death.

The anxiety of Cullen to refer so many issues to Rome, including matters which appeared to be within his own competence, suggest a lack of confidence in his own abilities. So often on the defensive, so much misunderstood and misrepresented, Cullen was seriously handicapped in his efforts to contribute to the process of promoting the interests of the people within the existing structures. Nor did his secretive and sometimes devious personality enable him to cultivate the friendships which would have helped him in his many agonising dilemmas. His many episodes of sickness and depression must have seriously impaired him. Thus, disappointingly for him and for the people, many of the grievances that existed at the time of his appointment as archbishop were still present at the time of his death twenty-eight years later. The major exception, appropriately enough in view of his priorities, was the legal status of the Catholic Church and the Catholic religion.

By the 1916-22 period, when the next armed rising took place, both Church and nationalism had learned from Cullen's experience with the Fenians. A generation of bishops, themselves imbued with the distinctive Irish cultural ethos of the early twentieth century, found it possible to accommodate the struggle for self-determination to the declarations of the Vatican. Confrontation and condemnation were avoided, despite the participation of secret oath-bound groups, and it was found that the revolutionary movement, though dominated by the lineal descendants of the Fenian brotherhood, could work with the Catholic Church when a separate state was established in 1922.

With regard to the legacy of Cullen in the sacred area of religion and the Catholic Church, he is still acknowledged as the towering figure that made Catholic Ireland what it remained for over one hundred years. The structures established during his era in the areas of health care and education endured for a similar length of time. Religious dominance in these authoritarian systems of care facilitated the development of a structure which was inherently flawed, in that those in care had no voice and remained invisible in the event of injustice or cruelty.

As far as the question of national independence is concerned, the image of the cardinal archbishop has become enveloped in a fog of confusion and disbelief. In seeking to explain the apparent dichotomy of Cullen's legacy, one must understand the dilemma of the theologian, schooled in the certainties of Church dogma, who sought to apply such principles and disciplines in the confused Ireland in which he operated. This helps explain his prepardness to ally with the British government and his readiness to excommunicate political radicals.

Many of Cullen's controversial actions are long forgotten. These include his tolerance of the defection of Sadleir and Keogh, his ambivalence in regard to the Tenant League and his support for certain election candidates while ordering his priests to keep out of politics. His escutcheon may still not be without stain, but Paul Cullen's monument deservedly occupies a prominent place in Dublin's Pro-Cathedral.

14

The 'Brick Palace' at Drumcondra: Archbishop Walsh and the building of Archbishop's House

David C. Sheehy

For over a century, Archbishop's House in Drumcondra has served as the official residence of the Roman Catholic archbishop of Dublin and as the administrative headquarters for the archdiocese. During that time the 'Palace', as it has been popularly known to Dubliners, has been a prominent landmark on the main route north out of the city of Dublin. A fixed residence for the archbishop is today taken for granted, but during penal times and later, those elevated to the see of Dublin lacked such a facility. The first archiepiscopal residence in Dublin was that of St Laurence O'Toole, the patron of the archdiocese, which was located in the precincts of Christ Church cathedral. His successor, John Cumin, established residences at Swords and Finglas and, in 1190, the palace of St Sepulchre adjoining St Patrick's cathedral.[1] In 1324, Alexander de Bicknor began the construction of a castle in Tallaght on the endangered frontier of the Anglo-Norman Pale.[2]

In the wake of the Reformation in Ireland and with the later turbulent upheavals of the Cromwellian and Williamite eras, Roman Catholic episcopal organisation suffered severe disruption. archbishops of Dublin lived either in exile or on the run at home, issuing letters '*e loco nostri refugii*' (from our place of refuge).[3] Edmund Byrne, in the early part of the eighteenth century, was the last archbishop to be hunted down by a 'priest-catcher' as active persecution gradually gave way to toleration. However, Byrne's successors continued to keep a low profile in the capital. As late as 1776, John Carpenter requested the nuncio, when writing from Brussels, to address him merely as 'Dr Carpenter, living at Usher's Island, Dublin'.[4]

1 Margaret Holmes, 'The Palace of St Sepulchre', *Dublin Historical Record*, 46, no. 4 (1989), p. 122.   2 F. Elrington Ball, *History of the county of Dublin*, Part III (Dublin, 1905), p. 6.   3 John Meagher, 'Edmund Byrne (1656-1723) archbishop of Dublin', *Reportorium Novum*, 3, no. 2 (1963-4), p. 378.   4 Carpenter to Cmesnos, 18 May 1776

Between 1740 and 1890, nine archbishops resided at approximately fourteen different locations within the Dublin metropolis. Each prelate had to make his own arrangements with regard to accommodation and few seem to have given much thought to the needs of their successors. Many accepted the hospitality of the Franciscans in Cook Street and Francis Street.[5] John Linegar lived with his mother in Church Street in the 1740s and John Troy spent the opening years of his episcopate residing with his brother in Smithfield. The opening of the nineteenth century found Troy living in North King Street, though some years later he moved to 3 Cavendish Row, where he resided until his death in 1823. His successor, Daniel Murray, resided firstly at 39 North Cumberland Street before relocating to 44 Mountjoy Square in 1827.

Following the death of Murray in February 1852, Paul Cullen was translated from the Armagh archbishopric to Dublin. Upon his arrival in the capital in June, Cullen rented apartments at 3 Belvedere Place – a mere stone's throw from the former residence of his immediate predecessor in Mountjoy Square, which had been sold after Murray's demise. In December of the same year, thanks to the generous bequest of the Reverend Michael Doyle, deceased parish priest of St Michan's, Cullen came into possession of a more secure and commodious home. 'He left me a fine house, furniture and library for myself,' Cullen wrote to a friend in Rome. 'The house is at 55 Eccles Street, quite close to Marlboro' Street but not in my parish. This however will not interfere with me as I suppose it is sufficient for me to reside in the diocese.'[6]

One of Cullen's chief ambitions was to provide the archdiocese of Dublin with its own seminary. In looking for a site for this important undertaking, Cullen focused his attention on the north city suburb of Clonliffe. In medieval times, the name 'Clonliffe' was applied to a substantial tract of land on Dublin's north side.[7] The exact derivation of the place-name is still a matter of scholarly dispute;[8] it has been rendered by some experts as 'the meadow of the herbs' (Cluain Luibheanna) but, perhaps more plausibly, by others as 'the plain of the Liffey' (Cluain Liffe). What is certain is that the name 'Clonliffe' was linked to a large area lying between the Liffey and Tolka

(Dublin Diocesan Archives (henceforth DDA), Carpenter Papers, AB/4/1 f. 110).   5 The parish of St Nicholas of Myra (Francis Street) served as the mensal parish of the archbishop of Dublin for much of the seventeenth and eighteenth centuries. See Nicholas Donnelly, *A short history of some Dublin parishes* (17 parts, Dublin, [1904-17]) (henceforth Donnelly, *Parishes*), part 6, pp 18-19.   6 Cullen to Abbot Bernard Smith, 17 Dec. 1852, cited in Peadar Mac Suibhne, *Paul Cullen and his contemporaries*, iii (Naas, 1965), pp 148-9.   7 *Holy Cross College, Clonliffe, Dublin: college history and centenary record 1859-1959* (Dublin, 1962), pp 20-1.   8 Ibid., pp 17-19; Father Colmcille, 'The lands of St Mary's Abbey, Dublin, at the dissolution of the abbey', *Reportorium Novum*, 3, no. 1 (1961-2), pp 97-9.

rivers. In this fertile and estuarine setting, an area encompassing the modern Clonliffe, that is, roughly between Blessington Street/North Frederick Street and the Tolka, served as the 'Grange' or farm of St Mary's abbey, an important monastic foundation begun by the White Benedictines in 1139 and soon afterwards taken over and greatly expanded by the Cistercians.

With the suppression of religious houses in Ireland in the sixteenth century, the Cistercians lost control of St Mary's abbey and its extensive possessions, including the 'Grange of Clonliffe'. The 'Grange' then passed through a number of hands before, in 1730, it came into the ownership of Luke Gardiner, the pre-eminent developer of Georgian Dublin.[9] Over time the modern townland of Clonliffe evolved, comprising a much smaller area than the old 'Grange'. The townland was divided into three parts: Clonliffe East, West and South. Its territory was bounded by the Tolka to the north, Cabra to the west, Ballybough to the east, and by the North Circular Road to the south. Drumcondra Road divided Clonliffe East from Clonliffe West and the Royal Canal served as their common boundary with Clonliffe South. In Clonliffe East, between Drumcondra Road and Ballybough Road, stood 'the great house of the Grange of Clonliffe'. This was located on the site of the present 'Red House' which was built in the last quarter of the eighteenth century. Its first occupant, Frederick Edward Jones, a colourful theatre impresario, gave it the name 'Clonliffe House'.[10]

The name, Drumcondra, derives from Drumcondraighe or 'the tribe of the Condraighe', a tribe who inhabited the district in the second century AD. Drumcondra shares with Clonliffe an early monastic history.[11] Part of the 'Grange' of St Mary's abbey stretched north across the Tolka to lands which are today the site of St Patrick's college. In addition, the area east of Upper Drumcondra Road served as the 'home farm' of the Augustinian priory of All Saints, which flourished on the site of the present Trinity College. After the suppression of the monasteries, the 'home farm' of Drumcondra came into the possession of Dublin Corporation.[12]

Drumcondra Road, linking Clonliffe with Drumcondra, has traditionally been part of the main route north out of the city of Dublin. As early as the fifteenth century it was called the 'Royal Way'.[13] By the middle of the nineteenth century this was too grand a title for a thoroughfare which was criticised in 1846 for being in a very bad state of repair, with numerous potholes and a thin surface. This was in spite of the presence of a turnpike on the junction between Drumcondra Road and St Alphonsus Road, which proved irksome to local residents, passing travellers and developers alike.[14]

9 *Clonliffe centenary history*, pp 23-4. 10 Ibid., p. 29. 11 *Church of Corpus Christi, golden jubilee 1941-91* (Dublin, 1991), pp. 5-6. 12 John Kingston, *The parish of Fairview* (Dundalk, 1953), p. 17. 13 Ibid., p. 14. 14 Patrick Kelly, 'Drumcondra, Clonliffe and

At this time, the area embraced by the districts of Drumcondra and Clonliffe was still essentially rural in character. Father John Kingston has described it thus:

> A large village with a thriving farming community in the neighbourhood, narrow roads through rich fields, a few large houses for the gentry, and, between the village and Dublin, a scattered number of cabins and small shops.[15]

If, as John Henry Newman asserted, the north side of Dublin was 'the specially Catholic side of Dublin', then the Clonliffe/Drumcondra district exemplified the burgeoning catholicity of the area north of the Liffey.[16] Here a cluster of ecclesiastical establishments was located from the 1830s onwards – so many, indeed, that the locality came to be known as the 'The Holy Land'.[17]

In 1833, Father John Smith opened St Mary's Asylum for 'female penitents' at 2 Lower Drumcondra Road.[18] From 1853, this institution was administered by the sisters of the French congregation of Our Lady of Charity of Refuge. In 1858, the Magdalen and laundry was relocated to larger premises at High Park on Grace Park Road. Meanwhile, in 1842, Father John Hand founded All Hallows missionary college in Drumcondra House.[19] Adjacent to All Hallows, the monastery of the Incarnation was established by the Carmelite Sisters in Hampton Lodge in 1858. The following year, the Redemptoristines opened a monastery in the former Magdalen on Drumcondra Road.

It was, then, to this rural, thinly-populated and yet increasingly Catholic area on the unfashionable north side of Dublin that Archbishop Cullen looked for a site for a seminary for the archdiocese. In 1858, Cullen purchased Clonliffe House and its grounds, twelve acres in all, from the Inland Revenue Commissioners. The following year Clonliffe House became home to the newly established Holy Cross College. This was not the high-water mark of Cullen's ambition, however, as he was determined to erect a purpose-built seminary. To this end, in 1860, he purchased a plot of land adjoining the Clonliffe House property from the estate of the last earl of Blessington. The

Glasnevin township, 1878-1900' in James Kelly and Uaitear Mac Gearailt (eds), *Dublin and Dubliners: essays in the history and literature of Dublin city* (Dublin, 1990), p. 36.   15 Kingston, *The parish of Fairview*, p. 54.   16 Newman to Woodlock, 19 Nov. 1861 (DDA, Woodlock Papers, cited in Liam Rigney, 'Bartholomew Woodlock and the Catholic University of Ireland, 1861-79' (National University of Ireland, Ph.D. thesis, 1995), p. 243).   17 Dillon Cosgrave, *North Dublin city and environs* (Dublin, n.d.), p. 79.   18 John Kingston, 'Rev. John Smyth, C.C. (1791-1858)', *Reportorium Novum*, 4, no. 1 (1971), p. 20.   19 Kevin Condon, *The Missionary College of All Hallows, 1842-1891* (Dublin, 1986), pp 53-60.

new seminary building was completed in 1863 and the church of the Holy Cross was added a little over a decade later.

Meanwhile, in 1861, the archbishop had acquired, through the Landed Estates Court, a third segment of land at Clonliffe East – the very land on which Archbishop's House would later be constructed.[20] The L-shaped property consisted of a field of one acre, three roods and ten perches, partly bordering Drumcondra Road and rising from there to the east to a ridge called Drumcondra Hill; and another larger plot of land running to the south, parallel with Drumcondra Road, as far as Turnpike Lane, and encompassing what would later become known as 'the Archbishop's Garden'. The whole property was held under four separate leases and, on 2 August 1861, Cullen paid £1,020 for the four lessee interests.[21] A further acquisition of five acres in 1866 completed the portfolio of property at Clonliffe which Cullen assembled with great foresight.[22] Now there was ample space not only for the future expansion of the diocesan seminary but also for such other building projects as Cullen or his successors might contemplate.

In 1866, Cullen became the first Irishman to be nominated to the college of cardinals. Whilst in Rome to collect the 'red hat', he received a letter from Patrick Moran, his nephew and secretary, at home in Dublin, informing him that some of the Dublin clergy had discussed a proposal to raise funds to build a residence for Cullen 'where the old house stands to the back of Clonliffe', to mark the unprecedented honour bestowed upon their archbishop. 'They were determined', Moran reported, 'that you will maintain the *dignitá Cardinalizia* with all due state in this country.'[23] In his reply, Cullen indicated that he himself had already decided to embark upon such a project and had even selected his own preferred site on the Clonliffe property – a garden area between the seminary and Drumcondra Road – adjacent to the one chosen by the Dublin clergy. He described it thus:

> The site is most eligible – high, outside fog and smoke, and still quite close to the City – we could sell or let the house in Eccles Street. The new house would have a library, archives and rooms for a strange bishop and four or five priests. A fixed home for the Archbishop and for the archives would be most important.[24]

Most likely because of finance, Cullen never got round to building his episcopal residence. It was a project left to his successors. However, he was

20 *Clonliffe Centenary history*, pp 46-47. **21** Registry of Deeds, Deed no. 1861-24-273. **22** *Clonliffe centenary history*, p. 47. **23** Moran to Cullen, 4 June 1866 (DDA, Cullen Papers, AB4/327/5/V[2]). **24** Cullen to Moran, 28 June 1866 (DDA, Cullen Papers, AB4/40/VII[30]).

instrumental in laying the groundwork to enable the undertaking to come to fruition eventually; he purchased the site on which Archbishop's House would later be constructed and he delineated the functional priorities which the house's design would follow in large measure.

Cullen died in October 1878 and Edward McCabe, his auxiliary, was appointed as his successor in May of the following year. McCabe declined to live in Cullen's house in Eccles Street but instead leased 4 Rutland Square East as his residence in the city, retaining a parochial house in Kingstown as a weekend and holiday retreat.[25] McCabe died in February 1885, and on 25 June, William Joseph Walsh was provided to the see of Dublin. Walsh's appointment, in spite of British intrigue in Rome, was hailed as a triumph by Irish nationalists.[26] A man of strongly held, if moderate, nationalist views, Walsh was the pre-eminent prelate in the Roman Catholic Church in Ireland during his thirty-six year reign.

Walsh was born in 1841, at 11 Essex Quay, Dublin, the only child of Ralph Walsh, a watchmaker and repeal activist, of County Kerry, and Mary Pierce of Galway.[27] He attended Newman's Catholic University of Ireland before entering St Patrick's College, Maynooth, in 1858. A brilliant student, he was appointed professor of dogmatic and moral theology within a year of his ordination in 1866. He was made vice-president of the college in 1878 and president in 1880. Walsh first came to national prominence through demonstrating his skills as an expert witness on canon law in the celebrated *O'Keefe* law case in 1875. He further consolidated a growing reputation with an equally brilliant display as an expert witness on land law before the Bessborough Commission in 1880.[28]

As archbishop, Walsh assiduously nurtured the substantial pastoral infrastructure of the Dublin archdiocese which had been carefully constructed by his predecessors. He built numerous churches and schools and increased the number of parishes from 65 to 76. His greatest accomplishments, however, were in the sphere of education, where he proved an able champion of Catholic interests. His chief contributions were in the fields of teacher-training, intermediate education and university education, culminating in his appointment in 1908 as the first chancellor of the National University of Ireland.[29]

In the political sphere, Walsh strove to forge an enduring alliance between the Roman Catholic Church and the main force of the constitutional nationalist movement in Ireland, from the Irish Parliamentary Party to Sinn Fein and from the Land League to the Gaelic League. His outspoken support for

---

25 Donnelly, *Parishes*, part 1, p. 166.   **26** Emmet Larkin, *The Roman Catholic Church and the creation of the modern Irish state 1878-1886* (Philadelphia, 1975), especially chapter 9.   **27** Patrick Walsh, *William J. Walsh, archbishop of Dublin* (Dublin, 1928), p. 1.   **28** Ibid., chapters 3 and 5.   **29** Ibid., p. 564.

the 'Plan of Campaign' resulted in his humiliation at the hands of Pope Leo XIII, then anxious to promote Anglo-Vatican diplomacy, and cost Dublin the 'red hat'. This Walsh bore with great dignity and fortitude.[30]

He promoted the use of arbitration to resolve land and labour disputes, advocated the establishment of a Board of Conciliation, and was often called upon to utilise his own considerable forensic skills to help resolve seemingly intractable *imbroglios* between unions and employers. He learned the art of photography, mastered the Pitman script and various methods to aid memory, and famously deciphered cablegrams, variously encoded, which fortuitously came into the hands of Parnell's lawyers during the *Times* Special Commission, but had left them baffled.[31] On the debit side, Walsh was too much the desk-bound administrator and a rather remote figure for his priests.[32] Writing after his death, in 1921, his former secretary, Michael Curran, noted that 'the dread of entanglement and loss of time contributed to make him shun society and discourage visitors'.[33]

On his return to Dublin from Rome, in September 1885, to take up his new post as archbishop, Walsh took up residence in the house in Rutland Square bequeathed to him by Cardinal McCabe. However, he found life in the centre of the bustling metropolis disagreeable. [34] Though a child of Dublin's innercity, he had spent all of his adult life in the sylvan tranquillity of Maynooth – so conducive to academic study and reflection. Living in Rutland Square, Walsh found himself easy prey for casual callers who interrupted his work schedule. He found this so distracting he placed a notice in the *Irish Catholic Directory* for 1887 advising visitors to write in advance for an appointment and advertising restricted hours 'at home'.[35] Seeking a weekend retreat from the burdens of office and the stresses of city life, Walsh leased 'Thorncliffe', a large house in Rathgar, set in its own grounds overlooking the Dodder river, in March 1886. The Rathgar residence served as a mere stop-gap, however, for the archbishop was determined to quit Rutland Square entirely and relocate to the suburbs. Walsh shared Cullen's ambition to erect a suitable, permanent home for the archbishop of Dublin.[36] Thanks to his predecessor's strategic land purchases at Clonliffe, a site was available for just such an undertaking.

30 See Emmet Larkin, *The Roman Catholic Church and the Plan of Campaign, 1886-1888* (Cork, 1978), especially chapter 6 and Walsh, pp 317-70 and 430-2.   31 Tim Healy, *Letters and leaders of my day* (2 vols, London, 1928), i, 296-7; Walsh, *Walsh*, p. 393.   32 *Clonliffe centenary history*, p. 120.   33 Michael Curran, 'The late archbishop of Dublin, 1841-1921', *Dublin Review*, July-Sept. 1921, p. 104.   34 Ibid., p. 104.   35 *Irish Catholic Directory*, 1887, p. 143.   36 Cardinal Patrick Moran, nephew of Cardinal Paul Cullen, told Archbishop Walsh of his uncle's desire to erect an archiepiscopal residence in the grounds of Clonliffe College (*Clonliffe centenary history*, p. 71 n.).

To build his new home Walsh turned to William Hague Jr, a leading Roman Catholic architect. Hague was born in 1840, in Cavan town, where his father was a successful building contractor.[37] In 1863, Hague moved to Dublin where he practised as an architect with offices successively at 175 Great Brunswick Street, 44 Westland Row and 50 Dawson Street. Hague built up an extensive practice as an ecclesiastical architect. Stylistically, he was a pupil of J.J. McCarthy, the pre-eminent Roman Catholic architect in Ireland from the 1840s to the 1860s and the principal exponent of the Gothic Revival school of architecture.[38] Hague was imbued with the same fervour for this style, which became the orthodoxy in ecclesiastical architecture in mid-Victorian Ireland, and he adorned a number of dioceses, especially his native Kilmore, with a series of finely executed cutstone Gothic churches.[39]

On the death of McCarthy in 1882, Hague succeeded to much of his practice, finishing several of McCarthy's prestigious projects, most notably the chapel of St Patrick's College, Maynooth. It was through this Maynooth connection that Walsh would first come to know Hague. After the fire of 1878, the year Walsh became vice-president of the college, Hague was commissioned to reconstruct St Mary's Wing.[40] In 1887, Walsh, now archbishop of Dublin, was nominated to a sub-committee of the trustees of Maynooth to oversee the completion of McCarthy's chapel. A competition was held, which Hague won ahead of such distinguished contemporaries as George C. Ashlin, W.H. Byrne and J.L. Robinson.[41]

Dispensing with an open competition, Walsh decided that Hague was the right man to build Dublin's new archiepiscopal residence. They first met to discuss the project on 29 September 1888, at Rutland Square.[42] Though Hague did not often turn his hand to building private dwellings he had, in 1873, erected a Gothic Revival palace for the bishop of Meath on a site in Mullingar adjacent to where St Finian's cathedral would later be constructed.[43] In January 1889, Hague submitted a detailed estimate for 'a new residence at Clonliffe,

---

37 Terence P. Cunningham, *St Patrick's College, Cavan, a centenary history* (Cavan, 1974), p. 45. 38 Jeanne Sheehy has suggested that Hague was in fact a pupil of McCarthy's. See Jeanne Sheehy, *J.J. McCarthy and the Gothic Revival in Ireland* (London, 1975), p. 19. 39 Daniel Gallogly, 'Kilmore Churches', *Breifne*, 8, no. 30 (1994), p. 464. 40 Valerie Seymour, 'Architectural plans & drawings' in Agnes Neligan (ed.), *Maynooth library treasures* (Dublin, 1995), pp 186-87. 41 Ibid.; Patrick Corish, *Maynooth College 1795-1995* (Dublin, 1995), p. 195. 42 Walsh's diary for 1888 (DDA, Walsh Papers). 43 Jeremy Williams, *A companion guide to architecture in Ireland, 1838-1921* (Dublin, 1994), p. 372. Williams also attributes to Hague the building of the residence of the bishop of Clogher in Monaghan (p. 320). However, evidence is wanting to support this attribution and its tentative date of construction corresponds with the date of Hague's death. Hague *was* responsible for the erection of the cathedral chapter house, in Monaghan in or about 1882, and this may account for the confusion. Williams' reference to Archbishop's House (p. 159) is both inaccurate

County Dublin, for His Grace the Archbishop of Dublin'.[44] The estimate was accepted and Hague then began work in earnest. He appointed William Connolly & Son as contractor and Henry McConnell as surveyor. Connolly had premises at 37-39 Upper Dominick Street and had partnered Hague on a number of commissions for the Dublin archdiocese. Walsh chose to build Archbishop's House on the site previously selected by Cardinal Cullen. The location was a ridge overlooking Drumcondra Road called 'Drumcondra Hill', situated on part of the property of Holy Cross College. A joint inspection by Walsh and Hague of the 'Clonliffe site' took place on 9 February 1889, and shortly thereafter, building work commenced. Walsh kept an interested eye on developments and occasionally forayed out to Drumcondra to consult with the architect or to inspect the workshops of Connolly the builder. Progress was precisely recorded in the Archbishop's diary:

17 April	Clonliffe, new house, first joists]
18 May	Girders laid, joists partly
27 May	Window sills laid except at large room [drawing room]
8 June	Hall etc. up to lintels of doors – outside walls not so high
6 July	First storey of north side practically finished; some cap[ital]s on at south side; dining room not so far advanced.[45]

The building activity at Drumcondra did not escape the attention of the press. In September 1889, one journal noted that 'a splendid palace' was being erected at Drumcondra for the archbishop of Dublin. Its readers were thus further enlightened:

The palace will afford a vast amount of accommodation, and will contain a special hall for the conferences of the Roman Catholic Bishops of Ireland and the Archbishop's receptions. The oratory will be exceptionally beautiful, and the whole building will be illuminated by the electric light.[46]

As work on this new home continued apace, Walsh wrote to his auxiliary, Nicholas Donnelly:

The new house at Clonliffe is making great progress; the grounds are now laid out, you would not know the place.[47]

and unflattering. **44** DDA, Walsh Papers. **45** Walsh's diary, 1889 (DDA, Walsh Papers). **46** 'Newspaper Extracts', iv, p. 91 (D.D.A., Walsh Papers). **47** Walsh to Donnelly, 25

In November 1889, it was reported in the press that the new 'palace' would be lit from top to bottom by electric light. This was reportedly the ninety-eighth such installation by Edmundson of Capel Street, Dublin, and was stated to be the same system as that which had been recently installed in the town house of Sir Edward Guinness on St Stephen's Green. The electricity was to be generated by a gas motor supplemented by a storage battery on the 'Fame' principle and the newspaper praised the apparatus for being economic, efficient and smoke and odour free.[48]

The building of Archbishop's House was not without its troubles. Towards the end of July 1889, a short, stark entry appears in the archbishop's diary: 'men on strike'.[49] The exact nature of the dispute is not recorded but it was quickly resolved and work resumed. In November, a deputation from the plasterers' union met with William Connolly, the contractor, to request that 'none other than regular plasterers would be employed in the erection of the new palace at Clonliffe'.[50] The required assurance was given and the deputation departed happy. Trouble, however, was still brewing.

In February 1890, at a meeting of the United Trades Council and Labour League, John M. Shannon, delegate of the Stucco Plasterers' Society, alleged that 'ornamental plaster casts' for Archbishop's House were being ordered from London instead of the work being placed at home in Dublin.[51] As the proceedings of the Council were open to the press, this charge was given wide publicity. Acrimonious letters were then exchanged between the contractor and the secretary of the Trades Council before the matter was referred to Michael Davitt MP, the founder of the Land League, for arbitration.[52] Davitt found that there was no foundation to the claim that the plaster-work for Archbishop's House was to come from England, but he found that the Plasterers' Society delegate had only asserted the claim on account of a misunderstanding and, in particular, on the basis of information supplied to him by an unsuccessful and disgruntled local bidder for the contract. Davitt reserved his chief criticism, however, for the Trades Council, which he found had acted in violation of its own rules in allowing a statement to be made at one of its public meetings before the accuracy of it had been determined.[53]

The building trade experienced fluctuating fortunes during the 1890s in Dublin.[54] Skilled tradesmen were, not surprisingly, hostile to the notion that work might be contracted abroad at their expense. However, it is still a little ironic that the construction of Archbishop's House should have encountered

Nov. 1889 (DDA, Walsh Papers).   48 'Newspaper Extracts', v, p. 19 (DDA, Walsh Papers).   49 Walsh's diary, 1889 (DDA, Walsh Papers).   50 'Newspaper Extracts', v, p. 16 (DDA, Walsh Papers).   51 Ibid., v, p. 118.   52 Ibid., v, pp 133-6.   53 Ibid., vi, p. 25.   54 Mary Daly, *Dublin, the deposed capital, a social and economic history, 1860-1914* (Dublin, 1984), pp 53-63.

labour troubles, given that the Archbishop himself was a nationally renowned arbitrator who enjoyed the confidence of both unions and employers. In August 1889, Walsh's mediation was successful in bringing to an end a protracted strike by builders' labourers in Dublin and, in April 1890, a similar intervention helped to resolve a bitter and costly dispute on the Great Southern & Western Railway. For the latter contribution, Walsh was honoured with the Freedom of the city of Cork.[55]

Of all the design aspects of the construction of Archbishop's House, the one which interested Archbishop Walsh the most was the building of the library. For a man possessing such an intellectually curious mind it was essential that he have ready access to a large and comprehensive body of books. But how was Walsh going to accommodate his own voluminous collection in his new home? This was a conundrum which the archbishop had not yet resolved by the spring of 1890. Quite fortuitously, in March 1890, William Ewart Gladstone published an article in the periodical *The Nineteenth Century* on the arrangement and shelving of books in large private libraries.[56] Gladstone, the pre-eminent politician in Victorian Britain, shared certain interests with the archbishop of Dublin. As Roy Jenkins, a recent biographer, has noted, Gladstone 'throughout his life ... had both a physical and an intellectual obsession with books'.[57] Immediately upon reading the article, Walsh wrote to Gladstone to tell him how useful he had found his ideas and stating that he would adopt his scheme, with certain alterations, when erecting his own library.[58] In May 1890, Walsh took up an invitation from Gladstone to visit his north Wales retreat at Hawarden and inspect his newly-built library holding some thirty thousand volumes. Writing to Gladstone on his return to Dublin, Walsh declared that he was satisfied that he could make use of 'your plan to a large extent' when it came to constructing the Drumcondra library.[59] In the event, Walsh used a modified version of Gladstone's shelving scheme, featuring projecting bookcases, and confined their installation to one end of the room.[60] The reason for this was that Walsh wished the library in Archbishop's House to fulfil a dual function; to accommodate books in wall-mounted and projecting bookcases and to provide space for the holding of meetings of the episcopal standing committee.

Aside from the library, Walsh intended, when resident in his new house, to pursue his interest in astronomy. To that end, he ordered a telescope from

55 'Newspaper Extracts', vi, p. 78 (DDA, Walsh Papers). 56 William Gladstone, 'On books and the housing of them', *The nineteenth century*, Mar. 1890, pp 3-15. 57 Roy Jenkins, *Gladstone* (London, 1995), p. 178. 58 Walsh to Gladstone, 5 March 1890 (British Library (henceforth BL), Gladstone Papers, Add. Ms. 44509). 59 Walsh to Gladstone, 20 May 1890 (BL, Gladstone Papers, Add. Ms. 44510 f. 29). 60 This portion of the library came to be known as the 'Gladstone Wing'.

the Dublin workshop of the brothers, Thomas and Howard Grubb, world renowned designers and manufacturers of telescopes.[61] In June 1890, Walsh visited Grubb's Observatory and Astronomical Instrument Works in Rathmines where he saw his own piece, a three-inch achromatic telescope in a brass lacquered tube on a combined alt-azimuth and equatorial mounting, with a tripod stand, then being assembled. To utilise the instrument, Walsh erected a metal stand on the roof of Archbishop's House and installed a staircase which gave access to the roof. The attention which Walsh gave to the details of the construction and the fitting out of his new home ensured that, as with Thomas Jefferson's 'Monticello', Archbishop's House came to reflect the man who built it.

The districts of Clonliffe and Drumcondra underwent considerable change in the period between the first purchase of the land at Clonliffe by Archbishop Cullen and the construction of Archbishop's House. The introduction of the tram and the provision of street lighting, an improved water supply, and a limited sewerage system all contributed to the growth of the locality. The mid-1860s witnessed the excitement associated with the laying of the foundation stone for a proposed new campus for the Catholic University of Ireland at Clonliffe West.[62] However, lack of funds forced the University Board to abandon this hugely ambitious scheme before much further progress had been made. Subsequently the Redemptoristines built a monastery on part of the site, the remaining land being sold to developers.[63] In 1875, St Patrick's College for the training of national school teachers opened in the Drumcondra premises lately vacated by the Redemptoristines. In 1883, the College was re-located across the Tolka to Belvedere House.[64]

Though Clonliffe experienced more rapid growth in development and population than Drumcondra in the second half of the nineteenth century, it gradually began to lose its own identity, finding itself inexorably subsumed into that of its neighbour as the latter rose in prominence.[65] This process was accelerated by the achievement of township status for Drumcondra in 1878, a proposition which enjoyed the personal backing of Cardinal Cullen.[66] Clonliffe never developed a village to underpin its identity and, in the process of transition from rural backwater to dormitory suburb, found itself squeezed between the demands of an expanding metropolis and the burgeoning Drumcondra.

61 'Newspaper Extracts', vi, p. 101 (DDA, Walsh Papers).   62 This solemn ceremony on 20 July 1862 drew a crowd of some 130,000, the largest Catholic demonstration in Dublin in the nineteenth century (Breandan Mac Giolla Choille, 'Fenian documents in the State Paper Office', *Irish Historical Studies*, 16, no. 63 (1969), p. 264 n.).   63 Rigney, 'Woodlock', pp 246-7.   64 *St Patrick's College of Education, Drumcondra, centenary booklet, 1875-1975* (Dublin, 1975), pp 7-12.   65 Cosgrave, *North Dublin city*, p. 76 and Kingston, *Parish of Fairview*, p. 52.   66 Kelly, 'Drumcondra', p. 39.

The building of Archbishop's House proved a boon to the township of Drumcondra. In November 1889, it was announced that the archbishop would contribute three shillings a yard towards the cost of flagging the footpath opposite Archbishop's House with the product of the Ferrumite Company of Belfast. A contemporary journal noted that 'this patriotic encouragement of Irish manufacture on the part of His Grace sets an excellent example for us all'.[67] The following January, Thomas Connolly, son of the contractor for the new 'palace', announced at a meeting of the Drumcondra town commissioners that Walsh had promised to have the slope on Drumcondra Road opposite his new home planted with trees. The chairman declared that the commissioners should all feel much obliged to the archbishop for the interest he had taken in the township. The meeting then passed a motion thanking the archbishop 'for his kindness and generosity in giving a sufficient supply of healthy trees to plant both sides of Drumcondra Road' and expressing the hope that the residents 'would evince their appreciation of the gift by exercising due vigilance in protecting the trees from injury'.[68]

The same town commissioners, meeting in August 1890 in premises close to the almost complete archiepiscopal residence, fulsomely congratulated themselves on the progress made in the twelve years since the township's establishment. Since most of the commissioners were developers and builders with major financial interests in the township, they had undoubtedly prospered themselves during the period in question. The chairman, Maurice Butterly JP, a leading developer in the area, stated that they had made Drumcondra 'one of the most prosperous townships in the country'. Edward McMahon MP asserted that since the formation of the township, the population of Drumcondra had doubled. The working class had been 'looked after', as there were two hundred houses which were let at 6 shillings a week each, and there was still plenty of ground to build more. Many houses for the 'better classes' had also been erected and in their township they had some of the finest houses in or near Dublin. There was no doubt that when the archbishop came to live amongst them it would be the means of still further benefiting their township. St Patrick had stood on the hill of Drumcondra, and blessed the place and said it would be the centre of Dublin, and this prediction was now being realised.[69]

We do not know if Archbishop Walsh was in the least bit charmed by such flummery. Even as the commissioners were meeting in Drumcondra, the archbishop was departing for the Continent on his annual vacation. Whilst he was abroad, Walsh was kept abreast by post of developments at home in Ireland. In mid-September, William Hague wrote to assure him that a big

67 'Newspaper Extracts', v, p. 26 (DDA, Walsh Papers).   68 Ibid., v, p. 99.   69 Ibid., vii, p. 8.

push was on to complete the construction and fitting out of Archbishop's House in time for his return early the following month. Rapid progress was made and Connolly, the contractor, had 'every man possible engaged ... plastering and painting, etc.'.[70] Thomas McGrath, professor of science and philosophy at Holy Cross College, also put pen to paper to enthuse about the impressive-looking edifice nearing completion:

> The other evening for the first time I saw the house lit up by the electric light. The transformation wrought in the appearance of the largest room was almost magical. It was a perfect luxury to linger and look. All parts make rapid progress except the Entrance Piers.[71]

Upon his return to Dublin on 7 October 1890, Walsh moved immediately into his new abode. A notice to this effect appeared in the *Freeman's Journal* advising readers to address letters to 'his Grace at Archbishop's House, Drumcondra'.[72]

It must have been with a mixture of excitement and pride that Walsh finally took possession of his new home. Hague had built a substantial, detached, two-storey over basement residence, set in its own grounds. The external surface of the upper storeys of the building was largely clad in red brick, in the 'dutch' style, while the basement level was covered externally with rock-faced squared ashlars of Dalkey granite. The distinctive terracotta brick in the upper storeys gave warmth and character to the appearance of the house, earning it the contemporary sobriquet, 'the brick palace'.[73] The windows and corners of the upper levels were plainly dressed in stone. Black calp stone was used in the foundations and the roof was clad in Bangor slate. At the first storey, a tower-covered entrance porch, with pilasters of Drumfries stone and Portland stone, and stained glass panels, gave way, through the front door, to a vestibule. A reception room and parlour led off from the vestibule, to the left and right respectively. Then, through an inner doorway, a long hall which ran almost the full length of the house, dividing it in two, gave access to a drawing room, a dining room, a sitting room, the archbishop's study, and the secretary's study. These first floor rooms were generally spacious, many with tall windows drawing in natural light. The largest and most elegant of the reception rooms was the drawing room.[74]

---

70 Hague to Walsh, 15 Sept. 1890 (DDA, Walsh Papers).   71 McGrath to Walsh, 14 Sept. 1890 (DDA, Walsh Papers).   72 *Freeman's Journal*, 8 Oct. 1890.   73 *Piccadilly*, 28 Aug. 1890.   74 Walsh, at a later date, possibly to facilitate his work, interchanged the locations of the library and the drawing room. The exchange was made easier by the fact that the rooms are of equivalent size. Wall-mounted bookcases in what is now the drawing room are a reminder of the room's original purpose (Contractor's invoices for refurbishment works in Archbishop's House (DDA, Walsh Papers).

The upper storey contained the library, featuring the 'Gladstone Wing', a beautifully decorated oratory, and several bedrooms. The basement level comprised a kitchen, scullery, servants' dining room, butler's pantry, housekeeper's bedroom, bedrooms for other servants, an engine room for the power supply and several small storerooms.

The interior of the house was richly outfitted and furnished using materials of high quality. Wood furnishings utilised Riga wood, Spanish, Honduran and Baywood mahogany, stripped and red pine, and white and red deal.[75] Tabasco panelled mahogany doors were taken from Walsh's former residence in Rutland Square, along with three fireplaces, and installed in the new house.[76] Floors in the upper levels of Archbishop's House were covered with Axminster, Persian, Brussels, Kidder and Wilton carpets, supplied by Todd Burns & Company of Mary Street and Henry Street.[77]

The London journal, *Piccadilly*, declared that 'the brick palace ... at Clonliffe, while externally one of the ugliest of edifices, is internally a most beautiful and commodious residence.' It described the library as being 'an especially noble apartment' with the 'Gladstone Wing' holding 'some thousands of volumes ... shelved in a space which would seem to accommodate only some hundreds.' The journal concluded by discussing the merits of the lighting system in rather impish fashion:

> The whole building is fitted with the most improved forms of electric lighting. The arrangement on the fine staircase, by which one ascending may light any of the bedrooms or other apartments in advance by turning a switch, is particularly novel and convenient. Awkward, rather, if a wag of a cleric turned on one's illumination in the course of one's beauty sleep![78]

After a month's residence at Drumcondra, Walsh wrote to Tobias Kirby, rector of the Irish College in Rome, to express his satisfaction with his new abode:

> I am now in a grand new home, where I have, for the first time since I left Maynooth, the advantage and comfort of a library. This facilitates my work enormously.[79]

Yet Walsh's great project was, in one respect, incomplete. So keen had he been to satisfy his bibliophilic requirements when building Archbishop's House

---

75 Receipts and invoices (DDA, Walsh Papers).   **76** Later, additional doors, in the same Georgian style, were procured from Richmond Works of North Richmond Street, Dublin. **77** Receipts and invoices (DDA, Walsh Papers).   **78** *Piccadilly*, 28 Aug. 1890.   **79** Walsh to Kirby, 12 Nov. 1890, quoted in Emmet Larkin, *The Roman Catholic Church in Ireland and the fall of Parnell* (Chapel Hill, 1979), pp 208-9.

that he had failed entirely to make any provision for the diocesan archives. This omission, which would have been regarded as a major transgression by his predecessor, Cardinal Cullen, had now to be rectified. Hague, more archivally aware than his client, deflected a hasty proposal from Archbishop's House that the diocesan archives be stored in a converted coal-cellar, or in an out-house, arguing that the archives should be housed in a better standard of accommodation so as to be 'securely dry and free from condensation which is prejudicial to documents'.[80] Hague came up with a scheme for a two-storey extension to the side and rere of Archbishop's House, fronted with red brick and granite to keep its appearance in sympathy with the main building. The lower storey of the extension featured a muniment room with walls clad with eighteen-inch thick fire-resistant bricks, and the upper storey consisted of a breakfast parlour. This extension was completed in 1891, along with other improvements and additions such as a formal entrance from Drumcondra Road, a gatelodge, a coach house, harness room and stables, a greenhouse, carriageway, a planted garden and landscaped grounds.[81]

How much did Archbishop's House cost to build? It is not possible today to determine the exact figure but surviving records permit the calculation of an approximate costing. Aside from the cost of demolition and site clearance, the site came without charge as it belonged to the diocesan seminary. Hague and Connolly submitted bills amounting to roughly £18,000, which covered fees, labour, materials, furnishings and fittings, the 1891 extension, and the laying out of the grounds.[82] Additional costs, for which no record survives, may have raised the final total to over £20,000. In any event, the true cost appears to have been a great deal less than the figure of £75,000 alleged by an anonymous correspondent of the London journal *John Bull* in March 1890.[83] Though Archbishop Walsh sold his old residence in Rutland Square, he still had to borrow the greater part of the cost of the building of Archbishop's House. The loan was soon repaid, however, as increased British exchequer funding for St Patrick's Training College from 1891 allowed that institution in turn to repay loans it had received from general diocesan funds.[84]

After Walsh moved into his new home in October 1890, the first callers to sign their names in the visitor's book were a group of Jesuits from Gardiner Street, led by their provincial, Thomas Kenny SJ, and including William Delaney SJ, former president of University College, Dublin. Further distinguished visitors were received following the announcement of the verdict in the O'Shea divorce case in November, which occasioned a crisis in

80 Hague to Father Dennis Pettit, 1 Nov. 1890 (DDA, Walsh Papers).   81 Receipts and invoices (DDA, Walsh Papers).   82 Calculation based on receipts and invoices in the Walsh Papers.   83 Letter from 'Shamrock' to the editor of *John Bull*, 1 Mar. 1890 (DDA, Walsh Papers).   84 Walsh, *Walsh*, pp 501-4.

the leadership of the Irish Parliamentary Party.[85] Walsh had several interviews at Archbishop's House with Dr Joseph Edward Kenny MP, a staunch supporter of Parnell, and through him sought, unavailingly, to persuade Parnell to stand down as leader.[86] On 3 December 1890, Walsh hosted a meeting of the Irish episcopal standing committee in the library as the Irish Parliamentary Party was meeting in Committee Room 15 in the Palace of Westminster.[87] This was the first opportunity the Bishops had had to meet and adjudicate on the crisis, and a telegram which Walsh sent from Archbishop's House at the conclusion of the meeting neatly, if starkly, summarised their fuller statement to the press:

> Mr Parnell unfit for leadership, first of all on moral grounds, social and personal discredit as a result of divorce court proceedings, also in view of inevitable disruption, with defeat at elections, wreck of Home Rule hopes, and sacrifice of tenants' interests.[88]

In spite of this, in a bid to save the party from destruction, Walsh, unbeknownst to his fellow prelates, met with a representative of Parnell, Edward Byrne, editor of the *Freeman's Journal*, in the week leading up to the bitterly fought Kilkenny by-election in mid-December 1890.[89] However, the resulting proposals proved impossible for Parnell to accept.[90] This extraordinary *démarche* on the part of the 'lone wolf' archbishop demonstrated his political naivety and willingness to embark alone upon a risky, if secret, undertaking. It also showed his keen appreciation of what was at stake for nationalist Ireland and his remarkable residual goodwill towards Parnell himself. [91] As the political drama continued to unfold, Walsh consulted with senior figures on the anti-Parnellite side at his home in Drumcondra.[92] The Parnell 'Split' was the first of many episodes in recent Irish history in which Archbishop's House would witness important scenes and play host to leading players on the political stage.

Three-quarters of a century after his death, the place of Archbishop Walsh in Irish history is assured. In the ecclesiastical sphere, he was the outstand-

---

85 See Larkin, *Fall*, chapter 5.   86 Walsh diary, 1890 (DDA, Walsh Papers); Larkin, *Fall*, pp 213-14 and 216.   87 In calling this meeting of the Standing Committee, Walsh was, for the first time, utilising powers conferred upon him by the hierarchy in October 1890 (Larkin, *Fall*, p. 220).   88 DDA, Walsh Papers.   89 Walsh diary, 1890 (DDA, Walsh Papers).   90 Manuscript entitled 'Notes of conversation, 16 Dec. 1890' (DDA, Walsh Papers).   91 Frank Callanan, *The Parnell split 1890-91* (Cork, 1992), pp 55-9; F.S.L. Lyons, *Charles Stewart Parnell* (London, 1978), pp 540-1.   92 These included the following members of the Irish Parliamentary party: William Martin Murphy, T.M. Healy, T.D. Sullivan, E.D. Gray, P.A. Chance, John Dillon, Henry Gill and David Sheehy (DDA, Walsh Papers, diaries for 1890, 1891 and 1892).

ing personality of his day in the Roman Catholic Church in Ireland. In the political sphere, he made a significant contribution to the birth of the Irish nation-state. Perhaps the most overlooked aspect of his legacy is the 'brick palace' at Drumcondra. With the erection of Archbishop's House, Dublin became one of the first Roman Catholic dioceses in Ireland to settle on a fixed and appropriate episcopal residence. This provided an essential pre-requisite for the upholding of the dignity of the episcopal office, for the good administration of the diocese, and for the continuity of preservation of the diocesan archives. It was a significant achievement that had eluded Walsh's predecessors and that proved a boon to his successors in office. The building of Archbishop's House brought an end to a long era of peripatetic archiepiscopal wanderings in Dublin and laid the foundation for the later development of a sophisticated curial bureaucracy to serve the changing needs of an expanding archdiocese.

Today, the imposing edifice on 'Drumcondra Hill', half-hidden amidst mature trees above a busy approach road to Dublin city, is a familiar land-mark to the citizens of the capital. Recently restored, refurbished and rid of the harmful, if character-enhancing, embrace of a Virginia creeper, it is now in appearance much as it must first have looked when built a century ago – a lasting testament to the vision of one archbishop and the accomplishment of another.

15

The religious life of the Catholic laity of Dublin, 1920-40

Maurice Hartigan

The religious zeal of the Catholic laity of Dublin city in the modern era was at its strongest during the 1920s and 1930s when the impact of the so-called 'devotional revolution' of the nineteenth century and the augmented pastoral capacity of the Church were at their height. The scale and depth of popular devotion was manifested most spectacularly by the mass displays of religious fervour that took place during the centenary celebrations of Catholic Emancipation in 1929 and the Eucharistic Congress in 1932, but the 1920s and 1930s in Dublin also witnessed a sustained attempt to forge a co-ordinated Catholic Action movement. This was spearheaded by a revived Catholic Young Men's Society, a newly-formed Legion of Mary, an expanded Society of St Vincent de Paul and recently established Catholic scout and guide organisations. Underpinning these organisational developments was the continued consolidation and reinforcement by the Church of the devotional command it had established over its people since the mid-nineteenth century.

In broad terms, with the exception of the growth of pilgrimages, the retreat movement and the initiation of new cults such as that centred on Matt Talbot, popular devotional practice among the Catholics of Dublin differed little after 1920 from what had gone before. Taking attendance at Sunday Mass as the basic measures of religiosity among Catholics, the annual reports of the Society of St Vincent de Paul suggest that non-attendance was the exception rather than the rule. In the course of its visitation work, the Society encountered city poor whose religious practice was irregular. Their number is difficult to quantify, but reliable evidence that the non-practice or irregular practice of the faith was unusual among those with whom the society dealt is provided by its report for 1931. In a year in which it carried out 70,000 visits in Dublin, only seven city conferences out of seventy-seven reported instances of irregular practice, and only one reported on a case of persistent non-attendance at Sunday Mass.[1] Moreover, where such lapses in prac-

1 *Report of the Council of Ireland 1931* (Dublin, 1932), p. 73.

tice did occur, the Society was usually successful bringing them to an end through intensive visitation and through close liaison with parish clergy after which recalcitrants frequently enrolled in local sodalities.

SODALITIES AND CONFRATERNITIES

It was among the sodalities and confraternities that the more devotionally active of the Catholic laity of Dublin was to be found. These had been established for the most part as part of the reorganisation of the Catholic Church that took place in the nineteenth century, and those organised by religious orders proved to be the strongest and most influential. On the city's northside, the Jesuits at St Francis Xavier's, Lower Gardiner Street, the Dominicans at St Saviour's, Dominic Street, and the Vincentians at St Peter's, Phibsborough held sway. On the south side, the Franciscans at Merchant's Quay, the Augustinians of John's Lane and the Carmelites of Whitefriar Street were equally dominant.

At St Francis Xavier's, the Jesuits were responsible for a number of specialist sodalities which catered for, among others, groups such as civic guards and night workers. One exception is the Working Men's Sodality, and it offers some insight into sodality life under the Jesuits. Founded in 1872 under the auspices of Cardinal Cullen to counteract the influence of Fenianism in Dublin, like all sodalities its chief purpose was to ensure the regular attendance of its members at the sacraments. No figures are available as to its membership until 1939, when it numbered nine hundred.[2] We have less information on the other sodalities based at St Francis Xavier's, but it is clear that these generated a high level of devotion at Gardiner Street church since it alone had 450,000 communicants in 1928.[3]

In nearby St Saviour's, the Dominicans also played host to a number of confraternities and sodalities; the most significant of which were the Holy Name Sodality and the Rosary Confraternity. Both of these were open to men and women but, in practice, the men of the locality joined the Holy Name and the women joined the Rosary Confraternity. The Holy Name Sodality was founded by Father Joseph Slattery OP in 1884 and it had 1,800 members by the 1920s.[4] It reached its peak in 1934 when 3,000 members marched to celebrate its Golden Jubilee.[5] The Rosary Confraternity also possessed a large membership, but the lack of records precludes any analysis of

2 Minute Book, Men's Sodality (St Francis Xavier's Church, Gardiner Street). The figure is based on statistics put before general meeting of prefects, 23 Jan. 1939.   3 *Irish Jesuit Directory*, 1928, p. 99.   4 *Irish Catholic*, 20 Sept. 1924 p. 6.   5 Chronicon Conventus SS Salvatoris, 9 Sept. 1934 (St Saviour's Church, Dublin).

its activities.[6] Members of both groups were also enrolled in the White Star League founded by Father Finbar Ryan OP to encourage respect for the Holy Name and to eliminate profane speech. In addition, for those who wished to sample the rigours of religious life there was the St Saviour's Chapter of Brothers which was affiliated to the Dominican Third Order. No register is existent for this body but it seems to have been small. Successful sodalities were also established at St Saviour's for children: the Imeldist Sodality for girls and the Angelic Warfare Sodality for boys catered for some 1,600 members in 1933.[7]

The Vincentians at St Peter's, Phibsborough, operated successful sodalities and confraternities in the form of the Archconfraternity of the Sacred Heart and St Patrick's Juvenile Temperance Sodality. Of the two, the Archconfraternity was the more significant. One of the pioneer confraternities in Ireland (it was formally established in 1874), it grew out of the need that the Vincentians identified to consolidate the work of the parish missions by securing regular attendance by the laity at the sacraments. Although established throughout the British Isles, it was particularly strong in Phibsborough where, in 1924, it had an estimated membership of 4,000 men and women.[8] St Patrick's Temperance Sodality also had a strong following, with a membership of between 1,600 and 1,800 in 1938.[9]

On the south side of the city, sodality and confraternity life flourished in the churches of the Carmelites, Augustinians and Franciscans. In the absence of relevant records, it is difficult to comment for certain on their membership, but the Grand Carmelite Confraternity based in Whitefriar Street was a significant organisation; figures for the 1950s indicate forty sodality guilds for women, with thirty members each.[10] It is a similar story with the Augustinians at St John's Lane.[11] No figures for memberships are available for groups such as the Archconfraternity of the Cincture, the Knights of the Shrine of Our Lady of Good Counsel, the Sacred Heart Sodality or the

<hr />

6 *St Saviour's Church, Dublin – centenary 1861-1961* (Dublin, 1961), p.22. This provides information on the background of the sodalities and confraternities at St Saviour's. The main sources for the members are the registers at St Saviour's. These include: The Register of the Confraternity of the Holy Rosary of the Blessed Virgin; Societatas SS Nominis Dei Catalogus Generalis; Tertiariorium SOP Catalogus; Societatis Militiae Angelicae Catalogus. 7 Chronicon Conventus SS Salvatoris, 22 Oct. 1933. 8 *Irish Catholic*, 5 July 1924 p. 5. 9 Minute Book of Temperance Sodality, St Peter's, Phibsborough, 1932-1959 (Vincentian Archives, 4 Cabra Road, Dublin). 10 Figures compiled from the Minute Book, Grand Carmelite Confraternity (Carmelite Archives, Whitefriar Street). 11 The main source for the John's Lane Confraternities is Thomas C. Butler OSA, *History of John's Lane Augustinians in Dublin 1280-1980* (Dublin, 1983). There are no records for the period 1920 to 1940 in the Augustinian archives in the Provincial House, Ballyboden.

Augustinian Third Order. Fortunately the records of the Franciscan Third Order at Merchant's Quay survive and allow a clearer picture to be established of sodality and confraternity life during the 1920s and 1930s.

The Franciscan Third Order at Merchant's Quay had both a brothers' branch and a sisters' branch, drawn mainly from the working class of the city. It is difficult to calculate its appeal, but figures placed before the council of the order in January 1937 indicate a membership of 1,877.[12] The number of professions to the brothers' branch certainly grew steadily between 1920 and 1937 (Table 1). This pattern was replicated by the sisters' branch which expanded significantly during the 1930s. The 3,000 members that attended monthly devotions at Merchant's Quay in 1937 had climbed to 3,511 by 1939.[13]

Table 1: Professions – Franciscan Third Order Brothers 1920-1937[14]

1920	16	1926	215
1921	20	1927	211
1922	47	1928-34	n/a
1923	40	1935	239
1924	79	1936	148
1925	135	1937	35 (first quarter)

Both branches of the Third Order were governed by their own elected councils and by spiritual directors appointed by the Franciscans. In practice, as with other sodalities and confraternities, it was the spiritual director who had the final say in all matters. Tertiaries were expected to obey the rule of the Third order which involved reciting the Divine Office daily or, if this was not possible, the Office of the Twelve Paters and Aves. In general, discipline at Merchant's Quay was satisfactory, as the Franciscan visitor Father Jerome OFM observed in 1937. No doubt this was a factor behind the healthy growth of the Third Order. Its members were attracted by what it had to offer in the way of devotion and opportunities for personal sanctification. Membership of an order within the church was very attractive to the more devout among the Dublin laity. Significantly, in August 1936, the council of the sisters' branch noted that 'a large number of our sisters have left the order to join different convents '.[15]

12 Minute Book of the Council Meetings (Brothers), Third Order of St Francis, council meeting, 2 May 1937 (Franciscan Archives, Merchant's Quay, Dublin). 13 Council meeting, 12 Feb. 1937, 9 Jan. 1939. 14 Figures compiled from Congregational Book of Third Order Brothers, Merchant's Quay. 15 Ibid., Council meeting, 25 Aug. 1936.

Although sodalities were attached to all parish churches in Dublin city, diocesan records for the 1920s and 1930s cast little additional light on their activities or membership. The only exceptions are the parishes of St James (James' Street) and St Michan's (Halston Street) for which figures exist for 1932 (see Table 2).

Table 2: Parish Sodality membership –
St Michan's and St James' Parishes, 1932

St Michan's[16]

Men's Sodality of Sacred Heart	700
Women's Sodality of Sacred Heart	800
Boys' Sodality of Sacred Heart	900
Girls' Sodality of Sacred Heart	800

St James[17]

Men's Sodality of Sacred Heart	400
Women's Sodality of Sacred Heart	510
Boys' Sodality of Sacred Heart	592
Girls' Sodality of Sacred Heart	300
Christian Doctrine Confraternity	40

As Table 2 shows, parish sodalities could be significant bodies. However, caution must be exercised in attributing such figures to sodalities in general given the fitful nature of the surviving records. Nonetheless, it is clear that the sodalities active in Dublin between 1920 and 1940 attracted significant numbers into their ranks. When the combined confraternities of the city attended the official opening of the Lourdes Grotto at Inchicore in 1930, they numbered 6,000.[18]

The 1920s and 1930s were probably the last decades when the sodalities and confraternities of Dublin grew and flourished. They were certainly in decline by the 1950s, as the dispersal of the city population to the new working class suburbs that were constructed in the late 1940s and early 1950s cut off many of the laity, especially the more devotionally inclined, from the religious orders which were the mainstay of the confraternity movement in Dublin. Some orders moved to the suburbs in the 1970s but by then it was too late to revive either confraternities or sodalities. The impact of the Second Vatican Council, the introduction of television into Ireland and the embrace of a secular youth culture made it an impossibility.

16 Maurice Hartigan, 'The Catholic laity of Dublin 1920-1940' (Ph.D. thesis, St Patrick's College, Maynooth, 1992), p. 361.   17 Ibid., p. 366.   18 *Standard*, 17 May 1930, p. 5.

DEVOTIONS POPULAR AMONG THE LAITY

Confraternities and sodalities apart, how did ordinary Catholics express their faith? A useful insight into popular devotion can be provided by tabulating the promises submitted to the *Irish Messenger of the Sacred Heart* as thanksgivings for favours granted. Table 3 provides a national perspective for the period August 1927-July 1928, but there is no reason to believe the pattern was different in Dublin.

Table 3: Promises of good works sent to Irish Messenger
August 1927-July 1928[19]

Preference	Devotion	Totals	per cent of Total
1	Visit to Blessed Sacrament	644,750	20.26
2	Hour of Silence	480,998	15.11
3	Weekday Mass	379,670	11.93
4	Rosary	368,526	11.58
5	Spiritual Communion	354,166	11.13
6	Act of Charity	273,804	8.60
7	Stations of the Cross	201,502	6.33
8	Holy Communion	197,025	6.19
9	Spiritual Reading	179,570	5.64
10	Visit to the Poor	62,470	1.96
11	Work for the Poor	38,810	1.21

What it reveals is that visits to the Blessed Sacrament were far more common than the receiving of communion, which suggests that prayer in the presence of the Eucharist was seen as more spiritually satisfying than receiving the Eucharist itself. Furthermore, it also reveals that the laity preferred to demonstrate their faith through prayer and devotions rather than through acts of charity. This was in spite of the deeper awareness of social issues prompted by the growth of the Catholic Action Movement in Dublin after 1920.

DEVOTION TO THE SACRED HEART

For the Catholics of Dublin, devotion to the Sacred Heart of Jesus was a vital part of their religious lives, as a visitor to the tenements of the city during the 1920s confirms:

19 *Irish Messenger of the Sacred Heart*, Aug. 1927-July 1928.

I went into some of the rooms. One of them, I remember, was full of girls. God knows what they did or how they lived; through the mixture of unclean clothes and scraps of linen drying from strings, one could see the glow of a broken red lamp. There was a picture of the Sacred Heart behind it![20]

This devotion was given organisational form in the shape of sodalities and confraternities dedicated to the Sacred Heart, and they demonstrated their public confidence in 1925 by launching a campaign to have a permanent statue to the Sacred Heart erected in O'Connell Street.[21] On 3 June that year, 1,452 members of the Confraternity of the Sacred Heart and Apostleship of Prayer assembled in O'Connell Street, following the conclusion of the annual novena to the Sacred Heart at St Francis Xavier's, Gardiner Street, to recite the act of Consecration to the Sacred Heart. Each year thereafter, a similar gathering, led by the brothers William J. and Francis X. Larkin, the chief instigators of the campaign, took place at the same location and prayers were said for the building of a statue of the Sacred Heart. No subscription list was ever opened because the promoters expected the state or municipal authorities to be prompted by their show of enthusiasm and prayers to take the initiative. In the meantime, they erected a small temporary statue on Upper O'Connell Street.

The Sacred Heart statue campaign climaxed in the summer of 1930. In that year, on a number of consecutive Monday evenings, the Larkins and their supporters marched in procession from the temporary statue on O'Connell Street to churches about the city. Beginning on 7 July, they visited St Francis Xavier's, the Pro-Cathedral and Our Lady of Lourdes in Gloucester Street. On 14 July, they targeted Church Street, Adam and Eve's and SS Michael and John's. And, finally, on 21 July, they visited St Audoen's, the Augustinian church in Thomas Street, and St Nicholas of Myra's in Francis Street. Despite, or maybe because of, the previous gathering held for this purpose, the numbers that took part were distinctly modest with women, significantly, outnumbering men.

It was at this time also that the Larkins organised a pilgrimage to Matt Talbot's grave in Glasnevin to appeal for his intercession for their campaign. Both had known him through the Apostleship of Prayer based at St Francis Xavier's. The procession that took place on 27 July 1930 was the first such pilgrimage to Talbot's grave, and it is significant that no clergy took part,

---

20 Extract from John Gibbons, *Tramping through Ireland,* quoted in *Capuchin Annual* (1938), p. 87.   21 The files of the *Irish Catholic* represent the main source of material on the campaign conducted by the Larkin brothers to have a statue dedicated to the Sacred Heart built in O'Connell Street.

since autonomous lay activity was rare at the time. The Larkins and their supporters sustained their campaign throughout the 1930s, but without any real prospect of success. For most of the Dublin laity the Sacred Heart was a devotion which belonged in the church and in the home, not on the streets. The Larkins also failed because their obsessive campaign made then appear as religious cranks.

The Larkins' failure notwithstanding, devotion to the Sacred Heart remained strong. This is most vividly illustrated by the decision of the people of Gray Street, St Catherine's parish, to erect a small statue to the Sacred Heart beneath the canopy of a disused drinking fountain during the Catholic Emancipation centenary celebrations in 1929. Later, it was replaced by a full size statue set permanently in place. Like the 'temporary' statue in O'Connell Street, the Gray Street statue became an important local landmark and a visible reminder of the popularity of the devotion it was erected to honour.

MARIAN DEVOTION

As well as the strong devotion to the Sacred Heart, devotion to Mary was also alive in Dublin. This took many forms, of which the saying of the Rosary (especially during May and October, the two months most associated with Mary), the foundation by Frank Duff of the Legion of Mary in 1925, and the enthusiasm with which the laity responded to the building of a grotto by the Oblates at Inchicore are the most significant.

Frank Duff is an extreme example of an individual who chose to immerse himself in devotion to Mary. Yet he is not untypical of the impact which this devotion had upon some of the laity. The key influence in shaping his devotional outlook was the mariology of Saint Louis Marie Grignon de Montfort, particularly his *True devotion to the Blessed Virgin* and *The secret of Mary*. It was this, together with the appeal of de Montfort's teaching for a small group of women members of the Pioneer Total Abstinence Association whom he encountered at Myra House, which prompted him to form an Association of Our Lady of Mercy in 1921. This was the forerunner of the Legion of Mary which came into being four years later. This is not the place to write of the Legion's impact on prostitution in Dublin during the early years of its foundation, or of the hostility it encountered from Archbishop Edward Byrne and other senior churchmen between 1927 and 1935.[22] Nonetheless, these events are significant since they demonstrate that the survival and success of this organisation, in the face of vigorous opposition, owed

22 For an account of the Legion of Mary's early years and its difficulties with Archbishop Byrne see Hartigan, 'The Catholic Laity', chapter 6.

much to the fact that it was grafted on to an already strong devotion to Mary among the laity of Dublin.

An indication of the strength of Marian devotion in Dublin can be provided by the attraction of pilgrimages to Marian shrines. For a laity long accustomed to reciting the rosary and familiar with the Marian devotional literature produced by the Dominicans, Oblates and Jesuits, this was a natural progression in the manifestation of their faith in Mary. The problem was to secure an acceptable focus for this devotion. It is true that Lourdes was already well established within Catholic Dublin's imagination as the premier Marian shrine and that its fame and reputation were reinforced following the canonisation of St Bernadette in 1933. However, a visit to Lourdes was not a realistic option for the majority of the Catholic laity of Dublin. There were Irish national pilgrimages in 1913 and 1924 to Knock, County Mayo, but this suffered from the serious handicap of not enjoying episcopal sanction. Despite this, many Dublin pilgrims made the journey. Indeed, it may well be that a pilgrimage to the shrine organised by the St Michan's conference of St Vincent de Paul in Dublin in 1929 encouraged Archbishop Gilmartin of Tuam to give devotion at Knock his conditional approval.[23] Certainly, the evident desire of the Dublin laity for Marian worship caused Father Michael Sweeney, an Oblate based at Inchicore, to build what became known as the 'Irish Lourdes'.

Inspired by the fervour that he witnessed at the national pilgrimage to Lourdes in 1924, Father Sweeney undertook to build a full scale replica of the Massabiele grotto at Inchicore.[24] With the assistance of Brother Patrick McIntyre OMI, engineer for the project, and the free labour of men drawn from the Oblate confraternity and the nearby Great Southern Railway works,

---

23 See Catherine Rynne, *Knock 1879-1979* (Dublin, 1979) p. 131. Rynne shows that Archbishop Gilmartin chose the occasion of the first annual pilgrimage to Knock of the St Michan's conference of the Society of St Vincent de Paul to mark the first ever appearance of an archbishop of Tuam at the shrine during devotions there. Despite words of caution from the archbishop that his presence at Knock was not to be taken as giving official sanction 'to the apparition alleged to have taken place here fifty years ago', those present saw it as a move towards recognition of the legitimacy of devotion at the shrine. This was reflected in the growing popularity of Knock among lay pilgrims in the years that followed.   24 The Oblates have no documentary material appertaining to the construction of the 'Irish Lourdes'. Father Vincent Denny OMI proved to be a valuable source of information on the history of the Oblates at Inchicore. Mr Joe Sweeney was helpful with information on the building of the grotto and its effect on the local community. An important source is *The first fifty years* (Dublin, 1980), a booklet published to commemorate the jubilee of the opening of the grotto. The lack of documentary evidence can be attributed, in part at least, to the decision of Brother McIntyre to bury his plans for the scheme in the grotto.

the grotto was constructed at a cost of £6,000 and officially opened by Archbishop Edward Byrne on 11 May 1930 before a crowd of between 80,000 and 100,000 people.[25] In the week that followed, an estimated 5,000 prayed at the grotto daily, while in subsequent years significant numbers attended the annual novena in preparation for the feast of Our Lady of Lourdes each 11 February. During the 1932 novena, communion was distributed to 80,000 people, while a month later the *Lourdes Messenger* maintained that half a million people had prayed at the 'Irish Lourdes' since May 1930.[26] Attendance was boosted by the presence of seven overseas prelates at the Oblate house at Inchicore during the Eucharistic Congress in 1932, and by the upsurge in devotion to Bernadette of Lourdes following her canonisation in 1933. Imitation though the Inchicore grotto was, it proved to be a devotionally fulfilling experience for many.[27]

An important stimulus towards Marian devotion in Dublin and the country at large was the ready availability of Marian publications. The most notable of these were *Madonna* (1898), *Virgo Potens* (1922) and the *Lourdes Messenger* (1931). *Virgo Potens* was published by the Daughters of Charity, North William Street, and used to promote the Miraculous Medal Crusade. The Vincentians in Phibsborough also encouraged this devotion which originated with an apparition of Mary witnessed by Catherine Laboure at the chapel of the rue du Bac, Paris in 1830. *Madonna* was published by the Jesuits to promote the Sodality of Our Lady, more popularly known as the Children of Mary, while the *Lourdes Messenger* was launched by Father Michael Sweeney OMI to promote the 'Irish Lourdes' at Inchicore.

DEVOTION TO ST BRIGID

Marian devotion was paralleled by a devotion to St Brigid in certain parts of Dublin. Credit for this rests primarily with a group of priests attached to St Brigid's Chruch, Killester in the late 1920s. Father James McCarroll, Father Michael Troy and Father Thomas Traynor, through the offices of the Dominicans, successfully secured the return to Ireland from Portugal of a relic of St Brigid that purported to be a fragment of her skull. This led to an annual devotion to Brigid at Killester during which the relic was paraded through the church grounds.

In 1933, Father McCarroll was appointed parish priest of James' Street parish where he took further steps to promote devotion to Brigid. He commissioned a statue of her modelled on an Aran woman, and founded a group

25 *Irish Independent*, 12 May 1930, p. 8.   26 *Lourdes Messenger*, Mar. 1932, p. 79.   27 *Irish Catholic*, 11 July 1936, p. 3.

called the little Brigids composed of girls from the nearby Basin Lane School. About forty girls, each named Brigid, were involved. Each year, they formed a guard of honour on the occasion of Brigid's feast day (1 February), and participated in the annual pilgrimage to her birthplace at Faughart, County Louth. Some indication of the following this devotion had in Dublin is provided by the fact that 2,000 pilgrims made the journey from the capital in 1936.[28]

Among the more interesting features of popular devotion in Dublin during the period was the emergence of devotional cults centred on local figures of piety such as Matt Talbot, Father Charles of Mount Argus and Father John Sullivan SJ. The Talbot devotion, in particular, stands out for the speed with which it developed.

THE CULT OF MATT TALBOT

Matt Talbot was born in dire poverty at Aldborough Court, North Strand in 1856.[29] As a youth he was a casual labourer before he secured permanent work with the firm of T. & C. Martin, North Wall. During this time he developed a serious alcohol problem and in 1884 was prompted to take the pledge, following which he embarked on a life of prayer, fasting and self-mortification which he maintained until his sudden death in Granby Lane on 7 June 1925. When his body was taken to Jervis Street Hospital it was found to be bound with chains. During his lifetime he had few intimates, yet in a matter of years a cult of devotion grew up around him in Dublin. His emergence as a figure of devotional significance was aided and enhanced by a number of factors, of which the most important was his adoption by a number of influential champions.

Perhaps the most important was Sir Joseph Glynn, who, apart from being president of the Society of St Vincent de Paul, was a senior figure on the board of the CTSI. This gave him ready access to leading members of the hierarchy like Archbishop Harty of Cashel and leading politicians such as W.T. Cosgrave. Told of Talbot's religious life by one of his fellow sodalists at St Francis Xavier's, Glynn wrote a brief biography of him that sold 120,000 copies within two months of its publication in 1926. So great was the demand that Glynn published a larger life two years later that went through three printings in its first year. The intense interest in Glynn's biography both spurred on devotion to Matt Talbot and reflected a growing interest in him on the part of the laity.

28 *Irish Catholic*, 11 July 1936, p. 3.   29 See Mary Purcell, *Matt Talbot and his times* (Dublin, 1954).

Parallel with the publication of Glynn's pamphlet, a spontaneous devotion commenced at Talbot's grave in Glasnevin cemetery. This is attested to by an article in the *Standard* in June 1928, in which an unnamed correspondent wrote of making 'a pilgrimage to his grave'.[30] He also recalled visiting the grave in 1926 where he saw a tin box in which people left petitions. In the years that followed, Talbot's grave became a place of personal pilgrimage and prayer. The devotional cult that sprang from this high level of interest in the life and the perceived religious fervour of Matt Talbot was both fuelled and reinforced by a continuous stream of books, pamphlets and articles about him in the twenty or so years following his death. The most significant of these were Alice Curtayne's *Holy man of Dublin or the silence of Matt Talbot* (1936), an account of his life published in the *Capuchin Annual* in 1937, and Mary Purcell's biography, *Matt Talbot and his times*, which appeared in 1954.

The strength of domestic enthusiasm for the emerging cult of Matt Talbot was reinforced and given legitimacy by international interest. The Eucharistic Congress was particularly consequential in this respect since it brought overseas visitors to Dublin who were curious to know more. Of particular significance was Cardinal Verdier, archbishop of Paris, who visited and prayed in the tenement where Talbot had lived.

Clear evidence of the rapid growth and power of devotion to Talbot that developed in Dublin is provided by the swift response of the diocesan authorities. In 1931 Archbishop Byrne initiated a diocesan inquiry into his life, a mere six years after his death, citing his own personal admiration, the petitions he received and the evidence of widespread devotion to him here and in foreign lands as justification for his decision.[31]

FATHER CHARLES OF MOUNT ARGUS

Another cult figure popular with the Catholics of Dublin during this period was Father Charles of Mount Argus.[32] A priest of the Passionist order, he was born Andrew Houben in the Netherlands in 1821. He arrived in Dublin in 1857 where he developed a reputation for piety and healing of the sick. However, he was transferred to England in 1866, as the Church authorities became uneasy that his reputation was leading to abuses such as the sale of water that he had blessed. Eight years later he was sent back to Mount Argus where he remained until his death in 1893. The devotion that grew up around him in the later years of his life continued after his death, despite attempts by the Passionists

---

30 *Standard*, June 1928, p. 13.   31 Pastoral letter from Archbishop Byrne, 8 Nov. 1931, quoted in *Irish Directory*, 1932, pp 628-31.   32 For an account of his life see Dermot Carroll CP, *A knight of the crucified – Father Charles of Mount Argus* (Dublin, 1957).

to prevent people entering their cemetery at Mount Argus and praying at his grave. It was on foot of this devotion that the diocesan authorities decided in 1928 to initiate an inquiry into his life. In 1935 Pius XI signed the decree for the introduction of his cause and the start of the apostolic process. This was followed by the exhumation and examination of his remains in 1937.

Little documentary evidence is available to support an investigation into the cult of Father Charles, because of the success with which the Passionists played it down for nearly forty years following his death. Indeed, it was not until 1936 that official pilgrimages to his grave were organised. These offer some indication of the strength of the devotion. At the first pilgrimage in January of that year, 3,000 members of the combined confraternities of Dublin attended; and an estimated 6,000 took part at another in July.[33]

THE JESUITS: FATHER JOHN SULLIVAN, FATHER WILLIE DOYLE

Another figure in Dublin to excite devotional enthusiasm during the 1930s was the Jesuit, Father John Sullivan.[34] Born in Eccles Street, Dublin in 1861, he was the son of a mixed marriage: his father was a member of the Church of Ireland and his mother a Catholic. In accordance with the custom of the time, the male children of the marriage were brought up as Protestants and the females as Catholics. Accordingly, the young John Sullivan was educated at Portora Royal School, Enniskillen and in due course followed his father, Sir Edward Sullivan, into the legal profession and qualified as a barrister. However, he was so deeply impressed by the religious zeal of his mother that he converted to Catholicism in 1896 and subsequently entered the Jesuit order. In 1907, Archbishop Walsh ordained him to the priesthood after which he was appointed to the teaching staff of Clongowes Wood College, Clane, County Kildare where he spent most of his life. During this period, he gained a reputation in the surrounding area as a healer of the sick; people called upon him for help in much the same manner as they had appealed to Father Charles at Mount Argus. He died in 1933 at St Vincent's Nursing Home, Dublin, and contemporary accounts record the veneration in which he was held based on his reputation as a healer. His biographer, Fergal McGrath recalled in 1941 that on the day following his death:

> There was a continual stream of clergy and laity touching the body with rosaries and other pious objects. The nuns of a Carmelite

33 *Standard*, 10 Jan. 1936, p. 6; 11 July 1936, p. 6. 34 See Fergal McGrath, *Father John Sullivan SJ* (London, 1941).

Convent rang up and asked for a bit of bandage stained with blood from the operation. Some of the hospital students were found cutting off pieces of his hair.[35]

In the years that followed, devotion to him was particularly strong among the sick, who put great store by his relics. During the 1930s, there were reports from people who claimed they had been cured of serious illnesses by Father Sullivan's intercession. In 1941, Fergal McGrath cited a dozen or so such cases.

Another Jesuit to catch the laity's attention at this time was the war chaplain Father Willie Doyle SJ, who was killed near Ypres in 1917.[36] However, his following was limited to those who came into contact with the Jesuits at St Francis Xavier's, Gardiner Street. Indeed, it may be going too far to describe his following as a cult or devotion at all. A pioneer in providing retreats for workingmen in Dublin and a courageous and selfless chaplain on the battlefields of France where he administered the sacraments to wounded soldiers, Father Doyle had the makings of a figure of devotion. Although a successful biography by Alfred O'Rahilly had reached a fourth edition by 1930, he never enjoyed the same cult status of Father Sullivan or Matt Talbot. It would seem that part at least of the explanation for this lies in the politics of the time. The fact that Doyle's deeds of sanctity occurred in a war which was regarded with little favour in newly-independent Ireland contributed to his limited appeal.

THE BLESSING OF THE THROATS AT MERCHANT'S QUAY

A more time-honoured devotion, popular among the Catholic laity, was the annual celebration of the feast of St Blaise on 3 February. This was marked in Dublin, as in a number of other European countries, by the blessing of throats. St Blaise was an Armenian bishop, martyred in 317 AD, who was reputed to have saved a child from choking on a bone stuck in his throat, hence his invocation for all maladies of the throat. The devotion in Dublin was particularly popular at the Franciscan Church, Merchant's Quay. There the laity, on the day of the feast, brought strips of red flannel and bottles of olive oil to the church that they held aloft to be blessed along with scarves and mufflers. This was then followed by the blessing of the throats of all those present by the placing of two crossed candles in front of each individual. Later, the flannel was dipped into the oil and distributed among the sick. One observer present at the ceremony in February 1934 described it thus:

35 Ibid., p. 252.   36 See Alfred O'Rahilly, *Father William Doyle SJ* (London, 1930) and *Merry in God* (New York, 1939).

The Franciscan church was packed to the doors and from eight o'clock onwards a continual stream of people kept coming, everybody carrying a parcel of flannel and a bottle of oil. Some of them had enough flannel to make an entire costume. The poorer the owner the bigger the parcel, a lovely revelation of the generosity of those who have least; for the more flannel they brought to have blessed, the more they had to give to those in trouble.[37]

There is little doubt but that the popularity of this devotion, particularly among the poor, was really a reflection of the adverse social and economic conditions prevalent in Dublin during the 1920s and 1930s.

DEVOTION TO ST ANNE AT ST AUDOEN'S

An old devotion that was revived during this time was to St Anne, the mother of Mary. In 1923, Father Butler of St Audoen's, High Street attempted to revive this pre-reformation tradition by having a shrine built in the saint's honour at St Audoen's. That this was well received by the laity was revealed in 1926 when the *Irish Catholic* noted the 'large and ever increasing numbers [that go] to this ancient and popular devotion'.[38] Further evidence of a growth in the cult was attested to by the many letters of thanksgiving pinned to a board inside St Audoen's listing favours received which were attributed to the intercession of St Anne. However, the impact of the devotion seems to have been confined to the general district around High Street and there is little reference to it after 1926.

It is clear that devotions initiated by the diocesan clergy, such as those to St Anne and to St Brigid at Killester and James' Street, never enjoyed the same success as those initiated by the religious orders, such as the 'Irish Lourdes' at Inchicore. This was perhaps inevitable given the greater promotional resources that the orders had at their disposal, the devotional literature they published and their access to the wider laity through their involvement in parish retreats and missions.

MISSIONS AND RETREATS

Indeed, it was through parish missions that the clergy sought most vigorously to encourage a wider participation on the part of the laity in the practise of the faith. Parish missions in Ireland date from November 1842, when

37 *Irish Independent*, 9 Feb. 1934, p. 5.   38 *Irish Catholic*, 31 July 1926, p. 5.

the Vincentians inaugurated the phenomenon in Athy, County Kildare. Used by the clergy to establish devotion among the laity in the nineteenth century, they were a vital means for renewing religious favour by the 1920s. During Lent each year, missioners visited parishes in order to encourage the spiritually slack as well as the devotionally committed. In Dublin folk memory, parish missions are commonly perceived as occasions of fear, as Eamon Mac Thomais' description of them in the 1930s attests:

> And to chase the Devil out of the parish the missioners were coming. The first week for women, the second week for men, and the boys and girls in between. The missioners were the order priests. There was always a big missioner and a little missioner, or a fat missioner and a skinny missioner, or a funny missioner and a missioner that no one liked. I often remember being glued to the seat in the chapel, half-afraid to go home in case Old Nick, the Devil himself, was waiting outside to grab me. It was always the funny fella who roared like a bull and made the hairs stand out on the back of my neck. The final night of the mission we all bought a candle for shilling to renounce the world, the flesh and the Devil. Old Nick got it that night.[39]

Missioners were drawn mainly from the ranks of the Redemptorists, Jesuits, Vincentians, Franciscans, Capuchins and Dominicans. The appeal that the parish mission held for the laity is attested by the fact that they were generally well attended. The men's mission at Westland Row in 1930 attracted 4,000; 5,000 were present at the men's mission at the Pro-Cathedral in 1936, while in 1933 over 10,000 communion hosts were distributed during the men's and women's missions in the same church.[40] It was during this period also that a tradition developed whereby on the concluding night of the Pro-Cathedral mission, the men of the parish marched in procession to Archbishop's House in Drumcondra, as they accompanied their parish priest, Archbishop Byrne, to his home. Not alone did this demonstrate loyalty to the archbishop; it also reveals the emotional fervour which missions frequently engendered.

For those among the Dublin laity in search of further spiritual renewal there was also the option of enclosed retreats. During the 1920s, these were provided by the Jesuits at Milltown Park and Rathfarnham Castle. Milltown offered retreat facilities for the Catholic middle class in that it played host to groups drawn from the Land Commission, past pupils of Belvedere

39 Eamon MacThomais, *Janey Mack me shirt is black* (Dublin, 1982), p. 29.   40 *Irish Catholic Directory*, 1936, p. 595.

College, University College Dublin, the Knights of St Columbanus and the legal profession. Rathfarnham Castle, by contrast, focused on groups from the Dublin working class.

It was Father Willie Doyle who first proposed that a house of retreat be established for Dublin workingmen. The Jesuits purchased Rathfarnham Castle at a cost of £17,000 and had it converted into a retreat house in March 1922. Notwithstanding the difficulties caused in Dublin that summer by the Civil War, week-end retreats commenced immediately. In the first sixteen months of its existence, sixty-nine retreats were attended by 2,472 men; by 1933, 21,360 men had been on retreat at Rathfarnham.[41]

While the level of spiritual commitment varied among individuals, the outward practice of the Catholic faith remained identifiably strong among the laity of Dublin during the 1920s and 1930s. During the Eucharistic Congress in 1932, G.K. Chesterton cited the enthusiasm with which the Dublin poor decorated their tenements as evidence of their attachment to their religion.[42] This was a manifestation of an attitude of mind that regarded religious observance as integral to daily life, as Father John Rowe observed in 1938:

> The most 'unexpected' thing in Dublin to strange eyes is to see the churches crowded, not only on Sundays, but on weekdays, and the rich praying with the poor, and the men praying as well as the women. It is an inspiration to see a Dublin man on his way to work saying his prayers unconcernedly in the morning rain.[43]

It is true that occasionally there were complaints that things were not as they had been. One contributor to the *Irish Catholic* in November 1923 felt that there had been a decline in reverence during the previous decade:

> Many do not wait for the conclusion of Mass, and the Benediction, a still larger number are well underway for the door while the Gloria is being sung.[44]

But such complaints were more the exception than the rule. In general it was accepted that the laity adhered to the practice of the faith and attended at Mass and the sacraments faithfully and in large numbers. Indeed, it has been argued that they tended to view religion primarily in terms of devotional practise, and that this explains the failure of Catholic Action to emerge as a

---

41 Figures compiled from *Irish Jesuit Directory*, 1922-33.   **42** G.K. Chesterton, *Christendom in Ireland* (London, 1932), p. 16.   **43** *Capuchin Annual*, 1938, p. 85.   **44** *Irish Catholic*, 3 Nov. 1923, p. 2.

powerful movement in Ireland during this period. However, although autonomous activity on the part of the laity in the area of devotion was far from
the norm, among Dublin Catholics it was not non-existent. It can be seen in
the popular cults attached to Father Charles of Mount Argus, Matt Talbot
and Father John Sullivan SJ, and in the campaign to have a statue to the
Sacred Heart erected in O' Connell Street.

16

John Charles McQuaid, archbishop of Dublin, 1940-72

Deirdre McMahon

In his seminal study *Church and state in modern Ireland 1923-1979*, John Whyte, who interviewed Archbishop McQuaid for his book, described him, with some understatement, as the 'most talked-about Irish prelate of his time'.[1] Whyte's judicious treatment of McQuaid's career contrasts with the crude caricatures of hidebound Catholic reaction with which McQuaid has become identified since his death in 1973. He did not expect much from history. 'History in the modern sense', he declared in his celebrated 1953 address to the Eucharistic Congress in Sydney, 'is incapable of filling the intellectual soul of man when it is divorced from a philosophy that can truly interpret events and character'.[2] On other occasions he variously described history as 'the cold construction of past events' and 'the sad recital of the gradual corruption of man's natural inclination to worship the Supreme Being'.[3] For McQuaid modern history was symbolised by the French Revolution which he regarded 'in itself and in its effects [as] one of the most disastrous cataclysms of human history'.[4]

McQuaid expected even less from biography. In 1955, on the occasion of the Catholic University centenary, he gave a sermon during which he spoke with evident empathy about his distinguished predecessor, Cardinal Cullen. 'No writer', stated McQuaid, 'has done adequate justice to his character or stature ... Silent, magnanimous, farseeing, Cardinal Cullen would seem to be as heedless of self-justification after death, as he was intrepid in administration during life. Not his the multitude of letters and scrupulous autobiography that help a later age to reconstruct the picture of the unspeaking

1 J.H. Whyte, *Church and state in modern Ireland 1923-1979* (2nd ed. Dublin, 1980), p. 75. 2 'The influence of Europe on Australia', 20 April 1953. This is reprinted in a collection of McQuaid's pastorals and addresses, *Wellsprings of the faith* (Dublin, 1956), p. 218. 3 *The Holy Rosary* (Dublin, 1947) p. 11; *The Church's worship* (Dublin, 1956), p. 4. 4 *What is a General Council?* (Dublin, 1963), p. 12.

dead.'[5] The recent decision to open Dr McQuaid's papers will help historians to remedy this biographical deficiency.[6] The McQuaid archive reveals the extraordinary range of his work within the diocese and also sheds valuable new light on the post-independence Catholic Church, about which too little is known but far too much that is ill-informed has been written. McQuaid's papers are extensive and at the time of writing are still in the process of release, so this essay offers only an introduction to the main areas of his work inside and outside the diocese. Several areas of that work – health and social welfare, emigrant welfare, education – are so extensive that they deserve separate studies of their own. Church-state relations, which have been discussed in some detail elsewhere, have for the most part been excluded from this essay.

CAREER AND APPOINTMENT

McQuaid was born in Cootehill, County Cavan, in 1895, and was educated at St Patrick's College, Cavan, and later at Blackrock College and Clongowes where one of his teachers was Joseph P. Walshe, later the first Secretary of the Department of External Affairs. Of St Patrick's he later commented that he was not happy there 'but if I were to record the barbarities practised in most boys' boarding schools at that time, I might fly the country'.[7] Despite his negative memories, he later gave several large donations to St Patrick's. McQuaid entered the Holy Ghost novitiate at Kimmage Manor in 1913 and was professed in 1914. Since the Holy Ghost Order was a missionary order, McQuaid must have expected his vocation to lie in mission work but this was not to be. While at Kimmage Manor he studied at University College Dublin from where he graduated in 1917 with first class honours in Ancient Classics. The following year he was awarded a first class honours MA for a thesis on the Roman philosopher Seneca and also studied for the Higher

5 *Wellsprings of the faith*, p. 209.   6 At the time of writing there exists only one biography of McQuaid, a brief paperback *John Charles McQuaid: the man and the mask* written by the late John Feeney in 1974. In 1965, *Studies* published a tribute to McQuaid on the occasion of his silver jubilee which gave an overview of his life and career. In 1972-3, the late Mary Purcell interviewed McQuaid about his early years for a projected biography which never appeared. Her notes of these interviews are in his papers in the Dublin Diocesan Archives (henceforth DDA). In 1973, shortly after McQuaid's death, RTE Radio broadcast a valuable two-part documentary, 'McQuaid, Servant of God', on McQuaid's life and career which is in the RTE Sound Archives. In 1998 RTE Television broadcast a two-part documentary on McQuaid which focused on his life and career as revealed by the release of his papers.   7 Biographical notes by Mary Purcell (DDA, McQuaid Papers).

Diploma in Education. He then went to Rome where he took a doctorate in theology at the Gregorian University. He was ordained in 1924 and had just embarked on further post-graduate studies in oriental languages when he was recalled to Blackrock in November 1925 to take over as dean of studies.

He soon attracted attention. In 1929, he was a special delegate to the Department of Education's commission on the teaching of English. In 1930, he was the official delegate of the Catholic Headmasters' Association at the first international congress on free secondary education in Brussels, and attended in the same capacity at later congresses in The Hague, Luxembourg and Fribourg. In 1931 he became president of Blackrock, a post he held until 1939. He was also elected chairman of the Catholic Headmasters' Association and remained in that post until 1940. He was a popular teacher at Blackrock, where he had the reputation of being strict but fair. His classes were long remembered by former pupils in whom McQuaid sought to imbue not only his love of classics and the English language but also an understanding of the visual arts.

On his appointment as archbishop in 1940, McQuaid was only forty-five and was one of the youngest members of the hierarchy.[8] The appointment of a priest from the ranks of the regular clergy occasioned considerable surprise, not least because he was the first since John Thomas Troy in 1786. With the release of files from the Department of External Affairs it is now known (and was suspected at the time) that the taoiseach, Eamon de Valera, and the secretary of the department, Joseph P. Walshe, pressed McQuaid's candidacy on the Vatican where, as the Irish minister at the Vatican reported to Dublin, 'the need for a person of no ordinary attainments and character is realised as they realise the defects of the last incumbent, owing to ill health'.[9] McQuaid was a long-standing friend of the de Valera family; de Valera's sons attended Blackrock College and he advised de Valera on the 1937 constitution. However, he also possessed an outstanding reputation as a Catholic educationalist and had already been mentioned as a potential bishop of his native diocese of Kilmore.[10] It is doubtful whether the Vatican needed much persuasion to appoint McQuaid whose formidable adminis-

8 McQuaid and Michael Browne were the youngest members of the hierarchy. Browne, who was five months younger than McQuaid, was appointed bishop of Galway in 1937. 9 Dermot Keogh, *Ireland and the Vatican: the politics and diplomacy of Church-state relations, 1922-1960* (Cork, 1995), pp 145-46.   10 For McQuaid's time at Blackrock, see Sean P. Farragher CSSP, *Dev and his alma mater* (Dublin, 1984). On McQuaid and the drafting of the 1937 constitution see Dermot Keogh, 'The Irish constitutional revolution: an analysis of the making of the Irish constitution', *Administration*, 35 (1987-88) pp 4-84; Sean Faughnan, 'De Valera's constitution: the drafting of the Irish constitution of 1937' (M.A. thesis, UCD, 1988)

trative abilities had already come to the attention of the Irish nuncio, Paschal Robinson.

From the moment of his appointment, wrote a member of his former community at Blackrock, 'Dr McQuaid's total dedication to his high concept of the office he held as Metropolitan Archbishop and Primate of Ireland was to affect all his reactions from this time.'[11] McQuaid was fiercely loyal to his diocese, which he referred to as 'my city', and resented criticisms from outsiders, however justified. At the end of 1941 a series of articles on Ireland appeared in the *Catholic Herald* written by Dr (later Cardinal) J.C. Heenan. McQuaid took particular exception to the fourth article, 'Where Ireland makes an unfavourable impression', dealing mostly with Dublin. Heenan indicted the 'appalling poverty' of the capital, that was 'regarded in too many circles with complacency', and attacked the lack of medical services for the poor. He was also scathing about Irish politicians: 'most Irishmen are politicians [who] have learned from the English the greatest vice of Protestantism, private judgment. They will accept the ruling of the Church on what may broadly be termed sacristy issues but consider the Church unqualified to pronounce, even in the name of morality, upon those matters which bear on political life and action'. McQuaid did not quarrel with these comments, but he was incensed by Heenan's observation that 'Irish Catholics are not sufficiently instructed or thoughtful in the practice of their religion. There seems to be a certain formalism about their faith.'[12] McQuaid complained to the apostolic delegate in Britain, William Godfrey, that Heenan's article was 'scandalously offensive calumny in respect of Catholic thought and life in the diocese of Dublin'. Godfrey refused to get involved, citing his difficult position as wartime Vatican representative in London 'where are gathered so many of the Allied Governments'.[13] Despite this rebuff, McQuaid's combative response in defence of his diocese was a warning shot across the bows of other potential critics inside and outside Ireland.

THE DIOCESE

Because of the illness that had diminished the pastoral effectiveness of his predecessor, Edward J. Byrne, the administration of the Dublin diocese had become stagnant and urgently in need of a thorough overhaul by 1940. McQuaid's brisk new broom was soon felt in almost every area of the work

11 Farragher, *Dev's alma mater*, pp 193-4.   12 *Catholic Herald*, 12 Dec. 1941. Heenan was a parish priest in London at this time and was a well-known broadcaster, public speaker and writer on Catholic affairs.   13 McQuaid to Godfrey, 19 Dec., Godfrey to McQuaid, 26 Dec. 1941(DDA, McQuaid Papers, 523/2).

of the diocese. To permit this he greatly increased the number of staff at Archbishop's House, although it is worth noting that for most of his long episcopate there was only one auxiliary bishop.[14] McQuaid had a phenomenal capacity for work. As the *Irish Times* noted after his death, he personally answered thousands of letters annually, 'writing lapidary notes in his clear handwriting'.[15] He also had 'the great administrator's innovating gifts. He did not wait for problems to hit him, but sought them out and anticipated them.' For recreation, McQuaid would sometimes spend a week or two at Rockwell College, the Holy Ghost college in Tipperary, but this did not interrupt his administration of the Dublin diocese; it was arranged that the Dublin bus would drop off McQuaid's correspondence at the Rockwell gates in the morning and pick it up again in the evening with his replies and instructions.

McQuaid's private charity became legendary in the diocese. He showed compassion and generosity towards people who were in trouble of any kind; those who were sick, dying, in financial difficulties, priests who experiencing difficulties about their faith. To many people McQuaid was at his best when he was away from the diocese on the annual diocesan pilgrimages to Lourdes which he regularly attended, and during which he spent many hours with the sick. A historian working in the archives at Archbishop's House in 1964 was intrigued by the callers who arrived at the door: 'There were not many clergy or well-dressed laity; but there was a constant trickle of beggars, itinerants, and down-and-outs of every kind. Whoever else was afraid of the archbishop, these evidently were not.'[16]

A simple barometer of McQuaid's impact on the diocese is provided by the number of pages devoted to Dublin in the *Irish Catholic Directory*. In his first year, 1941, Dublin took up thirty-five pages; by 1957 this had risen to forty-four. In almost every year of McQuaid's episcopate the *Directory* published a detailed supplement listing the diocesan arrangements for each week of the year that, as well as attesting to McQuaid's administrative impact, bears ample witness also to the growing size of the diocese. Dublin was the most important and populous diocese in the country. Between 1901 and 1936, the Catholic population rose from 407,000 to over 580,000, while the non-Catholic population declined steeply from 115,000 to 76,600 between 1911 and 1936. There was a marked urban-rural divide in the diocese which comprised all of Dublin, most of Wicklow and parts of Kildare and Wexford. In

---

14 Dr Francis Wall was auxiliary from 1931 to 1947; Dr Patrick Dunne was auxiliary from 1946 to 1979. In 1968 McQuaid appointed a second auxiliary, Dr Joseph Carroll. 15 McQuaid eagerly investigated any new technology which would help to ease this burden. In 1961 he wrote to a friend in the Brentwood diocese in England enquiring about a new machine which was able to photocopy documents (DDA, McQuaid Papers 523/2).   16 Obituary, *Irish Times*, 9 Apr. 1973.

the 1930s, the Fianna Fáil administrations embarked on a comprehensive house-building programme which involved not only slum clearance in the inner city but the construction of new suburbs in Cabra, Crumlin, Drumcondra, Donnycarney and Marino. The Second World War severely restricted house-building, but this resumed in the late 1940s with extensive suburban development in such areas as Artane, Ballyfermot, Finglas, Coolock, Donnybrook, Dundrum, Stillorgan, Blackrock and Dun Laoghaire. By the time McQuaid retired in 1972 the Catholic population was almost 875,000.

This huge demographic and urban expansion put enormous pressure on every area of diocesan resources because it necessitated the creation of a network of new parishes, schools, hospitals and social services. In 1941, the diocese had eighty-one parishes, thirty-one in the city and fifty in suburban and rural areas. Despite the exigencies of wartime, McQuaid created eight new parishes during his first five years in office, seven of them in the city. Once house-building recommenced in the late 1940s, the creation of new parishes proceeded apace. By 1957, there was a total of ninety-eight parishes, forty-two in the city and fifty-six in the suburbs and the countryside. By 1972, the diocese had 115 parishes.[17] The capital commitment involved in the creation of so many new parishes was enormous and in the mid-1960s, in order to speed up the liquidation of parish debts, McQuaid controversially encouraged parish clergy to employ professional fund-raisers.[18] However, on the subject of one particular new building McQuaid was resolute: he refused to consider building a new Catholic cathedral for Dublin, on the grounds that there were more pressing priorities.[19]

New parishes created a parallel demand for new schools at primary and secondary levels. In 1946, there were 386 Catholic primary schools in the diocese; by 1972, this had risen to 518. The number of secondary schools rose from sixty-two to 150 during the same period. The increase in the number of technical/vocational schools from twenty-one to forty-seven in the same period also necessitated Catholic involvement. These demands were compounded by the demands of other Catholic institutions. In 1941, the Church administered a wide range of hospitals, convalescent homes, asylums for the deaf and blind, homes for widows and the aged, refuges, penitentiaries and industrial schools. It also had to supply chaplains to public institutions in the diocese, including county homes, lunatic asylums, prisons, and the army.[20]

Meeting these demands necessitated a considerable increase in the number of clergy, secular and regular. In 1941, there were seventy-seven parish priests

17 See Appendix. 18 *Business and Finance*, 3 Dec. 1965. 19 Roland Burke Savage SJ, 'The Church in Dublin: 1940-1965', *Studies*, 54 (1965), pp 306-7. 20 See Appendix.

and 241 administrators and curates in the diocese. By 1951, this had increased to eighty-seven and 355 respectively. By 1972, the total number of diocesan clergy was 567. However, the most spectacular increase was registered by the regular clergy whose number climbed from 423 in 1941 to 1,002 in 1972. This derived primarily from the large number of religious communities that McQuaid invited into the diocese. In 1941, there were only thirty-three communities of regular clergy in Dublin; in 1961 there were forty-nine, and in 1972 there were sixty. A similar increase was registered in the number of communities of brothers and nuns. In 1946, there were twenty-nine communities of brothers; by 1972, this had risen to fifty-three. The number of communities of nuns and sisters rose from 118 in 1941 to 184 in 1972. Nor were lay societies and sodalities neglected. Ten were listed in the *Irish Catholic Directory* in 1941; by 1972 there were twenty-one.[21]

THE CATHOLIC SOCIAL SERVICE CONFERENCE

In the 1920s and 1930s there existed, as Eamonn Dunne has noted, a close bond between the Catholic Church and the working class in Dublin.[22] This was strengthened under McQuaid whose early pastorals attested to his dislike of the Catholic middle classes. 'It is not ... among the past pupils of Primary Schools', he stated in his 1941 Lenten pastoral,

> that one may look for the exceptional and graver infidelity to Christian duties. Rather often those persons whose social position and higher education befit them to be examples of a life of Faith are precisely those who prove to be a scandal to the poor. They forget that the more abundant gifts of God are a serious responsibility, demanding the exercise of deeper Faith and more generous devotedness to the less fortunate.[23]

He returned to the subject in 1942: 'The poor of Christ are favoured, in that, by reason of their penury, they are less liable to the pride and cruelty and unchastity that are begotten of wealth'.[24] In his 1944 Lenten pastoral he warned that 'there can be but one code of morals from which no class, however gifted, is exempt'.[25]

Lay organisations such as the Legion of Mary and the St Vincent de Paul Society were particularly active among the Dublin working class. The pri-

---

21 Ibid.   22 Eamonn Dunne, 'Action and reaction: Catholic lay organisations in Dublin in the 1920s and 1930s', *Archivium Hibernicum* 48 (1994), p. 109.   23 'The Christian family' (Lenten Pastoral 1941) reprinted in *Wellsprings of the faith*, p. 61.   24 *The law of self-denial* (Dublin, 1942), p. 52.   25 *The gift of faith* (Dublin, 1944), pp 10-11.

mary aim of the Vincent de Paul Society was 'the santification of the members through the performance of works of charity, particularly the visitation and assistance of poor in their own homes'. The Society provided a comprehensive range of services to the poor in Dublin: orphanages, hostels, a labour yard for men who were disabled and unfit, prisoners' aid, boys' clubs, night schools and coal, clothing and boot funds.[26] Such services were much needed, as the war imposed great hardships on the poor and destitute of Dublin. Inflation increased the price of food and there were severe shortages of fuel, flour and tea. Late in 1941, the government imposed a wage freeze. All of this aggravated the already low standards of public health in the Dublin slums; lice infestation was rife, and diseases like tuberculosis and gastro-enteritis contributed to huge mortality rates, especially among children. As distress increased, several organisations stepped in to help, among them the Goodwill Restaurants run by Judge Wylie's Guilds, the Society of Friends, and the St John's Ambulance. They set up food centres around the city and provided hot meals at nominal prices.

Within weeks of his consecration McQuaid had determined that the various Catholic organisations needed to co-ordinate their activities. Forty of them were invited to a meeting at the Mansion House in January 1941 (no representatives were invited from Judge Wylie's Guilds or the Society of Friends), arising out of which a provisional committee was set up. It recruited the services of volunteers expert in various fields, many of them from local government and the civil service. Following this, the inaugural meeting of what became known as the Catholic Social Service Conference (CSSC) took place in April. Its principal aims were to supplement and support the state during the Emergency; to provide means of employment; to supply the needs of those in distress; to serve as an active agent in unifying public effort and goodwill; and to mobilise all available resources for the common good.[27]

Food was the most pressing need, and the CSSC established food centres run by sisters from various convents throughout the diocese. Food was obtained at below or at cost price and occasionally for free. A special booklet, *Food supplies, foods and dietetics*, was published as a guide both for the provision of food to the needy and for the general nutrition of the country. Twenty-seven CSSC food centres were set up, and in their first year they served over two million meals to sit-down callers. Arrangements were also made for take-home meals, which meant that well over seven million meals were served in that first year. By the following year, 1942, maternity centres

---

26 Dunne, 'Action and reaction', pp 107-18.   27 At the time of writing most of the voluminous CSSC files in the McQuaid Papers were still unavailable. For this section I have consulted the Golden Jubilee history by Mary Purcell, *The Catholic Social Service Conference: fifty years targetting care and justice* (Dublin, 1991).

were added to the food centres to provide meals for pregnant women and those with young babies. Mothers could bring their children to the centres for meals. McQuaid was also instrumental in setting up an ambulance service for pregnant women, a service much appreciated by those who lived at some distance from the hospitals; wartime public transport was very unreliable.

The clothing, fuel and housing committees also had considerable achievements to their credit. Baby and children's clothes, children's boots, First Communion and Confirmation outfits, and warm winter clothes were all distributed by various guilds. Stockpiles of turf were accumulated at depots around the city and were distributed not only to the poor but also to schools and orphanages. The introduction of the government's free fuel scheme in 1943 made this CSSC committee redundant. With regard to housing, the shortage of building materials proved a severe limitation but, despite this, forty flats were made available in renovated houses in Gardiner Street and Holles Street to young married couples with fewer than four children who were not eligible for houses on the new estates. The least successful area was unemployment, but this was hardly surprising. The construction industry virtually shut down and factories laid off employees because of the shortage of raw materials. It was a report drafted by this committee which alerted McQuaid to the huge numbers of people going to Britain for war work which will be considered below.

In 1943, the government appointed McQuaid head of the Youth Unemployment Commission, and the subject of youth welfare came increasingly to preoccupy him. He was alarmed by the rise in juvenile crime and urged the CSSC to organise youth clubs and to train youth leaders. Leadership courses for boys' and girls' clubs were set up and the CSSC co-ordinated the work of various groups involved in youth work – the St Vincent de Paul Society, the Catholic Young Men's Society, the Catholic Boy Scouts and Girl Guides and the St John Bosco Clubs. By 1954, there were almost 10,000 boys and girls in youth clubs throughout the city and as far north and south as Skerries and Dun Laoghaire.

The CSSC was equally active in the post-war period, since the end of the war in 1945 did not mean an end to shortages and destitution. The winter of 1946-47 was one of the worst on record: snow lay on the ground for months; bread was rationed for the first time; coal supplies were non-existent and the turf was sodden. The demand for meals at the food centres was highest during that winter. However, other CSSC activities were gradually taken over by local government and the state. In 1950, Dublin Corporation took over the houses renovated by the CSSC and, as families left the inner city for the new housing estates, many CSSC centres were closed down and relocated in the new suburbs of Ballyfermot, Coolock, Donnycarney and Finglas. As unemployment and emigration increased in the mid-1950s, these new centres were needed. The number of meals served in 1954-55 was almost double that served in 1950-51 and the centres in Ballyfermot and Finglas were unable to cope with the demand.

The main sources of the CSSC's income were an annual appeal (with McQuaid himself usually leading the list of subscribers) and grants from Dublin Corporation and central government. The administration costs were low and McQuaid was proud of the fact that they only came to 2.4 per cent of income. But in the 1950s inflation and, particularly, the rising cost of items such as petrol reduced the value of this income, while the demands from the new suburbs prompted the closure of some inner city food and maternity centres. In any event, the state had begun to move into many of the areas in which the CSSC had been active and the new prosperity of the 1960s made some of these activities redundant. Although the CSSC was no longer involved in housing, McQuaid warned Dublin Corporation in the early 1960s against building complexes like Sheriff Street and Ballymun on the grounds that they were unsuitable for families. He also became concerned by new social problems such as itinerant resettlement and drug addiction. In 1969, he mobilised the CSSC to provide relief for refugees when the Northern Ireland troubles broke.

EMIGRANT WELFARE

In February 1944, the Statistics Branch of the Department of Industry and Commerce submitted a report to the Department of the Taoiseach pointing out that between September 1939 and December 1943 the number of people who had gone to Britain and Northern Ireland for employment was 181,565. Of these 125,411 were men and 56,154 women.[28] The departure of such huge numbers caused great anxiety among the members of the Irish and British hierachies. Emigrants received no advice either before departure or on arrival about accommodation, work and religious practice and had to rely instead on word-of-mouth from relatives and friends. Working conditions in some industries were poor, while the moral laxness of some of the emigrants was the subject of hostile comment. Barely two weeks after his consecration in December 1940, McQuaid received an angry letter from Cardinal Hinsley of Westminster protesting that he had been unfairly censured in the Irish press and portrayed as a British propagandist for drawing attention to this problem though he had 'spent money – my own and that of charitable persons ... in an endeavour to prevent the

28 National Archives Ireland (NAI), Department of the Taoiseach (DT), S12728A, February 1944.

scandal of Irish girls and Irishmen who have left their unwanted babies to be maintained by us.'[29]

To redress this problem McQuaid set up the Catholic Social Welfare Bureau (CSWB) in 1942. Financed by the CSSC, its primary remit was the care of emigrants whom it advised both before and after departure on their future welfare in British industrial cities. Most of the work was undertaken by the Legion of Mary. Bernard Griffin, the auxiliary bishop of Birmingham, wrote to McQuaid praising his new initiatives with the CSSC and the CSWB and expressing the hope that the Irish, English and Scottish hierarchies could undertake joint action on social matters after the war. The archbishop of Birmingham, Thomas Williams, told McQuaid that he had sent a chaplain to a workers' camp on a big contracting job in his diocese. The camp had been a disgrace but was now a model one. British firms employing large numbers of Irish workers realised the value of having chaplains attached to work sites and, in 1943, the British Sugar Corporation asked McQuaid for his assistance in providing chaplains for their Irish employees.[30] British government ministries, notably the ministries of Labour and of Fuel and Power, did the same and liaised with the English hierarchy over chaplains for Irish workers.

The problem, as McQuaid was aware, was that this was just a drop in the ocean compared to the scale of the problem as emigration escalated after the war. In the period 1946-1951 the annual rate of emigration was approximately 25,000. Emigrant welfare was the subject which forged close links between the Irish and English hierarchies. When Cardinal Griffin (as he had by then become) expressed his wish for such links, McQuaid agreed warmly in a letter which offers an interesting sidelight on his own political views:

> Formerly, we had a definite link in the presence at Westminster of the Irish Party. That link, which in my view benefited both countries from the point of view of the Faith, has been broken by a series of historical events that future generations may not judge altogether desirable. In our own day we can only accept the Providence of God which has permitted these events, and, if I may say it, repair the break in our Catholic association.[31]

One of the results of these contacts was a meeting in May 1948 of seventy Irish priests in Westminster Cathedral Hall to discuss the plight of newly

29 Hinsley to McQuaid, 9 Jan. 1941 (DDA, McQuaid Papers 523/2).   30 Griffin to McQuaid, 5 Sept. 1942; Williams to McQuaid, 16 Sept. 1942; McQuaid to Bishop Thomas Parker (Northampton), 16 Oct. 1943 (DDA, McQuaid Papers, 523/2).   31 McQuaid to Griffin, 1 Nov. 1952 (DDA, McQuaid Papers 523/2).

arrived emigrants. It was decided to set up an Irish Centre in London. In the winter of 1948-49, Father Leonard Sheil SJ travelled throughout Britain visiting oil refineries, steel works and camps for agricultural workers. He found many workers who were unable to attend Mass or who had given up their religion. On his return to Ireland he and another Jesuit, Father Robert Stevenson, decided to organise missions to Irish workers. McQuaid welcomed this move, and at his instigation the Irish hierarchy established the Episcopal Committee for Emigrants in June 1953 which liaised with the hierarchy of England and Wales. In a letter to Cardinal Griffin in January 1955, McQuaid frankly admitted the failures on his side of the Irish Sea. 'So far, we have not reached out to our own people, I believe, with the zeal that would have to some extent prevented very many from becoming a heart-ache to the bishops and priests of England and Wales'. He told Griffin that the Irish hierarchy had agreed to two of his proposals: firstly, that religious orders which gave missions should extend their activities to England and, later in the year, McQuaid met the provincials of the various orders and a small committee, consisting of priests with experience of mission work in Britain, was established for this purpose; and secondly, to the appointment of a Columban priest, Father Aedan McGrath, who had recently been released from a Chinese prison, to further the work of the Legion of Mary among Irish emigrants. McQuaid believed that McGrath's experiences would help to counter the activities of groups like the Connolly Clubs which were having some success in recruiting Irish emigrants, particularly in Birmingham.[32]

McGrath and his fellow priests aimed to integrate Irish emigrants within local parish structures; and they achieved much by extending the lay apostolate through the Legion of Mary and its subsidiary, the Patrician Movement. They also linked the various chaplaincy schemes together. McGrath and his groups travelled throughout England and Wales; legionaries met boat trains; and missions were targetted at construction works and London hotels. There was much to be achieved, as at one construction site near Carlisle the contractors, Wimpey's, who supported the appointment of chaplains, employed 300 Catholics (out of a workforce of 700), not just recent Irish immigrants but second and third-generation Irish from Glasgow and Newcastle. Thousands of Irish workers were also employed on motorway construction from the late 1950s. In London it was estimated that there were at least 15,000 Irish working in the hotel trade, most of them women. At the Cumberland Hotel, one of the largest in central London, 90 per cent of the staff were Irish and the management cooperated with the chaplains who established the Hotel and Catering Workers' Guild.

32 Kieran O'Shea, *The Irish emigrant chaplaincy scheme in Britain 1957-1962* (Dublin, 1985), pp 11-15.

'With regard to the building trade employees', wrote one mission priest to McQuaid in 1958, 'we all now feel that the best way of getting and keeping in contact with these is at parish level – intensive visitation of Irish homes, "digs" etc. by a few priests strategically located in the predominantly Irish "belt" of the archdiocese of Westminster'. McQuaid agreed 'wholeheartedly' and secured the appointment of five Irish priests to the so-called 'Irish' parishes of north London. He insisted that these priests were not 'mere curates' and that they were freed of ordinary parochial duties.[33] One class of emigrant which caused major problems for the chaplains in Britain was the young boys released from Irish orphanages and industrial schools aged fourteen and upwards who went to England with no preparation whatever. Many of them subsequently got into trouble with the law. Young men arrived on a Friday night, wrote Cardinal Griffin to McQuaid, with a week's wages which they immediately proceeded to drink away. 'Whilst we do not wish to take any step which may appear to encourage emigration from Ireland we feel strongly that some means must be adopted to inform those who are coming of the facilities which we shall be pleased to provide. Our task will be rendered easier if only those boys and girls will let us know in advance of their coming.'[34] By the mid-1960s, the shortage of vocations had begun seriously to affect the provision of chaplains in Britain and only eight were left by 1965. At this point the religious orders stepped into the breach and made twenty-eight priests available.[35] It was still not enough and right up to his retirement McQuaid was appealed to constantly by members of the English and Scottish hierarchies for more Irish priests to look after parishes with large Irish populations.

HEALTH AND SOCIAL WELFARE

At the time of McQuaid's appointment in 1940, there were five major Catholic hospitals in Dublin: the Mater, Jervis Street, St Vincent's, Temple Street Children's Hospital, and the National Maternity Hospital at Holles Street. Smaller Catholic institutions included St Michael's in Dun Laoghaire, a TB hospital at Kill o' the Grange, the Harold's Cross Hospice, and the St John of God hospital for mental and nervous disorders in south County Dublin. McQuaid was chairman of the Mater, Jervis Street, the NMH, and St Michael's. During the war, as the work of the CSSC demonstrated, McQuaid was particularly concerned about maternity care. After the war he began to focus attention on paediatrics and mental health. A training school

33 Ibid. pp 17-37.   34 Cardinal Griffin to McQuaid, 12 Apr. 1956 (DDA, McQuaid Papers 523/2).   35 O'Shea, *Emigrant chaplaincy scheme*, p. 48.

for nursery nurses was established towards the end of the war, but his most cherished project, one with which he had been involved since the 1930s, was Our Lady's Hospital for Sick Children in Crumlin, which finally opened in 1956 and quickly established a reputation as one of the best paediatric hospitals in Europe. McQuaid made sure that it had the latest equipment for cardiac treatment and advanced pathology and he later founded a research institute on children's diseases within the hospital which had links with the medical schools of Georgetown University and the National University of Ireland. Other hospitals also benefited fom his generosity; he presented a student medical library to the Mater and donated the funds to found a department of encephalography.

The plight of physically and mentally handicapped children was also of great concern to McQuaid. The Dominican Sisters and Christian Brothers ran two linked institutes for the deaf in Cabra. At his instigation, the Daughters of the Cross founded a boarding school for young deaf boys in the early 1950s. It was also at his instigation that the Order of St John of God expanded their work for the mentally handicapped at their institutions in Drumcar (County Meath) and Celbridge in Kildare. New homes for mentally handicapped women were also established at his request by the Sisters of Charity of St Vincent de Paul. The work of the CSSC also alerted McQuaid to the problem of disturbed children and young offenders. In the mid-1950s the Order of St John of God opened a clinic in Rathgar for emotionally disturbed children, one of the first of its kind in the Republic. He was also instrumental in setting up a special remand home for young boys, run by the De La Salle Brothers, and in establishing St Patrick's Institution for Young Offenders.

Alcoholism was a disease about which McQuaid felt particularly strongly. Its prevalence and the devastation it wrought on family life had been consistently reported by the CSSC and the CSWB but McQuaid believed that throughout Irish society, but especially at political level, there was supine complacency about the extent of the problem. The 1957 report of the commission of inquiry into the licensing laws was the basis for the government's 1959 Intoxicating Liquor Bill which proposed more uniform licensing hours throughout the country. Eager to curb the problems associated with alcoholism, McQuaid drafted the hierarchy's memorandum on the Bill which was presented to de Valera and the Minister for Justice on 8 May 1959. The memorandum criticised the emphasis which the 1957 report placed on drunkenness rather than alcoholism. It noted the increase in the consumption of alcohol since 1935 and was firmly of the opinion that the law had not been enforced: 'There exists among the Bishops ... a very uneasy feeling that the failure to enforce the law is to be explained, in great part, by the fact that, in our country, District Justices, officers of the Gardai ... are too closely linked in social life with the offenders'. Arising out of this, McQuaid was pessimistic about any major changes being effected in the bill as a result of the hierarchy's lobbying. He wrote to Cardinal D'Alton: 'we may well be obliged to content ourselves with a solution that cannot be ideally perfect but only good and practicable'.[36]

In view of the formidable list of McQuaid's achievements in the field of health and social welfare, the rumpus created by the Mother and Child Scheme, the most controversial episode of McQuaid's career, seems puzzling. This is not the place to examine the controversy in detail [37] but it is worth looking at some aspects of the crisis as they pertain to McQuaid. *In Church and state in modern Ireland*, John Whyte commented on the oddness of the controversy. Expanded medical services and social welfare systems were intro-duced in most of western Europe after the war without anything like the con-vulsions they occasioned in Ireland. The Mother and Child Scheme was, Whyte noted, the only instance in which a Catholic hierarchy sought to influ-ence the precise provisions of a country's social services.[38] Why? For McQuaid himself there were strong personal influences at work, as he came from a family with a strong medical tradition. His father was a doctor and medical officer for Cootehill in Cavan, in which position he had clashed with the local Board of Guardians over conditions in the local workhouse. McQuaid's paternal uncle was also a doctor and medical officer for Bally-jamesduff. His half-brother Eugene was approaching the end of his medical studies when he was killed in the Civil War in 1923. For McQuaid doctors, like teachers, were one of the privileged professions, a fact recognised in the 1944 Vocational Organisation Report.

Moreover, if one assesses the controversy in the wider historical context, the Irish reaction was not so unusual. Catholic social thought, as enshrined in such papal encyclicals as *Rerum Novarum* (1891) and *Quadragesimo Anno* (1931), came late to Ireland and reflected the priorities, fears and insecuri-ties of the Irish Catholic middle-class which was more rootless than histo-rians have assumed. Moreover, Catholic social thinkers in Ireland were pre-occupied with state power as represented by the 'bureaucracy' and central government.[39] The Church's suspicion of state bureaucracy pre-dated inde-

36 Intoxicating liquor bill. Memorandum by hierarchy, 8 May 1959; McQuaid to D'Alton, 30 Apr. 1959 (DDA, McQuaid Papers. Government: Box 2).   37 The Mother and Child crisis has been discussed by Whyte, *Church and state*, pp 236ff; Ruth Barrington, *Health, medicine and politics in Ireland 1900-1970* (Dublin, 1987); Eamonn McKee, 'Church-state relations and the development of Irish health policy: the mother-and-child scheme, 1944-1953', *Irish Historical Studies*, 25 no. 98 (1986), pp 159-94.   38 Whyte, *Church and state*, pp 300-1.   39 This has been discussed in Diarmaid Ferriter, ' "A peculiar people in their own land": Catholic social theory and the plight of rural Ireland 1930-1955' (Ph.D. thesis,

pendence and ran very deep. Its hostility to the state-funded national schools in the nineteenth century is a classic instance, but there was also considerable opposition to the Congested Districts Board set up in 1891. As one commentator noted, the papal encyclicals, for all their willingness to confront the social problems of the day,

> formulated the fundamental issue in terms inherited from Pius IX – the times were out of joint, humanity had taken the wrong road ... A secular solution is not sufficient and therefore a state solution is not possible ... where the State attempted a solution it had led to Communism, Fascism, or an over-bureaucractic State ... The Church must, therefore, be ever active in reminding men of their rights and duties, ever vocal in insisting on the moral rather than the economic root of the problem, and ever vigilant in combatting the modern heresy of seeing remedy in wholesale State activity.[40]

Put simply, the problem was that the respective developments of the Irish Catholic Church and the Irish state were out of historical kilter, as a result of which McQuaid's formidable endeavours were taking place at a time when the state was taking a more interventionist role in social and economic policies. Following the election of de Valera in 1932, successive Fianna Fail administrations pursued more dirigiste social and economic programmes to which the Emergency gave even greater impetus. The publication of the Beveridge Report in Britain at the end of 1942 received extensive coverage in Irish newspapers and periodicals. Two years later the first children's allowances act was introduced and the government embarked on an expansion and reform of the Irish health services, culminating in the 1947 health act. McQuaid opposed the Mother and Child provisions of the 1947 act because he regarded them as an unwarranted intrusion by the state into the sacred relationship between doctor and patient. He also believed there was a danger that contraception and abortion would be introduced under the cover of state health services. McQuaid and the hierarchy were later accused of adopting an obfuscatory attitude towards the Minister of Health, Noël Browne, when he attempted to bring in the Mother and Child provisions of the 1947 health act. However, the most cursory scrutiny of McQuaid's pastorals and addresses since 1941 would have amply revealed his views on the role of the state.[41]

UCD, 1996); Finín O'Driscoll, 'The Search for a Christian State: Irish Social Catholicism 1913-1939' (M.A. thesis, UCC, 1994). **40** Liam Ryan, 'The Church and politics: the last twenty-five years', *The Furrow*, 30, no. 1 (1979), pp 5-6. **41** See especially his 1944 Lenten Pastoral *The gift of faith* (Dublin, 1944). McQuaid's views were unaffected by the

The victory over Browne was a Pyrrhic one. In 1953, when a new health bill was under discussion, de Valera and his health minister, James Ryan, prevented McQuaid and the hierarchy from using the same divide-and-rule tactics they had employed so successfully in prising Noel Browne apart from the Inter-Party government. The hierarchy, and particularly McQuaid, did enormous damage to themselves by lining up with the conservative medical profession in fulminating against socialised medicine. With Irish tuberculosis and infant mortality statistics among the highest in the world, health was an issue of major popular concern. McQuaid was as knowledgeable about the import of these statistics as many in the medical profession and the government. It was one of the sad ironies of the controversy that he, who attracted most of the lightning hurled at the hierarchy, was accused of being out of touch with harsh social realities.

CULTURE AND EDUCATION

As a teacher in Blackrock, McQuaid was remembered by former pupils for his attempts to educate their interests outside the prescribed curriculum, not just in literature but in the visual arts. With his senior students he combined the teaching of film appreciation with his teaching of English literature. McQuaid took a keen interest in literature, music, drama, film and art and when he spoke on these subjects he usually did so knowledgeably, unlike other members of the hierarchy. In 1945, he founded Our Lady's Choral Society which, unlike the Palestrina Choir at the Pro-Cathedral, accepted women. In the visual arts, even before he became archbishop, he was a patron of Michael Healy, Evie Hone and Mainie Jellett. Michael Healy designed two fine windows for the Blackrock College chapel and it was in the same chapel that McQuaid received Evie Hone into the Church in 1937. When McQuaid was consulted by Lord Crawford and Sir Jasper Ridley about commissioning an artist to replace the great stained-glass windows at Eton College, which had been destroyed by German bombs, McQuaid recommended Hone, which led to one of her finest works. He always maintained an interest in good craftsmanship and one woodcarver recalled that McQuaid insisted on placing a small brass plaque on his work so that people would know in a hundred years that he had been responsible for it.[42]

events of 1951-3. In 1954 he addressed the International Congress of Catholic Doctors in Dublin: 'Your profession has great need in every country to close its ranks in face of theories and practices that are but a cancellation of human nature ... Only in recent times has your profession encountered the open or subtle violence that would destroy the liberty of free men to fulfil the personal and social responsibility of their vocation' (*Wellsprings of the faith*, p. 223). **42** Interview with Tom Doody, 'McQuaid, servant of God', 1973

When abroad, McQuaid liked to study church architecture, but he was constrained in what he could achieve architecturally, in the large number of new churches which were built in Dublin during his episcopate, by the conservatism of his flock and the economics of church building. In the late 1950s he authorised a competition for a new church at Bird Avenue in Clonskeagh. Although the winning design was controversial at the time, the church has since been recognised as one of the most important churches of the post-war period. Some of the older churches, Blackrock, Kilmacud and Terenure for example, were simply too small and were extended or replaced completely. However, the economics of church building favoured one large church rather than several small ones, a fact which McQuaid often regretted.[43]

It is one of the great paradoxes of his career that McQuaid, who was notoriously media-shy, was fascinated by film and television. In 1943 he founded the National Film Institute and helped to establish its journal *Vision*. In 1955 the Scottish Franciscan Father Agnellus Andrew, who was appointed to the BBC's religious broadcasting staff, published an article in the *Irish Ecclesiastical Record* describing the work of communications and media departments in US Catholic universities in producing programmes for radio and television.[44] McQuaid was deeply impressed by this and, in preparation for the opening of the Irish television service, he sent a group of priests to Britain and the US to train in television techniques and technology. They became the nucleus of the famous *Radharc* documentary team, which was one of the first independent production companies in Ireland. One of those priests, Father Joseph Dunn, wrote in his account of *Radharc* that McQuaid ensured that they had the necessary training, financial support and manpower; with one or two exceptions he also never interfered. When Dunn first mooted the idea of *Radharc* to McQuaid in 1961, the latter told him 'to go ahead, not to worry about failure, and offered £300 towards meeting our expenses'. The Archbishop's successor was not so accommodating.[45]

McQuaid's tastes were decisively shaped by his time in Rome. His deep love and reverence for Latin culture were expressed most memorably in the address he gave to the Eucharistic Congress in Sydney in April 1953. That culture, MacQuaid explained, was the Graeco-Roman culture conserved by the Catholic Church which flowered during the Italian Renaissance. For two centuries, Italy was the leader and teacher of civilised Europe until it succumbed to the military power of Spain and ceded cultural hegemony to France.

(RTE Sound Archives 326/73).   43 'The Church in Dublin', *Studies*, 54 (1965), pp 298, 328-9.   44 Father Agnellus Andrew, 'Television and religion', *Irish Ecclesiastical Record*, 83 (1955).   45 Joseph Dunn, *No tigers in Africa! Recollections and reflections on 25 years of Radharc* (Dublin, 1986), pp 18, 24, 35. Dunn also recalled McQuaid's fascination with the technical details of cameras and other equipment.

One of the most topical sections of this address was McQuaid's discussion of modern art and particularly Pablo Picasso, whose recent style he deplored but whose gifts he appreciated: 'Let us allow at once that Picasso can draw with a purity of line that rivals the perfection of the old Greek vases.'[46] McQuaid's artistic tastes, as this comment indicates, were educated but conservative; the same can be said also of his literary preferences. When Bishop David Mathew asked him in 1942 for permission to publish an article in Sean O'Faolain's journal *The Bell*, McQuaid was dismissive and suggested that Mathew should publish instead in the *Dublin Review*. 'My belief is that the group [around *The Bell*] is infected with the liberalism that considers it may give rein to "realistic expression"; that is, to the unworthy aspects of life in books. They suffer much from the disregard of the Irish Catholic public. To be attacked would give publicity, but, for the most part, no one notices and that hurts much.'[47] McQuaid, as this episode reveals, preferred to work behind the scenes. However, in 1958 his intervention in the Dublin Theatre Festival, which led to the withdrawal of a stage adaptation of Joyce's *Ulysses* and a new play by Sean O'Casey, *The drums of Father Ned*, and the eventual collapse of the festival, aroused huge controversy. Over the following decade there was a gradual easing of censorship which McQuaid was powerless to prevent. More enduring, however, was the Vigilance Committee which McQuaid established early in his episcopate to monitor left-wing and liberal personalities and organisations in the diocese, and which remained active until the 1970s.

The importance which McQuaid assigned to education was not surprising, given his career at Blackrock College and his involvement with the Catholic Headmasters' Association. In 1938, two years before his appointment, he had written a pamphlet on Catholic education in which he set out his views with clarity and vigour:

> He who expresses surprise at what is sometimes called the exclusiveness of the demand of Catholic education to rule all branches of human training, has failed to grasp both the sovereignty of God, the primal Truth, and the philosophy of the composite being who is to be educated ... Catholic education is not only supremely scientific in its certitude, but is also ... given possession of a unique and priceless instrument of human training.[48]

Given this conclusion, it is hardly surprising that when he became archbishop, McQuaid reserved some of his severest strictures for middle-class

46 *Wellsprings of the faith*, pp 214-19.   47 McQuaid to Mathew, 3 Dec. 1942 (DDA, McQuaid Papers, 523/2).   48 *Catholic education* (Dublin, 1938). This is reprinted in *Wellsprings of the faith*, p. 195.

Catholic parents who sent their children to non-Catholic schools: 'No consideration of mere wealth or social exclusiveness or pretended culture can justify the sending of a child to a school which the Church does not sanction as approved and safe.'[49]

During McQuaid's episcopate the number of primary schools in the diocese increased by a third. In 1954, McQuaid appointed three diocesan inspectors of schools and, in 1958, he set up the Council of Administration for Primary Schools. The Council was responsible for a number of important functions: the planning of new school buildings, the maintenance of existing ones, and the supply of up-to-date equipment. The Council also compiled a management handbook for all school managers in which they were directed to submit annual audited accounts. Despite this, the primary school system remained blighted by the low priority accorded to education by successive governments with the concomitant problems of lack of funding, inadequate resources and facilities, and poor pay and conditions for teachers. McQuaid held particularly strong views on the latter subject, and in 1946 his support for the primary teachers during a damaging seven-month strike (which was confined to Dublin) was glacially received by the government, which rejected his offer to mediate. The Irish National Teachers' Organisation (INTO) was jubilant about McQuaid's support for their case: 'At this fateful juncture it was a source of encouragement and inspiration to all the teachers, in city and country alike; an intimation, also, to all concerned of the justice of their reasonable claims and a strengthening of their determination to enter and continue the fight.' In the event the strike petered out in the face of government intransigence and the teachers returned to work after an appeal from McQuaid.[50] Another issue of concern to the INTO was the marriage bar on women teachers. The Minister of Education 1957-9, Jack Lynch, was anxious to remove it because of the growing shortage of female primary teachers but was advised that the hierarchy would never agree. In fact, when he broached the issue with McQuaid, the archbishop strongly supported lifting the ban and this was done in July 1958.[51]

Although free secondary education was not introduced until 1967, this sector grew fastest of all the education sectors during the period of McQuaid's epis-

49 *The gift of faith* (Dublin, 1944), p. 12.   **50** T.J. O'Connell, *A history of the INTO* (Dublin, 1968) pp 218-40. The strike soured relations between de Valera and McQuaid. Soon after this de Valera sent McQuaid a report criticising the state of the national school at Ballybrack which was in the neighbourhood of McQuaid's private house at Killiney, in south County Dublin. De Valera suggested that McQuaid could discuss how to improve the school with the Chief Medical Officer of the Department of Health, Dr James Deeny. McQuaid replied that he did not deal with 'junior civil servants' (Barrington, *Health, medicine and politics*, pp 190-1).   **51** Tribute by Jack Lynch, *Irish Times*, 9 Apr. 1973.

copate. The number of secondary schools more than doubled from 62 in 1946 to 129 in 1966, of which eighty were girls' secondary schools and forty-nine were for boys. In 1965 McQuaid established an advisory committee on secondary education to ensure that secondary school managers and teachers were kept in touch with the latest teaching methods and with research being carried out abroad. He felt that many of them were too focused on the affairs of their own schools and did not possess a sufficiently wide educational vision. However, the government had already embarked on a number of important reforms which signalled the beginning of a decisive shift in the administration of education. In May 1963, the Minister of Education, Dr Patrick Hillery, announced that comprehensive schools would be established under the control of the Department to provide a broader curriculum and to improve access to education. Building grants for secondary schools were also introduced in 1964. McQuaid welcomed the introduction of free secondary education, but the huge increase in the number of secondary school students after 1967 placed considerable pressure on existing schools and there was justified criticism that the introduction of free education was not followed up with adequate resources.[52]

There was also a major expansion of vocational education after 1945 as a consequence of the doubling of vocational schools during McQuaid's episcopate. These were controlled by the vocational education committees of the local authorities, to which McQuaid appointed representatives. Special courses in religious instruction were drawn up for these schools in the early 1940s and by 1947, there were forty-one priests working in vocational schools in the diocese. In 1958, he appointed a special diocesan director for vocational schools. McQuaid was also keen to expand opportunities for adult education, and in the period 1948-1955 he was behind four main initiatives in this area: the founding of the Catholic Workers' College under the directorship of Father Edward J. Coyne SJ in 1948; the establishment of the first Department of Extra-Mural Studies in University College Dublin in 1949; the setting up of the Dublin Institute of Catholic Sociology in 1950; and the creation of the Dublin Adult Education Committee in 1955.

These areas of McQuaid's educational endeavours were uncontroversial in the main. The same could not be said for his policies on third-level education. Almost immediately after he was appointed he took a hardline stand against the attendance of Catholic students at Trinity College Dublin and encouraged other members of the hierarchy to do the same. In June 1942, David Mathew, auxiliary bishop of Westminster, wrote to McQuaid asking for permission to accept an LLD from TCD with which his family had long connections. When McQuaid replied that 'the acceptance of a degree can only help to strengthen the mentality that I profoundly deplore', Mathew

52 J.J. Lee, *Ireland 1912-1985: politics and society* (Cambridge, 1989), pp 362-3.

did not proceed.[53] McQuaid's perception of Trinity as a kind of contagion that needed to be quarantined did not diminish with age, and he was particularly irked by the fact that Fianna Fáil administrations established friendly relations with Trinity and gave the College its first government grant in 1947. In 1959-60, McQuaid effectively vetoed the proposal of Dr Richard Hayes, Director of the National Library of Ireland, that the Library be relocated to a new site in the grounds of TCD.[54] In 1961 he produced one of his most outspoken attacks on the institution in the pamphlet *Higher education for Catholics*. TCD, he declared, 'has never been acceptable, and is not now acceptable, to Catholics'. He resolutely dismissed arguments that university education should embrace Irish youth of any religion:

> Common blood is not the one sign of unity that God made Man declared to be essential. Above every natural tie of blood or country, He exacts one unity alone; membership of the one, true Church ... We may not for any human consideration rate the natural ties of blood or country above the supernatural claims of Jesus Christ and the Church that He has founded.[55]

University College Dublin was, McQuaid emphasised, the institution which gave Catholic parents 'guarantees of both academic excellence and of Catholic inspiration' and he praised 'its convinced and consistent reverence for the Catholic faith'. McQuaid's lauding of UCD and his olympian view of university teachers and their functions struck many interested observers at the time, even in UCD, as excessive. It is hardly surprising, therefore, that the issue of McQuaid's influence and power in UCD should become a matter of controversy in the 1960s or that it was accorded a special section in the silver jubilee tribute to McQuaid published in the Jesuit periodical *Studies* in 1965. The author of the tribute, Father Roland Burke Savage SJ, attempted to refute charges of excessive interference by McQuaid but there was a defensive and occasionally obscure quality about his comments that failed to convince critics. 'Not everything that is said and done in University College in the name of the Archbishop is in fact his wish', wrote Father Burke Savage. From time

53 Mathew to McQuaid, 25 June 1942 (DDA, McQuaid Papers, 523/2). McQuaid's reply is not on file but in a subsequent letter from Mathew on 23 July 1942 he refers to McQuaid's views on the matter. Mathew had been awarded a Litt.D. by Trinity in 1933. He was related to the Fine Gael TD, James Dillon.   54 John Bowman, '"The wolf in sheep's clothing": Richard Hayes' proposal for a new National Library of Ireland, 1959-1960' in Ronald J. Hill and Michael Marsh (eds), *Modern Irish democracy: essays in honour of Basil Chubb* (Dublin, 1993) pp 44-61.   55 *Higher education for Catholics* (Dublin, 1961), pp 15-17.

to time there had been 'a breakdown in direct communication', but such was UCD's anomalous position that there was no direct communication between the Archbishop and the College as such, 'only informal communication with individuals'. Such 'non-formalised relationships' often led to misunderstandings and apparent conflict. The Philosophy Faculty (over which most of the controversy centred) was, as Burke Savage acknowledged, McQuaid's special interest and concern as were its offshoots, the Departments of Psychology and Social Science, that he had been instrumental in establishing.[56] The non-partisan theological journal *Herder Correspondence* certainly considered that the Philosophy Faculty, which was 'predominantly manned and attended by clerics', was susceptible to McQuaid's influence: 'Its dull record has not helped to distinguish a university that is, in certain other aspects, intellectually alive.'[57]

As the 1960s progressed the winds of change blew with gale force through third-level education. The establishment of regional technical colleges was announced in 1963. In 1967-68 there was not only student unrest in UCD with demands for reform of the creaking college administration, but also the bombshell proposal for a merger between Trinity and UCD put forward by the Minister of Education, Donogh O'Malley. The merger was stillborn but it was an unmistakable sign that with the reforms in secondary education, the introduction of grants for third-level education, and the consequent rise in student numbers, the Trinity 'ban' was no longer sustainable. McQuaid acceded reluctantly and it was lifted in 1970.

THE VATICAN COUNCIL AND AFTER

In retrospect, the faultlessly organised Patrician Year celebrations in 1961, in which McQuaid played a prominent part, were the apotheosis of his episcopate and of the Tridentine, post-Cullenite Church in which he had lived most of his life. The following year, Pope John XXIII summoned the Second Vatican Council which transformed both the religious environment and the institutional Church in a manner that McQuaid found uncongenial. As a result, many concluded that he should have retired then or, perhaps, on the occasion of his silver jubilee in 1965, but McQuaid failed to gauge the true extent of the seismic shifts taking place in the structures of the Church at either date. He believed that his role was to act as a base of certainty in a very uncertain world, though there were many in the clergy and the laity who increasingly disputed the validity of that role.

---

56 'The Church in Dublin', pp 329-31. McQuaid's relations with UCD will be discussed in Professor Donal McCartney's forthcoming official history of the College.   **57** *Herder Correspondence*, July 1965.

In November 1964, the monthly theological journal *Herder Correspondence* published an article entitled 'Time of decision for Irish Catholicism' in which it was observed that the new mood of self-criticism detectable among the Catholic clergy and laity in Ireland antedated the Vatican Council. One indication of this was provided by the tightening up of ecclesiastical censorship, with the appointment by McQuaid of a special vicar general in 1956. Paradoxically, despite his interest in the media, McQuaid was not a good communicator; he was a shy and reserved man whose dry sense of humour was revealed only rarely. Like many others in his position, he increasingly felt the isolation of his office. McQuaid tended to keep aloof from the rest of the hierarchy; during the bishops' meetings at Maynooth he never stayed overnight in the college but travelled each day from Dublin. In the decade or so after his appointment, his pastorals and addresses had vigour and clarity. The wartime ones were particularly trenchant while others such as *Prayer* (1948) and *Death* (1953) had a lucid, simple style. The pastorals and addresses bore testimony to McQuaid's devotion to the Mass and to Marian rituals but they became increasingly formulaic and abstract, with the exception of the pastorals dating from the 1960s on the Vatican Council. *Atonement* (1952) was accompanied by eighty-seven footnotes; *Jesus Christ whom thou has sent* (1971) had 135 footnotes! McQuaid's pastoral letters, which were his main form of communication with his flock, were, according to one critic in 1965, 'masterly expositions of doctrinal themes' but their language assumed 'a devoted audience with earnest theological interests rather than the multifarious laity of a capital city ... involved in rapidly changing conditions'.[58]

No significant reforms were expected from the Vatican Council by the Irish hierarchy, which maintained a cloistered existence at the Irish College in Rome. To Louis McRedmond, who reported on the Council for the *Irish Independent*, 'it was regrettable how rarely we saw a face from the Irish College except at an occasional briefing'. He found McQuaid personally helpful while Archbishop (later Cardinal) Conway was excellent at press conferences, but 'they never seemed to realise the pastoral value – not to mention the sheer public relations – of the social contacts that flourished in conciliar Rome'. The result was that neither the clergy nor the laity were prepared for the impact of the Council on the Irish Church: 'they were asked to contribute their prayers, not their understanding'.[59]

58 'Curial mentality in Dublin archdiocese?', *Herder Correspondence*, July 1965, pp 195-9. It was reprinted as 'Dublin's archbishop' in *The changing face of Catholic Ireland* (London, 1968), pp 109-20. This book was edited by Desmond Fennell who was also the editor of *Herder Correspondence*.   59 Louis McRedmond, *The Council reconsidered* (Dublin, 1966) p. 186.

McQuaid issued an explanatory pastoral in 1963 entitled *What is a general council?* in which he gave a potted history of previous councils and explained revealingly that 'they are not essential to the nature of the Church'. It is quite clear that McQuaid did not see the need for a Council because, as he emphasised, with quotations from the pope himself, 'nothing that the Council may enact can exceed the faith ... that we already loyally profess. No measure of discipline can alter the basic law of Jesus Christ'. He laid particular emphasis on the role of the pope and the bishops, especially the latter: bishops 'have direct, immediate jurisdiction over their proper territory, for, in the Church they alone are the judges of the Faith. As successors of the apostles, they are the pastors who ... are the authority that teaches, rules and sanctifies the Church'.[60] As the deliberations of the Council proceeded, this was a subject about which McQuaid became increasingly preoccupied and he insisted that bishops must be free to administer their dioceses without interference. It was an unwelcome portent of what was to come once the Council had concluded. In November 1965, the month before the Council closed, Father Joseph Dunn of *Radharc* asked McQuaid for permission to attend the final sessions. McQuaid's reply made it clear what he thought of the proceedings: 'I am quite willing that you come to Rome for a brief period to meet missionary bishops – and journalists. The facile ignorance of some of the latter will enable you to understand the Council if not the Catholic Church.'[61]

In *The Sacred Liturgy*, a pastoral published in 1964, McQuaid seemed relatively content with the Constitution on the Sacred Liturgy passed by the Council in December 1963. However, this was not the case, because in his 1965 pastoral, *The Sacrifice of the Mass*, which explained the new liturgy, he concluded pessimistically: 'It can avail us little to use the more simple ceremonies and a language that we more easily understand, if, in the performance of the Holy Sacrifice, our dispositions have not been exactly those of Jesus Christ'.[62] A year later, he was even more forthright: 'It is not to be thought that, as a consequence of the Council, we are bidden to expect the radical and immediate transformation of the members of the Church ... Only the spirit of God, who dwells in the Church, can re-create our times.'[63] His evident displeasure at the direction of events notwithstanding, McQuaid did not set his face against change *per se*. He established a diocesan liturgical commission, and special commissions on sacred art and architecture, and sacred music, which drew on such distinguished lay experts as Thomas McGreevy, James White, J.F. Larchet, Anthony Hughes and Gerard Gillen. The creation of a diocesan press office in March 1965, headed by Osmond

60 *What is a general council?* (Dublin, 1963) pp 12-18.   61 Dunn, *No tigers in Africa!*, p. 32.   62 *The sacrifice of the Mass* (Dublin, 1965), p. 15.   63 *The people of God* (Dublin, 1966), p. 12.

Dowling, surprised many in the Dublin media. In 1965, the first post-ordination course for priests was held, a recognition that pastoral training had been neglected. 'You will not take a narrow view of the word "pastoral"', McQuaid told the assembled priests. 'Education in all its forms, literary, moral, physical, is pastoral. Pastoral, too, every form of care for the aged, the sick, the young, the neglected.'[64]

But there were other developments which indicate the limits to McQuaid's tolerance for reforms. He discouraged progressive theologians from lecturing in the diocese, notably Father John Courtney Murray SJ whose views on the pluralist state were diametrically opposed to his own.[65] His commitment to ecumenism was also less than wholehearted, as his *maladroit* handling of the issue amply revealed. In 1961, he refused to meet the archbishop of Canterbury when he visited Dublin. In 1964, he asked his flock to pray for Church Unity Week but then advised them to pray that separated Christian brethren would return to the one, true Church. He sought to discourage the Pax Romana ecumenical society in UCD. In January 1966 there was the incident of the 'empty chair' at a meeting in the Mansion House during Church Unity Week; Dr Simms, the Church of Ireland archbishop of Dublin, sat in the body of the hall while McQuaid and other Catholic dignitaries sat on the platform. The episode attracted considerable press attention and McQuaid became the scapegoat, although the seating arrangements were not his responsibility.[66] His discomfort with greater lay participation was equally obvious. From the early years of his episcopate he discouraged lay discussion groups, such as the Mercier Society and the Pillar of Fire Society, that sought to foster dialogue with the Protestant Churches and the Jewish community.

Following Vatican II, McQuaid's personality and policies came under increasing scrutiny from a more assertive laity. McQuaid was very sensitive to criticism but never replied to it, preferring to regard it as another cross to be borne, though much of what was said about him was hurtful as well as ill-informed. Thus, when Michael Serafian (a pseudonym of Malachi Martin) drew a critical portrait of McQuaid in his book *The Pilgrim* (1964) in which he accused him, among other things, of stifling dissent, of having an 'innate hatred of Protestants', and of substituting 'juridical norms for the one irre-

64 Press release, 15 July 1965 (DDA, McQuaid Papers).   65 The case of Father Courtney Murray and of Father Gregory Baum OSA, who were both accredited theologians at the Vatican Council, had attracted criticism in Britain and the US. But *Herder Correspondence* observed in July 1965 that Father Baum was interviewed on RTE television, and gave lectures in Maynooth, the Milltown Institute in Dublin, Carlow, Cork, Glenstal, and Belfast. Father Courtney Murray was 'indirectly discouraged' and did not come to Ireland. 'Curial mentality in Dublin Archdiocese?', p. 196.   66 Lesley Whiteside, *George Otto Simms: a biography* (Gerrard's Cross, 1990) pp 95-8.

placeable quality of a Christian – genuine charity',[67] McQuaid made no formal reply. The criticisms were addressed in an article published in July 1965 by *Herder Correspondence* where it was pointed out that while parish clergy had certainly found their freedom of initiative and expression stifled, it was non-sense to claim that McQuaid hated Protestants; moreover, his private char-itable works were well-known in the diocese. More telling were the author's criticisms of McQuaid's reserved style; he never appeared on radio or tele-vision and there was no diocesan newspaper. More importantly, he displayed a lack of leadership on the subject of the Vatican Council.[68]

December 1965 was McQuaid's silver jubilee and he made it known that he wanted it to be observed privately. However, public controversy was guar-anteed when *Studies* published a jubilee tribute to McQuaid's episcopate enti-tled 'The Church in Dublin: 1940-1965'.[69] The tribute was characterised by an uneasy mix of adulation and defensiveness which was particularly evident in the special section devoted to McQuaid's critics. Inevitably, controversy followed. *Herder Correspondence* deemed the tribute 'well-informed and charm-ingly written' but pointed out that it had concentrated only on those aspects of Catholic life which interested McQuaid. It acknowledged his charity and administrative skill, but criticised his failure to inspire the clergy and the laity and ascribed this to McQuaid's 'unconquered shyness, ...martyr com-plex, ... dislike of public occasions, [and] ... penchant for the unnecessary harsh or humiliating phrase'. The article concluded: 'Perhaps it does not matter quite so much to Christians what their bishop is like; but one of the boomerang effects of a century and more of clergy identifying the Church with themselves alone is that it matters very much what the bishop is like – it matters inordinately.'[70]

Following the conclusion of the Vatican Council in December 1965, it became increasingly clear in Ireland that McQuaid was dragging his feet on the reforms instituted by the Council, especially in the areas of liturgical change, greater lay participation, and ecumenism. This perception was con-firmed with the publication in 1968 of *Our Faith* in which McQuaid took issue with the way that sections of the clergy and laity interpreted the work of the Council and chose, once again, to emphasise the role of the bishop:

> The emphasis on reform that springs from merely human considera-tions can deflect one completely from the genuine aims of the Vatican

---

67 Michael Serafian, *The pilgrim: Pope Paul VI, the council, and the Church in a time of deci-sion* (London, 1964) pp 38-9.   68 'Curial mentality in Dublin archdiocese?', *Herder Correspondence*, July 1965.   69 'The Church in Dublin', *Studies* 54 (December, 1965), pp 297-346.   70 *Herder Correspondence*, Apr. 1966, p. 126. This criticism of McQuaid prompted two correspondents to cancel their subscriptions, *Herder Correspondence*, June 1966, p. 188.

Council. Many have chosen to make reform consistent, not in a change of their inner life, but in a concern for the outer life of social framework and activity ... Thus, many are preoccupied with accidental structures, particularly, in the Church. The supernatural structure of their own life would not seem to have at all the same interest for them as the deficiencies that they profess to discover in the members of the Church, especially her rulers, the Bishops. Far from returning to a humble, assiduous study of God's word in Sacred Scripture and Tradition, many have sought to put forward unusual and personal explanations of accepted doctrine. Terms consecrated by definition of the Church have been wrested from their traditional and obvious meaning. Faltering human theories are being substituted for the unerring, constant teaching of the Church ...

It is not a renewal in the spirit of the Second Vatican Council to exchange the certain teaching of the Church of Christ for the partial vision of a private judgement. One may not tamper with the doctrine of the Church. Some knowledge of how the tragic revolt (which is incorrectly called the Reformation) succeeded in breaking the unity of the Church could help in preventing many modern publicists from again wounding gravely the Church of Christ ...

When ... a Bishop, in union with the pope and all the Bishops of the Church, in virtue of his pastoral office, declares to his flock the authentic doctrine of the Church, it is as if Jesus Christ were teaching once again on earth. To him are owed the reverence and submission that are due to one who, by God's appointment declares, in the person of Christ, the revealed truth of God.[71]

Members of McQuaid's clergy who failed to show due reverence and submission increasingly felt the weight of his displeasure. Advancement and promotion were blocked and some non-compliant priests found themselves despatched to outlying parishes; for instance, Father Dermod McCarthy was removed from the *Radharc* team in 1970 and sent to Athy in County Kildare because of McQuaid's disapproval of programmes he made for RTE about the delays in implementing Vatican II reforms.[72] McCarthy's colleague, Father Joseph Dunn, wrote perceptively about this aspect of McQuaid, for though he had considerable affection for the archbishop, he frankly admitted that 'there was no man I feared more'.

He was most supportive of those he trusted and least likely to interfere with them. On the other hand, if he felt anyone was taking ini-

71 *Our faith* (Dublin, 1968), pp 3-4, 14.   72 'Mediascope' interview with Father Dermod McCarthy, *Irish Times*, 14 Jan. 1998.

tiatives without his knowledge or permission then the fur could fly. He was a master of the karate chop in written form. One of his secretaries told me that they dreaded a morning when some visitor failed to turn up. John Charles would seize the opportunity to toss off letters at a rate of about one a minute in his unique spidery hand, all of which the secretaries had to photocopy and file. And because he tossed out comments so fast, he couldn't have have fully considered the shock effect that some of them would have on the recipients ... Undoubtedly many people were hurt by his sarcasm, though I often felt that much of this sarcasm was meant to be humorous rather than hurtful ...

He exercised absolute power over his priests which nobody in their right mind would dare question. The theology we were taught placed the bishop as pastor of the diocese and priests as extra arms and mouths and legs of the bishops. If it were possible to have clones of the bishop, then priests would be unnecessary. The bishop received his mission as a successor of the apostles directly from Christ. To question a bishop's ruling was to question Christ. Perhaps the theology books didn't go quite that far, but certainly that was the conclusion which underlay a lot of the practice ...

The successful priest made John Charles the patron of his enterprise, kept him fully informed, and attributed all success to him. This led to sycophancy of a kind that I found most distasteful in others but which I felt forced at times to practise myself ... It's easy to be critical of this attitude, until one remembers that one careless move might mean that a life's work could be undone.[73]

Assertive lay voices could not be silenced so easily. The renewal and reform of the Second Vatican Council, Seán Mac Réamoinn wrote in 1969, were being stifled within the Irish Church, thus rendering it unable to meet the challenges of the time. No one doubted McQuaid's immense integrity, genuine pastoral concern and commitment but what was in doubt was 'his position in a changing Church and a changing Ireland, or more specifically, his awareness of and attitude to change'.[74] In a historical survey of the relationship of priests and people in Ireland, Professor John A. Murphy observed that while some of the clergy 'may privately regret that they can no longer say with Canon Sheehan "we have the lead and we must hold it"', the majority 'will be glad of a new relationship of equality, enhancing the dignity of both priest and layman'.[75] Desmond Costello, who was Fine Gael TD for

73 Dunn, *No tigers in Africa!*, pp 25-6, 28-35.   74 Seán MacRéamoinn, 'The religious position' in Owen Dudley Edwards (ed.), *Conor Cruise O'Brien introduces Ireland* (London, 1969), pp 61-70.   75 John A. Murphy, 'Priests and people in modern Irish history',

Dublin North-West, observed that while there was a good deal of evidence to suggest a failure of effective communication between bishops and priests in the Irish Church, 'the communication between the laity and the clergy has been negligible'. He concluded with a prophetic warning: 'The Church has the allegiance of the vast majority of the Irish people. It would, however, be a mistake to depend on an unswerving allegiance in the future.'[76]

Evidence of declining religious observance had already begun to appear. A survey of UCD students revealed in 1969 that while 83 per cent were attending Mass on all days of obligation, 11 per cent were attending sometimes, and 6 per cent were not attending at all. Only 38 per cent of those surveyed identified religious beliefs as the basis of Christian responsibility to the community while 26 per cent believed that matters of faith or doctrine were the most important part of the Church's demands.[77] Five years later another survey of UCD students found that regular religious practice had fallen to 59 per cent. Among male students 40 per cent were no longer practising their religion while for women students the figure was 30 per cent. 'Many young people', this survey concluded, 'even in recent years, seem to have been taught their faith in school in an authoritarian and aggressive way. More seriously still, they have been taught in a highly impersonal way as if it were like mathematics, or the vocabulary of some foreign language, or something to be learned by heart.'[78]

The reaction to the 1968 papal encyclical on birth control, *Humanae vitae*, represented a watershed in relations between clergy and laity in Ireland. In Dublin it caused open rebellion, the force of which caught McQuaid unawares. It provoked his last pastoral *Contraception and conscience: three statements* (1971) whose terse, shrill tone betrayed his anger, frustration, and bemusement at the response to *Humanae vitae* in the diocese. He began with a forthright attack on the media. 'For some time past, in this diocese', he declared, 'statements have been made by various categories of people in the daily press and in magazines concerning the regulation of birth. In a Diocese there is only one teaching authority, who, under the pope and in union with him, is competent, by virtue of his sacred office, to declare the authentic and objective moral law that is binding on all the Faithful of his Diocese, both priests and lay-folk. That authority is the Bishop.' Much was being written about conscience 'as if conscience can make right that which is wrong in itself. Conscience is a judgement ... But [this] judgement, if it is to be right accord-

Christus Rex, 23, no. 4 (1969), p. 259.   76 Desmond Costello, 'The priest and public affairs', *Christus Rex*, 23, no. 4 (1969), pp 293-8.   77 Katherine O'Doherty, 'Where have all the faithful gone? a survey of religion in the university', *The Furrow*, 20, no. 11 (Nov. 1969), pp 575-91.   78 Michael Paul Gallagher, 'Atheism Irish style', *The Furrow*, 25, no. 4 (Apr. 1974), pp 183-92.

ing to the objective moral law, must agree with that law.' McQuaid was concerned that the debate over birth control was a cover for other issues such as divorce. Both were being presented as issues of minorities' rights but both were 'evil' and 'there cannot be, on the part of any person, a right to know what is evil'. McQuaid stressed that the availability of contraceptives was a matter of public morality for which politicians were responsible. If they passed any measure promoting contraceptives, he warned, 'they ought to know clearly the meaning of their action, when it is judged by the norms of objective morality and the certain consequences of such a law'. McQuaid was scathing about arguments which contrasted the practices of Irish society with other countries: 'One can conceive no worse fate for Ireland than that it should, by the legislation of our elected representatives, be now made conform to the patterns of sexual conduct in other countries.' As an Ulsterman, he was equally dismissive about the argument that the introduction of divorce and contraception would assist the reunification of the country: 'One must know little of the Northern people to realise the indignant ridicule with which good Northern people would treat such an argument. It would indeed be a foul basis on which to attempt to construct the unity of our people.' The pastoral ended as it began, with a statement on the function and power of the bishops, in this case an extract from the Vatican Council's Dogmatic Constitution of the Church: 'Bishops, teaching in communion with the Roman Pontiff, are to be respected by all as witnesses to divine and Catholic truth. In matters of faith and morals, the bishops speak in the name of Christ and the faithful are to accept their teaching and to adhere to it with a religious assent of soul.'

This was McQuaid's swansong, his elegy to the kind of Catholicism in which he had been brought up and which was now disintegrating around him. Of course, it was not just the Church which had changed; Irish society was experiencing a profound social, economic, and cultural transformation, the implications of which both disturbed and baffled him. In 1970, aged seventy-five, he submitted his resignation to the Vatican, apparently not anticipating that it would be accepted. However, it was and his resignation was announced on 4 January 1972. That night there was a special programme on RTE to mark the event. The attacks made on McQuaid by several of the participants incensed the taoiseach, Jack Lynch, who urged him to complain to RTE. McQuaid replied that history would be the judge.[79] Given his views on history and biography, McQuaid must have been pessimistic about history's verdict. He died fifteen months later in April 1973. Thousands of Dubliners, who cared little about doctrinal arguments or Church-state controversies but who had benefited from McQuaid's public and private charity, turned out to pay their final respects. It was estimated that over 50,000 filed past his coffin.

79 Jack Lynch quoted in *Mission Outlook*, June 1973.

McQuaid lived and worked in an era of great change in Ireland that coincided with the first five decades of independence. His achievements, and his failures, cannot be understood without encompassing this context of change in the life of his Church and his country. Historians and biographers ignore this at their peril. Twenty-five years after his death, the career of one of the most remarkable figures in post-independence Irish history is long overdue for serious assessment.

STATISTICAL APPENDIX

	1941	1946	1951	1957	1961	1966	1972
Number of parishes							
City	31	38	38	42	42	46	54
Suburban & rural	50	51	52	56	56	61	61
Parish priests	77	84	87	95	95	*	*
Curates & administrators	241	367	355	380	421	*546	*567
Regular clergy	423	523	569	721	737	850	1,002
No. of communities	33	34	40	42	49	53	60
Communities of brothers	**	29	34	43	44	48	53
Communities of nuns & sisters	118	127	142	158	159	169	184
Schools							
Primary	**	386	481	491	485	500	518
Secondary	**	62	69	80	109	129	150
Vocational	**	21	21	27	34	34	47
Institutions							
Hospitals & homes	14	16	16	19	14	14	14
Asylums for deaf & blind	3	3	3	4	3	6	6
Orphanages	14	13	13	13	12	12	12
Homes for aged & widows	3	4	4	4	4	5	6
Refuges	5	5	5	5	3	5	4
Penitentiaries/homes for girls	4	4	4	4	4	4	3
Industrial schools	7	7	7	6	6	6	6
Societies & sodalities	10	15	15	18	18	20	23

* The ICD in these years made no distinction between parish priests and curates.
** Not published in 1941.
Source: *Irish Catholic Directory*, 1941-72.

Index